ETHICAL ISSUES IN BUSINESS

Sixth Edition

ETHICAL ISSUES IN BUSINESS

A Philosophical Approach

Edited by

Thomas Donaldson
University of Pennsylvania

Patricia H. Werhane
University of Virginia

Prentice Hall, Upper Saddle River, New Jersey 07458

Library of Congress Cataloging-in-Publication Data

Ethical issues in business : a philosophical approach / [edited by]
  Thomas Donaldson, Patricia H. Werhane. — 6th ed.
      p.   cm.
  Includes bibliographical references.
  ISBN 0-13-290628-7
    1. Business ethics—Case studies.   2. Social responsibility of
business—Case studies.   I. Donaldson, Thomas (date).
II. Werhane, Patricia Hogue.
HF5387.E8   1999
174'.4—dc21   98–31341
                                                                CIP

Editorial/Production Supervision and Interior Design: Barbara De Vries
Acquisitions Editor: Karita France
Assistant Editor: Emsal Hasan
Editorial Director: Charlyce Jones Owen
Editorial Assistant: Jennifer Ackerman
Cover Photo: "Hands Bridge." Curtis Parker/Scott Hull Associates
Cover Design: Bruce Kenselaar
Cover Design Director: Jayne Conte
Manufacturing Buyer: Tricia Kenny
Line Art Coordinator: Guy Ruggiero

This book was set 10/11 New Baskerville by Pub-Set Inc.,
and was printed by Courier Companies Inc.
The cover was printed by Phoenix Color Corp.

 © 1999, 1996, 1993, 1988, 1983, 1979 by Prentice-Hall, Inc.
Simon & Schuster / A Viacom Company
Upper Saddle River, New Jersey 07458

Printed in the United States of America
10 9 8 7 6 5 4 3 2 1

ISBN 0-13-290628-7

PRENTICE-HALL INTERNATIONAL (UK) LIMITED, London
PRENTICE-HALL OF AUSTRALIA PTY. LIMITED, Sydney
PRENTICE-HALL CANADA INC., Toronto
PRENTICE-HALL HISPANOAMERICANA, S.A., Mexico
PRENTICE HALL OF INDIA PRIVATE LIMITED, New Delhi
PRENTICE-HALL OF JAPAN, INC., Tokyo
SIMON & SCHUSTER ASIA PTE. LTD., Singapore
EDITORA PRENTICE-HALL DO BRASIL, LTDA., Rio de Janeiro

Contents

‑ PART TWO ‑
Property, Profit, and Justice

➤ PART THREE ➤
Corporations, Persons, and Morality

━ PART FOUR ━
International Business

━ PART FIVE ━
Contemporary Business Themes

Preface

Ethical Issues in Business was first published two decades ago in 1979. Since then the field of business ethics has grown into an academic discipline bristling with research and practical implications for managers. Textbooks as well as research have multiplied. In 1979, *Ethical Issues in Business* was one of only three textbooks in the field. Now at least fifty are available. Along with the growth of course offerings and college teaching materials has occurred an explosion of new articles, cases, and journals. Meanwhile, outside colleges and universities, hundreds of business firms have now created positions of "corporate ethics officer," and thousands more have instituted ethics training programs for managers and employees. The sixth edition reflects these dramatic changes that the field has undergone.

Some theoretical perspectives preserve their importance over the decades. Indeed, many are foundational materials for the study of business ethics. The insights of Adam Smith and John Locke about markets and human rights, or the radical claims made by Karl Marx that capitalism affects the minds of its participants, are no less relevant today than they were in earlier centuries. You will find those perspectives included in this edition, just as in the earlier ones. Yet other issues are clearly time-bound. When the last edition appeared, the hot issue of business conversation was Merrill Lynch's sale of derivatives to Orange County, California. At that time also, Bhopal, India, and the chemical disaster at its Union Carbide plant was still on the minds of many managers.

Since the publication of that fifth edition new events have posed new ethical challenges. Since then a financial crisis has erupted in Asia, and child labor issues have become central concerns for transnational corporations. The U.S. tobacco industry's cigarette marketing practices, including its public assurances that tobacco is nonaddictive, have been slammed by the media and public opinion. Meanwhile, Europe's largest company, Shell, has become entangled in human rights issues in Nigeria and in environmental controversy over its plan to sink its Brent Spar oil rig in the North Atlantic ocean. Still further, in the increasingly competitive commercial environment of global business, corporate leaders have been faced with new challenges in employment, in corporate restructuring, and training. Readings that focus on some of the ethical issues raised by these new kinds of challenges are included in this sixth edition.

The present edition, like earlier ones, has not been simply the product of its editors, but owes greatly to those whose suggestions, criticism, and editorial assistance made it a better book. We especially want to thank Margaret

Cording, Thomas Dunfee, R. Edward Freeman, Henry Tulloch, and Donna Wood for their helpful revision suggestions. Thanks also goes to the reviewers who accepted Prentice Hall's invitation to evaluate changes planned for this edition: Ronald Glass, University of Wisconsin, La Crosse, Krishna Mallick, Salem State College, Laura C. Morgan, University of North Carolina, Chapel Hill, and Joseph J. Tarala, Ocean City College. Most important, we want to thank Cynthia Rudolph again for her excellent organizational and editorial skills without which there would not have been a second, a third, a fourth, a fifth, and now a sixth edition.

T. D. and P. H. W.

General Introduction

Introduction to Ethical Reasoning

THOMAS DONALDSON ➤ PATRICIA H. WERHANE

What is the basis for making ethical decisions? Should Joan challenge Fred the next time he cracks a sexist joke? Should John refrain from lying on his job application despite his temptation to do so? What, if anything, should make Hillary decide that eating meat is corrupting, whereas vegetarianism is uplifting? It is obvious that the kind of evidence required for an ethical decision is different from that needed to make a nonethical one; but what is the nature of the difference? These questions give rise to a search for a *method* of ethical justification and decision making, a method that will specify the conditions that any good ethical decision should meet.

To see how such questions arise concretely, consider the following case.[1]

Some years ago, a large German chemical firm, BASF, decided to follow the lead of many other European firms and build a factory in the United States. BASF needed land, lots of it (1,800 acres), an inexpensive labor pool, almost 5 million gallons of fresh water every day, a surrounding area free of import taxes, and a nearby railroad and ocean port. Obviously, only a handful of locations could meet all these requirements. The spot the company finally picked seemed perfect, an area near the coast of South Carolina called Beaufort County. It purchased 1,800 acres.

South Carolina and Beaufort County were pleased with BASF's decision. The surrounding area, from which the company would pick its workers, was economically depressed and per capita income stood well below the national average. Jobs of any kind were desperately needed. Even the Governor of South Carolina and his staff were eager for BASF to build in South Carolina, and although BASF had not yet finalized its exact production plans, the State Pollution Central Authority saw no problems with meeting the State pollution laws. BASF itself said that although it would dump chemical byproducts into the local Colleton River, it planned not to lower the river's quality.

But trouble started immediately. To see why, one needs to know that Beaufort County is the home of the internationally famous resort area called "Hilton Head." Hilton Head attracts thousands of vacationers every year—most of them with plenty of money—and its developers worried that the scenic splendor of the area might be marred by the air and water pollution. Especially concerned about water pollution, resort developers charged that the proposed chemical plant would pollute the Colleton River. They argued that BASF plants in Germany had polluted the Rhine and, in Belgium, the Schelde River. Further, they noted that on BASF's list of proposed expenditures, pollution control was allocated only one million dollars.

The citizens of Beaufort County, in contrast to the Hilton Head Developers, welcomed BASF. They presented the company with a petition bearing over 7,000 signatures endorsing the new plant. As one local businessman commented, "I would say 80 percent of the people in Beaufort County are in favor of BASF.

Those who aren't rich." (William D. McDonald, "Youth Corps Looking for Jobs," *The State*, February 23, 1970.)

The manager of BASF's U.S. operations was clearly confronted by an economic and moral dilemma. He knew that preventing massive pollution was virtually impossible and, in any case, outrageously expensive. The eagerness of South Carolina officials for new industry suggested that pollution standards might be "relaxed" for BASF. If it decided to go ahead and build, was the company to push for the minimum pollution control it could get away with under the law? Such a policy might maximize corporate profits and the financial interests of the shareholders, while at the same time it would lower the aesthetic quality of the environment. It might make jobs available to Beaufort County while ignoring the resort industry and the enjoyment of vacationers. Moreover, the long-term effects of dumping chemicals was hard to predict, but past experience did not give the manager a feeling of optimism. Pollution seemed to be not only a business issue but a *moral* one. But how should the manager sort out, and eventually decide upon, such a moral issue?

To solve his moral problem, BASF's manager might try a variety of strategies. He might, for example, begin by assuming that he has three basic options: (1) Build with minimal pollution control; (2) build with maximal pollution control; or (3) do not build.

Then, he might reason:

> The consequences of option 1 will be significant but tolerable water pollution, hostility from the Hilton Head Developers, high short-term corporate profits, and satisfied shareholders.
>
> The consequences of option 2 will be unnoticeable pollution, no complaints from the Hilton Head Developers, high pollution-control costs, low profits, and unsatisfied stockholders.
>
> The consequences of option 3 will be approval from the Hilton Head Developers, low short-term profits (while a search for a new location is underway), and strong disapproval from the local townspeople.
>
> My job from a *moral* perspective is to weigh these consequences and consider which of the alternatives constitutes a maximization of good. Who will benefit from each decision? How many people will be adversely affected and in what ways?

Or the manager might reason:

> Both BASF Corporation and I are confronted with a variety of *duties, rights,* and *obligations.* First there is the company's obligation to its stockholders, and my duty as manager is to protect the economic interests and rights of our stockholders. Next there are the rights of those Beaufort residents and visitors in the area to clean air and water. Finally there are the rights of other property owners in the area, including the Hilton Head Developers, not to be harmed unreasonably by other industries. There is an implied obligation to future generations to protect the river. And finally, there are broader considerations: Is this an act I would want others to do? What kind of moral example will I be setting?
>
> My job from a *moral* perspective is to balance and assess these duties, rights, and obligations, and determine which have priority.

Finally, the manager might reason:

> I cannot confront a moral problem from either the abstract perspective of "consequences," or of "duties, rights, and obligations." Instead, I must use a concrete

concept of *human nature* to guide my deliberations. Acts that aid persons to develop their potential human nature are morally good; ones that do the opposite are bad.

I believe that crucial potentialities of human nature include such things as health, knowledge, moral maturity, meaningful employment, political freedom, and self-respect.

My job from a *moral* perspective is to assess the situation in terms of its harmony or disharmony with these basic concepts of human potential.

Notice how different each of these approaches is. The first focuses on the concept of *consequences;* the second on *duties, rights* and *obligations;* and the third on *human nature.* Of course, the three methods may overlap; for example, applying the concept of "human nature" in the third approach may necessitate referring to concepts drawn from the first and second, such as "consequences" and "rights," and vice versa. Even so, the approaches reflect three classical types of ethical theory in the history of philosophy. Each has been championed by a well-known traditional philosopher, and most ethical theories can be categorized under one of the three headings. The first may be called *consequentialism,* the second, *deontology,* and the third, *human nature ethics.*

CONSEQUENTIALISM

As its name implies, a consequentialist theory of ethical reasoning concentrates on the consequences of human actions, and all actions are evaluated in terms of the extent to which they achieve desirable results. Such theories are also frequently labeled *teleological,* a term derived from the Greek word *telos,* which means "end" or "purpose." According to consequential theories, the concepts of right, wrong, and duty are subordinated to the concept of the end or purpose of an action.

There are at least two types of consequential theory. The first—advocated by only a few consequentialists—is a version of what philosophers call ethical egoism. It construes right action as action whose consequences, considered among all the alternatives, maximizes *my* good—that is, action that benefits *me* the most or harms *me* the least. The second type—advocated by most consequentialists—denies that right action concerns only *me.* Rather, right action must maximize *overall* good; that is, it must maximize good (or minimize bad) from the standpoint of the entire human community. The best-accepted label for this type of consequentialism is *utilitarianism.* This term was coined by the eighteenth-century philosopher Jeremy Bentham, although its best-known proponent was the nineteenth-century English philosopher John Stuart Mill. As Bentham formulated it, the principle of utility states that an action is right if it produces the greatest balance of pleasure or happiness and unhappiness in light of alternative actions. Mill supported a similar principle, using what he called the "proof" of the principle of utility—namely, the recognition that the only proof for something's being desirable is that someone actually desires it. Since everybody desires pleasure or happiness, it follows, according to Mill, that happiness is the most desirable thing. The purpose of moral action is to achieve greatest overall happiness, and actions are evaluated in terms of the extent to which they contribute to this end. The most desirable state of affairs, the greatest good and the goal of morality, said Mill, is the "greatest happiness for the greatest number."

While later utilitarians accept the general framework of Mill's argument, not all utilitarians are hedonists. That is, not all utilitarians equate "the good" with pleasure or happiness. Some utilitarians have argued that in maximizing the "good," one must be concerned not only with maximizing pleasure, but with maximizing other things, such as knowledge, moral maturity, and friendship. Although it could be claimed that such goods also bring pleasure and happiness to their possessor, it is arguable whether their goodness is ultimately *reducible* to whatever pleasure they bring. These philosophers are sometimes called pluralistic utilitarians. Still other philosophers have adapted utilitarianism to modern methods of economic theory by championing what is known as preference utilitarianism. Instead of referring to the maximization of specific goods, such as pleasure or knowledge, preference utilitarians understand the ultimate foundation of goodness to be the set of preferences people actually possess. One person prefers oysters to strawberries; another prefers rock music to Mozart. Each person has a set of preferences, and so long as the set is internally consistent, it makes no sense to label one set morally superior to another. Preference utilitarianism thus interprets right action as that which is optimal among alternatives in terms of everyone's preferences. Disputes, however, rage among preference utilitarians and their critics over how to specify the meaning of *optimal*.

Bentham and Mill thought that utilitarianism was a revolutionary theory, both because it accurately reflected human motivation and because it had clear application to the political and social problems of their day. If one could measure the benefit or harm of any action, rule or law, they believed, one could sort out good and bad social and political legislation as well as good and bad individual actions.

But how, specifically, does one apply the traditional principle of utility? To begin with, one's race, religion, intelligence, or condition of birth is acknowledged to be irrelevant in calculating one's ultimate worth. Each person counts for "one," and no more than "one." Second, in evaluating happiness, one must take into account not only present generations, but ones in the future. In calculating the effects of pollution, for instance, one must measure the possible effects pollution might have on health, genetics, and the supply of natural resources for future generations. Third, pleasure or happiness is measured *in toto* so that the thesis does not reduce to the idea that "one ought to do what makes the most persons happy." Utilitarianism does not reduce to a dictatorship of majority interests. One person's considerable unhappiness might outweigh the minor pleasures of many other persons added together. Utilitarians also consider the long-term consequences for single individuals. For instance, it might be pleasurable to drink a full bottle of wine every evening, but the long-term drawbacks of such a habit might well outweigh its temporary pleasures.

Finally, according to many utilitarians (such as Mill), some pleasures are *qualitatively* better than others. Intellectual pleasure, for example, is said to be higher than physical pleasure. "Better to be Socrates unsatisfied," writes Mill, "than a pig satisfied." The reasons that drove Mill to formulate this qualitative distinction among pleasures are worth noting. Since Mill believed that the optimal situation was one of "greatest happiness for the greatest number," then what was he to say about a world of people living at the zenith of merely *physical* happiness? If science could invent a wonder drug, like the "soma" in Aldous Huxley's *Brave New World*, that provided a permanent state of drugged happiness (without even a hangover), would the consequence be a perfect world? Mill believed not, and to remedy this difficulty in his theory, he introduced *qualitative levels* of happiness. For example, he said that the happiness of understanding Plato is "higher" than that of drinking three martinis. But how was Mill to say *which* pleasures were higher? Here he retreated to an ingenious proposal: When deciding which of two pleasures is higher, one should poll the group of persons who are experienced—that is, who know *both* pleasures. Their decision will indicate which is the higher pleasure. Ah, but might the majority decision not be wrong? Here Mill provides no clear answer.

Modern-day utilitarians divide themselves roughly into two groups: *act utilitarians* and *rule utilitarians*. An *act utilitarian* believes that the principle of utility should be applied to individual acts. Thus one measures the consequences of each *individual action* according to whether it maximizes good. For example, suppose a certain community were offered the opportunity to receive a great deal of wealth in the form of a gift. The only stipulation was that the community force some of its citizens with ugly, deteriorated homes to repair and beautify them. Next, suppose the community held an election to decide whether to accept the gift. An act utilitarian would analyze the problem of whether to vote for or against the proposal from the standpoint of the *individual voter*. Would an individual's vote to accept the gift be more likely to maximize the community's overall good than would a vote to the contrary?

A *rule utilitarian*, on the other hand, believes that instead of considering the results of specific actions, one must weigh the consequences of adopting a *general rule* exemplified by that action. According to the rule utilitarian, one should act according to a general rule which, if adopted, would maximize good. For example, in the hypothetical case of the community deciding whether to accept a gift, a rule utilitarian might adopt the rule "Never vote in a way that lowers the self-respect of a given class of citizens." She might accept this rule because of the general unhappiness that would ensue if society systematically treated some persons as second-class citizens. Here the focus is on the general rule and not on the individual act.

Critics raise objections to utilitarianism. Perhaps the most serious objection is that it is unable to account for justice. Because the utilitarian concentrates on the consequences of an action for a majority, the employment of the principle of utility can be argued to allow injustice for a small minority. For example, if overall goodness were maximized in the long run by making slaves of 2 percent of the population, utilitarianism seemingly is forced to condone slavery. But clearly this is unjust. Utilitarianism's obvious response is that such slavery will not, as a matter of empirical fact, maximize goodness. Rule utilitarians, as we have seen, can argue that society should embrace the rule "Never enslave others," because following such a principle will, in the long run, maximize goodness. Even so, the battle continues between utilitarians and their critics. Can utilitarianism account for the widely held moral conviction that injustice to a minority is wrong *regardless* of the consequences? The answer is hotly contested.

Another criticism concerns the determination of the good to be maximized. Any consequentialist has the problem of identifying and ranking whatever is to be maximized. For a utilitarian such as Mill, as we have seen, the problem involves distinguishing between higher and lower pleasures. But for pluralistic utilitarians, a similar problem exists: What is the basis for selecting, for example, friendship and happiness as goods to be maximized and not, say, aesthetic sensitivity? And even granted that this problem can be solved, there is the future problem of arbitrating trade-offs between goods such as happiness and friendship when they *conflict*. When one is forced to choose between enhancing happiness and enhancing friendship, which gets priority? And under what conditions?

An interesting fact about consequentialist reasoning is that most of us employ it to some degree in ordinary decisions. We weigh the consequences of alternatives in choosing colleges, in deciding on a career, in hiring and promoting others, and in many other judgments. We frequently weigh good consequences over bad ones and predict the long- and short-term effects of our choices. We often even cite consequentialist-style principles—for example, "No one should choose a college where he or she will be unhappy," or, "No one should pollute the environment when his or her action harms others."

However, for a variety of reasons, including the objections to utilitarianism mentioned earlier, some philosophers refuse to acknowledge consequentialism as an adequate theory of ethics. They argue that the proper focus for ethical judgments should not be consequences, but moral *precepts*—that is, the rules, norms, and principles we use to guide our actions. Such philosophers are known as deontologists, and the next section will examine their views.

DEONTOLOGY

The term *deontological* comes from the Greek word for "duty," and what is crucial according to the deontologist are the rules and principles that guide actions. We shall discuss here two approaches to deontological ethical reasoning that have profoundly influenced ethics. The first is that of the eighteenth-century philosopher Immanuel Kant and his followers. This approach focuses on duty and universal rules to determine right actions. The second—actually a subspecies of deontological reasoning—is known as the "social contract" approach. It focuses not on individual decision making, but on the general social principles that rational persons in certain ideal situations would agree upon and adopt.

Kantian Deontology

Kant believed that ethical reasoning should concern activities that are rationally motivated and should utilize precepts that apply universally to all human actions. To this end, he opens his treatise on ethics by declaring

> It is impossible to conceive anything at all in the world, . . . which can be taken as good without qualification except a *good* will.[2]

This statement sums up much of what Kant wants to say about ethics and is worth unraveling. What Kant means is that the only thing that can be good or worthwhile without any provisos or stipulations is an action of the will freely motivated for the right reasons. Other goods such as wealth, beauty, and intelligence are certainly valuable, but they are not good *without qualification* because they have the potential to create both good and bad effects. Wealth, beauty, and intelligence can be bad when they are used for purely selfish ends. Even human happiness—which Mill held as the highest good—can, according to Kant, create complacency, disinterest, and excessive self-assurance under certain conditions.

According to Kant, reason is the faculty that can aid in the discovery of correct moral principles; thus it is *reason,* not *inclination,* that should guide the will. When reason guides the will, Kant calls the resulting actions ones done from "duty." Kant's use of the term *duty* turns out to be less formidable than it first appears. Kant is simply saying that a purely good and free act of the will is one done not merely because you have an *inclination* to do it, but because you have the right reasons for doing it. For example, suppose you discover a wallet belonging to a stranger. Kant would say that despite one's inclination to keep the money (which the stranger may not even need), one should return it. This is an act you know is right despite your inclinations. Kant also believes you should return the wallet even when you believe the *consequences* of not returning it are better. Here his views are at sharp odds with consequentialism. Suppose that the stranger is known for her stinginess, and you plan to donate the money to a children's hospital. No matter. For Kant, you must return the wallet. Thus the moral worth lies in the act itself and not in either your happiness or the consequences brought about by the act. Acts are good because they are done for the sake of what is right and not because of the consequences they might produce.

But how do I know what my duty is? While it may be clear that one should return a wallet, there are other circumstances in which one's duty is less evident. Suppose you are in a six-person lifeboat at sea with five others and a seventh person swims up? What is one's duty here? And how does one even know that what one *thinks* is right *is* right? To settle such problems, Kant claims that duty is more than doing merely what you "feel" is right. Duty is acting with *respect for other rational beings.* It almost goes without saying, then, that "acting from duty" is not to be interpreted as action done in obedience to local, state, or national laws, since these can be good or bad. Instead, "duty" is linked to the idea of universal principles that should govern all our actions.

But is there any principle that can govern *all* human beings? Kant believes the answer is yes, and he calls the highest such principle the "categorical imperative." He formulates the categorical imperative in three ways (although we shall consider only two formulations here). The first formulation, roughly translated, is

> One ought only to act such that the principle of one's act could become a universal law of human action in a world in which one would hope to live.

For example, one would want to live in a world where people followed the principle "Return property that belongs to others." Therefore one should return the stranger's wallet. We do not, however, want to live in a world where everyone lies. Therefore, one should not adopt the principle "Lie whenever it seems helpful."

The second formulation of the categorical imperative is

One ought to treat others as having intrinsic value in themselves, and *not* merely as means to achieve one's ends.

In other words, one should respect every person as a rational and free being. Hitler treated one group of persons as nonpersons in order to achieve his own ends, and thus he acted contrary to the categorical imperative. Another instance of treating persons as means would occur if a teacher looked up the grade records of new students to determine how to assign grades in her own class. She would be treating students as if they had no control over their destinies. Such actions are immoral according to Kant because they fail to respect the inherent dignity of rational beings.

Ethical reasoning for Kant implies adopting principles of action and evaluating one's actions in terms of those principles. Even Kant grants that the evaluation is sometimes difficult. For example, there is the problem of striking the proper level of generality in choosing a principle. A principle that read, "If one is named John Doe and attends Big State University and has two sisters, then he should borrow fifty dollars without intending to repay it" is far too specific. On the other hand, the principle "You should always pay your debts" might be too general, since it would require that a starving man repay the only money he possesses to buy a loaf of bread. Because of the problem of striking the proper degree of generality, many modern deontologists have reformulated Kant's basic question to read: "Could I wish that everyone in the world would follow this principle *under relevantly similar conditions?*"

As with utilitarianism, critics challenge deontological reasoning. Some assert that fanatics such as Hitler could at least *believe* that the rule "Persecute Jews whenever possible" is one that the world should live by. Similarly, a thief might universalize the principle "Steal whenever you have a good opportunity." Moreover, a strict interpretation of deontological ethical reasoning is said to allow no exceptions to a universal principle. Such strict adherence to universal principles might encourage moral rigidity and might fail to reflect the diversity of responses required by complex moral situations. Finally, critics argue that, in a given case, two principles may conflict without there being a clear way to decide which principle or rule should take precedence. Jean-Paul Sartre tells of his dilemma during World War II when he was forced to choose between staying to comfort his ill and aging mother, and fighting for the freedom of France. Two principles seemed valid: "Give aid to your father and mother," and "Contribute to the cause of freedom." But with conflicting principles, how is one to choose? Nevertheless, deontological ethical reasoning represents a well-respected and fundamentally distinctive mode of ethical reasoning, one which, like consequentalism, appears in the deliberations of ordinary persons as well as philosophers. We have all heard actions condemned by the comment, "what would it be like if everyone did that?"

The Contractarian Alternative

Kant assumes that the categorical imperative is something all rational individuals can discover and agree upon. A different version of deontology is offered by many philosophers who focus less on the actions of individuals, and more on the principles that govern society at large. These include two philosophers whose writings appear in our book: the seventeenth-century political philosopher John Locke and the twentieth-century American philosopher John Rawls. They and others try to establish universal principles of a just society through what might be called "social contract thought experiments." They ask us to imagine what it would be like to live in a situation where there are no laws, no social conventions, and no political state. In this so-called state of nature, we imagine that rational persons gather to formulate principles or rules to govern political and social communities. Such rules would resemble principles derived through the categorical imperative in that they are presumably principles to which every rational person would agree and which would hold universally.

Locke and Rawls differ in their approach to establishing rules or principles of justice, and the difference illustrates two distinct forms of contractarian reasoning. Locke argues from a "natural rights" position, while Rawls argues from a "reasonable person" position. Locke claims that every person is born with, and possesses, certain basic rights that are "natural." These rights are inherent to a person's nature, and they are possessed by every one equally. Like other inherent traits, they cannot be taken away. They are, in the words of the Declaration of Independence, "inalienable." When rational persons meet to formulate principles to govern the formation of social and political communities, they construct a social contract that is the basis for an agreement between themselves and their government, and whose rules protect natural rights. Rights, then, become deontological precepts by which one forms and evaluates rules, constitutions, government, and socioeconomic systems. While many philosophers disagree with Locke's view that each of us has inherent or *natural* rights, many do utilize a theory of human rights as the basis for justifying and evaluating political institutions.

Rawls adopts a different perspective. He does not begin from a natural rights position. Instead, he asks which principles of justice rational persons would formulate if they were behind a "veil of ignorance"—that is, if each person knew nothing about who he or she was. That is, one would not know whether one were old or young, male or female, rich or poor, highly motivated or lazy, or anything about one's personal status in society. Unable to predict which principles, if picked, will favor them personally, Rawls argues, persons will be forced to choose principles that are fair to all.

Rawls and Locke are not in perfect agreement about which principles would be adopted in such hypothetical situations, and more will be said about their views later in the book. For now it is important to remember that the social contract approach maintains a deontological character. It is used to formulate principles of justice that apply universally. Some philosophers note, however, that from an original position in a "state of nature" or behind a "veil of ignorance," rational persons *could* adopt consequentialist principles as rules for a just society. Thus, while the social contract approach is deontological in style, the principles it generates are not necessarily ones that are incompatible with consequentialism.

In the moral evaluations of business, all deontologists—contractarians included—would ask questions such as the following:

1. Are the rules fair to everyone?
2. Do the rules hold universally even with the passage of time?
3. Is every person treated with equal respect?

What may be missing from a deontological approach to ethical reasoning is a satisfactory means of coping with valid exceptions to general rules. Under what circumstances, if any, are exceptions allowed? Deontologists believe that they can answer this question, but their solutions vary. Suffice it to say that deontologists, just as utilitarians, have not convinced everyone.

HUMAN NATURE ETHICS

According to some contemporary philosophers, the preceding two modes of ethical reasoning exhaust all possible modes. That is to say, all theories can be classified as either teleological or deontological. Whether this is true cannot be settled here, but it will be helpful to introduce briefly what some philosophers consider to be a third category, namely the *human nature* approach.

A *human nature* approach assumes that all humans have inherent capacities that constitute the ultimate basis for all ethical claims. Actions are evaluated in terms of whether they promote or hinder, coincide with or conflict with, these capacities. One of the most famous proponents of this theory was the Greek philosopher Aristotle. In Aristotle's opinion, human beings have inherent *potentialities,* and thus human development turns out to be the struggle for self-actualization, or in other words, the perfection of inherent human nature. Consider the acorn. It has the natural potential to become a sturdy oak tree. Its natural drive is not to become an elm or a cedar or even a stunted oak, but to become the most robust oak tree possible. Diseased or stunted oak trees are simply deficient; they are instances of things in nature whose potential has not been fully developed. Similarly, according to Aristotle, persons are born with inherent potentialities. Persons, like acorns, naturally are oriented to actualize their potentialities, and for them this means more than merely developing their physical potential. It also means developing their mental, moral, and social potential. Thus, human beings in this view are seen as basically good; evil is understood as a deficiency that occurs when one is unable to fulfill one's natural capacities.

It is important to understand that the concept of human nature need not be an individualistic one. According to Aristotle, persons are "social" by nature and cannot be understood apart from the larger community in which they participate. "Man," Aristotle wrote, is a "social animal." For Aristotle, then, fulfilling one's natural constitution implies developing wisdom, generosity, and self-restraint, all of which help to make one a good member of the community.

The criterion for judging the goodness of any action is whether or not the action is compatible with one's inherent human capacities. Actions that enhance human capacities are good; those that deter them are bad unless they are the best among generally negative alternatives. For example, eating nothing but starches is unhealthy, but it is clearly preferable to starving.

Because this theory puts great emphasis on the nature of persons, how one undersands that "nature" will obviously be the key to determining both what counts as a right action and how one defines the proper end of human action in general. Aristotle argued that intelligence and wisdom are uniquely human potentialities and consequently that intellectual virtue is the highest virtue. The life of contemplation, he believed, is the best sort of life, in part because it represents the highest fulfillment of human nature. Moral virtue, also crucial in Aristotle's theory, involves the rational control of one's desires. In action where a choice is possible, one exercises moral virtue by restraining harmful desires and cultivating beneficial ones. The development of virtue requires the cultivation of good habits, and this in turn leads Aristotle to emphasize the importance of good upbringing and education.

One problem said to affect human nature theories is that they have difficulty justifying the supposition that human beings *do* have specific inherent capacities and that these capacities are the same for all humans. Further, critics claim that it is difficult to warrant the assumption that humans are basically good. Perhaps the famous psychoanalyst Sigmund Freud is correct in his assertion that at bottom we are all naturally aggressive and selfish. Finally, critics complain that it is difficult to employ this theory in ethical reasoning, since it appears to lack clear-cut rules and principles for use in moral decision making. Obviously, any well-argued human nature ethic will take pains to spell out the aspects of human nature which, when actualized, constitute the ultimate ground for moral judgments.

CONCLUSION

The three approaches to ethical reasoning we have discussed—consequentialism, deontology, and human nature ethics—all present theories of ethical reasoning distinguished in terms of their basic methodological elements. Each represents a type or model of moral reasoning that is applicable to practical decisions in concrete situations. Consider, for example, the case study with which we began our discussion, involving BASF and its proposed new plant. As it happened, BASF chose option 3 and decided to build elsewhere. In making his decision, did the BASF manager actually use any or all of the methods described above? Although we cannot know the answer to this question, it is clear, as we saw earlier, that each method was applicable to his problem. Indeed, the three methods of moral reasoning are sufficiently broad that each is applicable to the full range of problems confronting human moral experience. The question of which method, if any, is superior to the others must be left for another time. The intention of this essay is not to substitute for a thorough study of traditional ethical theories—something for which there is no substitute—but to introduce the reader to basic modes of ethical reasoning that will help to analyze the ethical problems in business that arise in the remainder of the book.

Notes

1. "BASF Corporation vs. The Hilton Head Island Developers," in *Business and Society,* Robert D. Hay, et al., eds. (Cincinnati: South-Western Publishing Co., 1984). pp. 100–12.
2. Immanuel Kant, *Groundwork of the Metaphysic of Morals,* trans. H. J. Paton (New York: Harper & Row, 1948, 1956), p. 61.

Does Business Ethics Make Economic Sense?

AMARTYA SEN[1]

1. Introduction

I begin not with the need for business ethics, but at the other end—the idea that many people have that there is no need for such ethics. That conviction is quite widespread among practitioners of economics, though it is more often taken for granted implicitly rather than asserted explicitly. We have to understand better what the conviction rests on, to be able to see its inadequacies. Here, as in many other areas of knowledge, the importance of a claim depends to a great extent on what it denies.

How did this idea of the redundancy of ethics get launched in economics? The early authors on economic matters, from Aristotle and Kautilya (in ancient Greece and ancient India respectively—the two were contemporaries, as it happens) to medieval practitioners (including Aquinas, Ockham, Maimonides, and others), to the economists of the early modern age (William Petty, Gregory King, François Quesnay, and others) were all much concerned, in varying degrees, with ethical analysis. In one way or another, they saw economics as a branch of "practical reason," in which concepts of the good, the right and the obligatory were quite central.

What happened then? As the "official" story goes, all this changed with Adam Smith, who can certainly be described—rightly—as the father of modern economics. He made, so it is said, economics scientific and hardheaded, and the new economics that emerged in the 19th and 20th centuries was all ready to do business, with no ethics to keep it tied to "morals and moralizing." That view of what happened—with Smith doing the decisive shooting of business and economic ethics—is not only reflected in volumes of professional economic writings, but has even reached the status of getting into the English literature via a limerick by Stephen Leacock, who was both a literary writer and an economist:

> Adam, Adam, Adam Smith
> Listen what I charge you with!
> Didn't you say
> In a class one day
> That selfishness was bound to pay?
> Of all doctrines that was the Pith.
> Wasn't it, wasn't it, wasn't it, Smith?[2]

The interest in going over this bit of history—or alleged history—does not lie, at least for this conference, in scholastic curiosity. I believe it is important to see how that ethics-less view of economics and business emerged in order to understand what it is that is being missed out. As it happens, that bit of potted history of "who killed business ethics" is altogether wrong, and it is particularly instructive to understand how that erroneous identification has come about.

A paper presented at the International Conference on the Ethics of Business in a Global Economy, held in Columbus, Ohio, in March 1992. Reprinted by permission of the author, Amartya Sen, University of Cambridge, and *Business Ethics Quarterly*, January 1993, Vol. 3, Issue 1.

2. Exchange, Production and Distribution

I get back, then, to Adam Smith. Indeed, he did try to make economics scientific, and to a great extent was successful in this task, within the limits of what was possible then. While that part of the alleged history is right (Smith certainly did much to enhance the scientific status of economics), what is altogether mistaken is the idea that Smith demonstrated—or believed that he had demonstrated—the redundancy of ethics in economic and business affairs. Indeed, quite the contrary. The Professor of Moral Philosophy at the University of Glasgow—for that is what Smith was—was as interested in the importance of ethics in behavior as anyone could have been. It is instructive to see how the odd reading of Smith—as a "no-nonsense" sceptic of economic and business ethics—has come about.

Perhaps the most widely quoted remark of Adam Smith is the one about the butcher, the brewer and the baker in *The Wealth of Nations:* "It is not from the benevolence of the butcher, the brewer, or the baker that we expect our dinner, but from their regard to their own interest. We address ourselves, not to their humanity but to their self-love. . . ."[3] The butcher, the brewer and the baker want our money, and we want their products, and the exchange benefits us all. There would seem to be no need for any ethics—business or otherwise—in bringing about this betterment of all the parties involved. All that is needed is regard for our own respective interests, and the market is meant to do the rest in bringing about the mutually gainful exchanges.

In modern economics this Smithian tribute to self-interest is cited again and again—indeed with such exclusivity that one is inclined to wonder whether this is the only passage of Smith that is read these days. What did Smith really suggest? Smith did argue in this passage that the pursuit of self-interest would do fine to motivate the exchange of commodities. But that is a very limited claim, even though it is full of wonderful insights in explaining why it is that we seek exchange and how come exchange can be such a beneficial thing for all. But to understand the limits of what is being claimed here, we have to ask, first: Did Smith think that economic operations and business activities consist only of exchanges of this kind? Second, even in the context of exchange, we have to question: Did Smith think that the result would be just as good if the businesses involved, driven by self-interest, were to try to defraud the consumers, or the consumers in question were to attempt to swindle the sellers?

The answers to both these questions are clearly in the negative. The butcher-brewer-baker simplicity does not carry over to problems of production and distribution (and Smith never said that it did), nor to the problem as to how a system of exchange can flourish institutionally. This is exactly where we begin to see why Smith could have been right in his claim about *the motivation for exchange* without establishing or trying to establish *the redundancy of business or ethics* in general (or even in exchange). And this is central to the subject of this conference.

The importance of self-interest pursuit is a helpful part of understanding many practical problems, for example, the supply problems in the Soviet Union and East Europe. But it is quite unhelpful in explaining the success of, say, Japanese economic performance *vis-à-vis* West Europe or North America (since behavior modes in Japan are often deeply influenced by other conventions and pressures). Elsewhere in *The Wealth of Nations,* Adam Smith considers other problems which call for a more complex motivational structure. And in his *The Theory of Moral Sentiments,* Smith goes extensively into the need to go beyond profit maximization, arguing that "humanity, justice, generosity, and public spirit, are the qualities most useful to others."[4] Adam Smith was very far from trying to deny the importance of ethics in behavior in general and business behavior in particular.[5]

Overlooking everything else that Smith said in his wide-ranging writings and concentrating only on this one butcher-brewer-baker passage, the father of modern economics is too often made to look like an ideologue. He is transformed into a partisan exponent of an ethics-free view of life which would have horrified Smith. To adapt a Shakespearian aphorism, while some men are born small and some achieve smallness, the unfortunate Adam Smith has had much smallness thrust upon him.

It is important to see how Smith's whole tribute to self-interest as a motivation for exchange (best illustrated in the butcher-brewer-baker passage) can co-exist peacefully with Smith's advocacy of ethical behavior elsewhere. Smith's concern with ethics was, of course, extremely extensive and by no means confined to economic and business matters. But since this is not the occasion to review Smith's ethical beliefs, but only to get insights from his combination of economic and ethical expertise to understand better the exact role of business ethics, we have to point our inquiries in that particular direction.

The butcher-brewer-baker discussion is all about *motivation for exchange,* but Smith was—as any good economist should be—deeply concerned also with *production* as well as *distribution*. And to understand how exchange might itself actually work in practice, it is not adequate to concentrate only on the motivation that makes people *seek* exchange. It is necessary to look at the behavior patterns that could sustain a flourishing system of mutually profitable exchanges. The positive role of intelligent self-seeking in motivating exchange has to be supplemented by the motivational demands of production and distribution, and the systemic demands on the organization of the economy.

These issues are taken up now, linking the general discussion with practical problems faced in the contemporary world. In the next three sections I discuss in turn (1) the problem of organization (especially that of exchange), (2) the arrangement and performance of production, and (3) the challenge of distribution.

3. Organization and Exchange: Rules and Trust

I come back to the butcher-brewer-baker example. The concern of the different parties with their own interests certainly can adequately *motivate* all of them to take part in the exchange from which each benefits. But whether the exchange would operate well would depend also on organizational conditions. This requires institutional development which can take quite some time to work—a lesson that is currently being learned rather painfully in East Europe and the former Soviet Union. That point is now being recognized, even though it was comprehensively ignored in the first flush of enthusiasm in seeking the magic of allegedly automatic market processes.

But what must also be considered now is the extent to which the economic institutions operate on the basis of common behavior patterns, shared trusts, and a mutual confidence in the ethics of the different parties. When Adam Smith pointed to the motivational importance of "regard to their own interest," he did not suggest that this motivation is all that is needed to have a flourishing system of exchange. If he cannot trust the householder, the baker may have difficulty in proceeding to produce bread to meet orders, or in delivering bread without prepayment. And the householder may not be certain whether he would be sensible in relying on the delivery of the ordered bread if the baker is not always altogether reliable. These problems of mutual confidence—discussed in a very simple form here—can be incomparably more complex and more critical in extended and multifarious business arrangements.

Mutual confidence in certain rules of behavior is typically implicit rather than explicit—indeed so implicit that its importance can be easily overlooked in situations in which confidence is unproblematic. But in the context of economic development across the Third World, and also of institutional reform now sweeping across what used to be the Second World, these issues of behavioral norms and ethics can be altogether central.

In the Third World there is often also a deep-rooted scepticism of the reliability and moral quality of business behavior. This can be directed both at local businessmen and the commercial people from abroad. The latter may sometimes be particularly galling to well-established business firms including well-known multinationals. But the record of some multinationals and their unequal power in dealing with the more vulnerable countries have left grounds for much suspicion, even though such suspicion may be quite misplaced in many cases. Establishing high standards of business ethics is certainly one way of tackling this problem.

There is also, in many Third World countries, a traditional lack of confidence in the moral behavior of particular groups of traders, for example merchants of food grains. This is a subject on which—in the context of the then- Europe—Adam Smith himself commented substantially in *The Wealth of Nations,* though he thought these suspicions were by and large unjustified. In fact, the empirical record on this is quite diverse, and particular experiences of grain trade in conditions of scarcity and famine have left many questions to be answered.

This is an issue of extreme seriousness, since it is now becoming increasingly clear that typically the best way of organizing famine prevention and relief is to create additional incomes for the destitute (possibly through employment schemes) and then to rely on normal trade to meet (through standard arrangements of transport and sales) the resulting food demand.[6] The alternative of bureaucratic distribution of food in hastily organized relief camps is often much slower, more wasteful, seriously disruptive of family life and normal economic operations, and more conducive to the spread of epidemic diseases. However, giving a crucial role to the grain traders at times of famine threats (as a complement to state-organized employment schemes to generate income) raises difficult issues of trust and trustworthiness, in particular, that the traders will not manipulate the precarious situation in search of unusual profit. The issue of business ethics, thus, becomes an altogether vital part of the arrangement of famine prevention and relief.

The problem can be, to some extent, dealt with by skillful use of the threat of government intervention in the market. But the credibility of that threat depends greatly on the size of grain reserves the government itself has. It can work well in some cases (generally it has in India), but not always. Ultimately, much depends on the extent to which the relevant business people can establish exacting standards of behavior, rather than fly off in search of unusual profits to be rapidly extracted from manipulated situations.

I have been discussing problems of organization in exchange, and it would seem to be right to conclude this particular discussion by noting that the need for business ethics is quite strong even in the field of exchange (despite the near-universal presence of the butcher-brewer-baker motivation of "regard to their own interest"). If we now move on from exchange to production and distribution, the need for business ethics becomes even more forceful and perspicuous. The issue of trust is central to all economic operations. But we now have to consider other problems of interrelation in the process of production and distribution.

4. Organization of Production: Firms and Public Goods

Capitalism has been successful enough in generating output and raising productivity. But the experiences of different countries are quite diverse. The recent experiences of Eastern Asian economies—most notably Japan—raise deep questions about the modeling of capitalism on traditional economic theory. Japan is often seen—rightly in a particular sense—as a great example of successful capitalism, but it is clear that the motivation patterns that dominate Japanese business have much more content than would be provided by pure profit maximization.

Different commentators have emphasized distinct aspects of Japanese motivational features. Michio Morishima has outlined the special characteristics of "Japanese ethos" as emerging from its particular history of rule-based behavior pattern.[7] Ronald Dore has seen the influence of "Confucian ethics."[8] Recently, Eiko Ikegami has pointed to the importance of the traditional concern with "honor"—a kind of generalization of the Samurai code—as a crucial modifier of business and economic motivation.[9]

Indeed, there is some truth, oddly enough, even in the puzzlingly witty claim made by *The Wall Street Journal* that Japan is "the only communist nation that works" (30 January 1989, p. 1). It is, as one would expect, mainly a remark about the non-profit motivations underlying many economic and business activities in Japan. We have to understand and interpret the peculiar fact that the most successful capitalist nation in the world flourishes economically with a motivation structure that departs firmly—and often explicitly—from the pursuit of self-interest, which is meant to be the bedrock of capitalism.

In fact, Japan does not, by any means, provide the only example of a powerful role of business ethics in promoting capitalist success. The productive merits of selfless work and devotion to enterprise have been given much credit for economic achievements in many countries in the world. Indeed, the need of capitalism for a motivational structure more complex than pure profit maximization has been acknowledged in various forms, over a long time, by various social scientists (though typically not by any "mainstream" economists): I have in mind Marx, Weber, Tawney, and others.[10] The basic point about the observed success of non-profit motives is neither unusual nor new, even though that wealth of historical and conceptual insights is often thoroughly ignored in professional economics today.

It is useful to try to bring the discussion in line with Adam Smith's concerns, and also with the general analytical approaches successfully developed in modern microeconomic theory. In order to understand how motives other than self-seeking can have an important role, we have to see the limited reach of the butcher-brewer-baker argument, especially in dealing with what modern economists call "public good." This becomes particularly relevant because the overall success of a modern enterprise is, in a very real sense, a public good.

But what *is* a public good? That idea can be best understood by contrasting it with a "private good," such as a toothbrush or a shirt or an apple, which either you can use or I, but not both. Our respective uses would compete and be exclusive. This is not so with public goods, such as a livable environment or the absence of epidemics. All of us may benefit from breathing fresh air, living in an epidemic-free environment, and so on. When uses of commodities are non-competitive, as in the case of public goods, the rationale of the self-interest-based market mechanism comes under severe strain. The market system works by putting a price on a commodity and the allocation between consumers is done by the intensities of the respective willingness to buy it at the prevailing price. When "equilibrium prices" emerge, they balance demand with supply for each commodity. In contrast, in the case of public goods, the uses are—largely or entirely—non-competitive, and the system of giving a good to the highest bidder does not have much merit, since one person's consumption does not exclude that of another. Instead, optimum resource allocation would require that the *combined* benefits be compared with the costs of production, and here the market mechanism, based on profit maximization, functions badly.[11]

A related problem concerns the allocation of private goods involving strong "externalities," with interpersonal interdependencies working outside the markets. If the smoke from a factory makes a neighbor's home dirty and unpleasant, without the neighbor being able to charge the factory owner for the loss she suffers, then that is an "external" relation. The market does not help in this case, since it is not there to allocate the effects—good or bad— that work outside the market.[12] Public goods and externalities are related phenomena, and they are both quite common in such fields as public health care, basic education, environmental protection, and so on.

There are two important issues to be addressed in this context, in analysing the organization and performance of production. First, there would tend to be some failure in resource allocation when the commodities produced are public goods or involve strong externalities. This can be taken either (1) as an argument for having *publicly owned enterprises,* which would be governed by principles other than profit maximization, or (2) as a case for *public regulations* governing private enterprise, or (3) as establishing a need for the use of non-profit values—particularly of *social concern*—in private decisions (perhaps because of the goodwill that it might generate). Since public enterprises have not exactly covered themselves with glory in the recent years, and public regulations—while useful—are sometimes quite hard to implement, the third option has become more important in public discussions. It is difficult, in this context, to escape the argument for encouraging business ethics, going well beyond the traditional values of honesty and reliability, and taking on social responsibility as well (for example, in matters of environmental degradation and pollution).

The second issue is more complex and less recognized in the literature, but also more interesting. Even in the production of private commodities, there can be an important "public good" aspect in the production process itself. This is because production itself is typically a joint activity, supervisions are costly and often unfeasible, and each participant contributes to the overall success of the firm in a way that cannot be fully reflected in the private rewards that he or she gets.

The over-all success of the firm, thus, is really a public good, from which all benefit, to which all contribute, and which is not parcelled out in little boxes of person-specific rewards strictly linked with each person's *respective contribution*. And this is precisely where the motives other than narrow self-seeking become productively important. Even though I do not have the opportunity to pursue the point further here, I do believe that the successes of "Japanese ethos," "Confucian ethics," "Samurai codes of honor," etc., can be fruitfully linked to this aspect of the organization of production.

5. The Challenge of Distribution: Values and Incentives

I turn now to distribution. It is not hard to see that non-self-seeking motivations can be extremely important for *distributional* problems in general. In dividing a cake, one person's gain is another's loss. At a very obvious level, the contributions that can be made by ethics—business ethics and others—include the amelioration of misery through policies explicitly aimed at such a result. There is an extensive literature on donations, charity, and philanthropy in general, and also on the willingness to join in communal activities geared to social improvement. The connection with ethics is obvious enough in these cases.

What is perhaps more interesting to discuss is the fact that distributional and productional problems very often come mixed together, so that how the cake is divided influences the size of the cake itself. The so-called "incentive problem" is a part of this relationship. This too is a much discussed problem,[13] but it is important to clarify in the present context that the extent of the conflict between size and distribution depends crucially on the motivational and behavioral assumptions. The incentive problem is not an immutable feature of production technology. For example, the more narrowly profit-oriented an enterprise is, the more it would, in general, tend to resist looking after the interests of others—workers, associates, consumers. This is an area in which ethics can make a big difference.

The relevance of all this to the question we have been asked to address ("Does business ethics make economic sense?") does, of course, depend on how "economic sense" is defined. If economic sense includes the achievement of a good society in which one lives, then the distributional improvements can be counted in as parts of sensible outcomes even for business. Visionary industrialists and businesspersons have tended to encourage this line of reasoning.

On the other hand, if "economic sense" is interpreted to mean nothing other than achievement of profits and business rewards, then the concerns for others and for distributional equity have to be judged entirely instrumentally—in terms of how they indirectly help to promote profits. That connection is not to be scoffed at, since firms that treat its workers well are often very richly rewarded for it. For one thing, the workers are then more reluctant to lose their jobs, since more would be sacrificed if dismissed from this (more lucrative) employment, compared with alternative opportunities. The contribution of goodwill to team spirit and thus to productivity can also be quite plentiful.

We have then an important contrast between two different ways in which good business behavior could make economic sense. One way is to see the improvement of the society in which one lives as a reward in itself; this works directly. The other is to use ultimately a business criterion for improvement, but to take note of the extent to which good business behavior could in its turn lead to favorable business performance; this enlightened self-interest involves an indirect reasoning.

It is often hard to disentangle the two features, but in understanding whether or how business ethics make economic sense, we have to take note of each feature. If, for example, a business firm pays inadequate attention to the safety of its workers, and this results accidentally in a disastrous tragedy, like the one that happened in Bhopal in India some years ago (though I am not commenting at present on the extent to which Union Carbide was in fact negligent there), that event would be harmful both for the firm's profits and for the general objectives of social well-being in which the firm may be expected to take an interest. The two effects are distinct and separable and should act cumulatively in an overall consequential analysis. Business ethics has to relate to both.

6. A Concluding Remark

I end with a brief recapitulation of some of the points discussed, even though I shall not attempt a real summary. First, the importance of business ethics is not contradicted in any way by Adam Smith's pointer to the fact that our "regards to our own interest" provide adequate motivation for exchange (section 2). Smith's butcher-brewer-baker argument is concerned (1) directly with *exchanges* only (not production or distribution), and (2) only with the *motivational aspect* of exchange (not its organizational and behavioral aspects).

Second, business ethics can be crucially important in economic organization in general and in exchange operations in particular. This relationship is extensive and fairly ubiquitous, but it is particularly important, at this time, for the development efforts of the Third World and the reorganizational attempts in what used to be the Second World (section 3).

Third, the importance of business ethics in the arrangement and performance of production can be illustrated by the contrasting experiences of different economies, e.g., Japan's unusual success. The advantages of going beyond the pure pursuit of profit can be understood in different ways. To some extent, this question relates to the failure of profit-based market allocation in dealing with "public goods." This is relevant in two different ways:

(1) the presence of public goods (and of the related phenomenon of externalities) in the commodities produced (e.g., environmental connections), and (2) the fact that the success of the firm can itself be fruitfully seen as a public good (section 4).

Finally, distributional problems—broadly defined—are particularly related to behavioral ethics. The connections can be both direct and valuational, and also indirect and instrumental. The interrelations between the size of the cake and its distribution increase the reach and relevance of ethical behavior, e.g., through the incentive problem (section 5).

Notes

1. Lamont University Professor, and Professor of Economics and Philosophy, at Harvard University.
2. Stephen Leacock, *Hellements of Hickonomics* (New York: Dodd, Mead & Co., 1936), p. 75.
3. Adam Smith, *An Inquiry into the Nature and Causes of the Wealth of Nations* (1776; republished, London: Dent, 1910), vol. I, p. 13.
4. Adam Smith, *The Theory of Moral Sentiments* (revised edition, 1790; reprinted, Oxford: Clarendon Press, 1976), p. 189.
5. On this and related manners, see my *On Ethics and Economics* (Oxford: Blackwell, 1987); Patricia H. Werhane, *Adam Smith and His Legacy for Modern Capitalism* (New York: Oxford University Press, 1991); Emma Rothschild, "Adam Smith and Conservative Economics," *Economic History Review*, 45 (1992).
6. On this see Jean Drèze and Amartya Sen, *Hunger and Public Action* (Oxford: Clarendon Press, 1989).
7. Michio Morishima, *Why Has Japan 'Succeeded'? Western Technology and Japanese Ethos* (Cambridge: Cambridge University Press, 1982).
8. Ronald Dore, "Goodwill and the Spirit of Market Capitalism," *British Journal of Sociology*, 34 (1983), and *Taking Japan Seriously: A Confucian Perspective on Leading Economic Issues* (Stanford: Stanford University Press, 1987).
9. Eiko Ikegami, "The Logic of Cultural Change: Honor, State-Making, and the Samurai," mimeographed, Department of Sociology, Yale University, 1991.
10. Karl Marx (with F. Engels), *The German Ideology* (1845–46, English translation, New York: International Publishers, 1947); Richard Henry Tawney, *Religion and the Rise of Capitalism* (London: Murray, 1926); Max Weber, *The Protestant Ethic and the Spirit of Capitalism* (London: Allen & Unwin, 1930).
11. The classic treatment of public goods was provided by Paul A. Samuelson, "The Pure Theory of Public Expenditure," *Review of Economics and Statistics*, 35 (1954).
12. For a classic treatment of external effects, see A. C. Pigou, *The Economics of Welfare* (London: Macmillan, 1920). There are many different ways of defining "externalities," with rather disparate bearings on policy issues; on this see the wide-ranging critical work of Andreas Papandreou (*Jr.*, I should add to avoid an ambiguity, though I don't believe he uses that clarification), *Ideas of Externality*, to be published by Clarendon Press, Oxford, and Oxford University Press, New York.
13. A good general review of the literature can be found in A. B. Atkinson and J. E. Stiglitz, *Lectures on Public Economics* (New York: McGraw-Hill, 1980). On the conceptual and practical importance of the incentive problem and other sources of potential conflict between efficiency and equity, see my *Inequality Reexamined* (Cambridge, MA: Harvard University Press, 1992), Chapter 9.

PART ONE

General Issues in Ethics
Introduction

- As the newly appointed controller of a small family-held company, you are asked to approve a year-end financial statement that does not accurately represent the company's finances. The external auditors have approved the financial statement package. What should you do?
- If you were operating a branch of a U.S. company in a foreign country, would you follow that country's tax procedures if they conflicted with procedures in the United States and even required falsifying earnings reports?
- Suppose you were a manager of a corporation doing business in a country where bribery and extortion were acceptable practices in getting business contracts. Would you participate in that activity? Would you condone such activities in your foreign national managers?
- As an account executive, you think that one of the advertisements for which you are responsible presents misleading information about the product. Would you request a change in the advertisement?
- In seeking employment do you always tell the whole truth in an interview? Does your resume accurately represent yourself, even your weaknesses?

Each of these vignettes is drawn from an actual business situation, and, in fact, such incidents occur more frequently than one might expect. Understanding their ethical implications requires not only an awareness of concrete situations but also the ability to subsume business problems under categories of more general ethical concern. The philosophical material in Part One introduces two traditional ethical concerns: truth telling and virtue. Stated as questions, these concerns are as follows:

Truth telling: What obligations, if any, exist for individuals and organizations to communicate honestly? When, if ever, is not telling the truth justified?

Virtue: What role does personal character play in commercial activity? Does it make sense to talk about the virtuous manager, or is virtue an outmoded concept?

Truth Telling

The concept of truth telling can be used to investigate a wide variety of issues, including those relating to nondeceptive advertising, the accuracy of consumer information, and the responsibilities a business has to communicate honestly with its employees and stockholders. A philosopher well known for his vigorous defense of truth telling is the eighteenth-century German philosopher Immanuel Kant. In this section, selections from his *Lectures on Ethics* are presented in which Kant claims that truth telling is an essential feature of morally right communication. Kant equates honesty with both frankness and reserve and supports the principle of never telling a lie on three grounds. First, the principle of truth telling is one which each of us would like everyone else to follow. In other words, it is a principle that philosophers call "universalizable," meaning that each of us would like to see it universally followed by all human beings. Second, truth telling is a necessary element for society because all societies depend on mutual bonds of honesty and truthfulness to enforce their unity and orderly continuation. Finally, lying undermines one of the major sources of human development—knowledge acquisition—since, without underlying trust in the veracity of research, experimentation, reporting, and fact-gathering, it would be impossible to discover or evaluate truth claims in any field. Kant's famous example of an enemy trying to extort information challenges us to wonder whether there are extreme cases where it is morally permissible to lie. Kant argues that lies in these cases are not violations of trust between oneself and the enemy, since such an understanding does not exist. Nevertheless, even lying to an enemy violates a universal principle. It is "contrary to the general right of mankind" not to be deceived.

Questioning Kant's strict prohibitions on lying, Albert Carr, in his lively article, "Is Business Bluffing Ethical?" suggests that the moral requirement of telling the truth depends on the context in which the activity takes place. For example, in advertising, although few advertisers lie about their products, most engage in puffery or make unfair comparisons between their products and the competition. This is all right, according to Carr, because everyone understands the "game" of advertising, and no one is really fooled by the claims.

Similarly, according to Carr, in applying for a job, one does not tell a prospective employer all of one's past, nor detail one's weaknesses. It is part of the "game" of the hiring process and full disclosure is not expected nor warranted. Hiring is a form of negotiation, and like other negotiating practices in business the "game" is more akin to poker than to full disclosure. Because perfect market information, or in Kantian terms, the whole truth, is never obtainable, market imperfections are often to the advantage of business. Moreover, it is not always to the economic advantage of business to reveal the "whole truth" about a product or service, and it is often unprofitable not to engage in competitive bluffing in bargaining processes when other businesses are doing so.

Despite Carr's persuasive arguments, many advertisers as well as other business persons and philosophers are worried about the impact of the "game" analogy in business, and in particular its effect on those of us not "playing the game" or unaware of its rules. Is bluffing or puffery justified when some persons affected by them do not understand the game and are deceived or misled? Moreover, as Joseph Betz points out, business is part of our social life. Businesses cannot exist or thrive except in communities, thus the basic moral standards of those communities apply to business dealings as well. The convention of truth telling and the standard of trust are part of basic community mores. To question those conventions and standards is to separate business from the community and to invite regulation and restriction.

Focusing on the phenomena of bargaining and negotiation, Peter Cramton and J. Gregory Dees make a sustained argument that deception in negotiations, while practiced and often encouraged, is neither the right way to conduct business, on Kantian grounds, nor is such behavior in the self-interest of the bargainers. Cramton and Dees create a mythical community, Metopia, where people are self-centered, where they try only to act in their self-interests and seek only to maximize their own personal welfare. Even there, Cramton and Dees show, the reputation for honesty, truth-telling, and trust are in the self-interest of Metopians. In an ordinary society in which most of us are not merely self-centered, deception is even more destructive and reprehensible.

If Carr's game analogy is questionable in bargaining, negotiation, and advertising, the reader might want to consider its application to other aspects of business. Does the analogy ever justify making an exception to Kant's dictum that one should never lie? The case study "Italian Tax Mores" presents a situation in which truth telling, as well as relativism, are major issues. The case concerns an American executive managing a branch of a U.S. bank in Italy, who finds that typical Italian practices at that time encourage actions that he believes constitute both bribery and lying. Is it morally acceptable to misrepresent the bank's income tax figures if it appears that most other companies in Italy do the same thing, and if truth telling will do harm to the bank? As a matter of self-defense, should the executive "play the game" and adopt the practices of the Italian tax system when those practices involve outright lying? Or, can the manager justify providing the truth to the Italian tax authorities even when this might threaten the short-term well-being of his bank?

Virtues and the Virtuous Manager

Despite the individual managerial locus of decision making in business, it is often this individual—the individual manager—and his or her values and character, that are ignored in business ethics. In an age in which technological systems and complex organizational structures dominate business activity, what role can the integrity of the individual manager play? Large conglomerates, transnational corporations, and worldwide trading systems appear to mask the importance of the single business person, even though he or she is the final focal point of all business activities.

Finding inspiration in the philosophy of the ancient Greek thinker, Aristotle, Robert Solomon argues in "Corporate Roles, Personal Virtues: An Aristotelean Approach to Business Ethics" that individual character and virtue do matter in business. He asserts that the personal and community aspects of business are no less relevant today than they wee centuries ago. To neglect personal virtues, in turn, is to condemn business ethics to sterile irrelevance. In so doing, he reflects the late-twentieth-century trend toward what has been called "virtue ethics." Solomon's approach, however, is not merely an exposition of personal virtues that, ideally, every manager should exemplify. Solomon recognizes that each of us develops out of a set of communities, so who we are is created from and found only within a community or society. Solomon then locates the manager within the community of the corporation, which in turn is part of a larger set of communities: the local community, culture, the state, and, ultimately, the world. Thus, the Aristotelean virtues Solomon expounds are community, excellence, role identity, holism, integrity, and judgment, all virtues that involve relationships with others and with communities.

Solomon lays out a matrix for managerial moral excellence that takes into account the moral community of business. This approach has been criticized as being too contextual because it does not provide a moral framework for evaluating role responsibilities, excellence, business judgments, or community values; such evaluations are usually made from a Kantian, utilitarian, or human rights perspective. But Solomon's project may be of a different order. He is not merely extolling managerial virtues; he is also challenging each of us to rethink the way in which we often depict business as a separate, morally mute, community-independent enterprise of self-interested managers and entrepreneurs.

This view of business as morally "mute" is illustrated by Robert Jackall, who decries the hypocrisy of modern management culture. Jackall's research suggests that the connection between excellence of work and reward has become more capricious. The moral virtues, if they ever existed or were extolled in business, have been replaced by bureaucratic conventions in which loyalties and alliances, patronage, luck, and the ability to outrun one's mistakes contribute to managerial success. The problem is serious, writes Jackall, in that many men and women no longer see success as necessarily connected to excellence. The Protestant work ethic, characterized by self-reliance and devotion to work, has been replaced by administrative hierarchies, standardized work procedures, regularized timetables, uniform policies, office politics, and centralized control. It all adds up, believes Jackall, to office political games and the capriciousness of success. The result is what Jackall calls "the bureaucratic ethic," an "ethic" that belies what Solomon believes to be the exemplification of the Aristotelian virtues of managerial excellence. Solomon's challenge, then, is to reformulate managerial thinking in terms of managerial and corporate excellence, integrity, and civic virtue that will avoid what Jackall depicts as downsides to modern management and the contemporary business enterprise.

Truth Telling

— *Case Study* —

Italian Tax Mores

Arthur L. Kelly

The Italian federal corporate tax system has an official, legal tax structure and tax rates just as the U.S. system does. However, all similarity between the two systems ends there.

The Italian tax authorities assume that no Italian corporation would ever submit a tax return which shows its true profits but rather would submit a return which understates actual profits by anywhere between 30 percent and 70 percent; their assumption is essentially correct. Therefore, about six months after the annual deadline for filing corporate tax returns, the tax authorities issue to each corporation an "invitation to discuss" its tax return. The purpose of this notice is to arrange a personal meeting between them and representatives of the corporation. At this meeting, the Italian revenue service states the amount of corporate income tax which it believes is due. Its position is developed from both prior years' taxes actually paid and the current year's return; the amount which the tax authorities claim is due is generally several times that shown on the corporation's return for the current year. In short, the corporation's tax return and the revenue service's stated position are the opening offers for the several rounds of bargaining which will follow.

The Italian corporation is typically represented in such negotiations by its *commercialista,* a function which exists in Italian society for the primary purpose of negotiating corporate (and individual) tax payments with the Italian tax authorities; thus, the management of an Italian corporation seldom, if ever, has to meet directly with the Italian revenue service and probably has a minimum awareness of the details of the negotiation other than the final settlement.

Both the final settlement and the negotiation are extremely important to the corporation, the tax authorities, and the *commercialista.* Since the tax authorities assume that a corporation *always* earned more money this year than last year and *never* has a loss, the amount of the final settlement, i.e., corporate taxes which will actually be paid, becomes, for all practical

This case, based on an actual occurrence, was prepared by Arthur L. Kelly and was first presented at Loyola University in Chicago in April 1977 at a Mellon Foundation Symposium entitled "Foundations of Corporate Responsibility to Society." Mr. Kelly has served as Vice President–International of the management consulting firm A. T. Kearney, Inc., and as President of LaSalle Steel Company, and he is currently Managing Partner of KEL Enterprises Ltd., a Chicago holding and investment company. He serves as a member of the Board of Directors of corporations in the United States and Europe, including Deere & Company and BMW A.G.

purposes, the floor for the start of next year's negotiations. The final settlement also represents the amount of revenue the Italian government will collect in taxes to help finance the cost of running the country. However, since large amounts of money are involved and two individuals having vested personal interests are conducting the negotiations, the amount of *bustarella*—typically a substantial cash payment "requested" by the Italian revenue agent from the *commercialista*—usually determines whether the final settlement is closer to the corporation's original tax return or to the fiscal authority's original negotiating position.

Whatever *bustarella* is paid during the negotiation is usually included by the *commercialista* in his lump-sum fee "for services rendered" to his corporate client. If the final settlement is favorable to the corporation, and it is the *commercialista's* job to see that it is, then the corporation is not likely to complain about the amount of its *commercialista's* fee, nor will it ever know how much of that fee was represented by *bustarella* and how much remained for the *commercialista* as payment for his negotiating services. In any case, the tax authorities will recognize the full amount of the fee as a tax deductible expense on the corporation's tax return for the following year.

About ten years ago, a leading American bank opened a banking subsidiary in a major Italian city. At the end of its first year of operation, the bank was advised by its local lawyers and tax accountants, both from branches of U.S. companies, to file its tax return "Italian-style," i.e., to understate its actual profits by a significant amount. The American general manager of the bank, who was on his first overseas assignment, refused to do so both because he considered it dishonest and because it was inconsistent with the practices of his parent company in the United States.

About six months after its "American-style" tax return, the bank received an "invitation to discuss" notice for the Italian tax authorities. The bank's general manager consulted with his lawyers and tax accountants who suggested he hire a *commercialista*. He rejected this advice and instead wrote a letter to the Italian revenue service not only stating that his firm's corporate return was correct as filed but also requesting that they inform him of any specific items about which they had questions. His letter was never answered.

About sixty days after receiving the initial "invitation to discuss" notice, the bank received a formal tax assessment notice calling for a tax of approximately three times that shown on the bank's corporate tax return; the tax authorities simply assumed the bank's original return had been based on generally accepted Italian practices, and they reacted accordingly. The bank's general manager again consulted with his lawyers and tax accountants who again suggested he hire a *commercialista* who knew how to handle these matters. Upon learning that the *commercialista* would probably have to pay *bustarella* to his revenue service counterpart in order to reach a settlement, the general manager again chose to ignore his advisors. Instead, he responded by sending the Italian revenue service a check for the full amount of taxes due according to the bank's American-style tax return even though the due date for the payment was almost six months hence; he made no reference to the amount of corporate taxes shown on the formal tax assessment notice.

Ninety days after paying its taxes, the bank received a third notice form the fiscal authorities. This one contained the statement, "We have reviewed

your corporate tax return of 19__ and have determined that [the lira equivalent of] \$6,000,000 of interest paid on deposits is not an allowable expense for federal tax purposes. Accordingly, the total tax due for 19__ is lira ____."
Since interest paid on deposits is any bank's largest single expense item, the new tax assessment was for an amount many times larger than that shown in the initial tax assessment notice and almost fifteen times larger than the taxes which the bank had actually paid.

The bank's general manager was understandably very upset. He immediately arranged an appointment to meet personally with the manager of the Italian revenue service's local office. Shortly after the start of their meeting, the conversation went something like this:

> General Manager: "You can't really be serious about disallowing interest paid on deposits as a tax deductible expense."

> Italian Revenue Service: "Perhaps. However, we thought it would get your attention. Now that you're here, shall we begin our negotiations?"[1]

Note

1. For readers interested in what happened subsequently, the bank was forced to pay the taxes shown in the initial tax assessment, and the American manager was recalled to the United States and replaced.

Ethical Duties Towards Others: "Truthfulness"

IMMANUEL KANT

The exchange of our sentiments is the principal factor in social intercourse, and truth must be the guiding principle herein. Without truth social intercourse and conversation become valueless. We can only know what a man thinks if he tells us his thoughts, and when he undertakes to express them he must really do so, or else there can be no society of men. Fellowship is only the second condition of society, and a liar destroys fellowship. Lying makes it impossible to derive any benefit from conversation. Liars are, therefore, held in general contempt. Man is inclined to be reserved and to pretend. . . . Man is reserved in order to conceal his faults and shortcomings which he has; he pretends in order to make others attribute to him merits and virtues which he has not. Our proclivity to reserve and concealment is due to the will of Providence that the defects of which we are full should not be too obvious. Many of our propensities and peculiarities are objectionable to others, and if they became patent we should be foolish and hateful in their eyes. Moreover, the parading of these objectionable characteristics would so familiarize men with them that they would themselves acquire them. Therefore we arrange our conduct either to conceal our faults or to

From *Lectures on Ethics,* trans. Louis Infield (London: Methuen, 1930) rpt. Harper & Row, 1963. Pp. 224–35. Reprinted by permission of the publisher.

appear other than we are. We possess the art of simulation. In consequence, our inner weakness and error is revealed to the eyes of men only as an appearance of well-being, while we ourselves develop the habit of dispositions which are conducive to good conduct. No man in his true senses, therefore, is candid. Were man candid, were the request of Momus[1] to be complied with that Jupiter should place a mirror in each man's heart so that his disposition might be visible to all, man would have to be better constituted and possess good principles. If all men were good there would be no need for any of us to be reserved; but since they are not, we have to keep the shutters closed. Every house keeps its dustbin in a place of its own. We do not press our friends to come into our water-closet, although they know that we have one just like themselves. Familiarity in such things is the ruin of good taste. In the same way we make no exhibition of our defects, but try to conceal them. We try to conceal our mistrust by affecting a courteous demeanor and so accustom ourselves to courtesy that at last it becomes a reality and we set a good example by it. If that were not so, if there were none who were better than we, we should become neglectful. Accordingly, the endeavour to appear good ultimately makes us really good. If all men were good, they could be candid, but as things are they cannot be. To be reserved is to be restrained in expressing one's mind. We can, of course, keep absolute silence. This is the readiest and most absolute method of reserve, but it is unsociable, and a silent man is not only unwanted in social circles but is also suspected; every one thinks him deep and disparaging, for if when asked for his opinion he remains silent people think that he must be taking the worst view or he would not be averse from expressing it. Silence, in fact, is always a treacherous ally, and therefore it is not even prudent to be completely reserved. Yet there is such a thing as prudent reserve, which requires not silence but careful deliberation; a man who is wisely reserved weighs his words carefully and speaks his mind about everything excepting only those things in regard to which he deems it wise to be reserved.

We must distinguish between reserve and secretiveness, which is something entirely different. There are matters about which one has no desire to speak and in regard to which reserve is easy. We are, for instance, not naturally tempted to speak about and to betray our own misdemeanours. Everyone finds it easy to keep a reserve about some of his private affairs, but there are times about which it requires an effort to be silent. Secrets have a way of coming out, and strength is required to prevent ourselves betraying them. Secrets are always matters deposited with us by other people and they ought not to be placed at the disposal of third parties. But man has a great liking for conversation, and the telling of secrets adds much to the interest of conversation; a secret told is like a present given; how then are we to keep secrets? Men who are not very talkative as a rule keep secrets well, but good conversationalists, who are at the same time clever, keep them better. The former might be induced to betray something, but the latter's gift of repartee invariably enables them to invent on the spur of the moment something non-committal.

The person who is as silent as a mute goes to one extreme; the person who is loquacious goes to the opposite. Both tendencies are weaknesses. Men are liable to the first, women to the second. Someone has said that women are talkative because the training of infants is their special charge, and their talkativeness soon teaches a child to speak, because they can chatter to it all day long. If men had the care of the child, they would take much longer to learn to talk. However that may be, we dislike anyone who will not speak: he annoys us; his silence betrays his pride. On the other hand, loquaciousness in men is contemptible and contrary to the strength of the male. All this by the way; we shall now pass to more weighty matters.

If I announce my intention to tell what is in my mind, ought I knowingly to tell everything, or can I keep anything back? If I indicate that I mean to speak my mind, and instead of doing so make false declaration, what I say is an untruth, a *falsiloquium*. But there can be *falsiloquium* even when people have no right to assume that we are expressing our thoughts. It is possible to deceive without making any statement whatever. I can make believe, make a demonstration from which others will draw the conclusion I want, though they have no right to expect that my action will express my real mind. In that case I have not lied to them, because I had not undertaken to express my mind. I may, for instance, wish people to think that I am off on a journey, and so I pack my luggage; people draw the conclusion I want them to draw; but others have no right to demand a declaration of my will from me.

. . . Again, I may make a false statement (*falsiloquium*), when my purpose is to hide from another what is in my mind and when the latter can assume that such is my purpose, his own purpose being to make a wrong use of the truth. Thus, for instance, if my enemy takes me by the throat and asks where I keep my money, I need not tell him the truth, because he will abuse it; and my untruth is not a lie (*mendacium*) because the thief knows full well that I will not, if I can help it, tell him the truth and that he has no right to demand it of me. But let us assume that I really say to the fellow, who is fully aware that he has no right to demand it, because he is a swindler, that I will tell him the truth, and I do not, am I then a liar? He has deceived me and I deceive him in return; to him, as an individual, I have done no injustice and he cannot complain; but I am none the less a liar in that my conduct is an infringement of the rights of humanity. It follows that a *falsiloquium* can be a *mendacium*—a lie—especially when it contravenes the right of an individual. Although I do a man no injustice by lying to him when he has lied to me, yet I act against the right of mankind, since I set myself in opposition to the condition and means through which any human society is possible. If one country breaks the peace this does not justify the other in doing likewise in revenge, for if it did no peace would ever be secure. Even though a statement does not contravene any particular human right it is nevertheless a lie if it is contrary to the general right of mankind. If a man spreads false news, though he does no wrong to anyone in particular, he offends against mankind, because if such a practice were universal man's desire for knowledge would be frustrated. For, apart from speculation, there are only two ways in which I can increase my fund of knowledge, by experience or by what others tell me. My own experience must necessarily be limited, and if what others told me was false, I could not satisfy my craving for knowledge.

. . . Not every untruth is a lie; it is a lie only if I have expressly given the other to understand that I am willing to acquaint him with my thought. Every lie is objectionable and contemptible in that we purposely let people think that we are telling them our thoughts and do not do so. We have broken our pact and violated the right of mankind. But if we were to be at all times punctiliously truthful we might often become victims of the wickedness of others who were ready to abuse our truthfulness. If all men were well-intentioned it would not only be a duty not to lie, but no one would do so because there would be no point in it. But as men are malicious, it cannot be denied that to be punctiliously truthful is often dangerous. This has given rise to the conception of a white lie, the lie enforced upon us by necessity—a difficult point for moral philosophers. For if necessity is urged as an excuse it might be urged to justify stealing, cheating and killing, and the whole basis of morality goes by the board. Then, again, what is a case of necessity? Everyone will interpret it in his own way. And, as there is then no definite standard to judge by, the application of moral rules becomes uncertain. Consider, for example, the following case. A man who knows that I have money asks me: "Have you any money on you?" If I fail to reply, he will conclude that I have; if I reply in the affirmative he will take it from me; if I reply in the negative, I tell a lie. What am I to do? If force is used to extort a confession from me, if any confession is improperly used against me, and if I cannot save myself by maintaining silence, then my lie is a weapon of defence. The misuse of a declaration extorted by force justifies me in defending myself. For whether it is my money or a confession that is extorted makes no difference. The forcing of a statement from me under conditions which convince me that improper use would be made of it is the only case in which I can be justified in telling a white lie. But if a lie does no harm to anyone and no one's interests are affected by it, is it a lie? Certainly, I undertake to express my mind, and if I do not really do so, though my statement may not be to the prejudice of the particular individual to whom it was made, it is none the less in *praejudicium humanitatis*. Then, again, there are lies which cheat. To cheat is to make a lying promise, while a breach of faith is a true promise which is not kept. A lying promise is an insult to the person to whom it is made, and even if this is not always so, yet there is always something mean about it. If, for instance, I promise to send some one a bottle of wine, and afterwards make a joke of it, I really swindle him. It is true that he had no right to demand the present of me, but in Idea it is already a part of his own property.

. . . If a man tries to extort the truth from us and we cannot tell it [to] him and at the same time do not wish to lie, we are justified in resorting to equivocation in order to reduce him to silence and put a stop to his questionings. If he is wise, he will leave it at that. But if we let it be understood that we are expressing our sentiments and we proceed to equivocate we are in a different case; for our listeners might then draw wrong conclusions from our statements and we should have deceived them. . . . But a lie is a lie, and is in itself intrinsically base whether it be told with good or bad intent. For formally a lie is always evil; though if it is evil materially as well, it is a much meaner thing. There are no lies which may not be the source of evil. A liar is a coward; he is a man who has recourse to lying because he is unable to help himself and gain his ends by any other means. But a stout-hearted man will love truth and will not recognize a *casus necessitatis*. All expedients which take us off our guard are thoroughly mean. Such are lying, assassination, and poisoning. To attack a man on the highway is less vile than to attempt to poison him. In the former case he can at least defend himself, but, as he must eat, he is defenseless against the poisoner. A flatterer is not always a liar; he is merely lacking in self-esteem; he has no scruple in reducing his own worth and raising that of another in order to gain something by it. But there exists a form of flattery which springs from kindness of heart. Some kind souls flatter people whom they hold in high esteem. There are thus two kinds of flattery, kindly and treacherous; the first is weak, while the second is mean. People who are not given to flattery are apt to be fault-finders.

If a man is often the subject of conversation, he becomes a subject of criticism. If he is our friend, we ought not invariably to speak well of him or else we arouse jealousy and grudge against him; for people, knowing that he is only human, will not believe that he has only good qualities. We must, therefore, concede a little to the adverse criticism of our listeners and point out some of our friend's faults; if we allow him faults which are common and unessential, while extolling his merits, our friend cannot take it in ill part. Toadies are people who praise others in company in hope of gain. Men are meant to form opinions regarding their fellows and to judge them. Nature has made us judges of our neighbors so that things which are false but are outside the scope of the established legal authority should be arraigned before the court of social opinion. Thus, if a man dishonours some one, the authorities do not punish him, but his fellows judge and punish him, though only so far as it is within their right to punish him and without doing violence to him. People shun him, and that is punishment enough. If that were not so, conduct not punished by the authorities would go altogether unpunished. What then is meant by the enjoinder that we ought not to judge others? As we are ignorant of their dispositions we cannot tell whether they are punishable before God or not, and we cannot, therefore, pass an adequate moral judgment upon them. The moral dispositions of others are for God to judge, but we are competent judges of our own. We cannot judge the inner core of morality; no man can do that; but we are competent to judge its outer manifestations. In matters of morality we are not judges of our fellows, but nature has given us the right to form judgments about others and she also has ordained that we should judge ourselves in accordance with judgments that others form about us. The man who turns a deaf ear to other people's opinion of him is base and reprehensible. There is nothing that happens in this world about which we ought not to form an opinion, and we show considerable subtlety in judging conduct. Those who judge our conduct with exactness are our best friends. Only friends can be quite candid and open with each other. But in judging a man a further question arises. In what terms are we to judge him? Must we pronounce him either good or evil? We must proceed from the assumption that humanity is lovable, and, particularly in regard to wickedness, we ought never to pronounce a verdict either of condemnation or of acquittal. We pronounce such a verdict whenever we judge from his conduct that a man deserves to be condemned or acquitted. But though we are entitled to form opinions about our fellows, we have no right to spy upon them. Everyone has a right to prevent others from watching and scrutinizing his actions. The spy arrogates to himself the right to watch the doings of strangers; no one ought to presume to do such a thing. If I see two people whispering to each other so as to not be heard, my inclination ought to be to get farther away so that no sound may reach my ears. Or if I am left alone in a room and I see a letter lying open on the table, it would be contemptible to try to read it; a right-thinking man would not do so; in fact, in order to avoid suspicion and distrust he will endeavour not to be left alone in a room where money is left lying about, and he will be averse from learning other people's secrets in order to avoid the risk of the suspicion that he has betrayed them; other people's secrets trouble him, for even between the most intimate of friends suspicion might arise. A man who will let his inclination or appetite drive him to deprive his friend of anything, of his fiancée, for instance, is contemptible beyond a doubt. If he can cherish a passion for my sweetheart, he can equally well cherish a passion for my purse. It is very mean to lie in wait and spy upon a friend, or on anyone else, and to elicit information about him from menials by lowering ourselves to the level of our inferiors, who will thereafter not forget to regard themselves as our equals. Whatever militates against frankness lowers the dignity of man. Insidious, underhand conduct uses means which strike at the roots of society because they make frankness impossible; it is far viler than violence; for against violence we can defend ourselves, and a violent man who spurns meanness can be tamed to goodness, but the mean rogue, who has not the courage to come out into the open with his roguery, is devoid of every vestige of nobility of character. For that reason a wife who attempts to poison her husband in England is burnt at the stake, for if such conduct spread, no man would be safe from his wife.

As I am not entitled to spy upon my neighbour, I am equally not entitled to point out his faults to him; and even if he should ask me to do so he would feel hurt if I complied. He knows his faults better than I, he knows that he has them, but he likes to believe that I have not noticed them, and if I tell him of them he realizes that I have. To say, therefore, that friends ought to point out each other's faults, is not sound advice. My friend may know better than I whether my gait or deportment is proper or not, but if I will only examine myself, who can know me better than I can know myself? To point out his faults to a friend is sheer impertinence; and once fault finding begins between friends their friendship will not last long. We must turn a blind eye to the faults of others, lest they conclude that they have lost our respect and we lose theirs. Only if placed in positions of authority over others should we point out to them their defects. Thus a husband is entitled to teach and correct his wife, but his corrections must be well-intentioned and kindly and must be dominated by respect, for if they be prompted only by displeasure they result in mere blame and bitterness. If we must blame, we must temper the blame with a sweetening of love, good-will, and respect. Nothing else will avail to bring about improvement.

Note

1. CF. *Babrii fabulae Aesopeae*, ed. O. Cousins, 1897, Fable 59, p. 54.

Is Business Bluffing Ethical?

ALBERT CARR

A respected businessman with whom I discussed the theme of this article re-marked with some heat, "You mean to say you're going to encourage men to bluff? Why, bluffing is nothing more than a form of lying! You're advising them to lie!"

I agreed that the basis of private morality is a respect for truth and that the closer a businessman comes to the truth, the more he deserves respect. At the same time, I suggested that most bluffing in business might be regarded simply as game strategy—much like bluffing in poker, which does not reflect on the morality of the bluffer.

I quoted Henry Taylor, the British statesman who pointed out that "falsehood ceases to be falsehood when it is understood on all sides that the truth is not expected to be spoken"—an exact description of bluffing in poker, diplomacy, and business. I cited the analogy of the criminal court, where the criminal is not expected to tell the truth when he pleads "not guilty." Everyone from the judge down takes it for granted that the job of the defendant's attorney is to get his client off, not to reveal the truth; and this is considered ethical practice. I mentioned Representative Omar Burleson, the Democrat from Texas, who was quoted as saying, in regard to the ethics of Congress, "Ethics is a barrel of worms"[1]—a pungent summing up of the problem of deciding who is ethical in politics.

I reminded my friend that millions of businessmen feel constrained every day to say *yes* to their bosses when they secretly believe *no* and that this is generally accepted as permissible strategy when the alternative might be the loss of a job. The essential point, I said, is that the ethics of business are game ethics, different from the ethics of religion.

He remained unconvinced. Referring to the company of which he is president, he declared: "Maybe that's good enough for some businessmen, but I can tell you that we pride ourselves on our ethics. In 30 years not one customer has ever questioned my word or asked to check our figures. We're loyal to our customers and fair to our suppliers. I regard my handshake on a deal as a contract. I've never entered into price-fixing schemes with my competitors. I've never allowed my salesmen to spread injurious rumors about other companies. Our union contract is the best in our industry. And, if I do say so myself, our ethical standards are of the highest!"

He really was saying, without realizing it, that he was living up to the ethical standards of the business game—which are a far cry from those of private life. Like a gentlemanly poker player, he did not play in cahoots with others at the table, try to smear their reputations, or hold back chips he owed them.

But this same fine man, at that very time, was allowing one of his products to be advertised in a way that made it sound a great deal better than it actually was. Another item in his product line was notorious among dealers for its "built-in-obsolescence." He was holding back from the market a much-improved product because he did not want to interfere with sales of the inferior item it would have replaced. He had joined with certain of his competitors in hiring a lobbyist to push a state legislature, by methods that he preferred not to know too much about, into amending a bill then being enacted.

In his view these things had nothing to do with ethics; they were merely normal business practice. He himself undoubtedly avoided outright false-hood—never lied in so many words. But the entire organization that he ruled was deeply involved in numerous strategies of deception.

Pressure to Deceive

Most executives from time to time are almost compelled, in the interests of their companies or themselves, to practice some form of deception when negotiating with customers, dealers, labor unions, government officials, or even other departments of their companies. By conscious misstatements, concealment of pertinent facts, or exaggeration—in short, by bluffing—they seek to persuade others to agree with them. I think it is fair to say that if the individual executive refuses to bluff from time to time—if he feels ob-ligated to tell the truth, the whole truth, and nothing but the truth—he is ignoring opportunities permitted under the rules and is at a heavy disad-vantage in his business dealings.

But here and there a businessman is unable to reconcile himself to the bluff in which he plays a part. His conscience, perhaps spurred by religious idealism, troubles him. He feels guilty; he may develop an ulcer or a ner-vous tic. Before any executive can make profitable use of the strategy of the bluff, he needs to make sure that in bluffing he will not lose self-respect or become emotionally disturbed. If he is to reconcile personal integrity and high standards of honesty with the practical requirements of business, he must feel that his bluffs are ethically justified. The justification rests on the fact that business, as practiced by individuals as well as by corporations, has the impersonal character of a game—a game that demands both special strategy and an understanding of its special ethics.

The game is played at all levels of corporate life, from the highest to the lowest. At the very instant that a man decides to enter business, he may be forced into a game situation, as is shown by the recent experience of a Cor-nell honor graduate who applied for a job with a large company:

- This applicant was given a psychological test which included the statement, "Of the following magazines, check any that you have read either regularly or from time to time, and double-check those which interest you most. *Reader's Digest, Time, Fortune, Saturday Evening Post, The New Republic, Life, Look, Ram-parts, Newsweek, Business Week, U.S. News & World Report, The Nation, Playboy, Esquire, Harper's, Sports Illustrated.*"

His tastes in reading were broad, and at one time or another he had read almost all of these magazines. He was a subscriber to the *The New Re-public,* an enthusiast for *Ramparts,* and an avid student of the pictures in *Playboy.* He was not sure whether his interest in *Playboy* would be held against him, but he had a shrewd suspicion that if he confessed to an interest in

Ramparts and *The New Republic,* he would be thought a liberal, a radical, or at least an intellectual, and his chances of getting the job, which he needed, would greatly diminish. He therefore checked five of the more conservative magazines. Apparently it was a sound decision, for he got the job.

He had made a game player's decision, consistent with business ethics.

A similar case is that of a magazine space salesman who, owing to a merger, suddenly found himself out of a job:

- This man was 58, and, in spite of a good record, his chances of getting a job elsewhere in a business where youth is favored in hiring practice was not good. He was a vigorous, healthy man, and only a considerable amount of gray in his hair suggested his age. Before beginning his job search he touched up his hair with a black dye to confine the gray to his temples. He knew that the truth about his age might well come out in time, but he calculated that he could deal with that situation when it arose. He and his wife decided that he could easily pass for 45, and he so stated his age on his résumé.

This was a lie; yet within the accepted rules of the business game, no moral culpability attaches to it.

The Poker Analogy

We can learn a good deal about the nature of business by comparing it with poker. While both have a large element of chance, in the long run the winner is the man who plays with steady skill. In both games ultimate victory requires intimate knowledge of the rules, insight into the psychology of the other players, a bold front, a considerable amount of self-discipline and the ability to respond swiftly and effectively to opportunities provided by chance.

No one expects poker to be played on the ethical principles preached in churches. In poker it is right and proper to bluff a friend out of the rewards of being dealt a good hand. A player feels no more than a slight twinge of sympathy, if that, when—with nothing better than a single ace in his hand—he strips a heavy loser, who holds a pair, of the rest of his chips. It was up to the other fellow to protect himself. In the words of an excellent poker player, former President Harry Truman, "If you can't stand the heat, stay out of the kitchen." If one shows mercy to a loser in poker, it is a personal gesture, divorced from the rules of the game.

Poker has its special ethics, and here I am not referring to rules against cheating. The man who keeps an ace up his sleeve or who marks the cards is more than unethical; he is a crook, and can be punished as such—kicked out of the game or, in the Old West, shot.

In contrast to the cheat, the unethical poker player is one who, while abiding by the letter of the rules, finds ways to put the other players at an unfair disadvantage. Perhaps he unnerves them with loud talk. Or he tries to get them drunk. Or he plays in cahoots with someone else at the table. Ethical poker players frown on such tactics.

Poker's own brand of ethics is different from the ethical ideals of civilized human relationships. The game calls for distrust of the other fellow. It ignores the claim of friendship. Cunning deception and concealment of one's strength and intentions, not kindness and openheartedness, are vital in poker. No one thinks any the worse of poker on that account. And no one should think any the worse of the game of business because its standards of right and wrong differ from the prevailing traditions of morality in our society. . . .

We Don't Make the Laws

Wherever we turn in business, we can perceive the sharp distinction between its ethical standards and those of the churches. Newspapers abound with sensational stories growing out of this distinction:

- We read one day that Senator Philip A. Hart of Michigan has attacked food processors for deceptive packaging of numerous products.[2]
- The next day there is a Congressional to-do over Ralph Nader's book, *Unsafe At Any Speed,* which demonstrates that automobile companies for years have neglected the safety of car-owning families.[3]
- Then another Senator, Lee Metcalf of Montana, and journalist Vic Reinemer show in their book, *Overcharge,* the methods by which utility companies elude regulating government bodies to extract unduly large payments from users of electricity.[4]

These are merely dramatic instances of a prevailing condition; there is hardly a major industry at which a similar attack could not be aimed. Critics of business regard such behavior as unethical, but the companies concerned know that they are merely playing the business game.

Among the most respected of our business institutions are the insurance companies. A group of insurance executives meeting recently in New England was startled when their guest speaker, social critic Daniel Patrick Moynihan, roundly berated them for "unethical" practices. They had been guilty, Moynihan alleged, of using outdated actuarial tables to obtain unfairly high premiums. They habitually delayed the hearings of lawsuits against them in order to tire out the plaintiffs and win cheap settlements. In their employment policies they used ingenious devices to discriminate against certain minority groups.[5]

It was difficult for the audience to deny the validity of these charges. But these men were business game players. Their reaction to Moynihan's attack was much the same as that of the automobile manufacturers to Nader, of the utilities to Senator Metcalf, and of the food processors to Senator Hart. If the laws governing their business change, or if public opinion becomes clamorous, they will make the necessary adjustments. But morally they have in their view done nothing wrong. As long as they comply with the letter of the law, they are within their rights to operate their businesses as they see fit.

The small business is in the same position as the great corporation in this respect. For example:

- In 1967 a key manufacturer was accused of providing master keys for automobiles to mail-order customers, although it was obvious that some of the purchasers might be automobile thieves. His defense was plain and straightforward. If there was nothing in the law to prevent him from selling his keys to anyone who ordered them, it was not up to him to inquire as to his customers' motives. Why was it any worse, he insisted, for him to sell car keys by mail, than for mail-order houses to sell guns that might be used for murder?

> Until the law was changed, the key manufacturer could regard himself as being just as ethical as any other businessman by the rules of the business game.[6]

Violations of the ethical ideals of society are common in business, but they are not necessarily violations of business practices. Each year the Federal Trade Commission orders hundreds of companies, many of them of the first magnitude, to "cease and desist" from practices which, judged by ordinary standards, are of questionable morality but which are stoutly defended by the companies concerned.

In one case, a firm manufacturing a well-known mouthwash was accused of using a cheap form of alcohol possibly deleterious to health. The company's chief executive, after testifying in Washington, made this comment privately:

> We broke no law. We're in a highly competitive industry. If we're going to stay in business, we have to look for profit wherever the law permits. We don't make up the laws. We obey them. Then why do we have to put up with this 'holier than thou' talk about ethics? It's sheer hypocrisy. We're not in business to promote ethics. Look at the cigarette companies, for God's sake! If the ethics aren't embodied in the laws by the men who made them, you can't expect businessmen to fill the lack. Why, a sudden submission to Christian ethics by businessmen would bring about the greatest economic upheaval in history!

It may be noted that the government failed to prove its case against him.

Cast Illusions Aside

Talk about ethics by businessmen is often a thin decorative coating over the hard realities of the game:

- Once I listened to a speech by a young executive who pointed to a new industry code as proof that his company and its competitors were deeply aware of their responsibilities to society. It was a code of ethics, he said. The industry was going to police itself, to dissuade constituent companies from wrongdoing. His eyes shone with conviction and enthusiasm.

The same day there was a meeting in a hotel room where the industry's top executives met with the "czar" who was to administer the new code, a man of high repute. No one who was present could doubt their common attitude. In their eyes the code was designed primarily to forestall a move by the federal government to impose stern restrictions on the industry. They felt that the code would hamper them a good deal less than new federal laws would. It was, in other words, conceived as a protection for the industry, not for the public.

The young executive accepted the surface explanation of the code; these leaders, all experienced game players, did not deceive themselves for a moment about its purpose.

The illusion that business can afford to be guided by ethics as conceived in private life is often fostered by speeches and articles containing such phrases as, "It pays to be ethical," or, "Sound ethics is good business." Actually this is not an ethical question at all; it is a self-serving calculation in disguise. The speaker is really saying that in the long run a company can make more money if it does not antagonize competitors, suppliers, employees,

and customers by squeezing them too hard. He is saying that oversharp policies reduce ultimate gains. That is true, but it has nothing to do with ethics.
The underlying attitude is much like that in the familiar story of the shop-
keeper who finds an extra $20 bill in the cash register, debates with himself
the ethical problem—should he tell his partner?—and finally decides to
share the money because the gesture will give him an edge over the s.o.b.
the next time they quarrel.

I think it is fair to sum up the prevailing attitude of businessmen on
ethics as follows:

We live in what is probably the most competitive of the world's civilized
societies. Our customs encourage a high degree of aggression in the individual's striving for success. Business is our main area of competition, and it
has been ritualized into a game of strategy. The basic rules of the game have
been set by the government, which attempts to detect and punish business
frauds. But as long as a company does not transgress the rules of the game
set by law, it has the legal right to shape its strategy without reference to anything but its profits. If it takes a long-term view of its profits, it will preserve
amicable relations, so far as possible, with those with whom it deals. A wise
businessman will not seek advantage to the point where he generates dangerous hostility among employees, competitors, customers, government, or
the public at large. But decisions in this area are, in the final test, decisions
of strategy, not of ethics.

Playing to Win

. . . If a man plans to make a seat in the business game, he owes it to
himself to master the principles by which the game is played, including its
special ethical outlook. He can then hardly fail to recognize that an occasional bluff may well be justified in terms of the game's ethics and warranted
in terms of economic necessity. Once he clears his mind on this point, he
is in a good position to match his strategy against that of the other players.
He can then determine objectively whether a bluff in a given situation has
a good chance of succeeding and can decide when and how to bluff, without a feeling of ethical transgression.

To be a winner, a man must play to win. This does not mean that he
must be ruthless, cruel, harsh, or treacherous. On the contrary, the better
his reputation for integrity, honesty, and decency, the better his chances of
victory will be in the long run. But from time to time every businessman,
like every poker player, is offered a choice between certain loss or bluffing
within the legal rules of the game. If he is not resigned to losing, if he wants
to rise in his company and industry, then in such a crisis he will bluff—and
bluff hard.

Every now and then one meets a successful businessman who has conveniently forgotten the small or large deceptions that he practiced on his
way to fortune. "God gave me my money," old John D. Rockefeller once pi-
ously told a Sunday school class. It would be a rare tycoon in our time who
would risk the horse laugh with which such a remark would be greeted.

In the last third of the twentieth century even children are aware that if
a man has become prosperous in business, he has sometimes departed from
the strict truth in order to overcome obstacles or has practiced the more sub-

tle deceptions of the half-truth or the misleading omission. Whatever the form of the bluff, it is an integral part of the game, and the executive who does not master its techniques is not likely to accumulate much money or power.

Notes

1. *The New York Times,* March 9, 1967.
2. *The New York Times,* November 21, 1966.
3. New York, Grossman Publishers, Inc., 1965.
4. New York, David McKay Company, Inc., 1967.
5. *The New York Times,* January 17, 1967.
6. Cited by Ralph Nader in "Business Crime," *The New Republic,* July 1, 1967, p. 7.

Business Ethics and Politics

JOSEPH BETZ

I. THE QUESTION AND THE BASIC DISTINCTION

What is the relation of business ethics to politics? There is one sense in which business ethics should be kept quite distinct from politics, and a second sense in which business ethics and politics should be seen as united. In the first sense, it is foolish for those in business to act so as to invite political involvement in matters of business ethics. In the second sense, it is foolish for those in business to imagine that there is any solution to the problems of business ethics apart from political solutions.

The division of business ethics which allows for this dual relation to politics is quite simple. It is the distinction between the primary, basic, and settled issues and the secondary, unsettled, and controversial issues in the field of business ethics.

II. BASIC, SETTLED ETHICS

First, the settled issues. Business is a mode of human social interaction. When Aristotle defined humans as, in the Greek, *zoon politikon*, it was rendered later as *animal socialis* in Latin—humans are social animals.[1] This means that for the full development of human potential, humans need to live with other humans. Babies and children need their mothers and fathers, families need the institutions of the village, everyone needs the more extensive web of support provided by the state—schools and police and fire departments and hospitals and armies and roads and post offices. Support for the family comes from the parents' participation in the economic life made possible by the village and the state.[2] Thus does business exist as a part of human social life.

From a forthcoming issue of *Business Ethics Quarterly*. Reprinted by permission of the author.

To live together beneficially, we must act decently or morally with one another. There is no social, economic, or political institution that can exist if the participants in it restrainedly lie, cheat, steal, injure, threaten, or physically endanger one another. This is the settled, agreed-on, taken-for-granted kind of morality that business requires as much as other elementary social institutions. We do not want and will not tolerate locker-theft in our factories or in our schools. We cannot accept lying from clerks in our retail stores or from social workers in our welfare departments. There will be no getting one's way by bullying violence either in our church meetings or in our stockholders' meetings.

My claim that there is a basic, settled ethics might seem a naive claim to the experienced moral philosopher. Moral philosophers pride themselves in rendering the most unquestionable of beliefs questionable. What is settled by custom for the average person is a matter of critical investigation for the moral philosopher. And this is as it should be. Moral philosophy began to exist only when custom was rigorously criticized.

But the very words "ethics" and "morals" come from the ancient Greek and Latin words for custom. The first sense of ethical or moral is customary. Etymology is decisive here. What is customary is settled and basic. Even if not everything that is customary deserves to remain so, and even if everything that is customary and should endure benefits from critical scrutiny, the customary remains at the core of ethics, part of it an almost indestructible core. Much of this is in the "Thou shalt not's" of the Ten Commandments. Thou shalt not kill. Thou shalt not steal. Thou shalt not bear false witness against thy neighbor. Other parts are derivatives or closely related to these. Thou shalt not lie. Thou shalt not physically injure others. Thou shalt not sexually assault others. Thou shalt not commit fraud.

I do not claim that gray areas inviting discrimination and argumentation do not emerge from the black and white of this settled, core ethics, but that we judge of the gray by referring to the black and white of the background of settled, moral certainty.

We argue about the gray area of euthanasia only because it is normally required that we do not kill. We argue about the gray area of puffery in advertising only because we agree that it is normally required that we do not lie. Arguing about at what point an advertisement becomes a lie makes no sense unless we agree that lying is wrong. There is no point to arriving at a workable legal definition of sexual harassment unless we agree that sexual coercion and assault is wrong. We would not wrangle about privacy issues in our legislatures and courts unless we had already made a pre-legal and ethical determination that privacy is a basic value worthy of legal protection.

That there is a basic, settled ethics is proven by the widespread acceptance of justified civil disobedience. For the justified civil disobedient would never protest laws allowing sexual or racial wage discrimination by beating white, male legislators senseless with a baseball bat. That there is a basic, settled ethics is proven by both the ordinary person's and the philosopher's rejection of any moral theory or principle which has counterintuitive consequences. We reject any -ism that would require or allow torture, the sexual molestation of children, and bank robbery.

Business is the same as other parts of our social life, then, in supporting the basics of social morality. Politics does sustain this social morality but not in any special relation to business. Liars might be expelled from school and fired from businesses. And the penalized liars will usually accept this as morally justified. In some cases they will seek political redress in legislatures or courts, but rarely, and the political involvement they demand will be no different for businesses than it is for schools and clubs and neighbors. So it is that business, to be possible, needs a background of ordinary morality which is normally settled and secure and invites political attention only rarely. This sort of business ethics sustains itself and usually does not need politics.

III. FOOLISHLY UNSETTLING THE SETTLED

This is worth stressing, I think, because there occasionally arises a sort of position in business ethics that would unsettle this settled ethics. One example of this is a much-anthologized article by Albert Z. Carr, "Is Business Bluffing Ethical?"[3] which is also part of Carr's book, *Business As a Game.*[4]

Carr's thesis is that business does not accept or assume the morality basic to all social life which I have described. He claims that business is special and should not be judged by ordinary morality, by what he calls "private morality" or "the ethics of religion" (p. 21) or "ethics as conceived in private life." The difference is that business involves more competition than most spheres of social life and should thus be judged like a competitive game—"the ethics of business are game ethics" (p. 21). Games, of course, involve strategy, especially the strategy of bluffing, deceiving, faking. So the answer to the title question, "Is Business Bluffing Ethical?", is "Yes, just as in any other game."

In the course of his article, Carr thus claims the following behaviors are morally justified in the separate and "special" "ethics of business," an ethics far more permissive than basic, ordinary, settled social ethics: (1) a young-looking 58-year-old man gets a job by putting black dye on his hair and "Age: 45" on his resume (p. 23); a young college graduate gets a job by putting answers on a psychological-inventory test that he thinks his prospective employers want to see. The question was "Which of these magazines do you regularly read?" and, contrary to the truth, he checks off conservative magazines like *Fortune* and *Business Week* though he actually reads liberal ones like *The New Republic* and *Ramparts* (p. 22); (3) a business leader advertises his product "in a way that makes it sound a great deal better than it actually was" (p. 21); (4) a businessman supplies call girls to customers (p. 23); (5) another employs spies who work for his competitors (p. 24); and (6) another sells master keys for automobiles for mail-order customers (p. 24).

All these are permissible practices in Carr's business-or-game ethics. How then do we know the limits of this distinctive business ethics? Carr suggests both an informal answer and a formal one. The informal one is that we may do to others what experience teaches us that they might due to us. Since no one really expects the truth from others in business negotiations, one need not provide it for others (p. 23).

But this is an impossibly low standard which could overrule virtually all parts of basic, ordinary morality. And Carr is not willing to go this far. Thus his more formal standard saves basic business ethics from totally unraveling. The more formal limit, then, is the law. Carr writes of the business people who have done the sort of things in my examples:

If the laws governing their business change, or if public opinion becomes clamorous, they will make the necessary adjustments. But morally they have in their view done nothing wrong. As long as they comply with the letter of the law, they are within their rights to operate their businesses as they see fit (p. 24).

Carr, then, opposes my position that there is a basic settled area of business ethics that is normally indifferent to and ignored by politics. Since even basics like truth telling and respecting privacy and property are not assumed in business ethics, the political sphere in the society must carefully write laws that bind the game of business ethics. Carr is thus inviting constant political involvement in business ethics and a proliferation of laws regulating business.

Experienced business men and women reacted quite strongly to the publication of Carr's article. There had been no article in the *Harvard Business Review* up to that time that elicited so many disapproving letters to the editors as Carr's.[5] These business leaders rejected Carr's reasoning as inviting massive government intervention and regulation in business. But more basically, they denied his factual claims, they denied that business was the amoral game he claimed it was. They said that they practiced normal, basic, settled Judaeo-Christian ethics in their business lives and they expected the same from their partners, contacts, employees, customers, and even competitors. That breaches of this settled moral code occurred was no more reason for accepting breaches as nonsettling in business than the fact that cheating occurred in school was a reason for making it proper and accepted student behavior. It must be opposed and corrected when it occurs.

The point, then, is this. There is a part of business ethics that is settled and accepted. And because it is, business ethics remains apart from politics in this regard. Handshakes still cement deals, even if lawyers are first consulted, and the word of the representatives of two businesses bind their principals to perform and there need not, normally, be recourse to courts or legislatures to compel performance. Thus does a strong, settled moral code in basics make business possible and allow politics to deal with other more important things. Those like Carr who jeopardize this convention and division of labor are fools.

Notes

1. Hannah Arendt, *The Human Condition* (New York: Doubleday Anchor Books, 1959), p. 24.
2. Aristotle, *Politics*, Chapter I, Book I.
3. Albert Z. Carr, "Is Business Bluffing Ethical?" *Harvard Business Review* (Jan.–Feb. 1968). This article is widely reprinted in business ethics anthologies. For instance, pp. 33–39 in Thomas Donaldson and Patricia H. Werhane, eds., *Ethical Issues in Business: A Philosophical Approach*, 6th ed. (Upper Saddle River, N. J.: Prentice-Hall, Inc., 1999), and pp. 21–28 in Joseph R. DesJardins and John J. McCall, eds., *Contemporary Issues in Business Ethics*, 2d ed. (Belmont, Calif.: Wadsworth, 1990). My subsequent references to the pages of Carr's essay are to its reprinting in DesJardins and McCall and I give these in my text.
4. Albert Z. Carr, *Business As a Game* (New York: Mentor, New American Library, 1968).
5. Timothy B. Blodgett, "Showdown on Business Bluffing," *Harvard Business Review* (May–June, 1968).

Promoting Honesty in Negotiation: An Exercise in Practical Ethics

PETER C. CRAMTON ➤ J. GREGORY DEES

If business ethics is to have a significant impact on business practice, many of us working in the field will need to take a more pragmatic approach to our craft (Dees and Cramton, 1991). Our work should help ethically sensitive business people establish stable institutional arrangements that promote and protect ethically desirable conduct, and it should help individuals to develop strategies for effective ethical behavior in a competitive and morally imperfect world. This paper is offered as one model of more practical business ethics.

To illustrate the model, we have selected the topic of deception in negotiation. Negotiation is a pervasive feature of business life. Success in business typically requires successful negotiations. It is commonly believed that success in negotiation is enhanced by the skillful use of deceptive tactics, such as bluffing, exaggeration, posturing, stage-setting, and outright misrepresentation. As White (1980, p. 927) candidly states, "The critical difference between those who are successful negotiators and those who are not lies in this capacity both to mislead and not to be misled." Some shrewd practitioners have advanced the art of deception beyond prudent concealment of preferences to more aggressive forms of strategic misrepresentation.

Given the high value placed on honesty, the incentives for deception in negotiation create a serious moral tension for business people, as well as a public relations problem for business. The public relations problem is not new. In ancient Athens, Hermes, a trickster who stole his brother's (Apollo's) cattle on the day he was born and later lied about it, was the patron god of merchants. Anacharsis wrote in 600 B.C., "The market is the place set apart where men may deceive one another."

Not surprisingly, deception in negotiation is a widely discussed problem in business ethics. However, much of the attention has been devoted to the question of when (if ever) various deceptive tactics are ethically justified. Many writers have been highly critical of deception in business. Others, most notably Carr (1968) in his controversial piece on business bluffing, have argued that business has its own ethics, one that permits a wide range of deceptive practices that would not be acceptable outside of business.

We see little benefit from joining this debate. . . . Our premise is that, outside of a few recreational contexts, deception is a regrettable feature of business negotiations, even when it is justified (or commonplace). The Machiavellian gap between what is done and what (ideally) ought to be done is real when it comes to deception in business negotiations. A purely moralistic (or philosophical) response is likely to be ineffective. A Machiavellian response is likely to make things worse. . . . We prefer to

Reprinted by permission of the authors, Peter C. Cramton, University of Maryland, and J. Gregory Dees, Stanford University, *Business Ethics Quarterly*, October 1993, Vol. 3, Issue 4, the Journal of the Society for Business Ethics.

explore means of constructively narrowing the gap, thereby making the world more honest.

ETHICS, OPPORTUNISM, AND TRUST

In an ideal world, people would do the right thing simply because it is right. In the world in which we live, morality is more complex. People often disagree about what is right. Even when a consensus on moral values is reached, many find that they do not consistently live up to moral standards. One reason for falling short is that most people place a high value on their own welfare. They may have moral ideals and commitments, but concern about personal well-being is a powerful motivating factor. It is more powerful for some than it is for others, but few can claim to be indifferent to it. Any significant gap between the demands of ethics and the urging of self-interest, narrowly defined,[1] creates incentive problems for individuals and for societies wishing to maintain high ethical standards. The problems arise on two levels.

At the first level are the direct incentive problems of opportunism and desperation. Problems of opportunism arise when individuals willingly violate ethical norms in order to pursue opportunities for private gain. They yield to temptation. Problems of desperation arise when individuals violate ethical norms to avoid personal loss or hardship. Even if we grant that most people place some intrinsic value on doing the right thing, as they see it, sometimes the risk or the temptation is just too great. Philosophers refer to this problem as "weakness of the will." Weakness of the will is not limited to moral deviants. Too often we are presented with evidence from our daily lives, from news stories, and from academic research, that well-educated, apparently normal individuals can be tempted or pressured into compromising ethical standards.

The effects of opportunism and desperation are magnified by a second-level problem concerning trust and fair play. One of the reasons people are willing to behave ethically, even when their personal welfare is at risk, is that they expect others to behave likewise. It seems unfair for individuals with weaker ethical commitments to prosper materially, especially at the expense of individuals with stronger commitments. An atmosphere of mutual trust appears to play an important role in grounding ethical behavior for many people. Suspicion that others are profiting from misconduct can destroy that atmosphere and spoil the sense of satisfaction that might be gained from principled behavior. A sense of fair play can motivate individuals with strong ethical commitments to engage in what they would otherwise consider unacceptable behavior.

Individual integrity and social stability are difficult to maintain in a social setting in which there is serious conflict between ethics and personal welfare. Traditionally, moral philosophers have responded to this conflict in one of two ways. Some, particularly Kantians, acknowledge the gap between ethics and self-interest, but assert on philosophical grounds the dominance of moral considerations over those of personal welfare. Others argue that the gap is only apparent. By refining the definition of self-interest, they attempt to reconcile ethics and self-interest (Kavka, 1984). As philosophically interesting as these views are, neither holds much promise of improving conduct. Practical, not conceptual, solutions are needed.

INCENTIVES FOR DECEPTION IN NEGOTIATION

To illustrate the practical approach to ethical incentive problems, we have chosen to concentrate on the phenomenon of deception in negotiation. Negotiation offers a familiar setting in which individuals often feel a tension between ethics and self-interest. In particular, individuals frequently face a temptation to deceive the other party, in hopes of bettering the outcome for themselves.

We adopt the following definitions:

> A *negotiation* is any situation in which two or more parties are engaged in communications, the aim of which is agreement on terms affecting an exchange, or a distribution of benefits, burdens, roles, or responsibilities.
>
> *Deception* is any deliberate act or omission by one party taken with the intention of creating or adding support to a false belief in another party.
>
> *Honesty* is the absence of deception.[2]

Notice that lying is only one tactic that may be used to deceive a negotiation partner. Lying, strictly interpreted, requires making a false statement (or at least a statement believed to be false by its maker). The clever manipulation of verbal and non-verbal signals to create or support a false impression, without making a false statement, also counts as deception. Likewise, concealing information is a deceptive tactic if and only if the concealment is intended to create or support a false belief. In some cases, there is a fine line between allowing the other party to continue to hold a false belief and adding support to the belief.

To understand the incentives for deception in negotiation, we use some basic game theory[3] and a fictional world called Metopia. The simplified world of Metopia allows us to put aside temporarily some of the complexity of the real world, in order to analyze the incentives for deception. Metopia is a world much like ours, but populated exclusively with rational, self-centered individuals. We adopt the standard definition of self-interest from economics.

> An action is in a party's *self-interest* if, given the party's beliefs at the time of decision, the action yields greater expected utility for the party than any other available action.

Metopians always act in their self-interest. Their interests are even more self-centered and material, focused on their own personal welfare. Metopians' preferences are independent of the preferences of others. They have no specific preferences about the process of the negotiation. In particular, Metopians do not have an independent preference for honesty or dishonesty in the process of negotiation. They feel no guilt about deception, nor do they enjoy fooling others. Metopians have no interest in the opinions of others, except to the extent that such opinions are likely to inhibit or enhance their ability to satisfy their self-centered interests. Finally, Metopians do not have any religious belief system that provides moral rewards and punishments. These features characterize the narrow conception of self-interest in Metopia.

Opportunities for Deception in Metopia

The basis for deception in Metopia is the presence of (real or perceived)[4] informational differences among the parties. Negotiators often have private information about the item under discussion, about their ability and willingness to take future actions, and about their own settlement preferences. Private information, however, does not always present a profitable opportunity for deception. Often it is more prudent to be honest. In general, an opportunity for *A* to profitably deceive *B* arises only when *B* believes *A* has information that is of value to *B* in determining *B*'s negotiating position, *B* knows of no other cost-efficient way to get the information before making a commitment, and it is to *A*'s advantage if *B* acts on false beliefs about the matter. The opportunity will depend in part on the kind of information in question. . . . For this reason, bargainers in Metopia are skeptical of information that the other party presents that bears on that party's settlement preferences. This has its costs. To convince *B* of the strength of her position, *B* must take actions that a weaker *A* would not want to imitate, such as delaying agreement or risking disagreement, both of which involve bargaining inefficiencies. Indeed, so long as there is some uncertainty about whether gains from trade exist, some bargaining inefficiencies must occur regardless of the bargaining process adopted, if the parties act in their own self-interest and have only costly means of signaling strength.

Factors Inhibiting Deception in Metopia

One might think the Metopia would be riddled with attempted deception and bad faith, since Metopians exploit opportunities to misrepresent information in a negotiation. However, . . . several mechanisms work to inhibit deception. Metopians would rationally invest in processes and mechanisms to protect themselves from deception and its untoward social consequences. Even potential deceivers recognize the effect that the possibility of deception has in undermining even their true statements. To create a climate of confidence that would facilitate negotiations, Metopians would investigate claims, construct contractual mechanisms to enforce honesty, and work to ease the availability of reputation information.

Ex Ante Verification.   One remedy for the risk of deception is to verify claims and assumptions before making commitments that depend on those claims or assumptions. Negotiators could gather independent evidence themselves, or they might hire others to do it. Gathering it themselves is, generally, the most reliable method. However, an individual negotiator does not always have the expertise to verify claims efficiently. Accordingly, just as the use of house inspectors has become commonplace in residential real estate transactions, Metopians would employ auditors, testers, inspectors, and private detectives to verify the truth of claims made or implied in negotiations.[5]

One problem is that verification of every significant claim made in a negotiation would be quite costly. Often, it would not be justified. Metopians would be creative in reducing the costs of verification. Two mechanisms for doing so are the use of economies of scale and random verification. It would be highly inefficient, for instance, for everyone buying a refrigerator to hire a private inspector to evaluate different models. However, because refrigerators are standard products, we would expect to see information gathered by a third party who would sell it to those who need it. When economies of scale are not possible, Metopians could adopt random verification procedures to lower verification costs. This would work so long as the parties caught in a deceptive act could be punished harshly. For example, if the maximum penalty that A could apply to B is ten times B's individual net gain from deceiving A, then A's verifying information one out of ten times is sufficient to prevent deception by B. Verification is economical in this case, so long as the cost of verification is no more than ten times the net efficiency gain from honest behavior.

Contractual Mechanisms. Unfortunately, even with some creativity, ex ante verification is limited. Some claims are simply too difficult, or too costly to test ex ante with any confidence. Claims about the long-term reliability of a new product typically fall into this category, as do many claims about actions to be taken in the future and about settlement preferences. In such cases, Metopians would develop contractual mechanisms to add credibility to claims made or implied in a negotiation.

Ideally, the mechanisms would be self-enforcing. However, such mechanisms are limited in their applicability, and may be more costly than alternatives, even though the alternatives require third-party enforcement. Consequently, we would expect to find in Metopia systems of third-party enforcement and a high level of explicit contracting. . . .

Reputation Effects. To supplement ex ante verification and contractual mechanisms, Metopians would need to rely on reputation effects to induce honesty. A person's reputation affects future opportunities by influencing the other's belief about what the person will do in the future. A negotiator with a reputation for being deceitful is likely to be disadvantaged in future negotiations. She may have a hard time finding negotiating partners and when she finds them, they will be on their guard. This is not because Metopians are morally offended by deceit. It is simply that negotiations tend to go better, other things being equal, when one is dealing with a person who has a reputation for honesty to maintain. Thus, when deciding to deceive, a Metopian negotiator must consider not only the short-run consequence of the decision, but also how the decision affects her reputation and hence future negotiations. . . . An intelligent Metopian will know that some attempts at deception pose greater risks to one's reputation than others. Reputation works best when claims are explicit, ex post detection is likely, and information about deceptive practices can be credibly communicated to the culprit's future negotiating partners. . . .

Summary of Factors Affecting Deception in Metopia

Even in the self-centered world of Metopia, deception would be moderated by natural forces in a wide range of circumstances. To preserve fruitful transactions, Metopians will protect themselves (and their trading partners) from deception when they can do so in a cost-effective way. Since even the suspicion of deception can be harmful to potentially profitable negotiations, it is worthwhile for the negotiating parties to find means of reducing it.

Honesty, however, is not always the best policy by Metopian standards. Occasionally, Metopians will be able to gain from deceptive tactics. Based on the above analysis, we would predict that in Metopia, other things equal, deception is more likely to be a problem when the following conditions hold.

Information asymmetry is great.   The greater the information disparity between the two parties, the more opportunity at least one of the parties has for profitable deception. Every negotiation involves some asymmetry. Each negotiator possesses some private information, such as information about her preferences, or about her intentions to keep future commitments.

Verification is difficult.   Some questions, such as the physical condition of a simple, existing product, can be easily settled before the deal is consummated. Others, such as long-term maintenance costs for a new product, can only be confirmed afterwards. And some, such as a party's reservation price, are difficult to ever confirm. Deception is more likely with matters that are most difficult to verify, such as the other party's preferences, their commitment to future actions, and long-term performance claims about the good under negotiation. Because it makes verification to a third-party difficult, deception is also more likely to occur when claims are made verbally without independent witnesses.

The intention to deceive is difficult to establish.   Deliberate deception is often hard to distinguish from a mistake or oversight. Deception is more likely when the deceiver has a plausible alternative explanation for her behavior. Deception about something one should clearly know is less likely than deception about matters for which one could innocently claim to be the victim of misinformation. Subtle forms of deception are more likely to occur than explicit lying. The use of negotiating agents may also make it difficult to detect intentional deception. The principal can claim that the deception was the result of poor communication, or an unscrupulous negotiating agent who acted without authority. Finally, vague or sweeping claims that are open to alternative interpretations make it difficult to establish intentional deception. In such cases, a negotiator can more plausibly claim that she never meant to give a false impression.

The parties have insufficient resources to adequately safeguard against deception.   Depending on the expected gains from the negotiation and on the initial endowments of the negotiating parties, there will be limits on the resources available to protect the parties against deception. Warranties, collateral, hostages, and other insurance devices use up resources. They may be potentially useful, but not sensible in transactions promising small gains. In larger, more risky transactions, the negotiators may have too few assets to create bonding devices sufficient to eliminate incentive problems.

Interaction between the parties is infrequent.   Deception is more likely in one-shot negotiations than in long-term relationships. The expectation of continued interaction provides negotiators with more time and a greater incentive to confirm the reliability of information provided or signaled by the other party. It also provides more opportunities for retaliation in future transactions.

Ex post redress is too costly.   If deception is uncovered after the deal is done, there may be means of seeking redress, either individually or through third-parties. One could track down the offender and threaten harm, unless adequate compensation is provided. Alternatively, one could take the offender to court. The deceived party may prefer such an effort, even when the costs of it exceed the expected compensation, if the action has enough reputation value. Aggressive action in one case may dissuade future negotiating partners from attempting deception. Sometimes, however, the costs and risks of seeking redress are too high, even recognizing the reputation value. In other cases, such redress is not feasible, because the deceived party has little leverage over the deceiver, the deceiver cannot easily be found, or the deception cannot be adequately demonstrated to a third-party (a court, or future negotiators).

Reputation information is unavailable, unreliable, or very costly to communicate. When it is difficult to convey information about the past performance of negotiators, we can expect more deception. We should find less deception in small, close-knit communities, or in dense social networks, than we do in large, loosely connected populations. Even in Metopia, there may be situations in which handshake deals are possible, without formal contracting. We should also find less deception when there is a relatively low cost system for collecting and transmitting reputation information, such as a Better Business Bureau.

The circumstances are unusual in a way that limits inferences about future behavior. Some instances of deception are unlikely to damage future negotiations, because they occur in distinctly different circumstances. The question is whether future negotiating partners would regard a particular act of deception as relevant to predicting behavior in negotiations with them. For instance, deception in a game setting, such as bluffing in poker, may not be thought to have any bearing on expectations of behavior outside of the game setting. Deception of an enemy or of an outsider may not affect negotiations with a friend or an insider.

One party has little to lose (or much to gain) from attempting deception. The mechanisms discussed so far work only when each negotiator has expectations of a continuing economic life, places reasonably high value on future economic success, and has a reputation to protect. However, in some circumstances, a negotiator may not be concerned about the prospects of being caught at deception, provided she is not caught until after the deal is closed. The negotiator may have a reputation that is so bad that further deception would not hurt it. She may have a high discount rate, placing a low value on future transactions. She may be in desperate straits. Or, the payoff from this one negotiation may be sufficiently high.

These above conditions represent rough guidelines about when Metopians have greater incentives for profitable deception. Whether to attempt deception in a given situation requires a complex assessment of expected costs, benefits, and risks.

REAL WORLD DIFFERENCES

We have offered some specific hypotheses about incentives for deception in Metopia. To what extent do our findings about Metopia extend to the world we know? Human nature is not so simple or uniform as that of the Metopians.

People are not as self-centered as Metopians. They are capable of a wide range of sentiments and commitments not available to Metopians. Some of these sentiments work to promote honesty; others encourage more deception.

People often care about others. Most people have some benevolent motivations and ethical commitments. Individuals have sympathy for the pains of others and take pleasure in others' well-being. However, this care does not typically extend to all of humankind, but only to a referent group (Hirschleifer, 1982). The size and nature of that group varies significantly from person to person. The care also varies in intensity, depending on such things as the closeness of the relationship with the other person. In addition to this passive care for others, people care about how they affect others (Arrow, 1974). They generally do not want to cause harm, and do want to cause pleasure or satisfaction. Individuals typically do not want to benefit from the misfortune of others, even when they have not caused the misfortune (Nagel, 1975).

Beyond concerns about the welfare of others, most have internalized rules of behavior so that they feel pangs of conscience, guilt, or shame when they resort to certain objectionable behaviors such as deception. They have preferences about how they act as well as preferences about the results of their actions. Many take pride in their sense of personal integrity. They take offense at any suggestion that they are not trustworthy. On a social level, people feel and express moral approbation and disapprobation about the behavior of others, even when the other's behavior is not a direct threat to them. They are willing to incur costs to shame, ostracize, and punish others who engage in questionable behavior.

On the other hand, people also have preferences that may encourage deception. Benevolence and moral commitments typically have limits. People are concerned about their own well-being and generally place more weight on their own welfare than on that of others. Furthermore, people tend to be competitive. Relative standing matters. People want to win, to do better than their peers. The harm they are willing to commit on their way to winning may be limited—each will draw the line somewhere—but many are willing to cause harm to have an advantage. For many people, moral commitments are contingent upon a belief that others share the same commitments. Many individuals, especially in competitive settings, are moral pragmatists, willing to do their part, but concerned not to be taken as a sucker or a fool. At the extreme, some people actually appear to take pleasure in harming other parties in a negotiation. People can carry grudges and vendettas beyond reason. They are capable of malevolence and spite. Some even take a particular pleasure in successful deception. The evidence for this is the large number of games where bluffing and deception play a role in the enjoyment of the game and in determining success. Some individuals carry the thrill of fooling others out of the game setting into other more serious negotiations.

People are not as smart as Metopians. Individuals in the real world vary more in their ability to make rational calculations. None reach the level of intelligence found in Metopians. Consequently, people are more likely to make mistakes in reasoning about the costs and benefits of deception. Some opportunities for self-interested deception will be missed as a result of such mistakes. Also, because of the common affliction of myopia, the bias toward clear short-term gains, some individuals will see opportunities for deception even when they would disappear with a longer view. Hume (1751) identified the risk of opportunism by frail humans. Of those who attempt to selectively use deception only when it appears to be in their self-interest he says, "while they propose to cheat with moderation and secrecy, a tempting incident occurs, nature is frail, and they give in to the snare; whence they can never extricate themselves, without total loss of reputation, and the forfeiture of all future trust and confidence with mankind." Hume identifies a real risk, but exaggerates the repercussions of getting caught in a deception. As Bhide and Stevenson (1990, p. 192) observe, "Even unreconstructed scoundrels are tolerated in our world as long as they have something else to offer."

Because of the limits of human rationality and intelligence, judgments of trust may be made hastily without adequate supporting evidence. In some cases, individuals will not appreciate the powerful incentives for deception. As a result, individuals may be gullible and believe others when it would be more reasonable to discount their claims. This opens the door to more deception. However, sometimes people err in the other direction and exhibit more distrust than is rational. Bad experience in a negotiation can make people cynical about the trustworthiness of others. They may ignore the structural differences from one negotiation to the next, irrationally distrusting the other party regardless of the incentives. Such a person is likely to overinvest in protective measures.

What can we conclude from these differences? The main lessons can be summarized briefly. In the real world, mutual benevolence, moral commitment, and mutual trust are available as tools for promoting honesty in negotiations. However, there is so much variation in individual moral attitudes, characters, and abilities that it is hard to develop strategies for promoting honesty that are robust. People do not wear their characters on their sleeves. Negotiators often face significant uncertainty about the trustworthiness of the party on the other side of the table. The chances for honesty depend not only on the structural conditions that permit self-interested deception in Metopia, but also on the psychological forces in individuals and in the communities in which they live. A benevolent person supported by a community that reinforces that benevolence is less likely to engage in opportunistic deception than a Metopian would be. A more competitive person from a community of competitive persons is more likely to be deceptive. In either case, how the individual behaves may be a function of that individual's attitudes toward and expectations of the other party in the negotiation.

Despite the differences, we believe that the Metopian model presents a useful starting point for thinking about the problem of deception in real world negotiations. Self-interest plays an important role in the real world. Reputation, verification, and contractual mechanisms are viable means of reducing the inefficiencies caused by deception and providing a basis for trust.

PROMOTING HONESTY IN NEGOTIATION

Given that deception is a regrettable feature of negotiations, both morally and practically, what can be done by ethically concerned people to promote more honesty? Before describing individual strategies, it is useful to review how existing institutional arrangements work to support honesty.

Social and Institutional Support

Those who think social engineering for ethics is unwise or unnecessary should reflect on the many institutions (public and private) that already exist with this end in mind. Many of the mechanisms that we noticed in Metopia are part of standard practice in the real world.[6] Individuals deciding on strategies for promoting honesty should be aware of the support mechanisms already in place to promote honesty and trust. This is not to say that further institutional improvement is impossible. Something may be learned by reflecting on the strengths and weaknesses of existing mechanisms. Entrepreneurial extensions and innovations (both in the public and private sectors) may be possible.

Legal and Regulatory Protection. The most obvious social support mechanism is government enforcement of norms. Not only do we have civil and criminal law, but we have in this country elaborate regulatory mechanisms. Regulators not only set rules, but also do the research that individual consumers could ill afford. . . .

In addition to governmental regulation and adjudication, industries often have their own regulatory mechanisms. Sometimes it is in the interest of an industry to provide assurance of honorable dealings with its customers, suppliers, employees, and the communities in which it does business. For instance, in the securities industry, a form of arbitration is used to settle disputes between brokers and their clients. A negotiator should know whether any relevant industry regulations or dispute resolution procedures apply. . . .

Society has been remarkably creative in developing mechanisms to promote honesty and secure business transactions from the risks of deception. However, these institutional safeguards are not present, nor are they effective, in all arenas of negotiation. Sometimes individual negotiators have to develop strategies for promoting honesty and for protecting themselves from opportunism.

Tactics and Strategies for Individual Negotiators

What can be done by individuals who wish to promote honesty in their negotiations? We cannot recommend a single strategy that will work effectively in all negotiations. We can offer some strategic and tactical suggestions. They are directed to negotiators who see the value of honesty and mutual trust and are willing to make some investment in them. They are based on a rather extensive literature in the field of negotiation and conflict resolution, as well as our experiences teaching and studying negotiation and business ethics.

Negotiators face two kinds of risks: trusting too much and trusting too little. The first risk is all too familiar. Most people can think of situations in which their trust proved to be unfounded. Painful memories provide powerful lessons. The second risk is not so apparent, in part, because the cost, which may take the form of a foregone opportunity, is not so vivid. However, this risk is just as real. As the movie actress's agent in one of the Philip Marlowe detective stories comments, "One of these days . . . I'm going to make the mistake which a man in my business dreads above all other mistakes. I'm going to find myself doing business with a man I can trust and I'm going to be just too goddamn smart to trust him." (Chandler, 1955, p. 118; cited in Coleman, 1990). Coleman (1990, p. 100–101) points out that the mistake one should worry about most depends on the nature of the risks involved. A sensible strategy for dealing with the risks of deception is one that enhances trust in the negotiations and protects the participants from opportunistic exploitation. In specific situations, it is reasonable for one of these elements to be emphasized more than the other.

Assessing the Situation.   No matter what strategy one pursues, the place to start is by doing one's homework. This seems like an obvious point, but it is surprising how many people cut this step short. Admittedly, it is not always cost-effective to do in-depth pre-negotiation research, but rarely should this step be skipped. There are many low-cost mechanisms for gathering information. For our purposes, pre-negotiation homework can be broken down into four steps.

1.   Incentives for Deception. The questions here are based on what we learned about incentives in Metopia. The starting point in assessing vulnerabilities is to determine what sort of privileged information each side is likely to have. To what extent do you have to rely on them, and they on you, for important information? Are there natural incentives for either of you to exaggerate, deliberately suppress, or misrepresent any of this privileged information? Is there time pressure on either side? How important is a favorable outcome to each of the parties? This should be asked about principals and specific negotiating agents. It is generally thought to be a good thing if the other side in a negotiation is highly motivated to reach agreement. However, other things being equal, this creates a more powerful incentive for deception, both to cover up a weak bargaining position, and to persuade the other side to accept an agreement. It is also important to determine whether there are any factors to counterbalance these natural incentives. Are there easy means of verifying the information? How important is it for each of you to do business together in the future? How easy would it be for either of you to penalize or ruin the reputation of the other? These questions should be asked from your point of view and theirs. Do not expect them to fully appreciate the long-term and intangible benefits of honesty. Recognize that immediate payoffs can exert an inordinate amount of influence. Finally, you should assess how bad it would be for either side if the other attempts deception.

2.   Competence and Character of the Other Side. Whether you can trust the claims and signals from the other party is a function of your assessment of their character[7] and their competence. Competence, in this context, speaks to whether the other party would be a reliable source of information, even if they were honest. With regard to information about the item under negotiation, the party you are negotiating with may lack technical expertise, have access only to limited information, or be susceptible to a natural bias. With regard to future actions, the party may not have a realistic perception of her own (or her firm's) abilities to fulfill the promise. With regard to settlement issues, if one is dealing with a new company representative, for instance, she may not know just how flexible she

can be on price or terms. In cases of questionable competence, promoting honesty may not solve the problem of getting reliable information. Other steps my be required.

Evaluating the other party's character would not be necessary if we could simply observe when someone is attempting to deceive us. Though Ekman (1985) suggests that there are behavioral signs associated with lying, these are not so obvious and reliable as to relieve us of the need to think about the character of the parties with whom we are dealing. Assessing character is usually done first by reference to one's own past dealings with the other party, and second by checking on the other party's reputation in the marketplace. One should check not only for instances of dishonesty per se, but also for a general willingness to engage in objectionable behavior for selfish or competitive reasons. For the first, you must ask, how well do you know the other party? Are you really in a position to assess their character? If not, checking their reputation may be sensible. This can be done through any of the reputational sources of information mentioned in the previous section, or, more directly, by interviewing their prior negotiating partners. The latter step may help a great deal at little cost. It is important to attempt to get an unbiased list. Instead of asking for references in general, ask for a specific group that should be able to offer a fair and independent judgment, such as the landlord's last three tenants. In many cases, a candid assessment will be provided. However, in some situations, candor may be limited because of the fear of litigation or some other reason. For instance, one of the authors asked a group of mid-level executives whether they would provide an honest reference about a former employee who was dismissed for unethical conduct. The vast majority said they would not tell about the unethical conduct, unless the person requesting the information happened to be another manager within their company or a friend. . . .

3. Attitudes and Perspective of the Other Side. The other party will enter the negotiation with a set of expectations and attitudes. Some of these will bear directly on their willingness to engage in deceptive behavior. One important matter concerns their attitude and beliefs about you. What is the other party likely to believe about you and your character? Will they identify with you? Will they trust you to be honest? Is there a history of animosity between the two of you, or between the other party and people like you? You also need to find out what they expect in the negotiation. This is especially crucial in cross-cultural negotiations. How do they expect information to be shared? How do they build trust with other negotiators? How adversarial or competitive are their negotiations? How are they likely to respond to different techniques of checking their veracity? Will your status as an "outsider" be a barrier to building trust?

4. Critical Self-Reflection. Finally, you must assess the biases and attitudes that you bring into the negotiation. You have a set of attitudes and presumptions, some of which may not be justified. Ask whether your attitudes are fair to the other side. Without critical reflection, there is a tendency toward cognitive inertia. This is a tendency to persist in certain prior beliefs by selecting and ignoring evidence. Both trust and distrust can persist beyond a reasonable point. Significant effort must be made to question

your own beliefs and conclusions. Discussions with a third party whom you can trust to challenge your reasoning may be helpful.

The overall issue in all this "due diligence" is to establish a basis on which to craft an appropriate strategy. If the negotiating risks seem too high compared to the benefits, you may choose (if this is an option) not to negotiate with this particular party. On the other hand, if the risks are small, or the other side seems trustworthy and trusting, you may choose to simply negotiate in good faith. The costs of building trust or constructing protective mechanisms may not be justified. When the risks are moderate (or when they are high and you have no alternative but to negotiate), you must decide on a mix of building trust and protecting yourself from opportunistic, desperate, or defensive deception on the part of the other party. The mix will depend on the structure of the negotiation, time pressures, and whether you believe the other side is open to promoting honesty. If the other party is either highly opportunistic, or in desperate straits, attempting to build trust may be too risky.

Building Mutual Trust. In many cases, the incentive for deception in negotiation is defensive. It arises out of a suspicion that the other party is likely to be dishonest and out of a fear that the other party will unfairly exploit any weakness that is honestly revealed. This suspicion and fear may be overcome if a climate of mutual trust can be developed.

The level of trust with which a specific negotiation begins depends on the prior relationship of the parties, their individual reputations, their vulnerabilities to opportunism, and the established norms. We find some settings in which handshake deals are common, and others in which the distrust is so high that a lengthy and complex contracting process is required.[8]

The general principle behind the trust-building mechanisms is that one should demonstrate both trustworthiness and the ability to trust. The latter entails taking some moderate risks. As Adam Smith (1759, p. 531) observed. "We trust the [person] who seems willing to trust us." If we want to be trusted, we have to be able to show trust in return. In many cases, this trust will be reciprocated. It will promote honesty and reduce negotiating and contracting cost. In other cases, it will invite opportunistic exploitation. The process must be managed carefully. As long as the parties still have some divergent interests, it is unlikely that all deception, bluffing, or posturing can be eliminated.

The effort to build trust should match the opportunity. If the gains from trust are likely to be great and time and resources are available, a major investment in trust building may be justified. If not, trust-building activities may have to be constrained. The choice of techniques should also be tailored to the parties and the social context. Zucker (1986, p. 53) has identified three modes of trust production: "(1) process-based, where trust is tied to past or expected exchange such as in reputation or gift exchange; (2) characteristic-based, where trust is tied to a person, depending on characteristics such as family background or ethnicity; and (3) institutional-based, where trust is tied to formal societal structures depending on individual or firm-specific attributes, (e.g., certification as an accountant) or on intermediary mechanisms (e.g., use of escrow accounts)." Drawing on these modes, we outline some generic steps that might help business negotiators build trust.

1. Build Mutual Benevolence. One avenue available in the real world, but not in Metopia, is to build a personal or moral foundation for trust by creating a sense of mutual benevolence. The key here is to get each party to include the other in the reference group toward whom they feel good will, or a sense of moral commitment. It is easier to maintain distrust as long as the other party is seen as an adversary. One strategy for accomplishing this is to create more characteristic-based trust by highlighting any common religious, ethnic, family, or community ties shared by the parties. Another approach is to create opportunities for face-to-face meetings, either to discuss issues related to the negotiation, or simply to socialize. The use of preliminary meetings before the actual negotiation (or between negotiations) to discuss issues of mutual concern is becoming a more common element in labor-management relations. For instance, contracts between CBS and the IBEW now stipulate that the parties "shall meet at least once every three months, unless waived by mutual consent, to discuss subjects of mutual concern or interest . . ." The experimental gaming literature suggests that the possibility of communication between the parties typically enhances the probability of cooperation (Good, 1988). The use of pre-negotiation social contact and gift giving is common in Japanese (March, 1989) and Chinese negotiations. It serves to build trust and good will. If face-to-face meetings are to be arranged, the choice of site and arrangements can be crucial. For trust building, it would seem wise to hold the meetings at a neutral location, or on the home turf of the most vulnerable party.

This strategy is not suitable to all situations. Sometimes direct contact between the principles may be risky. It may provoke more conflict and animosity, or one party may manipulate the other into unreasonable concessions. The prospect for these untoward outcomes is a function of the prior relationship, relative power, and attitudes of the parties. Each has to be willing and able to treat the other with respect.

2. Create Opportunities for Displaying Trust. Taking Adam Smith's observation seriously, if you want to get the other side to trust you, you may want to show a willingness to trust them, within the bounds of prudence. If the negotiations will be on-going, or if the process can be broken into stages, this approach can be part of the early stages. Strategic trust building of this sort involves creating low (or moderate) risk opportunities, in the pre-contractual stage, to be trusting, and, thus, provide the other party with occasions to prove themselves trustworthy. This is a way of both testing their trustworthiness and sending a signal of respect. In creating these opportunities, it is important not to appear weak or naive. Mutual trust is not promoted by passively allowing yourself to be taken advantage of. The risk taken should be seen as reasonable, the other party's performance needs to be at least partially observable before final contracting, and you should be prepared to demonstrate dissatisfaction if the trust is abused. . . .

There are two risks, even with modest trusting steps. One risk is that the trust will be abused. If there were no risk of this, it would not be trust. However, if the abuse is observed before further commitments are made, this provides extremely valuable information for going forward. It may be worth the cost. A more serious risk is that you are dealing with a clever opportunist, who plays along until the stakes get high and then exploits the trust.

You have to rely on the due diligence process and your own judgment to help screen out extreme opportunists.

3. Demonstrate Trustworthiness. In addition to showing a willingness to trust, you should also show that you are trustworthy. This is best done in the early stages of the negotiation. Again, the trustworthiness must be at least partially observable before final contracting. To show your trustworthiness, you may have to facilitate the other party's verification. You may need to provide direct access to what would otherwise have been privileged information. Trustworthiness that will not be apparent until much later cannot help build mutual trust in the pre-contracting stage. One difficulty with this strategy is that you do not fully control the opportunities to demonstrate your trustworthiness. These opportunities will, in large part, be a function of the other party's decisions to trust you. It is essential for trust-building that negotiators create and vigilantly watch for opportunities to show that they can be trusted. It is wise to keep even small promises, and be candid about matters that the other side may already know (from their due diligence) or could verify before the deal is complete. Anything short of this could undermine a trust built to that point. As Dasgupta (1988, p.62) points out, "although a reputation for honesty may be acquired slowly, it can generally be destroyed very quickly."

Of course, there are risks in being fully trustworthy. In some cases, it is not possible to conceal your negotiating vulnerabilities without being deceptive. If you are under time pressure and are asked, "How soon do you need to close the deal on this building?", it is hard to conceal your vulnerability without seeming shifty and evasive. The question is not out of line if timing is an important matter for the other party. Being trustworthy may require you to be trusting.

A variation on the strategy of being trustworthy is to offer to stand behind your claims, by using some of the contractual devices we discussed in Metopia (warranties, collateral, etc.) to show that you are willing to protect the other party from the risk and uncertainty of relying on your word. In contrast to visible trustworthy behavior, this can be done with claims that cannot easily be verified before the other side makes a commitment. The point of doing this is not to set a precedent of always using contractual mechanisms to secure the trust. This would defeat the purpose of building the trust. Rather, the purpose of such an offer is to signal good faith, in hopes that a sincere show of good faith on one important issue will alleviate the need for further contractual protection.

4. Place the Negotiation in a Longer-Term Context. When negotiating with someone for the first time, it may be tempting for both parties to think of the negotiation as a one-shot deal. We have seen the incentive problems this can create. When business people develop norms of constantly shopping for the best deal, with no long-term commitment to specific suppliers or customers, they invite this risk. It has been claimed that many of the recent problems on Wall Street result from a breakdown in investment bank and client relations. As investment banks get more aggressive and clients shop around for specialized services, it increases the incentives for drawing a client into a deal that will generate large fees for the bank today, but that

might harm the client in the long run. A wiser long-term strategy may be to demonstrate a willingness to be a loyal negotiating partner. By placing the negotiation in the context of being first among many, the incentive problem may be removed. Within an on-going relationship, the parties can invoke a number of strategies to encourage honest behavior. The fact that these strategies are available should provide some comfort.

Demonstrating loyalty to a relationship takes time. This is hard to do credibly in an initial negotiation. However, some contractual devices can promote this. For instance, making a follow-on service contract part of the deal may help. Alternatively, providing and asking for references can emphasize the importance of reputations and convince the other that you are interested in the long run.

5.   Bring in Mutually Respected Intermediaries. A final possibility is to induce trust by involving a mutually trusted intermediary. This intermediary can serve as a conduit for trust and as a form of security. Though trust may not be perfectly transitive, finding an intermediary who can vouch for the reliability of each of the parties to the negotiation may provide some comfort. This comfort is strengthened when the third party is in a position to reward honest behavior, or punish dishonest behavior (Brams, 1990, pp. 29–61). This practice is common in cross-cultural negotiations when the party from country X hires a respected consultant or representative in country Y to facilitate negotiations with another party in country Y. . . .

Trust building requires time and puts the negotiator at some risk. By using a mutually trusted intermediary, one may be able to shorten the time requirements, but costs and risks remain. Accordingly, trust building is only suitable when additional trust could have significant value, the stakes are high, the risks of trust building can be effectively managed, and the negotiation can be structured to provide sufficient time.

Self-Protection.   Given the uncertainties associated with business negotiation, some element of self-protection and structuring of the incentives of the other party may be in order. *Caveat emptor* may not be a good legal rule, but it is reasonable advice for negotiators in many arm's length business transactions. In discussing Metopia, we identified several mechanisms that might be used to reduce the incentives for deception. Many of these will work just as effectively in the real world. However, when these mechanisms are proposed in the real world, the negotiator proposing them runs the risk of offending the other party: "Don't you trust me?" The offended party may respond irrationally by walking away or retaliating in some fashion. It may lead to an ever increasing spiral of mutual distrust. . . .

The following tactics can be effective in protecting against opportunistic deception when opportunities for trust-building are limited. Since many of these have been introduced earlier, we will keep our descriptions brief.

1. Select Your Negotiating Partners Wisely. The best protection is simply to avoid dealing with opportunists. Provide and ask for references. Consider their reputation, their relationship with you, and their incentives. When you decide to take a risk, do it with your eyes open.

2. Verify What You Can. Do your homework. Kick the tires. Tap into independent sources of information as available. Hire expert third-parties (e.g., inspectors,

assessors, auditors, etc.) to assist. In many instances where there are incentive problems, this will be common practice. Request direct access to information that you need.

3. Get Important Claims in Writing. What you think the other party said and what they think they said (or claim they said) can be two different things, especially when a conflict arises. You should identify those areas in which you are relying most heavily on their word and ask for written clarification. If a written commitment is not feasible, see if you can get them to make their claims in front of an independent audience. Push for some precision. Vague claims and verbal assurances made in private make it difficult to confirm bad faith in court or to reputation channels. The claim should be clear and easily verifiable.

4. Request Bonds and Warranties. Warranties at least provide a written document to appeal to if difficulties arise later. They may be written so as to provide strong incentives for reliability. If the other party has enough resources, it may be wise to ask for collateral (or some other bond) to secure commitments and claims where their good faith will not be evident until after you have made irreversible investments. As noted in the Metopia discussion, these contractual mechanisms must be carefully crafted if they are to be effective and are not to induce more opportunistic behavior.

5. Hire a Skilled Intermediary. A skilled intermediary can serve many purposes. She can provide reputation value, negotiating expertise, legal or technical expertise, and a buffer from the other's manipulative tactics. Finding a suitable intermediary for self-protection is especially hard when you also are interested in building trust. As with any third party, the challenge is to find the right party and to provide them with the right incentives. . . .

Each of the steps we recommend for self-protection is costly. As with trust building, you need to weigh the costs against the benefits. Even when you have little reason to trust the other party, establishing protective mechanisms may be too costly. When the stakes are low, the wise course may be to accept the risk. Nonetheless, in many business negotiations, the stakes are sufficiently high and the level of trust sufficiently low, so that an investment in self-protection is worthwhile.

Many negotiations, particularly those at arms-length with strangers, require both trust building and self-protection. The former works to raise the moral climate, the latter to take the other party out of the path of temptation. The challenge is to strike the right balance. Too much self-protection can undermine the trust-building effort.[9] Care must be taken not to present inconsistent signals.

SUMMARY AND CONCLUSION

Deception is a regrettable, but common element in negotiations. In this paper, we have provided a practical response to the problem of deception in negotiation. The foundation of the response is built on our analysis of a self-interested world, Metopia. This analysis reveals that deception is not monolithic. Different types of deception have different characteristics that need to be considered in promoting honesty. The analysis also illustrates the insidious nature of deception, showing how the mere possibility of deception can rob good faith claims of their credibility. Finally, our exploration of

Metopia suggests many steps that can be taken, even with amoral individuals, to promote honesty.

Real people have a wider range of sentiments and are less rational than Metopians. Accordingly, we propose options for promoting honesty that reflect the differences between Metopia and the real world. They are set within the context of social institutions, public and private, designed, at least in part, to promote honesty. The options draw heavily on a growing body of empirical and theoretical research on negotiation and conflict resolution.

Because of the diversity of negotiation contexts, it is not possible for us to offer a specific strategy that will be effective on all occasions. We hope that our presentation of options allows practitioners to craft strategies appropriate to their situations. These strategies cannot eliminate all deception in negotiation. It is not always wise to invest in building trust, or protecting oneself. Even when it is wise, strategies based on the options we have presented will not always achieve their objectives. Nonetheless, if we are to narrow the Machiavellian gap between the normative ideal of honesty and the practice of negotiation, we must encourage negotiators to identify and pursue opportunities for promoting trust and honesty. We must also encourage them to participate in and improve existing institutional support mechanisms. Some practitioners may even embark on institution building ventures, providing new and better support for doing the right thing. The fight to extend the moral frontier into remaining pockets of Hobbesian behavior (Dees and Cramton, 1991) is a difficult one. It requires creativity and prudent risk taking.

Notes

We are grateful to Howard Stevenson and Tom Piper for comments, and to the Harvard Business School, the National Science Foundation and the Hoover Institution for support.

1. We invoke a narrow notion of self-interest specifically to avoid two dangers inherent in broader notions. One danger is reflected in the meaningless conception of self-interest characterized by revealed preference theory, according to which even the most blatant self-sacrificial behavior is by definition self-interested. Sen (1977) exposes the weaknesses inherent in this definition. The other danger is that posed by some philosophers (see Kavka, 1984) who wish to broaden the notion of self-interest in a specific way, so as to guarantee that ethical behavior is self-interested. Ethical behavior becomes its own reward. Both of these views trivialize real incentive problems.

2. Some would suggest that honesty requires the disclosure of all relevant information, even when withholding that information would not qualify as deception on our account. We prefer to distinguish between honesty, i.e., the absence of deliberate deception, and candor, i.e., complete openness. For simplicity of analysis, we choose to focus on the former.

3. This may seem problematic, because the standard assumptions of game theory imply that deception is never successful. Game theory assumes that the agents are intelligent and rational. As a result, agents recognize when deception is in another's self-interest, and are not misled. By not allowing gullible negotiators, we understate the incentives to deceive. Nonetheless, game theory provides a rigorous and consistent framework for thinking about incentive problems.

4. For simplicity, we speak of one party having information that could be concealed, misrepresented, or truthfully shared. Technically, however, deception can occur even when the deceiver has no private information. It is enough that the other party to the negotiation believe that the first party has valuable private information.

5. For now, we set aside the problem of contracting with these third-parties in Metopia. In order to assure the reliability of a third-party verifier, Metopian negotiators would have to use the same mechanisms that they use for promoting honesty in their primary negotiations.

6. We concentrate here on secular mechanisms relevant to all in our pluralistic society. However, we would be remiss if we failed to note the importance of religion in inspiring and reinforcing the moral conduct of many individuals. Religion often relies not only on inspiration and moral exhortation, but also on powerful incentive systems, including monitoring of behavior by an all-knowing third party. For a discussion of the importance of moral retribution in religion, see Green (1988), especially pp. 12–16.

7. Fisher and Brown (1988) play down the importance of character, suggesting that reliability is largely a function of other things. We acknowledge other influences, but believe that perceptions of character are central to assessing the likelihood of honesty.

8. The practical difficulties of eliminating deception are seen in the distrust often present in labor negotiations. For example, according to *The New York Times* (28 October 1990, p. B1), "At the core of the stalled New York City municipal labor talks is the union leaders' growing distrust of the claims being made about the city's financial plight." This distrust persists despite the fact that the setting allows for reputations (labor and management deal with each other on a regular basis), contractual mechanisms (wage rates could be tied to financial performance) and verification (management can open its books).

9. Ring and Van de Ven (1989) found that, in attempts to build relationships to pursue innovations, too much attention to formal protections of the individual parties could undermine trust created in the informal sharing processes.

Bibliography

Arrow, Kenneth J.: 1974, "Gifts and Exchanges." *Philosophy and Public Affairs* 1, 343–362.

Axelrod, Robert: 1984, *The Evolution of Cooperation* (Basic Books, New York).

Baiman, Stanley and Barry Lewis: 1989, "An Experiment Testing the Behavioral Equivalence of Strategically Equivalent Employment Contracts." *Journal of Accounting Research* 27, 1–20.

Bhide, Amar and Howard H. Stevenson: 1990, "Why Be Honest if Honesty Doesn't Pay." *Harvard Business Review* September–October, 121–129.

Brams, Steven J.: 1990, *Negotiation Games: Applying Game Theory to Bargaining and Arbitration* (Foundation Press, New York).

Carr, Albert Z.: 1968, "Is Business Bluffing Ethical?" *Harvard Business Review* January–February, 143–159.

Chandler, R.: 1955, *The Little Sister* (Penguin Books, Harmondsworth).

Chisholm, Roderick, and Thomas D. Feehan: 1977, "The Intent to Deceive." *Journal of Philosophy* 74, 143–159.

Coleman, James S.: 1990, *Foundations of Social Theory* (Harvard University Press, Cambridge).

Cramton, Peter, Robert Gibbons, and Paul Klemperer: 1987, "Dissolving a Partnership Efficiently." *Econometrica* 55, 615–632.

Dasgupta, Partha: 1988, "Trust as a Commodity." In Diego Gambetta (ed.), *Trust: Making and Breaking Cooperative Relations* (Basil Blackwell Ltd., Oxford).

Dees, J. Gregory, and Peter C. Cramton: 1991, "Shrewd Bargaining on the Moral Frontier: Toward a Theory of Morality in Practice." *Business Ethics Quarterly* 1, 135–167.

Ekman, Paul: 1985, *Telling Lies* (W. W. Norton and Company, New York).

Etzioni, Amitai: 1988, *The Moral Dimension: Toward a New Economics* (The Free Press, New York).

Fried, Charles: 1978, *Right and Wrong* (Harvard University Press, Cambridge).

Good, David: 1988, "Individuals, Interpersonal Relations, and Trust." In Diego Gambetta (ed.), *Trust: Making and Breaking Cooperative Relations* (Basil Blackwell Ltd., Oxford).

Green, Ronald M.: 1988, *Religion and Moral Reason: A New Method for Comparative Study* (Oxford University Press, Oxford).

Hirschleifer, Jack: 1982, "Evolutionary Models in Economics and Law: Cooperation versus Conflict Strategies." In P. H. Rubin and R. O. Zerbe, Jr. (eds.), *Research in Law and Economics* 4, 1–60 (JAI Press, Greenwich).

Hume, David. 1751. *An Enquiry Concerning the Principle of Morals.* References are to the 1975 edition (Clarendon Press, Oxford).

Kavka, Gregory S.: 1984, "The Reconciliation Project." In D. Copp and D. Zimmerman (eds.), *Morality, Reason, and Truth* (Rowman and Allanheld, Totowa).

March, Robert M.: 1989, *The Japanese Negotiator: Subtlety and Strategy Beyond Western Logic* (Kodansha International, Tokyo).

Myerson, Roger B. and Mark A. Satterthwaite: 1983, "Efficient Mechanisms for Bilateral Trading." *Journal of Economic Theory* 28, 265–281.

Nagel, Thomas: 1975, "Comment." In E. S. Phelps (ed.), *Altruism, Morality, and Economic Theory* (Russell Sage Foundation, New York).

Pearce, David: 1992, "Repeated Games: Cooperation and Rationality." In J. J. Laffont (ed.), *Advances in Economic Theory: Sixth World Congress* (Cambridge University Press, Cambridge).

Ring, Peter Smith and Andrew Van de Ven: 1989, "Formal and Informal Dimensions of Transactions." In Andrew H. Van de Ven, Harold L. Angle, and Marshall Scott Poole (eds.), *Research on the Management of Innovation* (Ballinger Publishing Company, New York).

Sen, Amartya: 1977, "Rational Fools: A Critique of the Behavioural Foundations of Economic Theory." *Philosophy and Public Affairs* 6, 317–344.

Smith, Adam. 1759. *The Theory of Moral Sentiments.* Reprinted in 1976 (Liberty Classics, Indianapolis).

White, James J.: 1980, "Machiavelli and the Bar: Ethical Limitations on Lying in Negotiation." *American Bar Foundation Research Journal* 1980, 926–934.

Zucker, Lynne G.: 1986, "The Production of Trust: Institutional Sources of Economic Structure." *Research in Organizational Behavior* 8, 53–111.

Virtues
and
the Virtuous Manager

— *Case Study* —

RUN, Inc.

<small>Ａ<small>MERICAN</small> I<small>NSTITUTE OF</small> C<small>ERTIFIED</small> P<small>UBLIC</small> A<small>CCOUNTANTS</small></small>

The work of preparing the 1991 financial statements for RUN, Inc., was largely complete and the company's Controller, Martin Field, recognized that this final reading of the draft statements was a critical time. Once the statements were released to the printer and distribution was begun there would be no chance for second thoughts. He had been on the job at RUN, Inc. for only five months, but they had been the most tumultuous months of his career. Now all of that tumult was coming down to this single February afternoon. He was proud of the work he had done in cleaning up the Company's balance sheet, and he had satisfied himself that there would be no more unpleasant surprises in that area. He had also pretty well convinced himself that the compromise which had been developed by the CEO for the presentation of the Income Statement was acceptable, but compromises had always made him uncomfortable. It was soon going to be time to accept that compromise or do something else—although what the something else might be was not really clear.

The Company

RUN, Inc. manufactured and marketed a variety of products and parts for automobiles, from starters, alternators and brakes to complete replacement interiors. The Company had originally been known as Rebuilt and Used Auto Parts, Inc. but the acronym RUN had been adopted as the Company's name when the product line was expanded to include new replacement parts and other auto accessories. Sales had been good during the early 1980's as interest rates and credit problems discouraged people from buying new cars and encouraged them to repair and rehabilitate their existing cars. As consumer confidence waned in the later eighties and early nineties, even the upgrading process came under pressure and the company's spectacular sales curve began to flatten out. Still, the company had been well received by the financial markets and the stock traded (on NASDAQ) at an attractive multiple. (Earnings data and stock price activity for the period 1987–91 is detailed in Exhibit I.)

The company sold its products primarily to independent and chain auto parts retailers in the Southeast. Most of the products in the Company's line were either rebuilt from parts which had been scrapped or were manufactured by RUN to meet original equipment specifications. The Company also sold parts and accessories manufactured by offshore suppliers. There were several other companies in the field about the same size as RUN and there was very little to distinguish one firm's rebuilt starter (for example) from another. RUN stressed its distribution system and its prompt delivery as its competitive advantage. The company's primary facilities were in Montgomery, Alabama, but 12 warehouses had been established at strategic locations throughout the Southeast.

RUN's management team included The Chairman (and founder) Harry White; the Chief Executive Officer, John Harvey; the Sales VP, Joanne Jones; the Operations VP, Tex Armor; and the Secretary/Treasurer (and Harry's wife), Mary White. All of those people were members of the Board of Directors, together with a partner in the company's law firm, and a vice-president from the company's bank. Both of those men were long time friends of the Whites, and had been associated with the company since its earliest days. The management team was a close knit group and met frequently for working lunches. Because of the strength of that working relationship, and the strength of the White's personalities, the Board was not significant to the structure of the firm. Board meetings tended to be formalities, where the results of the previous period and plans for the next period were reviewed and approved.

The company's accounting functions were Mary White's responsibility, but the day-to-day accounting activities had been the primary responsibility of Lester Foote, until his retirement in the summer of 1991. Martin Field assumed those day-to-day responsibilities in October, 1991, with the title of Controller. He had taken the job with the understanding that he would become CFO and Treasurer in two years when the Whites were planning to step out of active involvement in the firm.

Earlier, Martin Field had been able to land a job with the Atlanta office of a major CPA firm as a junior auditor. He easily passed the CPA exam on the first try and moved through the ranks of his firm. As he moved up in the firm he found that he was measured against different and more intangible standards: he was expected to resolve accounting problems with client managements at higher and higher levels, and he was asked to look aggressively for opportunities where the firm's tax and consulting services might be brought to bear on clients' business problems. He didn't really like the new marketing-type responsibility he was being asked to undertake, and because he was uncomfortable in that role he did not do it very well. When one of the firm's partners pointed him to an assistant controller's job with one of Atlanta's most prestigious companies, Martin jumped at the chance.

In that new job, Martin was responsible for the preparation of the company's annual and quarterly filings with the SEC, and was the company's primary liaison with the external auditors. It was easy for him to learn the annual reporting process from the other side of the desk, and after several years he was bored. He decided that he wanted to get into the financing aspect of business and to move toward a CFO position.

Martin first heard about RUN when a headhunter, looking for a replacement for Lester Foote, called in early 1991. After some initial interviews, the Company expressed real interest in Martin and he was sorely tempted. The Company's suggestion, that he start as controller and then in two years move up to CFO, seemed to be exactly what he had in mind. Still, he wavered because he was uncomfortable with what he took to be a very unstructured management environment. He reasoned that that nonchalant environment was partly a reflection of the family-style management the company had experienced in its early years, and partly the shirt sleeve nature of the industry. John Harvey assured him that the company's management style was evolving and would continue to become more business-like as the Whites phased out into retirement and played a decreasing role in the firm. Martin understood that the industry would always be a little rough and tumble, but those concerns were somewhat offset by the company's very attractive salary offer. He was finally convinced to take the job when the Whites offered him a five year option to buy 5,000 shares of stock in the firm at $1.50 a share.

Earlier, when Martin had first left public practice, he had carefully weighed the cost of maintaining his membership in the AICPA and his state society. Ultimately he decided to retain those memberships because he was proud of his CPA status, and because those memberships gave him a network of professional associates and brought him journal subscriptions. He also complied with the Continuing Professional Education requirements imposed by his state society and the AICPA, because he felt it was important that he keep his skills up to date. He had joined the Institute of Management Accountants when he first took the assistant controller's job and he found their publications to be of interest as well. When he decided to take the job with RUN, he checked into the membership requirements for the Financial Executives Institute, but found that they would not consider him until he achieved the CFO position.

Problems With the Prior Financials

During Martin's first week on the job, in early October 1991, he studied the firm's systems and began to get into the details of the accounts. In one sense he was pleased that the year-end was fast approaching; he understood that the effort of pulling together the financial statements for the first time would force him to understand the numbers in depth, in a hurry. For example, he was concerned that the inventories seemed to be very high—even for a firm which prided itself on prompt service—and the receivables had been growing much faster than sales. The audit process would surely flush out any problems which might be lurking in those slow turn-over numbers.

After he had been on the job for about three weeks, Martin was invited to a working lunch staff meeting which included all of the other senior executives. He was asked for his impressions after his short time on board. He expressed his concern about the levels of inventory and receivables, and said that in preparation for the year-end audit he planned to visit the warehouses and study the receivables files. Mr. White broke in and told him that it would be better for him to stay around home for a while and be sure he had the lay of the land. He said, "We each take care of our own areas of expertise around here—that's what has gotten us to where we are today. Tex will worry about operations and the inventory, Joanne will worry about the customers and receivables, and you just worry about accounting. We'll all get along fine."

Martin decided to go along for a while but on his own began to do some analysis of the company's operating and balance sheet numbers, comparing them to industry data he was able to get from Dun and Bradstreet. What he saw heightened his concerns (See Exhibit II). He went to see John Harvey and showed him the ratio data he had developed. John expressed surprise at the company's performance against the industry, but said, "We have always been a customer-oriented firm, and we have not let financial details get in the way of service. It may be that we will have to exercise a little more control than we have in the past. And you can help us do that—we're glad you are here." Martin reminded him that the auditors would be in soon and that they would be looking at both receivables and inventory. Martin mused, "Maybe I'll ask them to really get into the details this year, to help us get a good understanding of where we are." John simply waved Martin on.

The next day, John Harvey called Martin into his office. All of the officers of RUN were there, even Mr. and Mrs. White. Mr. White led off, saying, "Martin, we think you are entitled to know what has been going on here. We have all been concerned about the slow-down in the economy caused by those idiots in Washington. Sales have been harder and harder to get, and we have been concerned that the stock price would be badly hurt by any drop-off in our results. I don't have to tell you that this is an important time for the firm, what with Mary and me planning to phase out and sell off some of our holdings. After all we have done to build this firm over the last 25 years we could not let the stock price slip at this critical juncture—I'm not sure you understand that. To keep the price where it belongs, we have been forced to work the books a bit. I'm not sure of the numbers, but some of those receivables you have been so concerned about are the result of sales that we are sure will happen, and some of that inventory is stuff that we have shipped but not yet recorded as cost of goods sold. We knew that eventually things would have to turn around—and they are beginning to do so now. In the next several years, as operations pick back up, we will work those borrowed profits out of receivables and inventories. We decided that you would figure it all out yourself soon enough, and so we thought we had better tell you what you will find."

Martin felt a little weak in the knees. His anger cleared his head however and he said, "Borrowed profits, indeed! You have to face up to those misstatements now. If you can't agree to clean up all of that stuff, I'm going to have to resign. Decide now!" There was an awkward silence, but John Harvey eventually spoke up; he told Martin to work with Tex and Joanne and figure out the dollar effect of the problems and prepare the 1991 financial statements on the assumption that all of those past misstatements would be resolved this year.

Over the next several weeks, Martin picked up worksheets from Tex and Joanne which suggested that the preliminary December 31, 1991 balance sheet included $10 million in receivables and inventory which would have to be written off. Neither of them was exactly sure as to when the results-inflating entries had been recorded but, based on some sketchy notes they had in their files, Tex and Joanne estimated that $5 million of the errors had been booked in the prior quarters of 1991; $3.5 million had been booked in 1990; and $1.5 million had been booked in 1989. Using the data Tex and Joanne provided, Martin prepared the three year income statements required for the 10-K showing these adjustments as "Corrections of Errors." (See Exhibit III.)

When he showed those results to John Harvey, John blanched. He said, "Martin we can't do that. No one is really sure which years are affected, in what amounts. Besides, if we report that we are adjusting the earnings we reported in prior years, we will lose all credibility with our stockholders. Because of the economy, the results we have been forced to report have been depressing anyway, and if we add a new insult to the existing injury, we will probably get sued. I can't let the Whites wrap up their careers here with that hanging over their heads. If we can't work out another way of putting that $10 million behind us, we'll have to find a way to bleed it in over the next several years. The economy *is* picking up you know." When Martin started to protest, John went on, "Why don't we just charge all of that stuff off this year as a restructuring charge and say that we are taking a belt-tightening approach to the business. If we do that right, the stock price might even go up—I've seen that happen to other companies."

John Harvey had Martin's draft re-typed, pulling the $10 million into 1991 as an unusual item. John also drafted a note which described that charge as a result of a fresh look at inventory and receivables (See the revised statements and the draft note in Exhibit IV), and took the package to show to Mr. and Mrs. White. Later, Mrs. White came to see Martin and told him how pleased she was that he had forced the company to clean house. She said that she was glad that these problems would be resolved now because she had always worried about what people would say if the company had been forced to take a big write-off the year after she retired. She commented that this was one year she would be happy to sign the 10-K, saying "Next year you can sign off as the person responsible for the statements, but please let me have this satisfaction this year." The income statement with the special charge in 1991 was presented to the CPA firm for their audit.

As the audit progressed, the partner and manager asked about the special charge, and Martin explained that because he was going to be responsible for the December 31, 1991 balance sheet as the starting point for 1992, he had insisted that that balance sheet be as clean as possible. He referred the auditors to John Harvey's draft footnote as a further explanation for the big write-off. However, he also took the CPAs to lunch at an out-of-the-way place and suggested that they look very carefully at the receivables and inventory items that were written off in that special charge. He reminded the auditors that he was new on the job and didn't have all of the details, but that "some of those things in that write-off don't pass the smell test." In a subsequent meeting with Martin and John Harvey, the CPAs challenged the special-item treatment for the write-offs. John explained his belt-tightening philosophy, and when the CPAs nodded sympathetically, Martin sat quietly, saying nothing.

That had been two weeks ago. The external audit team had completed their work and had reported that the balance sheet was as clean as Martin had said. They accepted the income statement presentation for the $10 million, treating it as a special charge—one of the staff people referred to it as a "change in estimate." All of the documentation for the audit was completed: the attorneys' letters were in, the important confirmations had all been returned and Mr. and Mrs. White and John Harvey had signed the usual representation letter for the CPA firm. The typed financial statement package was on Martin's desk ready for one final reading before being delivered to the printer. The statements were scheduled to be mailed to the shareholders the next day, and would be reviewed at the shareholders' meeting two weeks from today. Martin poured himself another cup of coffee and sat down to read the statements carefully one more time.

EXHIBIT I. RUN, Inc.: Five Year Income and Stock Price Data (000)

	1991*	1990	1989	1988	1987
SALES	$75,000	$68,000	$58,000	$45,000	$35,000
growth rate, ty/ly	10.3%	17.2%	28.9%	28.6%	
COST OF SALES	$39,500	$35,500	$30,000	$22,500	$17,000
% of sales	52.7%	52.2%	51.7%	50.0%	48.6%
EXPENSES	$18,500	$17,500	$16,250	$13,500	$11,000
EARNINGS PRE TAX	$17,000	$15,000	$11,750	$ 9,000	$ 7,000
% of sales	22.7%	22.1%	20.3%	20.0%	20.0%
growth rate, ty/ly	13.3%	27.7%	30.6%	28.6%	
EARNINGS AFTER TAX	$11,050	$ 9,300	$ 7,050	$ 5,220	$ 4,060
% of sales	14.7%	13.7%	12.2%	11.6%	11.6%
growth rate, ty/ly	18.8%	31.9%	35.1%	28.6%	
EARNINGS PER SHARE	$ 0.111	$ 0.095	$ 0.074	$ 0.055	$ 0.051
MIDDLE OF STOCK					
PRICE RANGE	$ 1.44	$ 1.33	$ 1.11	$ 0.77	$ 0.61
multiple	13	14	15	14	12

*The estimated results for 1991 are the numbers expected by the market, based on the results reported through the first nine months, and trends in the industry. The company's book numbers, before consideration of any adjustments discussed in the case, were very cose to these estimates.

ty/ly means that the ratio is the growth rate from last year to this.

EXHIBIT II. RUN Inc.: Comparative Ratio Analysis

	RUN data		Industry data	
	1991	*1990*	*1991*	*1990*
Return on sales, %	14.7%	13.7%	11.8%	10.7%
Asset turnover	.58	.54	.66	.58
Days sales outstanding	161	166	141	155
Inventory turn	.70	.65	.82	.74

EXHIBIT III. RUN, Inc.: Five Year Income Statement (000)

	1991		1990		1989		1988		1987	
SALES	$75,000		$68,000		$58,000		$45,000		$35,000	
growth rate, ty/ly		10.3%		17.2%		28.9%		28.6%		
COST OF SALES	$39,500		$35,500		$30,000		$22,500		$17,000	
% of sales		52.7%		52.2%		51.7%		50.0%		48.6%
EXPENSES	$18,500		$17,500		$16,250		$13,500		$11,000	
EARNINGS PRE TAX	$17,000		$15,000		$11,750		$ 9,000		$ 7,000	
% of sales		22.7%		22.1%		20.3%		20.0%		20.0%
growth rate, ty/ly		13.3%		27.7%		30.6%		28.6%		
EARNINGS AFTER TAX	$11,050		$ 9,300		$ 7,050		$ 5,220		$ 4,060	
% of sales		14.7%		13.7%		12.2%		11.6%		11.6%
growth rate, ty/ly		18.8%		31.9%		35.1%		28.6%		
CORRECTION OF ERROR (after tax)	$ 3,250		$ 2,170		900					
NET EARNINGS	$ 7,800		$ 7,130		$ 6,150		$ 5,220		$ 4,060	
EARNINGS PER SHARE:										
Before error correction	$ 0.110		$ 0.094		$ 0.074		$ 0.055		$ 0.051	
After error correction	$ 0.078		$ 0.073		$ 0.065		$ 0.055		$ 0.051	

71

EXHIBIT IV. RUN, Inc.: Five Year Income Statement (000)

	1991		1990		1989		1988		1987	
SALES	$75,000		$68,000		$58,000		$45,000		$35,000	
growth rate, ty/ly		10.3%		17.2%		28.9%		28.6%		48.6%
COST OF SALES	$39,500		$35,500		$30,000		$22,500		$17,000	
% of sales		52.7%		52.2%		51.7%		50.0%		48.6%
EXPENSES	$18,500		$17,500		$16,250		$13,500		$11,000	
SPECIAL CHARGE	$10,000		0		0		0			
EARNINGS PRE TAX	$ 7,000		$15,000		$11,750		$ 9,000		$ 7,000	
% of sales		9.3%		22.1%		20.3%		20.0%		20.0%
growth rate, ty/ly		−53.3%		27.7%		30.6%		28.6%		
EARNINGS AFTER TAX	$ 4,550		$ 9,300		$ 7,050		$ 5,220		$ 4,060	
% of sales		6.1%		13.7%		12.2%		11.6%		11.6%
growth rate, ty/ly		−51.1%		31.9%		35.1%		28.6%		
EARNINGS PER SHARE	$ 0.046		$ 0.095		$ 0.074		$ 0.055		$ 0.051	

Financial Statement Footnote

SPECIAL CHARGE
Because of the continued decline in the economy, the company determined to challenge the levels of the assets it would carry forward into the next year, and in fourth quarter of 1991 took an objective look at receivables and inventories. That fresh look, together with an understanding that business operations in the future will be more rigorous than they have been in the past years, resulted in a writedown of excess inventory and slow paying receivables. The company believes that the writedown was necessary to account for those assets at the lower of cost or market, as market conditions are perceived today.

EXHIBIT V. RUN, Inc.: Extracts from the AICPA Code, Applicable to the Case

ARTICLE II—THE PUBLIC INTEREST

Members should accept the obligation to act in a way that will serve the public interest, honor the public trust, and demonstrate commitment to professionalism.

.01 A distinguishing mark of a profession is acceptance of its responsibility to the public. The accounting profession's public consists of clients, credit grantors, governments, employers, investors, the business and financial community, and others who rely on the objectivity and integrity of certified public accountants to maintain the orderly functioning of commerce. This reliance imposes a public interest responsibility on certified public accountants. The public interest is defined as the collective well-being of the community of people and institutions the profession serves.

.02 In discharging their professional responsibilities, members may encounter conflicting pressures from among each of those groups. In resolving those conflicts, members should act with integrity, guided by the precept that when members fulfill their responsibility to the public, clients' and employers' interests are best served.

.03 Those who rely on certified public accountants expect them to discharge their responsibilities with integrity, objectivity, due professional care, and a genuine interest in serving the public. They are expected to provide quality services, enter into fee arrangements, and offer a range of services—all in a manner that demonstrates a level of professionalism consistent with these Principles of the Code of Professional Conduct.

.04 All who accept membership in the American Institute of Certified Public Accountants commit themselves to honor the public trust. In return for the faith that the public reposes in them, members should seek continually to demonstrate their dedication to professional excellence.

ARTICLE III—INTEGRITY

To maintain and broaden public confidence, members should perform all professional responsibilities with the highest sense of integrity.

.01 Integrity is an element of character fundamental to professional recognition. It is the quality from which the public trust derives and the benchmark against which a member must ultimately test all decisions.

.02 Integrity requires a member to be, among other things, honest and candid within the constraints of client confidentiality. Service and the public trust should not be subordinated to personal gain and advantage. Integrity can accommodate the inadvertent error and the honest difference of opinion; it cannot accommodate deceit or subordination of principle.

.03 Integrity is measured in terms of what is right and just. In the absence of specific rules, standards, or guidance, or in the face of conflicting opinions, a member should test decisions and deeds by asking: "Am I doing what a person of integrity would do? Have I retained my integrity?" Integrity requires a member to observe both the form and the spirit of technical and ethical standards; circumvention of those standards constitutes subordination of judgment.

.04 Integrity also requires a member to observe the principles of objectivity and independence and of due care.

ARTICLE IV—OBJECTIVITY AND INDEPENDENCE

A member should maintain objectivity and be free of conflicts of interest in discharging professional responsibilities. A member in public practice should be independent in fact and appearance when providing auditing and other attestation services.

.01 Objectivity is a state of mind, a quality that lends value to a member's services. It is a distinguishing feature of the profession. The principle of objectivity imposes the obligation to be impartial, intellectually honest, and free of conflicts of interest. Independence precludes relationships that may appear to impair a member's objectivity in rendering attestation services.

.02 Members often serve multiple interests in many different capacities and must demonstrate their objectivity in varying circumstances. Members in public practice render attest, tax, and management advisory services. Other members prepare financial statements in the employment of others, perform internal auditing services, and serve in financial and management capacities in industry, education, and government. They also educate and train those who aspire to admission into the profession. Regardless of service or capacity, members should protect the integrity of their work, maintain objectivity, and avoid any subordination of their judgment.

.03 For a member in public practice, the maintenance of objectivity and independence requires a continuing assessment of client relationships and public responsibility. Such a member who provides auditing and other attestation sevices should be independent in fact and appearance. In providing all other services, a member should maintain objectivity and avoid conflicts of interest.

.04 Although members not in public practice cannot maintain the appearance of independence, they nevertheless have the responsibility to maintain objectivity in rendering professional services. Members employed by others to prepare financial statements or to perform auditing, tax, or consulting services are charged with the same responsibility for objectivity as members in public practice and must be scrupulous in their application of generally accepted accounting principles and candid in all their dealings with members in public practice.

**EXHIBIT VA. RUN, Inc.: Extracts from the AICPA Ethics
Rules and Interpretations—Section 102**

INTEGRITY AND OBJECTIVITY

.01 Rule 102—Integrity and objectivity. In the performance of any professional service, a member shall maintain objectivity and integrity, shall be free of conflicts of interest, and shall not knowingly misrepresent facts or subordinate his or her judgment to others. [As adopted January 12, 1988.]

Interpretations under Rule 102—Integrity and Objectivity

Interpretations and Ethics Rulings which existed before the adoption of the Code of Professional Conduct on January 12, 1988, will remain in effect until further action is deemed necessary by the appropriate senior technical committee.

.02 102-1—Knowing misrepresentations in the preparation of financial statements or records. A member who knowingly makes, or permits or directs another to make, false and misleading entries in an entity's financial statements or records shall be considered to have knowingly misrepresented facts in violation of rule 102 [ET section 102.01].

.03 102-2—Conflicts of interest. A conflict of interest may occur if a member performs a professional service for a client or employer and the member or his or her firm has a significant relationship with another person, entity, product, or service that could be viewed as impairing the member's objectivity. If this significant relationship is disclosed to and consent is obtained from such client, employer, or other appropriate parties, the rule shall not operate to prohibit the performance of the professional service. When making the disclosure, the member should consider rule 301, "Confidential Client Information" [ET section 301.01].

Certain professional engagements require independence. Independence impairments under rule 101 [ET section 101.01] and its interpretations cannot be eliminated by such disclosure and consent. [Effective August 31, 1989.]

.04 102-3—Obligations of member to his or her employer's external accountant. Under rule 102 [ET section 102.01], a member must maintain objectivity and integrity in the performance of a professional service. In dealing with his or her employer's external accountant, a member must be candid and not knowingly misrepresent facts or knowingly fail to disclose material facts. This would include, for example, responding to specific inquiries for which his or her employer's external accountant requests written representation. [Effective November 30, 1993.]

.05 102-4—Subordination of judgment by a member. Rule 102 [ET section 102.01] prohibits a member from knowingly misrepresenting facts or subordinating his or her judgment when performing professional services. Under this rule, if a member and his or her supervisor have a disagreement or dispute relating to the preparation of financial statements or the recording of transactions, the member should take the following steps to ensure that the situation does not constitute a subordination of judgment:[1]

1. The member should consider whether (a) the entry or the failure to record a transaction in the records, or (b) the financial statement presentation or the nature or omission of disclosure in the financial statements, as proposed by the supervisor, represents the use of an acceptable alternative and does not materially misrepresent the facts. If, after appropriate research or consultation, the member concludes that the matter has authoritative support and/or does not result in a material misrepresentation, the member need do nothing further.

2. If the member concludes that the financial statements or records could be materially misstated, the member should make his or her concerns known to the appropriate higher level(s) of management within the organization (for example, the supervisor's immediate superior, senior management, the audit committee or equivalent, the board of directors, the company's owners). The member should consider documenting his or her understanding of the facts, the accounting principles involved, the application of those principles to the facts, and the parties with whom these matters were discussed.

3. If, after discussing his or her concerns with the appropriate person(s) in the organization, the member concludes that appropriate action was not taken, he or she should consider his or her continuing relationship with the employer. The member also should consider any responsibility that may exist to communicate to third parties, such as regulatory authorities or the employer's (former employer's) external accountant. In this connection, the member may wish to consult with his or her legal counsel.

4. The member should at all times be cognizant of his or her obligations under interpretation 102-3 [ET section 101.04].

[Effective November 30, 1993.]

ACCOUNTING PRINCIPLES

.01 Rule 203—Accounting principles. A member shall not (1) express an opinion or state affirmatively that the financial statements or other financial data of any entity are presented in conformity with generally accepted accounting principles or (2) state that he or she is not aware of any material modifications that should be made to such statements or data in order for them to be in conformity with generally accepted accounting principles, if such statements or data contain any departure from an accounting principle promulgated by bodies designated by Council to establish such principles that has a material effect on the statements or data taken as a whole. If, however, the statements or data contain such a departure and the member can demonstrate that due to unusual circumstances the financial statements or data would otherwise have been misleading, the member can comply with the rule by describing the departure, its approximate effects, if practicable, and the reasons why compliance with the principle would result in a misleading statement.

[As adopted January 12, 1988.]

Interpretations under Rule 203—Accounting Principles

Interpretations and Ethics Rulings which existed before the adoption of the Code of Professional Conduct on January 12, 1988, will remain in effect until further action is deemed necessary by the appropriate senior technical committee.

.02 203-1—Departures from established accounting principles. Rule 203 [ET section 203.01] was adopted to require compliance with accounting principles promulgated by the body designated by Council to establish such principles. There is a strong presumption that adherence to officially established accounting principles would in nearly all instances result in financial statements that are not misleading.

However, in the establishment of accounting principles it is difficult to anticipate all of the circumstances to which such principles might be applied. This rule therefore recognizes that upon occasion there may be unusual circumstances where the literal application of pronouncements on accounting principles would have the effect of rendering financial statements misleading. In such cases, the proper accounting treatment is that which will render the financial statements not misleading.

The question of what constitutes unusual circumstances as referred to in rule 203 [ET section 203.01] is a matter of professional judgment involving the ability to support the position that adherence to a promulgated principle would be regarded generally by reasonable men as producing a misleading result.

Examples of events which may justifiy departures from a principle are new legislation or the evolution of a new form of business transaction. An unusual degree of materiality or the existence of conflicting industry practices are examples of circumstances which would not ordinarily be regarded as unusual in the context of rule 203 [ET section 203.01].

.03 203-2—Status of FASB interpretations. Council is authorized under rule 203 [ET section 203.01] to designate a body to establish accounting principles and has designated the Financial Accounting Standards Board as such body. Council also has resolved that FASB Statements of Financial Accounting Standards, together with those Accounting Research Bulletins and APB Opinions which are not superseded by action of the FASB, constitute accounting principles as contemplated in rule 203 [ET section 203.01].

In determining the existence of a departure from an accounting principle established by a Statement of Financial Accounting Standards, Accounting Research Bulletin or APB Opinion encompassed by rule 203 [ET section 203.01], the division of professional ethics will construe such Statement, Bulletin or Opinion in the light of any interpretations thereof issued by the FASB.

[.04][203-3] [Deleted]

.05 203-4—Responsibility of employees for the preparation of financial statements in conformity with GAAP, Rule 203 [ET section 203.01] provides, in part, that a member shall not state affirmatively that financial statements or other financial data of an entity are presented in conformity with generally accepted accounting principles (GAAP) if such statements or data contain any departure from an accounting principle promulgated by a body designated by Council to establish such principles that has a material effect on the statements or data taken as a whole.

Rule 203 [ET section 203.01] applies to all members with respect to any affirmation that financial statements or other financial data are presented in conformity with GAAP. Represention regarding GAAP conformity included in a letter or other communication from a client entity to its auditor or others related to that entity's financial statements is subject to rule 203 [ET section 203.01] and may be considered an affirmative statement within the meaning of the rule with respect to members who signed the letter or other communication; for example, signing reports to regulatory authorities, creditors and auditors.
[Effective November 30, 1993.]

Note

1. A member in the practice of public accounting should refer to the Statements on Auditing Standards. For example, see SAS No. 22, *Planning and Supervision* [AU section 311], which discusses what the auditor should do when there are differences of opinion concerning accounting and auditing standards.

**EXHIBIT VI. RUN, Inc.: Standards of Ethical Conduct
for Management Accountants**

STANDARDS OF ETHICAL CONDUCT
FOR MANAGEMENT ACCOUNTANTS

Management accountants have an obligation to the organizations they serve, their profession, the public, and themselves to maintain the highest standards of ethical conduct. In recognition of this obligation, the National Association of Accountants has promulgated the following standards of ethical conduct for management accountants. Adherence to these standards is integral to achieving the *Objectives of Management Accounting.*[1] Management accountants shall not commit acts contrary to these standards nor shall they condone the commission of such acts by others within their organizations.

Competence

Management accountants have a responsibility to:

- Maintain an appropriate level of professional competence by ongoing development of their knowledge and skills.
- Perform their professional duties in accordance with relevant laws, regulations, and technical standards.
- Prepare complete and clear reports and recommendations after appropriate analyses of relevant and reliable information.

Confidentiality

Management accountants have a responsibility to:

- Refrain from disclosing confidential information acquired in the course of their work except when authorized, unless legally obligated to do so.
- Inform subordinates as appropriate regarding the confidentiality of information acquired in the course of their work and monitor their activities to assure the maintenance of that confidentiality.
- Refrain from using or appearing to use confidential information acquired in the course of their work for unethical or illegal advantage either personally or through third parties.

Integrity

Management accountants have a responsibility to:

- Avoid actual or apparent conflicts of interest and advise all appropriate parties of any potential conflict.
- Refrain from engaging in any activity that would prejudice their ability to carry out their duties ethically.
- Refuse any gift, favor, or hospitality that would influence or would appear to influence their actions.
- Refrain from either actively or passively subverting the attainment of the organization's legitimate and ethical objectives.
- Recognize and communicate professional limitations or other constraints that would preclude responsible judgment or successful performance of an activity.
- Communicate unfavorable as well as favorable information and professional judgments or opinions.
- Refrain from engaging in or supporting any activity that would discredit the profession.

Objectivity

Management accountants have a responsibility to:

- Communicate information fairly and objectively.
- Disclose fully all relevant information that could reasonably be expected to influence an intended user's understanding of the reports, comments, and recommendations presented.

Resolution of Ethical Conflict

In applying the standards of ethical conduct, management accountants may encounter problems in identifying unethical behavior or in resolving an ethical conflict. When faced with significant ethical issues, management accountants should follow the established policies of the organization bearing on the resolution of such conflict. If these policies do not resolve the ethical conflict, management accountants should consider the following course of action:

- Discuss such problems with the immediate superior except when it appears that the superior is involved, in which case the problem should be presented initially to the next higher managerial level. If satisfactory resolution cannot be achieved when the problem is initially presented, submit the issues to the next higher managerial level.

    If the immediate superior is the chief executive officer, or equivalent, the acceptable reviewing authority may be a group such as the audit committee, board of directors, board of trustees, or owners. Contact with levels above the immediate superior should be initiated only with the superior's knowledge, assuming the superior is not involved.

- Clarify relevant concepts by confidential discussion with an objective advisor to obtain an understanding of possible courses of action.

- If the ethical conflict still exists after exhausting all levels of internal review, the management accountant may have no other recourse on significant matters than to resign from the organization and to submit an informative memorandum to an appropriate representative of the organization.

Except where legally prescribed, communication of such problems to authorities or individuals not employed or engaged by the organization is not considered appropriate.

Note

1. National Association of Accountants. *Statements on Management Accounting: Objectives of Management Accounting.* Statement No. 1B, New York, N.Y., June 17, 1982.

EXHIBIT VII. RUN, Inc.: Code of Ethics for the Membership of the Financial Executives Institute

CODE OF ETHICS

To be eligible for active membership in Financial Executives Institute, applicants must possess those personal attributes such as character, personal integrity and business ability that will be an asset to the Institute. They must also meet pre-established criteria indicating a high degree of participation in the formulation of policies for the operation of the enterprises they represent and in the administration of the financial functions. Members of the Institute are expected to follow this Code of Ethics.

As a member of Financial Executives Institute, I will:

Conduct my business and personal affairs at all times with honesty and integrity.

Provide complete, appropriate and relevant information in an objective manner when reporting to management, stockholders, employees, government agencies, other institutions and the public.

Comply with rules and regulations of federal, state, provincial, and local governments, and other appropriate private and public regulatory agencies.

Discharge duties and responsibilities to my employer to the best of my ability, including complete communication on all matters within my jurisdiction.

Maintain the confidentiality of information acquired in the course of my work except when authorized or otherwise legally obligated to disclose. Confidential information acquired in the course of my work will not be used for my personal advantage.

Maintain an appropriate level of professional competence through continuing development of my knowledge and skills.

Refrain from committing acts discreditable to myself, my employer, FEI or fellow members of the Institute.

Corporate Roles, Personal Virtues:
An Aristotelean Approach to Business Ethics

ROBERT C. SOLOMON

Each of us is ultimately lonely. In the end, it's up to each of us and each of us alone to figure out who we are and who we are not, and to act more or less consistently on those conclusions.

—TOM PETERS "The Ethical Debate"
Ethics Digest, Dec 1989, p. 2.

THE ARISTOTELEAN APPROACH TO BUSINESS ETHICS

Economists and economic theorists naturally tend to look at systems and theories about systems, while ethicists tend to look at individual behavior, its motives and consequences. Neither of these approaches is suitable for business ethics. One of the problems in business ethics, accordingly, is the *scope* and *focus* of the disciplines and the proper unit of study and discourse. Much of the work in business ethics courses and seminars centers around "case studies," which almost always involve one or several particular people within the realm of a particular corporation in a particular industry facing

Reprinted by permission of the author, Robert C. Solomon, University of Texas at Austin, and *Business Ethics Quarterly*, The Journal of the Society for Business Ethics, July 1992, Vol. 2, Issue 3.

some particular crisis or dilemma. Individual ethical values are, of course, relevant here, but they are rarely the focus of attention. Economics, of course, is essential to the discussion—since the realm of the corporation is, after all, a business, but the desire to show a profit is virtually taken for granted while our attention is drawn to other values. Insofar as business ethics theories tend to be drawn from either individualistic ethics or economics they remain remote from the case study method which often seems so inadequate with regard to more general implications and conclusions in business and why business ethics theory lags so far behind theory in both ethics and economics. In this paper, I want to begin to develop a more appropriate focus for business ethics theory, one that centers on *the individual within the corporation*. For reasons that should be evident to anyone who has had the standard Philosophy 102 History of Ethics course, I call this the Aristotelean Approach to Business Ethics. . . .

Aristotle is the philosopher who is best known for this emphasis on the cultivation of the virtues. But isn't it inappropriate if not perverse to couple Aristotle and business ethics? True, he was the first economist. He had much to say about the ethics of exchange and so might well be called the first (known) business ethicist as well. But Aristotle distinguished two different senses of what I call economics, one of them "*oecinomicus*" or household trading, which he approved of and thought essential to the working of any even modestly complex society, and "*chrematisike*," which is trade for profit. Aristotle declared that latter activity wholly devoid of virtue and called those who engaged in such purely selfish practices "parasites." All trade, he believed, was a kind of exploitation. Such was his view of what I call "business." Indeed, Aristotle's attack on the unsavory and unproductive practice of "usury" and the personal vice of avarice held force virtually until the seventeenth century. Only outsiders at the fringe of society, not respectable citizens, engaged in such practices. (Shakespeare's Shylock, in *The Merchant of Venice*, was such an outsider and a usurer, though his idea of a forfeit was a bit unusual.) It can be argued that Aristotle had too little sense of the importance of production and based his views wholly on the aristocratically proper urge for acquisition, thus introducing an unwarranted zero-sum thinking into his economics.[1] And, of course, it can be charged that Aristotle, like his teacher Plato, was too much the spokesman for the aristocratic class and quite unfair to the commerce and livelihoods of foreigners and commoners.[2] It is Aristotle who initiates so much of the history of business ethics as the wholesale attack on business and its practices. Aristotelean prejudices underlie much of business criticism and the contempt for finance that preoccupies so much of Christian ethics even to this day, avaricious evangelicals notwithstanding. Even defenders of business often end up presupposing Aristotelean prejudices in such Pyrrhonian arguments as "business is akin to poker and apart from the ethics of everyday life"[3] (Albert Carr) and "the [only] social responsibility of business is to increase its profits" (Milton Friedman).[4] But if it is just this schism between business and the rest of life that so infuriated Aristotle, for whom life was supposed to fit together, in a coherent whole, it is the same holistic idea—that business people and corporations are first of all part of a larger community—that drives business ethics today. I can no longer accept the amoral idea that "business is business" (not a tautology but an excuse for insensitivity). According to

Aristotle, one has to think of oneself as a member of the larger community, the *Polis*, and strive to excel, to bring out what was best in ourselves and our shared enterprise. What is best in us—our virtues—are in turn defined by that larger community, and there is therefore no ultimate split of antagonism between individual self-interest and the greater public good. Of course, there were no corporations in those days, but Aristotle would certainly know what I mean when I say that most people in business now identify themselves—if tenuously—in terms of their companies, and corporate policies, much less corporate codes of ethics, are not by themselves enough to constitute an ethics. But corporations are not isolated city-states, not even the biggest and most powerful of the multi-nationals (contrast the image of "the sovereign state of ITT"). They are part and parcel of a larger global community. The people that work for them are thus citizens of two communities at once, and one might think of business ethics as getting straight about the dual citizenship. What I need to cultivate is a certain way of thinking about ourselves in and out of the corporate context, and this is the aim of ethical theory in business, as I understand it. It is not, I insist, anti-individualistic in any sense of "individualism" that is worth defending. The Aristotelean approach to business ethics rather begins with the idea that it is individual virtue and integrity that counts: good corporate and social policy will follow: good corporate and social policy are both the preconditions and the result of careful cultivation and encouragement.

With what is this Aristotelean approach to be contrasted? . . .

It is to be contrasted with that two hundred or so year old obsession in ethics that takes everything of significance to be a matter of *rational principles*, "morality" as the strict Kantian sense of duty to the moral law. This is not to say, of course, that Aristotelean ethics dispenses with rationality, or for that matter with principles or the notion of duty. But Aristotle is quite clear about the fact that it is cultivation of character that counts, long before we begin to "rationalize" our actions, and the formulation of general principles (in what he famously but confusingly calls his "practical syllogism") is not an explicit step in correct and virtuous behavior as such but rather a philosopher's formulation about what it means to act rationally.[5] And, most important for our purposes here, duties too are defined by our roles in a community, e.g. a corporation, and not by means of any abstract ratiocination, principle of contradiction or *a priori* formulations of the categorical imperative. Kant, magnificent as he was a thinker, has proved to be a kind of disease in ethics. It's all very elegant, even brilliant, until one walks into the seminar room with a dozen or so bright, restless corporate managers, waiting to hear what's new and what's relevant to them on the business ethics scene. And then we tell them: don't lie, don't steal, don't cheat—elaborated and supported by the most gothic non-econometric construction ever allowed in a company training center. But it's not just its impracticality and the fact that we don't actually do ethics that way; the problem is that the Kantian approach shifts our attention away from just what I would call the "inspirational" matters of business ethics (its "incentives") and the emphasis on "excellence" (a buzz-word for Aristotle as well as Tom Peters and his millions of readers). It shifts the critical focus from oneself as a full-blooded person occupying a significant role in a productive organization to an abstract role-transcendent morality that necessarily finds itself empty-handed when it comes to most of the matters and many of the motives that we hear so much about in any corporate setting.

The Aristotelean approach is also to be contrasted with that rival ethical theory that goes by the name of "utilitarianism." I have considerably more to say about utilitarianism, its continued vulgarization and its forgotten humanistic focus in John Stuart Mill, but not here. For now, I just want to point out that utilitarianism shares with Kant that special appeal to anal compulsives in its doting over principles and rationalization (in crass calculation) and its neglect of individual responsibility and the cultivation of character. (John Stuart Mill exempted himself from much of this charge in the last chapter of *Utilitarianism*, but I promised not to talk about that here.) But I can imagine a good existentialist complaining quite rightly that the point of all such "decision procedures" in ethics is precisely to neutralize the annoyance of personal responsibility altogether, appealing every decision to "the procedure" rather than taking responsibility oneself. Of course, I am not denying the importance of concern for the public good or the centrality of worrying, in any major policy decision, about the number of people helped and hurt. But I take very seriously the problems of measurement and incommensurability that have been standard criticisms of utilitarianism ever since Bentham, and there are considerations that often are more basic than public utility—if only because, in most of our actions, the impact on public utility is so small in contrast to the significance for our personal sense of integrity and "doing the right thing" that it becomes a negligible factor in our deliberations.

I would also distinguish the Aristotelean approach to business ethics from all of those approaches that primarily emphasize rights, whether the rights of free enterprise as such, the rights of the employee, the customer or the community and even civil rights. Again, I have no wish to deny the relevance of rights to ethics or the centrality of civil rights, but I think that we should remind ourselves that talk about rights was never intended to eclipse talk about responsibilities and I think the emphasis in business ethics should move from *having* rights oneself to *recognizing* the rights of others, but then, I'm not at all sure that all of this couldn't just as well or better be expressed by saying that there are all sorts of things that a virtuous person should or shouldn't ever do to others.[6] Of course, Aristotle's defense of slavery in his *Politics* should be more than enough to convince us that we would still need the language of rights even with a fully developed language of the virtues. The problem with virtue ethics is that it tends to be provincial and ethnocentric. It thereby requires the language of rights and some general sense of utility as a corrective.

It will be evident to most of you that I am arguing—or about to argue— for a version of what has recently been called "virtue ethics," but I do want to distance myself from much of what has been defended recently under that title. . . .

THE SIX DIMENSIONS OF VIRTUE ETHICS

So what defines the Aristotelean approach to business ethics? What are its primary dimensions? There is a great deal of ground to be covered, from the general philosophical questions "what is a virtue?" and "what is the role of the virtues in ethics and the good life?" to quite specific questions about virtues and supposed virtues in business, such as loyalty, dependability, integrity, shrewdness and "toughness." But I can only begin to answer these general questions or speak much of these particular virtues here, but what I want to do first is to very briefly circumscribe the discussion of the virtues in business ethics with a half dozen considerations not usually so highlighted in the more abstract and principle-bound discussions of ethics nor so personalized in the policy discussions that so dominate the field. Those six considerations make up the framework of virtue ethics in business, and for the sake of brevity I simply call them: *community, excellence, role identity, holism, integrity, judgment.*

Community

The Aristotelean approach and, I would argue, the leading question for business in the nineties begins with the idea that the corporation is first of all a community. We are all individuals, to be sure, but we find our identities and our meanings only within communities, and for most of us that means— at work in a company or an institution. The philosophical myth that has grown almost cancerous in many business circles, the neo-Hobbesian view that "it's every man[sic] for himself" and the newer Darwinian view that "it's all a jungle out there" are direct denials of the Aristotelean view that we are all *first of all* members of a community and our self-interest is for the most part identical to the larger interests of the group. Our individuality is socially constituted and socially situated. Furthermore, our seemingly all-important concept of competition presumes, it does not replace, an underlying assumption of mutual interest and cooperation. Whether we do well, whether we like ourselves, whether we lead happy productive lives, depends to a large extent on the companies we choose. As the Greeks used to say, "to live the good life one must live in a great city." To my business students today, who are all too prone to choose a job on the basis of salary and start-up bonus alone, I always say, "to live a decent life choose the right company." In business ethics the corporation is one's community, which is not to deny, of course, that there is always a larger community—as diverse as it may be—that counts even more.

Excellence

The Greek "*arete*" is often translated either "virtue" or "excellence," as opposed to the rather modest and self-effacing notion of "virtue" that we inherited from our Victorian ancestors (indeed, even Kant used the term). The dual translation by itself makes a striking point. It is not enough to do no wrong. "Knowingly do no harm" (*Primus non nocere*) is *not* the end of business ethics (as Peter Drucker suggests[7]). The hardly original slogan I sometimes use to sell what I do, "ethics and excellence" (the title of the book in which this essay finds its home) is not just a tag-along with Peters and Waterman. Virtue is doing one's best, excelling, and not merely "toeing the line" and "keeping one's nose clean." The virtues that constitute business ethics should not be conceived as purely ethical or moral virtues, as if (to come again) business ethics were nothing other than the general application of moral principles to one specific context (among others). Being a "tough negotiator" is a virtue in business but not in babysitting. It does not follow, however, that the virtues of business are therefore opposed to the ordinary virtues of civilized life—as Albert Carr famously argued in his *Harvard Business Review* polemic of several years ago. The virtues of business ethics are business virtues but they are nonetheless virtues, and the exercise of these virtues is aimed at both "the bottom line" and ethics.

Role Identity

Much has been written, for example, by Norman Bowie in his good little book *Business Ethics*, on the importance of "role morality" and "My Position and its Duties."[8] It is the situatedness of corporate roles that lends them their particular ethical poignancy, the fact that an employee or an executive is not just a person who happens to be in a place and is constrained by no more than the usual ethical prohibitions. To work for a company is to accept a set of particular obligations, to assume a *prima facie* loyalty to one's employer, to adopt a certain standard of excellence and conscientiousness that is largely defined by the job itself. There may be general ethical rules and guidelines that cut across most positions but as these get more general and more broadly applicable they also become all but useless in concrete ethical dilemmas. Robert Townsend's cute comment that "if a company needs an ethical code, use the Ten Commandments" is thus not only irreverent but irrelevant too.[9] The Aristotelean approach to business ethics presumes concrete situations and particular people and their place in organizations. There is little point to an ethics that tries to transcend all such particularities and embrace the chairman of the board as well as a middle manager, a secretary and a factory worker. All ethics is contextual, and one of the problems with all of those grand theories is that they try to transcend context and end up with vacuity. The problem, of course, is that people in business inevitably play several roles ("wear several hats") at once, and these roles may clash with one another as they may clash with more personal roles based on family, friendship and personal obligation. This, I will argue, is the pervasive problem in micro-business ethics, and it is the legitimacy of roles and their responsibilities, and the structures of the corporation that defines those roles and their responsibilities, that ought to occupy a good deal more of our time and attention.

Integrity

Integrity, accordingly, in the key to Aristotelean ethics, not, perhaps, as a virtue as such but rather as the linchpin of all of the virtues, the key to their unity or, in conflict and disunity, an anchor against personal disintegration. "Integrity" is a word, like "honor"—its close kin—that sometimes seems all but archaic in the modern business world. To all too many business executives, it suggests stubbornness and inflexibility, a refusal to be a "team player." But integrity seems to have at least two divergent meanings, one of them encouraging conformity, the other urging a belligerent independence.[10] Both of these are extreme and potentially dangerous. The very word suggests "wholeness," but insofar as one's identity is not that of an isolated atom but rather the product of a larger social molecule, that wholeness includes—rather than excludes—other people and one's social roles. A person's integrity on the job typically requires him or her to follow the rules and practices that define that job, rather than allow oneself to be swayed by distractions and contrary temptations. And yet, critical encounters sometimes require a show of integrity that is indeed antithetical to one's assigned role and duties. At that point some virtues, notably moral courage, become definitive and others, e.g. loyalty, may be jettisoned. (In other cases, of course, it is loyalty that might require moral courage.) But in harmony or in conflict, integrity represents the integration of one's roles and responsibilities and the virtues defined by them.

Judgment (*phronesis*)

The fact that our roles conflict and there are often no singular principles to help us decide on an ethical course of action shifts the emphasis away from our calculative and ratiocinative faculties and back towards an older, often ignored faculty called "judgment." Against the view that ethics consists primarily of general principles that get applied to particular situations, Aristotle thought that it was "good judgment" or *phronesis* that was of the greatest importance in ethics. Good judgment (which centered on "perception" rather than the abstract formulation and interpretation of general principles) was the product of a good up-bringing, a proper education. It was always situated, perhaps something like Joseph Fletcher's still much referred-to notion of a "situation ethics," and took into careful account the particularity of the persons and circumstances involved. But I think the real importance of *phronesis* is not just its priority to ethical deliberation and ratiocination; it has rather to do with the inevitable conflicts of both concerns and principles that define almost every ethical dilemma. Justice, for example, may sound (especially in some philosophers) as if it were a monolithic or hierarchically layered and almost mechanical process. But, as I have argued elsewhere, there are a dozen or more different considerations that enter into most deliberations about justice, including not only rights and prior obligations and the public good but questions of merit (which themselves break down into a variety of sometimes conflicting categories) and responsibility and risk.[11] I won't go into this here but the point is that there is *no* (non-arbitrary) mechanical decision procedure for resolving most disputes about justice, and what is required, in each and every particular case, is the ability to balance and weigh competing concerns and come to a "fair" conclusion. But what's fair is not the outcome of one or several preordained principles of justice; it is (as they say) a "judgment call," always disputable but nevertheless well or badly made. I have often thought that encouraging abstract ethical theory actually discourages and distracts us from the need to make judgments. I have actually heard one of my colleagues say (without qualms) that, since he's been studying ethical theory, he no longer has any sense of ethics. And if this sounds implausible, I urge you to remember your last department or faculty senate meeting, and the inverse relationship between high moral tone of the conversation and ridiculousness of the proposals and decisions that followed.

Holism

It more or less follows from what I've said above that one of the problems of traditional business thinking is our tendency to isolate our business or professional roles from the rest of our lives, a process that Marx, following Schiller, described as "alienation." The good life may have many facets, but they are facets and not mere components, much less isolated aspects despite the tiresome emphasis on tasks, techniques and "objectives," that a manager's primary and ultimate concern is *people*. It's gotten trite, but as I watch our more ambitious students and talk with more and more semi-successful but "trapped" middle managers and executives, I become more and more convinced that the tunnel-vision of business life encouraged by the too narrow business curriculum and the daily rhetoric of the corporate community is damaging and counter-productive. Good employees are good people, and to pretend that the virtues of business stand isolated from the virtues of the rest of our lives—and this is not for a moment to deny the particularity of either our business roles or our lives—is to set up that familiar tragedy in which a pressured employee violates his or her "personal values" because, from a purely business point of view, he or she "didn't really have any choice." It is the integration of our roles—or at least their harmonization—that is our ideal here, and that integration should not be construed as either the personal yielding to the corporate or the corporate giving in to the personal. The name of that integration is *ethics*, construed in an Aristotelean way.

BUSINESS AND THE VIRTUES

Business ethics is too often conceived as a set of impositions and constraints, obstacles to business behavior rather than the motivating force of that behavior. So conceived, it is no surprise that many people in business look upon ethics and ethicists with suspicion, as antagonistic if not antithetical to their enterprise. But properly understood, ethics does not and should not consist of a set of prohibitive principles or rules, and it is the virtue of an ethics of virtue to be rather an intrinsic part and the driving force of a successful life well lived. Its motivation need not depend on elaborate soul searching and deliberation but in the best companies moves along with the easy flow of interpersonal relations and a mutual sense of mission and accomplishment.

"The virtues" is a short-hand way of summarizing the ideals that define good character. There are a great many virtues that are relevant to business life; in fact, it would be a daunting task to try to even list them all. Just for a start, we have honesty, loyalty, sincerity, courage, reliability, trustworthiness, benevolence, sensitivity, helpfulness, cooperativeness, civility, decency, modesty, openness, cheerfulness, amiability, tolerance, reasonableness, tactfulness, wittiness, gracefulness, liveliness, magnanimity, persistence, prudence, resourcefulness, cool-headedness, warmth and hospitality.[12] Each of these has subtle sub-traits and related virtues, and there are a great many virtues of strength, energy and skill as well as attractiveness, charm and aesthetic appeal that I have not yet mentioned. There are "negative" virtues, that is, virtues that specify the absence of some annoying, inefficient or anti-social trait, such as non-negligence, non-vengefulness, non-vindictiveness and non-pretentiousness, and there are virtues of excess and superiority, such as super-conscientiousness and super-reliability. Then there are those virtues that seem peculiar (though not unique) to business, such as being shrewd and ruthless and "tough," which may well be vices in other aspects of life.

From the variety of virtues, one of the most important conclusions to be drawn immediately is the impoverished nature of ethical language when it limits itself to such terms as "good" and "bad," "right" and "wrong." To be sure, most of the virtues are "good" and lead to "right" action, and most of the contrary vices are "bad" and lead to "wrong"-doing. But not only does such ethical language lead us to ignore most of what is significant and subtle in our ordinary ethical judgments, it tends to lead us away from just that focus on personal character that is most essential to most of our interpersonal decisions, whether it is to trust a colleague, make a new friend, hire or fire a new assistant, respect a superior or invite the boss over to the house for dinner. Ethics is not the study of right and wrong, anymore than art and aesthetics are the study of beauty and ugliness.[13] Ethics (like art and aesthetics) is a colorful, multifaceted appreciation and engagement with other people in the world. In business ethics, it is only the extreme and sinister misdeed that we label simply "wrong"; more often, we invoke an artist's palette of imaginative descriptions such as "sleazy" and "slimy." Even the phrase "good character" (or "good person") strikes us as uninteresting and vacuous; it is the details that count, not the gloss. And there are many, many details, any of which might become more or less significant in some particular situation.

A virtue, according to Aristotle, is an excellence. It is not, however, a very specialized skill or talent (like being good with numbers or a brilliant researcher) but an exemplary way of getting along with other people, a way of manifesting in one's own thoughts, feelings and actions the ideals and aims of the entire community. Thus honesty is a virtue not because it is a skill necessary for any particular endeavor or because it represents the ideal of straight dealing, fair play, common knowledge and open inquiry. What is public is probably approved of and what is hidden is probably dangerous. So, too, courage is a virtue not just because it requires a special talent or because "somebody's got to do it" but because we all believe (with varying degrees of commitment) that a person should stand up for what he or she cares about and what he or she believes in. But not all virtues need to be so serious or so central to our idea of integrity. Aristotle listed charm, wit and a good sense of humor as virtues, and with corporate life in particular I think that we would probably agree. To be sure, the circumstances in which congeniality is a central virtue and in which courage becomes cardinal will be very different, but it is a troubled organization that requires the more heroic virtues all the time and does not have the relative security and leisure to enjoy those virtues that make life worthwhile rather than those that are necessary for mere survival. Indeed, part of the folly of the familiar military, machine and jungle metaphors in business is that they all make business life out to be something threatening and relentless. But the truth (even in the military and in the jungle) is that there are long and sometimes relaxed respites and a need for play and playfulness as well as diligence. There is welcome camaraderie and the virtues of "getting along" are just as important to group survival as the coordination needed for fighting together. There are reasons why we want to survive—apart from sheer Darwinian obstinacy— and the fact that we relish and enjoy the social harmony of our life and our jobs is one of them. One of the most powerful but most ignored arguments against hostile takeovers and unfriendly mergers is the desire on the part of the members of a corporate community to maintain that community, and this is not the same as executives "fighting to keep their jobs." . . .

If business life was like the brutal and heroic world of Homer's *Iliad*, corporations in mortal conflict with one another, we would expect the business virtues to be those warrior virtues most closely associated with combat, not only strength and prowess but courage, imperviousness to pain or pity, frightfulness (that is, causing fright in others, not being frightened oneself). We would expect the warrior to have an appropriately insensitive personality, rather clumsy social habits, and an enormous ego. Not surprising, these are precisely the virtues often praised and attributed to top business executives, summarized (badly) in the single word, "toughness." But, of course, warrior metaphors depend on a war-like situation, but business ethicists have taken considerable pains to dismiss that picture of corporate business life as pathological and misleading. Most CEOs, however "tough," do not fit this picture at all. Consider, instead, a very different and usually more representative picture of the corporation, the corporation as a wealthy and prosperous "polis," a free and sophisticated city-state with considerable pride in its products, philosophy, and corporate culture. There will still be external threats and an occasional battle, but this is not the day-to-day concern of the community. Courage might still be an important virtue, but most of the other warrior virtues and the typical characteristics of the warrior personality will seem boorish and bullish, inappropriate in most social settings and downright embarrassing in some. The virtues, in such a society, will tend to be the genteel, congenial virtues, those which lubricate a rich, pleasant social life. And these will be just as applicable to the CEO as to the boy at the loading dock or the teller at the check-out window. . . .

One might insist, just to waylay the argument I seem to be developing here, that warrior virtues, congeniality (Aristotelean) virtues and moral virtues are in fact quite compatible, and there is no reason why a James Burke or a Warren Buffett, for example, can't display warrior toughness, Aristotelean gentility and Christian righteousness. And indeed, this is the case. But my argument is not that three sets of virtues are incompatible as such, but rather that they present us with three quite distinct contexts and three different ethical frameworks, and to understand business ethics is to understand the confluence, the priorities and the potential conflicts between these. Excessive attention paid to a corporation may become a screaming alliance of desperation and one's personal sense of integrity can be threatened or fatally damaged. Excessive attention to the congenial virtues may in fact "soften" a company so that it becomes less competitive, and an exaggerated sense of righteousness to the detriment of congeniality and competitiveness may well cause a company to shatter into a thousand rigid little moralists, incapable of working together. But the Aristotelean framework tells us that it is cooperation and not an isolated individual sense of self-worth that defines the most important virtues, in which the warrior virtues play an essential but diminished role, in which the well-being of the community goes hand in hand with individual excellence, not by virtue of any "invisible hand" but precisely because of the social consciousness and public spirit of each and every individual.

Almost all of Aristotle's virtues are recognizable as business virtues, and this is, of course, not surprising. Business is, above all, a social activity, involving dealing with other people in both stressful and friendly situations (and trying to make the former into the latter). Despite our emphasis on hard-headedness and the bottom line, we do not praise and often despise tight-fistedness and we do praise great-souled generosity ("magnificence"). But such virtues may be misleading for us. We would not praise an executive who "gave away the store"; we would rather think that executive mentally unhinged. But the virtues for Aristotle do not involve radical demands on our behavior, and the sort of fanaticism praised if not preached in many religions ("give away all of your worldly goods") is completely foreign to Aristotle's insistence on "moderation." Thus the generous or "magnificent" person gives away only as much of wealth as will increase his or her status in the community. Here we would encounter the familiar charge that such giving is not true generosity, for it involves no personal sacrifice and includes a "selfish" motive, the quest for self-aggrandizement. But Aristotle would refuse to recognize this opposition between enlightened self-interest and virtue, and we continue to enforce it at our peril. The argument here, of course, is exactly the skeptical argument leveled against generous corporations when they give to the arts, to education, to social welfare programs: "They're only doing it for the P. R." But here executives (and everyone else) would be wise to follow Aristotle and reject the notion that "true" generosity is self-sacrifice and self-benefiting generosity is only "P.R." There are occasions that call for self-sacrifice, but to insist that such extreme action is essential to the virtues is to deny the virtues their relevance to business (and most of) life.

This brings us to the perhaps most misunderstood virtue in business life, the virtue of *toughness*. The word "tough" is typically used by way of admiration, though often coupled with a shake of the head and an expression of frustration. Sometimes, it is used as a euphemism, in place of or in conjunction with various synonyms for a nasty or odious human being. Not infrequently, it simply means stubborn, impossible or mean-spirited. But toughness is generally and genuinely perceived as virtue, albeit a virtue that is often misplaced and misconceived. Insofar as business consists of bargaining and dealing with other people, toughness is essential, and its opposite is not so much weakness as incompetence. But much of what is called toughness is neither a virtue nor a vice. It is not a character trait so much as it is a skill, whether cultivated or "natural." In certain central business practices, notably negotiating, toughness is not so much a personal virtue as it is a technique or set of techniques, an acquired manner and an accomplished strategy, "knowing when to hold 'em, knowing when to fold 'em." Toughness includes knowing how to bluff and when to keep silent, when to be cooperative and when not to be. But such a skill is not, contra Carr, unethical or divorced from ordinary morals; it is a legitimate part of a certain kind of obviously legitimate activity. Yet, as a specific skill or set of skills, being a tough negotiator is not sufficiently personal or general to count as a virtue, which is not to say, of course, that it is not therefore admirable or necessary. . . .

Toughness in an executive also has an ethically painful element. Sometimes it is necessary to do something wrong in order to do what is right. Powerful politicians, of course, face such dilemmas all of the time, giving rise to a substantial literature on the controversial virtues of toughness and "ruthlessness" and the allegedly opposed domains of public and private morality.[14] Sometimes, to reach a higher goal, one must do what one otherwise would not and should not even consider. For example, in the face of debts or deficiencies that will very likely capsize the company, a chairman may need to let go perfectly qualified, hard-working loyal employees. Viewed as an action isolated from the circumstances, letting people go for no reason whatever, that is, for no fault of their own, would be the height of injustice. But if it is a matter of saving the company, then this otherwise unjust act may nevertheless be necessary. Toughness is being able and willing to undertake such measures. This is not to say, however—and this cannot be emphasized enough—that such decisions can or should be made without guilt or pain or bad feelings. It does not mean that what one has done is not, despite its necessity, wrong. The chief executive of a large corporation once told me that "down-sizing" his company was the most painful thing he had ever had to do. His toughness lay not in callousness or indifference but in his willingness to do what was necessary and in his insistence on doing it as humanely as possible. Indeed, callousness and indifference are not themselves signs of toughness but the very opposite, indications of that form of weakness that can face moral issues only by denying them. Toughness is a virtue, but callousness and indifference are not, and the two should never be confused. . . .

THE BOTTOM LINE (Conclusion)

The bottom line of the Aristotelean approach to business ethics is that we have to get away from both traditional individualistic ethics and "bottom line" thinking. This does not in any way imply that the individual "checks his or her values at the office door" nor does it suggest that, except in the unusual and unfortunate case, there will be any thoroughgoing disharmony or incompatibility between one's personal and professional values. Quite to the contrary, the point of what I am arguing is that we are, as Aristotle famously insisted, social creatures who get our identity from our communities and measure our worth accordingly. And as much as many employees may feel the need to divorce themselves from their work and pretend that what they "do" is not indicative of their true selves, the truth is that most adults spend literally half of their waking adult life on the job, in the office, in the role or position that defines them as a citizen of the corporation. The Aristotelean approach to business ethics ultimately comes down to the idea that, while business life has its specific goals and distinctive practices and people in business have their particular concerns, loyalties, roles and responsibilities, there is no "business world" apart from the people who work in business and the integrity of those people determines the integrity of the organization as well as vice versa. The Aristotelean approach to business ethics is, perhaps, just another way of saying that people come before profits.

Notes

Earlier versions of this essay were presented at a number of conferences, the Ruffin conference at the University of Virginia, the Applied Ethics conference at the University of British Columbia and (with Nick Imparato) the International Association of Business and Society conference in Sundance, Utah, the Center of Ethics conference at the University of Melbourne. Some parts of this essay have been published in some of the proceedings of those conferences and I have benefited from comments and criticism from my colleagues there, most notably, from Patricia Werhane, Peter French, R. Edward Freeman and Tony Coady. Parts of this essay also appear in my book, *Ethics and Excellence* (Oxford: Oxford University Press, 1992).

1. Anthony Flew, "The Profit Motive," in *Ethics*, Vol. 86 (July 1976), pp. 312–22.
2. Manuel Velasquez, comment on Joanne Ciulla, Ruffin lectures, 1989.
3. Albert Carr, "Is Business Bluffing Ethical?" *Harvard Business Review* (Jan.–Feb. 1968).
4. Milton Friedman, "The Social Responsibility of Business Is to Increase Its Profits" *The New York Times Magazine* (1971).
5. This has been the topic of considerable debate. See, notably, G. E. M. Anscombe, *Intentionality*, and John Cooper, *Reason and Human Good in Aristotle* (Cambridge, 1975).
6. Elizabeth Wolgast, *A Grammar of Justice* (Cornell, 1989).
7. Peter Drucker, *Management* (Harper and Row, 1973), pp. 366f.
8. Norman Bowie, *Business Ethics* (NJ: Prentice-Hall, 1982), pp. 1–16.
9. Robert Townsend, *Up the Organization*.
10. Lynne McFall, "Integrity," in *Ethics* (October 1987).
11. Robert C. Solomon, *A Passion for Justice* (New York: Addison-Wesley, 1989), Chapter 2.
12. A complex taxonomy of the virtues is in Edmund Pincoffs, *Quandries and Virtues* (Kansas, 1986), p. 84.
13. See Frithjof Bergmann, "The Experience of Values," in Hauerwas and MacIntyre, eds., *Revisions* (Notre Dame 1983), pp. 127–59.
14. See, for example, Stuart Hampshire, ed., *Public and Private Morality* (Cambridge: Cambridge University Press, 1978) and his own *Innocence and Experience* (Cambridge: Harvard University Press, 1989). See also Bernard Williams, "Politics and Moral Character" in his moral *Luck* (Cambridge University Press, 1981) and Thomas Nagel, "Ruthlessness in Public Life" in the Hampshire Collection.

Moral Mazes:
Bureaucracy and Managerial Work

Robert Jackall

Corporate leaders often tell their charges that hard work will lead to success. Indeed, this theory of reward being commensurate with effort has been an enduring belief in our society, one central to our self-image as a people where the "main chance" is available to anyone of ability who has the gumption and the persistence to seize it. Hard work, it is also frequently asserted, builds character. This notion carries less conviction because businessmen, and our society as a whole, have little patience with those who make a habit of finishing out of the money. In the end, it is success that matters, that legitimate striving, and that makes work worthwhile.

What if, however, men and women in the big corporation no longer see success as necessarily connected to hard work? What becomes of the social morality of the corporation—I mean the everyday rules in use that people play by—when there is thought to be no "objective" standard of excellence to explain how and why winners are separated from also-rans, how and why some people succeed and others fail?

This is the puzzle that confronted me while doing a great many extensive interviews with managers and executives in several large corporations, particularly in a large chemical company and a large textile firm. I went into these corporations to study how bureaucracy—the prevailing organizational form of our society and economy—shapes moral consciousness. I came to see that managers' rules for success are at the heart of what may be called the bureaucratic ethic.

This article suggests no changes and offers no programs for reform. It is, rather, simply an interpretive sociological analysis of the moral dimensions of managers' work. Some readers may find the essay sharp-edged, others familiar. For both groups, it is important to note at the outset that my materials are managers' own descriptions of their experiences.[1] In listening to managers, I have had the decided advantages of being unencumbered with business reponsibilities and also of being free from the taken-for-granted views and vocabularies of the business world. As it happens, my own research in a variety of other settings suggests that managers' experiences are by no means unique; indeed they have a deep resonance with those of other occupational groups.

WHAT HAPPENED TO THE PROTESTANT ETHIC?

To grasp managers' experiences and the more general implications they contain, one must see them against the background of the great historical transformations, both social and cultural, that produced managers as an occupational group. Since the concern here is with the moral significance of work in business, it is important to begin with an understanding of the original Protestant Ethic, the world view of the rising bourgeois class that spearheaded the emergence of capitalism.

The Protestant Ethic was a set of beliefs that counseled "secular asceticism"—the methodical, rational subjection of human impulse and desire to God's will through "restless, continuous, systematic work in a worldly calling."[2] This ethic of ceaseless work and ceaseless renunciation of the fruits of one's toil provided both the economic and the moral foundations for modern capitalism.

On one hand, secular asceticism was a ready-made prescription for building economic capital; on the other, it became for the upward-moving bourgeois class—self-made industrialists, farmers, and enterprising artisans—the ideology that justified their attention to this world, their accumulation of wealth, and indeed the social inequities that inevitably followed such accumulation. This bourgeois ethic, with its imperatives for self-reliance, hard work, frugality, and rational planning, and its clear definition of success and failure, came to dominate a whole historical epoch in the West.

But the ethic came under assault from two directions. First, the very accumulation of wealth that the old Protestant Ethic made possible gradually stripped away the religious basis of the ethic, especially among the rising middle class that benefited from it. There were, of course, periodic reassertions of the religious context of the ethic, as in the case of John D. Rockefeller and his turn toward Baptism. But on the whole, by the late 1800s the religious roots of the ethic survived principally among the independent farmers and proprietors of small businesses in rural areas and towns across America.

In the mainstream of an emerging urban America, the ethic had become secularized into the "work ethic," "rugged individualism," and especially the "success ethic." By the beginning of this century, among most of the economically successful, frugality had become an aberration, conspicuous consumption the norm. And with the shaping of the mass consumer society later in this century, the sanctification of consumption became widespread, indeed crucial to the maintenance of the economic order.

Affluence and the emergence of the consumer society were responsible, however, for the demise of only aspects of the old ethic—namely, the imperatives for saving and investment. The core of the ethic, even in its later, secularized form—self-reliance, unremitting devotion to work, and a morality that postulated just rewards for work well done—was undermined by the complete transformation of the organizational form of work itself. The hallmarks of the emerging modern production and distribution systems were administrative hierarchies, standardized work procedures, regularized timetables, uniform policies, and centralized control—in a word, the bureaucratization of the economy.

This bureaucratization was heralded at first by a very small class of salaried managers, who were later joined by legions of clerks and still later by technicians and professionals of every stripe. In this century, the process spilled over from the private to the public sector and government bureaucracies came to rival those of industry. This great transformation produced the decline of the old middle class of entrepreneurs, free professionals, independent farmers, and small independent businessmen—the traditional carriers of the old Protestant Ethic—and the ascendance of a new middle class of salaried employees whose chief common characteristic was and is their dependence on the big organization.

Any understanding of what happened to the original Protestant Ethic and to the old morality and social character it embodied—and therefore any understanding of the moral significance of work today—is inextricably tied to an analysis of bureaucracy. More specifically, it is, in my view, tied to an analysis of the work and occupational cultures of managerial groups within bureaucracies. Managers are the quintessential bureaucratic work group; they not only fashion bureaucratic rules, but they are also bound by them. Typically, they are not just *in* the organization; they are *of* the organization. As such, managers represent the prototype of the white-collar salaried employee. By analyzing the kind of ethic bureaucracy produces in managers, one can begin to understand how bureaucracy shapes morality in our society as a whole.

PYRAMIDAL POLITICS

American businesses typically both centralize and decentralize authority. Power is concentrated at the top in the person of the chief executive officer and is simultaneously decentralized; that is, responsibility for decisions and profits is pushed as far down the organizational line as possible. For example, the chemical company that I studied—and its structure is typical of other organizations I examined—is one of several operating companies of a large and growing conglomerate. Like the other operating companies, the chemical concern has its own president, executive vice presidents, vice presidents, other executive officers, business area managers, entire staff divisions, and operating plants. Each company is, in effect, a self-sufficient organization, though they are all coordinated by the corporation, and each president reports directly to the corporate CEO.

Now, the key interlocking mechanism of this structure is its reporting system. Each manager gathers up the profit targets or other objectives of his or her subordinates, and with these formulates his commitments to his boss; this boss takes these commitments, and those of his subordinates, and in turn makes a commitment to *his* boss. (Note: henceforth only "he" or "his" will be used to allow for easier reading.) At the top of the line, the president of each company makes his commitment to the CEO of the corporation, based on the stated objectives given to him by his vice presidents. There is always pressure from the top to set higher goals.

This management-by-objectives system, as it is usually called, creates a chain of commitments from the CEO down to the lowliest product manager. In practice, it also shapes a patrimonial authority arrangement which is crucial to defining both the immediate experiences and the long-run career chances of individual managers. In this world, a subordinate owes fealty principally to his immediate boss. A subordinate must not overcommit his boss; he must keep the boss from making mistakes, particularly public ones; he must not circumvent the boss. On a social level, even though an easy, breezy informality is the prevalent style of American business, the subordinate must extend to the boss a certain ritual deference: for instance, he must follow the boss's lead in conversation, must not speak out of turn at meetings, and must laugh at the boss's jokes while not making jokes of his own.

In short, the subordinate must not exhibit any behavior which symbolizes parity. In return, he can hope to be elevated when and if the boss is elevated, although other important criteria also intervene here. He can also expect protection for mistakes made up to a point. However, that point is never exactly defined and always depends on the complicated politics of each situation.

Who Gets Credit?

It is characteristic of this authority system that details are pushed down and credit is pushed up. Superiors do not like to give detailed instructions to subordinates. The official reason for this is to maximize subordinates' autonomy; the underlying reason seems to be to get rid of tedious details and to protect the privilege of authority to declare that a mistake has been made.

It is not at all uncommon for very bald and extremely general edicts to emerge from on high. For example, "Sell the plant in St. Louis. Let me know when you've struck a deal." This pushing down of details has important consequences:

1. Because they are unfamiliar with entangling details, corporate higher echelons tend to expect highly successful results without complications. This is central to top executives' well-known aversion to bad news and to the resulting tendency to "kill the messenger" who bears that news.

2. The pushing down of detail creates great pressure on middle managers not only to transmit good news but to protect their corporations, their bosses, and themselves in the process. They become the "point men" of a given strategy and the potential "fall guys" when things go wrong.

Credit flows up in this structure and usually is appropriated by the highest ranking officer involved in a decision. This person redistributes credit as he chooses, bound essentially by a sensitivity to public perceptions of his fairness. At the middle level, credit for a particular success is always a type of refracted social honor; one cannot claim credit even if it is earned. Credit has to be given, and acceptance of the gift implicitly involves a reaffirmation and strengthening of fealty. A superior may share some credit with subordinates in order to deepen fealty relationships and induce greater future efforts on his behalf. Of course, a different system is involved in the allocation of blame, a point I shall discuss later.

Fealty to the 'King'

Because of the interlocking character of the commitment system, a CEO carries enormous influence in his corporation. If, for a moment, one thinks of the presidents of individual operating companies as barons, then the CEO of the parent company is the king. His word is law; even the CEO's wishes and whims are taken as commands by close subordinates on the corporate staff, who zealously turn them into policies and directives.

A typical example occurred in the textile company last year when the CEO, new at the time, expressed mild concern about the rising operating costs of the company's fleet of rented cars. The following day, a stringent system for monitoring mileage replaced the previous casual practice.

Great efforts are made to please the CEO. For example, when the CEO of the large conglomerate that includes the chemical company visits a plant, the most important order of business for local management is a fresh paint job, even when, as in several cases last year the cost of paint alone exceeds $100,000. I am told that similar anecdotes from other organizations have been in circulation since 1910; this suggests a certain historical continuity of behavior toward top bosses.

The second order of business for the plant management is to produce a complete book describing the plant and its operations, replete with photographs and illustrations, for presentation to the CEO; such a book costs about $10,000 for the single copy. By any standards of budgetary stringency, such expenditures are irrational. But by the social standards of the corporation, they make perfect sense. It is far more important to please the king today than to worry about the future economic state of one's fief, since if one does not please the king, there may not be a fief to worry about or indeed any vassals to do the worrying.

By the same token, all of this leads to an intense interest in everything the CEO does and says. In both the chemical and the textile companies, the most common topic of conversation among managers up and down the line is speculation about their respective CEOs' plans, intentions, strategies, actions, styles, and public images.

Such speculation is more than idle gossip. Because he stands at the apex of the corporation's bureaucratic and patrimonial structures and locks the intricate system of commitments between bosses and subordinates into place, it is the CEO who ultimately decides whether those commitments have been satisfactorily met. Moreover, the CEO and his trusted associates determine the fate of whole business areas of a corporation.

Shake-Ups & Contingency

One must appreciate the simultaneously monocratic and patrimonial character of business bureaucracies in order to grasp what we might call their contingency. One has only to read the *Wall Street Journal* or the *New York Times* to realize that, despite their carefully constructed "eternal" public image, corporations are quite unstable organizations. Mergers, buy-outs, divestitures, and especially "organizational restructuring" are commonplace aspects of business life. I shall discuss only organizational shake-ups here.

Usually, shake-ups occur because of the appointment of a new CEO and/or division president, or because of some failure that is adjudged to demand retribution; sometimes these occurrences work together. The first action of most new CEOs is some form of organizational change. On the one hand, this prevents the inheritance of blame for past mistakes; on the other, it projects an image of bareknuckled aggressiveness much appreciated on Wall Street. Perhaps most important, a shake-up rearranges the fealty structure of the corporation, placing in power those barons whose style and public image mesh closely with that of the new CEO.

A shake-up has reverberations throughout an organization. Shortly after the new CEO of the conglomerate was named, he reorganized the whole business and selected new presidents to head each of the five newly formed companies of the corporation. He mandated that the presidents carry out a thorough reorganization of their separate companies complete with extensive "census reduction"—that is, firing as many people as possible.

The new president of the chemical company, one of these five, had risen from a small but important specialty chemicals division in the former company. Upon promotion to president, he reached back into his former division, indeed back to his own past work in a particular product line, and systematically elevated many of his former colleagues, friends, and allies. Powerful managers in other divisions, particularly in a rival process chemicals division, were: (1) forced to take big demotions in the new power structure; (2) put on "special assignment"—the corporate euphemism for Siberia (the saying is: "No one ever comes back from special assignment"); (3) fired; or (4) given "early retirement," a graceful way of doing the same thing.

Up and down the chemical company, former associates of the president now hold virtually every important position. Managers in the company view all of this as an inevitable fact of life. In their view, the whole reorganization could easily have gone in a completely different direction had another CEO been named or had the one selected picked a different president for the chemical company, or had the president come from a different work group in the old organization. Similarly, there is the abiding feeling that another significant change in top management could trigger yet another sweeping reorganization.

Fealty is the mortar of the corporate hierarchy, but the removal of one well-placed stone loosens the mortar throughout the pyramid and can cause things to fall apart. And no one is ever quite sure, until after the fact, just how the pyramid will be put back together.

SUCCESS & FAILURE

It is within this complicated and ambiguous authority structure, always subject to upheaval, that success and failure are meted out to those in the middle and upper middle managerial ranks. Managers rarely spoke to me of objective criteria for achieving success because once certain crucial points in one's career are passed, success and failure seem to have little to do with one's accomplishments. Rather, success is socially defined and distributed. Corporations do demand, of course, a basic competence and sometimes specified training and experience; hiring patterns usually ensure these. A weeding-out process takes place, however, among the lower ranks of managers during the first several years of their experience. By the time a manager reaches a certain numbered grade in the ordered hierarchy—in the chemical company this is Grade 13 out of 25, defining the top 8½% of management in the company—managerial competence as such is taken for granted and assumed not to differ greatly from one manager to the next. The focus then switches to social factors, which are determined by authority and political alignments—the fealty structure—and by the ethos and style of the corporation.

Moving to the Top

In the chemical and textile companies as well as the other concerns I studied, five criteria seem to control a person's ability to rise in middle and upper middle management. In ascending order they are:

1. Appearance and dress. This criterion is so familiar that I shall mention it only briefly. Managers have to look the part, and it is sufficient to say that corporations are filled with attractive, well-groomed, and conventionally well-dressed men and women.

2. Self-control. Managers stress the need to exercise iron self-control and to have the ability to mask all emotion and intention behind bland, smiling, and agreeable public faces. They believe it is a fatal weakness to lose control of oneself, in any way, in a public forum. Similarly, to betray valuable secret knowledge (for instance, a confidential reorganization plan) or intentions through some relaxation of self-control—for example, an indiscreet comment or a lack of adroitness in turning aside a query—can not only jeopardize a manager's immediate position but can undermine others' trust in him.

3.   Perception as a team player. While being a team player has many meanings, one of the most important is to appear to be interchangeable with other managers near one's level. Corporations discourage narrow specialization more strongly as one goes higher. They also discourage the expression of moral or political qualms. One might object, for example, to working with chemicals used in nuclear power, and most corporations today would honor that objection. The public statement of such objections, however, would end any realistic aspirations for higher posts because one's usefulness to the organization depends on versatility. As one manager in the chemical company commented: "Well, we'd go along with his request but we'd always wonder about the guy. And in the back of our minds, we'd be thinking that he'll soon object to working in the soda ash division because he doesn't like glass."

Another important meaning of team play is putting in long hours at the office. This requires a certain amount of sheer physical energy, even though a great deal of this time is spent not in actual work but in social rituals—like reading and discussing newspaper articles, taking coffee breaks, or having informal conversations. These rituals, readily observable in every corporation that I studied, forge the social bonds that make real managerial work—that is, group work of various sorts—possible. One must participate in the rituals to be considered effective in the work.

4.   Style. Managers emphasize the importance of "being fast on your feet"; always being well organized; giving slick presentations complete with color slides; giving the appearance of knowledge even in its absence; and possessing a subtle, almost indefinable sophistication, marked especially by an urbane, witty, graceful, engaging, and friendly demeanor.

I want to pause for a moment to note that some observers have interpreted such conformity, team playing, affability, and urbanity as evidence of the decline of the individualism of the old Protestant Ethic.[3] To the extent that commentators take the public images that managers project at face value, I think they miss the main point. Managers up and down the corporate ladder adopt the public faces that they wear quite consciously; they are, in fact, the masks behind which the real struggles and moral issues of the corporation can be found.

Karl Mannheim's conception of self-rationalization or self-streamlining is useful in understanding what is one of the central social psychological processes of organizational life.[4] In a world where appearances—in the broadest sense—mean everything, the wise and ambitious person learns to cultivate assiduously the proper, prescribed modes of appearing. He dispassionately takes stock of himself, treating himself as an object. He analyzes his strengths and weaknesses, and decides what he needs to change in order to survive and flourish in his organization. And then he systematically undertakes a program to reconstruct his image. Self-rationalization curiously parallels the methodical subjection of self to God's will that the old Protestant Ethic counseled; the difference, of course, is that one acquires not moral virtues but a masterful ability to manipulate personae.

5. *Patron power.* To advance, a manager must have a patron, also called a mentor, a sponsor, a rabbi, or a godfather. Without a powerful patron in the higher echelons of management, one's prospects are poor in most corporations. The patron might be the manager's immediate boss or someone several levels higher in the chain of command. In either case the manager is still bound by the immediate, formal authority and fealty patterns of his position; the new—although more ambiguous—fealty relationships with the patron are added.

A patron provides his "client" with opportunities to get visibility, to showcase his abilities, to make connections with those of high status. A patron cues his client to crucial political developments in the corporation, helps arrange lateral moves if the client's upward progress is thwarted by a particular job or a particular boss, applauds his presentations or suggestions at meetings, and promotes the client during an organizational shake-up. One must, of course, be lucky in one's patron. If the patron gets caught in a political crossfire, the arrows are likely to find his clients as well.

Social Definitions of Performance

Surely, one might argue, there must be more to success in the corporation than style, personality, team play, chameleonic adaptability, and fortunate connections. What about the bottom line—profits, performance?

Unquestionably, "hitting your numbers"—that is, meeting the profit commitments already discussed—is important, but only within the social context I have described. There are several rules here. First, no one in a line position—that is, with responsibility for profit and loss—who regularly "misses his numbers" will survive, let alone rise. Second, a person who always hits his numbers but who lacks some or all of the required social skills will not rise. Third, a person who sometimes misses his numbers but who has all the desirable social traits will rise.

Performance is thus always subject to a myriad of interpretations. Profits matter, but it is much more important in the long run to be perceived as "promotable" by belonging to central political networks. Patrons protect those already selected as rising stars from the negative judgments of others; and only the foolhardy point out even egregious errors of those in power or those destined for it.

Failure is also socially defined. The most damaging failure is, as one middle manager in the chemical company puts it, "when your boss or someone who has the power to determine your fate says: 'You failed.'" Such a godlike pronouncement means, of course, out-and-out personal ruin; one must, at any cost, arrange matters to prevent such an occurrence.

As it happens, things rarely come to such a dramatic point even in the midst of an organizational crisis. The same judgment may be made but it is usually called "nonpromotability." The difference is that those who are publicly labeled as failures normally have no choice but to leave the organization; those adjudged nonpromotable can remain, provided they are willing to accept being shelved or, more colorfully, "mushroomed"—that is, kept in a dark place, fed manure, and left to do nothing but grow fat. Usually, seniors do not tell juniors they are nonpromotable (though the verdict may be common knowledge among senior peer groups). Rather, subordinates are expected to get the message after they have been repeatedly overlooked for promotions. In fact, middle managers interpret staying in the same job for more than two or three years as evidence of a negative judgment. This leads to a mobility panic at the middle levels which, in turn, has crucial consequences for pinpointing responsibility in the organization.

Capriciousness of Success

Finally, managers think that there is a tremendous amount of plain luck involved in advancement. It is striking how often managers who pride themselves on being hardheaded rationalists explain their own career patterns and those of others in terms of luck. Various uncertainties shape this perception. One is the sense of organizational contingency. One change at the top can create profound upheaval throughout the entire corporate structure, producing startling reversals of fortune, good or bad, depending on one's connections. Another is the uncertainty of the markets that often makes managerial planning simply elaborate guesswork, causing real economic outcome to depend on factors totally beyond organizational and personal control.

It is interesting to note in this context that a line manager's credibility suffers just as much from missing his numbers on the up side (that is, achieving profits higher than predicted) as from missing them on the down side. Both outcomes undercut the ideology of managerial planning and control, perhaps the only bulwark managers have against market irrationality.

Even managers in staff positions, often quite removed from the market, face uncertainty. Occupational safety specialists, for instance, know that the bad publicity from one serious accident in the workplace can jeopardize years of work and scores of safety awards. As one high-ranking executive in the chemical company says, "In the corporate world, 1,000 'Attaboys!' are wiped away by one 'Oh, shit!'"

Because of such uncertainties, managers in all the companies I studied speak continually of the great importance of being in the right place at the right time and of the catastrope of being in the wrong place at the wrong time. My interview materials are filled with stories of people who were transferred immediately before a big shake-up and, as a result, found themselves riding the crest of a wave to power; of people in a promising business area who were terminated because top management suddenly decided that the area no longer fit the corporate image desired; of others caught in an unpredictable and fatal political battle among their patrons; of a product manager whose plant accidentally produced an odd color batch of chemicals, who sold them as a premium version of the old product, and who is now thought to be a marketing genius.

The point is that managers have a sharply defined sense of the *capriciousness* of organizational life. Luck seems as good an explanation as any of why, after a certain point, some people succeed and others fail. The upshot is that many managers decide that they can do little to influence external events in their favor. One can, however, shamelessly streamline oneself, learn to wear all the right masks, and get to know all the right people. And then sit tight and wait for things to happen.

'GUT DECISIONS'

Authority and advancement patterns come together in the decision-making process. The core of the managerial mystique is decision-making prowess, and the real test of such prowess is what managers call "gut decisions," that is, important decisions involving big money, public exposure, or significant effect on the organization. At all but the highest levels of the chemical and textile companies, the rules for making gut decisions are, in the words of one upper middle manager: "(1) Avoid making any decisions if at all possible; and (2) if a decision has to be made, involve as many people as you can so that, if things go south, you're able to point in as many directions as possible."

Consider the case of a large coking plant of the chemical company. Coke making requires a gigantic battery to cook the coke slowly and evenly for long periods; the battery is the most important piece of capital equipment in a coking plant. In 1975, the plant's battery showed signs of weakening and certain managers at corporate headquarters had to decide whether to invest $6 million to restore the battery to top form. Clearly, because of the amount of money involved, this was a gut decision.

No decision was made. The CEO had sent the word out to defer all unnecessary capital expenditures to give the corporation cash reserves for other investments. So the managers allocated small amounts of money to patch the battery up until 1979, when it collapsed entirely. This brought the company into a breach of contract with a steel producer and into violation of various Environmental Protection Agency pollution regulations. The total bill, including lawsuits and now federally mandated repairs to the battery, exceeded $10 million. I have heard figures as high as $150 million, but because of "creative accounting," no one is sure of the exact amount.

This simple but very typical example gets to the heart of how decision making is intertwined with a company's authority structure and advancement patterns. As the chemical company managers see it, the decisions facing them in 1975 and 1979 were crucially different. Had they acted decisively in 1975—in hindsight, the only rational course—they would have salvaged the battery and saved their corporation millions of dollars in the long run.

In the short run, however, since even seemingly rational decisions are subject to widely varying interpretations, particularly decisions which run counter to a CEO's stated objectives, they would have been taking a serious risk in restoring the battery. What is more, their political networks might have unraveled, leaving them vulnerable to attack. They chose short-term safety over long-term gain because they felt they were judged, both by higher authority and by their peers, on their short-term performances. Managers feel that if they do not survive the short run, the long run hardly matters. Even correct decisions can shorten promising careers.

By contrast, in 1979 the decision was simple and posed little risk. The corporation had to meet its legal obligations; also it had to either repair the battery the way the EPA demanded or shut down the plant and lose several hundred million dollars. Since there were no real choices, everyone could agree on a course of action because everyone could appeal to inevitability. Diffusion of responsibility, in this case by procrastinating until total crisis, is intrinsic to organizational life because the real issue in most gut decisions is: Who is going to get blamed if things go wrong?

'Blame Time'

There is no more feared hour in the corporate world than "blame time." Blame is quite different from responsibility. There is a cartoon of Richard Nixon declaring: "I accept all of the responsibility, but none of the blame." To blame someone is to injure him verbally in public; in large organizations, where one's image is crucial, this poses the most serious sort of threat. For managers, blame—like failure—has nothing to do with the merits of a case; it is a matter of social definition. As a general rule, it is those who are or who become politically vulnerable or expendable who get "set up" and become blamable. The most feared situation of all is to end up inadvertently in the wrong place at the wrong time and get blamed.

Yet this is exactly what often happens in a structure that systematically diffuses responsibility. It is because managers fear blame time that they diffuse responsibility; however, such diffusion inevitably means that someone, somewhere is going to become a scapegoat when things go wrong. Big corporations encourage this process by their complete lack of any tracking system. Whoever is currently in charge of an area is responsible—that is, potentially blamable—for whatever goes wrong in the area, even if he has inherited others' mistakes. An example from the chemical company illustrates this process.

When the CEO of the large conglomerate took office, he wanted to rid his capital accounts of all serious financial drags. The corporation had been operating a storage depot for natural gas which it bought, stored, and then resold. Some years before the energy crisis, the company had entered into a long-term contract to supply gas to a buyer—call him Jones. At the time, this was a sound deal because it provided a steady market for a stably priced commodity.

When gas prices soared, the corporation was still bound to deliver gas to Jones at 20¢ per unit instead of the going market price of $2. The CEO ordered one of his subordinates to get rid of this albatross as expeditiously as possible. This was done by selling the operation to another party—call him Brown—with the agreement that Brown would continue to meet the contractual obligations to Jones. In return for Brown's assumption of these costly contracts, the corporation agreed to buy gas from Brown at grossly inflated prices to meet some of its own energy needs.

In effect, the CEO transferred the drag on his capital accounts to the company's operating expenses. This enabled him to project an aggressive, asset-reducing image to Wall Street. Several levels down the ladder, however, a new vice president for a particular business found himself saddled with exorbitant operating costs when, during a reorganization, those plants purchasing gas from Brown at inflated prices came under his purview. The high costs helped to undercut the vice president's division earnings and thus to erode his position in the hierarchy. The origin of the situation did not matter. All that counted was that the vice president's division was steadily losing big money. In the end, he resigned to "pursue new opportunities."

One might ask why top management does not institute codes or systems for tracking responsibility. This example provides the clue. An explicit system of accountability for subordinates would probably have to apply to top executives as well and would restrict their freedom. Bureaucracy expands the freedom of those on top by giving them the power to restrict the freedom of those beneath.

On the Fast Track

Managers see what happened to the vice president as completely capricious, but completely understandable. They take for granted the absence of any tracking of responsibility. If anything, they blame the vice president for not recognizing soon enough the dangers of the situation into which he was being drawn and for not preparing a defense—even perhaps finding a substitute scapegoat. At the same time, they realize that this sort of thing could easily happen to them. They see few defenses against being caught in the wrong place at the wrong time except constant wariness, the diffusion of responsibility, and perhaps being shrewd enough to declare the ineptitude of one's predecessor on first taking a job.

What about avoiding the consequences of their own errors? Here they enjoy more control. They can "outrun" their mistakes so that when blame time arrives, the burden will fall on someone else. The ideal situation, of course, is to be in a position to fire one's successors for one's own previous mistakes.

Some managers, in fact, argue that outrunning mistakes is the real key to managerial success. One way to do this is by manipulating the numbers. Both the chemical and the textile companies place a great premium on a division's or a subsidiary's return on assets. A good way for business managers to increase their ROA is to reduce their assets while maintaining sales. Usually they will do everything they can to hold down expenditures in order to decrease the asset base, particularly at the end of the fiscal year. The most common way of doing this is by deferring capital expenditures, from maintenance to innovative investments, as long as possible. Done for a short time, this is called "starving" a plant; done over a longer period, it is called "milking" a plant.

Some managers become very adept at milking businesses and showing a consistent record of high returns. They move from one job to another in a company, always upward, rarely staying more than two years in any post. They may leave behind them deteriorating plants and unsafe working conditions, but they know that if they move quickly enough, the blame will fall on others. In this sense, bureaucracies may be thought of as vast systems of organized irresponsibility.

FLEXIBLITY & DEXTERITY WITH SYMBOLS

The intense competition among managers takes place not only behind the agreeable public faces I have described but within an extraordinarily indirect and ambiguous linguistic framework. Except at blame time, managers do not publicly criticize or disagree with one another or with company policy. The sanction against such criticism or disagreement is so strong that it constitutes, in managers' view, a suppression of professional debate. The sanction seems to be rooted principally in their acute sense of organizational contingency; the person one criticizes or argues with today could be one's boss tomorrow.

This leads to the use of an elaborate linguistic code marked by emotional neutrality, especially in group settings. The code communicates the meaning one might wish to convey to other managers, but since it is devoid of any significant emotional sentiment, it can be reinterpreted should social relationships or attitudes change. Here, for example, are some typical phrases describing performance appraisals followed by their probable intended meanings:

Stock Phrase	Probable Intended Meaning
Exceptionally well qualified	Has commited no major blunders to date
Tactful in dealing with superiors	Knows when to keep his mouth shut
Quick thinking	Offers plausible excuses for errors
Meticulous attention to detail	A nitpicker
Slightly below average	Stupid
Unusually loyal	Wanted by no one else

For the most part, such neutered language is not used with the intent to deceive; rather, its purpose is to communicate certain meanings within specific contexts with the implicit understanding that, should the context change, a new, more appropriate meaning can be attached to the language already used. In effect, the corporation is a setting where people are not held to their word because it is generally understood that their word is always provisional.

The higher one gets in the corporate world, the more this seems to be the case; in fact, advancement beyond the upper middle level depends greatly on one's ability to manipulate a variety of symbols without becoming tied to or identified with any of them. For example, an amazing variety of organizational improvement programs marks practically every corporation. I am referring here to the myriad ideas generated by corporate staff, business consultants, academics, and a host of others to improve corporate structure; sharpen decision making; raise morale; create a more humanistic workplace; adopt Theory X, Theory Y, or, more recently, Theory Z of management; and so on. These programs become important when they are pushed from the top.

The watchword in the large conglomerate at the moment is productivity and, since this is a pet project of the CEO himself, it is said that no one goes into his presence without wearing a blue *Productivity!* button and talking about "quality circles" and "feedback sessions." The president of another company pushes a series of managerial seminars that endlessly repeats the basic functions of management: (1) planning, (2) organizing, (3) motivating, and (4) controlling. Aspiring young managers attend these sessions and with a seemingly dutiful eagerness learn to repeat the formulas under the watchful eyes of senior officials.

Privately, managers characterize such programs as the "CEO's incantations over the assembled multitude," as "elaborate rituals with no practical effect," or as "waving a magic wand to make things wonderful again." Publicly, of course, managers on the way up adopt the programs with great enthusiasm, participate in or run them very effectively, and then quietly drop them when the time is right.

Playing the Game

Such flexibility, as it is called, can be confusing even to those in the inner circles. I was told the following by a highly placed staff member whose work requires him to interact daily with the top figures of his company:

"I get faked out all the time and I'm part of the system. I come from a very different culture. Where I come from, if you give someone your *word*, no one ever questions it. It's the old hard-work-will-lead-to-success ideology. Small community, Protestant, agrarian, small business, merchant-type values. I'm disadvantaged in a system like this."

He goes on to characterize the system more fully and what it takes to succeed within it:

"It's the ability to play this system that determines whether you will rise. . . . And part of the adeptness [required] is determined by how much it bothers people. One thing you have to be able to do is to play the game, but you can't be disturbed by the game. What's the game? It's bringing troops home from Vietnam and declaring peace with honor. It's saying one thing and meaning another.

"It's characterizing the reality of a situation with *any* description that is necessary to make that situation more palatable to some group that matters. It means that you have to come up with a culturally accepted verbalization to explain why you are *not* doing what you are doing. . . . [Or] you say that we had to do what we did because it was inevitable; or because the guys at the [regulatory] agencies were dumb; [you] say we won when we really lost; [you] say we saved money when we squandered it; [you] say something's safe when it's potentially or actually dangerous. . . . Everyone knows that it's bullshit, but it's *accepted*. This is the game."

In addition, then, to the other characteristics that I have described, it seems that a prerequisite for big success in the corporation is a certain adeptness at inconsistency. This premium on inconsistency is particularly evident in the many areas of public controversy that face top-ranking managers. Two things come together to produce this situation. The first is managers' sense of beleaguerment from a wide array of adversaries who, it is thought, want to disrupt or impede management's attempts to further the economic interests of their companies. In every company that I studied, managers see themselves and their traditional prerogatives as being under siege, and they respond with a set of caricatures of their perceived principal adversaries.

For example, government regulators are brash, young, unkempt hippies in blue jeans who know nothing about the business for which they make rules; environmental activists—the bird and bunny people—are softheaded idealists who want everybody to live in tents, burn candles, ride horses, and eat berries; workers' compensation lawyers are out-and-out crooks who prey on corporations to appropriate exorbitant fees from unwary clients; labor activists are radical troublemakers who want to disrupt harmonious industrial communities; and the news media consist of rabble-rousers who propagate sensational antibusiness stories to sell papers or advertising time on shows like "60 Minutes."

Second, within this context of perceived harassment, managers must address a multiplicity of audiences, some of whom are considered adversaries. These audiences are the internal corporate hierarchy with its intricate and shifting power and status cliques, key regulators, key local and federal legislators, special publics that vary according to the issues, and the public at large, whose goodwill and favorable opinion are considered essential for a company's free operation.

Managerial adeptness at inconsistency becomes evident in the widely discrepant perspectives, reasons for action, and presentations of fact that explain, excuse, or justify corporate behavior to these diverse audiences.

Adeptness at Inconsistency

The cotton dust issue in the textile industry provides a fine illustration of what I mean. Prolonged exposure to cotton dust produces in many textile workers a chronic and eventually disabling pulmonary disease called byssinosis or, colloquially, brown lung. In the early 1970s, the Occupational Safety and Health Adminstration proposed a ruling to cut workers' exposure to cotton dust sharply by requiring textile companies to invest large amounts of money in cleaning up their plants. The industry fought the regulation fiercely but a final OSHA ruling was made in 1978 requiring full compliance by 1984.

The industry took the case to court. Despite an attempt by Reagan appointees in OSHA to have the case removed from judicial consideration and remanded to the agency they controlled for further cost/benefit analysis, the Supreme Court ruled in 1981 that the 1978 OSHA ruling was fully within the agency's mandate, namely, to protect workers' health and safety as the primary benefit exceeding all cost considerations.

During these proceedings, the textile company was engaged on a variety of fronts and was pursuing a number of actions. For instance, it intensively lobbied regulators and legislators and it prepared court materials for the industry's defense, arguing that the proposed standard would crush the industry and that the problem, if it existed, should be met by increasing workers' use of respirators.

The company also aimed a public relations barrage at special-interest groups as well as at the general public. It argued that there is probably no such thing as byssinosis; workers suffering from pulmonary problems are all heavy smokers and the real culprit is the government-subsidized tobacco industry. How can cotton cause brown lung when cotton is white? Further, if there is a problem, only some workers are afflicted, and therefore the solution is more careful screening of the work force to detect susceptible people and prevent them from ever reaching the workplace. Finally, the company claimed that if the regulation were imposed, most of the textile industry would move overseas where regulations are less harsh.[5]

In the meantime, the company was actually addressing the problem but in a characteristically indirect way. It invested $20 million in a few plants where it knew such an investment would make money; this investment automated the early stages of handling cotton, traditionally a very slow procedure, and greatly increased productivity. The investment had the side benefit of reducing cotton dust levels to the new standard in precisely those areas of the work process where the dust problem is greatest. Publicly, of course, the company claims that the money was spent entirely to eliminate dust, evidence of its corporate good citizenship. (Privately, executives admit that, without the productive return, they would not have spent the money and they have not done so in several other plants.)

Indeed, the productive return is the only rationale that carries weight within the corporate hierarchy. Executives also admit, somewhat ruefully and only when their office doors are closed, that OSHA's regulation on cotton dust has been the main factor in forcing technological innovation in a centuries-old and somewhat stagnant industry.

Such adeptness at inconsistency, without moral uneasiness, is essential for executive success. It means being able to say, as a very high-ranking official of the textile company said to me without batting an eye, that the industry has never caused the slightest problem in any worker's breathing capacity. It means, in the chemical company, propagating an elaborate hazard/benefit calculus for appraisal of dangerous chemicals while internally conceptualizing "hazards" as business risks. It means publicly extolling the carefulness of testing procedures on toxic chemicals while privately ridiculing animal tests as inapplicable to humans.

It means lobbying intensively in the present to shape government regulations to one's immediate advantage and, ten years later, in the event of a catastrophe, arguing that the company acted strictly in accordance with the standards of the time. It means claiming that the real problem of our society is its unwillingness to take risks, while in the thickets of one's bureaucracy avoiding risks at every turn; it means as well making every effort to socialize the risks of industrial activity while privatizing the benefits.

THE BUREAUCRATIC ETHIC

The bureaucratic ethic contrasts sharply with the original Protestant Ethic. The Protestant Ethic was the ideology of a self-confident and independent propertied social class. It was an ideology that extolled the virtues of accumulating wealth in a society organized around property and that accepted the stewardship responsibilities entailed by property. It was an ideology where a person's word was his bond and where the integrity of the handshake was seen as crucial to the maintenance of good business relationships. Perhaps most important, it was connected to a predictable economy of salvation—that is, hard work will lead to success, which is a sign of one's election by God—a notion also containing its own theodicy to explain the misery of those who do not make it in this world.

Bureaucracy, however, breaks apart substance from appearances, action from responsibility, and language from meaning. Most important, it breaks apart the older connection between the meaning of work and salvation. In the bureaucratic world, one's success, one's sign of election, no longer depends on one's own efforts and on an inscrutable God but on the capriciousness of one's superiors and the market; and one achieves economic salvation to the extent that one pleases and submits to one's employer and meets the exigencies of an impersonal market.

In this way, because moral choices are inextricably tied to personal fates, bureaucracy erodes internal and even external standards of morality, not only in matters of individual success and failure but also in all the issues that managers face in their daily work. Bureaucracy makes its own internal rules and social context the principal moral gauges for action. Men and women in bureaucracies turn to each other for moral cues for behavior and come to fashion specific situational moralities for specific significant people in their worlds.

As it happens, the guidance they receive from each other is profoundly ambiguous because what matters in the bureaucratic world is not what a person is but how closely his many personae mesh with the organizational ideal; not his willingness to stand by his actions but his agility in avoiding blame; not what he believes or says but how well he has mastered the ideologies that serve his corporation; not what he stands for but whom he stands with in the labyrinths of his organization.

In short, bureaucracy structures for managers an intricate series of moral mazes. Even the inviting paths out of the puzzle often turn out to be invitations to jeopardy.

Author's Note

I presented an earlier version of this paper in the Faculty Lecture Series at Williams College on March 18, 1982. The intensive field work done during 1980 and 1981 was made possible by a Fellowship for Independent Research from the National Endowment for the Humanities and by a Junior Faculty Leave and small research grant from Williams College.

References

1. There is a long sociological tradition of work on managers and I am, of course, indebted to that literature. I am particularly indebted to the work, both joint and separate, of Joseph Bensman and Arthur J. Vidich, two of the keenest observers of the new middle class. See especially their *The New American Society: The Revolution of the Middle Class* (Chicago: Quadrangle Books, 1971).
2. See Max Weber, *The Protestant Ethic and the Spirit of Capitalism,* translated by Talcott Parsons (New York: Charles Scribner's Sons, 1958), p. 172.
3. See William H. Whyte, *The Organization Man* (New York: Simon & Schuster, 1956), and David Riesman, in collaboration with Reuel Denney and Nathan Glazer, *The Lonely Crowd: A Study of the Changing American Character* (New Haven: Yale University Press, 1950).
4. Karl Mannheim, *Man and Society in an Age of Reconstruction* [London: Paul (Kegan), Trench, Trubner Ltd. 1940], p. 55.
5. On February 9, 1982, the Occupational Safety and Health Administration issued a notice that it was once again reviewing its 1978 standard on cotton dust for "cost-effectiveness." See *Federal Register,* vol. 47, p. 5906. As of this writing (May 1983), this review has still not been officially completed.

PART TWO

Property, Profit, and Justice
Introduction

TRADITIONAL THEORIES OF PROPERTY AND PROFIT

Issues about money and economics are often connected to those of ethics and values. If a friend borrows five dollars and later refuses to repay it, then the issue quickly becomes an ethical one. The friend *should* repay the money. At all levels of economics, ethics plays an important role. For example, to decide how society should distribute wealth, one must know what ethical standards distinguish fair from unfair distributions. Can society distribute nothing to those who are sick and disabled? If not, why not? Because issues of ethical philosophy arise so often in economics, it is not surprising that two well-known economists, Adam Smith and Karl Marx (both of whom are discussed in this section), began their careers as philosophers.

Two of the most volatile issues in economics have ethical implications: the importance of the profit motive, and whether restrictions should be placed on private ownership of property. The pursuit of profit and the existence of private property are said by some economists to be the foundations of a free society. The seventeenth-century philosopher John Locke argued that each person has a natural right to own property. However, others argue that the profit motive and private property are corrupting and result in labor abuses, unfair income distribution, monopolistic practices, and misuse of the environment.

A third issue involving both ethics and economics is the nature of justice. For example, is there such a thing as a *just distribution* of wealth, resources, and opportunities in society, and if so, what does that distribution look like? Is it fair that one person buys yachts and racehorses while another cannot even buy food? Or is it true, instead, that any time government attempts to insure "fairness" by interfering with the free accumulation of wealth, its attempt to redistribute wealth, resources, or opportunities commits a fundamental injustice by violating the liberty of those who have freely earned power, position, or property?

The Profit Motive

It is common today to hear a person or corporation condemned for being greedy. Such an attitude, which questions the morality of emphasizing profit, is not new. If anything, people today are more accepting of the profit motive than at any other time in history. Especially prior to the nineteenth-century, pursuing wealth, and sometimes even lending money, were targets of intense criticism. One of the great defenders of the profit motive was the eighteenth-century economist Adam Smith. Today, nearly two hundred years after Smith presented his ideas in *The Wealth of Nations* (excerpts of which are presented in this section), his name is almost synonymous with the defense of the free market or "laissez-faire" economic system. Smith asserted that the pursuit of profit, even for one's self-interest, is not always bad. In a famous quotation from *The Wealth of Nations* he writes,

> It is not from the benevolence of the butcher, the brewer, or the baker that we expect our dinner, but from their regard of their own interest. We address ourselves not to their humanity, but to their self-love and never talk to them of our own necessities, but of their advantage.

However, Smith did not believe that economic gain was our most noble goal; rather he claimed that justice, not self-interest nor even benevolence, is the crowning virtue of humanity. Smith emphasized the way in which pursuing one's own economic interests in the free marketplace could enhance public welfare so long as one acted with prudence, engaged in fair play, and respected the rights of others. Smith believed that an economic system could function such that people's pursuing their own economic ends could generate, in the absence of government intervention, great public economic good, so long as economic actors acted with restraint and respected basic principles of justice.

Criticisms of the Invisible Hand

By the time the Industrial Revolution was under way in the early nineteenth century, Smith's ideas dominated economic theory, and interestingly, many of the emerging social patterns of that era were justified by appealing to his philosophy. The increased specialization, the reduction of quotas and tariffs, and the decreased roles of government in business were all justified by appealing to a reading of Smith's *Wealth of Nations*. Smith himself, however, did not live to see the changes, nor the human miseries rampant during the Industrial Revolution, and his worries about the poor pay of workers indicate that he would not have approved of the treatment of labor as a result of industrialization. In fact, labor was poorly paid, working conditions deplorable, and working hours long. One of the most depressing sights of all was children working in factories for sixteen hours a day, six days a week. For the children, such work was necessary to supplement their family's meager income.

Many witnesses to the Industrial Revolution were persuaded that the real villain was the economic system. The German philosopher and economist Karl Marx argued that the "free market" Smith championed was little more than a convenient fiction for capitalist property owners. Whereas

Smith had praised the competitive market because of its ability to generate better products at lower prices, Marx argued that in the marketplace workers were mere commodities, available to the factory owners at the lowest possible wages. Indeed, he thought the pressures of the marketplace would force workers, who could not refuse to work without starving, to accept wages barely above a subsistence level. Meanwhile the owners of the means of production, the capitalists, could exploit workers by using their labor and then selling the resulting product at a profit. Marx identified the difference between the costs of production, including wages, and the selling price of products as "surplus value." For Marx, then, profits always meant exploitation of the worker by the capitalist. And he added that whenever technology develops, the economic gap between the capitalist and the worker must widen further, since technology allows products to be manufactured with less human labor and thus creates unemployment and lower wages.

In the selections taken from the *Economic and Philosophic Manuscripts of 1844*, Marx outlines his influential theory of alienation, in which he asserts that workers in capitalistic society are separated from, and deprived of, their own labor. When forced to work for the capitalist, workers are also forced to give the capitalist what most belongs to them: their own work. Factory employees toil away producing products that the factory owner will eventually sell, and they feel no connection to those products; rather, they have been alienated from the effects of their labor. Thus, through the concept of alienation, Marx offers a fundamental condemnation of the treatment of labor in early modern capitalism, a condemnation that was enormously influential in improving labor conditions, although less effective in its more revolutionary implications.

At the same time that Marx was developing his criticism of capitalism, there was another equally dramatic development occurring. In 1859 the English naturalist Charles Darwin published his monumental work on evolution, *The Origin of the Species*. Darwin argued, in short, that in the process of natural selection (1) organisms in the biological kingdom had evolved from simple to more complex species; and (2) during this process organisms less adaptable to the environment failed to survive, while the more adaptable ones flourished. This selection process maximizes benefits for individual organisms and species as well.

Darwin himself expressly stated that his ideas applied only to the biological kingdom, but many thinkers extended them to social and economic issues. The resulting theory of society, popularized by Herbert Spencer and industrialists such as Andrew Carnegie (whose article "Wealth" is reproduced in this section), was known as Social Darwinism.

Social Darwinism impacted issues dealt with by Adam Smith and Karl Marx, but in point of fact it agreed with neither. The Darwinists argued that the Industrial Revolution exemplified social evolution from simple to complex societies. In the evolution of capitalistic industrial systems then, some individuals may suffer; but the system itself enhances human welfare, since it weeds out the unsuccessful, weak competitors while allowing the tougher ones to flourish. Thus, both marketplace and nature operate according to the same "natural" laws. Those who can, survive; those who cannot, perish. In this way the thesis of Social Darwinism came to view the profit motive in business as the essential motivating force in the struggle for economic survival. Unfortunately, Social Darwinism was also touted by a few wealthy tycoons in the nineteenth century as a justification for deplorable working conditions and massive economic inequalities.

The key issues of Part Two—human motivation, human nature, and which economic system is preferable—are interrelated. For example, the ethical question of when, if at all, it is best for people to be motivated by profit is directly connected to the question of whether there is a common human nature. If, as some have argued, people must and will pursue their own self-interest because of their very *nature,* it is sometimes concluded that the pursuit of self-interest in the form of economic gain is often morally justified. In a similar fashion, both issues are tied to that of discovering the best economic system. If people are naturally self-interested and will inevitably act on the basis of self-interest in the marketplace, perhaps society needs an economic system that proscribes such economic pursuits. On the other hand, if self-interested people can regularly subordinate their interests to higher motives such as justice, then perhaps a free market can be a morally viable economic framework.

Private Ownership

Another issue closely connected to that of profit is public versus private ownership. A common argument used by those who criticize private property asserts that the elimination of private property makes it impossible for people to strive to accumulate wealth, and thus discourages them from acting from a bad motive, that is, the profit motive. Defenders of the institution of private property disagree, citing the incentive for hard work and creativity that private property provides. But by far the most ingenious argument in favor of private property is the classical one offered by the seventeenth-century English philosopher John Locke.

Locke believed that human beings have a fundamental right to own private property, and the basic premises that establish this right can be found in the selection from his *Second Treatise* on Government. Even today his "social contract" argument is commonly used in defending the right to own property. Locke asserts what he claims is a truism: in the absence of a formally structured society—that is, in the "state of nature"—all people may be said to own their bodies. It was upon this seemingly obvious premise that Locke rested his defense. If one admits that one has the right to own one's body, it follows that one owns the actions of that body, or in other words, one's own labor, and that one is free to do what one pleases with one's body, one's abilities, and one's labor. Finally, one may also be said to own, and to have a right to own, the things which one mixes with one's labor. For example, if in the state of nature a person picks fruit from wild bushes, that person may be said to own the fruit. And if we grant that property may be freely traded, given, and accumulated, we have the beginning of the basis for justification of vast ownership of capital and land.

In sharp contrast to Locke's seemingly benign defense of private property, Marx argued that it is actually an institution that perpetuates the class struggle. He believed that it is likely that no such state of nature as Locke described ever existed, and he tried to give an accurate historical account of the evolution of the institution of property. He attempted to show how at every stage in the struggle for private property, one class succeeds in exploiting and alienating another. He argued that the institution of private property in a capitalistic economic system is nothing other than the means by which the privileged class—the capitalists—exploits the class of the less privileged, the workers.

We should remind ourselves that the immediate question confronting most people in the Western world is probably not whether to adopt a purely communistic or a purely free-market economy. Moreover, one should be reminded that Marx's ideal was a communal society, not the more totalitarian socialist systems that the Soviet Union and other Communistic nations developed in his name. Of more immediate practical significance is the question of how community issues should be handled by private corporations. Can private corporations, such as the "Dorrence Corporation" described in this book, combine the drive for profit with a sensitivity to human issues? The practical challenges of doing so are illustrated in the case, when profit targets are established by Dorrence's CEO, yet meeting those profit targets *appears* to have human costs.

PROFIT AND PROPERTY: MODERN DISCUSSIONS

One of the most outspoken critics of public ownership in the twentieth century is the economist Milton Friedman. Strongly opposing Marx, Friedman argues that the maintenance of the economic institution of private property is necessary to ensure basic political rights and freedoms. In his article "The Social Responsibility of Business Is to Increase Its Profits," Friedman denies the claim that businesses have obligations to society over and above their obligation to make a profit. In the spirit of Adam Smith, Friedman believes that the free market works best, and makes its greatest contribution, when companies compete for consumers' business and for the maximation of profits. Consequently, says Friedman, if a company were to make ethics or social responsibility a primary goal, it would be failing in its duty and hence, ironically, would not be fulfilling its real "social responsibility." Rather, the social responsibility of a corporate manager is simply to maximize profits on behalf of the corporation's owners, the shareholders.

Friedman strongly objects to placing society's major economic institutions in public ownership. Not only would the competitive marketplace be undermined, resulting in poorer products and services for the consumer, but a basic freedom would be denied insofar as the government would be interfering with the right to own property. In other of his writings, Friedman even argues that certain institutions that are now public, such as the post office and national parks, should be turned over to private investors.

How seriously one takes either Friedman's arguments or arguments asserting the opposite—that the railroads or oil industry, for example, should become publicly owned—will hinge on how seriously one takes the arguments of Locke and Marx. Is Locke correct in arguing that there is a natural right to private property? And how does his argument relate to Marx's claim that private property makes it possible for one class to exploit another?

Not all economists share Friedman's concern about corporate social responsibility. In his article in this section, "Can Socially Responsible Firms

Survive in a Competitive Environment?" the economist Robert Frank describes ways in which socially responsible firms may sometimes make more money precisely *because* of their social responsibility. Socially responsible firms, for example, may solve "commitment" problems with employees, customers, and other firms in a way that promotes greater efficiency. For example, an ethically responsible law firm may be able to command a higher fee from its clients simply because the firm can be trusted not to overcharge. Or, an ethical company may have more productive employees because the employees believe that the company has made a commitment to them. The employees are willing to invest their time in developing *firm-specific* skills (rather than developing only skills they can sell on the open market), because they trust the company to treat them sympathetically and not to fire them at the first sign of an economic downturn. In his article Robert Frank describes five specific ways in which a socially responsible firm might prosper in a competitive environment.

In the case study "Merck & Co., Inc.," issues of profit and social welfare clash in the context of Merck's quandary over whether to test and produce a new drug designed to fight the disease, river blindness. Should Merck proceed with the development of a drug that promises to save hundreds of thousands from blindness, *even if* it will lose money in the process? Merck's corporate history stresses commitment to the health of the customer over profits (despite the fact that Merck has been enormously successful financially). But can it seriously pursue this philosophy in the instance of river blindness?

JUSTICE

The subject of social justice, both for traditional and modern philosophers, is directly connected to economics and ethical theory. One important subcategory of justice dealt with in this section—namely, distributive justice—concerns the issue of how, and according to what principles, society's goods should be distributed. When thinking about justice, it is important to remember that the concept of "justice" cannot include all ethical and political values. Thus, no matter how desirable it may be to have justice established in society, we must acknowledge other ideals such as benevolence and charity. Justice refers to a minimal condition that should exist in a good society, a condition that traditionally has been interpreted as "giving each individual his or her due."

The notion of distributive justice, i.e., what constitutes justice in distributing goods to persons, is an evasive concept, as is illustrated by the following story: Once a group of soldiers found themselves defending a fort against an enemy. The soldiers were in desperate need of water, and the only source was 200 yards from the fort in enemy territory. Courageously, a small group sneaked outside the fort, filled their canteens with water, and returned safely. After showing the water to their fellow soldiers, the successful adventurers proposed that it should be distributed in accordance with the principles of justice. Since justice requires distribution on the basis of merit, they said, they themselves should get the water because they risked their lives in obtaining it. There was considerable disagreement. Although agreeing that justice requires distribution on the basis of deserving characteristics, a different group of soldiers, which had been longest without water, claimed they deserved it more because they *needed* it more than the others. After all, they were the thirstiest. And still a different group, agreeing with the same general principle of justice, argued that everyone deserved equal amounts of water because all human beings, considered generally, have equal worth. The moral, obviously, is that interpretations of justice have difficulty specifying a particular characteristic or set of characteristics which, when possessed by human beings, will serve as the basis for "giving each person his or her due."

Although the subject of distributive justice is a popular topic among modern philosophers, some thinkers, such as Robert Nozick, claim that the idea is prejudicial and controversial. If society's goods are to be distributed, this implies the existence of a distributing agency such as the government to enforce certain principles of distribution, thus taking away from those who have acquired holdings through voluntary exchanges and desert and giving them to those who have and deserve less. In attacking any principles of distribution, Nozick is arguing that the very existence of such a process violates basic principles of individual liberty, because it denies individuals the opportunity to do as they please without interference, and thus to engage freely in exchanges of goods and property. In this way, Nozick maintains, distributive and redistributive practices necessitate the violation of basic liberties and therefore no willful distribution can itself be just.

Another modern writer presented in this section, John Rawls, also considers questions of justice and the social order. Rawls believes that the idea of distributive justice can be coordinated with principles of individual rights and liberties. He argues that a just society is one in which agreements are freely made, in which no one is left out, and in which deserving people are not shortchanged. Rawls argues that a just society is based on two principles: (1) ". . . each person engaged in an institution or affected by it has an equal right to the most extensive liberty compatible with a like liberty for all . . ." and (2) ". . . inequalities as defined by the institutional structure . . . are arbitrary unless it is reasonable to expect that they will work out to everyone's advantage and provided that the positions and offices to which they attach or from which they may be gained are open to all." Thus, Rawls is not arguing that in a just society things would be structured so as to give all people an equal number of goods—for example, money, education, or status; and he allows that some people may have a great deal more than others. However, for a society to be just, such inequalities are only acceptable if their existence is to the advantage of the least fortunate as well as to everybody else. Rawls further specifies that no form of distribution in any society is just unless it satisfies the first condition of justice: freedom. Rawls's article "Distributive justice," excerpts of which are presented in this section, first appeared in 1967 and is a precursor of his influential book *A Theory of Justice* (Harvard University Press, 1971) in which he more fully develops the views presented here.

The contemporary debate over the interpretation of justice begun by thinkers such as Rawls and Nozick in the 1970s was joined in the 1980s by a variety of voices, many of them critical of the very assumptions underlying the debate. Perhaps, many have argued, the modern political mind-set is preoccupied with individual liberty and fair procedures at the expense of a fuller and more positive concept of social-personal good.

Issues of justice arise not only in large social systems, but in corporate organizations. We take for granted a considerable amount of inequality in the modern work place; inequality in salaries, working conditions, and status. But which inequalities are to be tolerated, and which are not? If medical quality and availability of medical treatment are significantly different for managers than for ordinary workers, is the result unfair? To what extent should modern managers concerned with justice be attempting to "level" perks and advantages for all working in the corporation? In the case, "The Oil Rig," we encounter dramatic disparities between ex-patriates and hired Angolan workers on an oil rig. The Angolans have dramatically lower salaries, fewer privileges, different clothing, limited access to medical treatment, and smaller quarters. Does justice require that the Tool Pusher (the boss of the oil rig) eliminate or substantially reduce inequalities?

Traditional Theories
of
Property and Profit

➤ *Case Study* ➤

Plasma International

T. W. ZIMMERER ➤ P. L. PRESTON

The Sunday headline in the Tampa, Florida, newspaper read:

Blood Sales Result in Exorbitant Profits for Local Firm

The story went on to relate how the Plasma International Company, head-quartered in Tampa, Florida, purchased blood in underdeveloped countries for as little a 90 cents a pint[1] and resold the blood to hospitals in the United States and South America. A recent disaster in Nicaragua produced scores of injured persons and the need for fresh blood. Plasma International had 10,000 pints of blood flown to Nicaragua from West Africa and charged hospitals $150 per pint, netting the firm nearly 1.5 million dollars.

As a result of the newspaper story, a group of irate citizens, led by prominent civic leaders, demanded that the City of Tampa, and the State of Florida, revoke Plasma International's licenses to practice business. Others protested to their congressmen to seek enactment of legislation designed to halt the sale of blood for profit. The spokesperson was reported as saying, "What kind of people are these—selling life and death? These men prey on the needs of dying people, buying blood from poor, ignorant Africans for 90 cents worth of beads and junk, and selling it to injured people for $150 a pint. Well, this company will soon find out that the people of our community won't stand for their kind around here."

"I just don't understand it. We run a business just like any other business; we pay taxes and we try to make an honest profit," said Sol Levin as he responded to reporters at the Tampa International Airport. He had just returned home from testifying before the House Subcommittee on Medical Standards. The recent publicity surrounding his firm's activities during the recent earthquakes had once again fanned the flames of public opinion. An election year was an unfortunate time for the publicity to occur. The politicians and the media were having a field day.

Levin was a successful stockbroker when he founded Plasma International Company three years ago. Recognizing the world's need for safe,

"Plasma International," case prepared by T. W. Zimmerer and P. L. Preston, reprinted from *Business and Society: Cases and Text*, ed. by Robert D. Hay, Edmund R. Gray, and James E. Gates (Cincinnati: South-Western Publishing Co., 1976). Reprinted with permission of the authors.

uncontaminated, and reasonably priced whole blood and blood plasma, Levin and several of his colleagues pooled their resources and went into business. Initially, most of the blood and plasma they sold was purchased through store-front operations in the southeast United States. Most of the donors were, unfortunately, men and women who used the money obtained from the sale of their blood to purchase wine. While sales increased dramatically on the basis of an innovative marketing approach, several cases of hepatitis were reported in recipients. The company wisely began a search for new sources.

Recognizing their own limitations in the medical-biological side of the business they recruited a highly qualified team of medical consultants. The consulting team, after extensive testing, and a worldwide search, recommended that the blood profiles and donor characteristics of several rural West African tribes made them ideal prospective donors. After extensive negotiations with the State Department and the government of the nation of Burami, the company was able to sign an agreement with several of the tribal chieftains.

As Levin reviewed these facts, and the many costs involved in the sale of a commodity as fragile as blood, he concluded that the publicity was grossly unfair. His thoughts were interrupted by the reporter's question: "Mr. Levin, is it necessary to sell a vitally needed medical supply, like blood, at such high prices especially to poor people in such a critical situation?" "Our prices are determined on the basis of a lot of costs that we incur that the public isn't even aware of," Levin responded. However, when reporters pressed him for details of these "relevant" costs, Levin refused any further comment. He noted that such information was proprietary in nature and not for public consumption.

Note

1. Prices have been adjusted in this article to allow for inflation occurring since the article was written (ed.).

← *Case Study* →

Dorrence Corporation Trade-offs

HANS WOLF

Arthur Cunningham, Chief Executive Officer of the Dorrence Corporation, was reflecting on the presentations by the various divisions of the company of their operating plans and financial budgets for the next three years, which he had heard during the past several days. A number of critical decisions would have to be made at tomorrow's meeting of the nine senior executives who formed Dorrence's Corporate Operating Committee. Although Dorrence's tradition was one of consensus management, Cunningham knew that he was expected to exercise leadership and would have the final word, as well as the ultimate responsibility for the subsequent performance of the company.

Dorrence, a large U.S.-based pharmaceutical company with sales and operations throughout the world, had achieved an outstanding long-term record of growth in sales and profits. The company had not incurred a loss in any year since 1957 and profits had increased over the prior year in 28 out of the past 32 years. During the past 10 years, sales had grown at an average compound rate of 12% per year and profits had increased at a 15% average annual rate. Dorrence's profit as a percent of sales was considerably higher than that of the average U.S. industrial concern. (See Exhibit 1)

This growth had produced a huge increase in the value of Dorrence's stock. There are approximately 30,000 Dorrence shareholders, but as with many large American corporations, about 65% of Dorrence shares are held by a relatively small number of pension funds, mutual funds, university endowments and insurance companies. Dorrence grants stock options to its executives and permits employees in the U.S. and several other countries to purchase Dorrence stock through the company's savings plan. Dorrence executives own about 2% of the company's shares and all other employees about 1%. Thus, directly and indirectly, Dorrence is owned by millions of people who are affected to some degree by the marketplace of Dorrence shares.

Dorrence's fine record of growth had also brought benefits to the company's customers, employees and the communities in which the company had operations. Dorrence had steadily expanded its research expenditures at a greater rate than its sales growth and had developed important new products that extended life and improved the quality of life for millions of people. Because of its profitability, Dorrence was able to pay higher-than-average salaries to its employees, pay sizeable incentive awards to middle and upper management and bonuses to all employees based on the success of the company. Dorrence's growth also had provided unusual opportunities for career growth to many of its people. The company prided itself on being a good citizen in the communities in which its laboratories and factories were located. It contributed to local charities and encouraged its employees to work constructively in community organizations.

Cunningham felt that 1989 was, however, a very disappointing year. The company fell short of the goals management had established at the start of the year.

Growth in sales and profits was far below the rate of recent years and below the levels achieved by several of Dorrence's peers in the pharmaceutical industry. Management incentive awards and employee bonuses were, therefore, about 5% smaller than those distributed for 1988. The value of Dorrence stock was about 20% below its high point.

Consequently, Cunningham considered it important that Dorrence achieve at least a 13% profit growth in 1990, and higher rates in the two years beyond that. He recognized that such a goal would not be easy to reach. It would not only require the best efforts of the entire organization, but also force some tough decisions.

The 1990 budgets proposed by the divisions added up to a growth rate of only 8% in profit-after-taxes, five percentage points below what Cunningham considered a minimum acceptable level. As a rough rule of thumb he calculated that each percentage point increase in the profit growth rate required about $8 million additional profit-before-taxes. Thus, each percentage point improvement could be achieved in a number of ways: $13 million additional sales volume accompanied by normal incremental costs, or $8 million additional revenue from price increases, or $8 million reduction on expenditures. During the course of the three days of presentations he had identified several possibilities for such improvements about which decisions would have to be made. In his notes he had summarized them as follows.

1. Size of the research budget: Dorrence's total expenditures for research and development had climbed annually, not only in absolute dollars but also as a percent of sales. During the current year they totaled about 17% of sales, one of the higher levels in the pharmaceutical industry. The proposed budget included a further increase and Cunningham knew that many promising projects required additional funding if the company were to demonstrate the safety and efficacy of important new drugs in a timely manner.

Cunningham was keenly aware that pharmaceutical research and development was a very risky activity. The failure rate was high. Many years of effort were required before the success or failure of a new product could be known. Typically, it took seven to ten years from the identification of a potential new drug to receiving the approval to market it from the Food and Drug Administration and its sister bodies in other countries. On average, a pharmaceutical company brought to successful conclusion only one new drug development program for each $100 million of R&D expenditures.

Clearly, there was a trade-off between investing for future growth and achieving acceptable profits in the short run. On Cunningham's list of possible changes in the proposed 1990 budget was a $10 million reduction in the amount of money requested for R&D.

2. Export sales: The International Division had presented an opportunity for a $4 million sale to the Philippine government which was not included in the 1990 budget because of lack of product availability. It was for Savolene, a new Dorrence injectable drug for the treatment of serious viral infections, including measles. The drug was difficult and expensive to manufacture and had been in very short supply since its introduction.

A large lot, costing about $1 million, had been rejected for the U.S. market on the basis of a very sensitive new test for endotoxins recently required by the U.S. Food & Drug Administration in addition to another test that had been the FDA standard for many years. The new test had shown a very low level of endotoxins on this batch of Savolene, even though no endotoxins has been revealed by the older test.

Cunningham had asked whether this ruled out shipping the batch to the Philippines. The company's chief medical safety officer had answered: "Officially the Philippines and a lot of other countries still rely only on the old test. It always takes them a while to follow U.S. practice, and sometimes they never do. Endotoxins might cause a high fever when injected into patients, but I can't tell you that the level in this batch is high enough to cause trouble. But how can we have a double standard, one for the U.S. and one for Third World countries?"

However, when Cunningham asked Dorrence's export vice president the same question, she said, "It's not our job to over-protect other countries. The health authorities in the Philippines know what they're doing. Our FDA always takes an extreme position. Measles is a serious illness. Last year in the Philippines half the kids who had measles died. It's not only good business but also good ethics to send them the only batch of Savolene we have available."

3. *Capital investments:* Among the capital investments that had been included in the proposed budgets was a $200 million plant automation program for Dorrence's Haitian chemical plant. The purpose of the investment was to permit a dramatic reduction in the cost of Libam, Dorrence's principal product whose U.S. patent would expire in a couple of years. Patent protection had already ended in most other countries and chemical manufacturers in Italy, Hungary and India were selling Libam's active ingredient at very low prices. Once there was no longer patent protection in the U.S., these companies, and others, could capture a large share of Dorrence's existing sales unless Dorrence could match their low prices. Automating the Haitian plant was essential to achieving such lower cost. Successful implementation of the new technology would enable the plant to achieve the required output with far fewer people than currently employed at the plant. What to do about these surplus workers presented a difficult problem for which no solution had yet been worked out.

Dorrence was currently earning about 9% interest on its surplus funds. The proposed automation project would use up $200 million of those funds and thus reduce the interest income earned by the company. The 1990 impact of such a reduction was about $9 million. If the automation program were stretched out over a longer period, almost half of that interest income reduction would be postponed a year, thus adding $4 million to 1990 profits. The risk was that the automated plant would not be in operation in time to meet the expected competition.

4. *Employee health insurance costs:* Like all U.S. companies Dorrence was experiencing rapid escalation in the cost of its employee health insurance program. Dorrence paid 100% of the premium for its employees and 80% of the premiums for their dependents. After meeting certain deductibles, employees are reimbursed 80% to 90% of their medical and dental costs. The company's cost of maintaining the plan was budgeted to increase 22%, or $12 million in 1990. An important issue, therefore, was whether the plan should be changed to shift all or a portion of that cost increase to the employees through reducing the share of the premiums paid by the company, or increasing the deductibles, or reducing the percent reimbursement, or some combination of those changes.

5. *Closing Dorrence's plant in Argentina:* Dorrence had purchased a small pharmaceutical company in Argentina in the early 1950s when prospects for growth in the local market seemed excellent. However, in most years since then Argentina has been plagued by hyper-inflation. With rapidly rising

wage rates and other local costs on the one hand, and strictly controlled selling prices for pharmaceuticals on the other hand, Dorrence's Argentine subsidiary had consistently lost money. The 1990 budget projected a loss of $4 million.

For the past year Dorrence had tried to find a buyer for its Argentine subsidiary who would utilize the existing Dorrence 120-person sales force and continue to operate Dorrence's Buenos Aires factory with its 250 employees. No such buyer had been found, but recently a local company had offered to purchase the rights to Dorrence's product line. It would manufacture them in its under-utilized plant and distribute them through its own sales force. If Dorrence accepted this offer, the 370 Dorrence employees in Argentina would be laid off. Dorrence had already created a financial reserve for the government-mandated severance payments. Thus if Dorrence decided to end its operations in Argentina, corporate profits would improve by $4 million in 1990.

6. *Price increase on principal product sold in the U.S.:* The budget proposed by Dorrence's U.S. pharmaceutical division already assumed a 5% price increase on all its current products at the end of the first quarter of the year, producing a $40 million increase in sales revenues. A substantially higher price increase on Libam, its largest selling product, could probably be implemented without adversely affecting sales volume. For example, if the budgeted price increase were 10% instead of 5%, an additional $12 million would be generated. Alternately, if two 5% price increases were implemented six months apart, Dorrence would earn $4 million above the proposed budget. Libam is used by chronically ill patients, many of them elderly. (See Exhibit 2 for a comparison of Libam's price with the prices of other drugs in the same therapeutic class.)

In most countries pharmaceutical prices are controlled by the government. The United States is one of the few countries in which pharmaceutical companies are free to decide what prices to charge for their drugs. Physicians generally prescribe the drug which they feel will be most beneficial to their patients regardless of price. Unless the patent on a drug has expired and a generic equivalent is available, the demand for a prescription drug is not very sensitive to its price. Consequently, drug prices in the United States are substantially higher than in most other countries. (See Exhibit 3)

Cunningham was, however, very conscious of the growing public concern about health care costs. Although drugs constitute only a small fraction of the nation's total health care bill, drug prices are an easily identified target and drug companies were coming increasingly under attack for their price increases. (See Exhibit 4)

7. *New Costa Rican manufacturing plant:* $10 million in sales of a new life-saving drug developed by Dorrence had been removed from the budget because of an unexpected problem at the new plant that had been constructed to produce the product.

Three years earlier Dorrence had chosen a small town in Costa Rica after evaluating various possible sites for the plant. The town had won the competition for the new plant because of the availability of inexpensive land, relatively low wages, certain tax concessions, and a promise by the local government to build a new municipal waste-treatment facility by the time the plant would be completed. In addition Dorrence felt it would be fulfilling its social responsibilities by providing jobs in an area of high unemployment.

A few days before Dorrence's budget meeting the company had learned that the completion of the municipal waste-treatment plant was delayed at least a year. Although Costa Rica's environmental regulations are less stringent than those of industrialized countries, local law does prohibit the discharge of untreated factory waste water into streams. Without a means of disposing of its waste water, the Dorrence plant could not operate.

A message from the Dorrence plant manager received yesterday seemed to solve the problem. The city sanitation commissioner had given Dorrence a special exemption which would allow it to discharge its waste water into a stream behind the plant until the city's waste-treatment facility was completed. Cunningham had immediately asked for a fuller report on the situation. The plant manager had sent the following additional details:

> The stream is used to irrigate sugarcane fields and small vegetable plots on which people in this area depend. There is, therefore, a chance that substances in the waste water would be absorbed by the crops that people are going to eat. I wonder if that is acceptable. On the other hand, I fear that all the good we have accomplished here will go down the drain if we don't begin manufacturing operations. Construction of the plant was completed on schedule three months ago. Building our own waste-treatment facility now would add $5 million to the cost of the plant and would take at least 12 months. I've already hired over 100 workers and have given them extensive training. We obviously can't pay the workers for a year to sit around in an idle plant. Losing their jobs would be devastating to them and the whole community. Besides, there is no other Dorrence facility or plant of another company which could accomplish the synthesis required for this product. Lots of people in the United States are anxiously waiting for this new drug.

8. Pricing of an important new product: Finally, there was the issue of what price to charge for another new Dorrence drug, Miracule, which was expected to be introduced late in the year. In most cases patients for whom Miracule was prescribed would require the drug for the rest of their lives, unless an even more effective drug became available. The budget had assumed a price which would result in a daily cost of $1.75 (including wholesaler and drugstore markups) for the average patient. A price of $2.50 would yield an additional $8 million profit to Dorrence during 1990 and far greater sums in subsequent years.

Despite the difficulties surrounding each of the issues Cunningham had identified, he felt it was critical that the 1990 budget be improved to call for 13% profit growth over 1989. He believed that a second year in a row of below-average profit growth would be viewed very negatively by the investment community, be demoralizing to the company's management, and could result in a substantial drop in the value of the company's stock as investors switched to pharmaceutical companies with better 1990 results. He also recognized that large institutional investors, such as pension funds, were taking a more active role in demanding better performance from the managements of the companies in which they invested the funds entrusted to them.

EXHIBIT 1. Dorrence Corporation: Financial & Other Data

	1979	1980	1981	1982	1983	1984	1985	1986	1987	1988	1989
Sales—$Millions	826	1,074	1,181	1,259	1,333	1,453	1,466	1,703	2,063	2,404	2,572
Profit*—$Millions	132	164	175	204	224	222	241	312	413	524	558
Profit* as % of Sales	16.0	15.3	14.8	16.2	16.8	15.3	16.4	18.3	20.0	21.8	21.7
Employees	12,500	12,900	13,500	13,600	13,800	14,000	13,300	13,100	13,500	13,900	14,700
Stockholders of Record	26,500	25,000	23,900	23,300	22,300	21,700	20,300	21,200	24,500	28,900	29,800

*After taxes.

126

EXHIBIT 2. Average* Daily Cost in the U.S. at Retail of Prescription Anti-inflammatory Drugs

Drug	Company	Average Daily Cost at Retail
Clinoril	Merck	$1.92
Ansaid	Upjohn	1.76
Feldene	Pfizer	1.67
Libam	Dorrence	1.61
Naprosyn	Syntex	1.59
Indocin	Merck	1.54
Voltaren	Ciba-Geigy	1.50
Motrin**	Upjohn	1.06
Ibuprofen (generic)	Boots	.67

*Assuming mid-range dosages.
**Branded form of ibuprofen.

EXHIBIT 3. Average Daily Cost of Libam at Retail in 10 Countries

United States	$1.61
Sweden	.96
Canada	.89
Italy	.86
Great Britain	.70
Japan	.70
France	.51
Spain	.40
Australia	.27
Mexico	.20

EXHIBIT 4. Price Increases for Major Drugs in the U.S. for the Past 12 Months

Company	Product	Price Versus One Year Ago ($ increase)
Pfizer	Procardia	20
Pfizer	Feldene	10
SmithKline Beecham	Dyazide	10
SmithKline Beecham	Tagamet	15
SmithKline Beecham	Augmentin	8
Syntex	Naprosyn	11
Merck	Vasotec	12
Merck	Mevacor	6
Marion	Cardizem	9
Marion	Carafate	7
Monsanto (Searle)	Calan SR	10
Bristol-Myers Squibb	Capoten	12
Bristol-Myers Squibb	Buspar	8
Ciba-Geigy	Voltaren	6
Glaxo	Zantac	6
Lilly	Prozac	19
Lilly	Ceclor	9
Upjohn	Xanax	22
Upjohn	Halcion	22
Warner-Lambert	Lopid	6

Source: Bear, Stearns & Co., Inc.

The Justification of Private Property

JOHN LOCKE

. . . God, who hath given the world to men in common, hath also given them reason to make use of it to the best advantage of life and convenience. The earth and all that is therein is given to men for the support and comfort of their being. And though all the fruits it naturally produces, and beasts it feeds, belong to mankind in common, as they are produced by the spontaneous hand of nature; and nobody has originally a private dominion exclusive of the rest of mankind in any of them as they are thus in their natural state; yet being given for the use of men, there must of necessity be a means to appropriate them some way or other before they can be of any use at all beneficial to any particular man. The fruit or venison which nourishes the wild Indian, who knows no enclosure, and is still a tenant in common, must be his, and so his, i.e., a part of him, that another can no longer have any right to it, before it can do any good for the support of his life.

From John Locke, *The Second Treatise of Government* (1764; rpt. New York, Macmillan, 1956).

Though the earth and all inferior creatures be common to all men, yet every man has a property in his own person; this nobody has any right to but himself. The labor of his body and the work of his hands we may say are properly his. Whatsoever, then, he removes out of the state that nature hath provided and left it in, he hath mixed his labor with, and joined to it something that is his own, and thereby makes it his property. It being by him removed from the common state nature placed it in, it hath by this labor something annexed to it that excludes the common right of other men. For this labor being the unquestionable property of the laborer, no man but he can have a right to what this is once joined to, at least where there is enough, and as good left in common for others.

He that is nourished by the acorns he picked up under an oak, or the apples he gathered from the trees in the wood, has certainly appropriated them to himself. Nobody can deny but the nourishment is his. I ask, then, When did they begin to be his—when he digested, or when he ate, or when he boiled, or when he brought them home, or when he picked them up? And 'tis plain if the first gathering made them not his, nothing else could. That labor put a distinction between them and common; that added something to them more than nature, the common mother of all, had done, and so they became his private right. And will anyone say he had no right to those acorns or apples he thus appropriated, because he had not the consent of all mankind to make them his? Was it robbery thus to assume to himself what belonged to all in common? If such a consent as that was necessary, man had starved, notwithstanding the plenty God had given him. We see in common which remains so by compact that 'tis the taking any part of what is common and removing it out of the state nature leaves it in, which begins the property; without which the common is of no use. And the taking of this or that does not depend on the express consent of all the commoners. Thus the grass my horse has bit, the turfs my servant has cut, the ore I have dug in any place where I have a right to them in common with others, become my property without the assignation or consent of anybody. The labor that was mine removing them out of that common state they were in, hath fixed my property in them. . . .

It will perhaps be objected to this, that if gathering the acorns, or other fruits of the earth, etc., makes a right to them, then anyone may engross as much as he will. To which I answer, Not so. The same law of nature that does by this means give us property, does also bound that property too. "God has given us all things richly" (1 Tim. vi. 17), is the voice of reason confirmed by inspiration. But how far has He given it us? To enjoy. As much as anyone can make use of any advantage of life before it spoils, so much he may by his labor fix a property in; whatever is beyond this, is more than his share, and belongs to others. Nothing was made by God for man to spoil or destroy. And thus considering the plenty of natural provisions there was a long time in the world, and the few spenders, and to how small a part of that provision the industry of one man could extend itself, and engross it to the prejudice of others—especially keeping within the bounds, set by reason, of what might serve for his use—there could be then little room for quarrels or contentions about property so established.

But the chief matter of property being now not the fruits of the earth, and the beasts that subsist on it, but the earth itself, as that which takes in and carries with it all the rest, I think it is plain that property in that, too, is acquired as the former. As much land as a man tills, plants, improves, cultivates, and can use the product of, so much is his property. He by his labor does as it were enclose it from the common. Nor will it invalidate his right to say, everybody else has an equal title to it; and therefore he cannot appropriate, he cannot enclose, without the consent of all his fellow-commoners, all mankind. God, when He gave the world in common to all mankind, commanded man also to labor, and the penury of his condition required it of him. God and his reason commanded him to subdue the earth, i.e., improve it for the benefit of life, and therein lay out something upon it that was his own, his labor. He that, in obedience to this command of God, subdued, tilled, and sowed any part of it, thereby annexed to it something that was his property, which another had no title to, nor could without injury take from him.

Nor was this appropriation of any parcel of land, by improving it, any prejudice to any other man, since there was still enough and as good left; and more than the yet unprovided could use. So that in effect, there was never the less left for others because of his enclosure for himself. For he that leaves as much as another can make use of, does as good as take nothing at all. Nobody could think himself injured by the drinking of another man, though he took a good draught, who had a whole river of the same water left him to quench his thirst; and the case of land and water, where there is enough of both, is perfectly the same.

God gave the world to men in common; but since He gave it them for their benefit, and the greatest conveniences of life they were capable to draw from it, it cannot be supposed He meant it should always remain common and uncultivated. He gave it to the use of the industrious and rational (and labor was to be his title to it), not to the fancy or coveteousness of the quarrelsome and contentious. He that had as good left for his improvement as was already taken up, needed not complain, ought not to meddle with what was already improved by another's labor; if he did, it is plain he desired the benefit of another's pains, which he had no right to, and not the ground which God had given him in common with others to labor on, and whereof there was as good left as that already possessed, and more than he knew what to do with, or his industry could reach to.

It is true, in land that is common in England, or any other country where there is plenty of people under Government, who have money and commerce, no one can enclose or appropriate any part without the consent of all his fellow-commoners: because this is left common by compact, i.e., by the law of the land, which is not to be violated. And though it be common in respect of some men, it is not so to all mankind; but is the joint property of this country, or this parish. Besides, the remainder, after such enclosure, would not be as good to the rest of the commoners as the whole was, when they could all make use of the whole, whereas in the beginning and first peopling of the great common of the world it was quite otherwise. The law man was under was rather for appropriating. God commanded, and his wants forced him, to labor. That was his property, which could not be taken from him wherever he had fixed it. And hence subduing or cultivating the earth, and having dominion, we see are joined together. The one gave title to the other. So that God, by commanding to subdue, gave authority so far to appropriate. And the condition of human life, which requires labor and materials to work on, necessarily introduces private possessions.

The measure of property nature has well set by the extent of men's labor and the conveniency of life. No man's labor could subdue or appropriate all, nor could his enjoyment consume more than a small part; so that it was impossible for any man, this way, to entrench upon the right of another or acquire to himself a property to the prejudice of his neighbor, who would still have room for as good and as large a possession (after the other had taken out his) as before it was appropriated. Which measure did confine every man's possession to a very moderate proportion, and such as he might appropriate to himself without injury to anybody in the first ages of the world, when men were more in danger to be lost, by wandering from their company, in the then vast wilderness of the earth than to be straitened for want of room to plant in. . . .

And thus, without supposing any private dominion and property in Adam over all the world, exclusive of all other men, which can no way be proved, nor any one's property be made out from it, but supposing the world, given as it was to the children of men in common, we see how labor could make men distinct titles to several parcels of it for their private uses, wherein there could be no doubt of right, no room for quarrel.

Nor is it so strange, as perhaps before consideration it may appear, that the property of labor should be able to overbalance the community of land. For it is labor indeed that puts the difference of value on everything; and let anyone consider what the difference is between an acre of land planted with tobacco or sugar, sown with wheat or barley, and an acre of the same land lying in common without any husbandry upon it, and he will find that the improvement of labor makes the far greater part of the value. I think it will be but a very modest computation to say that of the products of the earth useful to the life of man nine-tenths are the effects of labor; nay, if we will rightly estimate things as they come to our use, and cast up the several expenses about them—what in them is purely owing to nature, and what to labor—we shall find that in most of them ninety-nine hundredths are wholly to be put on the account of labor. . . .

From all which it is evident that, though the things of nature are given in common, yet man, by being master of himself and proprietor of his own person and the actions or labor of it, had still in himself the great foundation of property; and that which made up the great part of what he applied to the support or comfort of his being, when invention and arts had improved the conveniences of life, was perfectly his own, and did not belong in common to others.

Thus labor, in the beginning, gave a right of property, wherever anyone was pleased to employ it upon what was common, which remained a long while the far greater part, and is yet more than mankind makes use of. Men at first, for the most part, contented themselves with what unassisted nature offered to their necessities; and though afterwards, in some parts of the world (where the increase of people and stock, with the use of money, had made land scarce, and so of some value), the several communities settled the bounds of their distinct territories, and by laws within themselves, regulated the properties of the private men of their society, and so, by compact and agreement, settled the property which labor and industry began—and the leagues that have been made between several states and kingdoms, either expressly or tacitly disowning all claim and right to the land in the other's possession, have, by common consent, given up their pretenses to their natural common right, which originally they had to those countries; and so have, by positive agreement, settled a property amongst themselves in distant parts of the world—yet there are still great tracts of ground to be found which, the inhabitants thereof not having joined with the rest of mankind in the consent of the use of their common money, lie waste, and more than the people who dwell on it do or can make use of, and so still lie in common; though this can scarce happen amongst that part of mankind that have consented to the use of money.

The greatest part of things really useful to the life of man, and such as the necessity of subsisting made the first commoners of the world look after, as it doth the Americans now, are generally things of short duration, such as, if they are not consumed by use, will decay and perish of themselves: gold, silver, and diamonds are things that fancy or agreement have put the value on more than real use and the necessary support of life. Now of those good things which nature hath provided in common, everyone hath a right, as hath been said, to as much as he could use, and had a property in all he could effect with his labor—all that his industry could extend to, to alter from the state nature had put it in, was his. He that gathered a hundred bushels of acorns or apples had thereby a property in them; they were his goods as soon as gathered. He was only to look that he used them before they spoiled, else he took more than his share, and robbed others; and, indeed, it was a foolish thing, as well as dishonest, to hoard up more than he could make use of. If he gave away a part to anybody else, so that it perished not uselessly in his possession, these he also made use of; and if he also bartered away plums that would have rotted in a week, for nuts that would last good for his eating a whole year, he did no injury; he wasted not the common stock, destroyed no part of the portion of goods that belonged to others, so long as nothing perished uselessly in his hands. Again, if he would give his nuts for a piece of metal, pleased with its color, or exchange his sheep for shells, or wool for a sparkling pebble or a diamond, and keep those by him all his life, he invaded not the right of others; he might heap up as much as these durable things as he pleased, the exceeding of the bounds of his just property not lying in the largeness of his possessions, but the perishing of anything uselessly in it.

And thus came in the use of money—some lasting thing that men might keep without spoiling, and that, by mutual consent, men would take in exchange for the truly useful but perishable supports of life.

And as different degrees of industry were apt to give men possessions in different proportions, so this invention of money gave them the opportunity to continue and enlarge them; for supposing an island, separate from all possible commerce with the rest of the world, wherein there were but a hundred families—but there were sheep, horses, and cows, with other useful animals, wholesome fruits, and land enough for corn for a hundred thousand times as many, but nothing in the island, either because of its commonness or perishableness, fit to supply the place of money—what reason could anyone have there to enlarge his possessions beyond the use of his family and a plentiful supply to its consumption, either in what their own industry produced, or they could barter for like perishable useful commodities with others? Where there is not something both lasting and scarce, and so valuable to be hoarded up, there men will not be apt to enlarge their possessions of land, were it never so rich, never so free for them to take; for I ask, what would a man value ten thousand or a hundred thousand acres of excellent land, ready cultivated, and well stocked too with cattle, in the middle of the inland parts of America, where he had no hopes of commerce with other parts of the world, to draw money to him by the sale of the product? It would not be worth the enclosing, and we should see him give up again to the wild common of nature whatever was more than would supply the conveniences of life to be had there for him and his family.

Thus in the beginning all the world was America, and more so than that is now, for no such thing as money was anywhere known. Find out something that hath the use and value of money amongst his neighbors, you shall see the same man will begin presently to enlarge his possessions.

But since gold and silver, being little useful to the life of man in proportion to food, raiment, and carriage, has its value only from the consent of men, whereof labor yet makes, in great part, the measure, it is plain that the consent of men have agreed to a disproportionate and unequal possession of the earth—I mean out of the bounds of society and compact; for in governments the laws regulate it; they having, by consent, found out and agreed in a way how a man may rightfully and without injury possess more than he himself can make use of by receiving gold and silver, which may continue long in a man's possession, without decaying for the overplus, and agreeing those metals should have a value.

And thus, I think, it is very easy to conceive without any difficulty how labor could at first begin a title of property in the common things of nature, and how the spending it upon our uses bounded it; so that there could then be no reason of quarrelling about title, nor any doubt about the largeness of possession it gave. Right and conveniency went together; for as a man had a right to all he could employ his labor upon, so he had no temptation to labor for more than he could make use of. This left no room for controversy about the title, nor for encroachment on the right of others; what portion a man carved to himself was easily seen, and it was useless, as well as dishonest, to carve himself too much, or take more than he needed.

Alienated Labour

KARL MARX

We shall begin from a *contemporary* economic fact. The worker becomes poorer the more wealth he produces and the more his production increases in power and extent. The worker becomes an ever cheaper commodity the

From *Karl Marx: Early Writings, The Economic and Philosophic Manuscripts of 1844*, trans. T. B. Bottomore. Copyright © 1963 by McGraw-Hill Book Company. Used with permission of McGraw-Hill Book Co., New York, and Pitman Publishing, London.

more goods he creates. The *devaluation* of the human world increases in direct relation with the *increase in value* of the world of things. Labour does not only create goods; it also produces itself and the worker as a *commodity*, and indeed in the same proportion as it produces goods. . . .

All these consequences follow from the fact that the worker is related to the *product of his labour* as to an *alien* object. For it is clear on this presupposition that the more the worker expends himself in work the more powerful becomes the world of objects which he creates in face of himself, the poorer he becomes in his inner life, and the less he belongs to himself. It is just the same as in religion. The more of himself man attributes to God the less he has left in himself. The worker puts his life into the object, and his life then belongs no longer to himself but to the object. The greater his activity, therefore, the less he possesses. What is embodied in the product of his labour is no longer his own. The greater this product is, therefore, the more he is diminished. The *alienation* of the worker in his product means not only that his labour becomes an object, assumes an *external* existence, but that it exists independently, *outside himself,* and alien to him, and that it stands opposed to him as an autonomous power. The life which he has given to the object sets itself against him as an alien and hostile force.

. . . The worker becomes a slave of the object; first, in that he receives an *object of work,* i.e. receives *work,* and secondly, in that he receives *means of subsistence.* Thus the object enables him to exist, first as a *worker* and secondly as a *physical subject.* The culmination of this enslavement is that he can only maintain himself as a *physical subject* so far as he is a *worker,* and that it is only as a *physical subject* that he is a worker. . . .

What constitutes the alienation of labour? First, that the work is *external* to the worker, and that it is not part of his nature; and that, consequently, he does not fulfill himself in his work but denies himself, has a feeling of misery rather than well-being, does not develop freely his mental and physical energies but is physically exhausted and mentally debased. The worker, therefore, feels himself at home only during his leisure time, whereas at work he feels homeless. His work is not voluntary but imposed, *forced labour.* It is not the satisfaction of a need, but only a *means* for satisfying other needs. Its alien character is clearly shown by the fact that as soon as there is no physical or other compulsion it is avoided like the plague. External labour, labour in which man alienates himself, is a labour of self-sacrifice, of mortification. Finally, the external character of work for the worker is shown by the fact that it is not his own work but work for someone else, that in work he does not belong to himself but to another person. . . .

We arrive at the result that man (the worker) feels himself to be freely active only in his animal functions—eating, drinking, and procreating, or at most also in his dwelling and in personal adornment—while in his human functions he is reduced to an animal. The animal becomes human and the human becomes animal.

Eating, drinking, and procreating are of course also genuine human functions. But abstractly considered, apart from the environment of human activities, and turned into final and sole ends, they are animal functions.

We have now considered the act of alienation of practical human activity, labour, from two aspects: (1) the relationship of the worker to the *product of labour* as an alien object which dominates him. This relationship is at the same time the relationship to the sensuous external world, to natural objects, as an alien and hostile world; (2) the relationship of labour to the *act of production* within *labour*. This is the relationship of the worker to his own activity as something alien and not belonging to him, activity as suffering (passivity), strength as powerlessness, creation as emasculation, the *personal* physical and mental energy of the worker, his personal life (for what is life but activity?), as an activity which is directed against himself, independent of him and not belonging to him. This is *self-alienation* as against the above-mentioned alienation of the *thing*.

We have now to infer a third characteristic of *alienated labour* from the two we have considered.

Man is a species-being not only in the sense that he makes the community (his own as well as those of other things) his object both practically and theoretically, but also (and this is simply another expression for the same thing) in the sense that he treats himself as the present, living species, as a *universal* and consequently free being.[1]

Species-life, for man as for animals, has its physical basis in the fact that man (like animals) lives from inorganic nature, and since man is more universal than an animal so the range of inorganic nature from which he lives is more universal. . . . The universality of man appears in practice in the universality which makes the whole of nature into his inorganic body: (1) as a direct means of life; and equally (2) as the material object and instrument of his life activity. Nature is the inorganic body of man; that is to say nature, excluding the human body itself. To say that man *lives* from nature means that nature is his *body* with which he must remain in a continuous interchange in order not to die. The statement that the physical and mental life of man, and nature, are interdependent means simply that nature is interdependent with itself, for man is a part of nature.

Since alienated labour: (1) alienates nature from man; and (2) alienates man from himself, from his own active function, his life activity; so it alienates him from the species. It makes *species-life* into a means of individual life. In the first place it alienates species-life and individual life, and secondly, it turns the latter, as an abstraction, into the purpose of the former, also in its abstract and alienated form.

For labour, *life activity, productive life*, now appear to man only as *means* for the satisfaction of a need, the need to maintain his physical existence. Productive life is, however, species-life. It is life creating life. In the type of life activity resides the whole character of a species, its species-character; and free, conscious activity is the species-character of human beings. Life itself appears only as a *means of life*.

The animal is one with its life activity. It does not distinguish the activity from itself. It is *its activity*. But man makes his life activity itself an object of his will and consciousness. He has a conscious life activity. It is not a determination with which he is completely identified. Conscious life activity distinguishes man from the life activity of animals. Only for this reason is he a species-being. Or rather, he is only a self-conscious being, i.e., for his own life is an object for him, because he is a species-being. Only for this reason is his activity free activity. Alienated labour reverses the relationship, in that man because he is a self-conscious being makes his life activity, his *being*, only a means for his *existence*.

The practical construction of an *objective world*, the *manipulation* of inorganic nature, is the confirmation of man as a conscious species-being, i.e., a being who treats the species as his own being or himself as a species-being. . . .

It is just in his work upon the objective world that man really proves himself as a *species-being*. This production is his active species-life. By means of it nature appears as *his* work and his reality. The object of labour is, therefore, the *objectification of man's species-life:* for he no longer reproduces himself merely intellectually, as in consciousness, but actively and in a real sense, and he sees his own reflection in a world which he has constructed. While, therefore, alienated labour takes away the object of production from man, it also takes away his *species-life*, his real objectivity as a species-being, and changes his advantage over animals into a disadvantage in so far as his inorganic body, nature, is taken from him.

Just as alienated labour transforms free and self-directed activity into a means, so it transforms the species-life of man into a means of physical existence.

Consciousness, which man has from his species, is transformed through alienation so that species-life becomes only a means for him. (3) Thus alienated labour turns the *species-life of man*, and also nature as his mental species-property, into an *alien* being and into a *means* for his *individual existence*. It alienates from man his own body, external nature, his mental life and his *human* life. (4) A direct consequence of the alienation of man from the product of his labour, from his life activity and from his species-life, is that *man is alienated* from other *men*. When man confronts himself he also confronts *other* men. What is true of man's relationship to his work, to the product of his work and to himself, is also true of his relationship to other men, to their labour and to the objects of their labour.

In general, the statement that man is alienated from his species-life means that each man is alienated from others, and that each of the others is likewise alienated from human life.

Human alienation, and above all the relation of man to himself, is first realized and expressed in the relationship between each man and other men. Thus in the relationship of alienated labour every man regards other men according to the standards and relationships in which he finds himself placed as a worker.

We began with an economic fact, the alienation of the worker and his production. We have expressed this fact in conceptual terms as *alienated labour*, and in analysing the concept we have merely analysed an economic fact. . . .

The *alien* being to whom labour and the product of labour belong, to whose service labour is devoted, and to whose enjoyment the product of labour goes, can only be *man* himself. If the product of labour does not belong to the worker, but confronts him as an alien power, this can only be because it belongs to *a man other than the worker*. . . .

Thus, through alienated labour the worker creates the relation of another man, who does not work and is outside the work process, to this labour. The relation of the workers to work also produces the relation of the capitalist (or whatever one likes to call the lord of labour) to work. *Private property* is, therefore, the product, the necessary result, of *alienated labour*, of the external relation of the worker to nature and to himself.

Private property is thus derived from the analysis of the concept of *alienated labor;* that is, alienated man, alienated labour, alienated life, and estranged man.

We have, of course, derived the concept of *alienated labour* (*alienated life*) from political economy, from the analysis of the *movement of private property.* But the analysis of this concept shows that although private property appears to be the basis and cause of alienated labour, it is rather a consequence of the latter, just as the gods are *fundamentally* not the cause but the product of confusion of human reason. At a later stage, however, there is a reciprocal influence.

Only in the final state of the development of private property is its secret revealed, namely, that it is on one hand the *product* of alienated labour, and on the other hand the *means* by which labour is alienated, *the realization of this alienation.* . . .

Just as *private property* is only the sensuous expression of the fact that man is at the same time an *objective* fact for himself and becomes an alien and non-human object for himself; just as his manifestation of life is also his alienation of life and his self-realization a loss of reality, the emergence of an *alien* reality; so the positive supersession of private property, i.e., the *sensuous* appropriation of the human essence and of human life, of objective man and of human *creations,* by and for man, should not be taken only in the sense of *immediate,* exclusive *enjoyment,* or only in the sense of *possession* or *having.* Man appropriates his manifold being in an all-inclusive way, and thus as a whole man. All his *human* relations to the world—seeing, hearing, smelling, tasting, touching, thinking, observing, feeling, desiring, acting, loving—in short, all the organs of his individuality, like the organs which are directly communal in form, are in their objective action (their *action in relation to the object*) the appropriation of this object, the appropriation of human reality. The way in which they react to the object is the confirmation of *human reality.* It is human effectiveness and human *suffering,* for suffering humanly considered is an enjoyment of the self for man.

Private property has made us so stupid and partial that an object is only *ours* when we have it, when it exists for us as capital or when it is directly eaten, drunk, worn, inhabited, etc., in short, *utilized* in some way. But private property itself only conceives these various forms of possession as *means of life,* and the life for which they serve as means is the life of *private property*—labour and creation of capital.

The supersession of private property is, therefore, the complete *emancipation* of all the human qualities and senses. It is such an emancipation because these qualities and senses have become *human,* from the subjective as well as the objective point of view. The eye has become a *human* eye when its *object* has become a *human,* social object, created by man and destined for him. The senses have, therefore, become directly theoreticians in practice. They relate themselves to the thing for the sake of the thing, but the thing itself is an *objective human* relation to itself and to man, and vice versa. Need and enjoyment have thus lost their *egoistic* character and nature has lost its mere *utility* by the fact that its utilization has become *human* utilization. . . .

Note

1. In this passage Marx reproduces Feuerbach's argument in *Das Wesen des Christentums.*

Benefits of the Profit Motive

ADAM SMITH

BOOK I

Of the causes of improvement in the productive powers of labor and of the order according to which its produce is naturally distributed among the different ranks of the people

Chapter I   Of the Division of Labor

The greatest improvement in the productive powers of labor, and the greater part of the skill, dexterity, and judgment with which it is anywhere directed, or applied, seem to have been the effects of the division of labor. . . .

To take an example, therefore, from a very trifling manufacture; but one in which the division of labor has been very often taken notice of, the trade of the pin-maker; a workman not educated to this business (which the division of labor has rendered a distinct trade), nor acquainted with the use of the machinery employed in it (to the invention of which the same division of labor has probably given occasion), could scarce, perhaps, with his utmost industry, make one pin in a day, and certainly could not make twenty. But in the way in which this business is now carried on, not only the whole work is a peculiar trade, but it is divided into a number of branches, of which the greater part are likewise peculiar trades. One man draws out the wire, another straights it, a third cuts it, a fourth points it, a fifth grinds it at the top for receiving the head; to make the head requires two or three distinct operations; to put it on is a peculiar business, to whiten the pins is another; it is even a trade by itself to put them into the paper; and the important business of making a pin is, in this manner, divided into about eighteen distinct operations, which in some manufactories, are all performed by distinct hands, though in others the same man will sometimes perform two or three of them. I have seen a small manufactory of this kind where ten men only were employed, and where some of them consequently performed two or three distinct operations. But though they were very poor, and therefore but indifferently accommodated with the necessary machinery, they could, when they exerted themselves, make among them about twelve pounds of pins a day. There are in a pound upwards of four thousand pins of a middling size. Those ten persons, therefore, could make among them upwards of forty-eight thousand pins in a day. Each person, therefore, making a tenth part of forty-eight thousand pins, might be considered as making four thousand eight hundred pins in a day. But if they had all wrought separately and independently, and without any of them having been educated to this peculiar business, they certainly could not each of them have made twenty, perhaps not one pin in a day; that is, certainly, not the two hundred and fortieth, perhaps not the four thousand eight hundredth part, of what

From Adam Smith, *The Wealth of Nations*, Books I and IV (1776; rpt. Chicago: University of Chicago Press, 1976).

they are at present capable of performing in consequence of a proper division and combination of their different operations.

In every other art and manufacture, the effects of the division of labor are similar to what they are in this very trifling one; though in many of them, the labor can neither be so much subdivided, nor reduced to so great a simplicity of operation. The division of labor, however, so far as it can be introduced, occasions, in every art, a proportionate increase of the productive powers of labor. . . .

This great increase of the quantity of work, which in consequence of the division of labor, the same number of people are capable of performing, is owing to three different circumstances: first, to the increase of dexterity in every particular workman; secondly, to the saving of the time which is commonly lost in passing from one species of work to another; and lastly, to the invention of a great number of machines which facilitate and abridge labor, and enable one man to do the work of many.

First, the improvement of the dexterity of the workman necessarily increases the quantity of the work he can perform; and the division of labor, by reducing every man's business to some one simple operation and by making this operation the sole employment of his life, necessarily increases very much the dexterity of the workman. A common smith, who, though accustomed to handle the hammer, has never been used to make nails, if upon some particular occasion he is obliged to attempt it, will scarce, I am assured, be able to make about two or three hundred nails in a day, and those too very bad ones. A smith who has been accustomed to make nails, but whose sole or principal business has not been that of a nailer, can seldom with his utmost diligence make more than eight hundred or a thousand nails in a day. I have seen several boys under twenty years of age who had never exercised any other trade but that of making nails, and who, when they exerted themselves, could make, each of them, upwards of two thousand three hundred nails in a day. The making of a nail, however, is by no means one of the simplest operations. The same person blows the bellows, stirs or mends the fire as there is occasion, heats the iron, and forges every part of the nail: In forging the head too he is obliged to change his tools. The different operations into which the making of a pin or of a metal button is subdivided, are all of them much more simple; and the dexterity of the person, of whose life it has been the sole business to perform them, is usually much greater. The rapidity with which some of the operations of those manufacturers are performed exceeds what the human hand could, by those who had never seen them, be supposed capable of acquiring.

Secondly, the advantage which is gained by saving the time commonly lost in passing from one sort of work to another is much greater than we should at first view be apt to imagine it. It is impossible to pass very quickly from one kind of work to another, that is carried on in a different place, and with quite different tools. A country weaver who cultivates a small farm must lose a good deal of time in passing from his loom to the field, and from the field to his loom. When the two trades can be carried on in the same workhouse, the loss of time is no doubt much less. It is even in this case, however, very considerable. . . .

Thirdly, and lastly, every body must be sensible how much labor is facilitated and abridged by the application of proper machinery. . . .

. . . A great part of the machines made use of in those manufactures in which labor is most subdivided were originally the inventions of common workmen, who, being each of them employed in some very simple opera-tion, naturally turned their thoughts toward finding out easier and readier methods of performing it. Whoever has been much accustomed to visit such manufacturers must frequently have been shown very pretty machines which were inventions of such workmen in order to facilitate and quicken their own particular part of the work. In the first fire-engines, a boy was constantly employed to open and shut alternately the communication between the boiler and the cylinder, according as the piston either ascended or descended. One of those boys, who loved to play with his companions, observed that, by tying a string from the handle of the valve which opened this communi-cation to another part of the machine, the valve would open and shut with-out his assistance, and leave him at liberty to divert himself with his play-fellows. One of the greatest improvements that has been made upon this machine, since it was first invented, was in this manner the discovery of a boy who wanted to save his own labor. . . .

It is the great multiplication of the productions of all the different arts, in consequence of the division of labor, which occasions, in a well-governed society, that universal opulence which extends itself to the lowest ranks of the people. Every workman has a great quantity of his own work to dispose of beyond what he himself has occasion for; and every other workman being exactly in the same situation, he is enabled to exchange a great quantity of his own goods for a great quantity, or, what comes to the same thing, for the price of a great quantity of theirs. He supplies them abundantly with what they have occasion for, and they accommodate him as amply with what he has occasion for, and a general plenty diffuses itself through all the differ-ent ranks of the society. . . .

Chapter II   Of the Principle Which Gives Occasion to the Division of Labor

This division of labor, from which so many advantages are derived, is not originally the effect of any human wisdom which forsees and intends that general opulence to which it gives occasion. It is the necessary, though very slow and gradual, consequence of a certain propensity in human nature which has in view no such extensive utility: the propensity to truck, barter, and exchange one thing for another.

. . . In almost every other race of animals each individual, when it is grown up to maturity, is entirely independent, and in its natural state has occasion for the assistance of no other living creature. But man has almost constant occasion for the help of his brethren, and it is in vain for him to expect it from their benevolence only. He will be more likely to prevail if he can interest their self-love in his favor, and show them that it is for their own advantage to do for him what he requires of them. Whoever offers to an-other a bargain of any kind, proposes to do this. Give me that which I want, and you shall have this which you want, is the meaning of every such of-fer; and it is in the manner that we obtain from one another the far greater part of those good offices which we stand in need of. It is not from the benevolence of the butcher, the brewer, or the baker, that we expect our dinner, but from their regard to their own interest. We address ourselves, not to their humanity but to their self-love, and never talk to them of our own necessities but of their advantages. Nobody but a beggar chooses to depend chiefly upon the benevolence of his fellow-citizens. Even a beggar does not depend upon it entirely. The charity of well-disposed people, indeed, supplies him with the whole fund of his subsistence. But though this principle ultimately provides him with all the necessaries of life which he has occasion for, it neither does nor can provide him with them as he has occasion for them. The greater part of his occasional wants are supplied in the same manner as those of other people, by treaty, by barter, and by purchase. With the money which one man gives him he purchases food. The old clothes which another bestows upon him he exchanges for other old clothes which suit him better, or for lodging, or for food, or for money, with which he can buy either food, clothes, or lodging, as he has occasion.

As it is by treaty, by barter, and by purchase that we obtain from one another the greater part of those mutual good offices which we stand in need of, so it is this same trucking disposition which originally gives occasion to the division of labor. In a tribe of hunters or shepherds a particular person makes bows and arrows, for example, with more readiness and dexterity than any other. He frequently exchanges them for cattle or for venison with his companions; and he finds at last that he can in this manner get more cattle and venison than if he himself went to the field to catch them. From a regard to his own interest, therefore, the making of bows and arrows grows to be his chief business, and he becomes a sort of armorer. Another excels in making the frames and covers of their little huts or moveable houses. He is accustomed to be of use in this way to his neighbors, who reward him in the same manner with cattle and with venison till at last he finds it his interest to dedicate himself entirely to this employment, and to become a sort of house carpenter. In the same manner a third becomes a smith or a brazier; a fourth a tanner or dresser of hides or skins, the principal part of the clothing of savages. And thus the certainty of being able to exchange all that surplus part of the produce of his own labor, which is over and above his own consumption, for such parts of the produce of other men's labor as he may have occasion for, encourages every man to apply himself to a particular occupation, and to cultivate and bring to perfection whatever talent or genius he may possess for that particular species of business.

The difference of natural talents in different men is, in reality, much less than we are aware of; and the very different genius which appears to distinguish men of different professions, when grown up to maturity, is not upon many occasions so much the cause as the effect of the division of labor. The difference between the most dissimilar characters, between a philosopher and a common street porter, for example, seems to arise not so much from nature as from habit, custom, and education. When they came into the world, and for the first six or eight years of their existence, they were, perhaps, very much alike, and neither their parents nor play-fellows could perceive any remarkable difference. About that age, or soon after, they come to be employed in very different occupations. The difference of talents comes then to be taken notice of, and widens by degrees, till at last the vanity of the philosopher is willing to acknowledge scarce any resemblance. But without the disposition to truck, barter, and exchange, every man must have procured to himself every necessary and conveniency of life which he wanted. All must have had the same duties to perform, and the same work to do, and there could have been no such difference of employment as could alone give occasion to any great difference of talents. . . .

BOOK IV

Chapter II

Every individual is continually exerting himself to find out the most advantageous employment for whatever capital he can command. It is his own advantage, indeed, and not that of the society, which he has in view. But the study of his own advantage, naturally, or rather necessarily, leads him to prefer that employment which is most advantageous to the society. . . .

As every individual, therefore, endeavours as much as he can both to employ his capital in the support of domestic industry, and so to direct that industry that its produce may be of the greatest value, every individual necessarily labors to render the annual revenue of the society as great as he can. He generally, indeed, neither intends to promote the public interest, nor knows how much he is promoting it. By preferring the support of domestic to that of foreign industry, he intends only his own security: and by directing that industry in such a manner as its produce may be of the greatest value, he intends only his own gain, and he is in this, as in many other cases, led by an invisible hand to promote an end which was no part of his intention. Nor is it always the worse for society that it was no part of it. By pursuing his own interest he frequently promotes that of the society more effectually than when he really intends to promote it. I have never known much good done by those who affected to trade for the public good. It is an affectation, indeed, not very common among merchants, and very few words need be employed in dissuading them from it.

Wealth

ANDREW CARNEGIE

This article is one of the clearest attempts to justify Social Darwinism. Written in 1889, it defends the pursuit of wealth by arguing that society is strengthened and improved through the struggle for survival in the marketplace. Interestingly, it was written by one of the world's wealthiest men, Andrew Carnegie, who came to the United States as a poor immigrant boy and quickly rose to enormous power. He began his career as a minor employee in a telegraph company, but emerged in a few years as a superintendent of the Pennsylvania Railroad. After the Civil War he entered the iron and steel business, and by 1889 he controlled

First published in the *North American Review*, June 1889.

eight companies, which he eventually consolidated into the Carnegie Steel Corporation. Shortly before he died, he merged the Carnegie Steel Corporation with the United States Steel Company.

Carnegie took seriously the task of managing his vast fortune, and he made use of many of the ideas which are presented in the following article. He gave generously to many causes, including public libraries, public education, and the development of international peace.

The problem of our age is the proper administration of wealth, so that the ties of brotherhood may still bind together the rich and poor in harmonious relationship. The conditions of human life have not only been changed, but revolutionized, within the past few hundred years. In former days there was little difference between the dwelling, dress, food, and environment of the chief and those of his retainers. The Indians are today where civilized man then was. When visiting the Sioux, I was led to the wigwam of the chief. It was just like the others in external appearance, and even within the difference was trifling between it and those of the poorest of his braves. The contrast between the palace of the millionaire and the cottage of the laborer with us today measures the change which has come into civilization.

This change, however, is not to be deplored, but welcomed as highly beneficial. It is well, nay essential, for the progress of the race, that the houses of some should be homes for all that is highest and best in literature and art, and for all the refinements of civilization, rather than that none should be so. Much better this great irregularity than universal squalor. Without wealth there can be no Maecenases. When these apprentices rose to be masters, there was little or no change in their mode of life, and they, in turn, educated in the same routine succeeding apprentices. There was, substantially, social equality, and even political equality, for those engaged in industrial pursuits had then little or no political voice in the State.

But the inevitable result of such a mode of manufacture was crude articles at high prices. Today the world obtains commodities of excellent quality at prices which even the generation preceding this would have deemed incredible. In the commercial world similar causes have produced similar results, and the race is benefited thereby. The poor enjoy what the rich could not before afford. What were the luxuries have become the necessaries of life. The laborer has now more comforts than the farmer had a few generations ago. The farmer has more luxuries than the landlord had, and is more richly clad and better housed. The landlord has books and pictures rarer, and appointments more artistic, than the King could then obtain.

The price we pay for this salutary change is, no doubt, great. We assemble thousands of operatives in the factory, in the mine, and in the counting-house, of whom the employer can know little or nothing, and to whom the employer is little better than a myth. All intercourse between them is at an end. Rigid Castes are formed, and, as usual, mutual ignorance breeds mutual distrust. Each Caste is without sympathy for the other, and ready to credit anything disparaging in regard to it. Under the law of competition, the employer of thousands is forced into the strictest economies, among which the rates paid to labor figure prominently, and often there is friction between the employer and the employed, between capital and labor, between rich and poor. Human society loses homogeneity.

The price which society pays for the law of competition, like the price it pays for cheap comforts and luxuries, is also great; but the advantages of this law are greater still, for it is to this law that we owe our wonderful material development, which brings improved conditions in its train. But, whether the law be benign or not, we must say of it, as we say of the change in the conditions of men to which we have referred: It is here; we cannot evade it; no substitutes for it have been found; and while the law may be sometimes hard for the individual, it is best for the race, because it insures the survival of the fittest in every department. We accept and welcome, therefore, as conditions to which we must accommodate ourselves, great inequality of environment, the concentration of business, industrial and commercial, in the hands of a few, and the law of competition between these, as being not only beneficial, but essential for the future progress of the race. Having accepted these, it follows that there must be great scope for the exercise of special ability in the merchant and in the manufacturer who has to conduct affairs upon a great scale. That this talent for organization and management is rare among men is proved by the fact that it invariably secures for its possessor enormous rewards, no matter where or under what laws or conditions. The experienced in affairs always rate the man whose services can be obtained as a partner as not only the first consideration, but such as to render the question of his capital scarcely worth considering, for such men soon create capital; while, without the special talent required, capital soon takes wings. Such men become interested in firms or corporations using millions; and estimating only simple interest to be made upon the capital invested, it is inevitable that their income must exceed their expenditures, and that they must accumulate wealth. Nor is there any middle ground which such men can occupy, because the great manufacturing or commercial concern which does not earn at least interest upon its capital soon becomes bankrupt. It must either go forward or fall behind: to stand still is impossible. It is a condition essential for its successful operation that it should be thus far profitable, and even that, in addition to interest on capital, it should make a profit. It is a law, as certain as any of the others named, that men possessed of this peculiar talent for affairs, under the free play of economic forces, must, of necessity, soon be in receipt of more revenue than can be judiciously expended upon themselves, and this law is as beneficial for the race as the others.

Objections to the foundations upon which society is based are not in order, because the condition of the race is better with these than it has been with any others which have been tried. Of the effect of any new substitutes proposed we cannot be sure. The Socialist or Anarchist who seeks to overturn present conditions is to be regarded as attacking the foundation upon which civilization itself rests, for civilization took its start from the day that the capable, industrious workman said to his incompetent and lazy fellow, "If thou dost not sow, thou shalt not reap," and thus ended primitive Communism by separating the drones from the bees. One who studies this subject will soon be brought face to face with the conclusion that upon the sacredness of property civilization itself depends—the right of the laborer to his hundred dollars in the savings bank, and equally the legal right of the millionaire to his millions. To those who propose to substitute Communism for this intense Individualism the answer, therefore, is: The race has tried that. All progress from that barbarous day to the present time has resulted from its displacement. Not evil, but good, has come to the race from the accumulation of wealth by those who have the ability and energy that produce it. But even if we admit for a moment that it might be better for the race to discard its present foundations, Individualism—that it is a nobler ideal that man should labor, not for himself alone, but in and for a brotherhood of his fellows, and share with them all in common, realizing Swedenborg's idea of Heaven, where, as he says, the angels derive their happiness, not from laboring for self, but for each other—even admit all this, and a sufficient answer is, This is not evolution, but revolution. It necessitates the changing of human nature itself—a work of aeons, even if it were good to change it, which we cannot know. It is not practicable in our day or in our age. Even if desirable theoretically, it belongs to another and long-succeeding sociological stratum. Our duty is with what is practicable now; with the next step possible in our day and generation. It is criminal to waste our energies in endeavoring to uproot, when all we can profitably or possibly accomplish is to bend the universal tree of humanity a little in the direction most favorable to the production of good fruit under existing circumstances. We might as well urge the destruction of the highest existing type of man because he failed to reach our ideal as to favor the destruction of Individualism, Private Property, the Law of Accumulation of Wealth, and the Law of Competition; for these are the highest results of human experience, the soil in which society so far has produced the best fruit. Unequally or unjustly, perhaps, as these laws sometimes operate, and imperfect as they appear to the Idealist, they are nevertheless, like the highest type of man, the best and most valuable of all that humanity has yet accomplished.

We start, then, with a condition of affairs under which the best interests of the race are promoted, but which inevitably gives wealth to the few. Thus far, accepting conditions as they exist, the situation can be surveyed and pronounced good. The question then arises—and, if the foregoing be correct, it is the only question with which we have to deal—What is the proper mode of administering wealth after the laws upon which civilization is founded have thrown it into the hands of the few? And it is of this great question that I believe I offer the true solution. It will be understood that *fortunes* are here spoken of, not moderate sums saved by many years of effort, the returns from which are required for the comfortable maintenance and education of families. This is not *wealth*, but only *competence*, which it should be the aim of all to acquire.

. . . Indeed, it is difficult to set bounds to the share of a rich man's estate which should go at his death to the public through the agency of the state, and by all means such taxes should be graduated, beginning at nothing upon moderate sums to dependents, and increasing rapidly as the amounts swell, until of the millionaire's hoard, as of Shylock's at least

"_____The other half
Comes to the privy coffer of the state."

This policy would work powerfully to induce the rich man to attend to the administration of wealth during his life, which is the end that society should always have in view, as being that by far most fruitful for the people. Nor need it be feared that this policy would sap the root of enterprise and render men less anxious to accumulate, for to the class whose ambition it is to leave great fortunes and be talked about after their death, it will attract more attention, and, indeed, be a somewhat nobler ambition to have enormous sums paid over to the state from their fortunes.

There remains, then, only one mode of using great fortunes; but in this we have the true antidote for the temporary unequal distribution of wealth, the reconciliation of the rich and the poor—a reign of harmony—another ideal, differing, indeed, from that of the Communist in requiring only the further evolution of existing conditions, not the total overthrow of our civilization. It is founded upon the present most intense individualism, and the race is prepared to put it in practice by degrees whenever it pleases. Under its sway we shall have an ideal state, in which the surplus wealth of the few will become, in the best sense, the property of the many, because administered for the common good, and this wealth, passing through the hands of the few, can be made a much more potent force for the elevation of our race than if it had been distributed in small sums to the people themselves. Even the poorest can be made to see this, and to agree that great sums gathered by some of their fellow-citizens and spent for public purposes, from which the masses reap the principal benefit, are more valuable to them than if scattered among them through the course of many years in trifling amounts.

The best uses to which surplus wealth can be put have already been indicated. Those who would administer wisely must, indeed, be wise, for one of the serious obstacles to the improvement of our race is indiscriminate charity. It were better for mankind that the millions of the rich were thrown into the sea than so spent as to encourage the slothful, the drunken, the unworthy. Of every thousand dollars spent in so-called charity today, it is probable that $950 is unwisely spent; so spent, indeed, as to produce the very evils which it proposes to mitigate or cure. A well-known writer of philosophic books admitted the other day that he had given a quarter of a dollar to a man who approached him as he was coming to visit the house of his friend. He knew nothing of the habits of this beggar; knew not the use that would be made of this money, although he had every reason to suspect that it would be spent improperly. This man professed to be a disciple of Herbert Spencer; yet the quarter-dollar given that night will probably work more injury than all the money which its thoughtless donor will ever be able to give in true charity will do good. He only gratified his own feelings, saved himself from annoyance—and this was probably one of the most selfish and very worst actions of his life, for in all respects he is most worthy.

In bestowing charity, the main consideration should be to help those who will help themselves; to provide part of the means by which those who desire to improve may do so; to give those who desire to rise the aids by which they may rise; to assist, but rarely or never to do all. Neither the individual nor the race is improved by alms-giving. Those worthy of assistance, except in rare cases, seldom require assistance. The really valuable men of the race never do, except in cases of accident or sudden change. Everyone has, of course, cases of individuals brought to his own knowledge where temporary assistance can do genuine good, and these he will not overlook. But the amount which can be wisely given by the individual for individuals is necessarily limited by his lack of knowledge of the circumstance connected with each. He is the only true reformer who is as careful and as anxious not to aid the unworthy as he is to aid the worthy, and perhaps, even more so, for in alms-giving more injury is probably done by rewarding vice than by relieving virtue.

Thus is the problem of Rich and Poor to be solved. The laws of accumulation will be left free; the laws of distribution free. Individualism will continue, but the millionaire will be but a trustee for the poor; entrusted for a season with a great part of the increased wealth of the community, but administrating it for the community far better than it could or would have done for itself. The best minds will thus have reached a stage in the development of the race in which it is clearly seen that there is no mode of disposing of surplus wealth creditable to thoughtful and earnest men into whose hands it flows save by using it year by year for the general good. This day already dawns. But a little while, and although, without incurring the pity of their fellows, men may die sharers in great business enterprises from which their capital cannot be or has not been withdrawn, and is left chiefly at death for public uses, yet the man who dies leaving behind him millions of available wealth, which was his to administer during life, will pass away "unwept, unhonored, and unsung," no matter to what uses he leaves the dross which he cannot take with him. Of such as these the public verdict will then be: "The man who dies thus rich dies disgraced."

Such, in my opinion, is the true Gospel concerning Wealth, obedience to which is destined some day to solve the problems of the Rich and the Poor, and to bring "Peace on earth, among men Good-Will."

Property and Profit:
Modern
Discussions

— *Case Study* —

Merck & Co., Inc.

The Business Enterprise Trust

In 1978, Dr. P. Roy Vagelos, then head of the Merck research labs, received a provocative memorandum from a senior researcher in parasitology, Dr. William C. Campbell. Dr. Campbell had made an intriguing observation while working with ivermectin, a new antiparasitic compound under investigation for use in animals.

Campbell thought that ivermectin might be the answer to a disease called river blindness that plagued millions in the Third World. But to find out if Campbell's hypothesis had merit, Merck would have to spend millions of dollars to develop the right formulation for human use and to conduct the field trials in the most remote parts of the world. Even if these efforts produced an effective and safe drug, virtually all of those afflicted with river blindness could not afford to buy it. Vagelos, originally a university researcher but by then a Merck executive, had to decide whether to invest in research for a drug that, even if successful, might never pay for itself.

River Blindness

River blindness, formally known as *onchocerciasis*, was a disease labeled by the World Health Organization (WHO) as a public health and socioeconomic problem of considerable magnitude in over 35 developing countries throughout the Third World. Some 85 million people in thousands of tiny settlements throughout Africa and parts of the Middle East and Latin America were thought to be at risk. The cause: a parasitic worm carried by a tiny black fly which bred along fast-moving rivers. When the flies bit humans— a single person could be bitten thousands of times a day—the larvae of a parasitic worm, *Onchocerca volvulus*, entered the body.

These worms grew to more than two feet in length, causing grotesque but relatively innocuous nodules in the skin. The real harm began when the adult worms reproduced, releasing millions of microscopic offspring, known as microfilariae, which swarmed through body tissue. A terrible itching resulted, so bad that some victims committed suicide. After several years, the microfilariae caused lesions and depigmentation of the skin. Eventually they invaded the eyes, often causing blindness.

The World Health Organization estimated in 1978 that some 340,000 people were blind because of onchocerciasis, and that a million more suffered from varying degrees of visual impairment. At that time, 18 million or more people were infected with the parasite, though half did not yet have serious symptoms. In some villages close to fly-breeding sites, nearly all residents were infected and a majority of those over age 45 were blind. In such places, it was said, children believed that severe itching, skin infections and blindness were simply part of growing up.

In desperate efforts to escape the flies, entire villages abandoned fertile areas near rivers, and moved to poorer land. As a result, food shortages were frequent. Community life disintegrated as new burdens arose for already impoverished families.

The disease was first identified in 1893 by scientists and in 1926 was found to be related to the black flies. But by the 1970s, there was still no cure that could safely be used for community-wide treatment. Two drugs, diethylcarbamazine (DEC) & Suramin, were useful in killing the parasite, but both had severe side effects in infected individuals, needed close monitoring, and had even caused deaths. In 1974, the Onchocerciasis Control Program was created to be administered by the World Health Organization, in the hope that the flies could be killed through spraying of larvacides at breeding sites, but success was slow and uncertain. The flies in many areas developed resistance to the treatment, and were also known to disappear and then reinfest areas.

Merck & Co., Inc.

Merck & Co., Inc. was, in 1978, one of the largest producers of prescription drugs in the world. Headquartered in Rahway, New Jersey, Merck traced its origins to Germany in 1668 when Friedrich Jacob Merck purchased an apothecary in the city of Darmstadt. Over three hundred years later, Merck, having become an American firm, employed over 28,000 people and had operations all over the world.

In the late 1970s, Merck was coming off a 10-year drought in terms of new products. For nearly a decade, the company had relied on two prescription drugs for a significant percentage of its approximately $2 billion in annual sales: Indocin, a treatment for rheumatoid arthritis, and Aldomet, a treatment for high blood pressure. Henry W. Gadsden, Merck's chief executive from 1965 to 1976, along with his successor, John J. Horan, were concerned that the 17-year patent protection on Merck's two big moneymakers would soon expire, and began investing an enormous amount in research.

Merck management spent a great deal of money on research because it knew that its success ten and twenty years in the future critically depended upon present investments. The company deliberately fashioned a corporate culture to nurture the most creative, fruitful research. Merck scientists were among the best-paid in the industry, and were given great latitude to pursue intriguing leads. Moreover, they were inspired to think of their work as a quest to alleviate human disease and suffering world-wide. Within certain proprietary constraints, researchers were encouraged to publish in academic journals and to share ideas with their scientific peers. Nearly a billion dollars was spent between 1975 and 1978, and the investment paid off. In that period, under the direction of head of research, Dr. P. Roy Vagelos, Merck introduced Clinoril, a painkiller for arthritis; a general antibiotic called Mefoxin; a drug for glaucoma named Timoptic; and Ivomec (ivermectin, MSD), an antiparasitic for cattle.

In 1978, Merck had sales of $1.98 billion and net income of $307 million. Sales had risen steadily between 1969 and 1978 from $691 million to almost $2 billion. Income during the same period rose from $106 million to over $300 million. (See Exhibit 1 for a 10-year summary of performance.)

At that time, Merck employed 28,700 people, up from 22,200 ten years earlier. Human and animal health products constituted 84% of the company's sales, with environmental health products and services representing an additional 14% of sales. Merck's foreign sales had grown more rapidly during the 1970s than had domestic sales, and in 1978 represented 47% of total sales. Much of the company's research operations were organized separately as the Merck Sharp & Dohme Research Laboratories, headed by Vagelos. Other Merck operations included the Merck Sharp & Dohme Division, the Merck Sharp & Dohme International Division, Kelco Division, Merck Chemical Manufacturing Division, Merck Animal Health Division, Calgon Corporation, Baltimore Aircoil Company, and Hubbard Farms.

The company had 24 plants in the United States, including one in Puerto Rico, and 44 in other countries. Six research laboratories were located in the United States and four abroad.

While Merck executives sometimes squirmed when they quoted the "unbusinesslike" language of George W. Merck, son of the company's founder and its former chairman, there could be no doubt that Merck employees found the words inspirational. "We try never to forget that medicine is for the people," Merck said. "It is not for the profits. The profits follow, and if we have remembered that, they have never failed to appear. The better we have remembered it, the larger they have been." These words formed the basis of Merck's overall corporate philosophy.

The Drug Investment Decision

Merck invested hundreds of millions of dollars each year in research. Allocating those funds amongst various projects, however, was a rather involved and inexact process. At a company as large as Merck, there was never a single method by which projects were approved or money distributed.

Studies showed that, on the average, it took 12 years and $200 million to bring a new drug to market. Thousands of scientists were continually working on new ideas and following new leads. Drug development was always a matter of trial and error; with each new iteration, scientists would close some doors and open others. When a Merck researcher came across an apparent breakthrough—either in an unexpected direction, or as a derivative of the original lead—he or she would conduct preliminary research. If the idea proved promising, it was brought to the attention of the department heads.

Every year, Merck's research division held a large review meeting at which all research programs were examined. Projects were coordinated and consolidated, established programs were reviewed and new possibilities were considered. Final approval on research was not made, however, until the head of research met later with a committee of scientific advisors. Each potential program was extensively reviewed, analyzed on the basis of the likelihood of success, the existing market, competition, potential safety problems, manufacturing feasibility and patent status before the decision was made whether to allocate funds for continued experimentation.

The Problem of Rare Diseases and Poor Customers

Many potential drugs offered little chance of financial return. Some diseases were so rare that treatments developed could never be priced high enough to recoup the investment in research, while other diseases afflicted only the poor in rural and remote areas of the Third World. These victims had limited ability to pay even a small amount for drugs or treatment.

In the United States, Congress sought to encourage drug companies to conduct research on rare diseases. In 1978 legislation had been proposed which would grant drug companies tax benefits and seven-year exclusive marketing rights if they would manufacture drugs for diseases afflicting fewer than 200,000 Americans. It was expected that this "orphan drug" program would eventually be passed into law.

There was, however, no U.S. or international program that would create incentives for companies to develop drugs for diseases like river blindness which afflicted millions of the poor in the Third World. The only hope was that some Third World government, foundation, or international organization might step in and partially fund the distribution of a drug that had already been developed.

The Discovery of Ivermectin

The process of investigating promising drug compounds was always long, laborious and fraught with failure. For every pharmaceutical compound that became a "product candidate," thousands of others failed to meet the most rudimentary pre-clinical tests for safety and efficacy. With so much room for failure, it became especially important for drug companies to have sophisticated research managers who could identify the most productive research strategies.

Merck had long been a pioneer in developing major new antibiotic compounds, beginning with penicillin and streptomycin in the 1940s. In the 1970s, Merck Sharp & Dohme Research Laboratories were continuing this tradition. To help investigate for new microbial agents of potential therapeutic value, Merck researchers obtained 54 soil samples from the Kitasato Institute of Japan in 1974. These samples seemed novel and the researchers hoped they might disclose some naturally occurring antibiotics.

As Merck researchers methodically put the soil through hundreds of tests, Merck scientists were pleasantly surprised to detect strong antiparasitic activity in Sample No. OS3153, a scoop of soil dug up at a golf course near Ito, Japan. The Merck labs quickly brought together an interdisciplinary team to try to isolate a pure active ingredient from the microbial culture. The compound eventually isolated—avermectin—proved to have an astonishing potency and effectiveness against a wide range of parasites in cattle, swine, horses and other animals. Within a year, the Merck team also began to suspect that a group of related compounds discovered in the same soil sample could be effective against many other intestinal worms, mites, ticks and insects.

After toxicological tests suggested that ivermectin would be safer than related compounds, Merck decided to develop the substance for the animal health market. In 1978 the first ivermectin-based animal drug, Ivomec, was nearing approval by the U.S. Department of Agriculture and foreign regulatory bodies. Many variations would likely follow: drugs for sheep and pigs, horses, dogs, and others. Ivomec had the potential to become a major advance in animal health treatment.

As clinical testing of ivermectin progressed in the late 1970s, Dr. William Campbell's ongoing research brought him face-to-face with an intriguing hypothesis. Ivermectin, when tested in horses, was effective against the microfilariae of an exotic, fairly unimportant gastrointestinal parasite, Onchocerca cervicalis. This particular worm, while harmless in horses, had characteristics similar to the insidious human parasite that causes river blindness, Onchocerca volvulus.

Dr. Campbell wondered: Could ivermectin be formulated to work against the human parasite? Could a safe, effective drug suitable for community-wide treatment of river blindness be developed? Both Campbell and Vagelos knew that it was very much a gamble that it would succeed. Furthermore, both knew that even if success were attained, the economic viability of such a project would be nil. On the other hand, because such a significant amount of money had already been invested in the development of the animal drug, the cost of developing a human formulation would be much less than that for developing a new compound. It was also widely believed at this point that ivermectin, though still in its final development stages, was likely to be very successful.

A decision to proceed would not be without risks. If a new derivative proved to have any adverse health effects when used on humans, its reputation as a veterinary drug could be tainted and sales negatively affected, no matter how irrelevant the experience with humans. In early tests, ivermectin had had some negative side effects on some specific species of mammals. Dr. Brian Duke of the Armed Forces Institute of Pathology in Washington, D.C., said the cross-species effectiveness of antiparasitic drugs are unpredictable, and there is "always a worry that some race or subsection of the human population" might be adversely affected.

Isolated instances of harm to humans or improper use in Third World settings might also raise some unsettling questions: Could drug residues turn up in meat eaten by humans? Would any human version of ivermectin distributed to the Third World be diverted into the black market, undercutting sales of the veterinary drug? Could the drug harm certain animals in unknown ways?

Despite these risks, Vagelos wondered what the impact might be of turning down Campbell's proposal. Merck had built a research team dedicated to alleviating human suffering. What would a refusal to pursue a possible treatment for river blindness do to morale?

Ultimately, it was Dr. Vagelos who had to make the decision whether or not to fund research toward a treatment for river blindness.

EXHIBIT 1. 10-Year Summary of Financial Performance

Merck & Co., Inc. and Subsidiaries (Dollar amounts in thousands except per-share figures)

Results for Year:	1978	1977	1976	1975	1974	1973	1972	1971	1970	1969
Sales	$1,981,440	$1,724,410	$1,561,117	$1,401,979	$1,260,416	$1,104,035	$942,631	$832,416	$761,109	$691,453
Materials and production costs	744,249	662,703	586,963	525,853	458,837	383,879	314,804	286,646	258,340	232,878
Marketing/administrative expenses	542,186	437,579	396,975	354,525	330,292	304,807	268,856	219,005	201,543	178,593
Research/development expenses	161,350	144,898	133,826	121,933	100,952	89,155	79,692	71,619	69,707	61,100
Interest expense	25,743	25,743	26,914	21,319	8,445	6,703	4,533	3,085	2,964	1,598
Income before taxes	507,912	453,487	416,439	378,349	361,890	319,491	274,746	252,061	228,555	217,284
Taxes on income	198,100	173,300	159,100	147,700	149,300	134,048	121,044	118,703	108,827	109,269
Net income**	307,534	277,525	255,482	228,778	210,492	182,681	151,180	131,381	117,878	106,645
Per common share**	$4.07	$3.67	$3.38	$3.03	$2.79	$2.43	$2.01	$1.75	$1.57	$1.43
Dividends declared on common stock	132,257	117,101	107,584	105,564	106,341	93,852	84,103	82,206	76,458	75,528
Per common share	$1.75	$1.55	$1.42-½	$1.40	$1.40	$1.23-⅓	$1.12	$1.10	$1.02-⅔	$1.02-½
Gross plant additions	155,853	177,167	153,894	249,015	159,148	90,194	69,477	67,343	71,540	48,715
Depreciation	75,477	66,785	58,198	52,091	46,057	40,617	36,283	32,104	27,819	23,973
Year-End Position:										
Working capital	666,817	629,515	549,840	502,262	359,591	342,434	296,378	260,350	226,084	228,296
Property, plant, and equipment (net)	924,179	846,784	747,107	652,804	459,245	352,145	305,416	274,240	239,638	197,220
Total assets	2,251,358	1,993,389	1,759,371	1,538,999	1,243,287	988,985	834,847	736,503	664,294	601,484
Stockholders' equity	1,455,135	1,277,753	1,102,154	949,991	822,782	709,614	621,792	542,978	493,214	451,030
Year-End Statistics:										
Average number of common shares outstanding (in thousands)	75,573	75,546	75,493	75,420	75,300	75,193	75,011	74,850	74,850	74,547
Number of stockholders	62,900	63,900	63,500	63,500	61,400	60,000	58,000	54,300	54,600	53,100
Number of employees	28,700	28,100	26,800	26,300	26,500	25,100	24,100	23,200	23,000	22,200

*The above data are as previously reported, restated for poolings-of-interests and stock splits.
**Net income for 1977 and related per-share amounts exclude gain on disposal of businesses of $13,225 and 18¢, respecively.

153

The Social Responsibility of Business Is to Increase Its Profits

MILTON FRIEDMAN

When I hear businessmen speak eloquently about the "social responsibilities of business in a free-enterprise system," I am reminded of the wonderful line about the Frenchman who discovered at the age of 70 that he had been speaking prose all his life. The businessmen believe that they are defending free enterprise when they declaim that business is not concerned "merely" with profit but also with promoting desirable "social" ends; that business has a "social conscience" and takes seriously its responsibilities for providing employment, eliminating discrimination, avoiding pollution and whatever else may be the catchwords of the contemporary crop of reformers. In fact they are—or would be if they or anyone else took them seriously—preaching pure and unadulterated socialism. Businessmen who talk this way are unwitting puppets of the intellectual forces that have been undermining the basis of a free society these past decades.

The discussions of the "social responsibilities of business" are notable for their analytical looseness and lack of rigor. What does it mean to say that "business" has responsibilities? Only people can have responsibilities. A corporation is an artificial person and in this sense may have artificial responsibilities, but "business" as a whole cannot be said to have responsibilities, even in this vague sense. The first step toward clarity to examining the doctrine of the social responsibility of business is to ask precisely what it implies for whom.

Presumably, the individuals who are to be responsible are businessmen, which means individual proprietors or corporate executives. Most of the discussion of social responsibility is directed at corporations, so in what follows I shall mostly neglect the individual proprietors and speak of corporate executives.

In a free-enterprise, private-property system, a corporate executive is an employee of the owners of the business. He has direct responsibility to his employers. That responsibility is to conduct the business in accordance with their desires, which generally will be to make as much money as possible while conforming to the basic rules of the society, both those embodied in law and those embodied in ethical custom. Of course, in some cases his employers may have a different objective. A group of persons might establish a corporation for an eleemosynary purpose—for example, a hospital or a school. The manager of such a corporation will not have money profit as his objectives but the rendering of certain services.

In either case, the key point is that, in his capacity as a corporate executive, the manager is the agent of the individuals who own the corporation or establish the eleemosynary institution, and his primary responsibility is to them.

Needless to say, this does not mean that it is easy to judge how well he is performing his task. But at least the criterion of performance is straightforward, and the persons among whom a voluntary contractual arrangement exists are clearly defined.

Of course, the corporate executive is also a person in his own right. As a person, he may have many other responsibilities that he recognizes or assumes voluntarily—to his family, his conscience, his feelings of charity, his church, his clubs, his city, his country. He may feel impelled by these responsibilities to devote part of his income to causes he regards as worthy, to refuse to work for particular corporations, even to leave his job, for example, to join his country's armed forces. If we wish, we may refer to some of these responsibilities as "social responsibilities." But in these respects he is acting as a principal, not an agent; he is spending his own money or time or energy, not the money of his employers or the time or energy he has contracted to devote to their purposes. If these are "social responsibilities," they are the social responsibilities of individuals, not of business.

What does it mean to say that the corporate executive has a "social responsibility" in his capacity as businessman? If this statement is not pure rhetoric, it must mean that he is to act in some way that is not in the interest of his employers. For example, that he is to refrain from increasing the price of the product in order to contribute to the social objective of preventing inflation, even though a price increase would be in the best interests of the corporation. Or that he is to make expenditures on reducing pollution beyond the amount that is in the best interests of the corporation or that is required by law in order to contribute to the social objective of improving the environment. Or that, at the expense of corporate profits, he is to hire "hardcore" unemployed instead of better qualified available workmen to contribute to the social objective of reducing poverty.

In each of these cases, the corporate executive would be spending someone else's money for a general social interest. Insofar as his actions in accord with his "social responsibility" reduce returns to stockholders, he is spending their money. Insofar as his actions raise the price to customers, he is spending customers' money. Insofar as his actions lower the wages of some employees, he is spending their money.

The stockholders or the customers or the employees could separately spend their own money on the particular action if they wished to do so. The executive is exercising a distinct "social responsibility," rather than serving as an agent of the stockholders or the customers or the employees, only if he spends the money in a different way than they would have spent it.

But if he does this, he is in effect imposing taxes, on the one hand, and deciding how the tax proceeds shall be spent, on the other.

This process raises political questions on two levels: principle and consequences. On the level of political principle, the imposition of taxes and the expenditure of tax proceeds are governmental functions. We have established elaborate constitutional, parliamentary and judicial provisions to control these functions, to assure that taxes are imposed so far as possible in accordance with the preferences and desires of the public—after all, "taxation without representation" was one of the battle cries of the American Revolution. We have a system of checks and balances to separate the legislative function of imposing taxes and enacting expenditures from the executive function of collecting taxes and administering expenditure programs and from the judicial function of mediating disputes and interpreting the law.

Here the businessman—self-selected or appointed directly or indirectly by stockholders—is to be simultaneously legislator, executive and jurist. He is to decide whom to tax by how much and for what purpose, and he is to spend the proceeds—all this guided only by general exhortations from on high to restrain inflation, improve the environment, fight poverty and so on and on.

The whole justification for permitting the corporate executive to be selected by the stockholders is that the executive is an agent serving the interests of his principal. This justification disappears when the corporate executive imposes taxes and spends the proceeds for "social" purposes. He becomes in effect a public employee, a civil servant, even though he remains in name an employee of a private enterprise. On grounds of political principle, it is intolerable that such civil servants—insofar as their actions in the name of social responsibility are real and not just window dressing—should be selected as they are now. If they are to be civil servants, then they must be elected through a political process. If they are to impose taxes and make expenditures to foster "social" objectives, then political machinery must be set up to make the assessment of taxes and to determine through a political process the objectives to be served.

This is the basic reason why the doctrine of "social responsibility" involves the acceptance of the socialist view that political mechanisms, not market mechanisms, are the appropriate way to determine the allocation of scarce resources to alternative uses.

On the grounds of consequences, can the corporate executive in fact discharge his alleged "social responsibilities"? On the one hand, suppose he could get away with spending the stockholders' or customers' or employees' money. How is he to know how to spend it? He is told that he must contribute to fighting inflation. How is he to know what action of his will contribute to that end? He is presumably an expert in running his company—in producing a product or selling it or financing it. But nothing about his selection makes him an expert on inflation. Will his holding down the price of his product reduce inflationary pressure? Or, by leaving more spending power in the hands of his customers, simply divert it elsewhere? Or, by forcing him to produce less because of the lower price, will it simply contribute to shortages? Even if he could answer these questions, how much cost is he justified in imposing on his stockholders, customers, and employees for this social purpose? What is his appropriate share and what is the appropriate share of others?

And, whether he wants to or not, can he get away with spending his stockholders', customers' or employees' money? Will not the stockholders fire him? (Either the present ones or those who take over when his actions in the name of social responsibility have reduced the corporation's profits and the price of its stock.) His customers and his employees can desert him for other producers and employers less scrupulous in exercising their social responsibilities.

This facet of "social responsibility" doctrine is brought into sharp relief when the doctrine is used to justify wage restraint by trade unions. The conflict of interest is naked and clear when union officials are asked to subordinate the interest of their members to some more general purpose. If union officials try to enforce wage restraint, the consequence is likely to be wildcat strikes, rank-and-file revolts and the emergence of strong competitors for their jobs. We thus have the ironic phenomenon that union leaders—at least in the U.S.—have objected to Government interference with the market far more consistently and courageously than have business leaders.

The difficulty of exercising "social responsibility" illustrates, of course, the great virtue of private competitive enterprise—it forces people to be responsible for their own actions and makes it difficult for them to "exploit" other people for either selfish or unselfish purposes. They can do good— but only at their own expense.

Many a reader who has followed the argument this far may be tempted to remonstrate that it is all well and good to speak of Government's having the responsibility to impose taxes and determine expenditures for such "social" purposes as controlling pollution or training the hard-core unemployed, but that the problems are too urgent to wait on the slow course of political processes, that the exercise of social responsibility by businessmen is a quicker and surer way to solve pressing current problems.

Aside from the question of fact—I share Adam Smith's skepticism about the benefits that can be expected from "those who affect to trade for the public good"—this argument must be rejected on the grounds of principle. What it amounts to is an assertion that those who favor the taxes and expenditures in question have failed to persuade a majority of their fellow citizens to be of like mind and that they are seeking to attain by undemocratic procedures what they cannot attain by democratic procedures. In a free society it is hard for "evil" people to do "evil," especially since one man's good is another's evil.

I have, for simplicity, concentrated on the special case of the corporate executive, except only for the brief digression on trade unions. But precisely the same argument applies to the newer phenomenon of calling upon stockholders to require corporations to exercise social responsibility (the recent G.M. crusade for example). In most of these cases, what is in effect involved is some stockholders trying to get other stockholders (or customers or employees) to contribute against their will to "social" causes favored by the activists. Insofar as they succeed, they are again imposing taxes and spending the proceeds.

The situation of the individual proprietor is somewhat different. If he acts to reduce the returns of his enterprise in order to exercise his "social responsibility," he is spending his own money, not someone else's. If he wishes to spend his money on such purposes, that is his right, and I cannot see that there is any objection to his doing so. In the process, he, too, may impose costs on employees and customers. However, because he is far less likely than a large corporation or union to have monopolistic power, any such side effects will tend to be minor.

Of course, in practice the doctrine of social responsibility is frequently a cloak for actions that are justified on other grounds rather than a reason for those actions.

To illustrate, it may well be in the long-run interest of a corporation that is a major employer in a small community to devote resources to providing amenities to that community or to improving its government. That may make it easier to attract desirable employees, it may reduce the wage bill or lessen losses from pilferage and sabotage or have other worthwhile effects. Or it may be that, given the laws about the deductibility of corporate charitable contributions, the stockholders can contribute more to charities they favor by having the corporation make the gift than by doing it themselves, since they can in that way contribute an amount that would otherwise have been paid as corporate taxes.

In each of these—and many similar—cases, there is a strong temptation to rationalize these actions as an exercise of "social responsibility." In the present climate of opinion, with its widespread aversion to "capitalism," "profits," and the "soulless corporation" and so on, this is one way for a corporation to generate goodwill as a by-product of expenditures that are entirely justified in its own self-interest.

It would be inconsistent of me to call on corporate executives to refrain from this hypocritical window-dressing because it harms the foundations of a free society. That would be to call on them to exercise a "social responsibility"! If our institutions, and the attitudes of the public make it in their self-interest to cloak their actions in this way, I cannot summon much indignation to renounce them. At the same time, I can express admiration for those individual proprietors or owners of closely held corporations or stockholders of more broadly held corporations who disdain such tactics as approaching fraud.

Whether blameworthy or not, the use of the cloak of social responsibility, and the nonsense spoken in its name by influential and prestigious businessmen, does clearly harm the foundations of a free society. I have been impressed time and again by the schizophrenic character of many businessmen. They are capable of being extremely far-sighted and clearheaded in matters that are internal to their businesses. They are incredibly short-sighted and muddle-headed in matters that are outside their businesses but affect the possible survival of business in general. This short-sightedness is strikingly exemplified in the calls from many businessmen for wage and price guidelines or controls or income policies. There is nothing that could do more in a brief period to destroy a market system and replace it by a centrally controlled system than effective governmental control of prices and wages.

The short-sightedness is also exemplified in speeches by businessmen on social responsibility. This may gain them kudos in the short run. But it helps to strengthen the already too prevalent view that the pursuit of profits is wicked and immoral and must be curbed and controlled by external forces. Once this view is adopted, the external forces that curb the market will not be the social consciences, however highly developed, of the pontificating executives; it will be the iron fist of Government bureaucrats. Here, as with price and wage controls, businessmen seem to me to reveal a suicidal impulse.

The political principle that underlies the market mechanism is unanimity. In an ideal free market resting on private property, no individual can coerce any other, all cooperation is voluntary, all parties to such cooperation benefit or they need not participate. There are no values, no "social" responsibilities in any sense other than the shared values and responsibilities of individuals. Society is a collection of individuals and of the various groups they voluntarily form.

The political principle that underlies the political mechanism is conformity. The individual must serve a more general social interest—whether that be determined by a church or a dictator or a majority. The individual may have a vote and say in what is to be done, but if he is overruled, he must conform. It is appropriate for some to require others to contribute to a general social purpose whether they wish to or not.

Unfortunately, unanimity is not always feasible. There are some respects in which conformity appears unavoidable, so I do not see how one can avoid the use of the political mechanism altogether.

But the doctrine of "social responsibility" taken seriously would extend the scope of the political mechanism to every human activity. It does not differ in philosophy from the most explicitly collectivist doctrine. It differs only by professing to believe that collectivist ends can be attained without collectivist means. That is why, in my book *Capitalism and Freedom*, I have called it a "fundamentally subversive doctrine" in a free society, and I have said that in such a society, "there is one and only one social responsibility of business—to use its resources and engage in activities designed to increase its profits so long as it stays within the rules of the game, which is to say, engages in open and free competition without deception or fraud."

Can Socially Responsible Firms Survive in a Competitive Environment?

Robert H. Frank

In his celebrated 1970 article, Milton Friedman wrote that "there is one and only one social responsibility of business—to use its resources and engage in activities designed to increase its profits so long as it stays within the rules of the game, which is to say, engages in open and free competition without deception or fraud" (p. 126). In Friedman's view, managers who pursue broader social goals—say, by adopting more stringent emissions standards than required by law, or by donating corporate funds to charitable organizations—are simply spending other people's money. Firms run by these managers will have higher costs than those run by managers whose goal is to maximize shareholder wealth. According to the standard theory of competitive markets, the latter firms will attract more capital and eventually drive the former firms out of business.

Of course, as Friedman himself clearly recognized, there are many circumstances in which the firm's narrow interests coincide with those of the broader community. He noted, for example, that "it may well be in the long-run interest of a corporation that is a major employer in a small community to devote resources to providing amenities to that community or to improving its government. That may make it easier to attract desirable employees, it may reduce the wage bill or lessen losses from pilferage and sabotage or have other worthwhile effects" (p. 124).

From David Messick and Ann Tenbrunsel, *Codes of Conduct: Behavioral Research into Business Ethics,* © 1996 Russell Sage Foundation, New York, New York, pp. 86–103.

Friedman argued against using the term *social responsibility* to characterize those activities of a firm that, while serving the broader community, also augment the firm's profits. He believes that this language has great potential to mislead politicians and voters about the proper role of the corporation in society and will foster excessive regulation.

In the years since Friedman wrote this article, the development of the theory of repeated games has given us ever more sophisticated accounts of the forces that often align self-interest with the interests of others. For example, Robert Axelrod (1984) suggests that firms pay their suppliers not because they feel a moral obligation to do so but because they require future shipments from them.

Clearly, repeated interactions often do give rise to behaviors that smack of social responsibility. Yet as Friedman suggested, it is erroneous—or at least misleading—to call these behaviors morally praiseworthy. After all, even a firm whose owners and managers had no concern about the welfare of the broader community would have ample motive to engage in them. When material incentives favor cooperation, it is more descriptive to call the cooperating parties prudent than socially responsible.

It is also an error to assume that repeated interactions always provide ready solutions to social dilemmas and other collective action problems. Even among parties who deal with one another repeatedly, one-shot dilemmas—opportunities for cheating and other opportunistic behavior—often arise. Even a longstanding client of a law firm, for example, has no way to verify that the firm has billed only the number of hours actually worked.

In many cases, the knowledge that opportunities to cheat will arise may preclude otherwise profitable business ventures. Consider a person whose mutual fund has just been taken over by new management. She wants advice about whether to stay with the fund under its new management or switch to a different fund. She considers seeking a consultation, for a fee, from a knowledgeable stockbroker—a mutually beneficial exchange. Yet the investor also knows that a broker's interests may differ from her own. Perhaps, for example, the broker will receive a large commission or finder's fee if the client switches to a new fund. Fearing the consequences of opportunistic behavior, the investor may refrain from seeking advice, in the process depriving both herself and an informed broker of the gains from trade.

When parties to a business transaction confront a one-shot dilemma, their profits will be higher if they defect—that is, if they cheat—than if they cooperate. Yet when each party defects, profits for each are lower than if both had cooperated. In this paper, I will refer to firms that cooperate in one-shot dilemmas as socially responsible firms.

The question I pose is whether such firms can survive in competitive environments. At first glance, it would appear that the answer must be no, for if defecting were indeed a dominant strategy, then socially responsible firms would always have lower returns than pure profit maximizers. Evolutionary models pertaining to individuals have recently shown, however, that conditions often exist in which cooperation in one-shot dilemmas is sustainable in competitive environments. I will review some of this work and suggest that many of its conclusions carry over to populations of competitive firms.

EVOLUTIONARY MODELS OF ONE-SHOT COOPERATION

One of the enduring questions in evolutionary biology is whether altruistic individuals can survive. In this framework, the design criterion for each component of human motivation is the same as for an arm or a leg or an eye: To what extent does it assist the individual in the struggle to acquire the resources required for survival and reproduction? If it works better than the available alternatives, selection pressure will favor it. Otherwise, selection pressure will work against it (see Dawkins 1976, especially chapter 3).

At first glance, this theoretical structure appears to throw its weight squarely behind the self-interest conception of human motivation. Indeed, if natural selection favors the traits and behaviors that maximize individual reproductive fitness, and if we *define* behaviors that enhance personal fitness as selfish, then self-interest becomes the only viable human motive by definition. This tautology was a central message of much of the sociobiological literature of the 1970s and 1980s.

On closer look, however, the issues are not so simple. There are many situations in which individuals whose only goal is self-interest are likely to be especially bad at acquiring and holding resources. Thomas Schelling (1960) provided a vivid illustration with his account of a kidnapper who gets cold feet and wants to set his victim free but fears that if he does so, the victim will go to the police. The victim promises to remain silent. The problem, however, is that both he and the kidnapper know that it will not be in the victim's narrow self-interest to keep this promise once he is free. And so the kidnapper reluctantly concludes that he must kill his victim.

Suppose, however, that the victim were not a narrowly self-interested person but rather a person of honor. If this fact could somehow be communicated to the kidnapper, their problem would be solved. The kidnapper could set the victim free, secure in the knowledge that even though it would then be in the victim's interests to go to the police, he would not want to do so.

Schelling's kidnapper and victim face a *commitment problem*, a situation in which they have an incentive to commit themselves to behave in a way that will later seem contrary to self-interest. Such problems are a common feature of social life. Consider, for example, the farmer who is trying to deter a transient thief from stealing his ox. Suppose this farmer is known to be a narrowly self-interested rational person. If the thief knows that the farmer's cost of pursuing him exceeds the value of the ox, he can then steal the ox with impunity. But suppose that the farmer cares also about not being victimized, quite independently of the effect of victimization on his wealth. If he holds this goal with sufficient force, and if the potential thief knows of the farmer's commitment, the ox will no longer be such an inviting target.

In the one-shot prisoner's dilemma, if the two players cooperate, each does better than if both defect, and yet each individual gets a higher payoff by defecting no matter which strategy the other player chooses. Both players thus have a clear incentive to commit themselves to cooperate. Yet a mere promise issued by a narrowly self-interested person clearly will not suffice, for his partner knows he will have no incentive to keep this promise. If both players know one another to be honest, however, both could reap the gains of cooperation.

In both these examples, note that merely having the relevant motivations or goals is by itself insufficient to solve the problem. It is also necessary that the presence of these goals be discernible by others. Someone with a predisposition to cooperate in the one-shot prisoner's dilemma, for instance, is in fact at a disadvantage unless others can identify that predisposition in him and he can identify similar predispositions in others.

Can the moral sentiments and other psychological forces that often drive people to ignore narrow self-interest be reliably discerned by outsiders? A recent study (Frank, Gilovich, and Regan 1993) found that subjects were surprisingly accurate at predicting who would cooperate and who would defect in one-shot prisoner's dilemmas played with near strangers.

In our study, the base rate of cooperation was 73.7 percent, the base rate of defection only 26.3 percent. A random prediction of cooperation would thus have been accurate 73.7 percent of the time, a random prediction of defection accurate only 26.3 percent of the time. The actual accuracy rates for these two kinds of prediction were 80.7 percent and 56.8 percent, respectively. The likelihood of such high accuracy rates occurring by chance is less than one in one thousand.

Subjects in this experiment were strangers at the outset and were able to interact with one another for only thirty minutes before making their predictions.[1] It is plausible to suppose that predictions would be considerably more accurate for people we have known for a long time. For example, consider a thought experiment based on the following scenario:

> An individual has a gallon jug of unwanted pesticide. To protect the environment, the law requires that unused pesticide be turned in to a government disposal facility located thirty minutes' drive from her home. She knows, however, that she could simply pour the pesticide down her basement drain with no chance of being caught and punished. She also knows that her one gallon of pesticide, by itself, will cause only negligible harm if disposed of in this fashion.

Now the thought experiment: Can you think of anyone who you feel certain would dispose of the pesticide properly? Most people respond affirmatively, and usually they have in mind someone they have known for a long time. If you answer yes, then you, too, accept the central premise of the commitment model—namely, that it is possible to identify non-self-interested motives in at least some other people.

The presence of such motives, coupled with the ability of others to discern them, makes it possible to solve commitment problems of the sort that have been presented. Knowing that others could discern her motives, even a rational, self-interested individual would have every reason to choose preferences that were not narrowly self-interested. Of course, people do not choose their preferences in any literal sense. The point is that if moral sentiments can be reliably discerned by others, the complex interaction of genes and culture that yields human preferences can sustain preferences that lead people to subordinate narrow self-interest in the pursuit of other goals.

AN EQUILIBRIUM MIX OF MOTIVES

It might seem that if moral sentiments help solve important commitment problems, then evolutionary forces would assure that everyone have a full measure of these sentiments. But a closer look at the interplay between selfish and other-regarding motives suggests that this is unlikely (see Frank 1988, chapter 3, for an extended discussion of this point). Imagine, for example, an environment populated by two types of people, cooperators and defectors. And suppose that people earn their livelihood by interacting in pairs, where the commitment problem they confront is the one-shot prisoner's dilemma.

If cooperators and defects were perfectly indistinguishable, interactions would occur on a random basis and the average payoffs would always be larger for the defectors (owing to the dominance of defection in all prisoner's dilemmas). In evolutionary models, the rule governing population dynamics is that each type reproduces in proportion to its material payoff relative to other types. This implies that if the two types were indistinguishable, the eventual result would be extinction for the cooperators. In highly simplified form, this is the Darwinian story that inclines many social scientists to believe that self-interest is the only important human motive.

But now suppose that cooperators were distinguishable at a glance from defectors. Then interaction would no longer take place on a random basis. Rather, the cooperators would pair off systematically with one another to reap the benefits of mutual cooperation. Defectors would be left to interact with one another, and would receive the lower payoff associated with these pairings. The eventual result this time is that the defectors would be driven to extinction.

Neither of these two polar cases seems descriptive of actual populations, which typically contain a mix of cooperators and defectors. Such a mixed population is precisely the result we get if we make one small modification to the original story. Again suppose that cooperators are observably different from defectors, but that some effort is required to make the distinction. If the population initially consisted almost entirely of cooperators, it would not pay to expand this effort because one would be overwhelmingly likely to achieve a high payoff merely by interacting at random with another person. In such an environment, cooperators would cease to be vigilant in their choice of trading partners. Defectors would then find a ready pool of victims, and their resulting higher payoffs would cause their share of the total population to grow.

As defectors became more numerous, however, it would begin to pay cooperators to exercise greater vigilance in their choice of partners. With sufficient defectors in the population, cooperators would be vigilant in the extreme, and we would again see pairings among like types only. That, in turn, would cause the prevalence of cooperators to grow. At some point, a stable balance would be struck in which cooperators were just vigilant enough to prevent further encroachment by defectors. The average payoff to the two types would be the same, and their population shares would remain constant. There would be, in other words, a stable niche for each type.

FIVE WAYS A SOCIALLY RESPONSIBLE FIRM MIGHT PROSPER

The commitment model just described shows how it is possible for cooperative individuals to survive in competitive environments. What does this model have to say about the possibilities for survival of socially responsible firms? Recall that the socially responsible firm's problem is that by cooperating in one-shot dilemmas, it receives a lower payoff than do firms that defect. In the sections that follow, I will describe five possible areas in which the socially responsible firm might compensate for that disadvantage. The first three involve the recognition of potential commitment problems that arise within firms and between firms and the outside world. The last two involve the fact that people value socially responsible action and are willing to pay for it in the marketplace, even when they do not benefit from it directly in a material sense.

By Solving Commitment Problems with Employees

Just as commitment problems arise between independent individuals, so too do they arise among owners, managers, and employees. Many of these problems, like those among independent individuals, hinge on perceptions of trustworthiness and fairness. Some examples:

Shirking and Opportunism. The owner of a business perceives an opportunity to open a branch in a distant city. He knows that if he can hire an honest manager, the branch will be highly profitable. He cannot monitor the manager, however, and if the manager cheats, the branch will be unprofitable. By cheating, the manager can earn three times as much as he could by being honest. This situation defines a commitment problem. If the owner lacks the ability to identify an honest manager, the venture cannot go forward, but if he has that ability, he can pay the manager well and still earn an attractive return.

Piece Rates. In cases where individual productivity can be measured with reasonable accuracy, economic theory identifies piece-rate pay schemes as a simple and attractive way to elicit effort from workers. Workers, however, are notoriously suspicious of piece rates. They fear that if they work as hard as they can and do well under an existing piece rate, management will step in and reduce the rate. There is indeed a large literature that describes the elaborate subterfuges employed by workers to prevent this from happening and numerous cases in which piece rates were abandoned although they had led to significant increases in productivity. If piece-rate decisions were placed in the hands of someone who had earned the workers' trust, both owners and workers would gain.

Career Lock-In. Many of the skills one acquires on the job are firm-specific. By accepting long-term employment with a single firm, a worker can anticipate that the day will come when her particular mix of skills, although still of value to her employer, will be of relatively little value in the market at large. And with her outside opportunities diminished, she will find herself at her employer's mercy. Firms have a narrow self-interest, of course, in establishing a reputation for treating workers fairly under these circumstances, for a good reputation will aid them in their recruiting efforts.

But many workers will find that the firm's self-interest alone may not provide adequate security. A firm may determine, for example, that its employment base will shift overseas during the coming years, and therefore that diminished recruiting ability in the domestic market is not a serious problem. Any firm believed to be motivated only by economic self-interest would thus have been at a recruiting disadvantage from the very beginning. By contrast, a firm whose management can persuade workers that fair treatment of workers is a goal valued for its own sake will have its pick of the most able and attractive workers.

Rising Wage Profiles. It is a common pattern in industrial pay schemes for pay to rise more rapidly than productivity. A worker's pay is less than the value of his productivity early in his career, and it rises until it is more than the value of his productivity later in his career. Various reasons are offered for this pattern. One is that it discourages shirking, for the worker knows that if he is caught shirking, he may not survive to enjoy the premium pay of the out years. A second rationale is that workers simply like upward-sloping wage profiles. Given a choice between two jobs with the same present value of lifetime income, one with a flat wage profile and the other with a rising profile, most people opt for the second. Whatever the reason for upward-sloping wage profiles, they create an incentive for opportunistic behavior on the part of employers, who stand to gain by firing workers once their pay begins to exceed their productivity. Given the advantages of upward-sloping wage profiles, a firm whose management can be trusted not to renege on its implicit contract stands at a clear advantage.

Other Implicit Contracts. A firm with a skilled legal department might be able to devise some formal contractual arrangement whereby it could commit itself not to fire older workers. But such a contract would entail a potentially costly loss of flexibility. No firm can be certain of the future demand for its product, and the time may come when its survival may depend on its ability to reduce its work force. Both the firm and its workers would pay a price if this flexibility were sacrificed.

There are a host of other contingencies that might seriously affect the terms of the bargain between employers and workers. Many of these contingencies are impossible to foresee and hence impossible to resolve in advance by formal contractual arrangements. Any firm whose management can persuade workers that these contingencies will be dealt with in an equitable manner will have a clear advantage in attracting the most able workers.

By Solving Commitment Problems with Customers

A variety of commitment problems arise between firms and their customers, and at least some of these are amenable to solution along lines similar to those just discussed. Quality assurance is a clear example.

George Akerlof's celebrated paper on lemons (1970) describes a commitment problem in which sellers and buyers alike would benefit if the seller could somehow commit to providing a product or service of high quality. A variety of means have been suggested for solving this problem through reliance on material incentives. Firms can guarantee their products, for example, or they can develop public reputations for supplying high quality (see Klein and Leffler 1981).

Many forms of the quality assurance problem, however, cannot be resolved by manipulating material incentives. Consider a law firm that could provide the legal services a client wants at a price the client would be willing to pay. But suppose that the client has no way to evaluate the quality of his lawyer's services. The outcome of his case by itself is not diagnostic. He might win despite having received shoddy legal help, or he might lose despite having received the best possible help. In such situations, clients are willing to pay premium fees to a firm run by someone they feel they can trust.

By Solving Commitment Problems with Other Firms

Commitment problems also arise in the context of business transactions between firms, and here too solutions that rely on character assessment often play a role.

The Subcontractor Holdup Problem. Consider the familiar example of the subcontractor that does most of its business with a single buyer. To serve this buyer at the lowest possible price, much of the subcontractor's human and physical capital has to be tailored to the buyer's specific needs. Having made those investments, however, the subcontractor is vulnerable to the holdup problem; because the buyer knows that the subcontractor's customized assets cost more than they would bring in the open market, it can pay its subcontractor a price that is above the subcontractor's marginal cost but lower than its average cost. Anticipating this problem, subcontractors will be willing to invest in the capital that best serves their customers' needs only if they believe their partners can be trusted not to exploit them.

In a recent study, Edward Lorenz (1988) spelled out why material incentives are inadequate to solve the commitment problems that arise between small French manufacturing firms and their subcontractors. He described in detail how parties shop for trustworthy partners. For example, all the respondents in his sample emphasized the heavy weight they placed on personal relationships in this process.

Quality Assurance. The problem of quality assurance arises not just between firms and consumers but also between one firm and another. Consider, for example, the relationship between a parent company and its franchisees. When a franchise owner provides high-quality service to the public he enhances not just his own reputation with local consumers but also the reputations of other outlets. The parent firm would like him to take both these benefits into account in setting his service levels, but his private incentives are to focus only on how good service affects his own customers. Accordingly, it is common for franchise agreements to call on franchisees to provide higher quality service than would otherwise be in their interests to provide. Franchisers incur costs in the attempt to enforce these agreements, but their ability to monitor service at the local level is highly imperfect. The franchiser thus has a strong incentive to recruit franchisees who assign intrinsic value to living up to their service agreements. And prospective franchisees so identified are at a competitive advantage over those motivated by self-interest alone.

Maintaining Confidentiality. Many consulting firms provide services that require access to competitively sensitive information. Clearly no firm could succeed in this line of work if it acquired a reputation for making such information available to rivals. When employees leave these firms, however, their material incentives to maintain confidentiality fall considerably. In some cases, material incentives to maintain confidentiality are weakened by the fact that a number of people have had access to the sensitive information, so that it is much harder to trace the source of a leak. With these possibilities in mind, a client would be much more willing to deal with a consulting firm that is able to identify and attract employees who assign intrinsic value to honoring confidentiality agreements.

In the examples just discussed, firms compensate for the higher costs of socially responsible behavior by their ability to solve commitment problems. In addition, socially responsible firms benefit from a match with the moral values of socially responsible consumers and recruits.

By Reflecting Consumers' Moral Values

The standard free-rider model suggests that buyers will not be willing to pay a premium for products produced by socially responsible firms. For example, consumers may not like the fact that Acme Tire Corporation pollutes the air, but they are said to realize that their own purchase of Acme tires will have a virtually unmeasurable effect on air quality. Accordingly, the theory predicts, if Acme tires sell for even a little less than those produced by a rival with a cleaner technology, consumers will buy from Acme.

The commitment model challenges this account by showing that many people have come to develop a taste for socially responsible behavior. People with such a taste will prefer dealing with socially responsible firms even when they realize that their own purchases are too small to affect the outcomes they care about. Conventional free-rider theory predicted that Star Kist Tuna's sales and profits would fall when it raised its prices to cover the added cost of purchasing tuna only from suppliers who used dolphin-safe nets. Star Kist's sales and profits went up, however, not down. Any consumer who stopped to ponder the matter would know that a single household's tuna purchase would have no discernible impact on the fate of dolphins. Even so, it appears that many consumers were willing to pay higher prices in the name of a cause they cared about. There is also evidence that Ben & Jerry's sells more ice cream because of its preservation efforts on behalf of Amazon rain forests, that The Body Shop sells more cosmetics because of its environmentally friendly packaging, and that McDonald's sells more hamburgers because of its support for the parents of seriously ill children.

Experimental evidence from the "dictator game" provides additional evidence of consumers' willingness to incur costs on behalf of moral values. The dictator game is played by two players. The first is given a sum of money—say, $20—and is then asked to choose one of two ways of dividing it with the second player: either $10 each or $18 for the first player and $2 for the second. One study (Kahneman, Knetsch, and Thaler 1986) found that more than three-quarters of subjects chose the $10–$10 split. The researchers then described this experiment to a separate group of subjects, to whom they then gave a choice between splitting $10 with one of the subjects who had chosen the $10–$10 split or splitting $12 with one of the subjects who had chosen the $18–$2 split. More than 80 percent of these subjects chose the first option, which the authors of the study interpreted as a willingness to spend $1 to punish an anonymous stranger who had behaved unfairly in the earlier experiment.

Taken together, the market data and experimental evidence appears to shift the burden of proof to proponents of the free-rider hypothesis.

By Reflecting Prospective Employees' Moral Values

A fifth and final benefit that accrues to socially responsible firms is the relative advantage they enjoy in recruiting. Jobs differ in countless dimensions, one of which is the degree to which the worker contributes to the well-being of others. Consider two jobs identical along all dimensions except this one. (For example, one job might involve writing advertising copy for a product known to cause serious health problems, while the other involves writing advertising copy for the United Way.) If people derive satisfaction from engaging in altruistic behavior, it follows that if the wages in these two jobs were the same, there would be an excess supply of applicants to the second job, a shortage of applicants to the first. In equilibrium, we would therefore expect a compensating wage premium for the less altruistic job. A job applicant who wants to occupy the moral high ground can do so only by accepting lower wages. And these lower wages, in turn, help balance the higher costs of socially responsible operations.

In a recent study (Frank 1993), I attempted to quantify this advantage. The study included both experimental and empirical components; the results are described in the sections that follow.

Salary Differentials in the Cornell Employment Survey. Cornell University's career center recently completed an employment survey of recent graduates of the university's College of Arts and Sciences. This survey provided information on the current activities of respondents nine months after their graduation from Cornell. For those who were gainfully employed, the survey recorded information on annual salary, job title, and name and location of employer. Taking special steps to protect the anonymity of respondents, I was able to match the individual survey response forms with the college transcript of each respondent. Thus, unlike standard employment survey data sets, my data made it possible to control for the respondent's degree field as well as a rich variety of other details related to academic performance. And since almost all these data pertained to first jobs, I had access to almost as much information as did the employers who did the actual hiring.

By examining annual reports and other available records for each employer presented in the survey, I was able to categorize the employers as belonging to either the for-profit, the nonprofit, or the government sector of the economy. These categories provided at least a crude measure of the degree of social responsibility associated with the respondents' jobs, with employment in the nonprofit sector rated highest, government next, and the for-profit sector last on the social responsibility scale.

In the Cornell sample, a person employed by a private, for-profit firm earned a salary more than 13 percent larger than she would have if she were employed by government. A person working for a nonprofit firm, by contrast, earned almost 29 percent less than she would have in a government job. Thus, even after controlling for gender, curriculum, and academic performance, employees of for-profit firms in our sample earned roughly 59 percent more, on average, than did employees of nonprofit firms.

This is an enormous salary gap. Of course, the entire gap is not necessarily attributable to compensating differentials for social responsibility in the nonprofit sector. For example, some of the difference may be the result of unmeasured productivity differences between nonprofit and for-profit workers. But given the relative homogeneity of graduating classes at universities like Cornell, and given our ability to control for curriculum and academic performance, it would be difficult to maintain that unmeasured productivity differences could account for a large share of the nonprofit wage deficit. There is certainly no evidence in our data that nonprofit workers were any less motivated or capable as undergraduate students. In fact, nonprofit employees in our sample had slightly higher grade point averages than did for-profit employees. Nonprofit workers also had taken an average of almost five more science courses than had for-profit employees.

Another possibility is that dimensions of job satisfaction other than social responsibility may differ systematically between the nonprofit and for-profit sectors. At least some of these differences, however, seemed to favor the for-profit sector. For example, the average level of office space and other physical amenities in the workplace was higher in the for-profit than in the nonprofit sector, as were travel allowances and other nonsalary compensation items. Such differences suggest that the true compensation gap between nonprofit and for-profit firms may be even larger than suggested by the data.

In a second study using the Cornell data, I had a panel of second-year graduate students in a business ethics course rate the subjects' occupations and employers on a 7-point social responsibility scale ranging from least responsible (−3) to most responsible (+3).

Figure 1 summarizes the estimated compensating differentials for social responsibility thus measured. (For details on how the social responsibility measures were compressed to form the intervals shown in the diagram, see my paper.) As the figure shows, salaries fall dramatically with increases in social responsibility, even after controlling for gender, curriculum, academic performance, and sector of employment.

These estimates are remarkably large. As noted, they are based on fragmentary measures of occupational and employer social responsibility and should for this reason be regarded as tentative. But as the sections to follow suggest, they are broadly consistent with evidence from a variety of sources.

Salary Differentials between Corporate and Public-Interest Law. Another source of evidence on the strength of unselfish motives comes in the form of salary differentials between public-interest lawyers and corporate lawyers. When the public-interest law movement expanded rapidly in the 1960s, the salary differences between public-interest lawyers and other attorneys were small, on the order of only a few thousand dollars per year. In the intervening years, however, salaries in public-interest law have risen only modestly, while compensation in other areas of the law has mushroomed. As a result,

FIGURE 1. Compensating Salary Differentials for Social Responsibility

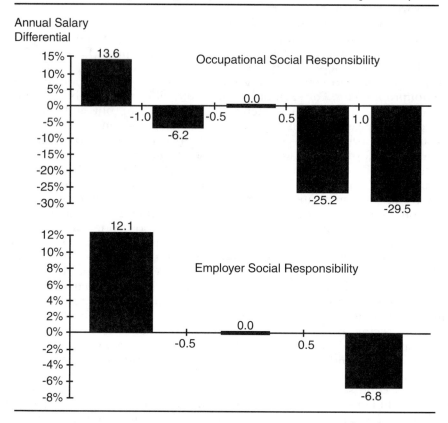

there is now a very large gap between public-interest and other legal salaries. For example, the average starting salary for public-interest lawyers in 1987 was only $23,843, as compared with $39,847 for all other lawyers in their first year of private practice (The National Law Journal, March 27, 1989, 18).[2]

The gap between starting salaries for public-interest lawyers and first-year associates in private law firms is even larger. Table 1 shows 1989 starting salaries for a small sample of institutions in these two categories.

At least in the case of public-interest firms in large cities, there is no indication that the lower salaries in public-interest law reflect inferior talent. Writing in the *National Law Journal,* a trade newspaper for the legal profession, Jamienne Studley (1989) reported that "well-known policy and advocacy organizations are typically deluged with excellent applicants" (p. 16). Indeed, such groups are often able to attract law review graduates from the nation's elite law schools, people who could have had their pick from among the choicest entry-level jobs in the legal profession and earned a far higher salary (see Table 1).

Fees for Expert Witness Testimony. During the past several decades, a series of legislative hearings has been held concerning public policy issues related to tobacco smoke. Many of the early hearings focused on whether

TABLE 1. 1989 Starting Salaries for Private and Public-Interest Lawyers

First-Year Public-Interest Lawyers	First-Year Associates in Private Law Firms
American Civil Liberties Union, New York: $28,000	Millbank, Tweed, Hadley & McCoy, New York: $83,000
Center for Constitutional Rights, New York: $29,000	Skadden, Arps, Slate, Meagher & Flom, New York: $83,000
People for the American Way, Washington, D.C.: $25,000	Arent, Fox, Kintner, Plotkin & Kahn, Washington, D.C.: $66,000 + $2,000 signing bonus
Public Citizen Litigation Group, Washington, D.C.: $21,000	Dow, Lohnes & Albertson, Washington, D.C.: $67,000

Source: National Law Journal, March 26, 1990.

people who smoke cigarettes are more likely than others to contract various pulmonary and cardiovascular diseases. More recently, the hearings have focused on whether exposure to "second-hand" smoke in the environment is a public health hazard. Throughout all these hearings, there is a common pattern of expert witness testimony. On one side, witnesses associated with the American Cancer Society, the American Heart Association, the American Lung Association, and other public-interest groups testify to the effect that tobacco smoke is a significant causal factor in the health problems at issue. On the opposing side, witnesses sponsored by the Tobacco Institute and other industry groups testify that the health risks associated with tobacco smoke are either unproved or highly exaggerated. Since 1964, when the first Surgeon General's report appeared identifying cigarette smoke as a major public health hazard, there has been a growing perception that advocates of the industry's position in these hearings are morally suspect. By now it seems fair to say that a large percentage of the population shares the perception that witnesses for the public-interest groups occupy the moral high ground in the tobacco hearings.

The compensation differentials for the expert witnesses associated with the two sides reflect this perception. Almost without exception, expert witnesses for the public-interest groups appear without charge, in many cases even paying their own travel expenses. Industry witnesses, by contrast, are compensated handsomely. One source, a senior scientific research professional formerly associated with the tobacco industry, reported that the current "official" rate for industry expert witnesses was in the range of $200 to $250 per hour. This source, who asked not to be identified, also reported that because the industry has an obvious interest in keeping its official witness fees low, the actual rate of compensation in many cases far exceeds the official hourly rate. The difference is achieved in a variety of ways. For instance, witnesses might be paid at the official hourly rate for activities only peripherally related to their testimony, such as "keeping up with the literature" or attending professional meetings and conferences. Whatever the total compensation for industry witnesses may be, it is substantial by any standard, certainly far in excess of the payments received by witnesses who appear on behalf of public-interest groups (again, in most cases, these are zero).

Tobacco industry sources make no pretense that the higher fees received by their witnesses are necessitated by superior professional credentials. On the contrary, all available evidence suggests that the volunteer witnesses for the public interest groups are much more professionally distinguished than their tobacco industry counterparts. Most members of the volunteer group are active scientific researchers who hold faculty positions at prestigious universities and medical schools. Most tobacco industry witnesses, by contrast, describe themselves as affiliates of private consulting firms and do not conduct ongoing programs of scientific research. As one former tobacco industry expert witness told me, "At this point, I know of only a few academics who still testify on behalf of the industry. All the others are consultants whose scientific thought process stopped years ago."

Reservation Pay Premium Survey. The final component of my 1993 study is based on a survey of the employment preferences of a sample of Cornell graduating seniors. In this survey, students were asked to consider six pairs of hypothetical job descriptions. Within each pair of jobs, the pay, working conditions, and specific tasks involved were described as being essentially the same, but the nature of the two businesses differed (for example, "write advertisements for the American Cancer Society" versus "write advertisements for Camel cigarettes"). The six pairs of jobs are listed in Table 2.

Subjects were first asked which of the two jobs in each pair they would choose if each paid a salary of $30,000 per year. They were then asked how much higher the salary would have to be in the job not chosen for them to reverse their decision.[3] As expected, the overwhelming majority of subjects indicated a preference for the jobs in the right column of Table 2.[4] The proportions choosing these jobs and the average and median pay premiums required for switching are reported in Table 3.

The reservation pay premiums reported by these subjects are large by almost any standard. Of course, it is hard to know whether subjects would really require premiums this large when confronted with an actual opportunity to switch to a less morally attractive but higher-paying job. It is possible, for example, that people might report high premiums when asked to consider such job changes in the abstract and yet be willing to switch for significantly smaller amounts when confronted with the reality of personal budget problems. Bear in mind, however, that we saw compensating differentials on an even larger scale in the case of public-interest lawyers and their counterparts in private law firms. And even if the actual reservation premiums

TABLE 2. Six Hypothetical Career Decisions

Ad copywriter for Camel cigarettes	Ad copywriter for the American Cancer Society
Accountant for a large petrochemical company	Accountant for a large art museum
Language teacher for the CIA	Language teacher for a local high school
Recruiter for Exxon	Recruiter for the Peace Corps
Lawyer for the National Rifle Association	Lawyer for the Sierra Club
Chemist for Union Carbide	Chemist for Dow Chemical

TABLE 3. Reservation Pay Premiums for Sacrificing the Moral High Ground

	Percent Choosing	Median Pay Premium for Switching ($)	Average Pay Premium for Switching ($)
Amer. Cancer Society	88.2	15,000/yr	24,333/yr
Art museum	79.4	5,000/yr	14,185/yr
High school	82.4	8,000/yr	18,679/yr
Peace Corps	79.4	5,000/yr	13,037/yr
Sierra Club	94.1	10,000/yr	37,129/yr*
Dow Chemical	79.4	2,000/yr	11,796/yr

*Excludes one response of $1,000,000,000,000/yr.

were only one-tenth as large as those reported by our survey respondents, they would still constitute a highly significant feature of the contemporary labor market.

CONCLUSIONS

When a business confronts an ethical dilemma, it must incur higher costs if it takes the high road. For example, in the process of refusing to supply master automobile keys to mail-order customers he believes to be car thieves, a locksmith sustains a penalty on the bottom line. Indeed, if the morally preferred action involved no such penalty, there would be no moral dilemmas.

In this chapter, I have described five advantages that help a socially responsible firm to compensate for the higher direct costs of its actions. Three of these involve the ability to avoid commitment problems and other one-shot dilemmas. The socially responsible firm is better able than its opportunistic rivals to solve commitment problems that might arise with employees, with customers, and with other firms. A fourth advantage is that buyers are often willing to pay more for the products of socially responsible firms. And finally, the socially responsible firm often enjoys an advantage when recruiting against its less responsible rivals. Taken together, these advantages often appear to be sufficient to offset the higher costs of socially responsible action.

This claim may invite the complaint that what I am calling socially responsible behavior is really just selfishness by another name. Consider this trenchant commentary by Albert Carr, an economic advisor to Harry Truman:

> The illusion that business can afford to be guided by ethics as conceived in private life is often fostered by speeches and articles containing such phrases as "It pays to be ethical," or, "Sound ethics is good business." Actually this is not an ethical question at all; it is a self-serving calculation in disguise. The speaker is really saying that in the long run a company can make more money if it does not antagonize competitors, suppliers, employees, and customers by squeezing them too hard. He is saying that oversharp policies reduce ultimate gains. That is true, but it has nothing to do with ethics (Carr 1968, 148).

This line of reasoning implies that any business behavior consistent with survival is selfish by definition. Such a definition, however, is completely at odds with our everyday understanding of the concept. Cooperation in one-shot dilemmas is costly in both the short run and the long run, and for that reason it is properly called unselfish. I have argued that because traits of character are discernible by others, the kinds of people who cooperate in one-shot dilemmas enjoy advantages in other spheres, and these advantages may help them survive in competition with less scrupulous rivals. It simply invites confusion to call the cooperative behaviors themselves self-serving.

Notes

1. In the version of the experiment reported here, subjects were permitted to discuss the PD game itself, and, if they chose, to make promises concerning their strategy choices.
2. One apparent effect of this growing salary gap has been a steady reduction in the proportion of law graduates accepting employment in the public interest sector. According to surveys done by the National Association for Law Placement, the percentage of law graduates taking public-interest jobs fell from 5.9 percent in 1978 to 3.0 percent in 1986.
3. The exact wording of the instructions to subjects was as follows:

   > Several pairs of jobs are described on the list below. All of these jobs offer a starting salary of $30,000/year. The jobs in each pair are located in the same city, and both involve working the same number of hours each week. The actual tasks you perform in each job are essentially the same, as are all relevant fringe benefits (pensions, paid vacations, insurance, etc.). The *only real difference* between the jobs in each pair involves the nature of the employer's line of business. In one of the blank spaces provided next to each job, check the member of each pair of jobs that you would accept if you had to choose one or the other. Then in the blank space below the job you did *not* choose, write the minimum annual salary required for you to switch your job choice. To illustrate, suppose that in the first pair of jobs you choose to work for The American Cancer Society when both jobs pay $30,000/year. You should then use the blank space below the Camel Cigarettes job to indicate how high its salary would have to be for you to switch. For example, if you say $40,000, that means that if Camel paid $39,999 or less you would still choose The American Cancer Society, but that for $40,000 or more you would choose Camel.

4. On the actual survey form completed by subjects, the more attractive job for a given pair sometimes appeared on the right, sometimes on the left.

References

Akerlof, G. 1970. "The Market for Lemons," *Quarterly Journal of Economics* 84: 488–500.

Axelrod, R. 1984. *The Evolution of Cooperation.* New York: Basic Books.

Carr, A. 1968. "Is Business Bluffing Ethical?" In *Ethical Issues in Business*, 4th ed., Thomas Donaldson and Patricia Werhane (eds.). (Englewood Cliffs, NJ.: Prentice Hall.)

Dawkins, R. 1976. *The Selfish Gene.* (New York: Oxford University Press.)

Frank, R.H. 1993. "What Price the Moral High Ground?" Unpublished manuscript, Cornell University.

Frank, R.H. 1988. "Passions Within Reason: The Strategic Role of the Emotions." (New York: Norton.)

Frank, R.H., T. Gilovich, and D. Regan. 1993. "The Evolution of One-Shot Cooperation," *Ethology and Sociobiology 14* (July): 247–56.

Friedman, M. 1970. "The Social Responsibility of Business Is to Increase Its Profits." *New York Times Magazine* 33 (September 13): 116–29.

Kahneman, D., J. Knetsch, and R. Thaler. 1986. "Perceptions of Unfairness: Constraints on Wealth Seeking," *American Economic Review* 76: 728–41.

Klein, B., and K. Leffler. 1981. "The Role of Market Forces in Assuring Contractual Performance." *Journal of Political Economy* 89: 615–41.

Lorenz, E. 1988. "Neither Friends Nor Strangers: Informal Networks of Subcontracting in French Industry." In *Trust: The Making and Breaking of Cooperative Relations*, Diego Gambetta (ed.). (New York: Basil Blackwell.)

Schelling, T.C. 1960. *Strategy and Conflict.* (Cambridge: Harvard University Press.)

Studley, J. 1989. "Financial Sacrifice Outside the Private Sector." *National Law Journal*, March 27, 1989, 16.

The Moral Muteness of Managers

Frederick B. Bird — James A. Waters

Many managers exhibit a reluctance to describe their actions in moral terms even when they are acting for moral reasons. They talk as if their actions were guided exclusively by organizational interests, practicality, and economic good sense even when in practice they honor morally defined standards codified in law, professional conventions, and social mores. They characteristically defend morally defined objectives such as service to customers, effective cooperation among personnel, and utilization of their own skills and resources in terms of the long-run economic objectives of their organizations. Ostensibly moral standards regarding colleagues, customers, and suppliers are passed off as "street smarts" and "ways to succeed."[1]

Many observers have called attention to this reluctance of managers to use moral expressions publicly to identify and guide their decision making even when they are acting morally. A century and a half ago, de Tocqueville noted the disinclination of American business people to admit they acted altruistically even when they did.[2] More recently, McCoy has observed that managers are constantly making value choices, privately invoking moral standards, which they in turn defend in terms of business interests. Silk and Vogel note that many managers simply take for granted that business and ethics have little relation except negatively with respect to obvious cases of illegal activities, like bribery or price-fixing. Solomon and Hanson observe that, although managers are often aware of moral issues, the public discussion of these issues in ethical terms is ordinarily neglected.[3]

Current research based on interviews with managers about how they experience ethical questions in their work reveals that mangers seldom discuss with their colleagues the ethical problems they routinely encounter.[4] In a very real sense, "Morality is a live topic for individual managers but it is close to a non-topic among groups of managers."[5]

This article explores this phenomenon of moral muteness and suggests ways that managers and organizations can deal openly with moral questions.

Actions, Speech, and Normative Expectations

To frame the exploration of moral muteness, it is useful to consider in general terms the relationships among managers' actions, their communicative exchanges, and relevant normative expectations. Normative expectations are standards for behavior that are sufficiently compelling and authoritative that people feel they must either comply with them, make a show of complying with them, or offer good reasons why not.

While normative expectations influence conduct in many areas of life from styles of dress to standards of fair treatment, in most societies certain types of activities are considered to be morally neutral. Choices of how to act with respect to morally neutral activities are considered to be matters of personal preference, practical feasibility, or strategic interest.[6]

Although managers often disagree regarding the extent to which business activities are morally neutral, their interactions in contemporary industrial societies are influenced by a number of normative expectations. These expectations are communicated by legal rulings, regulatory agencies' decrees, professional codes, organizational policies, and social mores.[7] Considerable consensus exists with respect to a number of general ethical principles bearing upon management regarding honest communication, fair treatment, fair competition, social responsibility, and provision of safe and worthwhile services and products.[8]

Through verbal exchanges people identify, evoke, and establish normative expectations as compelling cultural realities. Moral expressions are articulated to persuade others, to reinforce personal convictions, to criticize, and to justify decisions. Moral expressions are also invoked to praise and to blame, to evaluate and to rationalize. Moral discourse plays a lively role communicating normative expectations, seeking cooperation of others, and rendering judgments.

For those decisions and actions for which moral expectations are clearly relevant, it is possible to conceive of four different kinds of relationship between managers' actions and their verbal exchanges. These are depicted in Figure 1. One pattern (Quadrant I) identifies those situations in which speaking and acting correspond with each other in keeping with moral expectations. A second congruent pattern (Quadrant III) is the mirror image of the first: no discrepancy exists between speech and action, but neither is guided by moral expectations.

The other two patterns represent incongruence between speech and action. In Quadrant II, actual conduct falls short of what is expected. Verbal exchanges indicate a deference for moral standards that is not evident in actual conduct. Discrepancy here represents hypocrisy, when people intentionally act contrary to their verbalized commitments.[9] Discrepancy may also assume the form of moral backsliding or moral weakness. In this case, the failure to comply with verbalized commitments occurs because of moral fatigue, the inability to honor conflicting standards, or excusable exceptions.[10] Because they are intuitively understandable, none of these three patterns are our concern in this article.

Rather, our focus is on the more perplexing fourth pattern (Quadrant IV) which corresponds with situations of moral muteness: managers avoid moral expressions in their communicative exchanges but would be expected

FIGURE 1. Relations Between Moral Action and Speech

	Actions Follow Normative Expectations	Actions Do Not Follow Normative Expectations
Moral Terms Used in Speech	I Congruent Moral Conduct	II Hypocrisy, Moral Weakness
Moral Terms Not Used in Speech	IV Moral Muteness	III Congruent Immoral or Amoral Conduct

to use them either because their actual conduct reveals deference to moral standards, because they expect others to honor such standards, or because they privately acknowledge that those standards influence their decisions and actions. In other words, with respect to those instances where the managers involved feel that how they and others act ought to be and is guided by moral expectations, why do they avoid moral references in their work-related communications?

For example, a given manager may argue that the only ethic of business is making money, but then describe at length the non-remunerative ways she fosters organizational commitment from her co-workers by seeking their identification with the organization as a community characterized by common human objectives and styles of operation. In another example, managers may enter into formal and informal agreements among themselves. In the process they necessarily make promises and undertake obligations. Implicitly, they must use moral terms to enter and confirm such understandings even though explicitly no such expressions are voiced. This discrepancy occurs most pervasively in relation to countless existing normative standards regarding business practices that are passed off as common sense or good management—e.g., taking care of regular customers in times of shortage even though there is opportunity to capture new customers, respecting the bidding process in purchasing even though lower prices could be forced on dependent suppliers, and ensuring equitable pricing among customers even though higher prices could be charged to less-knowledgeable or less-aggressive customers.

Causes of Moral Muteness

Interviews with managers about the ethical questions they face in their work indicate that they avoid moral talk for diverse reasons.[11] In the particular pattern of moral muteness, we observe that in general they experience moral talk as dysfunctional. More specifically, managers are concerned that moral talk will threaten organizational harmony, organizational efficiency, and their own reputation for power and effectiveness.

Threat to Harmony—Moral talk may, on occasion, require some degree of interpersonal confrontation. In extreme cases, this may take the form of blowing the whistle on powerful persons in the organization who are involved in illegal or unethical practices and may involve significant personal risk for the whistleblower.[12] Even in less-extreme cases, moral talk may involve raising questions about or disagreeing with practices or decisions of superiors, colleagues, or subordinates. Managers typically avoid any such confrontation, experiencing it as difficult and costly—as witnessed, for example, by the frequent avoidance of candid performance appraisals. Faced with a situation where a subordinate or colleague is involved in an unethical practice, managers may "finesse" a public discussion or confrontation by publishing a general policy statement or drawing general attention to an existing policy.

In the case of moral questions, managers find confrontations particularly difficult because they experience them as judgmental and likely to initiate cycles of mutual finger-pointing and recrimination. They are aware of the small and not-so-small deceits which are pervasive in organizations, e.g., juggling budget lines to cover expenditures, minor abuses of organizational perks, favoritism, nepotism, and fear that if they "cast the first stone" an avalanche may ensue.[13]

Many managers conclude that it is disruptive to bring up moral issues at work because their organizations do not want public discussion of such issues. We interviewed or examined the interviews of sixty managers who in turn talked about nearly 300 cases in which they had faced moral issues in their work. In only twelve percent of these cases had public discussion of moral issues taken place and more than half of these special cases were cited by a single executive. Give-and-take discussions of moral issues typically took place in private conversations or not at all.

Threat to Efficiency—Many managers avoid or make little use of moral expressions because moral talk is associated with several kinds of exchanges that obstruct or distract from responsible problem-solving. In these instances, moral talk is viewed as being self-serving and obfuscating. Thus, for example, while moral talk may be legitimately used to praise and blame people for their conduct, praising and blaming do not facilitate the identification, analysis, and resolution of difficult moral conundrums. Similarly, while moral talk in the form of ideological exhortations may function to defend structures of authority and to rally support for political goals, it does not facilitate problem solving among people with varied ideological commitments.[14]

Because of the prevalence of such usages, many managers are loath to use moral talk in their work. Blaming, praising, and ideological posturing do not help to clarify issues. Moreover, such moral talk frequently seems to be narrowly self-serving. Those who praise, blame, or express ideological convictions usually do so in order to protect and advance their own interests.

In addition, managers shun moral talk because such talk often seems to result in burdening business decisions with considerations that are not only extraneous, but at times antagonistic to responsible management. Moral talk may distract by seeking simplistic solutions to complicated problems. For example, discussions of justice in business often divert attention to theoretical formulas for distributing rewards and responsibilities without first considering how resources as a whole might be expanded and how existing contractual relations might already have built-in standards of fair transactions and allocations.

Moral talk may also be experienced as a threat to managerial flexibility. In order to perform effectively, managers must be able to adapt to changes in their organizations and environments. They are correspondingly wary of contractual relations that seem to be too binding, that too narrowly circumscribe discretionary responses. They therefore seek out working agreements, when they legally can, that are informal, flexible, and can be amended easily. They assume that if the stipulations are formally articulated in terms of explicit promises, obligations, and rights, then flexibility is likely to be reduced. In order to preserve flexibility in all their relations, managers frequently seek verbal, handshake agreements that make minimal use of explicit moral stipulations.[15]

Many managers also associate moral talk with rigid rules and intrusive regulations. Too often, public talk about moral issues in business is felt to precede the imposition of new government regulations that are experienced as arbitrary, inefficient, and meddlesome. Complaints about particular immoral practices too often seem to lead to government harassment through procedures and rules that make little economic sense. Managers may therefore avoid using moral expressions in their exchanges so that they do not invite moralistic criticisms and rigid restrictions.[16]

Threat to Image of Power and Effectiveness—Ambitious managers seek to present themselves as powerful and effective. They avoid moral talk at times because moral arguments appear to be too idealistic and utopian. Without effective power, the uses of moral expressions are like empty gestures. Many managers experience futility after they attempt unsuccessfully to change corporate policies which they feel are morally questionable. They privately voice their objections but feel neither able to mount organized protests within their organization nor willing to quit in public outcry. De facto they express a loyalty they do not wholeheartedly feel.[17]

This sense of futility may even be occasioned by management seminars on ethics. Within these workshops managers are encouraged to discuss hypothetical cases and to explore potential action alternatives. Many find these workshops instructive and stimulating. However, when managers begin to consider problems that they actually face in their organizations, then the character of these discussions often changes. Moral expressions recede and are replaced by discussions of organizational politics, technical qualifications, competitive advantages, as well as costs and benefits measured solely in economic terms. In the midst of these kinds of practical considerations, moral terms are abandoned because they seem to lack robustness. They suggest ideals and special pleadings without too much organizational weight.

Managers also shun moral talk in order to not expose their own ethical illiteracy. Most managers neither know nor feel comfortable with the language and logic of moral philosophy. At best they received instruction in juvenile versions of ethics as children and young adults in schools and religious associations. They have little or no experience using ethical concepts to analyze issues. They may more readily and less self-consciously use some ethical terms to identify and condemn obvious wrongdoings, but do not know how to use ethical terms and theories with intellectual rigor and sophistication to identify and resolve moral issues.

Finally, the "value of autonomy places great weight on lower managers' ability to solve creatively all their own problems they regularly face."[18] They observe how this valuing of autonomy actually decreases the likelihood that managers will discuss with their superiors the ethical questions they experience. Figure 2 summarizes these three causes of moral muteness.

Consequences of Moral Muteness

The short-term benefits of moral muteness as perceived by managers (i.e., preservation of harmony, efficiency, and image of self-sufficiency) produce significant long-term costs for organizations. These costly consequences include:

- creation of moral amnesia;
- inappropriate narrowness in conceptions of morality;
- moral stress for individual managers;
- neglect of moral abuses; and
- decreased authority of moral standards.

Moral Amnesia—The avoidance of moral talk creates and reinforces a caricature of management as an amoral activity, a condition we describe as moral amnesia. Many business people and critics of business seem to be unable to recognize the degree to which business activities are in fact regulated by moral expectations. Critics and defenders of current business practices often debate about the legitimacy of bringing moral considerations to bear

FIGURE 2. Causes of Moral Muteness

Moral talk is viewed as creating these negative effects . . .	. . . because of these assumed attributes of moral talk.
• Threat to Harmony	• Moral talk is intrusive and confrontational and invites cycles of mutual recrimination.
• Threat to Efficiency	• Moral talk assumes distracting moralistic forms (praising, blaming, ideological) and is simplistic, inflexible, soft and inexact.
• Threat to Image of Power and Effectiveness	• Moral talk is too esoteric and idealistic, and lacks rigor and force.

as if most business decisions were determined exclusively by considerations of profit and personal and organizational self-interest. In the process they ignore the degree to which actual business interactions are already guided by moral expectations communicated by law, professional codes, organizational conventions, and social mores.

When particular business practices seem not to honor particular standards, then it may be wrongly assumed that such actions are guided by no normative expectations whatsoever. Actually, specific business practices which are not, for example, guided primarily by particular standards such as social welfare and justice may in fact be determined in a large part by other moral expectations such as respect for fair contractual relations, the efficient and not wasteful use of human and natural resources, and responsiveness to consumer choices and satisfactions. Often, when businesses act in ways that are judged to be immoral, such as the unannounced closure of a local plant, they may well be acting in keeping with other normative standards, regarding, for example, organizational responsibility. To assume that conduct judged to be unethical because it is counter to particular standards necessarily springs solely from amoral consideration is to fail to grasp the extent to which such conduct may well be guided and legitimated by other, conflicting norms.

The moral amnesia regarding business practices is illustrated by the debate occasioned by an article by Friedman entitled "The Social Responsibility of Business Is to Increase its Profit."[19] To many, Friedman seemed to conclude that business people had no moral responsibility other than to use any legal means to increase the returns on the investments of stockholders. He did argue that business people were ill-equipped to become social reformers and that such moral crusading might well lead them to do harm both to those they sought to help and to their own organizations. Both defenders and critics assumed the Friedman was defending an amoral position. However, although cloaked in the language of economic self-interest, Friedman's article alluded in passing to eight different normative standards relevant for business practices: namely, businesses should operate without fraud, without deception in interpersonal communications, in keeping with conventions regarding fair competition, in line with existing laws, with respect to existing contractual agreements, recognizing the given rights of employees and investors, seeking to maximize consumer satisfactions, and always in ways that allow for the free choices of the individual involved. It can be argued that Friedman invited misunderstanding by polarizing issues of profit and social responsibility. It cannot be argued that according to his position profits can be pursued without any other moral criteria than legality.

It is characteristic of this moral amnesia that business people often feel themselves moved by moral obligations and ideals and find no way to refer explicitly to these pushes and pulls except indirectly by invoking personal preferences, common sense, and long-term benefits. They remain inarticulate and unself-conscious of their convictions.

Narrowed Conception of Morality—In order to avoid getting bogged down in moral talk which threatens efficiency, managers who are convinced they are acting morally may argue that their actions are a morally neutral matter. They "stonewall" moral questions by arguing that the issues involved are ones of feasibility, practicality, and the impersonal balancing of costs and benefits, and that decisions on these matters are appropriately made by relevant managers and directors without public discussion.

We interviewed a number of managers who made these kinds of claims with respect to issues that others might consider contentious. A utilities executive argued, for example, that studies had exaggerated the impact of steam plants on water supplies. He also contended that no moral issues were relevant to the decisions regarding the domestic use of nuclear power. A pharmaceutical company manager criticized those who attempted to make a moral issue out of a leak in a rinse water pipe. An accountant criticized a colleague for arguing that the procedure recently used with a customer involved moral improprieties. These managers attempted to treat issues that had been questioned as if they were not publicly debatable.

Insofar as it is thought that moral issues are posed only by deviance from acceptable standards of behavior, then managers have a legitimate case to shun moral discussions of their actions which are neither illegal nor deviant. However, while appropriately claiming that their actions are not morally improper, managers stonewall whenever they insist, in addition, that their actions are constituted not only by deviance, but also by dilemmas (when two or more normative standards conflict) and by shortfalls (from the pursuit of high ideals). In the examples cited above, the managers were correct in asserting that no illegal nor blatantly deviant actions were involved. However, they were incorrect to argue that these actions were morally neutral.

Moral muteness in the form of stonewalling thus perpetuates a narrow conception of morality, i.e., as only concerned with blatant deviance from moral standards. Most importantly, moral muteness in this case prevents creative exploration of action alternatives that might enable the organization to balance better conflicting demands or to approximate better the highest ideals.

Moral Stress—Managers experience moral stress as a result of role conflict and role ambiguity in connection with moral expectations.[20] They treat their responsibility to their organizations as a moral standard and, when confronted with an ethical question, they frequently have difficulty deciding what kinds of costs will be acceptable in dealing with the question (e.g., it costs money to upgrade toilet facilities and improve working conditions). Moreover, moral expectations (for example, honesty in communications) are often very general and the manager is frequently faced with a decision on what is morally appropriate behavior in a specific instance. He or she may have to decide, for example, when legitimate entertainment becomes bribery or when legitimate bluffing or concealment of basic positions in negotiations with a customer or supplier becomes dishonesty in communication.

A certain degree of such moral stress is unavoidable in management life. However, it can be exacerbated beyond reasonable levels by the absence of moral talk. If managers are unable to discuss with others their problems and questions, they absorb the uncertainty and stress that would more appropriately be shared by colleagues and superiors. In the absence of moral talk, managers may cope with intolerable levels of moral stress by denying the relevance or importance of particular normative expectations. This may take the form of inappropriate idealism in which the legitimacy of the organization's economic objectives is given inadequate attention. Conversely, and perhaps more frequently, managers may cope with excessive moral stress by treating decisions as morally neutral, responding only to economic concerns and organizational systems of reward and censure. In either case, moral muteness eliminates any opportunity that might exist for creative, collaborative problem solving that would be best for the manager, as well as for the organization and its stakeholders.

Neglect of Abuses—The avoidance of moral talk by managers also means that many moral issues are simply not organizationally recognized and addressed. Consequently, many moral abuses are ignored, many moral ideals are not pursued, and many moral dilemmas remain unresolved. Managers we interviewed readily cited moral lapses of colleagues and competitors.[21] The popular press continually cites examples of immoral managerial conduct, often failing in the process to credit the extent to which managers actually adhere to moral standards.

Just as norms of confrontation contribute to moral muteness, in circular fashion that muteness reinforces those norms and leads to a culture of neglect. Organizational silence on moral issues makes it more difficult for members to raise questions and debate issues. What could and should be ordinary practice—i.e., questioning of the propriety of specific decisions and actions—tends to require an act of heroism and thus is less likely to occur.

Decreased Authority of Moral Standards—Moral arguments possess compelling authority only if the discourse in which these arguments are stated is socially rooted. It is an idealistic misconception to suppose that moral reasons by virtue of their logic alone inspire the feelings of obligation and desire that make people willingly adhere to moral standards. Blake and Davis refer to this assumption as the "fallacy of normative determinism."[22] The pushes and pulls which lead people to honor normative standards arise as much, if not more, from social relationships as from verbal communication of moral ideas. The articulations of moral ideas gain compelling authority to the degree that these expressions call to mind existing feelings of social attachments and obligations, build upon tacit as well as explicit agreements and promises, seem to be related to realistic rewards and punishments, and connect feelings of self-worth to moral compliance.[23] That is, moral expressions become authoritative, and therefore genuinely normative, to the degree that they both arouse such feelings and reveal such agreements, and also connect these feelings and recollections with moral action.

Moral ideas communicated without being socially rooted simply lack compelling authority. Such expressions are like inflated currency: because they possess little real authority, there is a tendency to use more and more of them in order to create hoped-for effects. Such language, unless it has become socially rooted, is experienced as disruptive, distracting, inflexible, and overblown. Simply attempting to talk more about moral issues in business is not likely to make these conversations more weighty and authoritative. What is needed is to find ways of realistically connecting this language with the experiences and expectations of people involved in business.

Indeed, in an even more general effect, the resolution of organizational problems through cooperation becomes more difficult to the extent that managers shun moral talk. Cooperation may be gained in several ways. For example, it may be inspired by charismatic leadership or achieved by forceful commands. Charisma and command are, however, limited temporary devices for gaining cooperation. Many managers do not have the gift for charismatic leadership. In any case, such leadership is best exercised in relation to crises and not ordinary operations. Commands may achieve compliance, but a compliance that is half-hearted, foot-dragging, and resentful. Cooperation is realized more enduringly and more fully by fostering commitments to shared moral values. Shared values provide a common vocabulary for identifying and resolving problems. Shared values constitute common cultures which provide the guidelines for action and the justifications for decisions.[24]

It is impossible to foster a sense of ongoing community without invoking moral images and normative expectations. Moral terms provide the symbols of attachment and guidelines for interactions within communities.[25] In the absence of such images and norms, individuals are prone to defend their own interests more aggressively and with fewer compromises. Longer range and wider conceptions of self-interest are likely to be abandoned. Without moral appeals to industry, organizational well-being, team work, craftsmanship, and service, it is much more difficult to cultivate voluntary rather than regimented cooperation.[26]

The Nature of Change Interventions

Several factors must be taken into account by those who wish to reduce this avoidance of moral talk by managers. Those who wish to "institutionalize ethics" in business, "manage values in organizations," or gain "the ethical edge"[27] must take into account the factors which give rise to this avoidance. It is impossible to foster greater moral responsibility by business people and organizations without also facilitating more open and direct conversations about these issues by managers.

First, business people will continue to shun open discussions of actual moral issues unless means are provided to allow for legitimate dissent by managers who will not be personally blamed, criticized, ostracized, or punished for their views. From the perspective of the managers we interviewed, their organizations seemed to expect from them unquestioning loyalty and deference. Although many had privately spoken of their moral objections to the practices of other managers and their own firms, few had publicly voiced these concerns within their own organizations. Full discussions of moral issues are not likely to take place unless managers and workers feel they can openly voice arguments regarding policies and practices that will not be held against them when alternatives are adopted.

Business organizations often do not tolerate full, open debate of moral issues because they perceive dissent as assuming the form either of carping assaults or of factional divisiveness. Carping is a way of airing personal grievances and frustrations, often using moral expressions in order to find fault.[28] Ideally, managers ought to be able openly to voice dissent and then, once decisions have been made contrary to their views, either respectfully support such choices or formally protest. However, business organizations that stifle open discussions of moral concerns invite the carping they seek to avoid by limiting debate in the first place. Managers are most likely to complain, to express resentment, and to find personal fault in others if they feel they have no real opportunities to voice justifiable dissents.

Legitimate expressions of dissent may be articulated in ways that do not aggravate and reinforce factional divisiveness. Before considering recommendations for organizational change (about which various managers and workers are likely to have vested interests), it is useful to set aside time for all those involved to recognize the degree to which they both hold similar long-run objectives and value common ethical principles.[29] These exercises are valuable because they help to make shared commitments seem basic and the factional differences temporary and relative. In addition, factional differences are less likely to become contentious if these factions are accorded partial legitimacy as recognized functional sub-groups within larger organizations. Finally, legitimate dissent is less likely to aggravate factional divisiveness if ground rules for debate and dissent include mutual consultations with all those immediately involved. These rules can help reduce the chances of discussions turning into empty posturing and/or irresolute harangues.

Second, if business people are going to overcome the avoidance of moral talk, then they must learn how to incorporate moral expressions and arguments into their exchanges. Learning how to talk ethics is neither as simple nor as difficult as it seems to be to many managers. Initially, managers must learn to avoid as much as possible the ordinary abuses of moral talk. In particular, efforts must be made to limit the degree to which moral talk is used for publicly extolling the virtues or excoriating the vices of other managers. Evaluations of personal moral worth ought to remain as private as possible. Furthermore, the use of moral expressions to rationalize and to express personal frustrations ought to be censored. In addition, the use of moral expression to take ideological postures ought to be minimized. Moral talk ought to be used primarily to identify problems, to consider issues, to advocate and criticize policies, and to justify and explain decisions.

Managers should recognize and learn to use several of the typical forms in which moral arguments are stated. An elementary knowledge of moral logics as applied to business matters is a useful skill not only for defending one's own argument, but also for identifying the weaknesses and strengths in the arguments of others. It is important, however, to recognize that verbal skill at talking ethics is primarily a rhetorical and discursive skill and not a matter of philosophical knowledge. Like the skill of elocution, learning how to talk ethics involves learning how to state and criticize moral arguments persuasively. What is critical is that managers are able to use moral reasoning to deal with issues they actually face in their lives and to influence others to consider carefully their positions.

Managers must regularly and routinely engage with each other in reflection and dialogue about their own experiences with moral issues. The attempt to overcome the avoidance of moral talk by managers by introducing them to formal philosophical languages and logics not rooted in their social experiences is likely to fail. Philosophical ethics is indeed an instructive and critical tool that can be used to analyze moral arguments of business people and to propose creative solutions to perceived dilemmas. It is improbable, however, that many managers are likely to adopt philosophical discourse on a day-to-day basis to talk about moral issues. At best, this language might serve as a technical instrument, much like the specialized languages of corporate law and advanced accounting used by specialized experts in consultation with executives. Such technical use does not overcome the moral amnesia that infects ordinary communications among managers. To be compelling, moral discourse must be connected with, express, foster, and strengthen managers' feelings of attachment, obligation, promises, and agreements.

Moral ideas rarely possess compelling authority unless some group or groups of people so closely identify with these ideas as to become their articulate champions. Moral ideas are likely to gain widespread following by business people as smaller groups of managers and workers so closely identify with these ideas—which in turn express their own attachments, obligations, and desires—that they champion them. This identification is most likely to occur where business people with existing feelings of community, due to professional, craft, or organizational loyalties, begin to articulate their moral convictions and to discuss moral issues. It is precisely in these sorts of subgroups of people who have to work with each other as colleagues that managers will be willing to risk speaking candidly and see the benefits of such candor in fuller cooperation.

The role of senior managers in fostering such "good conversation" among managers in an organization cannot be overemphasized.[30] If they seek to provide moral leadership to an organization, senior managers must not only signal the importance they place on such conversations, but also demand that they take place. They need also to build such conversations into the fabric of organizational life through management mechanisms such as requiring that managers include in their annual plans a statement of the steps they will take to ensure that questionable practices are reviewed, or that new business proposals include an assessment of the ethical climate of any new business area into which entry is proposed.[31]

Finally, interventions require patience. Open conversations of the kind we have been describing will, in the short-run, be slow and time-consuming and thus reduce organizational efficiency. They will, in the short-run, be awkward and fumbling and appear futile, and thus they will be quite uncomfortable for managers used to smooth control of managerial discussions. Patience will be required to persevere until these short-run problems are overcome, until new norms emerge which encourage debate without carping and acrimony, until managers develop the skills necessary for efficient and reflective problem solving with respect to moral issues, until moral voices and commitments are heard clearly and strongly throughout their organizations.

Note

The research on which this article is based was made possible in part by a grant from the Social Science and Humanities Research Council of Canada. The Center for Ethics and Social Policy in Berkeley, California, aided this research by helping to arrange for interviews with executives. The authors wish to thank William R. Torbert and Richard P. Nielsen for their helpful comments on an earlier draft of this article.

References

1. Chester Barnard, *The Function of the Executive* (Cambridge, MA: Harvard University Press, 1938), p. 154; George E. Breen, "Middle Management Morale in the 80's," *An AMA Survey Report* (New York, NY: The American Management Association, 1983); Mark H. McCormick, *What They Don't Teach You at Harvard Business School* (Toronto: Bantam Books, 1984), chapter 2.
2. Alexis DeTocqueville, *Democracy in America*, Vol. 2., translated by Henry Reeve, revised by Francis Bowen (New York, NY: Mentor Books, 1945), pp. 129–132.
3. Charles McCoy, *Management of Values: The Ethical Differences in Corporate Policy and Performance* (Boston, MA: Pitman, 1985), pp. 8, 9, 16, 98; Leonard Silk and David Vogel, *Ethics and Profits: The Crisis of Confidence in American Business* (New York, NY: Simon and Schuster, 1976), chapter 8; Robert C. Solomon and Kristine R. Hanson, *It's Good Business* (New York, NY: Atheneum, 1985), p. xiv; see also, Mark Pastin, *The Hard Problems of Management: Gaining the Ethics Edge* (San Francisco, CA: Jossey-Bass, 1986), Introduction, Part One.
4. James A. Waters, Frederick Bird, and Peter D. Chant, "Everyday Moral Issues Experienced by Managers," *Journal of Business Ethics* (Fall 1986), pp. 373–384; Barbara Ley Toffler, *Tough Choices: Managers Talk Ethics* (New York, NY: John Wiley and Sons, 1986); Kathy E. Kram, Peter C. Yaeger, and Gary Reed, "Ethical Dilemmas in Corporate Context," paper presented at Academy of Management, August 1988; Robin Derry, "Managerial Perceptions of Ethical Conflicts and Conceptions of Morality: A Qualitative Interview Study," paper presented at Academy of Management, August 1988.
5. James A. Waters and Frederick B. Bird, "The Moral Dimension of Organizational Culture," *Journal of Business Ethics*, 6/1 (1987): 18.
6. Jurgen Habermas, *The Theory of Communicative Action*, Vol. I, translated by Thomas McCarthy (Boston, MA: The Beacon Press, 1984), Part I, chapter 3.
7. Mark L. Taylor, *A Study of Corporate Ethical Policy Statements* (Dallas, TX: The Foundation of the Southwestern Graduate School of Banking, 1980).
8. Frederick Bird and James A. Waters, "The Nature of Managerial Moral Standards," *Journal of Business Ethics*, 6 (1987): 1–13.
9. George Wilhelm Frederick Hegel, *Philosophy of Right*, translated by T.M. Knox (London: Oxford University Press, 1952, 1967), pp. 93–103.
10. Aristotle, *The Nichomachean Ethics*, translated by J. A. R. Rhomson (Middlesex, U.K.: Penguin Books, 1953), Book VII; Peter Winch, *Ethics and Action* (London: Routledge and Kegan Paul, 1972), chapters 4, 8.
11. Waters, Bird, and Chant, op. cit.; Frederick Bird, Frances Westley, and James A. Waters, "The Uses of Moral Talk: Why Do Managers Talk Ethics?" *Journal of Business Ethics* (1989).
12. Ralph Nader, Peter Petkas, and Kate Blackwell, eds., *Whistle Blowing* (New York, NY: Grossman, 1972); Richard P. Nielsen, "What Can Managers Do About Unethical Management?" *Journal of Business Ethics* 6/4 (1987).
13. Steven Kerr, "Integrity in Effective Leadership," in Suresh Srivastra and Associates, eds., *Executive Integrity* (San Francisco, CA: Jossey-Bass, 1988).
14. Clifford Geertz, *The Interpretation of Cultures* (New York, NY: Basic Books, 1973), chapter 9.
15. Oliver E. Williamson, "Transactional Cost Economics: The Governance of Contractual Relations," *Journal of Law and Economics* (1980), pp. 233–261.
16. Pastin, op. cit., chapter 3; Silk and Vogel, op. cit., chapter 2; Solomon and Hanson, op. cit., p. 5; Kerr, op. cit., p. 138.
17. Albert Hirschman, *Exit, Voice and Loyalty: Responses to Decline in Firms and States* (Cambridge, MA: Harvard University Press, 1970), chapter 7.
18. Kram, Yaeger, and Read, op. cit., p. 28.
19. Milton Friedman, "The Social Responsibility of Business Is to Increase its Profit," *New York Times Magazine*, September 13, 1970.
20. Waters and Bird, op. cit., pp. 16–18.
21. Waters, Bird, and Chant, op. cit.

22. Judith Blake and Kingsley Davis, "Norms, Values and Sanctions" in Dennis Wrong and Harry L. Gracey, *Readings in Introductory Sociology* (New York, NY: Macmillan Co., 1967).

23. Emile Durkheim, *Suicide*, translated by John A. Spaulding and George Simpson (New York, NY: The Free Press, 1974), chapter 2; Frederick Bird, "Morality and Society: An Introduction to Comparative Sociological Study of Moralities," unpublished manuscript, 1988, chapter 4.

24. Karl E. Weick, "Organizational Culture as a Source of High Reliability," *California Management Review*, 29/2 (Winter 1987): 112–127.

25. Basil Bernstein, *Class Codes, and Control* (St. Albans, NY: Palladin, 1973).

26. Frances Westley and Frederick Bird, "The Social Psychology of Organizational Commitment," unpublished paper, 1989.

27. Kirk Hanson, "Ethics and Business: A Progress Report," in Charles McCoy, ed., *Management of Values* (Boston, MA: Pitman, 1985), pp. 280–88; Fred Twining and Charles McCoy, "How to Manage Values in Organizations," unpublished manuscript, 1987; Pastin, op. cit.

28. Bird, Westley, and Waters, op. cit.

29. Twining and McCoy, op. cit.

30. James A. Waters, "Integrity Management: Learning and Implementing Ethical Principles in the Workplace," in S. Srivastva, ed., *Executive Integrity* (San Francisco, CA: Jossey-Bass, 1988).

31. James A. Waters and Peter D. Chant, "Internal Control of Management Integrity: Beyond Accounting Systems," *California Management Review*, 24/3 (Spring 1982): 60–66.

Justice

← Case Study →

The Oil Rig

JOANNE B. CIULLA

This description focuses on one of the three exploratory rigs which have been drilling for several years along the coast of Angola, under contract to a major U.S. multinational oil company. All three rigs are owned and operated by a large U.S. drilling company.

The "Explorer IV" rig is a relatively small jack-up (i.e., with legs) with dimensions of approximately 200 ft. by 100 ft. which houses a crew of 150 men. The crew comprises laborers, roustabouts (unskilled laborers) and maintenance staff, and 30 expatriate workers who work as roughnecks, drillers or in administrative or technical positions. The top administrator on the Explorer IV is the "tool pusher," an American Expat, who wields almost absolute authority over matters pertaining to life on the rig.

The crew quarters on the Explorer IV were modified for operations in Angola. A second galley was installed on the lower level and cabins on the upper level were enlarged to permit a dormitory style arrangement of 16 persons per room. The lower level is the "Angolan section" of the rig, where the 120 local workers eat, sleep, and socialize during their 28-day "hitch."

The upper level houses the 30 Expats in an area equal in square footage to that of the Angolan section. The Expat section's quarters are semi-private with baths and this section boasts its own galley, game room and movie room. Although it is nowhere explicitly written, a tacit regulation exists prohibiting Angolan workers from entering the Expat section of the rig, except in emergencies. The only Angolans exempt from this regulation are those assigned to the highly valued positions of cleaning or galley staff in the Expat section. These few positions are highly valued because of the potential for receiving gifts or recovering discarded razors, etc., from the Expats.

The separation of Angolan workers from Expats is reinforced by several other rig policies. Angolan laborers travel to and from the rig by boat (an eighteen-hour trip) whereas the Expats are transported by helicopter. Also, medical attention is dispensed by the British R.N. throughout the day for Expats, but only during shift changes for the Angolans (except in emergencies). When there are serious injuries, the response is different for the two groups. If, for example, a finger is severed, Expats are rushed to Luanda for reconstructive surgery, whereas Angolan workers have the amputation operation performed on the rig by a medic.

From *Business Ethics Module*, 1990, pages 13–14, by Dr. Joanne B. Ciulla, University of Richmond. Reprinted with permission.

Angolan workers are issued grey overalls and Expats receive red coveralls. Meals in the two galleys are vastly different; they are virtually gourmet in the Expat galley and somewhat more proletarian in the Angolan section. The caterers informed the author that the two galleys' budgets were nearly equal (despite the gross disparity in numbers served).

Communication between Expats and Angolans is notable by its absence on the Explorer IV. This is principally because none of the Expats speaks Portuguese and none of the Angolans speaks more than a few words of English. Only the chef of the Portuguese catering company speaks both English and Portuguese, and consequently, he is required to act as interpreter in all emergency situations. In the working environment, training and coordination of effort is accomplished via sign language or repetition of example.

From time to time an entourage of Angolan government officials visits the Explorer IV. These visits normally last only for an hour or so, but invariably, the officials dine with the Expats and take a brief tour of the equipment before returning to shore via helicopter. Never has an entourage expressed concern about the disparity in living conditions on the rig, nor have the officials bothered to speak with the Angolan workers. Observers comment that the officials seem disinterested in the situation of the Angolan workers, most of whom are from outside the capital city.

The rig's segregated environment is little affected by the presence of an American black. The American black is assigned to the Expat section and is, of course, permitted to partake of all Expat privileges. Nevertheless, it should be noted that there are few American blacks in the international drilling business and those few are frequently less than completely welcomed into the rig's social activities.

Distributive Justice

JOHN RAWLS

We may think of a human society as a more or less self-sufficient association regulated by a common conception of justice and aimed at advancing the good of its members.[1] As a co-operative venture for mutual advantage, it is characterized by a conflict as well as an identity of interests. There is an identity of interests since social co-operation makes possible a better life for all than any would have if everyone were to try to live by his own efforts; yet at the same time men are not indifferent as to how the greater benefits produced by their joint labours are distributed, for in order to further their own aims each prefers a larger to a lesser share. A conception of justice is a set of principles for choosing between the social arrangements which determine this division and for underwriting a consensus as to the proper distributive shares.

From John Rawls, "Distributive Justice," *Philosophy, Politics, and Society*, 3rd series, ed. by Peter Laslett and W. G. Runcimann (Blackwell Publishers, Oxford; Barnes & Noble Books, Div. Harper & Row, Publishers, New York, 1967). Reprinted by permission of the author and publisher.

Now at first sight the most rational conception of justice would seem to be utilitarian. For consider: each man in realizing his own good can certainly balance his own losses against his own gains. We can impose a sacrifice on ourselves now for the sake of a greater advantage later. A man quite properly acts, as long as others are not affected, to achieve his own greatest good, to advance his ends as far as possible. Now, why should not a society act on precisely the same principle? Why is not that which is rational in the case of one man right in the case of a group of men? Surely the simplest and most direct conception of the right, and so of justice, is that of maximizing the good. This assumes a prior understanding of what is good, but we can think of the good as already given by the interests of rational individuals. Thus just as the principle of individual choice is to achieve one's greatest good, to advance so far as possible one's own system of rational desires, so the principle of social choice is to realize the greatest good (similarly defined) summed over all the members of society. We arrive at the principle of utility in a natural way: by this principle a society is rightly ordered, and hence just, when its institutions are arranged so as to realize the greatest sum of satisfactions.

The striking feature of the principle of utility is that it does not matter, except indirectly, how this sum of satisfactions is distributed among individuals, any more than it matters, except indirectly, how one man distributes his satisfactions over time. Since certain ways of distributing things affect the total sum of satisfactions, this fact must be taken into account in arranging social institutions; but according to this principle the explanation of common-sense precepts of justice and their seemingly stringent character is that they are those rules which experience shows must be strictly respected and departed from only under exceptional circumstances if the sum of advantages is to be maximized. The precepts of justice are derivative from the one end of attaining the greatest net balance of satisfactions. There is no reason in principle why the greater gains of some should not compensate for the lesser losses of others; or why the violation of the liberty of a few might not be made right by a greater good shared by many. It simply happens, at least under most conditions, that the greatest sum of advantages is not generally achieved in this way. From the standpoint of utility the strictness of common-sense notions of justice has a certain usefulness, but as a philosophical doctrine it is irrational.

If, then, we believe that as a matter of principle each member of society has an inviolability founded on justice which even the welfare of everyone else cannot override, and that a loss of freedom for some is not made right by a greater sum of satisfactions enjoyed by many, we shall have to look for another account of the principles of justice. The principle of utility is incapable of explaining the fact that in a just society the liberties of equal citizenship are taken for granted, and the rights secured by justice are not subject to political bargaining nor to the calculus of social interests. Now, the most natural alternative to the principle of utility is its traditional rival, the theory of the social contract. The aim of the contract doctrine is precisely to account for the strictness of justice by supposing that its principles arise from an agreement among free and independent persons in an original position of equality and hence reflect the integrity and equal sovereignty of the rational persons who are the contractees. Instead of supposing that a conception of right, and so a conception of justice, is simply an extension of the principle of choice for one man to society as a whole, the contract doctrine assumes that the rational individuals who belong to society must choose together, in one joint act, what is to count among them as just and unjust. They are to decide among themselves once and for all what is to be their conception of justice. This decision is thought of as being made in a suitably defined initial situation one of the significant features of which is that no one knows his position in society, nor even his place in the distribution of natural talents and abilities. The principles of justice to which all are forever bound are chosen in the absence of this sort of specific information. A veil of ignorance prevents anyone from being advantaged or disadvantaged by the contingencies of social class and fortune; and hence the bargaining problems which arise in everyday life from the possession of this knowledge do not affect the choice of principles. On the contract doctrine, then, the theory of justice, and indeed ethics itself, is part of the general theory of rational choice, a fact perfectly clear in its Kantian formulation.

Once justice is thought of as arising from an original agreement of this kind, it is evident that the principle of utility is problematical. For why should rational individuals who have a system of ends they wish to advance agree to a violation of their liberty for the sake of a greater balance of satisfactions enjoyed by others? It seems more plausible to suppose that, when situated in an original position of equal right, they would insist upon institutions which returned compensating advantages for any sacrifices required. A rational man would not accept an institution merely because it maximized the sum of advantages irrespective of its effect on his own interests. It appears, then, that the principle of utility would be rejected as a principle of justice, although we shall not try to argue this important question here. Rather, our aim is to give a brief sketch of the conception of distributive shares implicit in the principles of justice which, it seems would be chosen in the original position. The philosophical appeal of utilitarianism is that it seems to offer a single principle on the basis of which a consistent and complete conception of right can be developed. The problem is to work out a contractarian alternative in such a way that it has comparable if not all the same virtues.

In our discussion we shall make no attempt to derive the two principles of justice which we shall examine; that is, we shall not try to show that they would be chosen in the original position.[2] It must suffice that it is plausible that they would be, at least in preference to the standard forms of traditional theories. Instead we shall be mainly concerned with three questions: first, how to interpret these principles so that they define a consistent and complete conception of justice; second, whether it is possible to arrange the institutions of a constitutional democracy so that these principles are satisfied, at least approximately; and third, whether the conception of distributive shares which they define is compatible with common-sense notions of justice. The significance of these principles is that they allow for the strictness of the claims of justice; and if they can be understood so as to yield a consistent and complete conception, the contractarian alternative would seem all the more attractive.

The two principles of justice which we shall discuss may be formulated as follows: first, each person engaged in an institution or affected by it has an equal right to the most extensive liberty compatible with a like liberty for all; and second, inequalities as defined by the institutional structure or fostered by it are arbitrary unless it is reasonable to expect that they will work out to everyone's advantage and provided that the positions and offices to which they attach or from which they may be gained are open to all. These principles regulate the distributive aspects of institutions by controlling the assignment of rights and duties throughout the whole social structure, beginning with the adoption of a political constitution in accordance with which they are then to be applied to legislation. It is upon a correct choice of a basic structure of society, its fundamental system of rights and duties, that the justice of distributive shares depends.

The two principles of justice apply in the first instance to this basic structure, that is, to the main institutions of the social system and their arrangement, how they are combined together. Thus, this structure includes the political constitution and the principal economic and social institutions which together define a person's liberties and rights and affect his life-prospects, what he may expect to be and how well he may expect to fare. The intuitive idea here is that those born into the social system at different positions, say in different social classes, have varying life-prospects determined, in part, by the system of political liberties and personal rights, and by the economic and social opportunities which are made available to these positions. In this way the basic structure of society favours certain men over others, and these are the basic inequalities, the ones which affect their whole life-prospects. It is inequalities of this kind, presumably inevitable in any society, with which the two principles of justice are primarily designed to deal.

Now the second principle holds that an inequality is allowed only if there is reason to believe that the institution with the inequality, or permitting it, will work out for the advantage of every person engaged in it. In the case of the basic structure this means that all inequalities which affect life-prospects, say the inequalities of income and wealth which exist between social classes, must be to the advantage of everyone. Since the principle applies to institutions, we interpret this to mean that inequalities must be to the advantage of the representative man for each relevant social position; they should improve each such man's expectation. Here we assume that it is possible to attach to each position an expectation, and that this expectation is a function of the whole institutional structure: it can be raised and lowered by reassigning rights and duties throughout the system. Thus the expectation of any position depends upon the expectations of the others, and these in turn depend upon the pattern of rights and duties established by the basic structure. But it is not clear what is meant by saying that inequalities must be to the advantage of every representative man. . . . [One] . . . interpretation [of what is meant by saying that inequalities must be to the advantage of every representative man] . . . is to choose some social position by reference to which the pattern of expectations as a whole is to be judged, and then to maximize with respect to the expectations of this representative man consistent with the demands of equal liberty and equality of opportunity. Now, the one obvious candidate is the representative man of those who are least favoured by the system of institutional inequalities. Thus we arrive at the following idea: the basic structure of the social system affects the life-prospects of typical individuals according to their initial places in society, say the various income classes into which they are born, or depending upon certain natural attributes, as when institutions make discriminations between men and women or allow certain advantages to be gained by those with greater natural abilities. The fundamental problem of distributive justice concerns the differences in life-prospects which come about in this way. We interpret the second principle to hold that these differences are just if and only if the greater expectations of the more advantaged, when playing a part in the working of the whole social system, improve the expectations of the least advantaged. The basic structure is just throughout when the advantages of the more fortunate promote the well-being of the least fortunate, that is, when a decrease in their advantages would make the least fortunate even worse off than they are. The basic structure is perfectly just when the prospects of the least fortunate are as great as they can be.

In interpreting the second principle (or rather the first part of it which we may, for obvious reasons, refer to as the difference principle), we assume that the first principle requires a basic equal liberty for all, and that the resulting political system, when circumstances permit, is that of a constitutional democracy in some form. There must be liberty of the person and political equality as well as liberty of conscience and freedom of thought. There is one class of equal citizens which defines a common status for all. We also assume that there is equality of opportunity and a fair competition for the available positions on the basis of reasonable qualifications. Now, given this background, the differences to be justified are the various economic and social inequalities in the basic structure which must inevitably arise in such a scheme. These are the inequalities in the distribution of income and wealth and the distinctions in social prestige and status which attach to the various positions and classes. The difference principle says that these inequalities are just if and only if they are part of a larger system in which they work out to the advantage of the most unfortunate representative man. The just distributive shares determined by the basic structure are those specified by this constrained maximum principle.

Thus, consider the chief problem of distributive justice, that concerning the distribution of wealth as it affects the life-prospects of those starting out in the various income groups. These income classes define the relevant representative men from which the social system is to be judged. Now, a son of a member of the entrepreneurial class (in a capitalist society) has a better prospect than that of the son of an unskilled labourer. This will be true, it seems, even when the social injustices which presently exist are removed and the two men are of equal talent and ability; the inequality cannot be done away with as long as something like the family is maintained. What, then, can justify this inequality in life-prospects? According to the second principle it is justified only if it is to the advantage of the representative man who is worse off, in this case the representative unskilled labourer. The inequality is permissible because lowering it would, let's suppose, make the working man even worse off than he is. Presumably, given the principle of open offices (the second part of the second principle), the greater expectations allowed to entrepreneurs has the effect in the longer run of raising the life-prospects of the labouring class. The inequality in expectation provides an incentive so that the economy is more efficient, industrial advance proceeds at a quicker pace, and so on, the end result of which is that greater material and other benefits are distributed throughout the system. Of course, all of this is familiar, and whether true or not in particular cases, it is the sort of thing which must be argued if the inequality in income and wealth is to be acceptable by the difference principle.

We should now verify that this interpretation of the second principle gives a natural sense in which everyone may be said to be made better off. Let us suppose that inequalities are chain-connected: that is, if an inequality raises the expectations of the lowest position, it raises the expectations of all positions in between. For example, if the greater expectations of the representative entrepreneur raises that of the unskilled labourer, it also raises that of the semi-skilled. Let us further assume that inequalities are close-knit: that is, it is impossible to raise (or lower) the expectation of any representative man without raising (or lowering) the expectations of every other representative man, and in particular, without affecting one way or the other that of the least fortunate. There is no loose-jointedness, so to speak, in the way in which expectations depend upon one another. Now with these assumptions, everyone does benefit from an inequality which satisfies the difference principle, and the second principle as we have formulated it reads correctly. For the representative man who is better off in any pair-wise comparison gains by being allowed to have his advantage, and the man who is worse off benefits from the contribution which all inequalities make to each position below. Of course, chain-connection and close-knitness may not obtain; but in this case those who are better off should not have a veto over the advantages available for the least advantaged. The stricter interpretation of the difference principle should be followed, and all inequalities should be arranged for the advantage of the most unfortunate even if some inequalities are not to the advantage of those in middle positions. Should these conditions fail, then, the second principle would have to be stated in another way.

It may be observed that the difference principle represents, in effect, an original agreement to share in the benefits of the distribution of natural talents and abilities, whatever this distribution turns out to be, in order to alleviate as far as possible the arbitrary handicaps resulting from our initial starting places in society. Those who have been favoured by nature, whoever they are, may gain from their good fortune only on terms that improve the well-being of those who have lost out. The naturally advantaged are not to gain simply because they are more gifted, but only to cover the costs of training and cultivating their endowments and for putting them to use in a way which improved the position of the less fortunate. We are led to the difference principle if we wish to arrange the basic social structure so that no one gains (or loses) from his luck in the natural lottery of talent and ability, or from his initial place in society, without giving (or receiving) compensating advantages in return. (The parties in the original position are not said to be attracted by this idea and so agree to it; rather, given the symmetries of their situation, and particularly their lack of knowledge, and so on, they will find it to their interest to agree to a principle which can be understood in this way.) And we should note also that when the difference principle is perfectly satisfied, the basic structure is optimal by the efficiency principle. There is no way to make anyone better off without making someone worse off, namely, the least fortunate representative man. Thus the two principles of justice define distributive shares in a way compatible with efficiency, at least as long as we move on this highly abstract level. If we want to say (as we do, although it cannot be argued here) that the demands of justice have an absolute weight with respect to efficiency, this claim may seem less paradoxical when it is kept in mind that perfectly just institutions are also efficient.

Our second question is whether it is possible to arrange the institutions of a constitutional democracy so that the two principles of justice are satisfied, at least approximately. We shall try to show that this can be done provided the government regulates a free economy in a certain way. More fully, if law and government act effectively to keep markets competitive, resources fully employed, property and wealth widely distributed over time, and to maintain the appropriate social minimum, then if there is equality of opportunity underwritten by education for all, the resulting distribution will be just. Of course, all of these arrangements and policies are familiar. The only novelty in the following remarks, if there is any novelty at all, is that this framework of institutions can be made to satisfy the difference principle. To argue this, we must sketch the relations of these institutions and how they work together.

First of all, we assume that the basic social structure is controlled by a just constitution which secures the various liberties of equal citizenship. Thus the legal order is administered in accordance with the principle of legality, and liberty of conscience and freedom of thought are taken for granted. The political process is conducted, so far as possible, as a just procedure for choosing between governments and for enacting just legislation. From the standpoint of distributive justice, it is also essential that there be equality of opportunity in several senses. Thus, we suppose that, in addition to maintaining the usual social overhead capital, government provides for equal educational opportunities for all either by subsidizing private schools or by operating a public school system. It also enforces and underwrites equality of opportunity in commercial ventures and in the free choice of occupation. This result is achieved by policing business behaviour and by preventing the establishment of barriers and restriction to the desirable positions and markets. Lastly, there is a guarantee of a social minimum which the government meets by family allowances and special payments in times of unemployment, or by a negative income tax.

In maintaining this system of institutions the government may be thought of as divided into four branches. Each branch is represented by various agencies (or activities thereof) charged with preserving certain social and economic conditions. These branches do not necessarily overlap with the usual organization of government, but should be understood as purely conceptual. Thus the allocation branch is to keep the economy feasibly competitive, that is, to prevent the formation of unreasonable market power. Markets are competitive in this sense when they cannot be made more so consistent with the requirements of efficiency and the acceptance of the facts of consumer preferences and geography. The allocation branch is also charged with identifying and correcting, say by suitable taxes and subsidies wherever possible, the more obvious departures from efficiency caused by the failure of prices to measure accurately social benefits and costs. The stabilization branch strives to maintain reasonably full employment so that there is no waste through failure to use resources and the free choice of occupation and the deployment of finance is supported by strong effective demand. These two branches together are to preserve the efficiency of the market economy generally.

The social minimum is established through the operations of the transfer branch. Later on we shall consider at what level this minimum should be set, since this is a crucial matter; but for the moment, a few general remarks will suffice. The main idea is that the workings of the transfer branch take into account the precept of need and assign it an appropriate weight with respect to the other common-sense precepts of justice. A market economy ignores the claims of need altogether. Hence there is a division of labour between the parts of the social system as different institutions answer to different common-sense precepts. Competitive markets (properly supplemented by government operations) handle the problem of the efficient allocation of labour and resources and set a weight to the conventional precepts associated with wages and earnings (the precepts of each according to his work and experience, or responsibility and the hazards of the job, and so on), whereas the transfer branch guarantees a certain level of well-being and meets the claims of need. Thus it is obvious that the justice of distributive shares depends upon the whole social system and how it distributes total income, wages plus transfers. There is with reason strong objection to the competitive determination of total income, since this would leave out of account the claims of need and of a decent standard of life. From the standpoint of the original position it is clearly rational to insure oneself against these contingencies. But now, if the appropriate minimum is provided by transfers, it may be perfectly fair that the other part of total income is competitively determined. Moreover, this way of dealing with the claims of need is doubtless more efficient, at least from a theoretical point of view, than trying to regulate prices by minimum wage standards and so on. It is preferable to handle these claims by a separate branch which supports a social minimum. Henceforth, in considering whether the second principle of justice is satisfied, the answer turns on whether the total income of the least advantaged, that is, wages plus transfers, is such as to maximize their long-term expectations consistent with the demands of liberty.

Finally, the distribution branch is to preserve an approximately just distribution of income and wealth over time by affecting the background conditions of the market from period to period. Two aspects of this branch may be distinguished. First of all, it operates a system of inheritance and gift taxes. The aim of these levies is not to raise revenue, but gradually and continually to correct the distribution of wealth and to prevent the concentrations of power to the detriment of liberty and equality of opportunity. It is perfectly true, as some have said,[3] that unequal inheritance of wealth is no more inherently unjust than unequal inheritance of intelligence; as far as possible the inequalities founded on either should satisfy the difference principle. Thus, the inheritance of greater wealth is just as long as it is to the advantage of the worst off and consistent with liberty, including equality of opportunity. Now by the latter we do not mean, of course, the equality of expectations between classes, since differences in life-prospects arising from the basic structure are inevitable, and it is precisely the aim of the second principle to say when these differences are just. Indeed, equality of opportunity is a certain set of institutions which assures equally good education and chances of culture for all and which keeps open the competition for positions on the basis of qualities reasonably related to performance, and so on. It is these institutions which are put in jeopardy when inequalities and concentrations of wealth reach a certain limit; and the taxes imposed by the distribution branch are to prevent this limit from being exceeded. Naturally enough where this limit lies is a matter for political judgment guided by theory, practical experience, and plain hunch; on this question the theory of justice has nothing to say.

The second part of the distribution branch is a scheme of taxation for raising revenue to cover the costs of public goods, to make transfer payments, and the like. This scheme belongs to the distribution branch since the burden of taxation must be justly shared. Although we cannot examine the legal and economic complications involved, there are several points in favour of proportional expenditure taxes as part of an ideally just arrangement. For one thing, they are preferable to income taxes at the level of common-sense precepts of justice, since they impose a levy according to how much a man takes out of the common store of goods and not according to how much he contributes (assuming that income is fairly earned in return for productive efforts). On the other hand, proportional taxes treat everyone in a clearly defined uniform way (again assuming that income is fairly earned) and hence it is preferable to use progressive rates only when they are necessary to preserve the justice of the system as a whole, that is, to prevent large fortunes hazardous to liberty and equality of opportunity, and the like. If proportional expenditure taxes should also prove more efficient, say because they interfere less with incentives, or whatever, this would make the case for them decisive provided a feasible scheme could be worked out.[4] Yet these are questions of political judgment which are not our concern; and, in any case, a proportional expenditure tax is part of an idealized scheme which we are describing. It does not follow that even steeply progressive income taxes, given the injustice of existing systems, do not improve justice and efficiency all things considered. In practice we must usually choose between unjust arrangements and then it is a matter of finding the lesser injustice.

Whatever form the distribution branch assumes, the argument for it is to be based on justice: we must hold that once it is accepted the social system as a whole—the competitive economy surrounded by a just constitutional legal framework—can be made to satisfy the principles of justice with the smallest loss in efficiency. The long-term expectations of the least advantaged are raised to the highest level consistent with the demands of equal liberty. In discussing the choice of a distribution scheme we have made no reference to the traditional criteria of taxation according to ability to pay or benefits received; nor have we mentioned any of the variants of the sacrifice principle. These standards are subordinate to the two principles of justice; once the problem is seen as that of designing a whole social system, they assume the status of secondary precepts with no more independent force than the precepts of common sense in regard to wages. To suppose otherwise is not to take a sufficiently comprehensive point of view. In setting up a just distribution branch these precepts may or may not have a place depending upon the demands of the two principles of justice when applied to the entire system. . . .

The sketch of the system of institutions satisfying the two principles of justice is now complete. . . .

In order . . . to establish just distributive shares a just total system of institutions must be set up and impartially administered. Given a just constitution and the smooth working of the four branches of government, and so on, there exists a procedure such that the actual distribution of wealth, whatever it turns out to be, is just. It will have come about as a consequence of a just system of institutions satisfying the principles to which everyone would agree and against which no one can complain. The situation is one of pure procedural justice, since there is no independent criterion by which the outcome can be judged. Nor can we say that a particular distribution of wealth is just because it is one which could have resulted from just institutions although it has not, as this would be to allow too much. Clearly there are many distributions which may be reached by just institutions, and this is true whether we count patterns of distributions among social classes or whether we count distributions of particular goods and services among particular individuals. There are definitely many outcomes and what makes one of these just is that it has been achieved by actually carrying out a just scheme of co-operation as it is publicly understood. It is the result which has arisen when everyone receives that to which he is entitled given his and others' actions guided by their legitimate expectations and their obligations to one another. We can no more arrive at a just distribution of wealth except by working together within the framework of a just system of institutions than we can win or lose fairly without actually betting.

This account of distributive shares is simply an elaboration of the familiar idea that economic rewards will be just once a perfectly competitive price system is organized as a fair game. But in order to do this we have to begin with the choice of a social system as a whole, for the basic structure of the entire arrangement must be just. The economy must be surrounded with the appropriate framework of institutions, since even a perfectly efficient price system has no tendency to determine just distributive shares when left to itself. Not only must economic activity be regulated by a just constitution and controlled by the four branches of government, but a just saving-function must be adopted to estimate the provision to be made for future generations. . . .

Notes

1. In this essay I try to work out some of the implications of the two principles of justice discussed in "Justice as Fairness," which first appeared in the *Philosophical Review*, 1958, and which is reprinted in *Philosophy, Politics and Society*, Series II, pp. 132–57.

2. This question is discussed very briefly in "Justice as Fairness," see pp. 138–41. The intuitive idea is as follows: Given the circumstances of the original position, it is rational for a man to choose as if he were designing a society in which his enemy is to assign him his place. Thus, in particular, given the complete lack of knowledge (which makes the choice one uncertainty), the fact that the decision involves one's life-prospects as a whole and is constrained by obligations to third parties (e.g., one's descendants) and duties to certain values (e.g., to religious truth), it is rational to be conservative and so to choose in accordance with an analogue of the maximum principle. Viewing the situation in this

way, the interpretation given to the principles of justice earlier is perhaps natural enough. Moreover, it seems clear how the principle of utility can be interpreted; it is the analogue of the Laplacean principle for choice uncertainty. (For a discussion of these choice criteria, see R. D. Luce and H. Raiffa, *Games and Decisions* [1957], pp. 275–98.)

3. Example F. von Hayek, *The Constitution of Liberty* (1960), p. 90.

4. See N. Kaldor, *An Expenditure Tax* (1955).

The Entitlement Theory

Robert Nozick

The minimal state is the most extensive state that can be justified. Any state more extensive violates people's rights. Yet many persons have put forth reasons purporting to justify a more extensive state. It is impossible within the compass of this book to examine all the reasons that have been put forth. Therefore, I shall focus upon those generally acknowledged to be most weighty and influential, to see precisely wherein they fail. In this chapter we consider the claim that a more extensive state is justified, because necessary (or the best instrument) to achieve distributive justice; in the next chapter we shall take up diverse other claims.

The term "distributive justice" is not a neutral one. Hearing the term "distribution," most people presume that some thing or mechanism uses some principle or criterion to give out a supply of things. Into this process of distributing shares some error may have crept. So it is an open question, at least, whether *re*distribution should take place; whether we should do again what has already been done once, though poorly. However, we are not in the position of children who have been given portions of pie by someone who now makes last-minute adjustments to rectify careless cutting. There is no *central* distribution, no person or group entitled to control all the resources, jointly deciding how they are to be doled out. What each person gets, he gets from others who give to him in exchange for something, or as a gift. In a free society, diverse persons control different resources, and new holdings arise out of the voluntary exchanges and actions of persons. There is no more a distributing or distribution of shares than there is a distributing of mates in a society in which persons choose whom they shall marry. The total result is the product of many individual decisions which the different individuals involved are entitled to make. Some uses of the term "distribution," it is true, do not imply a previous distributing appropriately judged by some criteron (for example, "probability distribution"); nevertheless, despite the title of this chapter, it would be best to use a terminology that clearly is neutral. We shall speak of people's holdings; a principle of justice in holdings describes (part of) what justice tells us (requires) about holdings. I shall state first what I take to be the correct view about justice in holdings, and then turn to the discussion of alternate views.

I

The Entitlement Theory

The subject of justice in holdings consists of three major topics. The first is the *original acquisition of holdings,* the appropriation of unheld things. This includes the issues of how unheld things may come to be held, the process, or processes, by which unheld things may come to be held, the things that may come to be held by these processes, the extent of what comes to be held by a particular process, and so on. We shall refer to the complicated truth about this topic, which we shall not formulate here, as the principle of justice in acquisition. The second topic concerns the *transfer of holdings* from one person to another. By what processes may a person transfer holdings to another? How may a person acquire a holding from another who holds it? Under this topic come general descriptions of voluntary exchange, and gift and (on the other hand) fraud, as well as reference to particular conventional details fixed upon in a given society. The complicated truth about this subject (with placeholders for conventional details) we shall call the principle of justice in transfer. (And we shall suppose it also includes principles governing how a person may divest himself of a holding, passing it into an unheld state.)

If the world were wholly just, the following inductive definition would exhaustively cover the subject of justice in holdings.

1. A person who acquires a holding in accordance with the principle of justice in acquisition is entitled to that holding.
2. A person who acquires a holding in accordance with the principle of justice in transfer, from someone else entitled to the holding, is entitled to the holding.
3. No one is entitled to a holding except by (repeated) applications of 1 and 2.

The complete principle of distributive justice would say simply that a distribution is just if everyone is entitled to the holdings they possess under the distribution.

A distribution is just if it arises from another just distribution by legitimate means. The legitimate means of moving from one distribution to another are specified by the principle of justice in transfer. The legitimate first "moves" are specified by the principle of justice in acquisition.[1] Whatever arises from a just situation by just steps is itself just. The means of change specified by the principle of justice in transfer preserve justice. As correct rules of inference are truth-preserving, and any conclusion deduced via repeated application of such rules from only true premises is itself true, so the means of transition from one situation to another specified by the principle of justice in transfer are justice-preserving, and any situation actually arising from repeated transitions in accordance with the principle from a just situation is itself just. The parallel between justice-preserving transformations and truth-preserving transformations illuminates where it fails as well as where it holds. That a conclusion could have been deduced by truth-preserving means from premises that are true suffices to show its truth. That from a just situation a situation *could* have arisen via justice-preserving means does *not* suffice to show its justice. The fact that a thief's victims voluntarily *could* have presented him with gifts does not entitle the thief to his ill-gotten gains. Justice in holdings is historical; it depends upon what actually has happened. We shall return to this point later.

Not all actual situations are generated in accordance with the two principles of justice in holdings: the principle of justice in acquisition and the principle of justice in transfer. Some people steal from others, or defraud them, or enslave them, seizing their product and preventing them from living as they choose, or forcibly exclude others from competing in exchanges. None of these are permissible modes of transition from one situation to another. And some persons acquire holdings by means not sanctioned by the principle of justice in acquisition. The existence of past injustice (previous violations of the first two principles of justice in holdings) raises the third major topic under justice in holdings: the rectification of injustice in holdings. If past injustice has shaped present holdings in various ways, some identifiable and some not, what now, if anything, ought to be done to rectify these injustices? What obligations do the performers of injustice have toward those whose position is worse than it would have been had the injustice not been done? Or, than it would have been had compensation been paid promptly? How, if at all, do things change if the beneficiaries and those made worse off are not the direct parties in the act of injustice, but, for example, their descendants? Is an injustice done to someone whose holding was itself based upon an unrectified injustice? How far back must one go in wiping clean the historical slate of injustices? What may victims of injustice permissibly do in order to rectify the injustices being done to them, including the many injustices done by persons acting through their government? I do not know of a thorough or theoretically sophisticated treatment of such issues. Idealizing greatly, let us suppose theoretical investigation will produce a principle of rectification. This principle uses historical information about previous situations and injustices done in them (as defined by the first two principles of justice and rights against interference), and information about the actual course of events that flowed from these injustices, until the present, and it yields a description (or descriptions) of holdings in the society. The principle of rectification presumably will make use of its best estimate of subjunctive information about what would have occurred (or a probability distribution over what might have occurred, using the expected value) if the injustice had not taken place. If the actual description of holdings turns out not to be one of the descriptions yielded by the principle, then one of the descriptions yielded must be realized.

The general outlines of the theory of justice in holdings are that the holdings of a person are just if he is entitled to them by the principles of justice in acquisition and transfer, or by the principle of rectification of injustice (as specified by the first two principles). If each person's holdings are just, then the total set (distribution) of holdings is just. To turn these general outlines into a specific theory we would have to specify the details of each of the three principles of justice in holdings: the principle of acquisition of holdings, the principle of transfer of holdings, and the principle of rectification of violations of the first two principles. I shall not attempt that task here. . . .

Historical Principles and End-Result Principles

The general outlines of the entitlement theory illuminate the nature and defects of other conceptions of distributive justice. The entitlement theory of justice in distribution is *historical;* whether a distribution is just depends upon how it came about. In contrast, *current time-slice principles* of justice hold that the justice of a distribution is determined by how things are distributed (who has what) as judged by some *structural* principle(s) of just distribution. A utilitarian who judges between any two distributions by seeing which has the greater sum of utility and, if the sums tie, applies some fixed equality criterion to choose the more equal distribution, would hold a current time-slice principle of justice. As would someone who had a fixed schedule of trade-offs between the sum of happiness and equality. According to a current time-slice principle, all that needs to be looked at, in judging the justice of a distribution, is who ends up with what; in comparing any two distributions one need look only at the matrix presenting the distributions. No further information need be fed into a principle of justice. It is a consequence of such principles of justice that any two structurally identical distributions are equally just. (Two distributions are structurally identical if they present the same profile, but perhaps have different persons occupying the particular slots. My having ten and your having five, and my having five and your having ten are structurally identical distributions.) Welfare economics is the theory of current time-slice principles of justice. The subject is conceived as operating on matrices representing only current information about distribution. This, as well as some of the usual conditions (for example, the choice of distribution is invariant under relabeling of columns), guarantees that welfare economics will be a current time-slice theory, with all of its inadequacies.

Most persons do not accept current time-slice principles as constituting the whole story about distributive shares. They think it relevant in assessing the justice of a situation to consider not only the distribution it embodies, but also how that distribution came about. If some persons are in prison for murder or war crimes, we do not say that to assess the justice of the distribution in the society we must look only at what this person has, and that person has, and that person has, . . . at the current time. We think it relevant to ask whether someone did something so that he *deserved* to be punished, deserved to have a lower share. Most will agree to the relevance of further information with regard to punishments and penalties. Consider also desired things. One traditional socialist view is that workers are entitled to the product and full fruits of their labor; they have earned it; a distribution is unjust if it does not give the workers what they are entitled to. Such entitlements are based upon some past history. No socialist holding this view would find it comforting to be told that because the actual distribution *A* happens to coincide structurally with the one he desires *D, A* therefore is no less just than *D;* it differs only in that the "parasitic" owners of capital receive under *A* what the workers are entitled to under *D,* and the workers receive under *A* what the owners are entitled to under *D,* namely very little. This socialist rightly, in my view, holds onto the notions of earning, producing, entitlement, desert, and so forth, and he rejects current time-slice principles that look only to the structure of the resulting set of holdings.

(The set of holdings resulting from what? Isn't it implausible that how holdings are produced and come to exist has no effect at all on who should hold what?) His mistake lies in his view of what entitlements arise out of what sorts of productive processes.

We construe the position we discuss too narrowly by speaking of *current* time-slice principles. Nothing is changed if structural principles operate upon a time sequence of current time-slice profiles and, for example, give someone more now to counterbalance the less he has had earlier. A utilitarian or an egalitarian or any mixture of the two over time will inherit the difficulties of his more myopic comrades. He is not helped by the fact that *some* of the information others consider relevant in assessing a distribution is reflected, unrecoverably, in past matrices. Henceforth, we shall refer to such unhistorical principles of distributive justice, including the current time-slice principles, as *end-result principles* or *end-state principles*.

In contrast to end-result principles of justice, *historical principles* of justice hold that past circumstances or actions of people can create differential entitlements or differential deserts to things. An injustice can be worked by moving from one distribution to another structurally identical one, for the second, in profile the same, may violate people's entitlements or deserts; it may not fit the actual history.

How Liberty Upsets Patterns

It is not clear how those holding alternative conceptions of distributive justice can reject the entitlement conception of justice in holdings. For suppose a distribution favored by one of these nonentitlement conceptions is realized. Let us suppose it is your favorite one and let us call this distribution D_1; perhaps everyone has an equal share, perhaps shares vary in accordance with some dimension you treasure. Now suppose that Wilt Chamberlain is greatly in demand by basketball teams, being a great gate attraction. (Also suppose contracts run only for a year, with players being free agents.) He signs the following sort of contract with a team: In each home game, twenty-five cents from the price of each ticket of admission goes to him. (We ignore the question of whether he is "gouging" the owners, letting them look out for themselves.) The season starts, and people cheerfully attend his team's games; they buy their tickets, each time dropping a separate twenty-five cents of their admission price into a special box with Chamberlain's name on it. They are excited about seeing him play; it is worth the total admission price to them. Let us suppose that in one season one million persons attend his home games, and Wilt Chamberlain winds up with $250,000, a much larger sum than the average income and larger even than anyone else has. Is he entitled to this income? Is this new distribution D_2, unjust? If so, why? There is *no* question about whether each of the people was entitled to the control over the resources they held in D_1; because that was the distribution (your favorite) that (for the purposes of argument) we assumed was acceptable. Each of these persons *chose* to give twenty-five cents of their money to Chamberlain. They could have spent it on going to the movies, or on candy bars, or on copies of *Dissent* magazine, or of *Monthly Review*. But they all, at least one million of them, converged on giving it to Wilt

Chamberlain in exchange for watching him play basketball. If D_1 was a just distribution, and people voluntarily moved from it to D_2, transferring parts of their shares they were given under D_1 (what was it for if not to do something with?), isn't D_2 also just? If the people were entitled to dispose of the resources to which they were entitled (under D_1), didn't this include their being entitled to give it to, or exchange it with, Wilt Chamberlain? Can anyone else complain on grounds of justice? Each other person already has his legitimate share under D_1. Under D_1, there is nothing that anyone has that anyone else has a claim of justice against. After someone transfers something to Wilt Chamberlain, third parties *still* have their legitimate shares; *their* shares are not changed. By what process could such a transfer among two persons give rise to a legitimate claim of distributive justice on a portion of what was transferred, by a third party who had no claim of justice on any holding of the others *before* the transfer? To cut off objections irrelevant here, we might imagine the exchanges occurring in a socialist society, after hours. After playing whatever basketball he does in his daily work, or doing whatever other daily work he does. Wilt Chamberlain decides to put in *overtime* to earn additional money. (First his work quota is set; he works time over that.) Or imagine it is a skilled juggler people like to see, who puts on shows after hours.

Why might someone work overtime in a society in which it is assumed their needs are satisfied? Perhaps because they care about things other than needs. I like to write in books that I read, and to have easy access to books for browsing at odd hours. It would be very pleasant and convenient to have the resources of Widener Library in my back yard. No society, I assume, will provide such resources close to each person who would like them as part of his regular allotment (under D_1). Thus, persons either must do without some extra things that they want, or be allowed to do something extra to get some of these things. On what basis could the inequalities that would eventuate be forbidden? Notice also that small factories would spring up in a socialist society, unless forbidden. I melt down some of my personal possessions (under D_1) and build a machine out of the material. I offer you, and others, a philosophy lecture once a week in exchange for your cranking the handle on my machine, whose products I exchange for yet other things, and so on. (The raw materials used by the machine are given to me by others who possess them under D_1, in exchange for hearing lectures.) Each person might participate to gain things over and above their allotment under D_1. Some persons even might want to leave their job in socialist industry and work full time in this private sector. I shall say something more about these issues in the next chapter. Here I wish merely to note how private property even in means of production would occur in a socialist society that did not forbid people to use as they wished some of the resources they are given under the socialist distribution D_1. The socialist society would have to forbid capitalist acts between consenting adults.

The general point illustrated by the Wilt Chamberlain example and the example of the entrepreneur in a socialist society is that no end-state principle or distributional patterned principle of justice can be continuously realized without continuous interference with people's lives. Any favored pattern would be transformed into one unfavored by the principle, by people choosing to act in various ways; for example, by people exchanging goods and services with other people, or giving things to other people, things the transferrers are entitled to under the favored distributional pattern. To maintain a pattern one must either continually interfere to stop people from transferring resources as they wish to, or continually (or periodically) interfere to take from some persons resources that others for some reason chose to transfer to them. (But if some time limit is to be set on how long people may keep resources others voluntarily transfer to them, why let them keep these resources for *any* period of time? Why not have immediate confiscation?) It might be objected that all persons voluntarily will choose to refrain from actions which would upset the pattern. This presupposes unrealistically (1) that all will most want to maintain the pattern (are those who don't, to be "reeducated" or forced to undergo "self-criticism"?), (2) that each can gather enough information about his own actions and the ongoing activities of others to discover which of his actions will upset the pattern, and (3) that diverse and far-flung persons can coordinate their actions to dove-tail into the pattern. Compare the manner in which the market is neutral among persons' desires, as it reflects and transmits widely scattered information via prices, and coordinates persons' activities.

It puts things perhaps a bit too strongly to say that every patterned (or end-state) principle is liable to be thwarted by the voluntary actions of the individual parties transferring some of their shares they receive under the principle. For perhaps some *very* weak patterns are not so thwarted. Any distributional pattern with any egalitarian component is overturnable by the voluntary actions of individual persons over time; as is every patterned condition with sufficient content so as actually to have been proposed as presenting the central core of distributive justice. Still, given the possibility that some weak conditions or patterns may not be unstable in this way, it would be better to formulate an explicit description of the kind of interesting and contentful patterns under discussion, and to prove a theorem about their instability. Since the weaker the patterning, the more likely it is that the entitlement system itself satisfies it, a plausible conjecture is that any patterning either is unstable or is satisfied by the entitlement system.

Note

1. Applications of the principle of justice in acquisition may also occur as part of the move from one distribution to another. You may find an unheld thing now and appropriate it. Acquisitions also are to be understood as included when, to simplify, I speak only of transitions by transfers.

Complex Equality

MICHAEL WALZER

PLURALISM

Distributive justice is a large idea. It draws the entire world of goods within the reach of philosophical reflection. Nothing can be omitted; no feature of our common life can escape scrutiny. Human society is a distributive community. That's not all it is, but it is importantly that: we come together to share, divide, and exchange. We also come together to make things that are shared, divided, and exchanged; but that very making—work itself—is distributed among us in a division of labor. My place in the economy, my standing in the political order, my reputation among my fellows, my material holdings: all these come to me from other men and women. It can be said that I have what I have rightly or wrongly, justly or unjustly; but given the range of distributions and the number of participants, such judgments are never easy.

The idea of distributive justice has as much to do with being and doing as with having, as much to do with production as with consumption, as much to do with identity and status as with land, capital, or personal possessions. Different political arrangements enforce, and different ideologies justify, different distributions of membership, power, honor, ritual eminence, divine grace, kinship and love, knowledge, wealth, physical security, work and leisure, rewards and punishments, and a host of goods more narrowly and materially conceived—food, shelter, clothing, transportation, medical care, commodities of every sort, and all the odd things (paintings, rare books, postage stamps) that human beings collect. And this multiplicity of goods is matched by a multiplicity of distributive procedures, agents, and criteria. There are such things as simple distributive systems—slave galleys, monasteries, insane asylums, kindergartens (though each of these, looked at closely, might show unexpected complexities); but no full-fledged human society has ever avoided the multiplicity. We must study it all, the goods and the distributions, in many different times and places.

There is, however, no single point of access to this world of distributive arrangements and ideologies. There has never been a universal medium of exchange. Since the decline of the barter economy, money has been the most common medium. But the old maxim according to which there are some things that money can't buy is not only normatively but also factually true. What should and should not be up for sale is something men and women always have to decide and have decided in many different ways. Throughout history, the market has been one of the most important mechanisms for the distribution of social goods; but it has never been, it nowhere is today, a complete distributive system.

Similarly, there has never been either a single decision point from which all distributions are controlled or a single set of agents making decisions. No

state power has ever been so pervasive as to regulate all the patterns of sharing, dividing, and exchanging out of which a society takes shape. Things slip
away from the state's grasp; new patterns are worked out—familial networks,
black markets, bureaucratic alliances, clandestine political and religious
organizations. State officials can tax, conscript, allocate, regulate, appoint,
reward, punish, but they cannot capture the full range of goods or substitute themselves for every other agent of distribution. Nor can anyone else
do that: there are market coups and cornerings, but there has never been
a fully successful distributive conspiracy.

And finally, there has never been a single criterion, or a single set of interconnected criteria, for all distributions. Desert, qualification, birth and
blood, friendship, need, free exchange, political loyalty, democratic decision: each has had its place, along with many others, uneasily coexisting, invoked by competing groups, confused with one another.

In the matter of distributive justice, history displays a great variety of
arrangements and ideologies. But the first impulse of the philosopher is to
resist the displays of history, the world of appearances, and to search for
some underlying unity: a short list of basic goods, quickly abstracted to a single good; a single distributive criterion or an interconnected set; and the
philosopher himself standing, symbolically at least, at a single decision
point. I shall argue that to search for unity is to misunderstand the subject
matter of distributive justice. Nevertheless, in some sense the philosophical
impulse is unavoidable. Even if we choose pluralism, as I shall do, that choice
still requires a coherent defense. There must be principles that justify the
choice and set limits to it, for pluralism does not require us to endorse every
proposed distributive criteria or to accept every would-be agent. Conceivably,
there is a single principle and a single legitimate kind of pluralism. But this
would still be a pluralism that encompassed a wide range of distributions. By
contrast, the deepest assumption of most of the philosophers who have written about justice, from Plato onward, is that there is one, and only one, distributive system that philosophy can rightly encompass.

Today this system is commonly described as the one that ideally rational
men and women would choose if they were forced to choose impartially,
knowing nothing of their own situation, barred from making particularist
claims, confronting an abstract set of goods.[1] If these constraints on knowing and claiming are suitably shaped, and if the goods are suitably defined,
it is probably true that a singular conclusion can be produced. Rational men
and women, constrained this way or that, will choose one, and only one, distributive system. But the force of that singular conclusion is not easy to measure. It is surely doubtful that those same men and women, if they were
transformed into ordinary people, with a firm sense of their own identity,
with their own goods in their hands, caught up in everyday troubles, would
reiterate their hypothetical choice or even recognize it as their own. The
problem is not, most importantly, with the particularism of interest, which
philosophers have always assumed they could safely—that is, uncontrover-
sially—set aside. Ordinary people can do that too, for the sake, say, of the
public interest. The greater problem is with the particularism of history,
culture, and membership. Even if they are committed to impartiality, the
question most likely to arise in the minds of the members of a political community is not, What would rational individuals choose under universalizing

conditions of such-and-such a sort? But rather, What would individuals like us choose, who are situated as we are, who share a culture and are determined to go on sharing it? And this is a question that is readily transformed into, What choices have we already made in the course of our common life? What understandings do we (really) share?

Justice is a human construction, and it is doubtful that it can be made in only one way. At any rate, I shall begin by doubting, and more than doubting, this standard philosophical assumption.The questions posed by the theory of distributive justice admit of a range of answers, and there is room within the range for cultural diversity and political choice. It's not only a matter of implementing some singular principle or set of principles in different historical settings. No one would deny that there is a range of morally permissible implementations. I want to argue for more than this: that the principles of justice are themselves pluralistic in form; that different social goods ought to be distributed for different reasons, in accordance with different procedures, by different agents; and that all these differences derive from different understandings of the social goods themselves—the inevitable product of historical and cultural particularism.

A THEORY OF GOODS

Theories of distributive justice focus on a social process commonly described as if it had this form:

> *People distribute goods to (other) people.*

Here, "distribute" means give, allocate, exchange, and so on, and the focus is on the individuals who stand at either end of these actions: not on producers and consumers, but on distributive agents and recipients of goods. We are as always interested in ourselves, but, in this case, in a special and limited version of ourselves, as people who give and take. What is our nature? What are our rights? What do we need, want, deserve? What are we entitled to? What would we accept under ideal conditions? Answers to these questions are turned into distributive principles, which are supposed to control the movement of goods. The goods, defined by abstraction, are taken to be movable in any direction.

But this is too simple an understanding of what actually happens, and it forces us too quickly to make large assertions about human nature and moral agency—assertions unlikely, ever, to command general agreement. I want to propose a more precise and complex description of the central process.

> *People conceive and create goods, which they then distribute among themselves.*

Here, the conception and creation precede and control the distribution. Goods don't just appear in the hands of distributive agents who do with them as they like or give them out in accordance with some general principle.[2] Rather, goods with their meanings—because of their meanings—are the crucial medium of social relations; they come into people's minds before they come into their hands; distributions are patterned in accordance with shared conceptions of what the goods are and what they are for.

Distributive agents are constrained by the goods they hold; one might almost say that goods distribute themselves among people.

> Things are in the saddle
> And ride mankind.[3]

But these are always particular things and particular groups of men and women. And, of course, we make the things—even the saddle. I don't want to deny the importance of human agency, only to shift our attention from distribution itself to conception and creation: the naming of the goods, and the giving of meaning, and the collective making. What we need to explain and limit the pluralism of distributive possibilities is a theory of goods. For our immediate purposes, that theory can be summed up in six propositions.

1.   All the goods with which distributive justice is concerned are social goods. They are not and they cannot be idiosyncratically valued. I am not sure that there are any other kinds of goods; I mean to leave the question open. Some domestic objects are cherished for private and sentimental reasons, but only in cultures where sentiment regularly attaches to such objects. A beautiful sunset, the smell of new-mown hay, the excitement of an urban vista: these perhaps are privately valued goods, though they are also, and more obviously, the objects of cultural assessment. Even new inventions are not valued in accordance with the ideas of their inventors; they are subject to a wider process of conception and creation. God's goods, to be sure, are exempt from this rule—as in the first chapter of Genesis: "and God saw every thing that He had made, and, behold, it was very good" (1:31). That evaluation doesn't require the agreement of mankind (who might be doubtful), or of a majority of men and women, or of any group of men and women meeting under ideal conditions (though Adam and Eve in Eden would probably endorse it). But I can't think of any other exemptions. Goods in the world have shared meanings because conception and creation are social processes. For the same reason, goods have different meanings in different societies. The same "thing" is valued for different reasons, or it is valued here and disvalued there. John Stuart Mill once complained that "people like in crowds," but I know of no other way to like or to dislike social goods.[4] A solitary person could hardly understand the meaning of the goods or figure out the reasons for taking them as likable or dislikable. Once people like in crowds, it becomes possible for individuals to break away, pointing to latent or subversive meanings, aiming at alternative values—including the values, for example, of notoriety and eccentricity. An easy eccentricity has sometimes been one of the privileges of the aristocracy: it is a social good like any other.

2.   Men and women take on concrete identities because of the way they conceive and create, and then possess and employ social goods. "The line between what is me and mine," wrote William James, "is very hard to draw."[5] Distributions can not be understood as the acts of men and women who do not yet have particular goods in their minds or in their hands. In fact, people already stand in a relation to a set of goods; they have a history of transactions, not only with one another but also with the moral and material world in which they live. Without such a history, which begins at birth, they

wouldn't be men and women in any recognizable sense, and they wouldn't have the first notion of how to go about the business of giving, allocating, and exchanging goods.

3. There is no single set of primary or basic goods conceivable across all moral and material worlds—or, any such set would have to be conceived in terms so abstract that they would be of little use in thinking about particular distributions. Even the range of necessities, if we take into account moral as well as physical necessities, is very wide, and the rank orderings are very different. A single necessary good, and one that is always necessary— food, for example—carries different meanings in different places. Bread is the staff of life, the body of Christ, the symbol of the Sabbath, the means of hospitality, and so on. Conceivably, there is a limited sense in which the first of these is primary, so that if there were twenty people in the world and just enough bread to feed the twenty, the primacy of bread-as-staff-of-life would yield a sufficient distributive principle. But that is the only circumstance in which it would do so; and even there, we can't be sure. If the religious uses of bread were to conflict with its nutritional uses—if the gods demanded that bread be baked and burned rather than eaten—it is by no means clear which use would be primary. How, then, is bread to be incorporated into the universal list? The question is even harder to answer, the conventional answers less plausible, as we pass from necessities to opportunities, powers, reputations, and so on. These can be incorporated only if they are abstracted from every particular meaning—hence, for all practical purposes, rendered meaningless.

4. But it is the meaning of goods that determines their movement. Distributive criteria and arrangements are intrinsic not to the good-in-itself but to the social good. If we understand what it is, what it means to those for whom it is a good, we understand how, by whom, and for what reasons it ought to be distributed. All distributions are just or unjust relative to the social meanings of the goods at stake. This is in obvious ways a principle of legitimation, but it is also a critical principle.* When medieval Christians, for example, condemned the sin of simony, they were claiming that the meaning of a particular social good, ecclesiastical office, excluded its sale and purchase. Given the Christian understanding of office, it followed—I am inclined to say, it necessarily followed—that office holders should be chosen for their knowledge and piety and not for their wealth. There are presumably things that money can buy, but not this thing. Similarly, the

---

*Aren't social meanings, as Marx said, nothing other than "the ideas of the ruling class," "the dominant material relationships grasped as ideas"?[6] I don't think that they are ever only that or simply that, though the members of the ruling class and the intellectuals they patronize may well be in a position to exploit and distort social meanings in their own interests. When they do that, however, they are likely to encounter resistance, rooted (intellectually) in those same meanings. A people's culture is always a joint, even if it isn't an entirely cooperative, production; and it is always a complex production. The common understanding of particular goods incorporates principles, procedures, conceptions of agency, that the rulers would not choose if they were choosing *right now*—and so provides the terms of social criticism. The appeal to what I shall call "internal" principles against the usurpations of powerful men and women is the ordinary form of critical discourse.

words *prostitution* and *bribery*, like *simony*, describe the sale and purchase of goods that, given certain understandings of their meaning, ought never to be sold or purchased.

5. Social meanings are historical in character; and so distributions, and just and unjust distributions, change over time. To be sure, certain key goods have what we might think of as characteristic normative structures, reiterated across the lines (but not all the lines) of time and space. It is because of this reiteration that the British philosopher Bernard Williams is able to argue that goods should always be distributed for "relevant reasons"—where relevance seems to connect to essential rather than to social meanings.[7] The idea that offices, for example, should go to qualified candidates—though not the only idea that has been held about offices—is plainly visible in very different societies where simony and nepotism, under different names, have similarly been thought sinful or unjust. (But there has been a wide divergence of views about what sorts of position and place are properly called "offices.") Again, punishment has been widely understood as a negative good that ought to go to people who are judged to deserve it on the basis of a verdict, not of a political decision. (But what constitutes a verdict? Who is to deliver it? How, in short, is justice to be done to accused men and women? About these questions there has been significant disagreement.) These examples invite empirical investigation. There is no merely intuitive or speculative procedure for seizing upon relevant reasons.

6. When meanings are distinct, distributions must be autonomous. Every social good or set of goods constitutes, as it were, a distributive sphere within which only certain criteria and arrangements are appropriate. Money is inappropriate in the sphere of ecclesiastical office; it is an intrusion from another sphere. And piety should make for no advantage in the marketplace, as the marketplace has commonly been understood. Whatever can rightly be sold ought to be sold to pious men and women and also to profane, heretical, and sinful men and women (else no one would do much business). The market is open to all comers; the church is not. In no society, of course, are social meanings entirely distinct. What happens in one distributive sphere affects what happens in the others; we can look, at most, for relative autonomy. But relative autonomy, like social meaning, is a critical principle—indeed, as I shall be arguing throughout this book, a radical principle. It is radical even though it doesn't point to a single standard against which all distributions are to be measured. There is no single standard. But there are standards (roughly knowable even when they are also controversial) for every social good and every distributive sphere in every particular society; and these standards are often violated, the goods usurped, the spheres invaded, by powerful men and women.

DOMINANCE AND MONOPOLY

In fact, the violations are systematic. Autonomy is a matter of social meaning and shared values, but it is more likely to make for occasional reformation and rebellion than for everyday enforcement. For all the complexity of their distributive arrangements, most societies are organized on what we might think of as a social version of the gold standard: one good or one set of goods is dominant and determinative of value in all the spheres of distribution. And that good or set of goods is commonly monopolized, its value upheld by the strength and cohesion of its owners. I call a good dominant if the individuals who have it, because they have it, can command a wide range of other goods. It is monopolized whenever a single man or woman, a monarch in the world of value—or a group of men and women, oligarchs—successfully hold it against all rivals. Dominance describes a way of using social goods that isn't limited by their intrinsic meanings or that shapes those meanings in its own image. Monopoly describes a way of owning or controlling social goods in order to exploit their dominance. When goods are scarce and widely needed, like water in the desert, monopoly itself will make them dominant. Mostly, however, dominance is a more elaborate social creation, the work of many hands, mixing reality and symbol. Physical strength, familial reputation, religious or political office, landed wealth, capital, technical knowledge: each of these, in different historical periods, has been dominant; and each of them has been monopolized by some group of men and women. And then all good things come to those who have the one best thing. Possess that one, and the others come in train. Or, to change the metaphor, a dominant good is converted into another good, into many others, in accordance with what often appears to be a natural process but is in fact magical, a kind of social alchemy.

No social good ever entirely dominates the range of goods; no monopoly is ever perfect. I mean to describe tendencies only, but crucial tendencies. For we can characterize whole societies in terms of the patterns of conversion that are established within them. Some characterizations are simple: in a capitalist society, capital is dominant and readily converted into prestige and power; in a technocracy, technical knowledge plays the same part. But it isn't difficult to imagine, or to find, more complex social arrangements. Indeed, capitalism and technocracy are more complex than their names imply, even if the names do convey real information about the most important forms of sharing, dividing, and exchanging. Monopolistic control of a dominant good makes a ruling class, whose members stand atop the distributive system—much as philosophers, claiming to have the wisdom they love, might like to do. But since dominance is always incomplete and monopoly imperfect, the rule of every ruling class is unstable. It is continually challenged by other groups in the name of alternative patterns of conversion.

Distribution is what social conflict is all about. Marx's heavy emphasis on productive processes should not conceal from us the simple truth that the struggle for control of the means of production is a distributive struggle. Land and capital are at stake, and these are goods that can be shared, divided, exchanged, and endlessly converted. But land and capital are not the only dominant goods; it is possible (it has historically been possible) to come to them by way of other goods—military or political power, religious office and charisma, and so on. History reveals no single dominant good and no naturally dominant good, but only different kinds of magic and competing bands of magicians.

The claim to monopolize a dominant good—when worked up for public purposes—constitutes an ideology. Its standard form is to connect legitimate possession with some set of personal qualities through the medium of a philosophical principle. So aristocracy, or the rule of the best, is the principle of those who lay claim to breeding and intelligence: they are commonly the monopolists of landed wealth and familial reputation. Divine supremacy is the principle of those who claim to know the word of God: they are the monopolists of grace and office. Meritocracy, or the career open to talents, is the principle of those who claim to be talented: they are most often the monopolists of education. Free exchange is the principle of those who are ready, or who tell us they are ready, to put their money at risk: they are the monopolists of movable wealth. These groups—and others, too, similarly marked off by their principles and possessions—compete with one another, struggling for supremacy. One group wins, and then a different one; or coalitions are worked out, and supremacy is uneasily shared. There is no final victory, nor should there be. But that is not to say that the claims of the different groups are necessarily wrong, or that the principles they invoke are of no value as distributive criteria; the principles are often exactly right within the limits of a particular sphere. Ideologies are readily corrupted, but their corruption is not the most interesting thing about them.

It is in the study of these struggles that I have sought the guiding thread of my own argument. The struggles have, I think, a paradigmatic form. Some group of men and women—class, caste, strata, estate, alliance, or social formation—comes to enjoy a monopoly or a near monopoly of some dominant good; or, a coalition of groups comes to enjoy, and so on. This dominant good is more or less systematically converted into all sorts of other things—opportunities, powers, and reputations. So wealth is seized by the strong, honor by the wellborn, office by the well educated. Perhaps the ideology that justifies the seizure is widely believed to be true. But resentment and resistance are (almost) as pervasive as belief. There are always some people, and after a time there are a great many, who think the seizure is not justice but usurpation. The ruling group does not possess, or does not uniquely possess, the qualities it claims; the conversion process violates the common understanding of the goods at stake. Social conflict is intermittent, or it is endemic; at some point, counterclaims are put forward. Though these are of many different sorts, three general sorts are especially important:

1. The claim that the dominant good, whatever it is, should be redistributed so that it can be equally or at least more widely shared: this amounts to saying that monopoly is unjust.
2. The claim that the way should be opened for the autonomous distribution of all social goods: this amounts to saying that dominance is unjust.
3. The claim that some new good, monopolized by some new group, should replace the currently dominant good: this amounts to saying that the existing pattern of dominance and monopoly is unjust.

The third claim is, in Marx's view, the model of every revolutionary ideology—except, perhaps, the proletarian or last ideology. Thus, the French Revolution in Marxist theory: the dominance of noble birth and blood and of feudal landholding is ended, and bourgeois wealth is established in its stead. The original situation is reproduced with different subjects and objects (this is never unimportant), and then the class war is immediately renewed. It is not my purpose here to endorse or to criticize Marx's view. I suspect, in fact, that there is something of all three claims in every revolutionary ideology, but that, too, is not a position that I shall try to defend here. Whatever its sociological significance, the third claim is not philosophically interesting—unless one believes that there is a naturally dominant good, such that its possessors could legitimately claim to rule the rest of us. In a sense, Marx believed exactly that. The means of production is the dominant good throughout history, and Marxism is a historicist doctrine insofar as it suggests that whoever controls the prevailing means legitimately rules.[8] After the communist revolution, we shall all control the means of production: at that point, the third claim collapses into the first. Meanwhile, Marx's model is a program of ongoing distributive struggle. It will matter, of course, who wins at this or that moment, but we won't know why or how it matters if we attend only to the successive assertions of dominance and monopoly.

SIMPLE EQUALITY

It is with the first two claims that I shall be concerned, and ultimately with the second alone, for that one seems to me to capture best the plurality of social meanings and the real complexity of distributive systems. But the first is the more common among philosophers; it matches their own search for unity and singularity; and I shall need to explain its difficulties at some length.

Men and women who make the first claim challenge the monopoly but not the dominance of a particular social good. This is also a challenge to monopoly in general; for if wealth, for example, is dominant and widely shared, no other good can possibly be monopolized. Imagine a society in which everything is up for sale and every citizen has as much money as every other. I shall call this the "regime of simple equality." Equality is multiplied through the conversion process, until it extends across the full range of social goods. The regime of simple equality won't last for long, because the further progress of conversion, free exchange in the market, is certain to bring inequalities in its train. If one wanted to sustain simple equality over time, one would require a "monetary law" like the agrarian laws of ancient times or the Hebrew sabbatical, providing for a periodic return to the original condition. Only a centralized and activist state would be strong enough to force such a return; and it isn't clear that state officials would actually be able or willing to do that, if money were the dominant good. In any case, the original condition is unstable in another way. It's not only that monopoly will reappear, but also that dominance will disappear.

In practice, breaking the monopoly of money neutralizes its dominance. Other goods come into play, and inequality takes on new forms. Consider again the regime of simple equality. Everything is up for sale, and everyone has the same amount of money. So everyone has, say, an equal ability to buy an education for his children. Some do that, and others don't. It turns out to be a good investment: other social goods are, increasingly, offered for sale only to people with educational certificates. Soon everyone invests in education; or, more likely, the purchase is universalized through the tax system.

But then the school is turned into a competitive world within which money is no longer dominant. Natural talent or family upbringing or skill in writing examinations is dominant instead, and educational success and certification are monopolized by some new group. Let's call them (what they call themselves) the "group of the talented." Eventually the members of this group claim that the good they control should be dominant outside the school: offices, titles, prerogatives, wealth too, should all be possessed by themselves. This is the career open to talents, equal opportunity, and so on. This is what fairness requires; talent will out; and in any case, talented men and women will enlarge the resources available to everyone else. So Michael Young's meritocracy is born, with all its attendant inequalities.[9]

What should we do now? It is possible to set limits to the new conversion patterns, to recognize but constrain the monopoly power of the talented. I take this to be the purpose of John Rawls's difference principle, according to which inequalities are justified only if they are designed to bring, and actually do bring, the greatest possible benefit to the least advantaged social class.[10] More specifically, the difference principle is a constraint imposed on talented men and women, once the monopoly of wealth has been broken. It works in this way: Imagine a surgeon who claims more than his equal share of wealth on the basis of the skills he has learned and the certificates he has won in the harsh competitive struggles of college and medical school. We will grant the claim if, and only if, granting it is beneficial in the stipulated ways. At the same time, we will act to limit and regulate the sale of surgery—that is, the direct conversion of surgical skill into wealth.

This regulation will necessarily be the work of the state, just as monetary laws and agrarian laws are the work of the state. Simple equality would require continual state intervention to break up or constrain incipient monopolies and to repress new forms of dominance. But then state power itself will become the central object of competitive struggles. Groups of men and women will seek to monopolize and then to use the state in order to consolidate their control of other social goods. Or, the state will be monopolized by its own agents in accordance with the iron law of oligarchy. Politics is always the most direct path to dominance, and political power (rather than the means of production) is probably the most important, and certainly the most dangerous, good in human history.* Hence the need to constrain the agents of constraint, to establish constitutional checks and balances. There are limits imposed on political monopoly, and they are all the

---

*I should note here what will become more clear as I go along, that political power is a special sort of good. It has a twofold character. First, it is like the other things that men and women make, value, exchange, and share: sometimes dominant, sometimes not; sometimes widely held, sometimes the possession of very few. And, second, it is unlike all the other things because, however it is had and whoever has it, political power is the regulative agency for social goods generally. It is used to defend the boundaries of all the distributive spheres, including its own, and to enforce the common understandings of what goods are and what they are for. (But it can also be used, obviously, to invade the different spheres and to override those understandings.) In this second sense, we might say, indeed, that political power is always dominant—at the boundaries, but not within them. The central problem of political life is to maintain that crucial distinction between "at" and "in." But this is a problem that cannot be solved given the imperatives of simple equality.

more important once the various social and economic monopolies have been broken.

One way of limiting political power is to distribute it widely. This may not work, given the well-canvassed dangers of majority tyranny; but these dangers are probably less acute than they are often made out to be. The greater danger of democratic government is that it will be weak to cope with re-emerging monopolies in society at large, with the social strength of plutocrats, bureaucrats, technocrats, meritocrats, and so on. In theory, political power is the dominant good in a democracy, and it is convertible in any way the citizens choose. But in practice, again, breaking the monopoly of power neutralizes its dominance. Political power cannot be widely shared without being subjected to the pull of all the other goods that the citizens already have or hope to have. Hence democracy is, as Marx recognized, essentially a reflective system, mirroring the prevailing and emerging distribution of social goods.[11] Democratic decision making will be shaped by the cultural conceptions that determine or underwrite the new monopolies. To prevail against these monopolies, power will have to be centralized, perhaps itself monopolized. Once again, the state must be very powerful if it is to fulfill the purposes assigned to it by the difference principle or by any similarly interventionist rule.

Still, the regime of simple equality might work. One can imagine a more or less stable tension between emerging monopolies and political constraints, between the claim to privilege put forward by the talented, say, and the enforcement of the difference principle, and then between the agents of enforcement and the democratic constitution. But I suspect that difficulties will recur, and that at many points in time the only remedy for private privilege will be statism, and the only escape from statism will be private privilege. We will mobilize power to check monopoly, then look for some way of checking the power we have mobilized. But there is no way that doesn't open opportunities for strategically placed men and women to seize and exploit important social goods.

These problems derive from treating monopoly, and not dominance, as the central issue in distributive justice. It is not difficult, of course, to understand why philosophers (and political activists, too) have focused on monopoly. The distributive struggles of the modern age begin with a war against the aristocracy's singular hold on land, office, and honor. This seems an especially pernicious monopoly because it rests upon birth and blood, with which the individual has nothing to do, rather than upon wealth, or power, or education, all of which—at least in principle—can be earned. And when every man and woman becomes, as it were, a smallholder in the sphere of birth and blood, an important victory is indeed won. Birthright ceases to be a dominant good; henceforth, it purchases very little; wealth, power, and education come to the fore. With regard to these latter goods, however, simple equality cannot be sustained at all, or it can only be sustained subject to the vicissitudes I have just described. Within their own spheres, as they are currently understood, these three tend to generate natural monopolies that can be repressed only if state power is itself dominant and if it is monopolized by officials committed to the repression. But there is, I think, another path to another kind of equality.

TYRANNY AND COMPLEX EQUALITY

I want to argue that we should focus on the reduction of dominance—not, or not primarily, on the break-up or the constraint of monopoly. We should consider what it might mean to narrow the range within which particular goods are convertible and to vindicate the autonomy of distributive spheres. But this line of argument, though it is not uncommon historically, has never fully emerged in philosophical writing. Philosophers have tended to criticize (or to justify) existing or emerging monopolies of wealth, power, and education. Or, they have criticized (or justified) particular conversions—of wealth into education or of office into wealth. And all this, most often, in the name of some radically simplified distributive system. The critique of dominance will suggest instead a way of reshaping and then living with the actual complexity of distributions.

Imagine now a society in which different social goods are monopolistically held—as they are in fact and always will be, barring continual state intervention—but in which no particular good is generally convertible. As I go along, I shall try to define the precise limits on convertibility, but for now the general description will suffice. This is a complex egalitarian society. Though there will be many small inequalities, inequality will not be multiplied through the conversion process. Nor will it be summed across different goods, because the autonomy of distributions will tend to produce a variety of local monopolies, held by different groups of men and women. I don't want to claim that complex equality would necessarily be more stable than simple equality, but I am inclined to think that it would open the way for more diffused and particularized forms of social conflict. And the resistance to convertibility would be maintained, in large degree, by ordinary men and women within their own spheres of competence and control, without large-scale state action.

This is, I think, an attractive picture, but I have not yet explained just why it is attractive. The argument for complex equality begins from our understanding—I mean, our actual, concrete, positive, and particular understanding—of the various social goods. And then it moves on to an account of the way we relate to one another through those goods. Simple equality is a simple distributive condition, so that if I have fourteen hats and you have fourteen hats, we are equal. And it is all to the good if hats are dominant, for then our equality is extended through all the spheres of social life. On the view that I shall take here, however, we simply have the same number of hats, and it is unlikely that hats will be dominant for long. Equality is a complex relation of persons, mediated by the goods we make, share, and divide among ourselves; it is not an identity of possessions. It requires, then, a diversity of distributive criteria that mirrors the diversity of social goods.

The regime of complex equality is the opposite of tyranny. It establishes a set of relationships such that domination is impossible. In formal terms, complex equality means that no citizen's standing in one sphere or with regard to one social good can be undercut by his standing in some other sphere, with regard to some other good. Thus, citizen X may be chosen over citizen Y for political office, and then the two of them will be unequal in the sphere of politics. But they will not be unequal generally so long as X's office gives him no advantages over Y in any other sphere—superior medical care, access to better schools for his children, entrepreneurial opportunities, and so on. So long as office is not a dominant good, is not generally convertible, office holders will stand, or at least can stand, in a relation of equality to the men and women they govern.

But what if dominance were eliminated, the autonomy of the spheres established—and the same people were successful in one sphere after another, triumphant in every company, piling up goods without the need for illegitimate conversions? This would certainly make for an inegalitarian society, but it would also suggest in the strongest way that a society of equals was not a lively possibility. I doubt that any egalitarian argument could survive in the face of such evidence. Here is a person whom we have freely chosen (without reference to his family ties or personal wealth) as our political representative. He is also a bold and inventive entrepreneur. When he was younger, he studied science, scored amazingly high grades in every exam, and made important discoveries. In war, he is surpassingly brave and wins the highest honors. Himself compassionate and compelling, he is loved by all who know him. Are there such people? Maybe so, but I have my doubts. We tell stories like the one I have just told, but the stories are fictions, the conversion of power or money or academic talent into legendary fame. In any case, there aren't enough such people to constitute a ruling class and dominate the rest of us. Nor can they be successful in every distributive sphere, for there are some spheres to which the idea of success doesn't pertain. Nor are their children likely, under conditions of complex equality, to inherit their success. By and large, the most accomplished politicians, entrepreneurs, scientists, soldiers, and lovers will be different people; and so long as the goods they possess don't bring other goods in train, we have no reason to fear their accomplishments.

The critique of dominance and domination points toward an open-ended distributive principle. *No social good* x *should be distributed to men and women who possess some other good* y *merely because they possess* y *and without regard to the meaning of* x. This is a principle that has probably been reiterated, at one time or another, for every y that has ever been dominant. But it has not often been stated in general terms. Pascal and Marx have suggested the application of the principle against all possible y's, and I shall attempt to work out that application. I shall be looking, then, not at the members of Pascal's companies—the strong or the weak, the handsome or the plain—but at the goods they share and divide. The purpose of the principle is to focus our attention; it doesn't determine the shares or the division. The principle directs us to study the meaning of social goods, to examine the different distributive spheres from the inside. . . .

THREE DISTRIBUTIVE PRINCIPLES

The theory that results is unlikely to be elegant. No account of the meaning of a social good, or of the boundaries of the sphere within which it legitimately operates, will be uncontroversial. Nor is there any neat procedure for generating or testing different accounts. At best, the arguments will be rough, reflecting the diverse and conflict-ridden character of the social life that we seek simultaneously to understand and to regulate—but not to regulate until we understand. I shall set aside, then, all claims made on behalf of any single distributive criteron, for no such criterion can possibly match the diversity of social goods. Three criteria, however, appear to meet the requirements of the open-ended principle and have often been defended as the beginning and end of distributive justice, so I must say something about each of them. Free exchange, desert, and need: all three have real force, but none of them has force across the range of distributions. They are part of the story, not the whole of it.

Free Exchange

Free exchange is obviously open-ended; it guarantees no particular distributive outcome. At no point in any exchange process plausibly called "free" will it be possible to predict the particular division of social goods that will obtain at some later point.[12] (It may be possible, however, to predict the general structure of the division.) In theory at least, free exchange creates a market within which all goods are convertible into all other goods through the neutral medium of money. There are no dominant goods and no monopolies. Hence the successive divisions that obtain will directly reflect the social meanings of the goods that are divided. For each bargain, trade, sale, and purchase will have been agreed to voluntarily by men and women who know what that meaning is, who are indeed its makers. Every exchange is a revelation of social meaning. By definition, then, no x will ever fall into the hands of someone who possesses y, merely because he possesses y and without regard to what x actually means to some other member of society. The market is radically pluralistic in its operations and its outcomes, infinitely sensitive to the meanings that individuals attach to goods. What possible restraints can be imposed on free exchange, then, in the name of pluralism?

But everyday life in the market, the actual experience of free exchange, is very different from what the theory suggests. Money, supposedly the neutral medium, is in practice a dominant good, and it is monopolized by people who possess a special talent for bargaining and trading—the green thumb of bourgeois society. Then other people demand a redistribution of money and the establishment of the regime of simple equality, and the search begins for some way to sustain that regime. But even if we focus on the first untroubled moment of simple equality—free exchange on the basis of equal shares—we will still need to set limits on what can be exchanged for what. For free exchange leaves distributions entirely in the hands of individuals, and social meanings are not subject, or are not always subject, to the interpretative decisions of individual men and women.

Consider an easy example, the case of political power. We can conceive of political power as a set of goods of varying value, votes, influence, offices, and so on. Any of these can be traded on the market and accumulated by individuals willing to sacrifice other goods. Even if the sacrifices are real, however, the result is a form of tyranny—petty tyranny, given the conditions of simple equality. Because I am willing to do without my hat, I shall vote twice; and you who value the vote less than you value my hat, will not vote at all. I suspect that the result is tyrannical even with regard to the two of us, who have reached a voluntary agreement. It is certainly tyrannical with regard to all the other citizens who must now submit to my disproportionate power. It is not the case that votes can't be bargained for; on one interpretation, that's what democratic politics is all about. And democratic politicians have certainly been known to buy votes, or to try to buy them, by promising public expenditures that benefit particular groups of voters. But this is done in public, with public funds, and subject to public approval. Private trading is ruled out by virtue of what politics, or democratic politics, is—that is, by virtue of what we did when we constituted the political community and of what we still think about what we did.

Free exchange is not a general criterion, but we will be able to specify the boundaries within which it operates only through a careful analysis of particular social goods. And having worked through such an analysis, we will come up at best with a philosophically authoritative set of boundaries and not necessarily with the set that ought to be politically authoritative. For money seeps across all boundaries—this is the primary form of illegal immigration; and just where one ought to try to stop it is a question of expediency as well as of principle. Failure to stop it at some reasonable point has consequences throughout the range of distributions, but consideration of these belongs in a later chapter.

Desert

Like free exchange, desert seems both open-ended and pluralistic. One might imagine a single neutral agency dispensing rewards and punishments, infinitely sensitive to all the forms of individual desert. Then the distributive process would indeed be centralized, but the results would still be unpredictable and various. There would be no dominant good. No *x* would ever be distributed without regard to its social meaning; for, without attention to what *x* is, it is conceptually impossible to say that *x* is deserved. All the different companies of men and women would receive their appropriate reward. How this would work in practice, however, is not easy to figure out. It might make sense to say of this charming man, for example, that he deserves to be loved. It makes no sense to say that he deserves to be loved by this (or any) particular woman. If he loves her while she remains impervious to his (real) charms, that is his misfortune. I doubt that we would want the situation corrected by some outside agency. The love of particular men and women, on our understanding of it, can only be distributed by themselves, and they are rarely guided in these matters by considerations of desert.

The case is exactly the same with influence. Here, let's say, is a woman widely thought to be stimulating and encouraging to others. Perhaps she deserves to be an influential member of our community. But she doesn't deserve that I be influenced by her or that I follow her lead. Nor would we want my followership, as it were, assigned to her by any agency capable of making such assignments. She may go to great lengths to stimulate and encourage me, and do all the things that are commonly called stimulating or encouraging. But if I (perversely) refuse to be stimulated or encouraged, I am not denying her anything that she deserves. The same argument holds by extension for politicians and ordinary citizens. Citizens can't trade their votes for hats; they can't individually decide to cross the boundary that separates the sphere of politics from the marketplace. But within the sphere of politics, they do make individual decisions; and they are rarely guided, again, by considerations of desert. It's not clear that offices can be deserved—another issue that I must postpone; but even if they can be, it would violate our understanding of democratic politics were they simply distributed to deserving men and women by some central agency.

Similarly, however we draw the boundaries of the sphere within which free exchange operates, desert will play no role within those boundaries. I am skillful at bargaining and trading, let's say, and so accumulate a large number of beautiful pictures. If we assume, as painters mostly do, that pictures are appropriately traded in the market, then there is nothing wrong with my having the pictures. My title is legitimate. But it would be odd to say that I deserve to have them simply because I am good at bargaining and trading. Desert seems to require an especially close connection between particular goods and particular persons, whereas justice only sometimes requires a connection of that sort. Still, we might insist that only artistically cultivated people, who deserve to have pictures, should actually have them. It's not difficult to imagine a distributive mechanism. The state could buy all the pictures that were offered for sale (but artists would have to be licensed, so that there wouldn't be an endless number of pictures), evaluate them, and then distribute them to artistically cultivated men and women, the better pictures to the more cultivated. The state does something like this, sometimes, with regard to things that people need—medical care, for example—but not with regard to things that people deserve. There are practical difficulties here, but I suspect a deeper reason for this difference. Desert does not have the urgency of need, and it does not involve having (owning and consuming) in the same way. Hence, we are willing to tolerate the separation of owners of paintings and artistically cultivated people, or we are unwilling to require the kinds of interference in the market that would be necessary to end the separation. Of course, public provision is always possible alongside the market, and so we might argue that artistically cultivated people deserve not pictures but museums. Perhaps they do, but they don't deserve that the rest of us contribute money or appropriate public funds for the purchase of pictures and the construction of buildings. They will have to persuade us that art is worth the money; they will have to stimulate and encourage our own artistic cultivation. And if they fail to do that, their own love of art may well turn out to be "impotent and a misfortune."

Even if we were to assign the distribution of love, influence, offices, works of art, and so on, to some omnipotent arbiters of desert, how would we select them? How could anyone deserve such a position? Only God, who knows what secrets lurk in the hearts of men, would be able to make the necessary distributions. If human beings had to do the work, the distributive mechanism would be seized early on by some band of aristocrats (so they would call themselves) with a fixed conception of what is best and most deserving, and insensitive to the diverse excellences of their fellow citizens. And then desert would cease to be a pluralist criterion; we would find ourselves face to face with a new set (of an old sort) of tyrants. We do, of course, choose people as arbiters of desert—to serve on juries, for example, or to award prizes; it will be worth considering later what the prerogatives of a juror are. But it is important to stress here that he operates within a narrow range. Desert is a strong claim, but it calls for difficult judgments; and only under very special conditions does it yield specific distributions.

Need

Finally, the criterion of need. "To each according to his needs" is generally taken as the distributive half of Marx's famous maxim: we are to distribute the wealth of the community so as to meet the necessities of its members.[13] A plausible proposal, but a radically incomplete one. In fact, the first half of the maxim is also a distributive proposal, and it doesn't fit the rule of the second half. "From each according to his ability" suggests that jobs should be distributed (or that men and women should be conscripted to work) on the basis of individual qualifications. But individuals don't in any obvious sense need the jobs for which they are qualified. Perhaps such jobs are scarce, and there are a large number of qualified candidates: which candidates need them most? If their material needs are already taken care of, perhaps they don't need to work at all. Or if, in some non-material sense, they all need to work, then that need won't distinguish among them, at least not to the naked eye. It would in any case be odd to ask a search committee looking, say, for a hospital director to make its choice on the basis of the needs of the candidates rather than on those of the staff and the patients of the hospital. But the latter set of needs, even if it isn't the subject of political disagreement, won't yield a single distributive decision.

Nor will need work for many other goods. Marx's maxim doesn't help at all with regard to the distribution of political power, honor and fame, sailboats, rare books, beautiful objects of every sort. These are not things that anyone, strictly speaking, needs. Even if we take a loose view and define the verb *to need* the way children do, as the strongest form of the verb *to want,* we still won't have an adequate distributive criterion. The sorts of things that I have listed cannot be distributed equally to those with equal wants because some of them are generally, and some of them are necessarily, scarce, and some of them can't be possessed at all unless other people, for reasons of their own, agree on who is to possess them.

Need generates a particular distributive sphere, within which it is itself the appropriate distributive principle. In a poor society, a high proportion of social wealth will be drawn into this sphere. But given the great variety of goods that arises out of any common life, even when it is lived at a very low material level, other distributive criteria will always be operating alongside of need, and it will always be necessary to worry about the boundaries that mark them off from one another. Within its sphere, certainly, need meets the general distributive rule about x and y. Needed goods distributed to needy people in proportion to their neediness are obviously not dominated by any other goods. It's not having y, but only lacking x that is relevant. But we can now see, I think, that every criterion that has any force at all meets the general rule within its own sphere, and not elsewhere. This is the effect of the rule: different goods to different companies of men and women for different reasons and in accordance with different procedures. And to get all this right, or to get it roughly right, is to map out the entire social world.

Notes

1. See John Rawls, *A Theory of Justice* (Cambridge, Mass., 1971); Jürgen Habermas, *Legitimation Crisis*, trans. Thomas McCarthy (Boston, 1975), esp. p. 113; Bruce Ackerman, *Social Justice in the Liberal State* (New Haven, 1980).
2. Robert Nozick makes a similar argument in *Anarchy, State, and Utopia* (New York, 1974), pp. 149–50, but with radically individualistic conclusions that seem to me to miss the social character of production.
3. Ralph Waldo Emerson, "Ode," in *The Complete Essays and Other Writings*, ed. Brooks Atkinson (New York, 1940), p. 770.
4. John Stuart Mill, *On Liberty*, in *The Philosophy of John Stuart Mill*, ed. Marshall Cohen (New York, 1961), p. 255. For an anthropological account of liking and not liking social goods, see Mary Douglas and Baron Isherwood, *The World of Goods* (New York, 1979).
5. William James, quoted in C. R. Snyder and Howard Fromkin, *Uniqueness: The Human Pursuit of Difference* (New York, 1980), p. 108.
6. Karl Marx, *The German Idology*, ed. R. Pascal (New York, 1947), p. 89.
7. Bernard Williams, *Problems of the Self: Philosophical Papers, 1956–1972* (Cambridge, England, 1973), pp. 230–49 ("The Idea of Equality"). This essay is one of the starting points of my own thinking about distributive justice. See also the critique of Williams's argument (and of an earlier essay of my own) in Amy Gutmann, *Liberal Equality* (Cambridge, England, 1980), chap. 4.
8. See Alan W. Wood, "The Marxian Critique of Justice," *Philosophy and Public Affairs* 1 (1972): 244–82.
9. Michael Young, *The Rise of the Meritocracy, 1870–2033* (Hammondsworth, England, 1961)—a brilliant piece of social science fiction.
10. Rawls, *Theory of Justice* [1], pp. 75ff.
11. See Marx's comment, in his "Critique of the Gotha Program," that the democratic republic is the "form of state" within which the class struggle will be fought to a conclusion: the struggle is immediately and without distortion reflected in political life (Marx and Engels, *Selected Works* [Moscow, 1951], vol. II, p. 31).
12. Cf. Nozick on "patterning," *Anarchy, State, and Utopia* [2], pp. 155 ff.
13. Marx, "Gotha Program" [11], p. 23.

PART THREE

Corporations, Persons, and Morality
Introduction

People eat, sleep, vote, love, hate, and suffer guilt. They also go to work for, and manage, corporations that do none of these. Yet corporations are considered "persons" under the law and have many of the same rights as humans: to sue, to own property, to conduct business and conclude contracts, and to enjoy freedom of speech, of the press, and freedom from unreasonable searches and seizures. Corporations are legal citizens of the state in which they are chartered. They even possess two rights not held by humans: unlimited longevity and limited liability. Corporations in the United States have unlimited charters, they never "die" in the ordinary sense of the term, although some companies go bankrupt, and their shareholders are liable for corporate debts only up to the extent of their personal investments. Are corporations, then, morally responsible in the ways in which people are?

The Moral Responsibility of Corporations

One of the most stubborn ethical issues surrounding the corporation is not what it should do, but how it should be understood. *What* is a corporation? Is it a distinct individual in its own right, or merely an aggregate of individuals, for example, its stockholders, managers, and employees? The answer to this question is crucial for understanding corporations and their activities. We already know that individual members of a corporation can be held morally responsible. For example, if a chemical engineer intentionally puts a dangerous chemical in a new cosmetic product, he or she is morally blameworthy. But can we hold the corporation, considered as something distinct from its individual members, morally blameworthy too?

The very concept of a corporation seems to involve more than the individual actions of specific persons. The corporation is understood to exist even after all its original members are deceased; it is said to hire or fire employees when only a handful of the corporate members are involved in the decision; and it is said to have obligations through its charter that override the desires of its individual members. Let us grant that the corporation is a distinct entity whose actions are not reducible, at least in a straightforward way, to the actions of individuals. Does it follow that the corporation has moral characteristics that are not reducible to the moral characteristics of its members? Philosophers have addressed this issue by asking whether the corporation is a moral agent. Rocks, trees, and machines are clearly not moral agents. People clearly are. What are we to say about corporations?

When discussing whether corporations are moral agents, a good place to begin is with corporate legal history, that is, with the series of legislative acts and court decisions that have defined the corporation's existence. From its beginning in the Middle Ages, the corporation has been subject to differing legal interpretations. In the Middle Ages, the law did not recognize any profit-making organizations as corporations; instead, it granted corporate status only to guilds, boroughs, and the church. In some instances, the law decreed that corporations follow strict guidelines; for example, in 1279 the French Statute of Mortmain declared that a corporation's property could not exceed a specified amount. Even hundreds of years after its beginning, the corporation remained subject to strict legal sanctions on the conditions of its charter. As late as the nineteenth century, some U.S. corporations were granted charters only on the condition that they restrict land purchases to a certain geographic location and to a maximum number of acres. Thus corporations were viewed merely as artificial beings, created by the state and owing their very existence to a decree by the government.

But in the latter part of the nineteenth century and in the twentieth century, especially in the United States, this view changed dramatically. Instead of treating corporations as mere creations of the state, the courts began to see them as natural outcomes of the habits of businesspersons. It saw them as the predictable results of the actions of business persons who, exercising their inalienable right to associate freely with others, gathered together to conduct business and pursue a profit. As such, incorporation came to be seen less as a privilege granted by the state and more as a right to be protected by the state. Chartering a corporation became easier, and government restrictions less severe. Even so, the traditional view of a corporation continues to influence the law. The most accepted legal definition of a corporation remains the one offered by Chief Justice John Marshall in 1819: "A corporation is an artificial being, invisible, intangible, and existing only in the contemplation of law. Being the mere creation of law, it possesses only those properties which the charter of its creation confers upon it. . . ."

Throughout the evolution of corporation law, the problem of whether and how to ascribe responsibility to the corporation has persisted. In the sixteenth century, the large trading corporations were not held responsible when one ship collided with another; instead, the individual boat owners, who participated in the corporation only to secure special trading rights, were held individually responsible. By the seventeenth century, the notion of corporate responsibility was thoroughly established in the law, but some sticky issues remained. Could a corporation be criminally liable? What rights, if any, did corporations share with ordinary persons? In the early twentieth century and again in recent years, U.S. corporations have been charged with homicide. One such case involved the Ford Pinto's exploding gas tank. But in every instance so far, the court has stopped short of entering a verdict of homicide, although it has been willing to impose stiff fines.

In 1978 the U.S. Supreme Court delivered a landmark verdict in the case of *First National Bank of Boston v. Bellotti.* The fundamental issue was whether a corporation should be allowed the right to free speech even when exercising that right by spending corporate money to promote political causes not directly related to corporate profits. Should corporations have full-fledged first amendment rights to free speech even when that means that they can use their vast financial reserves to support partisan political ends? In a split decision the Supreme Court decided in favor of recognizing such a right, although the decision itself remains controversial.

Whatever the courts eventually decide about the legal status of a corporation, questions about its moral status will remain. While courts have upheld corporate rights to free speech, the federal government has tried to devise ways to hold corporations accountable for wrongdoing. As the article "The 'New' U.S. Sentencing Commission Guidelines" explains, in 1991 the United States Sentencing Commission instituted guidelines in order to encourage corporate compliance through the institution of ethics programs, establishing codes of conduct, the installation of ombudspeople, and other activities within the corporation to elicit appropriate managerial behavior. The idea is to encourage good corporate citizenship through internal standards of compliance. The Sentencing Guidelines pressure companies to develop standards of conduct, and they also help to protect other stakeholders and the public from corporate wrongdoing by imposing stiff financial penalties for noncompliance. In the years to follow, their effectiveness will be tested, demonstrated, and challenged.

Whether or not a corporation is a moral agent, it must adhere to certain norms of behavior. For example, at a minimum, a corporation must not deliberately kill or systematically harm others. But beyond specifying a bare minimum, what can one say? How can one *evaluate* corporate behavior from a moral perspective?

The case study "H. B. Fuller in Honduras" illustrates this issue. H. B. Fuller, a Minneapolis-based multinational corporation, is a well-managed company with the highest ethical standards. In 1995 it received a *Forbes* award for corporate ethics. But when what Fuller thought was an innocent product, glue, that it manufactures in Honduras, became the "sniffing drug of choice" by street children in Honduras, they were challenged, as a company, to reconsider their moral and social responsibilities.

How are we to understand the moral responsibility of a corporation? Does it extend to creating exemplary programs to deal with broad problems of public interest such as homelessness and child neglect in countries in which one operates? Does it extend to fighting proposed laws that the corporation opposes? In this section, we find three articles that help answer such questions. R. Edward Freeman's article, "Stakeholder Theory of the Modern Corporation," develops an increasingly popular concept in business ethics literature. Broadly defined, a stakeholder is any group or individual who can affect or is affected by a business. More narrowly conceived, stakeholders are individuals or groups of individuals who have defined role-relationships with the corporation or business in question. Under this more restricted definition, ordinarily primary stakeholders include shareholders, employees, and customers. Suppliers, other individuals or groups, and/or the community play a primary or secondary role, depending upon the particular firm and context. Notice that the stakeholder concept conflicts with the assumption that the moral responsibility of business is nothing other than profit maximization for shareholders (a view associated with Milton Friedman and examined in the previous section). It assumes, rather, that the firm has equal responsibilities to all its primary stakeholders. Thus the job of the manager is to weigh and balance the interests of a variety of stakeholders including, but not limited to, those of investors. Moreover, accountability relationships between an organization and its stakeholders are reciprocal; that is, "each can affect the other in terms of harms and benefits as well as rights and duties." So stakeholder relationships are normative relationships that entail, at a minimum, mutual respect between both parties.

In an article challenging Freeman's depiction of stakeholders, Kenneth Goodpaster argues that stakeholder *analysis* merely identifies stakeholders. He suggests that one must engage in stakeholder *synthesis;* that is, processes of moral reasoning that elicit moral judgment. Moreover, Goodpaster questions Freeman's multifiduciary approach to stakeholder analysis. Returning to Milton Friedman's argument that managers have fiduciary responsibilities to shareholders, Goodpaster enriches that analysis by claiming that managers have equally important nonfiduciary obligations to other stakeholders. This division of fiduciary and nonfiduciary responsibilities, Goodpaster contends, preserves the differences between various stakeholder relationships while enriching the moral dialogue that stakeholder analysis is designed to encourage.

One of the inevitable questions that arise in stakeholder theory is whether, or how, or on what grounds one evaluates stakeholder relationships. Freeman argues that stakeholder relationships entail a normative core, a set of normative theories that spell out how corporations should be governed and how managers should act. While refusing to commit himself to one set of moral considerations, Freeman acknowledges that respect for individuals and value creation are part of the normative core of all stakeholder relationships.

In retelling a dramatic true-to-life episode in which he played a role, Wall Street financier Bowen McCoy attempts to establish an analogy between personal and corporate ethics. When mountain climbing in the Himalaya Mountains, McCoy and his climbing party left a Sadhu, an Indian holy man, behind in the snow in order to achieve their goal of reaching the summit. What similarities, he asks, are there between this episode and decisions facing corporate managers? Equally important, what lessons from the behavior of McCoy's climbing party extend to the corporate organization and its obligations to its stakeholders?

Employee Rights and Responsibilities

A number of years ago the B. F. Goodrich Corporation became involved in serious ethical problems over the testing procedures it used in the fulfillment of a government contract for jet aircraft brakes. According to an account written by one of the company's employees, the pressures in this incident upon corporate employees, including those of job security and advancement, were so strong that they resulted in the falsifying of engineering specifications so that Goodrich could market dangerous and defective aircraft brakes. The dilemma of Kermit Vandivier, who finally "blew the whistle" on Goodrich, is a revealing illustration of some of the conflicts that can occur between self-interest, job responsibility, and one's sense of right and wrong.

This case illustrates a pressing contemporary concern: the relationship between employers and employees, especially in the area of employee rights. Do employees have rights in the workplace despite having voluntarily entered into a formal employee-employer relationship? For example, does a worker have the right to blow the whistle on a dangerous product without reprisal from management? Does he or she have a right to refuse a lie detector or polygraph test without being fired? Does he or she have the right to participate, directly or indirectly, in the management of the organization for which he or she works? And, what are the concomitant rights of employers vis-à-vis their employees? What might an employer justifiably and reasonably expect in terms of loyalty and trust from his or her employees? These questions are among those falling under the heading of "employee rights," and their discussion has become one of the most heated and controversial in the field of business ethics.

When talking about employee rights, a few philosophical distinctions about the concept of rights are in order. We take the concept of rights for granted, often forgetting that it was unknown only a few centuries ago. The first instance of the word in English appeared during the sixteenth century in the phrase "the rights of Englishmen." But these "rights" referred literally to Englishmen, not Englishwomen, and included only those who owned property. History waited for the English philosopher John Locke to provide the word "right" with its present, far-reaching significance. In Locke's writings, the word came to refer to something that, by definition, is possessed unconditionally by all rational adult human beings. The talk of rights in our own Declaration of Independence and Constitution owes much to Locke's early doctrine of rights.

Philosophers disagree about the precise definition of a *right*. Three of the most widely used definitions are (1) a right is a justified claim (for example, the right to freedom); (2) a right is an entitlement to something, held against someone else (for example, the right to equal protection is an entitlement which requires positive action on the part of others, including government); and (3) a right is a "trump" over a collective goal. The right to worship as one pleases, for example, overrides or trumps the collective goal of ideological unity within our society, and thus overrides any claims by certain groups or by a government that certain religions must be suppressed for the sake of the common good.

Rights may be divided into legal rights and moral rights. The former are rights that are either specified formally by law or protected by it. In the United States, the right to sue, to have a jury trial, to own property, and to have a free public education are legal rights. Not all such rights were included in the founding documents of the U.S. government: The right to free publication, the right of women and blacks to vote, and the right of workers to form unions were historical additions made in the nineteenth and twentieth centuries. Moral rights, on the other hand, are rights that are not necessarily protected and specified by the law. Moral rights are rights everyone has or should have, that is, they are normative claims about what people are entitled to, but they may not be universally recognized or incorporated into law. They would include, for example, the right to be treated with equal respect, the right to equal freedom, and the right not to be systematically deceived or harmed. The law might stop short of preventing private clubs, for instance, from excluding Jews and blacks, yet most of us would agree that Jews and blacks have a moral right in such situations not to be excluded. Similarly, for many years South African law perpetuated the apartheid system, yet few of us think that those laws were morally correct.

Turning to employee rights, although the Constitution and Bill of Rights protect the political rights of citizens, as late as 1946 the Supreme Court argued that the protection of the right to due process under the Fourteenth Amendment does not extend to private industry unless that particular business is performing a public function.[1] It is not that some rights are denied to employees in private industry, but rather that they are not always explicitly protected, nor are employers always restrained when rights are abrogated.

One of the most controversial issues in the area of employee rights, then, is whether, given that employees have some moral rights, those rights should remain only as *moral* rights or also be protected as *legal* rights. Until recently, the lack of protection of employee rights has been rationalized by appealing to the common-law doctrine of the principle of Employment at Will (EAW). This principle states that, in the absence of law or a specific contract, an employer may hire, fire, demote, or promote an employee whenever the employer wishes, and without having to give reasons or justify that action. In raising some issues about EAW in the article "Employment at Will and Due Process," Patricia Werhane and Tara Radin assert that the three grounds upon which EAW is typically defended are also grounds on which it can be attacked. As Richard Epstein argues, considerations of equal freedom, efficiency, and freedom of contract are often introduced in support of the prerogative of employers to fire "at will." But the grounds for defending EAW, inequality of freedom and power between employee and employer, inefficient outcomes, and violations of an employee's or employer's freedom of contract are also grounds on which it can be attacked. The problem is not so much the doctrine of EAW, per se, but the way in which it is interpreted to imply that managers, when dealing with "at will" employees, can act without having to give reasons for their actions, a phenomenon that is inexcusable in the exercise of other managerial decision making. At a minimum, Werhane and Radin argue, the reasonable free exercise of management requires that employees be given reasons, publicly stated and verifiable, for firing decisions. Due process is a means to institutionalize that requirement while protecting the employer from not being able to fire someone for *good* reasons.

Sissela Bok takes a hard look at one of the most difficult issues affecting Employment at Will and workplace freedom: whistleblowing. While she notes that the topic is rife with moral conflicts, she concludes that whistleblowing is often the only course available to a concerned employee. It is important, in turn, for any potential whistleblower to understand the broader panorama of issues against which whistleblowing occurs; for example, group loyalty, openness, authority, and the public interest. Equally important is the need for the employee to first exhaust less dramatic remedies before crying "foul" to the world. Only with such understanding, and by exploring alternative remedies, can an employee make an informed and correct decision about whether or not to blow the whistle.

One of the most serious issues facing late-twentieth-century business is the question of job security. It has often been argued that long-time good employees and managers have rights to their jobs. In a number of European countries and in Japan, companies often grant these rights, whereas in the United States "at will" employment has been the norm. In an interesting short article, Rosabeth Moss Kanter, an early defender of employee rights, introduces a new and challenging concept: "employability." While she does not make the case for lifetime employment in any one corporation, she argues that companies have obligations to train and retrain employees and managers so that they are *employable* in the changing markets of this and the next century. Thus, while managers may move from company to company with skills enhancement, they become flexible and adaptable to changing work environments.

Diversity

One important moral right that directly concerns business is the right of every person to be treated equally in matters of hiring, pay, and promotion. If a person may be said to have such rights, business managers presumably have corresponding obligations not to pursue discriminatory policies. For example, business organizations should be obliged to hire on the basis of applicant competence without being swayed by irrelevant factors such as gender, religion, race, or ethnic origin. Most business people today recognize this obligation, one that is enforced fully in the law. By the year 2000 less than 25 percent of all new hires will be white men. So how one integrates the workforce and treats an increasingly diverse population of employees is no longer merely a matter of philosophical or legal interest.

A more controversial issue is whether business has an obligation to go beyond the point of merely not discriminating, to take more positive steps of creating equal opportunities through policies of affirmative action. Affirmative action programs are of at least three sorts:

1. Those that pursue a policy of deliberately hiring and promoting equally qualified minorities and women when considering candidates for a position;
2. Those that pursue a policy of deliberately favoring qualified, but not necessarily equally qualified, minorities and women when hiring or promoting; and
3. Those that establish quota systems to regulate the percentage of minority members, hired or promoted in accordance with an ideal distribution of race, sex, creed, or ethnicity.

Although affirmative action is often misidentified as (3) above—that is, as promoting quota systems—in fact, almost all policies of affirmative action seek (1), to hire *equally* qualified minorities and women.

Perhaps the most common objection to affirmative action programs is that they are inconsistent; that is, that they make the same mistakes they hope to remedy. If discrimination entails using a morally irrelevant characteristic, such as a person's skin color, as a factor in hiring, is affirmative action itself perpetuating unjust discrimination? In giving preference to, say, blacks over whites, are such programs using the same morally irrelevant characteristic previously used in discriminatory practices, thus themselves committing discrimination?

Defenders of affirmative action argue that these programs are, all things considered, fair and consistent. They are not merely necessary to compensate past injustices in employment practices, injustices that clearly damaged the well being and prospects of many members of society. Rather, they are also necessary to guarantee fairness in hiring and promotion for future generations. How will minority applicants ever seriously compete for positions in, say, medical school unless the educational and economic opportunities for minorities and nonminorities are equalized? And, how will educational and economic opportunities be equalized unless minorities are able to attain a fair share of society's highest level of jobs? The current legalized ban of affirmative action initiatives in states such as California and Texas presents new challenges to equal opportunity.

While extremely important, affirmative action is only one of the issues at the center of the constellation of concerns involving race and sex, and discussions of affirmative action tend to focus on a narrow range of equal opportunity, that of hiring. In a controversial article that sheds new light on affirmative action, Peggy McIntosh points out that affirmative action argues for the equalizing of disadvantages. Seldom, however, do we recognize how being white or male is an advantage. Being white gives one implicit privileges that are neither acknowledged nor taken into account when questioning affirmative action programs. Being white *and* male offers more such privileges, all of which are simply due to one's race or gender, none of which is earned or deserved. Privilege is often accompanied by power, thus creating inevitable advantages that are hard to dismantle. McIntosh argues that race and gender inequalities will persist even with affirmative action programs until or unless we recognize, acknowledge, and work at changing unearned privileges of being white or white and male. McIntosh's analysis of privilege can also explain how gays in our society are disadvantaged by the fact of sexual orientation. The case study "Is This the Right Time to Come Out?" illustrates that homosexuals are at a disadvantage in corporate America.

"Ellen Moore in Bahrain" illustrates the existence of male privilege in another culture, bringing up the thorny issue of cultural differences in the treatment of women in the workplace. This case raises another concern, the changing role of women in corporate America. Felice N. Schwartz's "Management Women and the New Facts of Life" discusses aspects of this problem. It is one of the most discussed and controversial pieces to appear in the *Harvard Business Review*. It quickly became known as the "mommy-track" article because of its recommendation that women managers should be identified early by upper management as falling into one of two tracks: "career primary" and "career and family." This way, argues Schwartz, everyone gets what she wants. Career-primary women are not blamed for the fact that some women have more family-oriented commitments, career-and-family women are not blamed for not putting in lots of overtime hours, and corporate managers are able effectively to tap the full talent of the labor pool. In the responses to Schwartz's view that were printed later in the *Harvard Business Review,* many people, including active feminists, criticized

Schwartz's view as reactionary and wrong-headed. Not the least of their concerns is that such a view mistakenly turns an issue that is properly a *parenting* issue into something that is only a *women's* issue.

Sexual harassment has probably existed since the advent of employment, and to imagine that men and women working together will never produce sexual tension is naive at best. The existence of sexual harassment has been identified as a women's issue, although male managers have been subject to this phenomenon as well. With more women entering the workplace and assuming management positions, awareness of the existence of harassment has received a great deal of attention. One of the problems is in defining sexual harassment and distinguishing it from friendliness or harmless but verbally suggestive behavior. The article "Sexual Harassment" gives a number of examples of possible harassment incidents and suggests that it is, at best, difficult to equate sexual harassment with motives, with whether or not the person allegedly being harassed objects to the act, or whether or not the harassment produces negative consequences. Rather, sexual harassment is best evaluated on what counts as acceptable or unacceptable behavior. By specifying this behavior, the activity of sexual harassment is clearly defined, thus avoiding many pitfalls of misunderstandings.

Note

1. *Marsh v. State of Alabama*, 66 S. Ct. 276 (1946).

The Moral Responsibility of Corporations

➤ *Case Study* ➤

H. B. Fuller in Honduras:
Street Children and Substance Abuse

NORMAN E. BOWIE ➤ STEFANIE ANN LENWAY

In the summer of 1985 the following news story was brought to the attention of an official of the H. B. Fuller Company in St. Paul, Minnesota.

Glue Sniffing Among Honduran Street Children in Honduras: Children Sniffing Their Lives Away

AN INTER PRESS SERVICE FEATURE
BY PETER FORD

Tegucigalpa July 16, 1985 (IPS)—They lie senseless on doorsteps and pavements, grimy and loose limbed, like discarded rag dolls.

Some are just five or six years old. Others are already young adults, and all are addicted to sniffing a commonly sold glue that is doing them irreversible brain damage.

Roger, 21, has been sniffing "Resistol" for eight years. Today, even when he is not high, Roger walks with a stagger, his motor control wrecked. His scarred face puckers with concentration, his right foot taps nervously, incessantly, as he talks.

Since he was 11, when he ran away from the aunt who raised him, Roger's home has been the streets of the capital of Honduras, the second poorest nation in the western hemisphere after Haiti.

Roger spends his time begging, shining shoes, washing car windows, scratching together a few pesos a day, and sleeping in doorways at night.

Sniffing glue, he says, "makes me feel happy, makes me feel big. What do I care if my family does not love me? I know it's doing me damage, but it's a habit I have got, and a habit's a habit. I can not give it up, even though I want to."

No one knows how many of Tegucigalpa's street urchins seek escape from the squalor and misery of their daily existence through the hallucinogenic fumes of "Resistol." No one has spent the time and money needed to study the question.

But one thing is clear, according to Dr. Rosalio Zavala, Head of the Health Ministry's Mental Health Department,

234

"these children come from the poorest slums of the big cities. They have grown up as illegal squatters in very disturbed states of mental health, tense, depressed, aggressive.

"Some turn that aggression on society, and start stealing. Others turn it on themselves, and adopt self destructive behavior . . ."

But, he understands the attraction of the glue, whose solvent, toluene, produces feelings of elation. "It gives you delusions of grandeur, you feel powerful, and that compensates these kids for reality, where they feel completely worthless, like nobodies."

From the sketchy research he has conducted, Dr. Zavala believes that most boys discover Resistol for the first time when they are about 11, though some children as young as five are on their way to becoming addicts.

Of a small sample group of children interviewed in reform schools here, 56 percent told Zavala that friends introduced them to the glue, but it is easy to find on the streets for oneself.

Resistol is a contact cement glue, widely used by shoe repairers, and available at household goods stores everywhere . . .

In some states of the United States, glue containing addictive narcotics such as toluene must also contain oil of mustard—the chemical used to produce poisonous mustard gas—which makes sniffing the glue so painful it is impossible to tolerate. There is no federal U.S. law on the use of oil of mustard, however . . .

But even for Dr. Zavala, change is far more than a matter of just including a chemical compound, such as oil of mustard, in a contact cement.

"This is a social problem," he acknowledges. "What we need is a change in philosophy, a change in social organization."

Resistol is manufactured by H. B. Fuller S. A., a subsidiary of Kativo Chemical Industries, S. A. which in turn is a wholly owned subsidiary of the H. B. Fuller Company of St. Paul, Minnesota.[1] Kativo sells more than a dozen different adhesives under the Resistol brand name in several countries in Latin America for a variety of industrial and commercial applications. In Honduras the Resistol products have a strong market position.

Three of the Resistol products are solvent-based adhesives designed with certain properties that are not possible to attain with a water-based formula. These properties include rapid set, strong adhesion, and water resistance. These products are similar to airplane glue or rubber cement and are primarily intended for use in shoe manufacturing and repair, leatherwork, and carpentry.

Even though the street children of each Central American country may have a different choice of a drug for substance abuse, and even though Resistol is not the only glue that Honduran street children use as an inhalant, the term "Resistolero" stuck and has become synonymous with all street children, whether they use inhalants or not. In Honduras Resistol is identified as the abused substance.

Edward Sheehan writes in *Agony in the Garden:*

> Resistol. I had heard about Resistol. It was a glue, the angel dust of Honduran orphans. . . . In Tegucigalpa, their addiction had become so common they were known as los Resistoleros. (p. 32)

Honduras[2]

The social problems that contribute to widespread inhalant abuse among street children can be attributed to the depth of poverty in Honduras. In 1989, 65 percent of all households and 40 percent of urban households in Honduras were living in poverty, making it one of the poorest countries in Latin America. Between 1950 and 1988, the increase in the Honduran gross domestic product (GDP) was 3.8 percent, only slightly greater than the average yearly increase in population growth. In 1986, the Honduran GDP was about U.S. $740 per capita and has only grown slightly since. Infant and child mortality rates are high, life expectancy for adults is 64 years, and the adult literacy rate is estimated to be about 60 percent.

Honduras has faced several economic obstacles in its efforts to industrialize. First, it lacks abundant natural resources. The mountainous terrain has restricted agricultural productivity and growth. In addition, the small domestic market and competition from more industrially advanced countries has prevented the manufacturing sector from progressing much beyond textiles, food processing, and assembly operations.

The key to the growth of the Honduran economy has been the production and export of two commodities—bananas and coffee. Both the vagaries in the weather and the volatility of commodity markets had made the foreign exchange earned from these products very unstable. Without consistently strong export sales, Honduras has not been able to buy sufficient fuel and other productive input to allow the growth of its manufacturing sector. It also had to import basic grains (corn and rice) because the country's traditional staples are produced inefficiently by small farmers using traditional technologies with poor soil.

In the 1970s the Honduran government relied on external financing to invest in physical and social infrastructures and to implement development programs intended to diversify the economy. Government spending increased 10.4 percent a year from 1973. By 1981, the failure of many of these development projects led the government to stop financing state-owned industrial projects. The public sector failures were attributed to wasteful administration, mismanagement, and corruption. Left with little increase in productivity to show for these investments, Honduras continues to face massive budgetary deficits and unprecedented levels of external borrowing.

The government deficit was further exacerbated in the early 1980s by increasing levels of unemployment. By 1983, unemployment reached 20–30 percent of the economically active population, with an additional 40 percent of the population underemployed, primarily in agriculture. The rising unemployment, falling real wages, and low level of existing social infrastructure in education and health care contributed to the low level of labor productivity. Unemployment benefits were very limited and only about 7.3 percent of the population was covered by social security.

Rural-to-urban migration has been a major contributor to urban growth in Honduras. In the 1970s the urban population grew at more than twice as fast a rate as the rural population. This migration has increased in part as a result of a high birth rate among the rural population, along with a move by large landholders to convert forest and fallow land, driving off subsistence farmers to use the land for big-scale cotton and beef farming. As more and more land was enclosed, an increasing number of landless sought the cities for a better life.

Tegucigalpa, the capital, has had one of the fastest population increases among Central American cities, growing by 178,000 between 1970 and 1980, with a projected population of 975,000 by the year 2000. Honduras' second largest city, San Pedro Sula, is projected to have a population of 650,000 by 2000.

The slow growth in the industrial and commercial sectors has not been adequate to provide jobs for those moving to the city. The migrants to the urban areas typically move first to cuarterias (rows) of connected rooms. The rooms are generally constructed of wood with dirt floors, and they are usually windowless. The average household contains about seven persons, who live together in a single room. For those living in the rooms facing an alley, the narrow passageway between buildings serves both as sewage and waste disposal area and as a courtyard for as many as 150 persons.

Although more than 70 percent of the families living in these cuarterias had one member with a permanent salaried job, few could survive on that income alone. For stable extended families, salaried income is supplemented by entrepreneurial activities, such as selling tortillas. Given migratory labor, high unemployment, and income insecurity many family relationships are unstable. Often the support of children is left to mothers. Children are frequently forced to leave school, helping support the family through shining shoes, selling newspapers, or guarding cars; such help often is essential income. If a lone mother has become sick or dies, her children may be abandoned to the streets.

Kativo Chemical Industries S.A.[3]

Kativo celebrated its 40th anniversary in 1989. It is now one of the 500 largest private corporations in Latin America. In 1989, improved sales in most of Central America were partially offset by a reduction of its sales in Honduras.

Walter Kissling, chairman of Kativo's board and senior vice president for H. B. Fuller's international operations, has the reputation of giving the company's local managers a high degree of autonomy. Local managers often have to respond quickly because of unexpected currency fluctuations. He comments that, "In Latin America, if you know what you are doing, you can make more money managing your balance sheet than by selling products." The emphasis on managing the balance sheet in countries with high rates of inflation has led Kativo managers to develop a distinctive competence in finance.

In spite of the competitive challenge of operating under unstable political and economic conditions Kativo managers emphasized in the annual report the importance of going beyond the bottom line:

> Kativo is an organization with a profound philosophy and ethical conduct, worthy of the most advanced firms. It carries out business with the utmost respect for ethical and legal principles and its orientation is not solely directed to the

customer, who has the highest priority, but also to the shareholders, and communities where it operates.

In the early 1980s the managers of Kativo, which was primarily a paint company, decided to enter the adhesive market in Latin America. Their strategy was to combine their marketing experience with H. B. Fuller's products. Kativo found the adhesive market potentially profitable in Latin America because it lacked strong competitors. Kativo's initial concern was to win market share. Resistol was the brand name for all adhesive products including the water-based school glue.

Kativo and the Street Children

In 1983, Honduran newspapers carried articles about police arrests of "Resistoleros"—street children drugging themselves by sniffing glue. In response to these newspaper articles, Kativo's Honduras advertising agency, Calderon Publicidad, informed the newspapers that Resistol was not the only substance abused by street children and that the image of the manufacturer was being damaged by using a prestigious trademark as a synonym for drug abusers. Moreover glue sniffing was not caused by something inherent in the product but was a social problem. For example, on one occasion the company complained to the editor, requesting that he "make the necessary effort to recommend to the editorial staff that they abstain from using the brand name Resistol as a synonym for the drug, and the adjective Resistolero as a synonym for the drug addict."

The man on the spot was Kativo's Vice President, Humberto Larach ("Beto"), a Honduran, who headed Kativo's North Adhesives Division. Managers in nine countries including all of Central America, Mexico, the Caribbean and two South American countries, Ecuador and Colombia, reported to him. He had became manager of the adhesive division after demonstrating his entrepreneurial talents managing Kativo's paint business in Honduras.

Beto had proven his courage and his business creativity when he was among 105 taken hostage in the Chamber of Commerce building in downtown San Pedro Sula by guerrillas from the Communist Popular Liberation Front. Despite fire fights between the guerrillas and government troops, threats of execution, and being used as a human shield, Beto had sold his product to two clients (fellow hostages) who had previously been buying products from Kativo's chief competitor! Beto also has a reputation for emphasizing the importance of "Making the bottom line," as a part of Kativo corporate culture.

By summer 1985, more than corporate image was at stake. As a solution to the glue sniffing problem social activists working with street children suggested that oil of mustard, allyl isothiocyanate, could be added to the product to prevent its abuse. They argued that a person attempting to sniff glue with oil of mustard added would find it too powerful to tolerate. Sniffing it has been described like getting an "overdose of horseradish." An attempt to legislate the addition of oil of mustard received a boost when Honduran Peace Corps volunteer, Timothy Bicknell, convinced a local group called the "Committee for the Prevention of Drugs at the National Level," of the necessity of adding oil of mustard to Resistol. All members of the committee were prominent members of Honduran society.

Beto, in response to the growing publicity about the "Resistoleros," requested staff members of H. B. Fuller's U.S. headquarters to look into the viability of oil of mustard as a solution with special attention to side effects and whether it was required or used in the U.S. H. B. Fuller's corporate industrial hygiene staff found 1983 toxicology reports that oil of mustard was a cancer-causing agent in tests run with rats. A 1986 toxicology report from the Aldrich Chemical Company described the health hazard data of allyl isothiocyanate as:

Acute Effects

May be fatal if inhaled, swallowed, or absorbed through skin.
Carcinogen.
Causes burns.
Material is extremely destructive to tissue of the mucous membranes and upper respiratory tract, eyes and skin.

Prolonged Contact Can Cause:

Nausea, dizziness and headache.
Severe irritation or burns.
Lung irritation, chest pain and edema which may be fatal.
Repeated exposure may cause asthma.

In addition the product had a maximum shelf-life of six months.

To the best of our knowledge, the chemical, physical and toxicological properties have not been thoroughly investigated.

In 1986, Beto contacted Hugh Young, president of Solvent Abuse Foundation for Education (SAFE), and gathered information on programs SAFE had developed in Mexico. Young, who believed that there was no effective deterrent, took the position that the only viable approach to substance abuse was education, not product modification. He argued that reformulating the product was an exercise in futility because "nothing is available in the solvent area that is not abusable." With these reports in hand, Beto attempted to persuade Resistol's critics, relief agencies, and government officials that adding oil of mustard to Resistol was not the solution to the glue sniffing problem.

During the summer of 1986 Beto had his first success in changing the mind of one journalist. Earlier in the year Mary Kawas, an independent writer, wrote an article sympathetic to the position of Timothy Bicknell and the Committee for the Prevention of Drugs in Honduras. In June, Beto met with her and explained how both SAFE and Kativo sought a solution that was not product-oriented but that was directed at changing human behavior. She was also informed of the research on the dangers of oil of mustard (about which additional information had been obtained). Kawas then wrote an article:

Education Is the Solution for Drug Addiction

LA CEIBA. (BY MARIE J. KAWAS).

A lot of people have been interested in combating drug addiction among youths and children, but few have sought solutions, and almost no one looks into the feasibility of the alternatives that are so desperately proposed . . .

Oil of mustard (allyl isothiocyanate) may well have been an irresponsible solution in the United States of America during the sixties and seventies, and the Hondurans want to adopt this as a panacea without realizing that their information sources are out of date. Through scientific progress, it has been found that the inclusion of oil of mustard in products which contain solvents, in order to prevent their perversion into use as an addictive drug, only causes greater harm to the consumers and workers involved in their manufacture . . .

Education is a primordial instrument for destroying a social cancer. An effort of this magnitude requires the cooperation of different individuals and organizations . . .

Future generations of Hondurans will be in danger of turning into human parasites, without a clear awareness of what is harmful to them. But if drugs and ignorance are to blame, it is even more harmful to sin by indifference before those very beings who are growing up in an environment without the basic advantages for a healthy physical and mental existence. Who will be the standard bearer in the philanthropic activities which will provide Honduras with the education necessary to combat drug addiction? Who will be remiss in their duty in the face of the nation's altruism?

At first, Beto did not have much success at the governmental level. In September 1986, Dr. Rosalio Zavala, Head of the Mental Health Division of the Honduran Ministry of Health, wrote an article attacking the improper use of Resistol by youth. Beto was unsuccessful in his attempt to contact Dr. Zavala. He had better luck with Mrs. Norma Castro, Governor of the State of Cortes, who after a conversation with Beto became convinced that oil of mustard had serious dangers and that glue sniffing was a social problem.

Beto's efforts continued into the new year. Early in 1987, Kativo began to establish Community Affairs Councils, as a planned expansion of the worldwide company's philosophy of community involvement. These employee committees had already been in place in the U.S. since 1978.

A company document gave the purpose of Community Affairs Councils:

To educate employees about community issues.

To develop understanding of, and be responsive to the communities near our facilities.

To contribute to Kativo/H. B. Fuller's corporate presence in the neighborhoods and communities we are a part of.

To encourage and support employee involvement in the community.

To spark a true interest in the concerns of the communities in which we live and work.

The document goes on to state, "We want to be more than just bricks, mortar, machines and people. We want to be a company with recognized values, demonstrating involvement, and commitment to the betterment of the communities we are a part of." Later that year, the Honduran community affairs committees went on to make contributions to several organizations working with street children.

In May 1987, Beto visited Jose Oqueli, Vice-Minister of Public Health, to explain the philosophy behind H. B. Fuller's Community Affairs program. He also informed him of the health hazards of oil of mustard; they discussed the cultural, family and economic roots of the problem of glue-sniffing among street children.

In June 1987, Parents Resource Institute for Drug Education (PRIDE) set up an office in San Pedro Sula. PRIDE's philosophy was that through adequate *parental* education on the drug problem, it would be possible to deal with the problems of inhalant use. PRIDE was a North American organization that had taken international Nancy Reagan's "just say no" approach to inhalant abuse. Like SAFE, PRIDE took the position that oil of mustard was not the solution to glue-sniffing.

Through PRIDE, Beto was introduced to Wilfredo Alvarado, the new Head of the Mental Health Division in the Ministry of Health. Dr. Alvarado, an advisor to the Congressional Committee on Health, was in charge of preparing draft legislation and evaluating legislation received by Congress. Together with Dr. Alvarado, the Kativo staff worked to prepare draft legislation addressing the problem of inhalant addicted children. At the same time, five Congressmen drafted a proposed law that required the use of oil of mustard in locally produced or imported solvent based adhesives.

In June 1988, Dr. Alvarado asked the Congressional Committee on Health to reject the legislation proposed by the five congressmen. Alvarado was given 60 days to present a complete draft of legislation. In August 1988, however, he retired from his position and Kativo lost its primary communication channel with the Committee. This was critical because Beto was relying on Alvarado to help insure that the legislation reflected the technical information that he had collected.

The company did not have an active lobbying or government monitoring function in Tegucigalpa, the capital, which tends to be isolated from the rest of the country. (In fact, the company's philosophy has generally been not to lobby on behalf of its own narrow self-interest.) Beto, located in San Pedro Sula, had no staff support to help him monitor political developments. Monitoring, unfortunately, was an addition to his regular, daily responsibilities. His ability to keep track of political developments were made more difficult by the fact that he traveled about 45 percent of the time outside of Honduras. It took over two months for Beto to learn of Alvarado's departure from government. When the legislation was passed in March, he was completely absorbed in reviewing strategic plans for the nine-country divisions which report to him.

On March 30, 1989, the Honduran Congress approved the legislation drafted by the five congressmen.

After the law's passage Beto spoke to the press about the problems with the legislation. He argued:

> This type of cement is utilized in industry, in crafts, in the home, schools, and other places where it has become indispensable; thus by altering the product,

he said, not only will the drug addiction problem not be solved, but rather, the country's development would be slowed.

In order to put an end to the inhalation of Resistol by dozens of people, various products which are daily necessities would have to be eliminated from the marketplace. This is impossible, he added, since it would mean a serious setback to industry at several levels . . .

There are studies that show that the problem is not the glue itself, but rather the individual. The mere removal of this substance would immediately be substituted by some other, to play the same hallucinogenic trip for the person who was sniffing it.

H. B. Fuller: The Corporate Response

In late April 1986, Elmer Andersen, H. B. Fuller Chairman of the Board, received the following letter:

4/21/86

Elmer L. Andersen
H. B. Fuller Co.

Dear Mr. Andersen

I heard part of your talk on public radio recently, and was favorably impressed with your philosophy that business should not be primarily for profit. This was consistent with my previous impression of H. B. Fuller Co. since I am a public health nurse and have been aware of your benevolence to the nursing profession.

However, on a recent trip to Honduras, I spent some time at a new home for chemically dependent "street boys" who are addicted to glue sniffing. It was estimated that there are 600 of these children still on the streets in San Pedro Sula alone. The glue is sold for repairing *tennis shoes* and I am told it is made by H. B. Fuller in *Costa Rica*. These children also suffer toxic effects of liver and brain damage from the glue . . .

Hearing you on the radio, I immediately wondered how this condemnation of H. B. Fuller Company could be consistent with the company as I knew it before and with your business philosophy.

Are you aware of this problem in Honduras, and, if so, how are you dealing with it?

That a stockholder should write the 76-year-old Chairman of the Board directly is significant. Elmer Andersen is a legendary figure in Minnesota. He is responsible for the financial success of H. B. Fuller from 1941–1971 and his values reflected in his actions as CEO are embodied in H. B. Fuller's mission statement.

H. B. Fuller Mission Statement

The H. B. Fuller corporate mission is to be a leading and profitable worldwide formulator, manufacturer, and marketer of quality specialty chemicals, emphasizing service to customers and managed in accordance with a strategic plan.

H. B. Fuller Company is committed to its responsibilities, in order of priority, to its customers, employees and shareholders. H. B. Fuller will conduct business legally and ethically, support the activities of its employees in their communities, and be a responsible corporate citizen.

It was also Elmer Andersen who, as President and CEO, made the decision that foreign acquisitions should be managed by locals. Concerning the 1967 acquisition of Kativo Chemical Industries Ltd. Elmer Andersen said:

We had two objectives in mind. One was directly business related and one was altruistic. Just as we had expanded in America, our international business strategy was to pursue markets where our competitors were not active. We were convinced that we had something to offer Latin America that the region did not have locally. In our own small way, we also wanted to be of help to that part of the world. We believed that by producing adhesives in Latin America and by employing only local people, we would create new jobs and help elevate the standard of living. We were convinced that the way to aid world peace was to help Latin America become more prosperous.

Three years later a stockholder dramatically raised the Resistol issue for a second time directly by a stockholder. On June 7, 1989, Vice President for Corporate Relations, Dick Johnson, received a call from a stockholder whose daughter was in the Peace Corps in Honduras. She asked, "How can a company like H. B. Fuller claim to have a social conscience and continue to sell Resistol which is 'literally burning out the brains' of children in Latin America?"

Johnson was galvanized into action. This complaint was of special concern because he was about to meet with a national group of socially responsible investors who were considering including H. B. Fuller's stock in their portfolio. Fortunately Karen Muller, Director of Community Affairs, had been keeping a file on the glue sniffing problem. Within 24 hours of receiving the call, Dick had written a memo to CEO Tony Andersen.

In that memo he set forth the basic values to be considered as H. B. Fuller wrestled with the problem. Among them were the following:

1. H. B. Fuller's explicitly stated public concern about substance abuse.
2. H. B. Fuller's "Concern for Youth" focus in its community affairs projects.
3. H. B. Fuller's reputation as a socially responsible company.
4. H. B. Fuller's history of ethical conduct.
5. H. B. Fuller's commitment to the intrinsic value of each individual.

Whatever "solution" was ultimately adopted would have to be consistent with these values. In addition, Dick suggested a number of options including the company's withdrawal from the market or perhaps altering the formula to make Resistol a water-based product, eliminating sniffing as an issue.

Tony responded by suggesting that Dick create a task force to find a solution and a plan to implement it. Dick decided to accept Beto's invitation to travel to Honduras to view the situation first hand. He understood that the problem crossed functional and divisional responsibilities. Given H. B. Fuller's high visibility as a socially responsible corporation, the glue sniffing problem had the potential for becoming a public relations nightmare. The brand name of one of H. B. Fuller's products had become synonymous with a serious social problem. Additionally, Dick understood that there was an issue larger than product misuse involved, and it had social and community ramifications. The issue was substance abuse by children, whether the substance is a H. B. Fuller product or not. As a part of the solution, a community relations response was required. Therefore, he invited Karen to join him on his trip to Honduras.

Karen recalled a memo she had written about a year earlier directed to Beto. In it she had suggested a community relations approach rather than Beto's government relations approach. In that memo Karen wrote:

> This community relations process involves developing a community-wide coalition from all those with a vested interest in solving the community issue—those providing services in dealing with the street children and drug users, other businesses, and the government. It does require leadership over the long-term both with a clear set of objectives and a commitment on the part of each group represented to share in the solution . . .

In support of the community relations approach Karen argued that:

1. It takes the focus and pressure off H. B. Fuller as one individual company.
2. It can educate the broader community and focus on the best solution, not just the easiest ones.
3. It holds everyone reponsible, the government, educators, H. B. Fuller's customers, legitimate consumers of our product, social service workers and agencies.
4. It provides H. B. Fuller with an expanded good image as a company that cares and will stay with the problem—that we are willing to go the second mile.
5. It can de-politicize the issue.
6. It offers the opportunity to counterbalance the negative impact of the use of our product named Resistol by re-identifying the problem.

Karen and Dick left on a four-day trip to Honduras September 18. Upon arriving they were joined by Beto, Oscar Sahuri, General Manager for Kativo's adhesives business in Honduras, and Jorge Walter Bolanos, Vice-President Director of Finance, Kativo. Karen had also asked Mark Connelly, a health consultant from an international agency working with street children, to join the group. They began the process of looking at all aspects of the situation. Visits to two different small shoe manufacturing shops and a shoe supply distributor helped to clarify the issues around pricing, sales, distribution, and the packaging of the product.

A visit to a well-run shelter for street children provided them with some insight into the dynamics of substance abuse among this vulnerable population in the streets of Tegucigalpa and San Pedro Sula. At a meeting with the officials at the Ministry of Health, they reviewed the issue of implementing the oil-of-mustard law, and the Kativo managers offered to assist the committee as it reviewed the details of the law. In both Tegucigalpa and San Pedro Sula, the National Commission for Technical Assistance to

Children in Irregular Situations (CONATNSI), a county-wide association of private and public agencies working with street children, organized meetings of its members at which the Kativo managers offered an explanation of the company's philosophy and the hazards involved in the use of oil of mustard.

As they returned from their trip to Honduras, Karen and Dick had the opportunity to reflect on what they had learned. They agreed that removing Resistol from the market would not resolve the problem. However, the problem was extremely complex. The use of inhalants by street children was a symptom of Honduras' underlying economic problems—problems with social, cultural, and political aspects as well as economic dimensions.

Honduran street children come from many different circumstances. Some are true orphans while others are abandoned. Some are runaways, while others are working the streets to help support their parents. Children working at street jobs or begging usually earn more than the minimum wage. Nevertheless, they are often punished if they bring home too little. This creates a vicious circle; they would rather be on the street than take punishment at home—a situation that increases the likelihood they will fall victim to drug addiction. The street children's problems are exacerbated by the general lack of opportunities and a lack of enforcement of school attendance laws. In addition, the police sometimes abuse street children.

Karen and Dick realized that Resistol appeared to be the drug of choice for young street children, and children were able to obtain it in a number of different ways. There was no clear pattern, and hence the solution could not be found in simply changing some features of the distribution system. Children might obtain the glue from legitimate customers, small shoe repair stalls, by theft, from "illegal" dealers or from third parties who purchased it from legitimate stores and then sold it to children. For some sellers the sale of Resistol to children could be profitable. The glue was available in small packages which made it more affordable, but the economic circumstances of the typical legitimate customer made packaging in small packages economically sensible.

The government had long been unstable. As a result there was a tendency for people working with the government to hope that new policy initiatives would fade away within a few months. Moreover there was a large continuing turnover of government, so that any knowledge of H. B. Fuller and its corporate philosophy soon disappeared. Government officials usually had to settle for a quick fix, for they were seldom around long enough to manage any other kind of policy. Although it was on the books for six months by the time of their trip, the oil-of-mustard law had not yet been implemented, and national elections were to be held in three months. During meetings with government officials, it appeared to Karen and Dick that no further actions would be taken as current officials waited for the election outcome.

Kativo company officers, Jorge Walter Bolanos and Humberto Larach discussed continuing the government relations strategy, hoping that the law might be repealed or modified. They were also concerned with the damage done to H. B. Fuller's image. Karen and Dick thought the focus should be on community relations. From their perspective, efforts directed toward changing the law seemed important but would do nothing to help with the long-term solution to the problems of the street children who abused glue.

Much of the concern for street children was found in private agencies. The chief coordinating association was CONATNSI, created as a result of a seminar sponsored by UNICEF in 1987. CONATNSI was under the direction of a general assembly and a Board of Directors elected by the General Assembly. It began its work in 1988; its objectives included a) improving the quality of services, b) promoting interchange of experiences, c) coordinating human and material resources, d) offering technical support, and e) promoting research. Karen and others believe that CONATNSI had a shortage of both financial and human resources, but it appeared to be well-organized and was a potential intermediary for the company.

As a result of their trip, they knew that a community relations strategy would be complex and risky. H. B. Fuller was committed to a community relations approach, but what would a community relations solution look like in Honduras? The mission statement did not provide a complete answer. It indicated the company had responsibilities to its Honduran customers and employees, but exactly what kind? Were there other responsibilities beyond that directly involving its product? What effect can a single company have in solving an intractable social problem? How should the differing emphases in perspective of Kativo and its parent, H. B. Fuller, be handled? What does corporate citizenship require in situations like this?

Notes

1. The Subsidiaries of the North Adhesives Division of Kativo Chemical Industries, S.A. go by the name "H. B. Fuller (Country of Operation)," e.g., H. B. Fuller S. A. Honduras. To prevent confusion with the parent company we will refer to H. B. Fuller S. A. Honduras by the name of its parent, "Kativo."
2. The following discussion is based on *Honduras: A Country Study*, 2nd ed., James D. Rudolph, ed. (Washington, D.C.: Department of the Army, 1984).
3. Unless otherwise indicated all references and quotations regarding H. B. Fuller and its subsidiary Kativo Chemical Industries S. A. are from company documents.

Sources

Acker, Alison, *The Making of a Banana Republic* (Boston: South End Press, 1988).

H. B. Fuller Company, *A Fuller Life: The Story of H. B. Fuller Company: 1887–1987* (St. Paul: H. B. Fuller Company, 1986).

Rudolph, James D., ed., *Honduras: A Country Study*, 2nd ed. (Washington, D.C.: Department of the Army, 1984).

Schine, Eric, "Preparing for Banana Republic U.S." *Corporate Finance* (December, 1987).

Sheehan, Edward, *Agony in the Garden: A Stranger in Central America* (Boston: Houghton Mifflin, 1989).

Stakeholder Theory of the Modern Corporation

R. Edward Freeman

INTRODUCTION

Corporations have ceased to be merely legal devices through which the private business transactions of individuals may be carried on. Though still much used for this purpose, the corporate form has acquired a larger significance. The corporation has, in fact, become both a method of property tenure and a means of organizing economic life. Grown to tremendous proportions, there may be said to have evolved a "corporate system"—which has attracted to itself a combination of attributes and powers, and has attained a degree of prominence entitling it to be dealt with as a major social institution.[1]

Despite these prophetic words of Berle and Means (1932), scholars and managers alike continue to hold sacred the view that managers bear a special relationship to the stockholders in the firm. Since stockholders own shares in the firm, they have certain rights and privileges, which must be granted to them by management, as well as by others. Sanctions, in the form of "the law of corporations," and other protective mechanisms in the form of social custom, accepted management practice, myth, and ritual, are thought to reinforce the assumption of the primacy of the stockholder.

The purpose of this chapter is to pose several challenges to this assumption, from within the framework of managerial capitalism, and to suggest the bare bones of an alternative theory, *a stakeholder theory of the modern corporation*. I do not seek the demise of the modern corporation, either intellectually or in fact. Rather, I seek its transformation. In the words of Neurath, we shall attempt to "rebuild the ship, plank by plank, while it remains afloat."[2]

My thesis is that I can revitalize the concept of managerial capitalism by replacing the notion that managers have a duty to stockholders with the concept that managers bear a fiduciary relationship to stakeholders. Stakeholders are those groups who have a stake in or claim on the firm. Specifically I include suppliers, customers, employees, stockholders, and the local community, as well as management in its role as agent for these groups. I argue that the legal, economic, political, and moral challenges to the currently received theory of the firm, as a nexus of contracts among the owners of the factors of production and customers, require us to revise this concept. That is, each of these stakeholder groups has a right not to be treated as a means to some end, and therefore must participate in determining the future direction of the firm in which they have a stake.

The crux of my argument is that we must reconceptualize the firm around the following question: For whose benefit and at whose expense should the firm be managed? I shall set forth such a reconceptualization in the form of a *stakeholder theory of the firm*. I shall then critically examine the stakeholder view and its implication for the future of the capitalist system.

THE ATTACK ON MANAGERIAL CAPITALISM

The Legal Argument

The basic idea of managerial capitalism is that in return for controlling the firm, management vigorously pursues the interests of stockholders. Central to the managerial view of the firm is the idea that management can pursue market transactions with suppliers and customers in an unconstrained manner.

The law of corporations gives a less clearcut answer to the question: In whose interest and for whose benefit should the modern corporation be governed? While it says that the corporations should be run primarily in the interests of the stockholders in the firm, it says further that the corporation exists "in contemplation of the law" and has personality as a "legal person," limited liability for its actions, and immortality, since its existence transcends that of its members. Therefore, directors and other officers of the firm have a fiduciary obligation to stockholders in the sense that the "affairs of the corporation" must be conducted in the interest of the stockholders. And stockholders can theoretically bring suit against those directors and managers for doing otherwise. But since the corporation is a legal person, existing in contemplation of the law, managers of the corporation are constrained by law.

Until recently, this was no constraint at all. In this century, however, the law has evolved to effectively constrain the pursuit of stockholder interests at the expense of other claimants on the firm. It has, in effect, required that the claims of customers, suppliers, local communities, and employees be taken into consideration, though in general they are subordinated to the claims of stockholders.

For instance, the doctrine of "privity of contract," as articulated in *Winterbottom v. Wright* in 1842, has been eroded by recent developments in products liability law. Indeed, *Greenman v. Yuba Power* gives the manufacturer strict liability for damage caused by its products, even though the seller has exercised all possible care in the preparation and sale of the product and the consumer has not bought the product from nor entered into any contractual arrangement with the manufacturer. Caveat emptor has been replaced, in large part, with caveat venditor.[3] The Consumer Product Safety Commission has the power to enact product recalls, and in 1980 one U.S. automobile company recalled more cars than it built. Some industries are required to provide information to customers about a product's ingredients, whether or not the customers want and are willing to pay for this information.[4]

The same argument is applicable to management's dealings with employees. The National Labor Relations Act gave employees the right to unionize and to bargain in good faith. It set up the National Labor Relations Board to enforce these rights with management. The Equal Pay Act of 1963 and Title VII of the Civil Rights Act of 1964 constrain management from discrimination in hiring practices; these have been followed with the Age Discrimination in Employment Act of 1967.[5] The emergence of a body of administrative case law arising from labor-management disputes and the historic settling of discrimination claims with large employers such as AT&T have caused the emergence of a body of practice in the corporation that is consistent with the legal guarantee of the rights of the employees. The law has protected the due process rights of those employees who enter into collective bargaining agreements with management. As of the present, however, only 30 percent of the labor force are participating in such agreements; this has prompted one labor law scholar to propose a statutory law prohibiting dismissals of the 70 percent of the work force not protected.[6]

The law has also protected the interests of local communities. The Clean Air Act and Clean Water Act have constrained management from "spoiling the commons." In an historic case, *Marsh v. Alabama*, the Supreme Court ruled that a company-owned town has subject to the provisions of the U.S. Constitution, thereby guaranteeing the rights of local citizens and negating the "property rights" of the firm. Some states and municipalities have gone further and passed laws preventing firms from moving plants or limiting when and how plants can be closed. In sum, there is much current legal activity in this area to constrain management's pursuit of stockholders' interests at the expense of the local communities in which the firm operates.

I have argued that the result of such changes in the legal system can be viewed as giving some rights to those groups that have a claim on the firm, for example, customers, suppliers, employees, local communities, stockholders, and management. It raises the question, at the core of a theory of the firm: In whose interest and for whose benefit should the firm be managed? The answer proposed by managerial capitalism is clearly "the stockholders," but I have argued that the law has been progressively circumscribing this answer.

The Economic Argument

In its pure ideological form managerial capitalism seeks to maximize the interests of stockholders. In its perennial criticism of government regulation, management espouses the "invisible hand" doctrine. It contends that it creates the greatest good for the greatest number, and therefore government need not intervene. However, we know that externalities, moral hazards, and monopoly power exist in fact, whether or not they exist in theory. Further, some of the legal apparatus mentioned above has evolved to deal with just these issues.

The problem of the "tragedy of the commons" or the free-rider problem pervades the concept of public goods such as water and air. No one has an incentive to incur the cost of clean-up or the cost of nonpollution, since the marginal gain of one firm's action is small. Every firm reasons this way, and the result is pollution of water and air. Since the industrial revolution, firms have sought to internalize the benefits and externalize the costs of their actions. The cost must be borne by all, through taxation and regulation; hence we have the emergence of the environmental regulations of the 1970s.

Similarly, moral hazards arise when the purchaser of a good or service can pass along the cost of that good. There is no incentive to economize, on the part of either the producer or the consumer, and there is excessive use of the resources involved. The institutionalized practice of third-party payment in health care is a prime example.

Finally, we see the avoidance of competitive behavior on the part of firms, each seeking to monopolize a small portion of the market and not compete with one another. In a number of industries, oligopolies have emerged, and while there is questionable evidence that oligopolies are not the most efficient corporate form in some industries, suffice it to say that the potential for abuse of market power has again led to regulation of managerial activity. In the classic case, AT&T, arguably one of the great technological and managerial achievements of the century, was broken up into eight separate companies to prevent its abuse of monopoly power.

Externalities, moral hazards, and monopoly power have led to more external control on managerial capitalism. There are de facto constraints, due to these economic facts of life, on the ability of management to act in the interests of stockholders.

A STAKEHOLDER THEORY OF THE FIRM

The Stakeholder Concept

Corporations have stakeholders, that is, groups and individuals who benefit from or are harmed by, and whose rights are violated or respected by, corporate actions. The concept of stakeholders is a generalization of the notion of stockholders, who themselves have some special claim on the firm. Just as stockholders have a right to demand certain actions by management, so do other stakeholders have a right to make claims. The exact nature of these claims is a difficult question that I shall address, but the logic is identical to that of the stockholder theory. Stakes require action of a certain sort, and conflicting stakes require methods of resolution.

Freeman and Reed (1983)[7] distinguish two senses of *stakeholder*. The "narrow definition" includes those groups who are vital to the survival and success of the corporation. The "wide-definition" includes any group or individual who can affect or is affected by the corporation. I shall begin with a modest aim: to articulate a stakeholder theory using the narrow definition.

Stakeholders in the Modern Corporation

Figure 1 depicts the stakeholders in a typical large corporation. The stakes of each are reciprocal, since each can affect the other in terms of harms and benefits as well as rights and duties. The stakes of each are not univocal and would vary by particular corporation. I merely set forth some general notions that seem to be common to many large firms.

Owners have financial stake in the corporation in the form of stocks, bonds, and so on, and they expect some kind of financial return from them. Either they have given money directly to the firm, or they have some historical claim made through a series of morally justified exchanges. The firm affects their livelihood or, if a substantial portion of their retirement income is in stocks or bonds, their ability to care for themselves when they can no longer work. Of course, the stakes of owners will differ by type of owner, preferences for money, moral preferences, and so on, as well as by type of firm. The owners of AT&T are quite different from the owners of Ford Motor Company, with stock of the former company being widely dispersed among 3 million stockholders and that of the latter being held by a small family group as well as by a large group of public stockholders.

FIGURE 1. A Stakeholder Model of the Corporation.

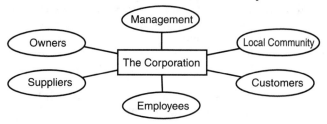

Employees have their jobs and usually their livelihood at stake; they often have specialized skills for which there is usually no perfectly elastic market. In return for their labor, they expect security, wages, benefits, and meaningful work. In return for their loyalty, the corporation is expected to provide for them and carry them through difficult times. Employees are expected to follow the instructions of management most of the time, to speak favorably about the company, and to be responsible citizens in the local communities in which the company operates. Where they are used as means to an end, they must participate in decisions affecting such use. The evidence that such policies and values as described here lead to productive company-employee relationships is compelling. It is equally compelling to realize that the opportunities for "bad faith" on the part of both management and employees are enormous. "Mock participation" in quality circles, singing the company song, and wearing the company uniform solely to please management all lead to distrust and unproductive work.

Suppliers, interpreted in a stakeholder sense, are vital to the success of the firm, for raw materials will determine the final product's quality and price. In turn the firm is a customer of the supplier and is therefore vital to the success and survival of the supplier. When the firm treats the supplier as a valued member of the stakeholder network, rather than simply as a source of materials, the supplier will respond when the firm is in need. Chrysler traditionally had very close ties to its suppliers, even to the extent that led some to suspect the transfer of illegal payments. And when Chrysler was on the brink of disaster, the suppliers responded with price cuts, accepting late payments, financing, and so on. Supplier and company can rise and fall together. Of course, again, the particular supplier relationships will depend on a number of variables such as the number of suppliers and whether the supplies are finished goods or raw materials.

Customers exchange resources for the products of the firm and in return receive the benefits of the products. Customers provide the lifeblood of the firm in the form of revenue. Given the level of reinvestment of earnings in large corporations, customers indirectly pay for the development of new products and services. Peters and Waterman (1982)[8] have argued that being close to the customer leads to success with other stakeholders and that a distinguishing characteristic of some companies that have performed well is their emphasis on the customer. By paying attention to customers' needs, management automatically addresses the needs of suppliers and owners. Moreover, it seems that the ethic of customer service carries over to the community. Almost without fail the "excellent companies" in Peters and

Waterman's study have good reputations in the community. I would argue that Peters and Waterman have found multiple applications of Kant's dictum, "Treat persons as ends unto themselves," and it should come as no surprise that persons respond to such respectful treatment, be they customers, suppliers, owners, employees, or members of the local community. The real surprise is the novelty of the application of Kant's rule in a theory of good management practice.

The local community grants the firm the right to build facilities and, in turn, it benefits from the tax base and economic and social contributions of the firm. In return for the provision of local services, the firm is expected to be a good citizen, as is any person, either "natural or artificial." The firm cannot expose the community to unreasonable hazards in the form of pollution, toxic waste, and so on. If for some reason the firm must leave a community, it is expected to work with local leaders to make the transition as smoothly as possible. Of course, the firm does not have perfect knowledge, but when it discovers some danger or runs afoul of new competition, it is expected to inform the local community and to work with the community to overcome any problem. When the firm mismanages its relationship with the local community, it is in the same position as a citizen who commits a crime. It has violated the implicit social contract with the community and should expect to be distrusted and ostracized. It should not be surprised when punitive measures are invoked.

I have not included "competitors" as stakeholders in the narrow sense, since strictly speaking they are not necessary for the survival and success of the firm; the stakeholder theory works equally well in monopoly contexts. However, competitors and government would be the first to be included in an extension of this basic theory. It is simply not true that the interests of competitors in an industry are always in conflict. There is no reason why trade associations and other multi-organizational groups cannot band together to solve common problems that have little to do with how to restrain trade. Implementation of stakeholder management principles, in the long run, mitigates the need for industrial policy and an increasing role for government intervention and regulation.

The Role of Management

Management plays a special role, for it too has a stake in the modern corporation. On the one hand, management's stake is like that of employees, with some kind of explicit or implicit employment contract. But, on the other hand, management has a duty of safeguarding the welfare of the abstract entity that is the corporation. In short, management, especially top management, must look after the health of the corporation, and this involves balancing the multiple claims of conflicting stakeholders. Owners want higher financial returns, while customers want more money spent on research and development. Employees want higher wages and better benefits, while the local community wants better parks and day-care facilities.

The task of management in today's corporation is akin to that of King Solomon. The stakeholder theory does not give primacy to one stakeholder group over another, though there will surely be times when one group will benefit at the expense of others. In general, however, management must keep the relationships among stakeholders in balance. When these relationships become imbalanced, the survival of the firm is in jeopardy.

When wages are too high and product quality is too low, customers leave, suppliers suffer, and owners sell their stocks and bonds, depressing the stock price and making it difficult to raise new capital at favorable rates. Note, however, that the reason for paying returns to owners is not that they "own" the firm, but that their support is necessary for the survival of the firm, and that they have a legitimate claim on the firm. Similar reasoning applies in turn to each stakeholder group.

A stakeholder theory of the firm must redefine the purpose of the firm. The stockholder theory claims that the purpose of the firm is to maximize the welfare of the stockholders, perhaps subject to some moral or social constraints, either because such maximization leads to the greatest good or because of property rights. The purpose of the firm is quite different in my view.

"The stakeholder theory" can be unpacked into a number of stakeholder theories, each of which has a "normative core," inextricably linked to the way that corporations should be governed and the way that managers should act. So, attempts to more fully define, or more carefully define, a stakeholder theory are misguided. Following Donaldson and Preston, I want to insist that the normative, descriptive, instrumental, and metaphorical (my addition to their framework) uses of 'stakeholder' are tied together in particular political constructions to yield a number of possible "stakeholder theories." "Stakeholder theory" is thus a genre of stories about how we could live. Let me be more specific.

A "normative core" of a theory is a set of sentences that includes among others, sentences like:

(1) Corporations ought to be governed . . .
(2) Managers ought to act to . . . .

where we need arguments or further narratives which include business and moral terms to fill in the blanks. This normative core is not always reducible to a fundamental ground like the theory of property, but certain normative cores are consistent with modern understandings of property. Certain elaborations of the theory of private property plus the other institutions of political liberalism give rise to particular normative cores. But there are other institutions, other political conceptions of how society ought to be structured, so that there are different possible normative cores.

So, one normative core of a stakeholder theory might be a feminist standpoint one, rethinking how we would restructure "value-creating activity" along principles of caring and connection.[9] Another would be an ecological (or several ecological) normative cores. Mark Starik has argued that the very idea of a stakeholder theory of the *firm* ignores certain ecological necessities.[10] Exhibit 1 is suggestive of how these theories could be developed.

In the next section I shall sketch the normative core based on pragmatic liberalism. But, any normative core must address the questions in columns A or B, or explain why these questions may be irrelevant, as in the ecological view. In addition, each "theory," and I use the word hesitantly, must place the normative core within a more full-fledged account of how we could understand value-creating activity differently (column C). The only way to get on with this task is to see the stakeholder idea as a metaphor. The attempt

EXHIBIT 1. A Reasonable Pluralism

	A. *Corporations ought to be governed . . .*	B. *Managers ought to act . . .*	C. *The background disciplines of "value creations" are . . .*
Doctrine of Fair Contracts	. . . in accordance with the six principles.	. . . in the interests of stakeholders.	—business theories —theories that explain stakeholder behavior
Feminist Standpoint Theory	. . . in accordance with the principles of caring/connection and relationships.	. . . to maintain and care for relationships and networks of stakeholders.	—business theories —feminist theory —social science understanding of networks
Ecological Principles	. . . in accordance with the principle of caring for the earth.	. . . to care for the earth.	—business theories —ecology —other

to prescribe one and only one "normative core" and construct "a stake-holder theory" is at best a disguised attempt to smuggle a normative core past the unsophisticated noses of other unsuspecting academics who are just happy to see the end of the stockholder orthodoxy.

If we begin with the view that we can understand value-creation activity as a contractual process among those parties affected, and if for simplicity's sake we initially designate those parties as financiers, customers, suppliers, employees, and communities, then we can construct a normative core that reflects the liberal notions of autonomy, solidarity, and fairness as articulated by John Rawls, Richard Rorty, and others.[11] Notice that building these moral notions into the foundations of how we understand value creation and con-tracting requires that we eschew separating the "business" part of the process from the "ethical" part, and that we start with the presumption of equality among the contractors, rather than the presumption in favor of fi-nancier rights.

The normative core for this redesigned contractual theory will capture the liberal idea of fairness if it ensures a basic equality among stakeholders in terms of their moral rights as these are realized in the firm, and if it rec-ognizes that inequalities among stakeholders are justified if they raise the level of the least well-off stakeholder. The liberal ideal of autonomy is cap-tured by the realization that each stakeholder must be free to enter agree-ments that create value for themselves, and solidarity is realized by the recognition of the mutuality of stakeholder interests.

One way to understand fairness in this context is to claim *à la* Rawls that a contract is fair if parties to the contract would agree to it in ignorance of their actual stakes. Thus, a contract is like a fair bet, if each party is willing to turn the tables and accept the other side. What would a fair contract among corporate stakeholders look like? If we can articulate this ideal, a sort of corporate constitution, we could then ask whether actual corporations measure up to this standard, and we also begin to design corporate struc-tures which are consistent with this Doctrine of Fair Contracts.

Imagine if you will, representative stakeholders trying to decide on "the rules of the game." Each is rational in a straightforward sense, looking out for its own self-interest. At least *ex ante*, stakeholders are the relevant parties since they will be materially affected. Stakeholders know how economic activity is organized and could be organized. They know general facts about the way the corporate world works. They know that in the real world there are or could be transaction costs, externalities, and positive costs of contracting. Suppose they are uncertain about what other social institutions exist, but they know the range of those institutions. They do not know if government exists to pick up the tab for any externalities, or if they will exist in the nightwatchman state of libertarian theory. They know success and failure stories of businesses around the world. In short, they are behind a Rawls-like veil of ignorance, and they do not know what stake each will have when the veil is lifted. What groundrules would they choose to guide them?

The first groundrule is "The Principle of Entry and Exit." Any contract that is the corporation must have clearly defined entry, exit, and renegotiation conditions, or at least it must have methods or processes for so defining these conditions. The logic is straightforward: each stakeholder must be able to determine when an agreement exists and has a chance of fulfillment. This is not to imply that contracts cannot contain contingent claims or other methods for resolving uncertainty, but rather that it must contain methods for determining whether or not it is valid.

The second groundrule I shall call "The Principle of Governance," and it says that the procedure for changing the rules of the game must be agreed upon by unanimous consent. Think about the consequences of a majority of stakeholders systematically "selling out" a minority. Each stakeholder, in ignorance of its actual role, would seek to avoid such a situation. In reality this principle translates into each stakeholder never giving up its right to participate in the governance of the corporation, or perhaps into the existence of stakeholder governing boards.

The third groundrule I shall call "The Principle of Externalities," and it says that if a contract between A and B imposes a cost on C, then C has the option to become a party to the contract, and the terms are renegotiated. Once again the rationality of this condition is clear. Each stakeholder will want insurance that it does not become C.

The fourth groundrule is "The Principle of Contracting Costs," and it says that all parties to the contract must share in the cost of contracting. Once again the logic is straightforward. Any one stakeholder can get stuck.

A fifth groundrule is "The Agency Principle" that says that any agent must serve the interests of all stakeholders. It must adjudicate conflicts within the bounds of the other principals. Once again the logic is clear. Agents for any one group would have a privileged place.

A sixth and final groundrule we might call, "The Principle of Limited Immortality." The corporation shall be managed as if it can continue to serve the interests of stakeholders through time. Stakeholders are uncertain about the future but, subject to exit conditions, they realize that the continued existence of the corporation is in their interest. Therefore, it would be rational to hire managers who are fiduciaries to their interest and the interest of the collective. If it turns out the "collective interest" is the empty set, then this principle simply collapses into the Agency Principle.

Thus, the Doctrine of Fair Contracts consists of these six groundrules or principles:

(1) The Principle of Entry and Exit
(2) The Principle of Governance
(3) The Principle of Externalities
(4) The Principle of Contracting Costs
(5) The Agency Principle
(6) The Principle of Limited Immortality

Think of these groundrules as a doctrine which would guide actual stakeholders in devising a corporate constitution or charter. Think of management as having the duty to act in accordance with some specific constitution or charter.

Obviously, if the Doctrine of Fair Contracts and its accompanying background narratives are to effect real change, there must be requisite changes in the enabling laws of the land. I propose the following three principles to serve as constitutive elements of attempts to reform the law of corporations.

The Stakeholder Enabling Principle

Corporations shall be managed in the interests of its stakeholders, defined as employees, financiers, customers, employees, and communities.

The Principle of Director Responsibility

Directors of the corporation shall have a duty of care to use reasonable judgment to define and direct the affairs of the corporation in accordance with the Stakeholder Enabling Principle.

The Principle of Stakeholder Recourse

Stakeholders may bring an action against the directors for failure to perform the required duty of care.

Obviously, there is more work to be done to spell out these principles in terms of model legislation. As they stand, they try to capture the intuitions that drive the liberal ideals. It is equally plain that corporate constitutions which meet a test like the doctrine of fair contracts are meant to enable directors and executives to manage the corporation in conjunction with these same liberal ideals.

Notes

1. Cf. A. Berle and G. Means, *The Modern Corporation and Private Property* (New York; Commerce Clearing House, 1932), 1. For a reassessment of Berle and Means' argument after 50 years, see *Journal of Law and Economics* 26 (June 1983), especially G. Stigler and C. Friedland, "The Literature of Economics: The Case of Berle and Means," 237–68; D. North, "Comment on Stigler and Friedland," 269–72; and G. Means, "Corporate Power in the Marketplace," 467–85.
2. The metaphor of rebuilding the ship while afloat is attributed to Neurath by W. Quine, *Word and Object* (Cambridge: Harvard University Press, 1960), and W. Quine and J. Ullian,

The Web of Belief (New York: Random House, 1978). The point is that to keep the ship afloat during repairs we must replace a plank with one that will do a better job. Our argument is that stakeholder capitalism can so replace the current version of managerial capitalism.

3. See R. Charan and E. Freeman, "Planning for the Business Environment of the 1980s," *The Journal of Business Strategy* 1 (1980): 9–19, especially p. 15 for a brief account of the major developments in products liability law.

4. See S. Breyer, *Regulation and Its Reform* (Cambridge: Harvard University Press, 1983), 133, for an analysis of food additives.

5. See I. Millstein and S. Katsh, *The Limits of Corporate Power* (New York: Macmillan, 1981), Chapter 4.

6. Cf. C. Summers, "Protecting All Employees Against Unjust Dismissal," *Harvard Business Review* 58 (1980): 136, for a careful statement of the argument.

7. See E. Freeman and D. Reed, "Stockholders and Stakeholders: A New Perspective on Corporate Governance," in C. Huizinga, ed., *Corporate Governance: A Definitive Exploration of the Issues* (Los Angeles: UCLA Extension Press, 1983).

8. See T. Peters and R. Waterman, *In Search of Excellence* (New York: Harper and Row, 1982).

9. See, for instance, A. Wicks, D. Gilbert, and E. Freeman, "A Feminist Reinterpretation of the Stakeholder Concept," *Business Ethics Quarterly*, Vol. 4, No. 4, October 1994; and E. Freeman and J. Liedtka, "Corporate Social Responsibility: A Critical Approach," *Business Horizons*, Vol. 34, No. 4, July–August 1991, pp. 92–98.

10. At the Toronto workshop Mark Starik sketched how a theory would look if we took the environment to be a stakeholder. This fruitful line of work is one example of my main point about pluralism.

11. J. Rawls, *Political Liberalism*, New York: Columbia University Press, 1993; and R. Rorty, "The Priority of Democracy to Philosophy" in *Reading Rorty: Critical Responses to Philosophy and the Mirror of Nature (and Beyond)*, ed. Alan R. Malachowski, Cambridge, MA: Blackwell, 1990.

Business Ethics and Stakeholder Analysis

KENNETH E. GOODPASTER

So we must think through what management should be accountable for; and how and through whom its accountability can be discharged. The stockholders' interest, both short- and long-term, is one of the areas. But it is only one.
PETER DRUCKER, 1988
Harvard Business Review

What is ethically responsible management? How can a corporation, given its economic mission, be managed with appropriate attention to ethical concerns? These are central questions in the field of business ethics. One approach to answering such questions that has become popular during the last

Reprinted by permission of the author Kenneth E. Goodpaster, University of St. Thomas, and *Business Ethics Quarterly*, January 1991, Vol. 1, No. 1, the Journal of the Society for Business Ethics.

two decades is loosely referred to as "stakeholder analysis." Ethically responsible management, it is often suggested, is management that includes careful attention not only to stockholders *but to stakeholders generally* in the decision-making process.

This suggestion about the ethical importance of stakeholder analysis contains an important kernel of truth, but it can also be misleading. Comparing the ethical relationship between managers and stockholders with their relationship to other stakeholders is, I will argue, almost as problematic as ignoring stakeholders (ethically) altogether—presenting us with something of a "stakeholder paradox."

Definition

The term "stakeholder" appears to have been invented in the early '60s as a deliberate play on the word "stockholder" to signify that there are other parties having a "stake" in the decision-making of the modern, publicly-held corporation in addition to those holding equity positions. Professor R. Edward Freeman, in his book *Strategic Management: A Stakeholder Approach* (Pitman, 1984), defines the term as follows:

> A stakeholder in an organization is (by definition) any group or individual who can affect or is affected by the achievement of the organization's objectives.(46)

Examples of stakeholder groups (beyond stockholders) are employees, suppliers, customers, creditors, competitors, governments, and communities. . . .

Another metaphor with which the term "stakeholder" is associated is that of a "player" in a game like poker. One with a "stake" in the game is one who plays and puts some economic value at risk.[1]

Much of what makes responsible decision-making difficult is understanding how there can be an ethical relationship between management and stakeholders that avoids being too weak (making stakeholders mere means to stockholders' ends) or too strong (making stakeholders quasi-stockholders in their own right). To give these issues life, a case example will help. So let us consider the case of General Motors and Poletown.

The Poletown Case[2]

In 1980, GM was facing a net loss in income, the first since 1921, due to intense foreign competition. Management realized that major capital expenditures would be required for the company to regain its competitive position and profitability. A $40 billion five-year capital spending program was announced that included new, state-of-the-art assembly techniques aimed at smaller, fuel-efficient automobiles demanded by the market. Two aging assembly plants in Detroit were among the ones to be replaced. Their closure would eliminate 500 jobs. Detroit in 1980 was a city with a black majority, an unemployment rate of 18% overall and 30% for blacks, a rising public debt and a chronic budget deficit, despite high tax rates.

The site requirements for a new assembly plant included 500 acres, access to long-haul railroad and freeways, and proximity to suppliers for "just-in-time" inventory management. It needed to be ready to produce 1983 model year cars beginning in September 1982. The only site in Detroit meeting GM's requirements was heavily settled, covering a section of the Detroit neighborhood of Poletown. Of the 3,500 residents, half were black. The whites were mostly of Polish descent, retired or nearing retirement. An alternative "green field" site was available in another midwestern state.

Using the power of eminent domain, the Poletown area could be acquired and cleared for a new plant within the company's timetable, and the city government was eager to cooperate. Because of job retention in Detroit, the leadership of the United Auto Workers was also in favor of the idea. The Poletown Neighborhood Council strongly opposed the plan, but was willing to work with the city and GM.

The new plant would employ 6,150 workers and would cost GM $500 million wherever it was built. Obtaining and preparing the Poletown site would cost an additional $200 million, whereas alternative sites in the midwest were available for $65–80 million.

The interested parties were many—stockholders, customers, employees, suppliers, the Detroit community, the midwestern alternative, the Poletown neighborhood. The decision was difficult. GM management needed to consider its competitive situation, the extra costs of remaining in Detroit, the consequences to the city of leaving for another part of the midwest, and the implications for the residents of choosing the Poletown site if the decision was made to stay. The decision about whom to talk to and *how* was as puzzling as the decision about *what* to do and *why*.

I. STAKEHOLDER ANALYSIS AND STAKEHOLDER SYNTHESIS

Ethical values enter management decision-making, it is often suggested, through the gate of stakeholder analysis. But the suggestion that introducing "stakeholder analysis" into business decisions is the same as introducing ethics into those decisions is questionable. To make this plain, let me first distinguish between two importantly different ideas: stakeholder analysis and stakeholder synthesis. I will then examine alternative kinds of stakeholder synthesis with attention to ethical content.

The decision-making process of an individual or a company can be seen in terms of a sequence of six steps to be followed after an issue or problem presents itself for resolution.[3] For ease of reference and recall, I will name the sequence PASCAL, after the six letters in the name of the French philosopher-mathematician Blaise Pascal (1623–62), who once remarked in reference to ethical decision-making that "the heart has reasons that reason knows not of."

(1) PERCEPTION or fact-gathering about the options available and their short- and long-term implications;

(2) ANALYSIS of these implications with specific attention to affected parties and to the decision-maker's goals, objectives, values, responsibilities, etc.;

(3) SYNTHESIS of this structured information according to whatever fundamental priorities obtain in the mindset of the decision-maker;

(4) CHOICE among the available options based on the synthesis;

(5) ACTION or implementation of the chosen option through a series of specific requests to specific individuals or groups, resource allocation, incentives, controls, and feedback;

(6) LEARNING from the outcome of the decision, resulting in either rein-
forcement or modification (for future decisions) of the way in which the
above steps have been taken.

We might simplify this analysis, of course, to something like "input," "decision," and "output," but distinguishing interim steps can often be helpful.
The main point is that the path from the presentation of a problem to its
resolution must somehow involve gathering, processing, and acting on relevant information.

Now, by *stakeholder analysis* I simply mean a process that does not go beyond the first two steps mentioned above. That is, the affected parties
caught up in each available option are identified and the positive and negative impacts on each stakeholder are determined. But questions having to
do with processing this information into a decision and implementing it are
left unanswered. These steps are not part of the *analysis* but of the *synthesis,
choice,* and *action.*

Stakeholder analysis may give the initial appearance of a decision-making
process, but in fact it is only a *segment* of a decision-making process. It represents the preparatory or opening phase that awaits the crucial application
of the moral (or nonmoral) values of the decision-maker. So, to be informed
that an individual or an institution regularly makes stakeholder analysis part
of decision-making or takes a "stakeholder approach" to management is to
learn little or nothing about the ethical character of that individual or institution. It is to learn only that stakeholders are regularly identified—*not
why and for what purpose.* To be told that stakeholders are or must be "taken
into account" is, so far, to be told very little. Stakeholder analysis is, as a
practical matter, morally *neutral.* It is therefore a mistake to see it as a substitute for normative ethical thinking.[4]

What I shall call "stakeholder synthesis" goes further into the sequence
of decision-making steps mentioned above to include actual decision-
making and implementation (S, C, A). The critical point is that stakeholder
synthesis offers *a pattern or channel by which to move from stakeholder identification to a practical response or resolution.* Here we begin to join stakeholder
analysis to questions of substance. But we must now ask: What kind of substance? And how does it relate to *ethics?* The stakeholder idea, remember, is
typically offered as a way of integrating *ethical* values into management decision-making. When and how does substance become *ethical* substance?

Strategic Stakeholder Synthesis

We can imagine decision-makers doing "stakeholder analysis" for different underlying reasons, not always having to do with ethics. A management
team, for example, might be careful to take positive and (especially) negative stakeholder effects into account for no other reason than that offended
stakeholders might resist or retaliate (e.g., through political action or opposition to necessary regulatory clearances). It might not be *ethical* concern
for the stakeholders that motivates and guides such analysis, so much as concern about potential impediments to the achievement of strategic objectives.
Thus positive and negative effects on relatively powerless stakeholders may
be ignored or discounted in the synthesis, choice, and action phases of the
decision process.[5]

In the Poletown case, General Motors might have done a stakeholder analysis using the following reasoning: our stockholders are the central stakeholders here, but other key stakeholders include our suppliers, old and new plant employees, the City of Detroit, and the residents of Poletown. These other stakeholders are not our direct concern as a corporation with an economic mission, but since they can influence our short- or long-term strategic interests, they must be taken into account. Public relation's costs and benefits, for example, or concerns about union contracts or litigation might well have influenced the choice between staying in Detroit and going elsewhere.

I refer to this kind of stakeholder synthesis as "strategic" since stakeholders outside the stockholder group are viewed instrumentally, as factors potentially affecting the overarching goal of optimizing stockholder interests. They are taken into account in the decision-making process, but as external environmental forces, as potential sources of either good will or retaliation. "We" are the economic principals and management; "they" are significant players whose attitudes and future actions might affect our short-term or long-term success. We must respect them in the way one "respects" the weather—as a set of forces to be reckoned with.[6]

It should be emphasized that managers who adopt the strategic stakeholder approach are not necessarily *personally* indifferent to the plight of stakeholders who are "strategically unimportant." The point is that *in their role as managers*, with a fiduciary relationship that binds them as agents to principals, their basic outlook subordinates other stakeholder concerns to those of stockholders. Market and legal forces are relied upon to secure the interests of those whom strategic considerations might discount. This reliance can and does take different forms, depending on the emphasis given to market forces on the one hand and legal forces on the other. A more conservative, market-oriented view acknowledges the role of legal compliance as an environmental factor affecting strategic choice, but thinks stakeholder interests are best served by minimal interference from the public sector. Adam Smith's "invisible hand" is thought to be the most important guarantor of the common good in a competitive economy. A more liberal view sees the hand of government, through legislation and regulation, as essential for representing stakeholders that might otherwise not achieve "standing" in the strategic decision process.

What both conservatives and liberals have in common is the conviction that the fundamental orientation of management must be toward the interests of stockholders. Other stakeholders (customers, employees, suppliers, neighbors) enter the decision-making equation either directly as instrumental economic factors or indirectly as potential legal claimants. Both see law and regulation as providing a voice for stakeholders that goes beyond market dynamics. They differ about how much government regulation is socially and economically desirable.

During the Poletown controversy, GM managers as individuals may have cared deeply about the potential lost jobs in Detroit, or about the potential dislocation of Poletown residents. But in their role as agents for the owners (stockholders) they could only allow such considerations to "count" if they served GM's strategic interests (or perhaps as legal constraints on the decision).

Professor Freeman (1984, cited above) appears to adopt some form of strategic stakeholder synthesis. After presenting his definition of stakeholders, he remarks about its application to any group or individual "who can *affect* or is *affected by*" a company's achievement of its purposes. The "affect" part of the definition is not hard to understand; but Freeman clarifies the "affected by" part:

> The point of strategic management is in some sense to chart a direction for the firm. Groups which can affect that direction and its implementation must be considered in the strategic management process. However, it is less obvious why "those groups who are affected by the corporation" are stakeholders as well . . . I make the definition symmetric because of the changes which the firm has undergone in the past few years. Groups which 20 years ago had no effect on the actions of the firm, can affect it today, largely because of the actions of the firm which ignored the effects on these groups. Thus, by calling those affected groups "stakeholders," the ensuing strategic management model will be sensitive to future change . . . (46)

Freeman might have said "who can actually or potentially affect" the company, for the mind-set appears to be one in which attention to stakeholders is justified in terms of actual or potential impact on the company's achievement of its strategic purposes. Stakeholders (other than stockholders) are actual or potential means/obstacles to corporate objectives. A few pages later, Freeman writes:

> From the standpoint of strategic management, or the achievement of organizational purpose, we need an inclusive definition. We must not leave out any group or individual who can affect or is affected by organizational purpose, *because that group may prevent our accomplishments.* (52) [Emphasis added.]

The sense of a strategic view of stakeholders is not that stakeholders are ignored, but that all but a special group (stockholders) are considered on the basis of their actual or potential influence on management's central mission. The basic normative principle is fiduciary responsibility (organizational prudence), supplemented by legal compliance.

Is the Substance Ethical?

The question we must ask in thinking about a strategic approach to stakeholder synthesis is this: Is it really an adequate rendering of the *ethical* component in managerial judgment? Unlike mere stakeholder *analysis,* this kind of synthesis does go beyond simply *identifying* stakeholders. It integrates the stakeholder information by using a single interest group (stockholders) as its basic normative touchstone. If this were formulated as an explicit rule or principle, it would have two parts and would read something like this: (1) Maximize the benefits and minimize the costs to the stockholder group, short- and long-term, and (2) Pay close attention to the interests of other stakeholder groups that might potentially influence the achievement of (1). But while expanding the list of stakeholders may be a way of "enlightening" self-interest for the organization, is it really a way of introducing ethical values into business decision-making?

There are really two possible replies here. The first is that as an account of how ethics enters the managerial mind-set, the strategic stakeholder approach fails not because it is *im*moral; but because it is *non*moral. By most accounts of the nature of ethics, a strategic stakeholder synthesis would not qualify as an ethical synthesis, even though it does represent a substantive view. The point is simply that while there is nothing necessarily *wrong* with strategic reasoning about the consequences of one's actions for others, the kind of concern exhibited should not be confused with what most people regard as *moral* concern. Moral concern would avoid injury or unfairness to those affected by one's actions because it is wrong, regardless of the retaliatory potential of the aggrieved parties.[7]

The second reply does question the morality (*vs.* immorality) of strategic reasoning as the ultimate principle behind stakeholder analysis. It acknowledges that strategy, when placed in a highly effective legal and regulatory environment and given a time-horizon that is relatively long-term, may well avoid significant forms of anti-social behavior. But it asserts that as an operating principle for managers under time pressure in an imperfect legal and regulatory environment, strategic analysis is insufficient. In the Poletown case, certain stakeholders (e.g., the citizens of Detroit or the residents of Poletown) may have merited more *ethical* consideration than the strategic approach would have allowed. Some critics charged that GM only considered these stakeholders *to the extent that* serving their interests also served GM's interests, and that as a result, their interests were undermined.

Many, most notably Nobel Laureate Milton Friedman, believe that market and legal forces are adequate to translate or transmute ethical concerns into straightforward strategic concerns for management. He believes that in our economic and political system (democratic capitalism), direct concern for stakeholders (what Kant might have called "categorical" concern) is unnecessary, redundant, and inefficient, not to mention dishonest:

> In many cases, there is a strong temptation to rationalize actions as an exercise of "social responsibility." In the present climate of opinion, with its widespread aversion to "capitalism," "profits," the "soulless corporation" and so on, this is one way for a corporation to generate good will as a by-product of expenditures that are entirely justified in its own self-interest. If our institutions, and the attitudes of the public make it in their self-interest to cloak their actions in this way, I cannot summon much indignation to denounce them. At the same time, I can express admiration for those individual proprietors or owners of closely held corporations or stockholders of more broadly held corporations who disdain such tactics as approaching fraud.

Critics respond, however, that absent a pre-established harmony or linkage between organizational success and ethical success, some stakeholders, some of the time, will be affected a lot but will be able to affect in only a minor way the interests of the corporation. They add that in an increasingly global business environment, even the protections of law are fragmented by multiple jurisdictions.

At issue then is (1) defining ethical behavior partly in terms of the (non-strategic) decision-making values *behind* it, and (2) recognizing that too much optimism about the correlation between strategic success and virtue runs the risk of tailoring the latter to suit the former.

Thus the move toward substance (from analysis to synthesis) in discussions of the stakeholder concept is not necessarily a move toward ethics. And it is natural to think that the reason has to do with the instrumental status accorded to stakeholder groups other than stockholders. If we were to treat all stakeholders by strict analogy with stockholders, would we have arrived at a more ethically satisfactory form of stakeholder synthesis? Let us now look at this alternative, what I shall call a "multi-fiduciary" approach.

Multi-Fiduciary Stakeholder Synthesis

In contrast to a strategic view of stakeholders, one can imagine a management team processing stakeholder information by giving the same care to the interests of, say, employees, customers, and local communities as to the economic interests of stockholders. This kind of substantive commitment to stakeholders might involve trading off the economic advantages of one group against those of another, e.g., in a plant closing decision. I shall refer to this way of integrating stakeholder analysis with decision-making as "multi-fiduciary" since all stakeholders are treated by management as having equally important interests, deserving joint "maximization" (or what Herbert Simon might call "satisficing").

Professor Freeman, quoted earlier, contemplates what I am calling the multi-fiduciary view at the end of his 1984 book under the heading *The Manager As Fiduciary To Stakeholders:*

> Perhaps the most important area of future research is the issue of whether or not a theory of management can be constructed that uses the stakeholder concept to enrich "managerial capitalism," that is, can the notion that managers bear a fiduciary relationship to stockholders or the owners of the firm, be replaced by a concept of management whereby the manager *must* act in the interests of the stakeholders in the organization? (249)

As we have seen, the strategic approach pays attention to stakeholders as to factors that might affect economic interests, so many market forces to which companies must pay attention for competitive reasons. They become actual or potential legal challenges to the company's exercise of economic rationality. The multi-fiduciary approach, on the other hand, views stakeholders apart from their instrumental, economic, or legal clout. It does not see them merely as what philosopher John Ladd once called "limiting operating conditions" on management attention.[8] On this view, the word "stakeholder" carries with it, by the deliberate modification of a single phoneme, a dramatic shift in managerial outlook.

In 1954, famed management theorist Adolf Berle conceded a long-standing debate with Harvard law professor E. Merrick Dodd that looks in retrospect very much like a debate between what we are calling strategic and multi-fiduciary interpretations of stakeholder synthesis. Berle wrote:

> Twenty years ago, [I held] that corporate powers were powers in trust for shareholders while Professor Dodd argued that these powers were held in trust for the entire community. The argument has been settled (at least for the time being) squarely in favor of Professor Dodd's contention. (Quoted in Ruder, see below.)

The intuitive idea behind Dodd's view, and behind more recent formulations of it in terms of "multiple constituencies" and "stakeholders, not just stockholders," is that by expanding the list of those in whose trust corporate management must manage, we thereby introduce ethical responsibility into business decision-making.

In the context of the Poletown case, a multi-fiduciary approach by GM management might have identified the same stakeholders. But it would have considered the interests of employees, the city of Detroit, and the Poletown residents *alongside* stockholder interests, not solely in terms of how they might *influence* stockholder interests. This may or may not have entailed a different outcome. But it probably would have meant a different approach to the decision-making process in relation to the residents of Poletown (talking with them, for example).

We must now ask, as we did of the strategic approach: How satisfactory is multi-fiduciary stakeholder synthesis as a way of giving ethical substance to management decision-making? On the face of it, and in stark contrast to the strategic approach, it may seem that we have at last arrived at a truly moral view. But we should be cautious. For no sooner do we think we have found the proper interpretation of ethics in management than a major objection presents itself. And, yes, it appears to be a *moral* objection!

It can be argued that multi-fiduciary stakeholder analysis is simply incompatible with widely held moral convictions about the special fiduciary obligations owed by management to stockholders. At the center of the objection is the belief that the obligations of agents to principals are stronger or different in kind from those of agents to third parties.

The Stakeholder Paradox

Managers who would pursue a multi-fiduciary stakeholder orientation for their companies must face resistance from those who believe that a strategic orientation is the only *legitimate* one for business to adopt, given the economic mission and legal constitution of the modern corporation. This may be disorienting since the word "illegitimate" has clear negative ethical connotations, and yet the multi-fiduciary approach is often defended on ethical grounds. I will refer to this anomalous situation as the *Stakeholder Paradox:*

> It seems essential, yet in some ways illegitimate, to orient corporate decisions by ethical values that go beyond strategic stakeholder considerations to multi-fiduciary ones.

I call this a paradox because it says there is an ethical problem whichever approach management takes. Ethics seems both to forbid and to demand a strategic, profit-maximizing mind-set. The argument behind the paradox focuses on management's *fiduciary* duty to the stockholder, essentially the duty to keep a profit-maximizing promise, and a concern that the "impartiality" of the multi-fiduciary approach simply cuts management loose from certain well-defined bonds of stockholder accountability. On this view, impartiality is thought to be a *betrayal of trust*. Professor David S. Ruder, a former chairman of the Securities and Exchange Commission, once summarized the matter this way:

> Traditional fiduciary obligation theory insists that a corporate manager owes an obligation of care and loyalty to shareholders. If a public obligation theory unrelated to profit maximization becomes the law, the corporate manager who is not able to act in his own self interest without violating his fiduciary obligation, may nevertheless act in the public interest without violating that obligation.[9] (226)

Ruder continued:

> Whether induced by government legislation, government pressure, or merely by enlightened attitudes of the corporation regarding its long range potential as a unit in society, corporate activities carried on in satisfaction of public obligations can be consistent with profit maximization objectives. In contrast, justification of public obligations upon bold concepts of public need without corporate benefit will merely serve to reduce further the owner's influence on his corporation and to create additional demands for public participation in corporate management. (228–9).

Ruder's view appears to be that (a) multi-fiduciary stakeholder synthesis *need not* be used by management because the strategic approach is more accommodating than meets the eye; and (b) multi-fiduciary stakeholder synthesis should not be invoked by management because such a "bold" concept could threaten the private (*vs.* public) status of the corporation.

In response to (a), we saw earlier that there were reasonable questions about the tidy convergence of ethics and economic success. Respecting the interests and rights of the Poletown residents might really have meant incurring higher costs for GM (short-term as well as long-term).

Appeals to corporate self-interest, even long-term, might not always support ethical decisions. But even on those occasions where they will, we must wonder about the disposition to favor economic and legal reasoning "for the record." If Ruder means to suggest that business leaders can often *reformulate* or *re-present* their reasons for certain morally grounded decisions in strategic terms having to do with profit maximization and obedience to law, he is perhaps correct. In the spirit of our earlier quote from Milton Friedman, we might not summon much indignation to denounce them. But why the fiction? Why not call a moral reason a moral reason?

This issue is not simply of academic interest. Managers must confront it in practice. In one major public company, the C.E.O. put significant resources behind an affirmative action program and included the following explanation in a memo to middle management:

> I am often asked why this is such a high priority at our company. There is, of course, the obvious answer that it is in our best interest to seek out and employ good people in all sectors of our society. And there is the answer that enlightened self-interest tells us that more and more of the younger people, whom we must attract as future employees, choose companies by their social records as much as by their business prospects. *But the one overriding reason for this emphasis is because it is right.* Because this company has always set for itself the objective of assuming social as well as business obligations. Because that's the kind of company we have been. And with your participation, that's the kind of company we'll continue to be.[10]

In this connection, Ruder reminds us of what Professor Berle observed over twenty-five years ago:

> The fact is that boards of directors or corporation executives are often faced with situations in which they quite humanly and simply consider that such and such is the decent thing to do and ought to be done . . . They apply the potential profits or public relations tests later on, a sort of left-handed justification in this curious free-market world where an obviously moral and decent or humane action has to be apologized for on the ground that, conceivably, you may somehow make money by it. *(Ibid.)*

The Problem of Boldness

What appears to lie at the foundation of Ruder's cautious view is a concern about the "boldness" of the multi-fiduciary concept [(b) above].[11] It is not that he thinks the strategic approach is always satisfactory; it is that the multi-fiduciary approach is, in his eyes, much worse. For it questions the special relationship between the manager as agent and the stockholder as principal.

Ruder suggests that what he calls a "public obligation" theory threatens the private status of the corporation. He believes that what we are calling multi-fiduciary stakeholder synthesis *dilutes* the fiduciary obligation to stockholders (by extending it to customers, employees, suppliers, etc.) and he sees this as a threat to the "privacy" of the private sector organization. If public obligations are understood on the model of public sector institutions with their multiple constituencies, Ruder thinks, the stockholders lose status.

There is something profoundly *right* about Ruder's line of argument here, I believe, and something profoundly *wrong*. What is right is his intuition that if we treat other stakeholders on the model of the fiduciary relationship between management and the stockholder, we will, in effect, make them into quasi-stockholders. We can do this, of course, if we choose to as a society. But we should be aware that it is a radical step indeed. For it blurs traditional goals in terms of entrepreneurial risk-taking, pushes decision-making towards paralysis because of the dilemmas posed by divided loyalties and, in the final analysis, represents nothing less than the conversion of the modern private corporation into a public institution and probably calls for a corresponding restructuring of corporate governance (e.g., representatives of each stakeholder group on the board of directors). Unless we believe that the social utility of a private sector has disappeared, not to mention its value for individual liberty and enterprise, we will be cautious about an interpretation of stakeholder synthesis that transforms the private sector into the public sector.

On the other hand, I believe Ruder is mistaken if he thinks that business ethics requires this kind of either/or: either a private sector with a strategic stakeholder synthesis (business without ethics) or the effective loss of the private sector with a multi-fiduciary stakeholder synthesis (ethics without business).

Recent debates over state laws protecting companies against hostile takeovers may illustrate Ruder's concern as well as the new challenge. According to one journalist, a recent Pennsylvania anti-takeover law

> does no less than redefine the fiduciary duty of corporate directors, enabling them to base decisions not merely on the interests of shareholders, but on the interests of customers, suppliers, employees and the community at large. Pennsylvania is saying that it is the corporation that directors are responsible to. Shareholders say they always thought they themselves were the corporation.[12]

Echoing Ruder, one legal observer quoted by Elias *(ibid.)* commented with reference to this law that it "undermines and erodes free markets and property rights. From this perspective, this is an anticapitalist law. The management can take away property from the real owners."

In our terms, the state of Pennsylvania is charged with adopting a multi-fiduciary stakeholder approach in an effort to rectify deficiencies of the strategic approach which (presumably) corporate raiders hold.

The challenge that we are thus presented with is to develop an account of the moral responsibilities of management that (i) avoids surrendering the moral relationship between management and stakeholders as the strategic view does, while (ii) not transforming stakeholder obligations into fiduciary obligations (thus protecting the uniqueness of the principal-agent relationship between management and stockholder).

II. TOWARD A NEW STAKEHOLDER SYNTHESIS

We all remember the story of the well-intentioned Doctor Frankenstein. He sought to improve the human condition by designing a powerful, intelligent force for good in the community. Alas, when he flipped the switch, his creation turned out to be a monster rather than a marvel! Is the concept of the ethical corporation like a Frankenstein monster?

Taking business ethics seriously need not mean that management bears *additional* fiduciary relationships to third parties (nonstockholder constituencies) as multi-fiduciary stakeholder synthesis suggests. It may mean that there are morally significant *nonfiduciary* obligations to third parties surrounding any fiduciary relationship (See Figure 1.) Such moral obligations may be owed by private individuals as well as private-sector organizations to those whose freedom and well-being is affected by their economic behavior. It is these very obligations in fact (the duty not to harm or coerce and duties not to lie, cheat, or steal) that are cited in regulatory, legislative, and judicial arguments for constraining profit-driven business activities. These obligations are not "hypothetical" or contingent or indirect, as they would be on the strategic model, wherein they are only subject to the corporation's interests being met. They are "categorical" or direct. They are not rooted in the *fiduciary* relationship, but in other relationships at least as deep.

It must be admitted in fairness to Ruder's argument that the jargon of "stakeholders" in discussions of business ethics can seem to threaten the notion of what corporate law refers to as the "undivided and unselfish loyalty" owed by managers and directors to stockholders. For this way of speaking can suggest a multiplication of management duties *of the same kind* as the duty to stockholders. What we must understand is that the responsibilities of management toward stockholders are of a piece with the obligations that *stockholders themselves* would be expected to honor in their own right. As an old Latin proverb has it, *nemo dat quod non habet,* which literally means "nobody gives what he doesn't have." Freely translating in this context we can say: No one can expect of an *agent* behavior that is ethically less responsible than what he would expect of himself. I cannot (ethically) *hire* done on my

	Fiduciary	Non-fiduciary
Stockholders	●	
Other Stakeholders		●

Figure 1. Direct Managerial Obligations

behalf what I would not (ethically) *do* myself. We might refer to this as the "Nemo Dat Principle" (NDP) and consider it a formal requirement of consistency in business ethics (and professional ethics generally):

> (NDP) Investors cannot expect of managers (more generally, principals cannot expect of their agents) behavior that would be inconsistent with the reasonable ethical expectations of the community.[13]

The NDP does not, of course, resolve in advance the many ethical challenges that managers must face. It only indicates that these challenges are of a piece with those that face us all. It offers a different kind of test (and so a different kind of stakeholder synthesis) that management (and institutional investors) might apply to policies and decisions.

The foundation of ethics in management—and the way out of the stakeholder paradox—lies in understanding that the conscience of the corporation is a logical and moral extension of the consciences of its principals. It is *not* an expansion of the *list* of principals, but a gloss on the principal-agent relationship itself. Whatever the structure of the principal-agent relationship, neither principal nor agent can ever claim that an agent has "moral immunity" from the basic obligations that would apply to any human being toward other members of the community.

Indeed, consistent with Ruder's belief, the introduction of moral reasoning (distinguished from multi-fiduciary stakeholder reasoning) into the framework of management thinking may *protect* rather than threaten private sector legitimacy. The conscientious corporation can maintain its private economic mission, but in the context of fundamental moral obligations owed by any member of society to others affected by that member's actions. Recognizing such obligations does *not* mean that an institution is a public institution. Private institutions, like private individuals, can be and are bound to respect moral obligations in the pursuit of private purposes.

Conceptually, then, we can make room for a moral posture toward stakeholders that is both *partial* (respecting the fiduciary relationship between managers and stockholders) and *impartial* (respecting the equally important non-fiduciary relationships between management and other stakeholders). As philosopher Thomas Nagel has said, "In the conduct of life, of all places, the rivalry between the view from within and the view from without must be taken seriously."[14]

Whether this conceptual room can be used *effectively* in the face of enormous pressures on contemporary managers and directors is another story, of course. For it is one thing to say that "giving standing to stakeholders" in managerial reasoning is conceptually coherent. It is something else to say that it is practically coherent.

Yet most of us, I submit, believe it. Most of us believe that management at General Motors *owed* it to the people of Detroit and to the people of Poletown to take their (nonfiduciary) interests very seriously, to seek creative solutions to the conflict, to do more than use or manipulate them in accordance with GM's needs only. We understand that managers and directors have a special obligation to provide a financial return to the stockholders, but we also understand that the word "special" in this context needs to be tempered by an appreciation of certain fundamental community norms that go beyond the demands of both laws and markets. There are certain class-action suits that stockholders ought not to win. For there is sometimes a moral defense.

CONCLUSION

The relationship between management and stockholders is ethically different in kind from the relationship between management and other parties (like employees, suppliers, customers, etc.), a fact that seems to go unnoticed by the multi-fiduciary approach. If it were not, the corporation would cease to be a private sector institution—and what is now called business ethics would become a more radical critique of our economic system than is typically thought. On this point, Milton Friedman must be given a fair and serious hearing.

This does not mean, however, that "stakeholders" lack a morally significant relationship to management, as the strategic approach implies. It means only that the relationship in question is different from a fiduciary one. Management may never have promised customers, employees, suppliers, etc., a "return on investment," but management is nevertheless obliged to take seriously its extra-legal obligations not to injure, lie to or cheat these stakeholders *quite apart from* whether it is in the stockholders' interests.

As we think through the *proper* relationship of management to stakeholders, fundamental features of business life must undoubtedly be recognized: that corporations have a principally economic mission and competence; that fiduciary obligations to investors and general obligations to comply with the law cannot be set aside; and that abuses of economic power and disregard of corporate stewardship in the name of business ethics are possible.

But these things must be recognized as well: that corporations are not solely financial institutions; that fiduciary obligations go beyond short-term profit and are in any case subject to moral criteria in their execution; and that mere compliance with the law can be unduly limited and even unjust.

The *Stakeholder Paradox* can be avoided by a more thoughtful understanding of the nature of moral obligation and the limits it imposes on the principal-agent relationship. Once we understand that there is a practical "space" for identifying the ethical values shared by a corporation and its stockholders—a space that goes beyond strategic self-interest but stops short of impartiality—the hard work of filling that space can proceed.

Notes

This paper derives from a conference in Applied Ethics, *Moral Philosophy in the Public Domain,* held at the University of British Columbia, in June 1990. It will also appear in an anthology currently in preparation at the UBC Centre of Applied Ethics.

1. Strictly speaking the historical meaning of "stakeholder" in this context is someone who literally *holds* the stakes during play.

2. See Goodpaster and Piper, *Managerial Decision Making and Ethical Values,* Harvard Business School Publishing Division, 1989.

3. See Goodpaster, PASCAL: A Framework For Conscientious Decision Making (1989).

4. Actually, there are subtle ways in which even the stakeholder identification or inventory process might have *some* ethical content. The very process of *identifying* affected parties involves the use of the imagination in a way that can lead to a natural empathetic or caring response to those parties in the synthesis, choice and action phases of decision-making. This is a contingent connection, however, not a necessary one.

5. Note that including powerless stakeholders in the analysis phase may indicate whether the decision-maker cares about "affecting" them or "being affected by" them. Also, the inclusion of what might be called secondary stakeholders as advocates for primary stakeholders (e.g., local governments on behalf of certain citizen groups) may signal the values that will come into play in any synthesis.

6. It should be mentioned that some authors, most notably Kenneth R. Andrews in *The Concept of Corporate Strategy* (Irwin, Third Edition, 1987), employ a broader and more social definition of "strategic" decision-making than the one implied here.

7. Freeman writes: "Theoretically, 'stakeholder' must be able to capture a broad range of groups and individuals, even though when we put the concept to practical tests we must be willing to ignore certain groups who will have little or no impact on the corporation at this point in time." (52–3).

8. Ladd observed in a now-famous essay entitled "Morality and the Ideal of Rationality in Formal Organizations" (*The Monist*, 54, 1970) that organizational "rationality" was defined solely in terms of economic objectives: "The interests and needs of the individuals concerned, as individuals, must be considered only insofar as they establish limiting operating conditions. Organizational rationality dictates that these interests and needs must not be considered in their own right or on their own merits. If we think of an organization as a machine, it is easy to see why we cannot reasonably expect it to have any moral obligations to people or for them to have any to it." (507)

9. "Public Obligations of Private Corporations," *U. of Pennsylvania Law Review*, 114 (1965). Ruder recently (1989) reaffirmed the views in his 1965 article.

10. "Business Products Corporation—Part 1," HBS Case Services 9-377-077.

11. "The Business Judgement Rule" gives broad latitude to officers and directors of corporations, but calls for reasoning on the basis of the long-term economic interest of the company. And corporate case law ordinarily allows exceptions to profit-maximization criteria only when there are actual or potential *legal* barriers, and limits charitable and humanitarian gifts by the logic of long-term self-interest. The underlying rationale is accountability to investors. Recent work by the American Law Institute, however, suggests a rethinking of these matters.

12. Christopher Elias, "Turning Up the Heat on the Top," *Insight*, July 23, 1990.

13. We might consider the NDP in broader terms that would include the relationship between "client" and "professional" in other contexts, such as law, medicine, education, government, and religion, where normally the community's expectations are embodied in ethical standards.

14. T. Nagel, *The View from Nowhere*, Oxford U. Press (1986), p. 163.

The "New" U.S. Sentencing Commission Guidelines: A Wake-Up Call for Corporate America

DAN R. DALTON ━ MICHAEL B. METZGER ━ JOHN W. HILL

We recognize that some will interpret the title of this article as a bit of hyperbole. Until recently—November 1, 1991, to be exact—we might have agreed. On that day the United States Sentencing Commission's[1] guidelines for sentencing organizations found guilty of violating federal law became

Reprinted with permission of Academy of Management, P.O. Box 3020, Briarcliff Manor, NY 10510-8020. *The "New" U.S. Sentencing Guidelines: A Wake-Up Call for Corporate America*, Dan R. Dalton, Michael B. Metzger, and John W. Hill, 1994, Vol. 8, No. 1. Reprinted by permission of the publisher via Copyright Clearance Center, Inc.

effective.[2] In our view, expectations for reasonable business conduct will never be the same. Perhaps more important, the potential consequences of behavior outside those expectations have never been greater. In fact, the ability of the U.S. Sentencing Commission to create such an emphatic threat to business organizations has been described as an "awesome power."[3] It has been reported, for example, that a number of lobbying groups tried—unsuccessfully—to have the sentencing guidelines abated or made voluntary.[4] Those efforts having failed, we believe that rational business organizations are now compelled to sharply intensify their attention to managerial ethics.

We focus here on what might be referred to as the pragmatics of the sentencing guidelines. By this focus, we do not abandon our view that ethical managerial practice has value that transcends purely prudential concerns. Neither do we indicate any sympathy with those who dismiss programs of managerial ethics and corporate social responsibility because they have not been positively associated with organizational performance. It is not that we disagree that the extant literature on this point is articulate, but that we view it as largely irrelevant.[5]

Suppose, for example, that it has been unequivocally determined that the number of capital crimes in a given geographical area was unrelated to the vitality of the local economy. At the risk of some understatement, we would be uncomfortable concluding from such a report that our concerns about capital crime rates were misplaced. In response to such arguments in a business context prior to November 1, 1991, we might have argued that "economists know the price of everything and the value of nothing."[6] or that ". . . there are now numerous examples illustrating the choice of whether or not to do good is a moral, and not an economic, decision."[7] We might also have recalled that:

> It is irresponsible to imply that acting responsibly is always costless, and it is unethical to base the case for ethics on economic self interest . . . *The market has many worthwhile features, but setting an appropriate price on virtue is not among them.*[8]

While the U.S. Sentencing Commission similarly failed to set a price on virtue, it plainly enhanced the economic value of organizational efforts to encourage virtuous behavior while, at the same time, increasing the potential costs of misbehavior. The new guidelines, therefore, are a virtual mandate for organizational investment in ethics and compliance programs. This is not to say that the Commission has ordered organizations to adopt such programs; it has not. It does suggest, however, that for an organization not to do so borders on recklessness. We, therefore, agree with the assertion that "any general counsel not now reviewing his company's compliance programs could be engaged in professional malpractice."[9]

U.S. Sentencing Commission Guidelines for Organizational Defendants

In early 1991, the U.S. Sentencing Commission sent Congress its proposed guidelines for the sentencing of organizational offenders. However, the imposition of these guidelines is not limited to corporations. Partnerships, labor unions, pension funds, trusts, joint stock companies, unincorporated organizations and associations, and non-profit organizations are included as well.[10] It would seem that no business enterprise is exempt. Since November 1, 1991, these guidelines have governed the sentencing of organizations in the federal courts. Perhaps the most prominent feature of these guidelines is their provision for more lenient sentencing if, at the time of the offense, the convicted organization had implemented an "effective program to prevent and detect violations of the law." In the absence of such a program, a substantially more severe sentence may be imposed. It is notable—and a matter to which we devote more attention in a succeeding section—that such a program need not actually detect, or prevent the violation. The very existence of a reasonable program may entitle the corporation to leniency in subsequent sentencing.[11]

How Much Leniency?[12]

The actual sentencing under the guidelines for an offense committed by an organization depends on a number of factors. There are elements that aggravate an offense; conversely, there are elements that mitigate an offense. Having considered these various factors, the court must determine the "offense level" under the guidelines. Associated with any given offense level is a corresponding range from which the penalty must be assessed.

The first exacerbating issue is the nature of the crime itself. The more serious the crime, the higher the offense level. A second consideration is the amount of loss suffered by the victim(s) of the crime. Fraud, for example, is a level six offense; a fraud causing harm in excess of $5 million is increased by fourteen levels—to a level twenty offense. The amount of planning evidenced by the offense is also at issue. Anything beyond minimal planning, for instance, will increase the level of the crime by two levels. For the fraud example, the crime is now at level twenty-two. The different in offense level is hardly trivial. Crimes at level six or lower involve a base fine of $5,000; offense levels of thirty-eight or higher involve a base fine of $72.5 million, a ruinous penalty for most organizations.

Having set the offense level, the court must determine the defendant's "culpability score." This culpability score is essentially a multiplier. A number of conditions associated with the crime can have the effect of increasing or decreasing this multiplier. First, if the organization employs more than 5,000 people, the multiplier is increased. Further, suppose that high-level organizational personnel were involved in or tolerated the criminal activity. Also, suppose that the organization had a prior history of similar criminal conduct. Assume, too, that the organization had violated a judicial order or injunction, or had obstructed justice during the investigation or prosecution stages of the offense. Activities such as these would almost certainly establish the multiplier at four, the maximum. The $72.5 million fine to which we earlier referred would now be $290 million (i.e., the base fine times the multiplier: $72.5 million × 4).

Consider, instead, an organization that—unlike the one previously profiled—did nothing to exacerbate the crime. Instead, this organization is aware of the only two circumstances that actually reduce the culpability score. One is the existence—prior to the crime—of an effective program to prevent and detect violations of the law. The second is self-reporting, cooperation, and acceptance of responsibility. The reduction for self-reporting of the crime assumes that the report is made on a timely basis—within a reasonable period after the discovery of the offense. Also, the self-report must not have been made in consideration of an imminent threat of governmental investigation, indictment, or some threat of exposure through other means.

A company that has such a program and does self-report an offense in a timely manner could have a culpability score of less than zero. The minimum multiplier in such a case would be 0.05; the maximum multiplier for a sub-zero culpability score would be 0.2. Consider a simple example. Suppose that a company faced a $40 million base fine. The worst-case scenario (a four multiplier) would result in the actual assessment of a $160 million fine (four multiplier times $40 million base fine). A company with an effective program and a self-reported crime could receive a 0.05 multiplier. This would result in a fine of $2 million (0.05 multiplier times $40 million base fine). The difference between $160 million and $2 million should persuasively illustrate the potential impact of ethical managerial practice and attention to factors which reduce culpability scores under the sentencing guidelines. Such practices and attention can be "the difference between bankruptcy and salvation for a company that gets into trouble."[13] Further, it should be obvious that an effective compliance program should reduce the probability that an organization would "get into trouble" in the first place.

Given the gross differences in these outcomes, it might be expected that organizations would have immediately embraced compliance programs. Curiously, there is some indication that this is not the case. A recent commentary on the federal sentencing guidelines suggested that "few companies seem to be responding," and that "several major companies, lawyers and executives said they hadn't heard about the guidelines."[14] A general counsel acknowledged only a "vague idea of the guidelines" and remarked of the guidelines, "I don't think it has had a high profile." Another corporate spokesperson noted that "everybody I have asked in our area said, 'Huh?'"

What Constitutes Compliance?

Fortunately, there is little need to speculate on what exactly is meant by an "effective program to prevent and detect violations of law." The Sentencing Commission's commentary suggests that to qualify for a reduction in the culpability score, a program must be "reasonably designed, implemented and enforced so that it will generally be effective in preventing criminal conduct."[15] Minimum standards for such a program include a number of elements:

- An organization must have established standards and procedures for its employees and agents which are "reasonably capable of reducing the prospect of criminal conduct."
- Specific high-level officer(s) of the organization must be assigned the responsibility for compliance.
- An organization must use due care not to assign substantial discretionary authority to any individual whom the organization knew, or should have known, might have a propensity to engage in criminal activities.
- An organization must effectively communicate its standards and procedures to all employees or agents through appropriate training programs and publications.
- An organization must take reasonable steps to ensure compliance with its standards and procedures. This might be accomplished through the use of

monitoring and auditing systems. Also, the organization should maintain and publicize a reporting system so that employees can disclose criminal activities without fear of retribution.

- Standards and procedures should be enforced through appropriate disciplinary mechanisms.
- Following detection of an offense, an organization should take all reasonable steps "to respond appropriately to the offense" and to prevent further, similar offenses.[16]

Clearly, there are ambiguous components in these guidelines. What exactly is "substantial discretionary authority"? What are "reasonable steps"? What is an "appropriate disciplinary mechanism"? Inasmuch as the sentencing guidelines became effective in November 1991, we know of no cases on which we could rely to answer such questions. The total lack of empirical data on trends in corporate sentencing has been noted.[17] Even so, it has been wisely suggested that ". . . while the letter of these guidelines may be indistinct in parts, their spirit is clear: to encourage organizations to establish, monitor, and enforce programs that detect and prevent violations of the law."

Given the consequences of criminal activity with and without such programs, we would strongly recommend being an early adopter. Consider an example:[18] A $25,000 bribe has been paid to a city official to ensure an award of a cable television franchise. This is a level eighteen offense with a base penalty of a $350,000 fine. Based on a variety of factors (e.g., culpability, multipliers), that penalty is now increased to $1.4 million. The minimum fine with mitigating circumstances (e.g., company has a compliance plan, no high-level involvement) would have placed this fine in the $17,500 to $70,000 range. We do not mean to trivialize such offenses or penalties in this range. We will note, however, that the comparison of a $1.4 million fine to one of $70,000 does provide a stark—and we think persuasive—contrast.

Accordingly, it appears that the cost of waiting for the courts to define in some detail what constitutes these various elements could be enormous. We cannot resist noting the irony of an organization waiting for such guidance becoming a participant—as a defendant—in the court's determination of these guidelines. Moreover, our guess would be that a defense based on "Well, we were not sure exactly what to do with regard to the sentencing guidelines, so we opted to do nothing" would be less than compelling.

Conclusion

In many ways we rue the necessity of—and the opportunity provided by—the sentencing guidelines. We are sensitive to the cynicism expressed by some about the motives of those companies that will adopt ethics programs to capitalize on the "rewards" provided by such compliance.[19] We confess, however, that we think it is more important that organizations adopt effective compliance programs than that they do so for altruistic reasons. While we would always have argued that the principles set forth by the Sentencing Commission for a responsible compliance program were exemplary from an ethical perspective, we suggest that adherence to these principles—as a practical matter—is now imperative. Managers should also be aware that the Justice Department has recently announced similar guidelines. Companies with in-place environmental compliance audits that promptly report violations will qualify for "prosecution leniency."[20]

The sentencing guidelines address criminal behavior and sanctions. For us, legal compliance is a necessary, but insufficient, standard for the conduct of the modern organization. It is possible that an organization could behave legally on every dimension, yet demonstrate a near total disregard for managerial ethics and social responsibility. This sentiment may never have been stated more definitively than by Alexander Solzhenitsyn:

> I have spent all my life under a communist regime, and I will tell you that society without any objective legal scale is a terrible one indeed. But, a society with no other scale but the legal one is not quite worthy of man either . . . Life organized legalistically has shown its inability to defend itself against the corrosion of evil.[21]

We would hope that the U.S. sentencing guidelines do provide an incentive for organizations to establish compliance programs or to review and amend existing programs. Also, we hope that attention to these opportunities will acquaint employees at all levels with the commitment of the organization to establish, monitor, and enforce these programs. Beyond that, we would hope that programs consistent with the culpability guidelines of the Sentencing Commission will produce ripple effects that go beyond curbing illegal behavior to reach behavior that is "only" unethical.

There may be another aspect of the sentencing guidelines which may lead—somewhat more indirectly—to improved attention to ethical outcomes in the organization. A fascinating, and troublesome, point has recently been made. It seems that many managers are reluctant to recount their actions in moral terms even when, in fact, they are morally motivated. Instead, they adopt postures that justify such moral behavior only on the basis of "organizational interests, practicality, and economic good sense."[22]

Such postures are evidently of long standing as they echo de Tocqueville's observation that Americans in business enterprise were disinclined to admit altruistic behavior, even while engaging in it.[23] Certainly, the sentencing guidelines afford ethically motivated managers with additional prudential arguments in favor of corporate attention to ethical concerns. Perhaps the sentencing guidelines, by establishing a pretext for the discussion of ethical issues, will help lure morality out of the organizational closet.

Perhaps three matters bear repeating. First, any programs which may entitle an organization to decreases in the critical culpability index must be in place prior to any infraction. Second, it is not necessary that these programs actually lead to the discovery of prohibited behavior to qualify for culpability reduction. The Sentencing Commission commentary emphasizes that the "hallmark" of a meaningful program is that the organization exercised "due diligence" in seeking to prevent and detect criminal conduct by its employees and other agents.[24] Judge William W. Wilkins, chairman of the Sentencing Commission, noted that "Even the best efforts to prevent crime may not be successful in every case. But we have to reward the corporation that was trying to be a good corporate citizen."[25] Last, if attention to these sentencing guidelines, multipliers, culpability scores, and related issues are not "imperative" for the contemporary organization as we have suggested, it must be something very close to it.

Notes

1. The Sentencing Reform Act of 1984 (U.S.C. §3551 & 28 U.S.C. §§991–998) established the U.S. Sentencing Commission. This commission was created as an independent body of the judicial branch and empowered to provide guidelines for federal judges to follow in the sentencing of criminals. It is fair to say that these "guidelines" are not advisory, but determinate and binding on federal courts. While always referred to as "guidelines," departures from the standards set forth by the Sentencing Commission are subject to appeal by either the defendant or the government. For general commentary on the Sentencing Commission, see M. A. Cohen, "Explaining Judicial Behavior or What's 'Unconstitutional' About the Sentencing Commission," *Journal of Law, Economics, & Organization,* 7, 1991. 183–199. In *Mistretta v. U.S.* (682 F. Supp. 1033) the Supreme Court upheld (8–1; January 18, 1989) the constitutionality of the Sentencing Commission.

2. U.S. Sentencing Commission, "Sentencing Guidelines for Organizational Defendants," *Federal Register,* 56, 1991, 22786–22797.

3. L. Chambliss, "Hang 'em High." *Financial World,* July 9, 1991, 20–21.

4. T. Smart, "The Crackdown on Crime in the Suites," *Business Week,* April 23, 1991, 102–104.

5. There is virtually no evidence that managerial ethics/social responsibility is associated with improved financial performance of the firm. See: K. E. Aupperle, A. B. Carroll, and J. D. Hatfield, *Academy of Management Journal,* 28, 1985, 446–463; P. L. Cochran and R. A. Wood, "Corporate Social Responsibility and Financial Performance," *Academy of Management Journal,* 27, 1984, 42–56; J. B. McGuire, A. Sundren, and T. Schneeweis, "Corporate Social Responsibility and Firm Financial Performance," *Academy of Management Journal,* 31, 1988, 854–872.

6. See Paul T. Mentzler in *Medical Costs, Moral Choices* (New Haven, CT: Yale University Press, 1987), vi. We should note, however, that it is cited there as an "aphorism." Despite our efforts, we do not know the original source of this comment. No disrespect is meant to economists as a group; our point is that all things may not be subject to cost/benefit analysis.

7. J. O'Toole, "Doing Good by Doing Well: The Business Enterprise Trust Awards," *California Management Review,* 33, 1991, 21.

8. D. Vogel, "Ethics and Profits Don't Always Go Hand in Hand," *Ethics: Easier Said than Done,* 2, 1988, 63 (emphasis is ours).

9. See J. M. Kaplan, "Now Is the Time to Review Corporate Compliance Programs," *Ethikos,* 5, 1991, 8–9; 11. The statement is by law professor John Coffee of Columbia University, p. 11.

10. Kaplan, *op.cit.*

11. For some discussion of this point, see G. J. Wallance, "Guidelines on Corporate Crime Emphasize Prevention Programs," *The National Law Journal,* July 1, 1991, 22–23.

12. See Wallance, *op.cit.*, and Kaplan, *op.cit.*, for more detail on the derivation of offense levels and multipliers on which we rely for the examples in the text.

13. A. W. Singer, "Ethics Programs Could Save Companies Millions under New Sentencing Guidelines," *Ethikos,* 4, 1991, 1.

14. A. S. Hayes, "Corporate Sentencing Guidelines Trigger Limited Initial Response," *Wall Street Journal,* Nov. 1, 1991, B1, col. 4–5.

15. See Sec. 8A1.2. Also, quoted text in this section is from the Sentencing Guidelines' commentary.

16. We derive these guidelines from Wallance, *op. cit.* and Kaplan, *op. cit.*

17. See, for example, A. J. Chaset, and B. B. Weintraub, "New Guidelines for Sentencing Corporations," *Trial,* 28, 4, 1992, 41–44.

18. See Chaset and Weintraub, *op.cit.* 42.

19. See B. Hager, "What's Behind Business' Sudden Fervor for Ethics?" *Business Week,* September 23, 1991, 65.

20. J. Moses and W. Lambert, "Companies Given Spur to Uncover Own Environmental Wrongdoing," *The Wall Street Journal,* Sept. 25, 1991, B2. Environmental violations are not included in the U.S. Sentencing Commission Guidelines. Therefore, this opinion of the Justice Department could be an important indicator of sentencing under the various

environmental statutes. See Wallance, *op.cit.* for more detail on sentencing under environmental statutes.

21. Alexander Solzhenitsyn, "A World Split Apart," commencement address delivered at Harvard University, June 8, 1983, from G. Starling, *The Changing Environment of Business* (Boston, MA: Kent Publishing Company, 1984).

22. F. B. Bird and J. A. Waters, "The Moral Muteness of Managers," *California Management Review, 32,* 1989, 73. This point is also nicely made in R. Jackall, *Moral Mazes: The World of Corporate Managers* (New York, NY: Oxford University Press, 1988), see especially, Ch. 4. It is noted, for example, that managers who attend to ethical/moral considerations not associated with pragmatism in the workplace are at serious risk of breaking a "cardinal rule" of managerial circles: "you . . . don't play holier than thou," p. 97.

23. Alexis de Tocqueville, *Democracy in America,* Vol. 2, translated by Henry Reeve, revised by Francis Bowen (New York, NY: Mentor Books, 1945), 129–132. We acknowledge Bird and Waters, *op.cit.* for bringing this insight to our attention.

24. See Wallance, *op.cit.*, Kaplan, *op.cit.*, and Singer, *op.cit.*, for more detail on this point.

25. See Hager, *op.cit.,* p. 65 for these comments by Judge Wilkins.

The Parable of the Sadhu

BOWEN H. McCOY

It was early in the morning before the sun rose, which gave them time to climb the treacherous slope to the pass at 18,000 feet before the ice steps melted. They were also concerned about their stamina and altitude sickness, and felt the need to press on. Into the chance collection of climbers on that Himalayan slope an ethical dilemma arose in the guise of an unconscious, almost naked sadhu, an Indian holy man. Each climber gave the sadhu help but none made sure he would be safe. Should somebody have stopped to help the sadhu to safety? Would it have done any good? Was the group responsible? Since leaving the sadhu on the mountain slope, the author, who was one of the climbers, has pondered these issues. He sees many parallels for business people as they face ethical decisions at work.

Last year, as the first participant in the new six-month sabbatical program that Morgan Stanley has adopted, I enjoyed a rare opportunity to collect my thoughts as well as do some traveling. I spent the first three months in Nepal, walking 600 miles through 200 villages in the Himalayas and climbing some 120,000 vertical feet. On the trip my sole Western companion was an anthropologist who shed light on the cultural patterns of the villages we passed through.

During the Nepal hike, something occurred that has had a powerful impact on my thinking about corporate ethics. Although some might argue that the experience has no relevance to business, it was a situation in which a basic ethical dilemma suddenly intruded into the lives of a group of individuals. How the group responded I think holds a lesson for all organizations no matter how defined.

The Sadhu

The Nepal experience was more rugged and adventuresome than I had anticipated. Most commercial treks last two or three weeks and cover a quarter of the distance we traveled.

My friend Stephen, the anthropologist, and I were halfway through the 60-day Himalayan part of the trip when we reached the high point, an 18,000-foot pass over a crest that we'd have to traverse to reach the village of Muklinath, an ancient holy place for pilgrims.

Six years earlier I had suffered pulmonary edema, an acute form of altitude sickness, at 16,500 feet in the vicinity of Everest base camp, so we were understandably concerned about what would happen at 18,000 feet. Moreover, the Himalayas were having their wettest spring in 20 years; hip-deep powder and ice had already driven us off one ridge. If we failed to cross the pass, I feared that the last half of our "once in a lifetime" trip would be ruined.

The night before we would try the pass, we camped at a hut at 14,500 feet. In the photos taken at that camp, my face appears wan. The last village we'd passed through was a sturdy two-day walk below us, and I was tired.

During the late afternoon, four backpackers from New Zealand joined us, and we spent most of the night awake, anticipating the climb. Below we could see the fires of two other parties, which turned out to be two Swiss couples and a Japanese hiking club.

To get over the steep part of the climb before the sun melted the steps cut in the ice, we departed at 3:30 A.M. The New Zealanders left first, followed by Stephen and myself, our porters and Sherpas, and then the Swiss. The Japanese lingered in their camp. The sky was clear, and we were confident that no spring storm would erupt that day to close the pass.

At 15,500 feet, it looked to me as if Stephen were shuffling and staggering a bit, which are symptoms of altitude sickness. (The initial stage of altitude sickness brings a headache and nausea. As the condition worsens, a climber may encounter difficult breathing, disorientation, aphasia, and paralysis.) I felt strong, my adrenaline was flowing, but I was very concerned about my ultimate ability to get across. A couple of our porters were also suffering from the height, and Pasang, our Sherpa sirdar (leader), was worried.

Just after daybreak, while we rested at 15,500 feet, one of the New Zealanders, who had gone ahead, came staggering down toward us with a body slung across his shoulders. He dumped the almost naked, barefoot body of an Indian holy man—a sadhu—at my feet. He had found the pilgrim lying on the ice, shivering and suffering from hypothermia. I cradled the sadhu's head and laid him out on the rocks. The New Zealander was angry. He wanted to get across the pass before the bright sun melted the snow. He said, "Look, I've done what I can. You have porters and Sherpa guides. You care for him. We're going on!" He turned and went back up the mountain to join his friends.

I took a carotid pulse and found that the sadhu was still alive. We figured he had probably visited the holy shrines at Muklinath and was on his way home. It was fruitless to question why he had chosen this desperately high route instead of the safe, heavily traveled caravan route through the Kali Gandaki gorge. Or why he was almost naked and with no shoes, or how long he had been lying in the pass. The answers weren't going to solve our problem.

Stephen and the four Swiss began stripping off outer clothing and opening their packs. The sadhu was soon clothed from head to foot. He was not able to walk, but he was very much alive. I looked down the mountain and spotted below the Japanese climbers marching up with a horse.

Without a great deal of thought, I told Stephen and Pasang that I was concerned about withstanding the heights to come and wanted to get over the pass. I took off after several of our porters who had gone ahead.

On the steep part of the ascent where, if the ice steps had given way, I would have slid down about 3,000 feet, I felt vertigo. I stopped for a breather, allowing the Swiss to catch up with me. I inquired about the sadhu and Stephen. They said that the sadhu was fine and that Stephen was just behind. I set off again for the summit.

Stephen arrived at the summit an hour after I did. Still exhilarated by victory, I ran down the snow slope to congratulate him. He was suffering from altitude sickness, walking 15 steps, then stopping, walking 15 steps, then stopping. Pasang accompanied him all the way up. When I reached them, Stephen glared at me and said: "How do you feel about contributing to the death of a fellow man?"

I did not fully comprehend what he meant.

"Is the sadhu dead?" I inquired.

"No," replied Stephen, "but he surely will be!"

After I had gone, and the Swiss had departed not long after, Stephen had remained with the sadhu. When the Japanese had arrived, Stephen had asked to use their horse to transport the sadhu down to the hut. They had refused. He had then asked Pasang to have a group of our porters carry the sadhu. Pasang had resisted the idea, saying that the porters would have to exert all their energy to get themselves over the pass. He had thought they could not carry a man down 1,000 feet to the hut, reclimb the slope, and get across safely before the snow melted. Pasang had pressed Stephen not to delay any longer.

The Sherpas had carried the sadhu down to a rock in the sun at about 15,000 feet and had pointed out the hut another 500 feet below. The Japanese had given him food and drink. When they had last seen him he was listlessly throwing rocks at the Japanese party's dog, which had frightened him.

We do not know if the sadhu lived or died.

For many of the following days and evenings Stephen and I discussed and debated our behavior toward the sadhu. Stephen is a committed Quaker with deep moral vision. He said, "I feel that what happened with the sadhu is a good example of the breakdown between the individual ethic and the corporate ethic. No one person was willing to assume ultimate responsibility for the sadhu. Each was willing to do his bit just so long as it was not too inconvenient. When it got to be a bother, everyone just passed the buck to someone else and took off. Jesus was relevant to a more individualistic stage of society, but how do we interpret his teaching today in a world filled with large, impersonal organizations and groups?"

I defended the larger group, saying, "Look, we all cared. We all stopped and gave aid and comfort. Everyone did his bit. The New Zealander carried him down below the snow line. I took his pulse and suggested we treat him for hypothermia. You and the Swiss gave him clothing and got him warmed up. The Japanese gave him food and water. The Sherpas carried him down to the sun and pointed out the easy trail toward the hut. He was well enough to throw rocks at a dog. What more could we do?"

"You have just described the typical affluent Westerner's response to a problem. Throwing money—in this case food and sweaters—at it, but not solving the fundamentals!" Stephen retorted.

"What would satisfy you?" I said. "Here we are, a group of New Zealanders, Swiss, Americans, and Japanese who have never met before and who are at the apex of one of the most powerful experiences of our lives. Some years the pass is so bad no one gets over it. What right does an almost naked pilgrim who chooses the wrong trail have to disrupt our lives? Even the Sherpas had no interest in risking the trip to help him beyond a certain point."

Stephen calmly rebutted, "I wonder what the Sherpas would have done if the sadhu had been a well-dressed Nepali, or what the Japanese would have done if the sadhu had been a well-dressed Asian, or what you would have done, Buzz, if the sadhu had been a well-dressed Western woman?"

"Where, in your opinion," I asked instead, "is the limit of our responsibility in a situation like this? We had our own well-being to worry about. Our Sherpa guides were unwilling to jeopardize us or the porters for the sadhu. No one else on the mountain was willing to commit himself beyond certain self-imposed limits."

Stephen said, "As individual Christians or people with a Western ethical tradition, we can fulfill our obligations in such a situation only if (1) the sadhu dies in our care, (2) the sadhu demonstrates to us that he could undertake the two-day walk down to the village, or (3) we carry the sadhu for two days down to the village and convince someone there to care for him."

"Leaving the sadhu in the sun with food and clothing, while he demonstrated hand-eye coordination by throwing a rock at a dog, comes close to fulfilling items one and two," I answered. "And it wouldn't have made sense to take him to the village where the people appeared to be far less caring than the Sherpas, so the third condition is impractical. Are you really saying that, no matter what the implications, we should, at the drop of a hat, have changed our entire plan?"

The Individual vs. the Group Ethic

Despite my arguments, I felt and continue to feel guilt about the sadhu. I had literally walked through a classic moral dilemma without fully thinking through the consequences. My excuses for my actions include a high adrenaline flow, a superordinate goal, and a once-in-a-lifetime opportunity—factors in the usual corporate situation, especially when one is under stress.

Real moral dilemmas are ambiguous, and many of us hike right through them, unaware that they exist. When, usually after the fact, someone makes an issue of them, we tend to resent his or her bringing it up. Often, when the full import of what we have done (or not done) falls on us, we dig into a defensive position from which it is very difficult to emerge. In rare circumstances we may contemplate what we have done from inside a prison.

Had we mountaineers been free of physical and mental stress caused by the effort and the high altitude, we might have treated the sadhu differently. Yet isn't stress the real test of personal and corporate values? The instant decisions executives make under pressure reveal the most about personal and corporate character.

Among the many questions that occur to me when pondering my experience are: What are the practical limits of moral imagination and vision? Is there a collective or institutional ethic beyond the ethics of the individual? At what level of effort or commitment can one discharge one's ethical responsibilities?

Not every ethical dilemma has a right solution. Reasonable people often disagree; otherwise there would be no dilemma. In a business context, however, it is essential that managers agree on a process for dealing with dilemmas.

The sadhu experience offers an interesting parallel to business situations. An immediate response was mandatory. Failure to act was a decision in itself. Up on the mountain we could not resign and submit our résumés to a headhunter. In contrast to philosophy, business involves action and implementation—getting things done. Managers must come up with answers to problems based on what they see and what they allow to influence their decision-making processes. On the mountain, none of us but Stephen realized the true dimensions of the situation we were facing.

One of our problems was that as a group we had no process for developing a consensus. We had no sense of purpose or plan. The difficulties of dealing with the sadhu were so complex that no one person could handle it. Because it did not have a set of preconditions that could guide its action to an acceptable resolution, the group reacted instinctively as individuals. The cross-cultural nature of the group added a further layer of complexity. We had no leader with whom we could all identify and in whose purpose we believed. Only Stephen was willing to take charge, but he could not gain adequate support to care for the sadhu.

Some organizations do have a value system that transcends the personal values of the managers. Such values, which go beyond profitability, are usually revealed when the organization is under stress. People throughout the organization generally accept its values, which, because they are not presented as a rigid list of commandments, may be somewhat ambiguous. The stories people tell, rather than printed materials, transmit these conceptions of what is proper behavior.

For 20 years I have been exposed at senior levels to a variety of corporations and organizations. It is amazing how quickly an outsider can sense the tone and style of an organization and the degree of tolerated openness and freedom to challenge management.

Organizations that do not have a heritage of mutually accepted, shared values tend to become unhinged during stress, with each individual bailing out for himself. In the great takeover battles we have witnessed during past years, companies that had strong cultures drew the wagons around them and fought it out, while other companies saw executives, supported by their golden parachutes, bail out of the struggles.

Because corporations and their members are interdependent, for the corporation to be strong the members need to share a preconceived notion of what is correct behavior, a "business ethic," and think of it as a positive force, not a constraint.

As an investment banker I am continually warned by well-meaning lawyers, clients, and associates to be wary of conflicts of interest. Yet if I were to run away from every difficult situation, I wouldn't be an effective investment banker. I have to feel my way through conflicts. An effective manager can't run from risk either; he or she has to confront and deal with risk. To feel "safe" in doing this, managers need the guidelines of an agreed-on process and set of values within the organization.

After my three months in Nepal, I spent three months as an executive-in-residence at both Stanford Business School and the Center for Ethics and Social Policy at the Graduate Theological Union at Berkeley. These six months away from my job gave me time to assimilate 20 years of business experience. My thoughts turned often to the meaning of the leadership role in any large organization. Students at the seminary thought of themselves as antibusiness. But when I questioned them they agreed that they distrusted all large organizations, including the church. They perceived all large organizations as impersonal and opposed to individual values and needs. Yet we all know of organizations where peoples' values and beliefs are respected and their expressions encouraged. What makes the difference? Can we identify the difference and, as a result, manage more effectively?

The word "ethics" turns off many and confuses more. Yet the notions of shared values and an agreed-on process for dealing with adversity and change—what many people mean when they talk about corporate culture—seem to be at the heart of the ethical issue. People who are in touch with their own core beliefs and the beliefs of others and are sustained by them can be more comfortable living on the cutting edge. At times, taking a tough line or a decisive stand in a muddle of ambiguity is the only ethical thing to do. If a manager is indecisive and spends time trying to figure out the "good" thing to do, the enterprise may be lost.

Business ethics, then, has to do with the authenticity and integrity of the enterprise. To be ethical is to follow the business as well as the cultural goals of the corporation, its owners, its employees, and its customers. Those who cannot serve the corporate vision are not authentic business people and, therefore, are not ethical in the business sense.

At this stage of my own business experience I have a strong interest in organizational behavior. Sociologists are keenly studying what they call corporate stories, legends, and heroes as a way organizations have of transmitting the value system. Corporations such as Arco have even hired consultants to perform an audit of their corporate culture. In a company, the leader is the person who understands, interprets, and manages the corporate value system. Effective managers are then action-oriented people who resolve conflict, are tolerant of ambiguity, stress, and change, and have a strong sense of purpose for themselves and their organizations.

If all this is true, I wonder about the role of the professional manager who moves from company to company. How can he or she quickly absorb the values and culture of different organizations? Or is there, indeed, an art of management that is totally transportable? Assuming such fungible managers do exist, is it proper for them to manipulate the values of others?

What would have happened had Stephen and I carried the sadhu for two days back to the village and become involved with the villagers in his care? In four trips to Nepal my most interesting experiences occurred in 1975 when I lived in a Sherpa home in the Khumbu for five days recovering from altitude sickness. The high point of Stephen's trip was an invitation to participate in a family funeral ceremony in Manang. Neither experience had to do with climbing the high passes of the Himalayas. Why were we so reluctant to try the lower path, the ambiguous trail? Perhaps because we did not have a leader who could reveal the greater purpose of the trip to us.

Why didn't Stephen with his moral vision opt to take the sadhu under his personal care? The answer is because, in part, Stephen was hard-stressed physically himself, and because, in part, without some support system that involved our involuntary and episodic community on the mountain, it was beyond his individual capacity to do so.

I see the current interest in corporate culture and corporate value systems as a positive response to Stephen's pessimism about the decline of the role of the individual in large organizations. Individuals who operate from a thoughtful set of personal values provide the foundation for a corporate culture. A corporate tradition that encourages freedom of inquiry, supports personal values, and reinforces a focused sense of direction can fulfill the need for individuality along with the prosperity and success of the group. Without such corporate support, the individual is lost.

That is the lesson of the sadhu. In a complex corporate situation, the individual requires and deserves the support of the group. If people cannot find such support from their organization, they don't know how to act. If such support is forthcoming, a person has a stake in the success of the group, and can add much to the process of establishing and maintaining a corporate culture. It is management's challenge to be sensitive to individual needs, to shape them, and to direct and focus them for the benefit of the group as a whole.

For each of us the sadhu lives. Should we stop what we are doing and comfort him; or should we keep trudging up toward the high pass? Should I pause to help the derelict I pass on the street each night as I walk by the Yale Club en route to Grand Central Station? Am I his brother? What is the nature of our responsibility if we consider ourselves to be ethical persons? Perhaps it is to change the values of the group so that it can, with all its resources, take the other road.

Employee Rights
and
Responsibilities

◆ *Case Study* ◆

The Aircraft Brake Scandal

KERMIT VANDIVIER

The B. F. Goodrich Company is what business magazines like to refer to as "a major American corporation." It has operations in a dozen states and as many foreign countries; and of these far-flung facilities, the Goodrich plant at Troy, Ohio, is not the most imposing. It is a small, one-story building, once used to manufacture airplanes. Set in the grassy flatlands of west-central Ohio, it employs only about six hundred people. Nevertheless, it is one of the three largest manufacturers of aircraft wheels and brakes, a leader in a most profitable industry. Goodrich wheels and brakes support such well-known planes as the F111, the C5A, the Boeing 727, the XB70, and many others.

Contracts for aircraft wheels and brakes often run into millions of dollars, and ordinarily a contract with a total value of less than $70,000, though welcome, would not create any special stir of joy in the hearts of Goodrich sales personnel. But purchase order P-237138—issued on June 18, 1967, by the LTV Aerospace Corporation, ordering 202 brake assemblies for a new Air Force plane at a total price of $69,417—was received by Goodrich with considerable glee. And there was good reason. Some ten years previously, Goodrich had built a brake for LTV that was, to say the least, considerably less than a rousing success. The brake had not lived up to Goodrich's promises, and after experiencing considerable difficulty, LTV had written off Goodrich as a source of brakes. Since that time, Goodrich salesmen had been unable to sell so much as a shot of brake fluid to LTV. So in 1967, when LTV requested bids on wheels and brakes for the new A7D light attack aircraft it proposed to build for the Air Force, Goodrich submitted a bid that was absurdly low, so low that LTV could not, in all prudence, turn it down.

Goodrich had, in industry parlance, "bought into the business." The company did not expect to make a profit on the initial deal; it was prepared, if necessary, to lose money. But aircraft brakes are not something that can be ordered off the shelf. They are designed for a particular aircraft, and once an aircraft manufacturer buys a brake, he is forced to purchase all replacement parts from the brake manufacturer. The $70,000 that Goodrich would get for making the brake would be a drop in the bucket when compared with the cost of the linings and other parts the Air Force would have to buy from Goodrich during the lifetime of the aircraft.

There was another factor, besides the low bid, that had undoubtedly influenced LTV. All aircraft brakes made today are of the disk type, and the bid submitted by Goodrich called for a relatively small brake, one containing four disks and weighing only 106 pounds. The weight of any aircraft is extremely important: the lighter a part is, the heavier the plane's payload can be.

The brake was designed by one of Goodrich's most capable engineers, John Warren. A tall, lanky, blond graduate of Purdue, Warren had come from the Chrysler Corporation seven years before and had become adept at aircraft brake design. The happy-go-lucky manner he usually maintained belied a temper that exploded whenever anyone ventured to offer criticism of his work, no matter how small. On these occasions, Warren would turn red in the face, often throwing or slamming something and then stalking from the scene. As his coworkers learned the consequences of criticizing him, they did so less and less readily, and when he submitted his preliminary design for the A7D brake, it was accepted without question.

Warren was named project engineer for the A7D, and he, in turn, assigned the task of producing the final production design to a newcomer to the Goodrich engineering stable, Searle Lawson. Just turned twenty-six, Lawson had been out of the Northrop Institute of Technology only one year when he came to Goodrich in January, 1967. He had been assigned to various "paper projects" to break him in, and after several months spent reviewing statistics and old brake designs, he was beginning to fret at the lack of challenge. When told he was being assigned to his first "real" project, he was elated and immediately plunged into his work.

The major portion of the design had already been completed by Warren, and major subassemblies for the brake had already been ordered from Goodrich suppliers. Naturally, however, before Goodrich could start making the brakes on a production basis, much testing would have to be done. Lawson would have to determine the best materials to use for the linings and discover what minor adjustments in the design would have to be made.

Then, after the preliminary testing and after the brake was judged ready for production, one whole brake assembly would undergo a series of grueling, simulated braking stops and other severe trials called qualification tests. These tests are required by the military, which gives very detailed specifications on how they are to be conducted, the criteria for failure, and so on. They are performed in the Goodrich plant's test laboratory, where huge machines called dynamometers can simulate the weight and speed of almost any aircraft.

Searle Lawson was well aware that much work had to be done before the A7D brake could go into production, and he knew that LTV had set the last two weeks of June 1968 as the starting dates for flight tests. So he decided to begin testing immediately. Goodrich's suppliers had not yet delivered the brake housing and other parts, but the brake disks had arrived, and using the housing from a brake similar in size and weight to the A7D brake,

Lawson built a prototype. The prototype was installed in a test wheel and placed on one of the big dynamometers in the plant's test laboratory. Lawson began a series of tests, "landing" the wheel and brake at the A7D's landing speed and braking it to a stop. The main purpose of these preliminary tests was to learn what temperatures would develop within the brake during the simulated stops and to evaluate lining materials tentatively selected for use.

During a normal aircraft landing the temperatures inside the brake may reach 1,000 degrees, and occasionally a bit higher. During Lawson's first simulated landings, the temperature of his prototype brake reached 1,500 degrees. The brake glowed a bright cherry-red and threw off incandescent particles of metal and lining material as the temperature reached its peak. After a few such stops, the brake was dismantled and the linings were found to be almost completely disintegrated. Lawson chalked this first failure up to chance, and ordering new lining materials, tried again.

The second attempt was a repeat of the first. The brake became extremely hot, causing the lining materials to crumble into dust.

After the third such failure, Lawson, inexperienced though he was, knew that the fault lay not in defective parts or unsuitable lining material but in the basic design of the brake itself. Ignoring Warren's original computations, Lawson made his own, and it didn't take him long to discover where the trouble lay—the brake was too small. There simply was not enough surface area on the disks to stop the aircraft without generating the excessive heat that caused the linings to fail.

The answer to the problem was obvious, but far from simple—the four-disk brake would have to be scrapped, and a new design, using five disks, would have to be developed. The implications were not lost on Lawson. Such a step would require junking the four-disk-brake subassemblies, many of which had now begun to arrive from the various suppliers. It would also mean several weeks of preliminary design and testing and many more weeks of waiting while the suppliers made and delivered the new subassemblies.

Yet, several weeks had already gone by since LTV's order had arrived, and the date for delivery of the first production brakes for flight testing was only a few months away.

Although John Warren had more or less turned the A7D over to Lawson, he knew of the difficulties Lawson had been experiencing. He had assured the younger engineer that the problem revolved around getting the right kind of lining material. Once that was found, he said, the difficulties would end.

Despite the evidence of the abortive tests and Lawson's careful computations, Warren rejected the suggestion that the four-disk brake was too light for the job. He knew that his superior had already told LTV, in rather glowing terms, that the preliminary tests on the A7D brake were very successful. Indeed, Warren's superiors weren't aware at this time of the troubles on the brake. It would have been difficult for Warren to admit not only that he had made a serious error in his calculations and original design but that his mistakes had been caught by a green kid, barely out of college.

Warren's reaction to a five-disk brake was not unexpected by Lawson, and, seeing that the four-disk brake was not to be abandoned so easily, he took his calculations and dismal test results one step up the corporate ladder.

At Goodrich, the man who supervises the engineers working on projects slated for production is called, predictably, the projects manager. The job was held by a short, chubby, bald man named Robert Sink. Some fifteen years before, Sink had begun working at Goodrich as a lowly draftsman. Slowly, he worked his way up. Despite his geniality, Sink was neither respected nor liked by the majority of the engineers, and his appointment as their supervisor did not improve their feelings toward him. He possessed only a high-school diploma, and it quite naturally rankled those who had gone through years of college to be commanded by a man whom they considered their intellectual inferior. But, though Sink had no college training, he had something even more useful: a fine working knowledge of company politics.

Puffing on a Meerschaum pipe, Sink listened gravely as young Lawson confided his fears about the four-disk brake. Then he examined Lawson's calculations and the results of the abortive tests. Despite the fact that he was not a qualified engineer, in the strictest sense of the word, it must certainly have been obvious to Sink that Lawson's calculations were correct and that a four-disk brake would never work on the A7D.

But other things of equal importance were also obvious. First, to concede that Lawson's calculations were correct would also mean conceding that Warren's calculations were incorrect. As projects manager, not only was he responsible for Warren's activities, but in admitting that Warren had erred he would also have to admit that he had erred in trusting Warren's judgment. It also meant that, as projects manager, it would be he who would have to explain the whole messy situation to the Goodrich hierarchy, not only at Troy but possibly on the corporate level at Goodrich's Akron offices. And having taken Warren's judgment of the four-disk brake at face value, he had assured LTV, not once but several times, that about all there was left to do on the brake was pack it in a crate and ship it out the door.

There's really no problem at all, he told Lawson. After all, Warren was an experienced engineer, and if he said the brake would work, it would work. Just keep on testing and probably, maybe even on the very next try, it'll work out just fine.

Lawson was far from convinced, but without the support of his superiors there was little he could do except keep on testing. By now, housings for the four-disk brake had begun to arrive at the plant, and Lawson was able to build a production model of the brake and begin the formal qualification tests demanded by the military.

The first qualification attempts went exactly as the tests on the prototype had. Terrific heat developed within the brakes, and after a few short, simulated stops the linings crumbled. A new type of lining material was ordered and once again an attempt to qualify the brake was made. Again, failure.

Experts were called in from lining manufacturers, and new lining "mixes" were tried, always with the same result. Failure.

It was now the last week of March 1968, and flight tests were scheduled to begin in seventy days. Twelve separate attempts had been made to qualify the brake, and all had failed. It was no longer possible for anyone to ignore the glaring truth that the brake was a dismal failure and that nothing short of a major design change could ever make it work.

On April 4, the thirteenth attempt at qualification was begun. This time no attempt was made to conduct the tests by the methods and techniques spelled out in the military specifications. Regardless of how it had to be done, the brake was to be "nursed" through the required fifty simulated stops.

Fans were set up to provide special cooling. Instead of maintaining pressure on the brake until the test wheel had come to a complete stop, the pressure was reduced when the wheel had decelerated to around 15 mph, allowing it to "coast" to a stop. After each stop, the brake was disassembled and carefully cleaned, and after some of the stops, internal brake parts were machined in order to remove warp and other disfigurations caused by the high heat.

By these and other methods, all clearly contrary to the techniques established by the military specifications, the brake was coaxed through the fifty stops. But even using these methods, the brake could not meet all the requirements. On one stop the wheel rolled for a distance of 16,000 feet, or over three miles, before the brake could bring it to a stop. The normal distance required for such a stop was around 3,500 feet.

On April 11, the day the thirteenth test was completed, I became personally involved in the A7D situation.

I had worked in the Goodrich test laboratory for five years, starting first as an instrumentation engineer, then later becoming a data analyst and technical writer. As part of my duties, I analyzed the reams and reams of instrumentation data that came from the many testing machines in the lab, then transcribed all of it to a more usable form for the engineering department. When a new-type brake had successfully completed the required qualification tests, I would issue a formal qualification report.

Qualification reports are an accumulation of all the data and test logs compiled during the qualification tests and are documentary proof that a brake has met all the requirements established by the military specifications and is therefore presumed safe for flight testing. Before actual flight tests are conducted on a brake, qualification reports have to be delivered to the customer and to various government officials.

On April 11, I was looking over the data from the latest A7D test, and I noticed that many irregularities in testing had been noted on the test logs.

Technically, of course, there was nothing wrong with conducting tests in any manner desired, so long as the test was for research purposes only. But qualification test methods are clearly delineated by the military, and I knew that this test had been a formal qualification attempt. One particular notation on the test logs caught my eye. For some of the stops, the instrument that recorded the brake pressure had been deliberately miscalibrated so that, while the brake pressure used during the stops was recorded as 1,000 psi (pounds per square inch)—the maximum pressure that would be available on the A7D aircraft—the pressure had actually been 1,100 psi.

I showed the test logs to the test lab supervisor, Ralph Gretzinger, who said he had learned from the technician who had miscalibrated the instrument that he had been asked to do so by Lawson. Lawson, said Gretzinger, readily admitted asking for the miscalibration, saying he had been told to do so by Sink.

I asked Gretzinger why anyone would want to miscalibrate the data-recording instrument.

"Why? I'll tell you why," he snorted. "That brake is a failure. It's way too small for the job, and they're not ever going to get it to work. They're getting desperate, and instead of scrapping the damned thing and starting over, they figure they can horse around down here in the lab and qualify it that way."

An expert engineer, Gretzinger had been responsible for several innovations in brake design. It was he who had invented the unique brake system used on the famous XB70. "If you want to find out what's going on," said Gretzinger, "ask Lawson; he'll tell you."

Curious, I did ask Lawson the next time he came into the lab. He seemed eager to discuss the A7D and gave me the history of his months of frustrating efforts to get Warren and Sink to change the brake design. "I just can't believe this is really happening," said Lawson, shaking his head slowly. "This isn't engineering, at least not what I thought it would be. Back in school, I thought that when you were an engineer you tried to do your best, no matter what it cost. But this is something else."

He sat across the desk from me, his chin propped in his hand. "Just wait," he warned. "You'll get a chance to see what I'm talking about. You're going to get in the act too, because I've already had the word that we're going to make one more attempt to qualify the brake, and that's it. Win or lose, we're going to issue a qualification report!"

I reminded him that a qualification report could be issued only after a brake had successfully met all military requirements, and therefore, unless the next qualification attempt was a success, no report would be issued.

"You'll find out," retorted Lawson. "I was already told that regardless of what the brake does on test, it's going to be qualified." He said he had been told in those exact words at a conference with Sink and Russell Van Horn.

This was the first indication that Sink had brought his boss, Van Horn, into the mess. Although Van Horn, as manager of the design engineering section, was responsible for the entire department, he was not necessarily familiar with all phases of every project, and it was not uncommon for those under him to exercise the what-he-doesn't-know-won't-hurt-him philosophy. If he was aware of the full extent of the A7D situation, it meant that Sink had decided not only to call for help but to look toward that moment when blame must be borne and, if possible, shared.

Also, if Van Horn had said, "regardless of what the brake does on test, it's going to be qualified," then it could only mean that, if necessary, a false qualification report would be issued. I discussed this possibility with Gretzinger, and he assured me that under no circumstances would such a report ever be issued.

"If they want a qualification report, we'll write them one, but we'll tell it just like it is," he declared emphatically. "No false data or false reports are going to come out of this lab."

On May 2, 1968, the fourteenth and final attempt to qualify the brake was begun. Although the same improper methods used to nurse the brake through the previous tests were employed, it soon became obvious that this too would end in failure.

When the tests were about half completed, Lawson asked if I would start preparing the various engineering curves and graphic displays that were normally incorporated in a qualification report. I flatly refused to have anything to do with the matter and immediately told Gretzinger what I had been asked to do. He was furious and repeated his previous declaration that under no circumstances would any false data or other matter be issued from the lab.

"I'm going to get this settled right now, once and for all," he declared. "I'm going to see Line [Russell Line, manager of the Goodrich Technical Services Section, of which the test lab was a part] and find out just how far this thing is going to go!" He stormed out of the room.

In about an hour, he returned and called me to his desk. He sat silently for a few moments, then muttered, half to himself, "I wonder what the hell they'd do if I just quit?" I didn't answer and I didn't ask him what he meant. I knew. He had been beaten down. He had reached the point when the decision had to be made. Defy them now while there was still time—or knuckle under, sell out.

"You know," he went on uncertainly, looking down at his desk, "I've been an engineer for a long time, and I've always believed that ethics and integrity were every bit as important as theorems and formulas, and never once has anything happened to change my beliefs. Now this . . . Hell I've got two sons I've got to put through school and I just . . ." His voice trailed off.

He sat for a few more minutes, then, looking over the top of his glasses, said hoarsely, "Well, it looks like we're licked. The way it stands now, we're to go ahead and prepare the data and other things for the graphic presentation in the report, and when we're finished, someone upstairs will actually write the report."

"After all," he continued, "we're just drawing some curves, and what happens to them after they leave here—well, we're not responsible for that."

I wasn't at all satisfied with the situation and decided that I too would discuss the matter with Russell Line, the senior executive in our section.

Tall, powerfully built, his teeth flashing white, his face tanned to a coffee-brown by a daily stint with a sunlamp, Line looked and acted every inch the executive. He had been transferred from the Akron offices some two years previously, and he commanded great respect and had come to be well liked by those of us who worked under him.

He listened sympathetically while I explained how I felt about the A7D situation, and when I had finished, he asked me what I wanted him to do about it. I said that as employees of the Goodrich Company we had a responsibility to protect the company and its reputation if at all possible. I said I was certain that officers on the corporate level would never knowingly allow such tactics as had been employed on the A7D.

"I agree with you," he remarked, "but I still want to know what you want me to do about it."

I suggested that in all probability the chief engineer at the Troy plant, H. C. "Bud" Sunderman, was unaware of the A7D problem and that he, Line, could tell him what was going on.

Line laughed, good-humoredly. "Sure, I could, but I'm not going to. Bud probably already knows about this thing anyway, and if he doesn't, I'm sure not going to be the one to tell him."

"But why?"

"Because it's none of my business, and it's none of yours. I learned a long time ago not to worry about things over which I had no control. I have no control over this."

I wasn't satisfied with this answer, and I asked him if his conscience wouldn't bother him if, say, during flight tests on the brake, something should happen resulting in death or injury to the test pilot.

"Look," he said, becoming somewhat exasperated. "I just told you I have no control over this. Why should my conscience bother me?"

His voice took on a quiet, soothing tone as he continued. "You're just getting all upset over this thing for nothing. I just do as I'm told, and I'd advise you to do the same."

I made no attempt to rationalize what I had been asked to do. It made no difference who would falsify which part of the report or whether the actual falsification would be by misleading numbers or misleading words. Whether by acts of commission or omission, all of us who contributed to the fraud would be guilty. The only question left for me to decide was whether or not I would become a party to the fraud.

Before coming to Goodrich in 1963, I had held a variety of jobs, each a little more pleasant, a little more rewarding than the last. At forty-two, with seven children, I had decided that the Goodrich Company would probably be my "home" for the rest of my working life. The job paid well, it was pleasant and challenging, and the future looked reasonably bright. My wife and I had bought a home and we were ready to settle down into a comfortable, middle-age, middle-class rut. If I refused to take part in the A7D fraud, I would have either to resign or be fired. The report would be written by someone anyway, but I would have the satisfaction of knowing I had had no part in the matter. But bills aren't paid with personal satisfaction, nor house payments with ethical principles. I made my decision. The next morning, I telephoned Lawson and told him I was ready to begin on the qualification report.

I had written dozens of qualification reports, and I knew what a "good" one looked like. Resorting to the actual test data only on occasion, Lawson and I proceeded to prepare page after page of elaborate, detailed engineering curves, charts, and test logs, which purported to show what had happened during the formal qualification tests. Where temperatures were too high, we deliberately chopped them down a few hundred degrees, and where they were too low, we raised them to a value that would appear reasonable to the LTV and military engineers. Brake pressure, torque values, distances, times—everything of consequence was tailored to fit.

Occasionally, we would find that some test either hadn't been performed at all or had been conducted improperly. On those occasions, we "conducted" the test—successfully, of course—on paper.

For nearly a month we worked on the graphic presentation that would be a part of the report. Meanwhile, the final qualification attempt had been completed, and the brake, not unexpectedly, had failed again.

We finished our work on the graphic portion of the report around the first of June. Altogether, we had prepared nearly two hundred pages of data, containing dozens of deliberate falsifications and misrepresentations. I delivered the data to Gretzinger, who said he had been instructed to deliver it personally to the chief engineer, Bud Sunderman, who in turn would assign someone in the engineering department to complete the written portion of the report. He gathered the bundle of data and left the office. Within minutes, he was back with the data, his face white with anger.

"That damned Sink's beat me to it," he said furiously. "He's already talked to Bud about this, and now Sunderman says no one in the engineering department has time to write the report. He wants us to do it, and I told him we couldn't."

The words had barely left his mouth when Russell Line burst in the door. "What the hell's all the fuss about this damned report?" he demanded.

Patiently, Gretzinger explained. "There's no fuss. Sunderman just told me that we'd have to write the report down here, and I said we couldn't. Russ," he went on, "I've told you before that we weren't going to write the report. I made my position clear on that a long time ago."

Line shut him up with a wave of his hand and, turning to me, bellowed "I'm getting sick and tired of hearing about this damned report. Now, write the goddamn thing and shut up about it!" He slammed out of the office.

Gretzinger and I just sat for a few seconds looking at each other. Then he spoke.

"Well, I guess he's made it pretty clear, hasn't he? We can either write the thing or quit. You know, what we should have done was quit a long time ago. Now, it's too late."

Somehow I wasn't at all surprised at this turn of events, and it didn't really make that much difference. As far as I was concerned, we were all up to our necks in the thing anyway, and writing the narrative portion of the report couldn't make me more guilty than I already felt myself to be.

Within two days, I had completed the narrative, or written portion, of the report. As a final sop to my own self-respect, in the conclusion of the report I wrote, "The B. F. Goodrich P/N 2–1162–3 brake assembly does not meet the intent or the requirements of the applicable specification documents and therefore is not qualified."

This was a meaningless gesture, since I knew that this would certainly be changed when the report went through the final typing process. Sure enough, when the report was published, the negative conclusion had been made positive.

One final and significant incident occurred just before publication.

Qualification reports always bear the signature of the person who has prepared them. I refused to sign the report, as did Lawson. Warren was later asked to sign the report. He replied that he would "when I receive a signed statement from Bob Sink ordering me to sign it."

The engineering secretary who was delegated the responsibility of "dogging" the report through publication told me later that after I, Lawson, and Warren had all refused to sign the report, she had asked Sink if he would sign. He replied, "On something of this nature, I don't think a signature is really needed."

On June 5, 1968, the report was officially published and copies were delivered by hand to the Air Force and LTV. Within a week flight tests were begun at Edwards Air Force Base in California. Searle Lawson was sent to California as Goodrich's representative. Within approximately two weeks, he returned because some rather unusual incidents during the tests had caused them to be canceled.

His face was grim as he related stories of several near crashes during landings—caused by brake troubles. He told me about one incident in which, upon landing, one brake was literally welded together by the intense heat developed during the test stop. The wheel locked, and the plane skidded for nearly 1,500 feet before coming to a halt. The plane was jacked up and the wheel removed. The fused parts within the brake had to be pried apart.

That evening I left work early and went to see my attorney. After I told him the story, he advised that, while I was probably not actually guilty of fraud, I was certainly part of a conspiracy to defraud. He advised me to go to the Federal Bureau of Investigation and offered to arrange an appointment. The following week he took me to the Dayton office of the FBI, and after I had been warned that I would not be immune from prosecution, I disclosed the A7D matter to one of the agents. The agent told me to say nothing about the episode to anyone and to report any further incidents to him. He said he would forward the story to his superiors in Washington.

A few days later, Lawson returned from a conference with LTV in Dallas and said that the Air Force, which had previously approved the qualification report, had suddenly rescinded that approval and was demanding to see some of the raw test data. I gathered that the FBI had passed the word.

Omitting any reference to the FBI, I told Lawson I had been to an attorney and that we were probably guilty of conspiracy.

"Can you get me an appointment with your attorney?" he asked. Within a week, he had been to the FBI and told them of his part in the mess. He too was advised to say nothing but to keep on the job reporting any new development.

Naturally, with the rescinding of Air Force approval and the demand to see raw test data, Goodrich officials were in a panic. A conference was called for July 27, a Saturday morning affair at which Lawson, Sink, Warren, and I were present. We met in a tiny conference room in the deserted engineering department. Lawson and I, by now openly hostile to Warren and Sink, ranged ourselves on one side of the conference table while Warren sat on the other side. Sink, chairing the meeting, paced slowly in front of a blackboard, puffing furiously on a pipe.

The meeting was called, Sink began, "to see where we stand on the A7D." What we were going to do, he said, was to "level" with LTV and tell them the "whole truth" about the A7D. "After all," he said, "they're in this thing with us, and they have the right to know how matters stand."

"In other words," I asked, "we're going to tell them the truth?"

"That's right," he replied. "We're going to level with them and let them handle the ball from there."

"There's one thing I don't quite understand," I interjected. "Isn't it going to be pretty hard for us to admit to them that we've lied?"

"Now, wait a minute," he said angrily. "Let's don't go off half-cocked on this thing. It's not a matter of lying. We've just interpreted the information the way we felt it should be."

"I don't know what you call it," I replied, "but to me it's lying, and it's going to be damned hard to confess to them that we've been lying all along."

He became very agitated at this and repeated, "We're not lying," adding, "I don't like this sort of talk."

I dropped the matter at this point, and he began discussing the various discrepancies in the report.

We broke for lunch, and afterward, I came back to the plant to find Sink sitting alone at his desk, waiting to resume the meeting. He called me over and said he wanted to apologize for his outburst that morning. "This thing has kind of gotten me down," he confessed, "and I think you've got the wrong picture. I don't think you really understand everything about this."

Perhaps so, I conceded, but it seemed to me that if we had already told LTV one thing and then had to tell them another, changing our story completely, we would have to admit we were lying.

"No," he explained patiently, "we're not really lying. All we were doing was interpreting the figures the way we knew they should be. We were just exercising engineering license."

During the afternoon session, we marked some forty-three discrepant points in the report; forty-three points that LTV would surely spot as occasions where we had exercised "engineering license."

After Sink listed those points on the blackboard, we discussed each one individually. As each point came up, Sink would explain that it was probably "too minor to bother about," or that perhaps it "wouldn't be wise to open that can of worms," or that maybe this was a point that "LTV just wouldn't understand." When the meeting was over, it had been decided that only three points were "worth mentioning."

Similar conferences were held during August and September, and the summer was punctuated with frequent treks between Dallas and Troy and demands by the Air Force to see the raw test data. Tempers were short, and matters seemed to grow worse.

Finally, early in October 1968, Lawson submitted his resignation, to take effect on October 25. On October 18, I submitted my own resignation, to take effect on November 1. In my resignation, addressed to Russell Line, I cited the A7D report and stated: "As you are aware, this report contains numerous deliberate and willful misrepresentations which, according to legal counsel, constitute fraud and expose both myself and others to criminal charges of conspiracy to defraud . . . The events of the past seven months have created an atmosphere of deceit and distrust in which it is impossible to work . . ."

On October 25, I received a sharp summons to the office of Bud Sunderman. Tall and graying, impeccably dressed at all times, he was capable of producing a dazzling smile or a hearty chuckle or immobilizing his face into marble hardness, as the occasion required.

I faced the marble hardness when I reached his office. He motioned me to a chair. "I have your resignation here," he snapped, "and I must say you have made some rather shocking, I might even say irresponsible, charges. This is very serious."

Before I could reply, he was demanding an explanation. "I want to know exactly what the fraud is in connection with the A7D and how you can dare accuse this company of such a thing!"

I started to tell some of the things that had happened during the testing, but he shut me off saying, "There's nothing wrong with anything we've done here. You aren't aware of all the things that have been going on behind the scenes. If you had known the true situation, you would never have made these charges." He said that in view of my apparent "disloyalty" he had decided to accept my resignation "right now," and said it would be better for all concerned if I left the plant immediately. As I got up to leave he asked me if I intended to "carry this thing further."

I answered simply, "Yes," to which he replied, "Suit yourself." With-in twenty minutes, I had cleaned out my desk and left. Forty-eight hours later, the B. F. Goodrich Company recalled the qualification report and the four-disk brake, announcing that it would replace the brake with a new, improved, five-disk brake at no cost to LTV.

Ten months later, on August 13, 1969, I was the chief government wit-ness at a hearing conducted before Senator William Proxmire's Economy in Government Subcommittee. I related the A7D story to the committee, and my testimony was supported by Searle Lawson, who followed me to the witness stand. Air Force officers also testified, as well as a four-man team from the General Accounting Office, which had conducted an investigation of the A7D brake at the request of Senator Proxmire. Both Air Force and GAO investigators declared that the brake was dangerous and had not been tested properly.

Testifying for Goodrich was R. G. Jeter, vice-president and general coun-sel of the company, from the Akron headquarters. Representing the Troy plant was Robert Sink. These two denied any wrongdoing on the part of the Goodrich Company, despite expert testimony to the contrary by Air Force and GAO officials. Sink was quick to deny any connection with the writing of the report or directing of any falsifications, claiming to have been on the West Coast at the time. John Warren was the man who had supervised its writing, said Sink.

As for me, I was dismissed as a high-school graduate with no technical training, while Sink testified that Lawson was a young, inexperienced engi-neer. "We tried to give him guidance," Sink testified, "but he preferred to have his own convictions."

About changing the data to figures in the report, Sink said: "When you take data from several different sources, you have to rationalize among those data what is the true story. This is part of your engineering know-how." He admitted that changes had been made in the data, "but only to make them more consistent with the overall picture of the data that is available."

Jeter pooh-poohed the suggestion that anything improper occurred, say-ing: "We have thirty-odd engineers at this plant . . . and I say to you that it is incredible that these men would stand idly by and see reports changed or falsified . . . I mean you just do not have to do that working for anybody . . . Just nobody does that."

The four-hour hearing adjourned with no real conclusion reached by the subcommittee. But the following day the Department of Defense made sweep-ing changes in its inspection, testing, and reporting procedures. A spokesman for the DOD said the changes were a result of the Goodrich episode.

The A7D is now in service, sporting a Goodrich-made five-disk brake, a brake that works very well, I'm told. Business at the Goodrich plant is good. Lawson is now an engineer for LTV and has been assigned to the A7D proj-ect, possibly explaining why the A7D's new brakes work so well. And I am now a newspaper reporter.

At this writing, those remaining at Goodrich—including Warren—are still secure in the same positions, all except Russell Line and Robert Sink.

Line has been rewarded with a promotion to production superinten-dent, a large step upward on the corporate ladder. As for Sink, he moved up into Line's old job.

Whistleblowing and Professional Responsibility

SISSELA BOK

"Whistleblowing" is a new label generated by our increased awareness of the ethical conflicts encountered at work. Whistleblowers sound an alarm from within the very organization in which they work, aiming to spotlight neglect or abuses that threaten the public interest.

The stakes in whistleblowing are high. Take the nurse who alleges that physicians enrich themselves in her hospital through unnecessary surgery; the engineer who discloses safety defects in the braking systems of a fleet of new rapid-transit vehicles; the Defense Department official who alerts Congress to military graft and overspending: all know that they pose a threat to those whom they denounce and that their own careers may be at risk.

Moral Conflicts

Moral conflicts on several levels confront anyone who is wondering whether to speak out about abuses or risks or serious neglect. In the first place, he must try to decide whether, other things being equal, speaking out is in fact in the public interest. This choice is often made more complicated by factual uncertainties: Who is responsible for the abuse or neglect? How great is the threat? And how likely is it that speaking out will precipitate changes for the better?

In the second place, a would-be whistleblower must weigh his responsibility to serve the public interest against the responsibility he owes to his colleagues and the institution in which he works. While the professional ethic requires collegial loyalty, the codes of ethics often stress responsibility to the public over and above duties to colleagues and clients. Thus the United States Code of Ethics for Government Servants asks them to "expose corruption wherever uncovered" and to "put loyalty to the highest moral principles and to country above loyalty to persons, party, or government."[1] Similarly, the largest professional engineering association requires members to speak out against abuses threatening the safety, health, and welfare of the public.[2]

A third conflict for would-be whistleblowers is personal in nature and cuts across the first two: even in cases where they have concluded that the facts warrant speaking out, and that their duty to do so overrides loyalties to colleagues and institutions, they often have reason to fear the results of carrying out such a duty. However strong this duty may seem in theory, they know that, in practice, retaliation is likely. As a result, their careers and their ability to support themselves and their families may be unjustly impaired.[3] A government handbook issued during the Nixon era recommends reassigning "undesirables" to places so remote that they would prefer to resign. Whistleblowers may also be downgraded or given work without responsibility or work for which they are not qualified; or else they may be given many

From Sissela Bok, "Whistleblowing and Professional Responsibility," *New York University Education Quarterly,* 11 (Summer 1980): 2–7. Reprinted with permission. Bok offers more extensive discussion of these issues in her book, *Secrets: On the Ethics of Concealment and Revelation* (Vantage, 1989).

more tasks than they can possibly perform. Another risk is that an outspoken civil servant may be ordered to undergo a psychiatric fitness-for-duty examination,[4] declared unfit for service, and "separated" as well as discredited from the point of view of any allegations he may be making. Outright firing, finally, is the most direct institutional response to whistleblowers.

Add to the conflicts confronting individual whistleblowers the claim to self-policing that many professions make, and professional responsibility is at issue in still another way. For an appeal to the public goes against everything that "self-policing" stands for. The question for the different professions, then, is how to resolve, insofar as it is possible, the conflict between professional loyalty and professional responsibility toward the outside world. The same conflicts arise to some extent in all groups, but professional groups often have special cohesion and claim special dignity and privileges.

The plight of whistleblowers has come to be documented by the press and described in a number of books. Evidence of the hardships imposed on those who chose to act in the public interest has combined with a heightened awareness of professional malfeasance and corruption to produce a shift toward greater public support of whistleblowers. Public service law firms and consumer groups have taken up their cause; institutional reforms and legislation have been proposed to combat illegitimate reprisals.[5]

Given the indispensable services performed by so many whistleblowers, strong public support is often merited. But the new climate of acceptance makes it easy to overlook the dangers of whistleblowing: of uses in error or in malice; of work and reputations unjustly lost for those falsely accused; of privacy invaded and trust undermined. There comes a level of internal prying and mutual suspicion at which no institution can function. And it is a fact that the disappointed, the incompetent, the malicious, and the paranoid all too often leap to accusations in public. Worst of all, ideological persecution throughout the world traditionally relies on insiders willing to inform on their colleagues or even on their family members, often through staged public denunciations or press campaigns.

No society can count itself immune from such dangers. But neither can it risk silencing those with a legitimate reason to blow the whistle. How then can we distinguish between different instances of whistleblowing? A society that fails to protect the right to speak out even on the part of those whose warnings turn out to be spurious obviously opens the door to political repression. But from the moral point of view there are important differences between the aims, messages, and methods of dissenters from within.

Nature of Whistleblowing

Three elements, each jarring, and triply jarring when conjoined, lend acts of whistleblowing special urgency and bitterness: dissent, breach of loyalty, and accusation.

Like all dissent, whistleblowing makes public a disagreement with an authority or a majority view. But whereas dissent can concern all forms of disagreement with, for instance, religious dogma or government policy or court decisions, whistleblowing has the narrower aim of shedding light on negligence or abuse, or alerting to a risk, and of assigning responsibility for this risk.

Would-be whistleblowers confront the conflict inherent in all dissent: between conforming and sticking their necks out. The more repressive the authority they challenge, the greater the personal risk they take in speaking out. At exceptional times, as in times of war, even ordinarily tolerant authorities may come to regard dissent as unacceptable and even disloyal.[6]

Furthermore, the whistleblower hopes to stop the game; but since he is neither referee nor coach, and since he blows the whistle on his own team, his act is seen as a violation of loyalty. In holding his position, he has assumed certain obligations to his colleagues and clients. He may even have subscribed to a loyalty oath or a promise of confidentiality. Loyalty to colleagues and to clients comes to be pitted against loyalty to the public interest, to those who may be injured unless the revelation is made.

Not only is loyalty violated in whistleblowing, hierarchy as well is often opposed, since the whistleblower is not only a colleague but a subordinate. Though aware of the risks inherent in such disobedience, he often hopes to keep his job.[7] At times, however, he plans his alarm to coincide with leaving the institution. If he is highly placed, or joined by others, resigning in protest may effectively direct public attention to the wrongdoing at issue.[8] Still another alternative, often chosen by those who wish to be safe from retaliation, is to leave the institution quietly, to secure another post, and then to blow the whistle. In this way, it is possible to speak with the authority and knowledge of an insider without having the vulnerability of that position.

It is the element of accusation, of calling a "foul," that arouses the strongest reactions on the part of the hierarchy. The accusation may be of neglect, of willfully concealed dangers, or of outright abuse on the part of colleagues or superiors. It singles out specific persons or groups as responsible for threats to the public interest. If no one could be held responsible—as in the case of an impending avalanche—the warning would not constitute whistleblowing.

The accusation of the whistleblower, moreover, concerns a present or an imminent threat. Past errors or misdeeds occasion such an alarm only if they still affect current practices. And risks far in the future lack the immediacy needed to make the alarm a compelling one, as well as the close connection to particular individuals that would justify actual accusations. Thus an alarm can be sounded about safety defects in a rapid-transit system that threaten or will shortly threaten passengers, but the revelation of safety defects in a system no longer in use, while of historical interest, would not constitute whistleblowing. Nor would the revelation of potential problems in a system not yet fully designed and far from implemented.[9]

Not only immediacy, but also specificity, is needed for there to be an alarm capable of pinpointing responsibility. A concrete risk must be at issue rather than a vague foreboding or a somber prediction. The act of whistleblowing differs in this respect from the lamentation or the dire prophecy. An immediate and specific threat would normally be acted upon by those at risk. The whistleblower assumes that his message will alert listeners to something they do not know, or whose significance they have not grasped because it has been kept secret.

The desire for openness inheres in the temptation to reveal any secret, sometimes joined to an urge for self-aggrandizement and publicity and the hope for revenge for past slights or injustices. There can be pleasure, too—

righteous or malicious—in laying bare the secrets of co-workers and in setting the record straight at last. Colleagues of the whistleblower often suspect his motives: they may regard him as a crank, as publicity-hungry, wrong about the facts, eager for scandal and discord, and driven to indiscretion by his personal biases and shortcomings.

For whistleblowing to be effective, it must arouse its audience. Inarticulate whistleblowers are likely to fail from the outset. When they are greeted by apathy, their message dissipates. When they are greeted by disbelief, they elicit no response at all. And when the audience is not free to receive or to act on the information—when censorship or fear of retribution stifles response—then the message rebounds to injure the whistleblower. Whistleblowing also requires the possibility of concerted public response: the idea of whistleblowing in an anarchy is therefore merely quixotic.

Such characteristics of whistleblowing and strategic considerations for achieving an impact are common to the noblest warnings, the most vicious personal attacks, and the delusions of the paranoid. How can one distinguish the many acts of sounding an alarm that are genuinely in the public interest from all the petty, biased, or lurid revelations that pervade our querulous and gossip-ridden society? Can we draw distinctions between different whistleblowers, different messages, different methods?

We clearly can, in a number of cases. Whistleblowing may be starkly inappropriate when in malice or error, or when it lays bare legitimately private matters having to do, for instance, with political belief or sexual life. It can, just as clearly, be the only way to shed light on an ongoing unjust practice such as drugging political prisoners or subjecting them to electroshock treatment. It can be the last resort for alerting the public to an impending disaster. Taking such clear-cut cases as benchmarks, and reflecting on what it is about them that weighs so heavily for or against speaking out, we can work our way toward the admittedly more complex cases in which whistleblowing is not so clearly the right or wrong choice, or where different points of view exist regarding its legitimacy—cases where there are moral reasons both for concealment and for disclosure and where judgments conflict. Consider the following cases[10]:

> A. As a construction inspector for a federal agency, John Samuels (not his real name) had personal knowledge of shoddy and deficient construction practices by private contractors. He knew his superiors received free vacations and entertainment, had their homes remodeled and found jobs for their relatives—all courtesy of a private contractor. These superiors later approved a multimillion no-bid contract with the same "generous" firm.
>
> Samuels also had evidence that other firms were hiring nonunion laborers at a low wage while receiving substantially higher payments from the government for labor costs. A former superior, unaware of an office dictaphone, had incautiously instructed Samuels on how to accept bribes for overlooking sub-par performance.
>
> As he prepared to volunteer this information to various members of Congress, he became tense and uneasy. His family was scared and the fears were valid. It might cost Samuels thousands of dollars to protect his job. Those who had freely provided Samuels with information would probably recant or withdraw their friendship. A number of people might object to his using a dictaphone to gather information. His agency would start covering up and vent its collective wrath upon him. As for reporters and writers, they would gather for a

few days, then move on to the next story. He would be left without a job, with fewer friends, with massive battles looming, and without the financial means of fighting them, Samuels decided to remain silent.

B. Engineers of Company "A" prepared plans and specifications for machinery to be used in a manufacturing process and Company "A" turned them over to Company "B" for production. The engineers of Company "B," in reviewing the plans and specifications, came to the conclusion that they included certain miscalculations and technical deficiencies of a nature that the final product might be unsuitable for the purposes of the ultimate users, and that the equipment, if built according to the original plans and specifications, might endanger the lives of persons in proximity to it. The engineers of Company "B" called the matter to the attention of appropriate officials of their employer who, in turn, advised Company "A." Company "A" replied that its engineers felt that the design and specifications for the equipment were adequate and safe and that Company "B" should proceed to build the equipment as designed and specified. The officials of Company "B" instructed its engineers to proceed with the work.

C. A recently hired assistant director of admissions in a state university begins to wonder whether transcripts of some applicants accurately reflect their accomplishments. He knows that it matters to many in the university community, including alumni, that the football team continue its winning tradition. He has heard rumors that surrogates may be available to take tests for a fee, signing the names of designated applicants for admission, and that some of the transcripts may have been altered. But he has no hard facts. When he brings the question up with the director of admissions, he is told that the rumors are unfounded and asked not to inquire further into the matter.

Individual Moral Choice

What questions might those who consider sounding an alarm in public ask themselves? How might they articulate the problem they see and weigh its injustice before deciding whether or not to reveal it? How can they best try to make sure their choice is the right one? In thinking about these questions it helps to keep in mind the three elements mentioned earlier: dissent, breach of loyalty, and accusation. They impose certain requirements—of accuracy and judgment in dissent; of exploring alternative ways to cope with improprieties that minimize the breach of loyalty; and of fairness in accusation. For each, careful articulation and testing of arguments are needed to limit error and bias.

Dissent by whistleblowers, first of all, is expressly claimed to be intended to benefit the public. It carries with it, as a result, an obligation to consider the nature of this benefit and to consider also the possible harm that may come from speaking out: harm to persons or institutions and, ultimately, to the public interest itself. Whistleblowers must, therefore, begin by making every effort to consider the effects of speaking out versus those of remaining silent. They must assure themselves of the accuracy of their reports, checking and rechecking the facts before speaking out; specify the degree to which there is genuine impropriety; consider how imminent is the threat they see, how serious, and how closely linked to those accused of neglect and abuse.

If the facts warrant whistleblowing, how can the second element—breach of loyalty—be minimized? The most important question here is whether the existing avenues for change within the organization have been explored. It is a waste of time for the public as well as harmful to the institution to sound the loudest alarm first. Whistleblowing has to remain a last alternative because of its destructive side effects: it must be chosen only when other alternatives have been considered and rejected. They may be rejected if they simply do not apply to the problem at hand, or when there is not time to go through routine channels or when the institution is so corrupt or coercive that steps will be taken to silence the whistleblower should he try the regular channels first.

What weight should an oath or a promise of silence have in the conflict of loyalties? One sworn to silence is doubtless under a stronger obligation because of the oath he has taken. He has bound himself, assumed specific obligations beyond those assumed in merely taking a new position. But even such promises can be overridden when the public interest at issue is strong enough. They can be overridden if they were obtained under duress or through deceit. They can be overridden, too, if they promise something that is in itself wrong or unlawful. The fact that one has promised silence is no excuse for complicity in covering up a crime or a violation of the public's trust.

The third element in whistleblowing—accusation—raises equally serious ethical concerns. They are concerns of fairness to the persons accused of impropriety. Is the message one to which the public is entitled in the first place? Or does it infringe on personal and private matters that one has no right to invade? Here, the very notion of what is in the public's best "interest" is at issue: "accusations" regarding an official's unusual sexual or religious experiences may well appeal to the public's interest without being information relevant to "the public interest."

Great conflicts arise here. We have witnessed excessive claims to executive privilege and to secrecy by government officials during the Watergate scandal in order to cover up for abuses the public had every right to discover. Conversely, those hoping to profit from prying into private matters have become adept at invoking "the public's right to know." Some even regard such private matters as threats to the public: they voice their own religious and political prejudices in the language of accusation. Such a danger is never stronger than when the accusation is delivered surreptitiously. The anonymous accusations made during the McCarthy period regarding political beliefs and associations often injured persons who did not even know their accusers or the exact nature of the accusations.

From the public's point of view, accusations that are openly made by identifiable individuals are more likely to be taken seriously. And in fairness to those criticized, openly accepted responsibility for blowing the whistle should be preferred to the denunciation or the leaked rumor. What is openly stated can more easily be checked, its source's motives challenged, and the underlying information examined. Those under attack may otherwise be hard put to defend themselves against nameless adversaries. Often they do not even know that they are threatened until it is too late to respond. The anonymous denunciation, moreover, common to so many regimes, places the burden of investigation on government agencies that may thereby gain the power of a secret police.

From the point of view of the whistleblower, on the other hand, the anonymous message is safer in situations where retaliation is likely. But it is also often less likely to be taken seriously. Unless the message is accompanied by indications of how the evidence can be checked, its anonymity, however safe for the source, speaks against it.

During the process of weighing the legitimacy of speaking out, the method used, and the degree of fairness needed, whistleblowers must try to compensate for the strong possibility of bias on their part. They should be scrupulously aware of any motive that might skew their message: a desire for self-defense in a difficult bureaucratic situation, perhaps, or the urge to seek revenge, or inflated expectations regarding the effect their message will have on the situation. (Needless to say, bias affects the silent as well as the outspoken. The motive for holding back important information about abuses and injustice ought to give similar cause for soul-searching.)

Likewise, the possibility of personal gain from sounding the alarm ought to give pause. Once again there is then greater risk of a biased message. Even if the whistleblower regards himself as incorruptible, his profiting from revelations of neglect or abuse will lead others to question his motives and to put less credence in his charges. If, for example, a government employee stands to make large profits from a book exposing the iniquities in his agency, there is danger that he will, perhaps even unconsciously, slant his report in order to cause more of a sensation.

A special problem arises when there is a high risk that the civil servant who speaks out will have to go through costly litigation. Might he not justifiably try to make enough money on his public revelations—say, through books or public speaking—to offset his losses? In so doing he will not strictly speaking have *profited* from his revelations: he merely avoids being financially crushed by their sequels. He will nevertheless still be suspected at the time of revelation, and his message will therefore seem more questionable.

Reducing bias and error in moral choice often requires consultation, even open debate[11]: methods that force articulation of the moral arguments at stake and challenge privately held assumptions. But acts of whistleblowing present special problems when it comes to open consultation. On the one hand, once the whistleblower sounds his alarm publicly, his arguments will be subjected to open scrutiny; he will have to articulate his reasons for speaking out and substantiate his charges. On the other hand, it will then be too late to retract the alarm or to combat its harmful effects, should his choice to speak out have been ill-advised.

For this reason, the whistleblower owes it to all involved to make sure of two things: that he has sought as much and as objective advice regarding his choice as he can *before* going public; and that he is aware of the arguments for and against the practice of whistleblowing in general, so that he can see his own choice against as richly detailed and coherently structured a background as possible. Satisfying these two requirements once again has special problems because of the very nature of whistleblowing: the more corrupt the circumstances, the more dangerous it may be to seek counsultation before speaking out. And yet, since the whistleblower himself may have a biased view of the state of affairs, he may choose not to consult others when in fact it would be not only safe but advantageous to do so; he may see corruption and conspiracy where none exists.

Notes

1. Code of Ethics for Government Service passed by the U.S. House of Representatives in the 85th Congress (1958) and applying to all government employees and office holders.
2. Code of Ethics of the Institute of Electrical and Electronics Engineers, Article IV.
3. For case histories and descriptions of what befalls whistleblowers, see Rosemary Chalk and Frank von Hippel, "Due Process for Dissenting Whistle-Blowers," *Technology Review* 81 (June–July 1979): 48–55; Alan S. Westin and Stephen Salisbury, eds., *Individual Rights in the Corporation* (New York: Pantheon, 1980); Helen Dudar, "The Price of Blowing the Whistle," *New York Times Magazine,* 30 October 1979, pp. 41–54; John Edsall, *Scientific Freedom and Responsibility* (Washington, D.C.: American Association for the Advancement of Science, 1975), p. 5; David Ewing, *Freedom Inside the Organization* (New York: Dutton, 1979); Ralph Nader, Peter Petkas, and Kate Blackwell, *Whistle Blowing* (New York: Grossman, 1972); Charles Peter and Taylor Branch, *Blowing the Whistle* (New York: Praeger, 1972).
4. Congressional hearings uncovered a growing resort to mandatory psychiatric examinations.
5. For an account of strategies and proposals to support government whistleblowers, see Government Accountability Project, *A Whistleblower's Guide to the Federal Bureaucracy* (Washington, D.C.: Institute for Policy Studies, 1977).
6. See, e.g., Samuel Eliot Morison, Frederick Merk, and Frank Friedel, *Dissent in Three American Wars* (Cambridge: Harvard University Press, 1970).
7. In the scheme worked out by Albert Hirschmann in *Exit, Voice and Loyalty* (Cambridge: Harvard University Press, 1970), whistleblowing represents "voice" accompanied by a preference not to "exit," though forced "exit" is clearly a possibility and "voice" after or during "exit" may be chosen for strategic reasons.
8. Edward Weisband and Thomas N. Franck, *Resignation in Protest* (New York: Grossman, 1975).
9. Future developments can, however, be the cause for whistleblowing if they are seen as resulting from steps being taken or about to be taken that render them inevitable.
10. Case A is adapted from Louis Clark, "The Sound of Professional Suicide," *Barrister,* Summer 1978, p. 10; Case B is Case 5 in Robert J. Baum and Albert Flores, eds., *Ethical Problems of Engineering* (Troy, N.Y.: Rensselaer Polytechnic Institute, 1978), p. 186.
11. I discuss these questions of consultation and publicity with respect to moral choice in chapter 7 of Sissela Bok, *Lying* (New York: Pantheon, 1978); and in *Secrets* (New York: Pantheon Books, 1982), Ch. IX and XV.

Employment at Will and Due Process

PATRICIA H. WERHANE   ➤   TARA J. RADIN

In 1980, Howard Smith III was hired by the American Greetings Corporation as a materials handler at the plant in Osceola, Arkansas. He was promoted to forklift driver and held that job until 1989, when he became involved in a dispute with his shift leader. According to Smith, he had a dispute with his shift leader at work. After work he tried to discuss the matter, but according to Smith, the shift leader hit him. The next day Smith was fired.

Smith was an "at will" employee. He did not belong to, nor was he protected by, any union or union agreement. He did not have any special legal protection, for there was no apparent question of age, gender, race, or handicap discrimination. And he was not alleging any type of problem with worker safety on the job. The American Greetings Employee Handbook stated that "We believe in working and thinking and planning to provide a stable and growing business, to give such service to our customers that we may provide maximum job security for our employees." It did not state that employees could not be fired without due process or reasonable cause. According to the common law principle of Employment at Will (EAW), Smith's job at American Greetings could, therefore, legitimately be terminated at any time without cause, by either Smith or his employer, as long as that termination did not violate any law, agreement, or public policy.

Smith challenged his firing in the Arkansas court system as a "tort of outrage." A "tort of outrage" occurs when employer engages in "extreme or outrageous conduct" or intentionally inflicts terrible emotional stress. If such a tort is found to have occurred, the action, in this case, the dismissal, can be overturned.

Smith's case went to the Supreme Court of Arkansas in 1991. In court the management of American Greetings argued that Smith was fired for provoking management into a fight. The Court held that the firing was not in violation of law or a public policy, that the employee handbook did not specify restrictions on at will terminations, and that the alleged altercation between Smith and his shift leader "did not come close to meeting" criteria for a tort of outrage. Howard Smith lost his case and his job.[1]

The principle of EAW is a common-law doctrine that states that, in the absence of law or contract, employers have the right to hire, promote, demote, and fire whomever and whenever they please. In 1877, the principle was stated explicitly in a document by H. G. Wood entitled *Master and Servant.* According to Wood, "A general or indefinite hiring is prima facie a hiring at will."[2] Although the term "master-servant," a medieval expression, was once used to characterize employment relationships, it has been dropped from most of the recent literature on employment.[3]

In the United States, EAW has been interpreted as the rule that, when employees are not specifically covered by union agreement, legal statute, public policy, or contract, employers "may dismiss their employees at will . . . for good cause, for no cause, *or even for causes morally wrong,* without being thereby guilty of legal wrong."[4] At the same time, "at will" employees enjoy rights parallel to employer prerogatives, because employees may quit their jobs for any reason whatsoever (or no reason) without having to give any notice to their employers. "At will" employees range from part-time contract workers to CEOs, including all those workers and managers in the private sector of the economy not covered by agreements, statutes, or contracts. Today at least 60% of all employees in the private sector in the United States are "at will" employees. These employees have no rights to due process or to appeal employment decisions, and the employer does not have any obligation to give reasons for demotions, transfers, or dismissals. Interestingly, while employees in the *private* sector of the economy tend to be regarded as "at will" employees, *public*-sector employees have guaranteed rights, including due process, and are protected from demotion, transfer, or firing without cause.

Due process is a means by which a person can appeal a decision in order to get an explanation of that action and an opportunity to argue against it. Procedural due process is the right to a hearing, trial, grievance procedure, or appeal when a decision is made concerning oneself. Due process is also substantive. It is the demand for rationality and fairness: for good reasons for decisions. EAW has been widely interpreted as allowing employees to be demoted, transferred or dismissed without due process, that is, without having a hearing and without requirement of good reasons or "cause" for the employment decision. This is not to say that employers do not have reasons, usually good reasons, for their decisions. But there is no moral or legal obligation to state or defend them. EAW thus sidesteps the requirement of procedural and substantive due process in the workplace, but it does not preclude the institution of such procedures or the existence of good reasons for employment decisions.

EAW is still upheld in the state and federal courts of this country, as the Howard Smith case illustrates, although exceptions are made when violations of public policy and law are at issue. According to the *Wall Street Journal,* the court has decided in favor of the employees in 67% of the wrongful discharge suits that have taken place during the past three years. These suits were won not on the basis of a rejection of the principle of EAW but, rather, on the basis of breach of contract, lack of just cause for dismissal when a company policy was in place, or violations of public policy. The court has carved out the "public policy" exception so as not to encourage fraudulent or wrongful behavior on the part of employers, such as in cases where employees are asked to break a law or to violate state public policies, and in cases where employees are not allowed to exercise fundamental rights, such as the rights to vote, to serve on a jury, and to collect worker compensation. For example, in one case, the court reinstated an employee who was fired for reporting theft at his plant on the grounds that criminal conduct requires such reporting.[5] In another case, the court reinstated a physician who was fired from the Ortho Pharmaceutical Corporation for refusing to seek approval to test a certain drug on human subjects. The court held that safety clearly lies in the interest of public welfare, and employees are not to be fired for refusing to jeopardize public safety.[6]

During the last ten years, a number of positive trends have become apparent in employment practices and in state and federal court adjudications of employment disputes. Shortages of skilled managers, fear of legal repercussions, and a more genuine interest in employee rights claims and reciprocal obligations have resulted in a more careful spelling out of employment contracts, the development of elaborate grievance procedures, and in general less arbitrariness in employee treatment.[7] While there has not been a universal revolution in thinking about employee rights, an increasing number of companies have qualified their EAW prerogatives with restrictions in firing without cause. Many companies have developed grievance procedures and other means for employee complaint and redress.

Interestingly, substantive due process, the notion that employers should give good reasons for their employment actions, previously dismissed as legal and philosophical nonsense, has also recently developed positive advocates. Some courts have found that it is a breach of contract to fire a long-term employee when there is not sufficient cause—under normal economic conditions even when the implied contract is only a verbal one. In California, for example, 50% of the implied contract cases (and there have been over 200) during the last five years have been decided in favor of the employee, again, without challenging EAW.[8] In light of this recognition of implicit contractual obligations between employees and employers, in some unprecedented court cases *employees* have been held liable for good faith breaches of contract, particularly in cases of quitting without notice in the middle of a project and/or taking technology or other ideas to another job.[9]

These are all positive developments. At the same time, there has been neither an across-the-board institution of due process procedures in all corporations nor any direct challenges to the *principle* (although there have been challenges to the practice) of EAW as a justifiable and legitimate approach to employment practices. Moreover, as a result of mergers, downsizing, and restructuring, hundreds of thousands of employees have been laid off summarily without being able to appeal those decisions.

"At will" employees, then, have no rights to demand an appeal to such employment decisions except through the court system. In addition, no form of due process is a requirement preceding any of these actions. Moreover, unless public policy is violated, the law has traditionally protected employers from employee retaliation in such actions. It is true that the scope of what is defined as "public policy" has been enlarged so that "at will" dismissals without good reason are greatly reduced. It is also true that many companies have grievance procedures in place for "at will" employees. But such procedures are voluntary, procedural due process is not *required,* and companies need not give any reasons for their employment decisions.

In what follows we shall present a series of arguments defending the claim that the right to procedural and substantive due process should be extended to all employees in the private sector of the economy. We will defend the claim partly on the basis of human rights. We shall also argue that the public/private distinction that precludes the application of constitutional guarantees in the private sector has sufficiently broken down so that the absence of a due process requirement in the workplace is an anomaly.

Employment at Will

EAW is often justified for one or more of the following reasons:

1. The proprietary rights of employers guarantee that they may employ or dismiss whomever and whenever they wish.
2. EAW defends employee and employer rights equally, in particular the right to freedom of contract, because an employee voluntarily contracts to be hired and can quit at any time.
3. In choosing to take a job, an employee voluntarily commits herself to certain responsibilities and company loyalty, including the knowledge that she is an "at will" employee.
4. Extending due process rights in the workplace often interferes with the efficiency and productivity of the business organization.
5. Legislation and/or regulation of employment relationships further undermine an already overregulated economy.

Let us examine each of these arguments in more detail. The principle of EAW is sometimes maintained purely on the basis of proprietary rights of employers and corporations. In dismissing or demoting employees, the employer is not denying rights to *persons*. Rather, the employer is simply excluding that person's *labor* from the organization.

This is not a bad argument. Nevertheless, accepting it necessitates consideration of the proprietary rights of employees as well. To understand what is meant by "proprietary rights of employees" it is useful to consider first what is meant by the term "labor." "Labor" is sometimes used collectively to refer to the workforce as a whole. It also refers to the activity of working. Other times it refers to the productivity or "fruits" of that activity. Productivity, labor in the third sense, might be thought of as a form of property or at least as something convertible into property, because the productivity of working is what is traded for remuneration in employee-employer work agreements. For example, suppose an advertising agency hires an expert known for her creativity in developing new commercials. This person trades her ideas, the product of her work (thinking), for pay. The ideas are not literally property, but they are tradable items because, when presented on paper or on television, they are sellable by their creator and generate income. But the activity of working (thinking in this case) cannot be sold or transferred.

Caution is necessary, though, in relating productivity to tangible property, because there is an obvious difference between productivity and material property. Productivity requires the past or present activity of working, and thus the presence of the person performing this activity. Person, property, labor, and productivity are all different in this important sense. A person can be distinguished from his possessions, a distinction that allows for the creation of legally fictional persons such as corporations or trusts that can "own" property. Persons cannot, however, be distinguished from their working, and this activity is necessary for creating productivity, a tradable product of one's working.

In dismissing an employee, a well-intentioned employer aims to rid the corporation of the costs of generating that employee's work products. In ordinary employment situations, however, terminating that cost entails terminating that employee. In those cases the justification for the "at will" firing is presumably proprietary. But treating an employee "at will" is analogous to considering her a piece of property at the disposal of the employer or corporation. Arbitrary firings treat people as things. When I "fire" a robot, I do not have to give reasons, because a robot is not a rational being. It has no use for reasons. On the other hand, if I fire a person arbitrarily, I am making the assumption that she does not need reasons either. If I have hired people, then, in firing them, I should treat them as such, with respect, throughout the termination process. This does not preclude firing. It merely asks employers to give reasons for their actions, because reasons are appropriate when people are dealing with other people.

This reasoning leads to a second defense and critique of EAW. It is contended that EAW defends employee and employer rights equally. An employer's right to hire and fire "at will" is balanced by a worker's right to accept or reject employment. The institution of any employee right that restricts "at will" hiring and firing would be unfair unless this restriction were balanced by a similar restriction controlling employee job choice in the workplace. Either program would do irreparable damage by preventing both employees and employers from continuing in voluntary employment arrangements. These arrangements are guaranteed by "freedom of contract," the right of persons or organizations to enter into any voluntary agreement with which all parties of the agreement are in accord.[10] Limiting EAW practices or requiring due process would negatively affect freedom of contract. Both are thus clearly coercive, because in either case persons and organizations are forced to accept behavioral restraints that place unnecessary constraints on voluntary employment agreements.[11]

This second line of reasoning defending EAW, like the first, presents some solid arguments. A basic presupposition upon which EAW is grounded is that of protecting equal freedoms of both employees and employers. The purpose of EAW is to provide a guaranteed balance of these freedoms. But arbitrary treatment of employees extends prerogatives to managers that are not equally available to employees, and such treatment may unduly interfere with a fired employee's prospects for future employment if that employee has no avenue for defense or appeal. This is also sometimes true when an employee quits without notice or good reason. Arbitrary treatment of employees *or* employers therefore violates the spirit of EAW—that of protecting the freedoms of both employees and employers.

The third justification of EAW defends the voluntariness of employment contracts. If these are agreements between moral agents, however, such agreements imply reciprocal obligations between the parties in question for which both are accountable. It is obvious that, in an employment contract, people are rewarded for their performance. What is seldom noticed is that, if part of the employment contract is an expectation of loyalty, trust, and respect on the part of an employee, the employer must, in return, treat the employee with respect as well. The obligations required by employment agreements, if these are free and noncoercive agreements, must be equally obligatory and mutually restrictive on both parties. Otherwise one party cannot expect—morally expect—loyalty, trust, or respect from the other.

EAW is most often defended on practical grounds. From a utilitarian perspective, hiring and firing "at will" is deemed necessary in productive organizations to ensure maximum efficiency and productivity, the goals of such organizations. In the absence of EAW unproductive employees, workers who are no longer needed, and even troublemakers, would be able to keep their jobs. Even if a business *could* rid itself of undesirable employees, the lengthy procedure of due process required by an extension of employee rights would be costly and time-consuming, and would likely prove distracting to other employees. This would likely slow production and, more likely than not, prove harmful to the morale of other employees.

This argument is defended by Ian Maitland, who contends,

> [I]f employers were generally to heed business ethicists and institute workplace due process in cases of dismissals and take the increased costs or reduced efficiency out of workers' paychecks—then they would expose themselves to the pirating of their workers by other employers who would give workers what they wanted instead of respecting their rights in the workplace. . . . In short, there is good reason for concluding that the prevalence of EAW does accurately reflect workers' preferences for wages over contractually guaranteed protections against unfair dismissal.[12]

Such an argument assumes (a) that due process increases costs and reduces efficiency, a contention that is not documented by the many corporations that have grievance procedures, and (b) that workers will generally give up some basic rights for other benefits, such as money. The latter is certainly sometimes true, but not always so, particularly when there are questions of unfair dismissals or job security. Maitland also assumes that an employee is on the same level and possesses the same power as her manager, so that an employee can choose her benefit package in which grievance procedures, whistleblowing protections, or other rights are included. Maitland implies that employers might include in that package of benefits their rights to practice the policy of unfair dismissals in return for increased pay. He also at least implicitly suggests that due process precludes dismissals and layoffs. But this is not true. Procedural due process demands a means of appeal, and substantive due process demands good reasons, both of which are requirements for other managerial decisions and judgments. Neither demands benevolence, lifetime employment, or prevents dismissals. In fact, having good reasons gives an employer a justification for getting rid of poor employees.

In summary, arbitrariness, although not prohibited by EAW, violates the managerial ideal of rationality and consistency. These are independent grounds for not abusing EAW. Even if EAW itself is justifiable, the practice of EAW, when interpreted as condoning arbitrary employment decisions, is not justifiable. Both procedural and substantive due process are consistent with, and a moral requirement of, EAW. The former is part of recognizing obligations implied by freedom of contract, and the latter, substantive due process, conforms with the ideal of managerial rationality that is implied by a consistent application of this common law principle.

Employment at Will, Due Process, and the Public/Private Distinction

The strongest reasons for allowing abuses of EAW and for not instituting a full set of employee rights in the workplace, at least in the private sector of the economy, have to do with the nature of business in a free society. Businesses are privately owned voluntary organizations of all sizes from small entrepreneurships to large corporations. As such, they are not subject to the restrictions governing public and political institutions. Political procedures such as due process, needed to safeguard the public against the arbitrary exercise of power by the state, do not apply to private organizations. Guaranteeing such rights in the workplace would require restrictive legislation and regulation. Voluntary market arrangements, so vital to free enterprise and guaranteed by freedom of contract, would be sacrificed for the alleged public interest of employee claims.

In the law, courts traditionally have recognized the right of corporations to due process, although they have not required due process for employees in the private sector of the economy. The justification put forward for this is that since corporations are public entities acting in the public interest, they, like people, should be afforded the right to due process.

Due process is also guaranteed for permanent full-time workers in the public sector of the economy, that is, for workers in local, state and national government positions. The Fifth and Fourteenth Amendments protect liberty and property rights such that any alleged violations or deprivation of those rights may be challenged by some form of due process. According to recent Supreme Court decisions, when a state worker is a permanent employee, he has a property interest in his employment. Because a person's productivity contributes to the place of employment, a public worker is entitled to his job unless there is good reason to question it, such as poor work habits, habitual absences, and the like. Moreover, if a discharge would prevent him from obtaining other employment, which often is the case with state employees who, if fired, cannot find further government employment, that employee has a right to due process before being terminated.[13]

This justification for extending due process protections to public employees is grounded in the public employee's proprietary interest in his job. If that argument makes sense, it is curious that private employees do not have similar rights. The basis for this distinction stems from a tradition in Western thinking that distinguishes between the public and private spheres of life. The public sphere contains that part of a person's life that lies within the bounds of government regulation, whereas the private sphere contains that part of a person's life that lies outside those bounds. The argument is that the portion of a person's life that influences only that person should remain private and outside the purview of law and regulation, while the portion that influences the public welfare should be subject to the authority of the law.

Although interpersonal relationships on any level—personal, family, social, or employee-employer—are protected by statutes and common law, they are not constitutionally protected unless there is a violation of some citizen claim against the state. Because entrepreneurships and corporations are privately owned, and since employees are free to make or break employment contracts of their choice, employee-employer relationships, like family relationships, are treated as "private." In a family, even if there are no due process procedures, the state does not interfere, except when there is obvious harm or abuse. Similarly, employment relationships are considered private relationships contracted between free adults, and so long as no gross violations occur, positive constitutional guarantees such as due process are not enforceable.

The public/private distinction was originally developed to distinguish individuals from the state and to protect individuals and private property from public—i.e., governmental—intrusion. The distinction, however, has been extended to distinguish not merely between the individual or the family and the state, but also between universal rights claims and national sovereignty, public and private ownership, free enterprise and public policy, publicly and privately held corporations, and even between public and private employees. Indeed, this distinction plays a role in national and international affairs. Boutros Boutros-Ghali, the head of the United Nations, recently confronted a dilemma in deciding whether to go into Somalia without an invitation. His initial reaction was to stay out and to respect Somalia's right to "private" national sovereignty. It was only when he decided that Somalia had fallen apart as an independent state that he approved U.N. intervention. His dilemma parallels that of a state, which must decide whether to intervene in a family quarrel, the alleged abuse of a spouse or child, the inoculation of a Christian Scientist, or the blood transfusion for a Seventh-Day Adventist.

There are some questions, however, with the justification of the absence of due process with regard to the public/private distinction. Our economic system is allegedly based on private property, but it is unclear where "private" property and ownership end and "public" property and ownership begin. In the workplace, ownership and control is often divided. Corporate assets are held by an ever-changing group of individual and institutional shareholders. It is no longer true that owners exercise any real sense of control over their property and its management. Some do, but many do not. Moreover, such complex property relationships are spelled out and guaranteed by the state. This has prompted at least one thinker to argue that "private property" should be defined as "certain patterns of human interaction underwritten by public power."[14]

This fuzziness about the "privacy" of property becomes exacerbated by the way we use the term "public" in analyzing the status of businesses and in particular corporations. For example, we distinguish between privately owned business corporations and government-owned or -controlled public institutions. Among those companies that are not government owned, we distinguish between regulated "public" utilities whose stock is owned by private individuals and institutions; "publicly held" corporations whose stock is traded publicly, who are governed by special SEC regulations, and whose financial statements are public knowledge; and privately held corporations and entrepreneurships, companies and smaller businesses that are owned by an individual or group of individuals and not available for public stock purchase.

There are similarities between government-owned, public institutions and privately owned organizations. When the air controllers went on strike in the 1980s, Ronald Reagan fired them, and declared that, as public employees, they could not strike because it jeopardized the public safety. Nevertheless, both private and public institutions run transportation, control banks, and own property. While the goals of private and public institutions differ in that public institutions are allegedly supposed to place the public good ahead of profitability, the simultaneous call for businesses to become socially responsible and the demand for governmental organizations to become efficient and accountable further question the dichotomy between "public" and "private."

Many business situations reinforce the view that the traditional public/private dichotomy has been eroded, if not entirely, at least in large part. For example, in 1981, General Motors (GM) wanted to expand by building a plant in what is called the "Poletown" area of Detroit. Poletown is an old Detroit Polish neighborhood. The site was favorable because it was near transportation facilities and there was a good supply of labor. To build the plant, however, GM had to displace residents in a nine-block area. The Poletown Neighborhood Council objected, but the Supreme Court of Michigan decided in favor of GM and held that the state could condemn property for private use, with proper compensation to owners, when it was in the public good. What is particularly interesting about this case is that GM is not a government-owned corporation; its primary goal is *profitability*, not the common good. The Supreme Court nevertheless decided that it was in the *public* interest for Detroit to use its authority to allow a company to take over property despite the protesting of the property owners. In this case the public/private distinction was thoroughly scrambled.

The overlap between private enterprise and public interests is such that at least one legal scholar argues that "developments in the twentieth century have significantly undermined the 'privateness' of modern business corporations, with the result that the traditional bases for distinguishing them from public corporations have largely disappeared."[15] Nevertheless, despite the blurring of the public and private in terms of property rights and the status and functions of corporations, the subject of employee rights appears to remain immune from conflation.

The expansion of employee protections to what we would consider just claims to due process gives to the state and the courts more opportunity to interfere with the private economy and might thus further skew what is seen by some as a precarious but delicate balance between the private economic sector and public policy. We agree. But if the distinction between public and private institutions is no longer clear-cut, and the traditional separation of the public and private spheres is no longer in place, might it not then be better to recognize and extend constitutional guarantees so as to protect all citizens equally? If due process is crucial to political relationships between the individual and the state, why is it not central in relationships between employees and corporations since at least some of the companies in question are as large and powerful as small nations? Is it not in fact inconsistent with our democratic tradition *not* to mandate such rights?

The philosopher T. M. Scanlon summarizes our intuitions about due process. Scanlon says,

> The requirement of due process is one of the conditions of the moral acceptability of those institutions that give some people power to control or intervene in the lives of others.[16]

The institution of due process in the workplace is a moral requirement consistent with rationality and consistency expected in management decision-making. It is not precluded by EAW, and it is compatible with the overlap between the public and private sectors of the economy. Convincing business of the moral necessity of due process, however, is a task yet to be completed.

Notes

1. *Howard Smith III* v. *American Greetings Corporation,* 304 Ark. 596; 804 S.W. 2d 683.
2. H. G. Wood, *A Treatise on the Law of Master and Servant* (Albany, N.Y.: John D. Parsons, Jr., 1877), p. 134.
3. Until the end of 1980 the *Index of Legal Periodicals* indexed employee-employer relationships under this rubric.
4. Lawrence E. Blades, "Employment at Will versus Individual Freedom: On Limiting the Abusive Exercise of Employer Power," *Columbia Law Review,* 67 (1967), p. 1405, quoted from *Payne* v. *Western,* 81 Tenn. 507 (1884), and *Hutton* v. *Watters,* 132 Tenn. 527, S.W. 134 (1915).
5. *Palmateer* v. *International Harvester Corporation,* 85 Ill. App. 2d 124 (1981).
6. *Pierce* v. *Ortho Pharmaceutical Corporation* 845 NJ 58 (NJ 1980), 417 A.2d 505. See also Brian Heshizer, "The New Common Law of Employment: Changes in the Concept of Employment at Will," *Labor Law Journal,* 36 (1985), pp. 95–107.
7. See David Ewing, *Justice on the Job: Resolving Grievances in the Nonunion Workplace* (Boston: Harvard Business School Press, 1989).
8. See R. M. Bastress, "A Synthesis and a Proposal for Reform of the Employment at Will Doctrine," *West Virginia Law Review,* 90 (1988), pp. 319–51.
9. See "Employees' Good Faith Duties," *Hastings Law Journal,* 39 (198). See also *Hudson* v. *Moore Business Forms,* 609 Supp. 467 (N.D. Cal. 1985).
10. See *Lockner* v. *New York,* 198 U.S. (1905), and Adina Schwartz, "Autonomy in the Workplace," in Tom Regan, ed., *Just Business* (New York: Random House, 1984), pp. 129–40.
11. Eric Mack, "Natural and Contractual Rights," *Ethics,* 87 (1977), pp. 153–59.

12. Ian Maitland, "Rights in the Workplace: A Nozickian Argument," in Lisa Newton and Maureen Ford, eds., *Taking Sides* (Guilford, CT: Dushkin Publishing Group), 1990, pp. 34–35.
13. Richard Wallace, "Union Waiver of Public Employees' Due Process Rights," *Industrial Relations Law Journal,* 8 (1986), pp. 583–87.
14. Morris Cohen, "Dialogue on Private Property," *Rutgers Law Review* 9 (1954), pp. 357. See also *Law and the Social Order* (1933) and Robert Hale, "Coercion and Distribution in a Supposedly Non-Coercive State," *Political Science Quarterly,* 38 (1923), pp. 470; John Brest, "State Action and Liberal Theory," *University of Pennsylvania Law Review* (1982), pp. 1296–1329.
15. Gerald Frug, "The City As a Legal Concept," *Harvard Law Review,* 93 (1980), p. 1129.
16. T. M. Scanlon, "Due Process," in J. Roland Pennock and John W. Chapman, eds., *Nomos XVIII: Due Process* (New York: New York University Press, 1977), p. 94.

In Defense of the Contract at Will

RICHARD A. EPSTEIN

The persistent tension between private ordering and government regulation exists in virtually every area known to the law, and in none has that tension been more pronounced than in the law of employer and employee relations. During the last fifty years, the balance of power has shifted heavily in favor of direct public regulation, which has been thought strictly necessary to redress the perceived imbalance between the individual and the firm. In particular the employment relationship has been the subject of at least two major statutory revolutions. The first, which culminated in the passage of the National Labor Relations Act in 1935, set the basic structure for collective bargaining that persists to the current time. The second, which is embodied in Title VII of the Civil Rights Act of 1964, offers extensive protection to all individuals against discrimination on the basis of race, sex, religion, or national origin. The effect of these two statutes is so pervasive that it is easy to forget that, even after their passage, large portions of the employment relation remain subject to the traditional common law rules, which when all was said and done set their face in support of freedom of contract and the system of voluntary exchange. One manifestation of that position was the prominent place that the common law, especially as it developed in the nineteenth century, gave to the contract at will. The basic position was sell set out in an oft-quoted passage from *Payne v. Western & Atlantic Railroad:*

> [M]en must be left, without interference to buy and sell where they please, and to discharge or retain employees at will for good cause or for no cause, or even for bad cause without thereby being guilty of an unlawful act *per se*. It is a right which an employee may exercise in the same way, to the same extent, for the same cause or want of cause as the employer.[1]

From "In Defense of the Contract at Will" by Richard A. Epstein, *University of Chicago Law Review* 34 (1984). Reprinted by permission of the University of Chicago Law Review.

In the remainder of this paper, I examine the arguments that can be made for and against the contract at will. I hope to show that it is adopted not because it allows the employer to exploit the employee, but rather because over a very broad range of circumstances it works to the mutual benefit of both parties, where the benefits are measured, as ever, at the time of the contract's formation and not at the time of dispute. To justify this result, I examine the contract in light of the three dominant standards that have emerged as the test of the soundness of any legal doctrine: intrinsic fairness, effects upon utility or wealth, and distributional consequences. I conclude that the first two tests point strongly to the maintenance of the at-will rule, while the third, if it offers any guidance at all, points in the same direction.

I. THE FAIRNESS OF THE CONTRACT AT WILL

The first way to argue for the contract at will is to insist upon the importance of freedom of contract as an end in itself. Freedom of contract is an aspect of individual liberty, every bit as much as freedom of speech, or freedom in the selection of marriage partners or in the adoption of religious beliefs or affiliations. Just as it is regarded as prima facie unjust to abridge these liberties, so too is it presumptively unjust to abridge the economic liberties of individuals. The desire to make one's own choices about employment may be as strong as it is with respect to marriage or participation in religious activities, and it is doubtless more pervasive than the desire to participate in political activity. Indeed for most people, their own health and comfort, and that of their families, depend critically upon their ability to earn a living by entering the employment market. If government regulation is inappropriate for personal, religious, or political activities, then what makes it intrinsically desirable for employment relations?

It is one thing to set aside the occasional transaction that reflects only the momentary aberrations of particular parties who are overwhelmed by major personal and social dislocations. It is quite another to announce that a rule to which vast numbers of individuals adhere is so fundamentally corrupt that it does not deserve the minimum respect of the law. With employment contracts we are not dealing with the widow who has sold her inheritance for a song to a man with a thin mustache. Instead we are dealing with the routine stuff of ordinary life; people who are competent enough to marry, vote, and pray are not unable to protect themselves in their day-to-day business transactions.

Courts and legislatures have intervened so often in private contractual relations that it may seem almost quixotic to insist that they bear a heavy burden of justification every time they wish to substitute their own judgment for that of the immediate parties to the transactions. Yet it is hardly likely that remote public bodies have better information about individual preferences than the parties who hold them. This basic principle of autonomy, moreover, is not limited to some areas of individual conduct and wholly inapplicable to others. It covers all these activities as a piece and admits no ad hoc exceptions, but only principled limitations.

This general proposition applies to the particular contract term in question. Any attack on the contract at will in the name of individual freedom is fundamentally misguided. As the Tennessee Supreme Court rightly stressed in *Payne,* the contract at will is sought by both persons.[2] Any limitation upon the freedom to enter into such contracts limits the power of workers as well as employers and must therefore be justified before it can be accepted. In this context the appeal is often to an image of employer coercion. To be sure, freedom of contract is not an absolute in the employment context, any more than it is elsewhere. Thus the principle must be understood against a backdrop that prohibits the use of private contracts to trench upon third-party rights, including uses that interfere with some clear mandate of public policy, as in cases of contracts to commit murder or perjury.

In addition, the principle of freedom of contract also rules out the use of force or fraud in obtaining advantages during contractual negotiations; and it limits taking advantage of the young, the feeble-minded, and the insane. But the recent wrongful discharge cases do not purport to deal with the delicate situations where contracts have been formed by improper means or where individual defects of capacity or will are involved. Fraud is not a frequent occurrence in employment contracts, especially where workers and employers engage in repeat transactions. Nor is there any reason to believe that such contracts are marred by misapprehensions, since employers and employees know the footing on which they have contracted: the phrase "at will" is two words long and has the convenient virtue of meaning just what it says, no more and no less.

An employee who knows that he can quit at will understands what it means to be fired at will, even though he may not like it after the fact. So long as it is accepted that the employer is the full owner of his capital and the employee is the full owner of his labor, the two are free to exchange on whatever terms and conditions they see fit, within the limited constraints just noted. If the arrangement turns out to be disastrous to one side, that is his problem; and once cautioned, he probably will not make the same mistake a second time. More to the point, employers and employees are unlikely to make the same mistake once. It is hardly plausible that contracts at will could be so pervasive in all businesses and at all levels if they did not serve the interests of employees as well as employers. The argument from fairness then is very simple, but not for that reason unpersuasive.

II. THE UTILITY OF THE CONTRACT AT WILL

The strong fairness argument in favor of freedom of contract makes short work of the various for-cause and good-faith restrictions upon private contracts. Yet the argument is incomplete in several respects. In particular, it does not explain why the presumption in the case of silence should be in favor of the contract at will. Nor does it give a descriptive account of *why* the contract at will is commonly found in all trades and professions. Nor does the argument meet on their own terms the concerns voiced most frequently by the critics of the contract at will. Thus, the commonplace belief today (at least outside the actual world of business) is that the contract at will is so unfair and one-sided that it cannot be the outcome of a rational set of bargaining processes any more than, to take the extreme case, a contract for total slavery. While we may not, the criticism continues, be able to observe them, defects in capacity at contract formation nonetheless must be present: the ban upon the contract at will is an effective way to reach abuses that are pervasive but difficult to detect, so that modest government interference only strengthens the operation of market forces.

In order to rebut this charge, it is necessary to do more than insist that individuals as a general matter know how to govern their own lives. It is also necessary to display the structural strengths of the contract at will that explain why rational people would enter into such a contract, if not all the time, then at least most of it. The implicit assumption in this argument is that contracts are typically for the mutual benefit of both parties. Yet it is hard to see what other assumption makes any sense in analyzing institutional arrangements (arguably in contradistinction to idiosyncratic, nonrepetitive transactions). To be sure, there are occasional cases of regret after the fact, especially after an infrequent, but costly, contingency comes to pass. There will be cases in which parties are naive, befuddled, or worse. Yet in framing either a rule of policy or a rule of construction, the focus cannot be on that biased set of cases in which the contract aborts and litigation ensues. Instead, attention must be directed to standard repetitive transactions, where the centralizing tendency powerfully promotes expected mutual gain. It is simply incredible to postulate that either employers or employees, motivated as they are by self-interest, would enter routinely into a transaction that leaves them worse off than they were before, or even worse off than their next best alternative.

From this perspective, then, the task is to explain how and why the at-will contracting arrangement (in sharp contrast to slavery) typically works to the mutual advantage of the parties. Here, as is common in economic matters, it does not matter that the parties themselves often cannot articulate the reasons that render their judgment sound and breathe life into legal arrangements that are fragile in form but durable in practice. The inquiry into mutual benefit in turn requires an examination of the full range of costs and benefits that arise from collaborative ventures. It is just at this point that the nineteenth-century view is superior to the emerging modern conception. The modern view tends to lay heavy emphasis on the need to control employer abuse. Yet, as the passage from *Payne* indicates, the rights under the contract at will are fully bilateral, so that the employee can use the contract as a means to control the firm, just as the firm uses it to control the worker.

The issue for the parties, properly framed, is not how to minimize employer abuse, but rather how to maximize the gain from the relationship, which in part depends upon minimizing the sum of employer and employee abuse. Viewed in this way the private-contracting problem is far more complex. How does each party create incentives for the proper behavior of the other? How does each side insure against certain risks? How do both sides minimize the administrative costs of their contracting practices? ...

1. *Monitoring Behavior.* The shift in the internal structure of the firm from a partnership to an employment relation eliminates neither bilateral opportunism nor the conflicts of interest between employer and employee. Begin for the moment with the fears of the firm, for it is the firm's right to maintain at-will power that is now being called into question. In all too many cases, the firm must contend with the recurrent problem of employee theft

and with the related problems of unauthorized use of firm equipment and employee kickback arrangement. . . . [The] proper concerns of the firm are not limited to obvious forms of criminal misconduct. The employee on a fixed wage can, at the margin, capture only a portion of the gain from his labor, and therefore has a tendency to reduce output. The employee who receives a commission equal to half the firm's profit attributable to his labor may work hard, but probably not quite as hard as he would if he received the entire profit from the completed sale, an arrangement that would solve the agency-cost problem only by undoing the firm. . . .

The problem of management then is to identify the forms of social control that are best able to minimize these agency costs. . . . One obvious form of control is the force of law. The state can be brought in to punish cases of embezzlement or fraud. But this mode of control requires extensive cooperation with public officials and may well be frustrated by the need to prove the criminal offense (including mens rea) beyond a reasonable doubt, so that vast amounts of abuse will go unchecked. Private litigation instituted by the firm may well be used in cases of major grievances, either to recover the property that has been misappropriated or to prevent the individual employee from further diverting firm business to his own account. But private litigation, like public prosecution, is too blunt an instrument to counter employee shirking or the minor but persistent use of firm assets for private business. . . .

Internal auditors may help control some forms of abuse, and simple observation by coworkers may well monitor employee activities. (There are some very subtle tradeoffs to be considered when the firm decides whether to use partitions or separate offices for its employees.) Promotions, bonuses, and wages are also critical in shaping the level of employee performance. But the carrot cannot be used to the exclusion of the stick. In order to maintain internal discipline, the firm may have to resort to sanctions against individual employees. It is far easier to use those powers that can be unilaterally exercised: to fire, to demote, to withhold wages, or to reprimand. These devices can visit very powerful losses upon individual employees without the need to resort to legal action, and they permit the firm to monitor employee performance continually in order to identify both strong and weak workers and to compensate them accordingly. The principles here are constant, whether we speak of senior officials or lowly subordinates, and it is for just this reason that the contract at will is found at all levels in private markets. . . .

In addition, within the employment context firing does not require a disruption of firm operations, much less an expensive division of its assets. It is instead a clean break with consequences that are immediately clear to both sides. The lower cost of both firing and quitting, therefore, helps account for the very widespread popularity of employment-at-will contracts. There is no need to resort to any theory of economic domination or inequality of bargaining power to explain at-will contracting, which appears with the same tenacity in relations between economic equals and subordinates and is found in many complex commercial arrangements, including franchise agreements, except where limited by statutes.

Thus far, the analysis generally has focused on the position of the employer. Yet for the contract at will to be adopted ex ante, it must work for the benefit of workers as well. And indeed it does, for the contract at will also contains powerful limitations on employers' abuses of power. To see the importance of the contract at will to the employee, it is useful to distinguish between two cases. In the first, the employer pays a fixed sum of money to the worker and is then free to demand of the employee whatever services he wants for some fixed period of time. In the second case, there is no fixed period of employment. The employer is free to demand whatever he wants of the employee, who in turn is free to withdraw for good reason, bad reason, or no reason at all.

The first arrangement invites abuse by the employer, who can now make enormous demands upon the worker without having to take into account either the worker's disutility during the period of service or the value of the worker's labor at contract termination. A fixed-period contract that leaves the worker's obligations unspecified thereby creates a sharp tension between the parties, since the employer receives all the marginal benefits and the employee bears all the marginal costs.

Matters are very different where the employer makes increased demands under a contract at will. Now the worker can quit whenever the net value of the employment contract turns negative. As with the employer's power to fire or demote, the threat to quit (or at a lower level to come late or leave early) is one that can be exercised without resort to litigation. Furthermore, that threat turns out to be most effective when the employer's opportunistic behavior is the greatest because the situation is one in which the worker has least to lose. To be sure, the worker will not necessarily make a threat whenever the employer insists that the worker accept a less favorable set of contractual terms, for sometimes the changes may be accepted as an uneventful adjustment in the total compensation level attributable to a change in the market price of labor. This point counts, however, only as an additional strength of the contract at will, which allows for small adjustments *in both directions* in ongoing contractual arrangements with a minimum of bother and confusion. . . .

2. *Reputational Losses.* Another reason why employees are often willing to enter into at-will employment contracts stems from the asymmetry of reputational losses. Any party who cheats may well obtain a bad reputation that will induce others to avoid dealing with him. The size of these losses tends to differ systematically between employers and employees—to the advantage of the employee. Thus in the usual situation there are many workers and a single employer. The disparity in number is apt to be greatest in large industrial concerns, where the at-will contract is commonly, if mistakenly, thought to be most unsatisfactory because of the supposed inequality of bargaining power. The employer who decides to act for bad reason or no reason at all may not face any legal liability under the classical common law rule. But he faces very powerful adverse economic consequences. If coworkers perceive the dismissal as arbitrary, they will take fresh stock of their own prospects, for they can no longer be certain that their faithful performance will ensure their security and advancement. The uncertain prospects created by arbitrary employer behavior is functionally indistinguishable from a reduction in wages unilaterally imposed by the employer. At the margin some workers will look elsewhere, and typically the best workers will have the greatest opportunities. By the same token the large employer has more to gain if he dismisses undesirable employees, for this ordinarily acts as an

implicit increase in wages to the other employees, who are no longer burdened with uncooperative or obtuse coworkers.

The existence of both positive and negative reputational effects is thus brought back to bear on the employer. The law may tolerate arbitrary behavior, but private pressures effectively limit its scope. Inferior employers will be at a perpetual competitive disadvantage with enlightened ones and will continue to lose in market share and hence in relative social importance. The lack of legal protection to the employees is therefore in part explained by the increased informal protections that they obtain by working in large concerns.

3. *Risk Diversification and Imperfect Information.* The contract at will also helps workers deal with the problem of risk diversification. . . . Ordinarily, employees cannot work more than one, or perhaps two, jobs at the same time. Thereafter the level of performance falls dramatically, so that diversification brings in its wake a low return on labor. The contract at will is designed in part to offset the concentration of individual investment in a single job by allowing diversification among employers *over time.* The employee is not locked into an unfortunate contract if he finds better opportunities elsewhere or if he detects some weakness in the internal structure of the firm. A similar analysis applies on the employer's side where he is a sole proprietor, though ordinary diversification is possible when ownership of the firm is widely held in publicly traded shares.

The contract at will is also a sensible private adaptation to the problem of imperfect information over time. In sharp contrast to the purchase of standard goods, an inspection of the job before acceptance is far less likely to guarantee its quality thereafter. The future is not clearly known. More important, employees, like employers, *know what they do not know.* They are not faced with a bolt from the blue, with an "unknown unknown." Rather they face a known unknown for which they can plan. The at-will contract is an essential part of that planning because it allows both sides to take a wait-and-see attitude to their relationship so that new and more accurate choices can be made on the strength of improved information. ("You can start Tuesday and we'll see how the job works out" is a highly intelligent response to uncertainty.) To be sure, employment relationships are more personal and hence often stormier than those that exists in financial markets, but that is no warrant for replacing the contract at will with a for-cause contract provision. The proper question is: will the shift in methods of control work a change for the benefit of both parties, or will it only make a difficult situation worse?

4. *Administrative Costs.* There is one last way in which the contract at will has an enormous advantage over its rivals. It is very cheap to administer. Any effort to use a for-cause rule will in principle allow all, or at least a substantial fraction of, dismissals to generate litigation. Because motive will be a critical element in these cases, the chances of either side obtaining summary judgment will be negligible. Similarly, the broad modern rules of discovery will allow exploration into every aspect of the employment relation. Indeed, a little imagination will allow the plaintiff's lawyer to delve into the general employment policies of the firm, the treatment of similar cases, and a review of the individual file. The employer for his part will be able to examine every aspect of the employee's performance and personal life in order to bolster the case for dismissal. . . .

III. DISTRIBUTIONAL CONCERNS

Enough has been said to show that there is no principled reason of fairness or utility to disturb the common law's longstanding presumption in favor of the contract at will. It remains to be asked whether there are some hitherto unmentioned distributional consequences sufficient to throw that conclusion into doubt. . . .

The proposed reforms in the at-will doctrine cannot hope to transfer wealth systematically from rich to poor on the mode of comprehensive systems of taxation or welfare benefits. Indeed it is very difficult to identify in advance any deserving group of recipients that stands to gain unambiguously from the universal abrogation of the at-will contract. The proposed rules cover the whole range from senior executives to manual labor. At every wage level, there is presumably some differential in workers' output. Those who tend to slack off seem on balance to be most vulnerable to dismissal under the at-will rule; yet it is very hard to imagine why some special concession should be made in their favor at the expense of their more diligent fellow workers.

The distributional issues, moreover, become further clouded once it is recognized that any individual employee will have interests on both sides of the employment relation. Individual workers participate heavily in pension plans, where the value of the holdings depends in part upon the efficiency of the legal rules that govern the companies in which they own shares. If the regulation of the contract at will diminishes the overall level of wealth, the losses are apt to be spread far and wide, which makes it doubtful that there are any gains to the worst off in society that justify somewhat greater losses to those who are better off. The usual concern with maldistribution gives us situations in which one person has one hundred while each of one hundred has one and asks us to compare that distribution with an even distribution of, say, two per person. But the stark form of the numerical example does not explain how the skewed distribution is tied to the concrete choice between different rules governing employment relations. Set in this concrete context, the choices about the proposed new regulation of the employment contract do not set the one against the many but set the many against each other, all in the context of a shrinking overall pie. The possible gains from redistribution, even on the most favorable of assumptions about the diminishing marginal utility of money, are simply not present.

If this is the case, one puzzle still remains: who should be in favor of the proposed legislation? One possibility is that support for the change in common law rules rests largely on ideological and political grounds, so that the legislation has the public support of persons who may well be hurt by it in their private capacities. Another possible explanation could identify the hand of interest-group politics in some subtle form. For example, the lawyers and government officials called upon to administer the new legislation may expect to obtain increased income and power, although this explanation seems insufficient to account for the current pressure. A more uncertain line of inquiry could ask whether labor unions stand to benefit from the creation of a cause of action for wrongful discharge. Unions, after all, have some skill in working with for-cause contracts under the labor statutes that prohibit firing for union activities, and they might be able to promote their own growth by selling their services to the presently nonunionized sector. In addition, the for-cause rule might give employers one less reason to resist unionization, since they would be unable to retain the absolute power to hire and fire in any event. Yet, by the same token, it is possible that workers would be less inclined to pay the costs of union membership if they received some purported benefit by the force of law without unionization. The ultimate weight of these considerations is an empirical question to which no easy answers appear. What is clear, however, is that even if one could show that the shift in the rule either benefits or hurts unions and their members, the answer would not justify the rule, for it would not explain why the legal system should try to skew the balance one way or the other. The bottom line therefore remains unchanged. The case for a legal requirement that renders employment contracts terminable only for cause is as weak after distributional considerations are taken into account as before. . . .

CONCLUSION

The recent trend toward expanding the legal remedies for wrongful discharge has been greeted with wide approval in judicial, academic, and popular circles. In this paper, I have argued that the modern trend rests in large measure upon a misunderstanding of the contractual processes and the ends served by the contract at will. No system of regulation can hope to match the benefits that the contract at will affords in employment relations. The flexibility afforded by the contract at will permits the ceaseless marginal adjustments that are necessary in any ongoing productive activity conducted, as all activities are, in conditions of technological and business change. The strength of the contract at will should not be judged by the occasional cases in which it is said to produce unfortunate results, but rather by the vast run of cases where it provides a sensible private response to the many and varied problems in labor contracting. All too often the case for a wrongful discharge doctrine rests upon the identification of possible employer abuses, as if they were all that mattered. But the proper goal is to find the set of comprehensive arrangements that will minimize the frequency and severity of abuses by employers and employees alike. Any effort to drive employer abuses to zero can only increase the difficulties inherent in the employment relation. Here, a full analysis of the relevant costs and benefits shows why the constant minor imperfections of the market, far from being a reason to oust private agreements, offer the most powerful reason for respecting them. The doctrine of wrongful discharge is the problem and not the solution. This is one of the many situations in which courts and legislatures should leave well enough alone.

Notes

1. *Payne v. Western & Atl. R.R.,* 81 Tenn. 507, 518–19 (1884), *overruled on other grounds, Hutton v. Watters,* 132 Tenn. 527, 544, 179 S.W. 134, 138 (1915). . . .
2. *Payne v. Western & Atl. R.R.,* 81 Tenn. 507, 518–19 (1884). . . .

Employability Security

ROSABETH MOSS KANTER

For many people in the twentieth century, careers were constituted by institutions. Large employers were expected to provide—and guarantee—jobs, benefits, and upward mobility. Long-term employment has long been considered a central component of high-commitment, high-productivity work systems. And corporate entitlements, from health benefits to pensions, were based on an assumption of longevity, especially as U.S. employers were expected to offer benefits guaranteed by governments in other countries.

Now recessionary pressures and sweeping industrial transformations are forcing large companies to downsize—a euphemism that masks the human turmoil involved. Even in Japan, the bastion of life-time employment in big businesses where nearly three quarters of the country's 60 million workers stayed with one employer throughout their working life, cutbacks and layoffs beginning in 1992 have been shaking the social contract.

The job-tenure ideal of the past is colliding with the job-insecurity reality of the present. Institutionally dependent careers are declining; self-reliant careers as professionals and entrepreneurs are proliferating, increasing the burdens on people. And women are joining men as peers in nearly every corner of the labor market, bringing new issues—inclusion, empowerment, accommodation to family needs—at a time when companies are struggling to stay afloat.

Churn and Displacement

The United States has been fortunate in not depending solely on large enterprises. America has a vibrant entrepreneurial economy, a small business sector that creates a higher proportion of jobs than are similarly created in European nations. But employment in smaller organizations is inherently less secure, especially given the high failure rate of new small businesses, and such jobs often come without the benefits and safeguards mandated for companies with more than fifty employees. Some Americans count on entrepreneurs to pull the country out of the economic doldrums as large companies sputter and downsize. But an entrepreneurial economy is full of churn and displacement—and the fate of small companies is often linked to the fate of big ones which they supply and service.

New policies must reflect new forms of security while embracing the emerging realities of flexibility, mobility, and change.

"We promise to increase opportunity and power for our entire, diverse work force. We will:

- Recruit for the potential to increase in competence, not simply for narrow skills to fill today's slots.
- Offer ample learning opportunities, from formal training to lunchtime seminars—the equivalent of three weeks a year.

- Provide challenging jobs and rotating assignments that allow growth in skills even without promotion to higher jobs.
- Measure performance beyond accounting numbers and share the data to allow learning by doing and continuous improvement—turning everyone into self-guided professionals.
- Retrain employees as soon as jobs become obsolete.
- Emphasize team building, to help our diverse work force appreciate and utilize fully each other's skills.
- Recognize and reward individual and team achievements, thereby building external reputations and offering tangible indicators of value.
- Provide three-month educational sabbaticals, external internships, or personal time-out every five years.
- Find growth opportunities in our network of suppliers, customers, and venture partners.
- Ensure that pensions and benefits are portable, so that people have safety nets for the future even if they seek employment elsewhere.
- Help people be productive while carrying family responsibilities, through flex-time, provision for sick children, and renewal breaks between major assignments.
- Measure the building of human capital and the capabilities of our people as thoroughly and frequently as we measure the building and use of financial capital.
- Encourage entrepreneurship—new ventures within our company or outside that help our people start businesses and create alternative sources of employment.
- Tap our people's ideas to develop innovations that lower costs, serve customers, and create new markets—the best foundation for business growth and continuing employment, and the source of funds to reinvest in continuous learning."

Policies like these could renew loyalty, commitment, and productivity for all men and women, of corporations both large and small, as they struggle to create jobs, wealth, and well-being in the global economy.

Diversity

Case Study

Ellen Moore (A): Living and Working in Bahrain

HENRY W. LANE   GAIL ELLEMENT   MARTHA MAZNEVSKI

> *The General Manager had offered me a choice of two positions in the Operations area. I had considered the matter carefully, and was about to meet with him to tell him I would accept the Accounts Control position. The job was much more challenging than the Customer Services post, but I knew I could learn the systems and procedures quickly and I would have a great opportunity to contribute to the success of the Operations area.*

It was November 1989, and Ellen Moore was just completing her second year as an expatriate manager at the offices of a large American financial institution in Manama, Bahrain. After graduating with an MBA from a leading business school, Ellen had joined her husband, who [was] working as an expatriate manager at an offshore bank in Bahrain. Being highly qualified and capable, she had easily found a demanding position and had worked on increasingly complex projects since she had begun at the company. She was looking forward to the challenges of the Accounts Control position.

ELLEN MOORE

Ellen graduated as the top female from her high school when she was 16 and immediately began working full time for the main branch of one of the largest banks in the country. By the end of four years, she had become a corporate accounts officer and managed over twenty large accounts.

> I remember I was always making everything into a game, a challenge. One of my first jobs was filing checks. I started having a competition with the woman at the adjacent desk who had been filing for years, except she didn't know I was competing with her. When she realized it, we both started competing in earnest. Before long, people used to come over just to watch us fly through these stacks of checks. When I moved to the next job, I used to see how fast I could add up columns of numbers while handling phone conversations. I always had to do something to keep myself challenged.

IVEY "Ellen Moore (A): Living and Working in Bahrain" was prepared by Research Associates Gail Ellement and Martha Maznevski under the supervision of Professor Henry W. Lane. The Richard Ivey School of Business, The University of Western Ontario. One time permission to reproduce granted by Ivey Management Services 6/10/98. Copyright 1990 by Ivey Management Services Inc.

While working full time at the bank, Ellen achieved a Fellowship in the Institute of Bankers after completing demanding courses and exams. She went on to work in banking and insurance with one of her former corporate clients from the bank. When she was subsequently promoted to manage their financial reporting department, she was both the first female and the youngest person the company had ever had in that position.

Since she had begun working full time, Ellen had been taking courses towards a bachelor's degree at night in one of the city's universities. In 1983 she decided to stop working for two years to complete her bachelor's degree. After she graduated with a major in accounting and minors in marketing and management, she entered the MBA program.

> I decided to go straight into the MBA program for several reasons. First, I wanted to update myself. I had taken my undergraduate courses over ten years and wanted to obtain knowledge on contemporary views. Second, I wanted to tie some pieces together—my night school degree left my ideas somewhat fragmented. Third, I wasn't impressed with the interviews I had after I finished the bachelor's degree, and fourth I was out of work anyway. Finally, my father had already told everyone that I had my MBA, and I decided I really couldn't disappoint him.

Just after Ellen had begun the two-year MBA program, her husband was offered a position with an affiliate of his bank, posted in Bahrain beginning the next spring. They sat down and examined potential opportunities that would be available for Ellen once she completed her MBA. They discovered that women could work and assume positions of responsibility in Bahrain, and decided they could both benefit from the move. Her husband moved to Bahrain in March, while Ellen remained to complete her masters. Ellen followed, with MBA in hand, 18 months later.

BAHRAIN

Bahrain is an archipelago of 33 islands located in the Persian Gulf (see Exhibit 1). The main island, Bahrain, comprises 85 per cent of the almost 700 square kilometres of the country and is the location of the capital city, Manama. Several of the islands are joined by causeways, and in 1987 the 25 kilometre King Fahad Causeway linked the principal island to the mainland of Saudi Arabia, marking the end of island isolation for the country. In 1971, Bahrain gained full independence from Britain, ending a relationship that had lasted for almost a century. Of the population of over 400,000 people, about one third were foreigners.

Bahrain has had a prosperous history. Historically, it has been sought after by many countries for its lush vegetation, fresh water, and pearls. Many traditional crafts and industries were still practiced, including pottery, basket-making, fabric-weaving, pearl-diving, *dhow* (fishing boat) building, and fishing. Bahrain was the pearl capital of the world for many centuries.

Fortunately, just as the pearl industry collapsed with the advent of cultured pearls from Japan, Bahrain struck its first oil.

Since the 1930s, the oil industry had been the largest contributor to Bahrain's gross national product. The country was the first in the Persian

Gulf to have an oil industry, established with a discovery in 1932. Production at that time was 9,600 barrels a day. Eventually, crude output had reached over 40,000 barrels a day. Bahrain's oil products included crude oil, natural gas, methanol, ammonia, and refined products like gasoline, jet fuels, kerosene, and asphalts.

The Bahraini government had been aware for several years that the oil reserves were being seriously depleted. It was determined to diversify the country's economy away from a dependence on one resource. Industries established since 1971 included aluminum processing, shipbuilding, iron and steel processing, and furniture and door manufacturing. Offshore banking began in 1975. Since Bahraini nationals did not have the expertise to develop these industries alone, expatriates from around the world, particularly from Western Europe and North America, were invited to conduct business in Bahrain. By the late 1980s, the country was a major business and financial centre, housing many Middle East branch offices of international firms.

Expatriates in Bahrain

Since Bahrain was an attractive base from which to conduct business, it was a temporary home to many expatriates. Housing compounds, schools, services, shopping and leisure activities all catered to many international cultures. Expatriates lived under residence permits, gained only on the basis of recruitment for a specialist position which could not be filled by a qualified and available Bahraini citizen.

To Ellen, one of the most interesting roles of expatriate managers was that of teacher. The Arab nations had been industrialized for little more than two decades, and had suddenly found themselves needing to compete in a global market. Ellen believed that one of her main reasons for working in Bahrain was to train its nationals eventually to take over her job.

> Usually the teaching part was very interesting. When I first arrived in the office, I was amazed to see many staff members with microcomputers on their desks, yet they did not know the first thing about operating the equipment. When I inquired about the availability of computer courses, I was informed by a British expatriate manager that "as these were personal computers, any person should be able to use them, and as such, courses aren't necessary." It was clear to me that courses were very necessary when the computer knowledge of most employees consisted of little more than knowing where the on/off switch was located on a microcomputer.

Although it was outside of office policy, I held "Ellen's Introduction to Computers" after office hours, just to get people comfortable with the machines and to teach them a few basics.

> Sometimes the amount of energy you had to put into the teaching was frustrating in that results were not immediately evident. I often worked jointly with one of the Bahraini managers who really didn't know how to develop projects and prepare reports. Although I wasn't responsible for him, I spent a great deal of time with him, helping him improve his work. Initially there was resistance on his part, because he was not prepared to subordinate himself to an expatriate, let alone a woman. But eventually he came around and we achieved some great results working together.

The range of cultures represented in Bahrain was vast. Expatriate managers interacted not only with Arabic nationals, but also with managers from other parts of the world, and with workers from developing countries who provided a large part of the unskilled labour force.

> The inequality among nationalities was one issue I found very difficult to deal with during my stay in Bahrain. The third world immigrants were considered to be the lowest level possible in the pecking order, just slightly lower than nationals from countries outside the Gulf. Gulf Arabs, being of Bedouin origin, maintained a suspicious attitude towards "citified" Arabs. Europeans and North Americans were regarded much more highly. These inequalities had a major impact on daily life, including the availability of jobs and what relations would develop or not develop between supervisors and subordinates. Although I was well acquainted with the racial problems in North America, I haven't seen anything compared to the situation in Bahrain. It wasn't unusual for someone to be exploited and discarded, as any expendable and easily replaceable resource would be, because of their nationality.

Although many expatriates and their families spent their time in Bahrain immersed in their own cultural compounds, social groups, and activities, Ellen believed that her interaction with the various cultures was one of the most valuable elements of her international experience.

MANAGING IN BAHRAIN

Several aspects of the Middle Eastern culture had tremendous impact on the way business was managed, even in Western firms located in Bahrain. It seemed to Ellen, for example, that "truth" to a Bahraini employee was subject to an Arab interpretation, which was formed over hundreds of years of cultural evolution. What Western managers considered to be "proof" of an argument or "factual" evidence could be flatly denied by a Bahraini: if something was not believed it did not exist. As well, it seemed that the concept of "time" differed between Middle Eastern and Western cultures. Schedules and deadlines, while sacred to Western managers, commanded little respect from Bahraini employees. The two areas that had the most impact on Ellen's managing in a company in Bahrain were the Islamic religion and the traditional attitude towards women.

Islam[1]

Most Bahrainis are practicing Muslims. According to the Muslim faith, the universe was created by Allah who prescribed a code of life called Islam, and the Qur'an is the literal, unchanged Word of Allah preserved exactly as transcribed by Muhammad. Muhammad's own acts as a prophet form the basis for Islamic law, and are second in authority only to the Qur'an. The five Pillars of Islam are belief, prayer, fasting, almsgiving and pilgrimage. Muslims pray five times a day. During Ramadan, the ninth month of the Islamic calendar, Muslims must fast from food, drink, smoking and sexual activity from dawn until dusk, in order to master the urges which sustain and procreate life. All Muslims are obliged to give a certain proportion of their wealth in alms for charitable purposes; the Qur'an stresses that the poor have a just claim on the wealth of the prosperous. Finally, if possible, all Muslims should make a pilgrimage to Mecca during their lives, in a spirit of total sacrifice of personal comforts, acquisition of wealth and other matters of worldly significance.

> Certainly the Muslim religion had a tremendous impact on my daily working life. The first time I walked into the women's washroom at work I noticed a tap about three inches off the floor over a drain. I found this rather puzzling; I wondered if it was for the cleaning crew. When a woman came in, I asked her about the tap, and she explained that before going to the prayer room, everyone had to wash all uncovered parts of their bodies. The tap was for washing their feet and legs.

> One time I was looking for one of my employees, Mohammed, who had a report due to me that afternoon. I searched for him at his desk and other likely spots throughout the office, but to no avail, he just wasn't around. I had had difficulties with Mohammed's work before, when he would submit documents long after deadlines, and I was certain he was attempting to slack off once again. I bumped into one of Mohammed's friends, and asked if he knew Mohammed's whereabouts. When he informed me that Mohammed was in the prayer room, I wasn't sure how to respond. I didn't know if this prayer room activity was very personal and if I could ask questions, such as the length of time one generally spends in prayer. But I needed to know how long Mohammed would be away from his desk. Throwing caution to the wind, I asked the employee how long Mohammed was likely to be in prayers and he told me it usually takes about ten minutes. It wasn't that I felt I didn't have the right to know where my employee was or how long he would be away, I just wasn't certain my authority as a manager allowed me the right to ask questions about such a personal activity as praying.

> During Ramadan, the hours of business are shortened by law. It is absolutely illegal for any Muslim to work past two o'clock in the afternoon, unless special permits are obtained from the Ministry of Labor. Unfortunately, business coming in to an American firm does not stop at two, and a majority of the non-Muslim workers are required to take up the slack.

Unlike religion in Western civilization, Islam permeates every function of human endeavor. There does not exist a separation of church, state and judiciary. Indeed, in purist circles, the question does not arise. The hybrid systems existing in certain Arab countries are considered aberrations created by Western colonial influences. Accordingly, to function successfully, the expatriate must understand and learn to accept a very different structuring of a society.

Women in Bahrain

Bahrain tended to be more progressive than many Middle Eastern countries in its attitude towards women. Although traditions were strong, Bahraini women had some freedom. For example, all women could work outside the home, although the hours they could work were restricted both by convention and by the labour laws. They could only work if their husbands, fathers, or brothers permitted them, and could not take potential employment away from men. Work outside the home was to be conducted in addition to, not instead of, duties performed inside the home, such as child-rearing and cooking. Most women who worked held secretarial or clerical positions; very few worked in management.

Bahraini women were permitted to wear a variety of outfits, from the conservative full-length black robe with head scarf which covers the head and hair, to below-the-knee skirts and dresses without head covering.

> Arabic women who sincerely want change and more decision-making power over their own lives face an almost impossible task, as the male influence is perpetuated not only by men, but also by women who are afraid to alter views they understand and with which they have been brought up all their lives. I once asked a female co-worker the reason why one of the women in the office, who had previously been "uncovered," was now sporting a scarf over her head. The response was that this woman had just been married, and although her husband did not request that she become "covered," she personally did not feel as though she was a married woman without the head scarf. So she simply asked her husband to demand that she wear a scarf on her head. It was a really interesting situation, some of the more liberal Bahraini women were very upset that she had asked her husband to make this demand. They saw it as negating many of the progressive steps the women's movement had made in recent years.

Although Bahrainis had been exposed to Western cultures for the two decades of industrial expansion, they were still uncomfortable with Western notions of gender equality and less traditional roles for women.

> One day a taxi driver leaned back against his seat and, while keeping one eye on the road ahead, turned to ask me, "How many sons do you have?" I replied that I didn't have any children. His heartfelt response of "I'm so sorry" and the way he shook his head in sympathy were something my North American upbringing didn't prepare me for. My taxi driver's response typifies the attitude projected towards women, whether they are expatriates from Europe or North America, or are Bahrainis. Women are meant to have children, preferably sons. Although Bahrain is progressive in many ways, attitudes on the role of women in society run long and deep, and it is quite unlikely these sentiments will alter in the near, or even distant, future.

> Another time I was greeted with gales of laughter when I revealed to the women in the office that my husband performed most of the culinary chores in our household. They assumed I was telling a joke, and when I insisted that he really did most of the cooking, they sat in silent disbelief. Finally, one woman spoke up and informed the group that she didn't think her husband even knew where the kitchen was in their house, let alone would ever be caught touching a cooking utensil. The group nodded in agreement. Although these women have successful business careers—as clerks, but in the workforce nonetheless—they believe women should perform all household tasks without the assistance of their husbands. The discovery that this belief holds true in Bahrain is not remarkable as I know many North American and European businesswomen who believe the same to be true. What is pertinent is these women allow themselves to be completely dominated by the men in their lives.

> The one concept I faced daily but never accepted was that my husband was regarded as the sole decision maker in our household. He and I view our marriage as a partnership in which we participate equally in all decisions. But when the maintenance manager for our housing compound came by, repairs were completed efficiently only if I preceded my request with "my husband wants the following to be completed." It's a phrase I hated to use as it went against every rational thought I possess, but I frequently had to resort to it.

These attitudes also affected how Ellen was treated as a manager by Bahraini managers:

> One manager, I'll call him Fahad, believed that women were only capable of fulfilling secretarial and coffee-serving functions. One day I was sitting at my desk, concentrating on some documents. I didn't notice Fahad having a discussion with another male manager nearby. When I looked up from my papers, Fahad noticed me and immediately began talking in French to the other manager. Although my French was a bit rusty, my comprehension was still quite serviceable. I waited for a few moments and then broke into their discussion in French. Fahad was completely dismayed. Over the next few years, Fahad and I worked together on several projects. At first, he was pompous and wouldn't listen to anything I presented. It was a difficult situation, but I was determined to remain above his negative comments. I ignored his obvious prejudice towards me, remained outwardly calm when he disregarded my ideas, and proceeded to prove myself with my work. It took a lot of effort and patience but, in time, Fahad and I not only worked out our differences, but worked as a successful team on a number of major projects. Although this situation had a happy ending, I really would have preferred to have directed all that energy and effort towards more productive issues.

Bahraini nationals were not the only ones who perpetuated the traditional roles of women in society. Many of the expatriates, particularly those from Commonwealth countries, tended to view their role as "the colonial charged with the responsibility to look after the developing country." This was reflected in an official publication for new expatriates that stated: "Wives of overseas employees are normally sponsored by their husbands' employers, and their Residence Permits are processed at the same time. . . ."[2] However, wives were not permitted to work unless they could obtain a work permit for themselves.

> The first question I was often asked at business receptions was "What company is your husband with?" When I replied that I worked as well, I received the glazed-over look as they assumed I occupied myself with coffee mornings, beach, tennis, and other leisure activities as did the majority of expatriate wives.
>
> Social gatherings were always risky. At typical business and social receptions the men served themselves first, after which the women selected their food. Then women and men positioned themselves on opposite sides of the room. The women discussed "feminine" topics, such as babies and recipes, while the men discussed the fall (or rise) of the dollar and the big deal of the day. At one Bahraini business gathering, I hesitated in choosing sides: should I conform and remain with the women? But most of these women did not work outside their homes, and, consequently, they spoke and understood very little English. I joined the men. Contrary to what I expected, I was given a gracious welcome.
>
> However, on another occasion I was bored with the female conversation, so I ventured over to the forbidden male side to join a group of bankers discussing correspondent banking courses. When I entered the discussion, a British bank general manager turned his nose up at me. He motioned towards the other side of the room, and told me I should join the women. He implied that their discussion was obviously over my head. I quickly informed him that although I personally had found the banking courses difficult to complete while holding a full-time banking position, I not only managed to complete the program and obtain my Fellowship, but at the time as the youngest employee of my bank ever to be awarded the diploma. The man did a quick turnabout, was thoroughly

embarrassed, and apologized profusely. Although it was nice to turn the tables on the man, I was more than a little frustrated with the feeling that I almost had to wear my resume on my sleeve to get any form of respect from the men, whether European, North American, or Arab.

A small percentage of Bahraini women had completed university degrees in North America and Europe. While residing in these Western cultures, they were permitted to function as did their Western counterparts. For example, they could visit or phone friends when they wished without first obtaining permission. After completing their education, many of these women were qualified for management positions; however, upon returning to Bahrain they were required to resume their traditional female roles.

> The notion of pink MBA diplomas for women and blue for men is very real. Although any MBA graduate in North America, male or female, is generally considered to have attained a certain level of business sense, I had to constantly "prove" myself to some individuals who appeared to believe that women attended a special segregated section of the university with appropriately tailored courses.

Ellen discovered that, despite being a woman, she was accepted by Bahrainis as a manager as a result of her Western nationality, her education, and her management position in the company.

> Many of my male Arabic peers accepted me as they would any expatriate manager. For example, when a male employee returned from a holiday, he would typically visit each department, calling upon the other male employees with a greeting and a handshake. Although he might greet a female coworker, he would never shake her hand. However, because of my management position in the company and my status as a Western expatriate, male staff members gave me the same enthusiastic greeting and handshake normally reserved for their male counterparts.

Ellen also found herself facilitating Bahraini women's positions in the workplace.

> As I was the only female in a senior management position in our office, I was often asked by the female employees to speak to their male superiors about problems and issues they experienced in their departments. I also had to provide a role model for the women because there were no female Bahraini managers. Some of them came to me not just to discuss career issues but to discuss life issues. There was just no one else in a similar position for them to talk to. On the other hand, male managers would ask me to discuss sensitive issues, such as hygiene, with their female staff members.

The government of Bahrain introduced legislation that restricted the amount of overtime hours women could work. Although the move was being praised by the (female) Director of Social Development as recognition of the contribution women were making to Bahraini industry, Ellen saw it as further discriminatory treatment restricting the choices of women in Bahrain. Her published letter to the editor of the *Gulf Daily News* read:

> . . . How the discriminatory treatment of women in this regulation can be seen as recognition of the immense contribution women make to the Bahrain workforce is beyond comprehension. Discrimination of any portion of the population in the labor legislation does not recognize anything but the obvious

prejudice. If the working women in Bahrain want to receive acknowledgement of their indispensable impact on the Bahrain economy, it should be through an increase in the number of management positions available to qualified women, not through regulations limiting the hours they work. All this regulation means is that women are still regarded as second class citizens who need the strong arm tactics of the government to help them settle disputes over working hours. Government officials could really show appreciation to the working women in Bahrain by making sure that companies hire and promote based on skill rather than gender. But there is little likelihood of that occurring.

The letter was signed with a pseudonym, but the day it was published one of Ellen's female employees showed her the letter and claimed "if I didn't know better, Ellen, I'd think you wrote this letter."

CAREER DECISIONS

When Ellen first arrived in Bahrain, she had great expectations that she would work somewhere where she could make a difference. She received several offers for positions and turned down, among others, a university and a high-profile brokerage house. She decided to take a position as a Special Projects Coordinator at a large American financial institution.

> In fact, the records will show I was actually hired as a "Financial Analyst," but this title was given solely because at that time, the government had decided that expatriate women shouldn't be allowed to take potential positions away from Bahraini nationals. The expertise required as a Financial Analyst enabled the company to obtain a work permit for me as I had the required experience and academic credentials, although I performed few duties as an analyst.

In her special projects role, Ellen learned a great deal about international finance. She conducted efficiency studies on various operating departments. She used her systems expertise to investigate and improve the company's micro computer usage, and developed a payroll program which was subsequently integrated into the company's international systems. She was a member of the Strategic Review Committee, and produced a report outlining the long-term goals for the Middle East market, which she then presented to the Senior Vice President of Europe, Middle East, and Africa.

After one year, Ellen was rewarded for her achievements by a promotion to manager of Business Planning and Development, a position which reported directly to the Vice President and General Manager. She designed the role herself, and was able to be creative and quite influential in the company. During her year in this role, she was involved in a diverse range of activities. She managed the Quality Assurance department, coordinated a product launch, developed and managed a senior management information system, was an active participant in all senior management meetings, and launched an employee newsletter.

At the end of her second year in Bahrain, Ellen was informed that two positions in Operations would soon be available, and the General Manager, a European expatriate, asked if she would be interested in joining the area. She had previously only worked in staff positions, and quickly decided to accept the challenge and learning experience of a line post. Both positions were in senior management, and both had responsibility for approximately thirty employees.

The first position was for Manager of Accounts Control, which covered the Credit, Collection, and Authorization departments. The manager's role was to ensure that appropriate information was used to authorize spending by clients, to compile results of client payment, and to inform management of nonpayment issues. The manager also supervised in-house staff and representatives in other Gulf countries for the collection of withheld payments.

The second post was Manager of Customer Services, New Accounts, and Establishment Services. The manager's role was to ensure that new clients were worthy and that international quality standards were met in all Customer Service activity. The manager also worked with two other departments: with marketing to ensure that budgets were met, and with Sales to manage relationships with the many affiliate outlets of the service.

After speaking with the two current managers and considering the options carefully, Ellen decided that she would prefer working in the Accounts Control area. The job was more oriented to financial information, the manager had more influence on operations at the company, and she would have the opportunity to travel to other countries to supervise staff. Although she was not familiar with the systems and procedures, she knew she could learn them quickly. Ellen went into her meeting with the General Manager excited about the new challenges.

Ellen Meets with the General Manager

Ellen told the General Manager she had decided to take the Accounts Control position, and outlined her reasons. Then she waited for his affirmation and for the details of when she would begin.

"I'm afraid I've reconsidered the offer," the General Manager announced. "Although I know you would probably do a terrific job in the Accounts Control position, I can't offer it to you. It involves periodic travel into Saudi Arabia, and women are not allowed to travel there alone." He went on to tell Ellen how she would be subject to discriminatory practices, would not be able to gain the respect of the company's Saudi Arabian clients, and would experience difficulty travelling there.

Ellen was astonished. She quickly pointed out to him that many businesswomen were representatives of American firms in Saudi Arabia. She described one woman she knew of who was the sole representative of a large American bank in the Eastern Province of Saudi Arabia who frequently travelled there alone. She explained that other women's experiences in Saudi Arabia showed professional men there treated professional women as neither male nor female, but as businesspeople. Besides, she continued, there were no other candidates in the company for either position. She reminded the General Manager of the pride the company took in its quality standards and how senior management salaries were in part determined by assuring quality in their departments. Although the company was an equal opportunity employer in its home country, the United States, she believed the spirit of the policy should extend to all international offices.

The General Manager informed her that his decision reflected his desire to address the interests of both herself and the company. He was worried, he said, that Ellen would have trouble obtaining entry visas to allow her to conduct business in Saudi Arabia, and that the customers would not accept her. Also, if there were ever any hostile outbreaks, he believed she would be in danger, and he could not have lived with that possibility.

Ellen stated that as a woman, she believed she was at lower risk of danger than her Western male counterparts since in the event of hostility, the Saudi Arabians would most likely secure her safety. There was much greater probability that a male representative of the firm would be held as a hostage.

The General Manager was adamant. Regardless of her wishes, the company needed Ellen in the Customer Service position. New Accounts had only recently been added to the department, and the bottom-line responsibility was thus doubled from what it had been in the past. The General Manager said he wanted someone he could trust and depend upon to handle the pressure of New Accounts, which had a high international profile.

Ellen was offered the Customer Service position, then dismissed from the meeting. In frustration, she began to consider her options.

Take the Customers Services Position

The General Manager obviously expected her to take the position. It would mean increased responsibility and challenge. Except for a position in high school where she managed a force of sixty student police, Ellen had not yet supervised more than four employees at any time in her professional career. On the other hand, it went against her values to accept the post since it had been offered as a result of gender roles when all consideration should have been placed on competence.

She knew she had the abilities and qualifications for the position. She viewed the entire situation as yet another example of how the business community in Bahrain had difficulty accepting and acknowledging the contributions of women to international management and didn't want to abandon her values by accepting the position.

Fight Back

There were two approaches which would permit Ellen to take the matter further. She could go to the General Manger's superior, the Senior Vice President of Europe, Middle East, and Africa. She had had several dealings with him, and had once presented a report to him with which he was very impressed. But she wasn't sure she could count on his sympathy regarding her travelling to Saudi Arabia as his knowledge of the region was limited, and he generally relied on local management's decisions on such issues. She could consider filing a grievance against the company. There were provisions in Bahraini Labor Law that would have permitted this option in her case. However, she understood that the Labor Tribunals, unlike those held in Western countries, did not try cases based on precedents or rules of evidence. In other words, the judge would apply a hodgepodge of his own subjective criteria to reach a decision.

Stay in the Business Planning and Development Job

Although the General Manager had not mentioned it as an option, Ellen could request that she remain in her current position. It would mean not giving in to the General Manager's prejudices. Since she had been considering the two Operations positions, though, she had been looking forward to moving on to something new.

Leave the Company

Ellen knew she was qualified for many positions in the financial centre of Bahrain and could likely obtain work with another company. She was not sure, though, whether leaving her present company under these circumstances would jeopardize her chances of finding work elsewhere. Furthermore, to obtain a post at a new company would require a letter of permission from her current employer, who, as her sponsor in Bahrain, had to sanction her move to a new employer who would become her new sponsor. She was not sure that she would be able to make those arrangements considering the situation.

> I always tell my employees: "If you wake up one morning and discover you don't like your job, come to see me immediately. If the problem is with the tasks of the job, I'll see if I can modify your tasks. If the problem is with the department or you want a change, I'll assist you in getting another position in the company. If the problem is with the company, then I'll help you write your resume." I have stated this credo to all my employees in every post I've held. Generally, they don't believe that their manager would actually assist with resume writing, but when the opportunity arises, and it has, and I do come through as promised, the impact on the remaining employees is priceless. Employees will provide much more effort towards a cause that is supported by someone looking out for their personal welfare.

Ellen's superior did not have the same attitude towards his employees. As she considered her options, Ellen realized that no move could be made without a compromise either in her career or her values. Which choice was she most willing to make?

Notes

1. *Resident in Bahrain,* Volume 1, 1987, *Gulf Daily News,* pp. 61–63.
2. *Resident in Bahrain,* Volume 1, 1987, *Gulf Daily News,* p. 57.

EXHIBIT 1. Maps of the Middle East

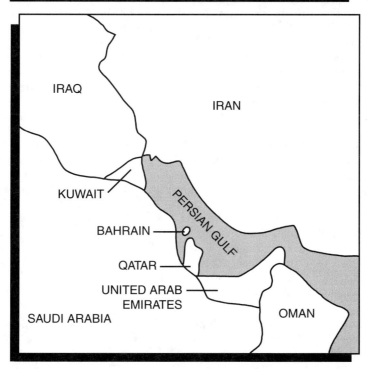

➤ *Case Study* ➤

Is This the Right Time to Come Out?

ALISTAIR D. WILLIAMSON

George Campbell, assistant vice president in mergers and acquisitions at Kirkham McDowell Securities, a St. Louis underwriting and financial advisory firm, looked up as Adam Lawson, one of his most promising associates, entered his office. Adam, 29 years old, had been with the firm for only two years but had already distinguished himself as having great potential. Recently, he had helped to bring in an extremely lucrative deal, and in six weeks, he and several other associates would be honored for their efforts at the firm's silver anniversary dinner.

As Adam closed the door and sat down, he said, "George, I'd like to talk to you about the banquet. I've thought about this very carefully, and I want you to know that I plan to bring my partner, Robert Collins, as my escort."

George was taken aback. "Well, Adam," he said, "I don't quite know what to say. I have to be honest with you; I'm a little surprised. I had no idea that you were gay. I would never have guessed." He looked at Adam for clues on how to proceed: his subordinate did seem nervous but not defiant or hostile.

Though only a 50-person operation, Kirkham McDowell had long since secured its status as one of the region's leading corporate financial advisers. The firm's client roster included established and successful regional companies as well as one of the country's largest defense contractors, a very conservative company for which the firm managed part of an impressive pension portfolio. Representatives of Kirkham McDowell's major clients and many of the area's most influential political and business leaders were expected to attend the banquet. All this raced through George's mind as he asked Adam, "Why do you want to do this? Why do you want to mix your personal and professional lives?"

"For the same reason that you bring your wife to company social events," Adam replied.

A look of confusion flickered across George's face while Adam continued. "Think about it for a moment, George. Success in this business depends in great part on the relationships you develop with your clients and the people you work with. An important part of those relationships is letting people know about your life away from the office, and that includes the people who are important to you. Some of the other associates already know Robert. Whenever his schedule permits, he accompanies me when I'm invited by one of my colleagues to have dinner with his or her spouse. Granted, that isn't very often—Robert is a corporate attorney, and his work is very demanding—but he joins me whenever he can."

"But, Adam, a wife isn't the same thing as a—"

"It *is* the same thing, George. Robert and I have made a commitment to each other. We have been together for almost five years now, and I would feel very uncomfortable telling him that I was going to a major social event alone—on a weekend, no less."

"Well, I'm sure you'd agree that it wouldn't be appropriate for an associate to bring a date—someone he barely knows—to such an event."

"Come on, George. I think you know me well enough to realize that I have better judgment than that. If Robert and I had known each other for only six months, I wouldn't be having this conversation with you right now. But, as I said, we've been together for over five years!"

George thought for a moment. "Adam," he said slowly, "I'm just not sure you should try to make an issue of this at such an important time for the company. Why bring it up now? Think of our clients. We work with some very conservative companies. They could very well decide to give their business to a firm whose views seem to agree more with their own. You're not just making a personal statement here. You're saying something about the culture at Kirkham McDowell, something that some of our clients might fundamentally oppose. How are they going to react?"

Adam leaned forward. "This is only an issue if people make it an issue," he said. "I have resolved never to lie about myself or about anything that is important to me—and that includes my sexuality. Since I joined the firm, as I've become comfortable sharing details of my personal life with certain colleagues, I've come out to them and often introduced them to Robert. If people ask me if I'm gay, I'm honest with them. Likewise, if people ask me if I have a girlfriend, I tell them about my relationship with Robert. With the silver anniversary celebration coming up, I thought the time was right to speak with you. This is the first large social event the company has held since I started working here. And after a lot of discussion with Robert and some of the associates here, I've decided that I need to be as open at the banquet as I have tried to be in other areas within the organization.

"It's not a decision that I've taken lightly. I've seen what has happened to some of my gay friends who have come out at work. Even at much less conservative companies, some are never invited to important social events with colleagues and customers, no matter how much business they bring in. They'll never know whether or not their bonuses have been affected by prejudice related to their sexuality. I know my career could be adversely influenced by this decision, but I believe that my work should stand on its own merits. George, I've been a top contributor at this firm since I walked in the door. I hope I can rely on you to back me up on this."

Adam stood up but waited for George to reply. "You've given me a lot to think about," George said. "And I don't want to say anything until I've had a chance to consider all the implications. I appreciate the confidence you've shown in me by being so open. I wish I had something conclusive to say at this point, but the fact of the matter is that I have never had to face this issue before. I am one of your biggest supporters here at the firm. Your work has been exemplary. And, until today, I would have said that you could look forward to a very successful career here. But I'm concerned about how this will play with our clients and, as a result, about how senior management will react. I personally don't have any problems with your being gay, but I'd hate to see you torpedo your career over this. It's possible that this could jeopardize some of our relationships with significant clients. Let me think about it for a few days. We can have lunch next week and map out a strategy."

After Adam left his office, George sat in silence for a few minutes, trying to make sense of the conversation. He was unsure of his next move. Adam clearly had *not* come into his office looking for permission to bring his lover to the banquet. George realized that he could do nothing and let events simply unfold. After all, Adam had not asked that Robert be included in his benefits coverage nor had he requested a specific managerial decision. There was no company policy on paper to guide him through his dilemma. But Adam wouldn't have come to him if he hadn't wanted a response of some kind. And shouldn't he at least tell his superior in order to head off any awkward moments at the banquet?

Just how negative an effect could Robert have on Adam's career with the firm and on the firm's relationship with its clients? Wasn't it possible, even likely, that the party would come off without incident? That the issue would blow over? That even the firm's most conservative clients wouldn't realize the significance of Adam's guest or would simply decide that it was a personal issue, not a business one? Or would George's worst fears be realized? Adam had to recognize that the potential risks were great. It was one thing for him to come out of the closet at the office. But wasn't he pushing things too far?

Management Women and the New Facts of Life

Felice N. Schwartz

The cost of employing women in management is greater than the cost of employing men. This is a jarring statement, partly because it is true, but mostly because it is something people are reluctant to talk about. A new study by one multinational corporation shows that the rate of turnover in management positions is 2½ times higher among top-performing women than it is among men. A large producer of consumer goods reports that one half of the women who take maternity leave return to their jobs late or not at all. And we know that women also have a greater tendency to plateau or to interrupt their careers in ways that limit their growth and development. But we have become so sensitive to charges of sexism and so afraid of confrontation, even litigation, that we rarely say what we know to be true. Unfortunately, our bottled-up awareness leaks out in misleading metaphors ("glass ceiling" is one notable example), veiled hostility, lowered expectations, distrust, and reluctant adherence to Equal Employment Opportunity requirements.

Career interruptions, plateauing, and turnover are expensive. The money corporations invest in recruitment, training, and development is less likely to produce top executives among women than among men, and the invaluable company experience that developing executives acquire at every level as they move up through management ranks is more often lost.

The studies just mentioned are only the first of many, I'm quite sure. Demographic realities are going to force corporations all across the country to analyze the cost of employing women in managerial positions, and what they will discover is that women cost more.

But here is another startling truth: The greater cost of employing women is not a function of inescapable gender differences. Women *are* different from men, but what increases their cost to the corporation is principally the clash of their perceptions, attitudes, and behavior with those of men, which is to say, with the policies and practices of male-led corporations.

It is terribly important that employers draw the right conclusions from the studies now being done. The studies will be useless—or worse, harmful—if all they teach us is that women are expensive to employ. What we need to learn is how to reduce that expense, how to stop throwing away the investments we make in talented women, how to become more responsive to the needs of the women that corporations *must* employ if they are to have the best and the brightest of all those now entering the work force.

The gender differences relevant to business fall into two categories: those related to maternity and those related to the differing traditions and expectations of the sexes. Maternity is biological rather than cultural. We can't alter it, but we can dramatically reduce its impact on the workplace and in many cases eliminate its negative effect on employee development. We can accomplish this by addressing the second set of differences, those between male and female socialization. Today, these differences exaggerate the real costs of maternity and can turn a relatively slight disruption in work schedule into a serious business problem and a career derailment for individual women. If we are to overcome the cost differential between male and female employees, we need to address the issues that arise when female socialization meets the male corporate culture and masculine rules of career development—issues of behavior and style, of expectation, of stereotypes and preconceptions, of sexual tension and harassment, of female mentoring, lateral mobility, relocation, compensation, and early identification of top performers.

The one immutable, enduring difference between men and women is maternity. Maternity is not simply childbirth but a continuum that begins with an awareness of the ticking of the biological clock, proceeds to the anticipation of motherhood, includes pregnancy, childbirth, physical recuperation, psychological adjustment, and continues on to nursing, bonding, and child rearing. Not all women choose to become mothers, of course, and among those who do, the process varies from case to case depending on the health of the mother and baby, the values of the parents, and the availability, cost, and quality of child care.

In past centuries, the biological fact of maternity shaped the traditional roles of the sexes. Women performed the home-centered functions that related to the bearing and nurturing of children. Men did the work that required great physical strength. Over time, however, family size contracted, the community assumed greater responsibility for the care and education of children, packaged foods and household technology reduced the work load in the home, and technology eliminated much of the need for muscle power at the workplace. Today, in the developed world, the only role still uniquely gender related is childbearing. Yet men and women are still socialized to perform their traditional roles.

Men and women may or may not have some innate psychological disposition toward these traditional roles—men to be aggressive, competitive, self-reliant, risk taking; women to be supportive, nurturing, intuitive, sensitive, communicative—but certainly both men and women are capable of the full range of behavior. Indeed, the male and female roles have already begun to expand and merge. In the decades ahead, as the socialization of boys and girls and the experience and expectations of young men and women grow steadily more androgynous, the differences in workplace behavior will continue to fade. At the moment, however, we are still plagued by disparities in perception and behavior that make the integration of men and women in the workplace unnecessarily difficult and expensive.

Let me illustrate with a few broadbrush generalizations. Of course, these are only stereotypes, but I think they help to exemplify the kinds of preconceptions that can muddy the corporate waters.

Men continue to perceive women as the rearers of their children, so they find it understandable, indeed appropriate, that women should renounce their careers to raise families. Edmund Pratt, CEO of Pfizer, once asked me in all sincerity, "Why would any woman choose to be a chief financial officer rather than a full-time mother?" By condoning and taking pleasure in women's traditional behavior, men reinforce it. Not only do they see parenting as fundamentally female, they see a career as fundamentally male—either an unbroken series of promotions and advancements toward CEOdom or stagnation and disappointment. This attitude serves to legitimize a woman's choice to extend maternity leave and even, for those who can afford it, to leave employment altogether for several years. By the same token, men who might want to take a leave after the birth of a child know that management will see such behavior as a lack of career commitment, even when company policy permits parental leave for men.

Women also bring counterproductive expectations and perceptions to the workplace. Ironically, although the feminist movement was an expression of women's quest for freedom from their home-based lives, most women were remarkably free already. They had many responsibilities, but they were autonomous and could be entrepreneurial in how and when they carried them out. And once their children grew up and left home, they were essentially free to do what they wanted with their lives. Women's traditional role also included freedom from responsibility for the financial support of their families. Many of us were socialized from girlhood to expect our husbands to take care of us, while our brothers were socialized from an equally early age to complete their educations, pursue careers, climb the ladder of success, and provide dependable financial support for their families. To the extent that this tradition of freedom lingers subliminally, women tend to bring to their employment a sense that they can choose to change jobs or careers at will, take time off, or reduce their hours.

Finally, women's traditional role encouraged particular attention to the quality and substance of what they did, specifically to the physical, psychological, and intellectual development of their children. This traditional focus may explain women's continuing tendency to search for more than monetary reward—intrinsic significance, social importance, meaning—in what they do. This too makes them more likely than men to leave the corporation in search of other values.

The misleading metaphor of the glass ceiling suggests an invisible barrier constructed by corporate leaders to impede the upward mobility of women beyond the middle levels. A more appropriate metaphor, I believe, is the kind of cross-sectional diagram used in geology. The barriers to women's leadership occur when potentially counterproductive layers of influence on women—maternity, tradition, socialization—meet management strata pervaded by the largely unconscious preconceptions, stereotypes, and expectations of men. Such interfaces do not exist for men and tend to be impermeable for women.

One result of these gender differences has been to convince some executives that women are simply not suited to top management. Other executives feel helpless. If they see even a few of their valued female employees fail to return to work from maternity leave on schedule or see one of their most promising women plateau in her career after the birth of a child, they begin to fear there is nothing they can do to infuse women with new energy and enthusiasm and persuade them to stay. At the same time, they know there is nothing they can do to stem the tide of women into management ranks.

Another result is to place every working woman on a continuum that runs from total dedication to career at one end to a balance between career and family at the other. What women discover is that the male corporate culture sees both extremes as unacceptable. Women who want the flexibility to balance their families and their careers are not adequately committed to the organization. Women who perform as aggressively and competitively as men are abrasive and unfeminine. But the fact is, business needs all the talented women it can get. Moreover, as I will explain, the women I call career-primary and those I call career-and-family each have particular value to the corporation.

———◦•◦———

Women in the corporation are about to move from a buyer's to a seller's market. The sudden, startling recognition that 80% of new entrants in the work force over the next decade will be women, minorities, and immigrants has stimulated a mushrooming incentive to "value diversity."

Women are no longer simply an enticing pool of occasional creative talent, a thorn in the side of the EEO officer, or a source of frustration to corporate leaders truly puzzled by the slowness of their upward trickle into executive positions. A real demographic change is taking place. The era of sudden population growth of the 1950s and 1960s is over. The birth rate has dropped about 40%, from a high of 25.3 live births per 1,000 population in 1957, at the peak of the baby boom, to a stable low of a little more than 15 per 1,000 over the last 16 years, and there is no indication of a return to a higher rate. The tidal wave of baby boomers that swelled the recruitment pool to overflowing seems to have been a one-time phenomenon. For 20 years, employers had the pick of a very large crop and were able to choose males almost exclusively for the executive track. But if future population remains fairly stable while the economy continues to expand, and if the new information society simultaneously creates a greater need for creative, educated managers, then the gap between supply and demand will grow dramatically and, with it, the competition for managerial talent.

The decrease in numbers has even greater implications if we look at the traditional source of corporate recruitment for leadership positions—white males from the top 10% of the country's best universities. Over the past decade, the increase in the number of women graduating from leading universities has been much greater than the increase in the total number of graduates, and these women are well represented in the top 10% of their classes.

The trend extends into business and professional programs as well. In the old days, virtually all MBAs were male. I remember addressing a meeting at the Harvard Business School as recently as the mid-1970s and looking out at a sea of exclusively male faces. Today, about 25% of that audience would be women. The pool of male MBAs from which corporations have traditionally drawn their leadership has shrunk significantly.

Of course, this reduction does not have to mean a shortage of talent. The top 10% is at least as smart as it always was—smarter, probably, since it's now drawn from a broader segment of the population. But it now consists increasingly of women. Companies that are determined to recruit the same number of men as before will have to dig much deeper into the male pool, while their competitors will have the opportunity to pick the best people from both the male and female graduates.

Under these circumstances, there is no question that the management ranks of business will include increasing numbers of women. There remains, however, the question of how these women will succeed—how long they will stay, how high they will climb, how completely they will fulfill their promise and potential, and what kind of return the corporation will realize on its investment in their training and development.

There is ample business reason for finding ways to make sure that as many of these women as possible will succeed. The first step in this process is to recognize that women are not all alike. Like men, they are individuals with differing talents, priorities, and motivations. For the sake of simplicity, let me focus on the two women I referred to earlier, on what I call the career-primary woman and the career-and-family woman.

Like many men, some women put their careers first. They are ready to make the same trade-offs traditionally made by the men who seek leadership positions. They make a career decision to put in extra hours, to make sacrifices in their personal lives, to make the most of every opportunity for professional development. For women, of course, this decision also requires that they remain single or at least childless or, if they do have children, that they be satisfied to have others raise them. Some 90% of executive men but only 35% of executive women have children by the age of 40. The *automatic* association of all women with babies is clearly unjustified.

The secret to dealing with such women is to recognize them early, accept them, and clear artificial barriers from their path to the top. After all, the best of these women are among the best managerial talent you will ever see. And career-primary women have another important value to the company that men and other women lack. They can act as role models and mentors to younger women who put their careers first. Since upwardly mobile career-primary women still have few role models to motivate and inspire them, a company with women in its top echelon has a significant advantage in the competition for executive talent.

Men at the top of the organization—most of them over 55, with wives who tend to be traditional—often find career women "masculine" and difficult to accept as colleagues. Such men miss the point, which is not that these women are just like men but that they are just like the *best* men in the organization. And there is such a shortage of the best people that gender cannot be allowed to matter. It is clearly counterproductive to disparage in a woman with executive talent the very qualities that are most critical to the business and that might carry a man to the CEO's office.

Clearing a path to the top for career-primary women has four requirements:

1. Identify them early.
2. Give them the same opportunity you give to talented men to grow and develop and contribute to company profitability. Give them client and customer responsibility. Expect them to travel and relocate, to make the same commitment to the company as men aspiring to leadership positions.
3. Accept them as valued members of your management team. Include them in every kind of communication. Listen to them.
4. Recognize that the business environment is more difficult and stressful for them than for their male peers. They are always a minority, often the only woman. The male perception of talented, ambitious women is at best ambivalent, a mixture of admiration, resentment, confusion, competitiveness, attraction, skepticism, anxiety, pride, and animosity. Women can never feel secure about how they should dress and act, whether they should speak out or grin and bear it when they encounter discrimination, stereotyping, sexual harassment, and paternalism. Social interaction and travel with male colleagues and with male clients can be charged. As they move up, the normal increase in pressure and responsibility is compounded for women because they are women.

Stereotypical language and sexist day-to-day behavior do take their toll on women's career development. Few male executives realize how common it is to call women by their first names while men in the same group are greeted with surnames, how frequently female executives are assumed by men to be secretaries, how often women are excluded from all-male social events where business is being transacted. With notable exceptions, men are still generally more comfortable with other men, and as a result women miss many of the career and business opportunities that arise over lunch, on the golf course, or in the locker room.

The majority of women, however, are what I call career-and-family women, women who want to pursue serious careers while participating actively in the rearing of children. These women are a precious resource that has yet to be mined. Many of them are talented and creative. Most of them are willing to trade some career growth and compensation for freedom from the constant pressure to work long hours and weekends.

Most companies today are ambivalent at best about the career-and-family women in their management ranks. They would prefer that all employees were willing to give their all to the company. They believe it is in their best interests for all managers to compete for the top positions so the company will have the largest possible pool from which to draw its leaders.

"If you have both talent and motivation," many employers seem to say, "we want to move you up. If you haven't got that motivation, if you want less pressure and greater flexibility, then you can leave and make room for a new generation." These companies lose on two counts. First, they fail to amortize the investment they made in the early training and experience of management women who find themselves committed to family as well as to career. Second, they fail to recognize what these women could do for their middle management.

The ranks of middle managers are filled with people on their way up and people who have stalled. Many of them have simply reached their limits, achieved career growth commensurate with or exceeding their capabilities, and they cause problems because their performance is mediocre but they still want to move ahead. The career-and-family woman is willing to trade off the pressures and demands that go with promotion for the freedom to spend more time with her children. She's very smart, she's talented, she's committed to her career, and she's satisfied to stay at the middle level, at least during the early child-rearing years. Compare her with some of the people you have there now.

Consider a typical example, a woman who decides in college on a business career and enters management at age 22. For nine years, the company invests in her career as she gains experience and skills and steadily improves her performance. But at 31, just as the investment begins to pay off in earnest, she decides to have a baby. Can the company afford to let her go home, take another job, or go into business for herself? The common perception now is yes, the corporation can afford to lose her unless, after six or eight weeks or even three months of disability and maternity leave, she returns to work on a full-time schedule with the same vigor, commitment, and ambition that she showed before.

But what if she doesn't? What if she wants or needs to go on leave for six months or a year or, heaven forbid, five years? In this worst-case scenario, she works full-time from age 22 to 31 and from 36 to 65—a total of 38 years as opposed to the typical male's 43 years. That's not a huge difference. Moreover, my typical example is willing to work part-time while her children are young, if only her employer will give her the opportunity. There are two rewards for companies responsive to this need: higher retention of their best people and greatly improved performance and satisfaction in their middle management.

The high-performing career-and-family woman can be a major player in your company. She can give you a significant business advantage as the competition for able people escalates. Sometimes too, if you can hold on to her, she will switch gears in mid-life and reenter the competition for the top. The price you must pay to retain these women is threefold: you must plan for and manage maternity, you must provide the flexibility that will allow them to be maximally productive, and you must take an active role in helping to make family supports and high-quality, affordable child care available to all women.

The key to managing maternity is to recognize the value of high-performing women and the urgent need to retain them and keep them productive. The first step must be a genuine partnership between the woman and her boss. I know this partnership can seem difficult to forge. One of my own senior executives came to me recently to discuss plans for her maternity leave and subsequent return to work. She knew she wanted to come back. I wanted to make certain that she would. Still, we had a somewhat awkward conversation, because I knew that no woman can predict with certainty when she will be able to return to work or under what conditions. Physical problems can lengthen her leave. So can a demanding infant, a difficult family or personal adjustment, or problems with child care.

I still don't know when this valuable executive will be back on the job full-time, and her absence creates some genuine problems for our organization. But I do know that I can't simply replace her years of experience with a new recruit. Since our conversation, I also know that she wants to come back, and that she *will* come back—part-time at first—unless I make it impossible for her by, for example, setting an arbitrary date for her full-time return or resignation. In turn, she knows that the organization wants and needs her and, more to the point, that it will be responsive to her needs in terms of working hours and child-care arrangements.

In having this kind of conversation it's important to ask concrete questions that will help to move the discussion from uncertainty and anxiety to some level of predictability. Questions can touch on everything from family income and energy level to child care arrangements and career commitment. Of course you want your star manager to return to work as soon as possible, but you want her to return permanently and productively. Her downtime on the job is a drain on her energies and a waste of your money.

━━━━◆◆◆━━━━

For all the women who want to combine career and family—the women who want to participate actively in the rearing of their children and who also want to pursue their careers seriously—the key to retention is to provide the flexibility and family supports they need in order to function effectively.

Time spent in the office increases productivity if it is time well spent, but the fact that most women continue to take the primary responsibility for child care is a cause of distraction, diversion, anxiety, and absenteeism—to say nothing of the persistent guilt experienced by all working mothers. A great many women, perhaps most of all women who have always performed at the highest levels, are also frustrated by a sense that while their children are babies they cannot function at their best either at home or at work.

In its simplest form, flexibility is the freedom to take time off—a couple of hours, a day, a week—or to do some work at home and some at the office, an arrangement that communication technology makes increasingly feasible. At the complex end of the spectrum are alternative work schedules that permit the woman to work less than full-time and her employer to reap the benefits of her experience and, with careful planning, the top level of her abilities.

Part-time employment is the single greatest inducement to getting women back on the job expeditiously and the provision women themselves most desire. A part-time return to work enables them to maintain responsibility for critical aspects of their jobs, keeps them in touch with the changes constantly occurring at the workplace and in the job itself, reduces stress and fatigue, often eliminates the need for paid maternity leave by permitting a return to the office as soon as disability leave is over, and, not least, can greatly enhance company loyalty. The part-time solution works particularly well when a work load can be reduced for one individual in a department or when a full-time job can be broken down by skill levels and apportioned to two individuals at different levels of skill and pay.

I believe, however, that shared employment is the most promising and will be the most widespread form of flexible scheduling in the future. It is feasible at every level of the corporation except at the pinnacle, for both the short and the long term. It involves two people taking responsibility for one job.

Two red lights flash on as soon as most executives hear the words "job sharing": continuity and client-customer contact. The answer to the continuity question is to place responsibility entirely on the two individuals sharing the job to discuss everything that transpires—thoroughly, daily, and on their own time. The answer to the problem of client-customer contact is yes, job sharing requires reeducation and a period of adjustment. But as both client and supervisor will quickly come to appreciate, two contacts means that the customer has continuous access to the company's representative, without interruptions for vacation, travel, or sick leave. The two people holding the job can simply cover for each other, and the uninterrupted, full-time coverage they provide together can be a stipulation of their arrangement.

Flexibility is costly in numerous ways. It requires more supervisory time to coordinate and manage, more office space, and somewhat greater benefits costs (though these can be contained with flexible benefits plans, prorated benefits, and, in two-paycheck families, elimination of duplicate benefits). But the advantages of reduced turnover and the greater productivity that results from higher energy levels and greater focus can outweigh the costs.

A few hints:

- Provide flexibility selectively. I'm not suggesting private arrangements subject to the suspicion of favoritism but rather a policy that makes flexible work schedules available only to high performers.
- Make it clear that in most instances (but not all) the rates of advancement and pay will be appropriately lower for those who take time off or who work part-time than for those who work full-time. Most career-and-family women are entirely willing to make that trade-off.
- Discuss costs as well as benefits. Be willing to risk accusations of bias. Insist, for example, that half time is half of whatever time it takes to do the job, not merely half of 35 or 40 hours.

The woman who is eager to get home to her child has a powerful incentive to use her time effectively at the office and to carry with her reading and other work that can be done at home. The talented professional who wants to have it all can be a high performer by carefully ordering her priorities and by focusing on objectives rather than on the legendary 15-hour day. By the time professional women have their first babies—at an average age of 31— they have already had nine years to work long hours at a desk, to travel, and to relocate. In the case of high performers, the need for flexibility coincides with what has gradually become the goal-oriented nature of responsibility.

Family supports—in addition to maternity leave and flexibility—include the provision of parental leave for men, support for two-career and single-parent families during relocation, and flexible benefits. But the primary ingredient is child care. The capacity of working mothers to function effectively and without interruption depends on the availability of good, affordable child care. Now that women make up almost half the work force and the growing percentage of managers, the decision to become involved in the personal lives of employees is no longer a philosophical question but a practical one. To make matters worse, the quality of child care has almost no relation to technology, inventiveness, or profitability but is more or less a pure function of the quality of child care personnel and the ratio of adults to children. These costs are irreducible. Only by joining hands with government and the public sector can corporations hope to create the vast quantity and variety of child care that their employees need.

Until quite recently, the response of corporations to women has been largely symbolic and cosmetic, motivated in large part by the will to avoid litigation and legal penalties. In some cases, companies were also moved by a genuine sense of fairness and a vague discomfort and frustration at the absence of women above the middle of the corporate pyramid. The actions they took were mostly quick, easy, and highly visible—child care information services, a three-month parental leave available to men as well as women, a woman appointed to the board of directors.

When I first began to discuss these issues 26 years ago, I was sometimes able to get an appointment with the assistant to the assistant in personnel, but it was only a courtesy. Over the past decade, I have met with the CEOs of many large corporations, and I've watched them become involved with ideas they had never previously thought much about. Until recently, however, the shelf life of that enhanced awareness was always short. Given pressing, short-term concerns, women were not a front-burner issue. In the past few months, I have seen yet another change. Some CEOs and top management groups now take the initiative. They call and ask us to show them how to shift gears from a responsive to a proactive approach to recruiting, developing, and retaining women.

I think this change is more probably a response to business needs—to concern for the quality of future profits and managerial talent—than to uneasiness about legal requirements, sympathy with the demands of women and minorities, or the desire to do what is right and fair. The nature of such business motivation varies. Some companies want to move women to higher positions as role models for those below them and as beacons for talented young recruits. Some want to achieve a favorable image with employees, customers, clients, and stockholders. These are all legitimate motives. But I think the companies that stand to gain most are motivated as well by a desire to capture competitive advantage in an era when talent and competence will be in increasingly short supply. These companies are now ready to stop being defensive about their experience with women and to ask incisive questions without preconceptions.

Even so, incredibly, I don't know of more than one or two companies that have looked into their own records to study the absolutely critical issue of maternity leave—how many women took it, when and whether they returned, and how this behavior correlated with their rank, tenure, age, and performance. The unique drawback to the employment of women is the physical reality of maternity and the particular socializing influence maternity has had. Yet to make women equal to men in the workplace we have chosen on the whole not to discuss this single most significant difference between them. Unless we do, we cannot evaluate the cost of recruiting, developing, and moving women up.

Now that interest is replacing indifference, there are four steps every company can take to examine its own experience with women:

1. Gather quantitative data on the company's experience with management-level women regarding turnover rates, occurrence of and return from maternity leave, and organizational level attained in relation to tenure and performance.

2. Correlate this data with factors such as age, marital status, and presence and age of children, and attempt to identify and analyze why women respond the way they do.

3. Gather qualitative data on the experience of women in your company and on how women are perceived by both sexes.

4. Conduct a cost-benefit analysis of the return on your investment in high-performing women. Factor in the cost to the company of women's negative reactions to negative experience, as well as the probable cost of corrective measures and policies. If women's value to your company is greater than the cost to recruit, train, and develop them—and of course I believe it will be—then you will want to do everything you can to retain them.

We have come a tremendous distance since the days when the prevailing male wisdom saw women as lacking the kind of intelligence that would allow them to succeed in business. For decades, even women themselves have harbored an unspoken belief that they couldn't make it because they couldn't be just like men, and nothing else would do. But now that women have shown themselves the equal of men in every area of organizational activity, now that they have demonstrated that they can be stars in every field of endeavor, now we can all venture to examine the fact that women and men are different.

On balance, employing women is more costly than employing men. Women can acknowledge this fact today because they know that their value to employers exceeds the additional cost and because they know that changing attitudes can reduce the additional cost dramatically. Women in management are no longer an idiosyncrasy of the arts and education. They have always matched men in natural ability. Within a very few years, they will equal men in numbers as well in every area of economic activity.

The demographic motivation to recruit and develop women is compelling. But an older question remains: Is society better for the change? Women's exit from the home and entry into the work force has certainly created problems—an urgent need for good, affordable child care; troubling questions about the kind of parenting children need; the costs and difficulties of diversity in the workplace; the stress and fatigue of combining work and family responsibilities. Wouldn't we all be happier if we could turn back the clock to an age when men were in the workplace and women in the home, when male and female roles were clearly differentiated and complementary?

Nostalgia, anxiety, and discouragement will urge many to say yes, but my answer is emphatically no. Two fundamental benefits that were unattainable in the past are now within our reach. For the individual, freedom of choice—

in this case the freedom to choose career, family, or a combination of the two. For the corporation, access to the most gifted individuals in the country. These benefits are neither self-indulgent nor insubstantial. Freedom of choice and self-realization are too deeply American to be cast aside for some wistful vision of the past. And access to our most talented human resources is not a luxury in this age of explosive international competition but rather the barest minimum that prudence and national self-preservation require.

White Privilege and Male Privilege: A Personal Account of Coming to See Correspondences Through Work in Women's Studies

PEGGY MCINTOSH

Through work to bring materials and perspectives from Women's Studies into the rest of the curriculum, I have often noticed men's unwillingness to grant that they are over-privileged in the curriculum, even though they may grant that women are disadvantaged. Denials which amount to taboos surround the subject of advantages which men gain from women's disadvantages. These denials protect male privilege from being fully recognized, acknowledged, lessened, or ended.

Thinking through unacknowledged male privilege as a phenomenon with a life of its own, I realized that since hierarchies in our society are interlocking, there was most likely a phenomenon of white privilege which was similarly denied and protected but alive and real in its effects. As a white person, I realized I had been taught about racism as something which puts others at a disadvantage, but had been taught not to see one of its corollary aspects, white privilege, which puts me at an advantage.

I think whites are carefully taught not to recognize white privilege, as males are taught not to recognize male privilege. So I have begun in an untutored way to ask what it is like to have white privilege. This paper is a partial record of my personal observations, and not a scholarly analysis. It is based on my daily experiences within my particular circumstances.

I have come to see white privilege as an invisible package of unearned assets which I can count on cashing in each day, but about which I was "meant" to remain oblivious. White privilege is like an invisible weightless knapsack of special provisions, assurances, tools, maps, guides, codebooks, passports, visas, clothes, compass, emergency gear, and blank checks.

Since I have had trouble facing white privilege and describing its results in my life, I saw parallels here with men's reluctance to acknowledge male privilege. Only rarely will a man go beyond acknowledging that women are disadvantaged to acknowledging that men have unearned advantage, or that unearned privilege has not been good for men's development as human beings, or for society's development, or that privilege systems might ever be challenged and *changed.*

I will review here several types or layers of denial which I see at work protecting, and preventing awareness about, entrenched male privilege. Then I will draw parallels, from my own experience, with the denials which veil the facts of white privilege. Finally, I will list 46 ordinary and daily ways in which I experience white privilege within my life and its particular social and political frameworks.

Writing this paper has been difficult, despite warm receptions for the talks on which it is based.[1] For describing white privilege makes one newly accountable. As we in Women's Studies work reveal male privilege and ask men to give up some of their power, so one who writes about having white privilege must ask, "Having described it, what will I do to lessen or end it?"

The denial of men's overprivileged status takes many forms in discussions of curriculum change work. Some claim that men must be central in the curriculum because they have done most of what is important or distinctive in life or in civilization. Some recognize sexism in the curriculum but deny that it makes male students seem unduly important in life. Others agree that certain *individual* thinkers are blindly male-oriented but deny that there is any systemic tendency in disciplinary frameworks or epistemology to overempower men as a group. Those men who do grant that male privilege takes institutionalized and embedded forms are still likely to deny that male hegemony has opened doors for them personally. Virtually all men deny that male overreward alone can explain men's centrality in all the inner sanctums of our most powerful institutions. Moreover, those few who will acknowledge that male privilege systems have overempowered them usually end up doubting that these privilege systems could ever be dismantled. They may say they will work to improve women's status in society or in the university, but they can't or won't support the idea of lessening men's. In curricular terms, this is the point at which men say that they regret they cannot use any of the interesting new scholarship on women because the syllabus is full. When the talk turns to giving men less cultural room, even the most thoughtful and fair-minded of the men I know well tend to reflect or fall back on conservative assumptions about the inevitability of present gender relations and distributions of power, calling on precedent or sociobiology and psychobiology to demonstrate that male domination is natural and follows inevitably from evolutionary pressures. Others resort to arguments from "experience," religion, social responsibility or wishing and dreaming.

After I realized, through faculty development work in Women's Studies, the extent to which men work from a base of unacknowledged privilege, I understood that much of their oppressiveness was unconscious. Then I remembered the frequent charges from women of color that white women whom they encounter are oppressive. I began to understand why we are justly seen as oppressive, even when we don't see ourselves that way. At the very least, obliviousness of one's privileged state can make a person or group irritating to be with. I began to count the ways in which I enjoy unearned skin privilege and have been conditioned into oblivion about its existence, unable to see that it put me "ahead" in any way, or put my people ahead, overrewarding us and yet also paradoxically damaging us, or that it could or should be changed.

My schooling gave me no training in seeing myself as an oppressor, as an unfairly advantaged person, or as a participant in a damaged culture. I was taught to see myself as an individual whose moral state depended on her individual moral will. At school, we were not taught about slavery in any depth; we were not taught to see slaveholders as damaged people. Slaves were seen as the only group at risk of being dehumanized. My schooling followed the pattern which Elizabeth Minnich has pointed out: whites are taught to think of their lives as morally neutral, normative, and average, and also ideal, so that when we work to benefit others, this is seen as work which will allow "them" to be more like "us." I think many of us know how obnoxious this attitude can be in men.

After frustration with men who would not recognize male privilege, I decided to try to work on myself at least by identifying some of the daily effects of white privilege in my life. It is crude work, at this stage, but I will give here a list of special circumstances and conditions I experience which I did not earn but which I have been made to feel are mine by birth, by citizenship, and by virtue of being a conscientious law-abiding "normal" person of good will. I have chosen those conditions which I think in my case *attach somewhat more to skin-color privilege* than to class, religion, ethnic status, or geographical location, though of course all these other factors are intricately intertwined. As far as I can see, my African-American co-workers, friends, and acquaintances with whom I come into daily or frequent contact in this particular time, place, and line of work cannot count on most of these conditions.

1. I can if I wish arrange to be in the company of people of my race most of the time.
2. I can avoid spending time with people whom I was trained to mistrust and who have learned to mistrust my kind or me.
3. If I should need to move, I can be pretty sure of renting or purchasing housing in an area which I can afford and in which I would want to live.
4. I can be pretty sure that my neighbors in such a location will be neutral or pleasant to me.
5. I can go shopping alone most of the time, pretty well assured that I will not be followed or harassed.
6. I can turn on the television or open to the front page of the newspaper and see people of my race widely represented.
7. When I am told about our national heritage or about "civilization," I am shown that people of my color made it what it is.
8. I can be sure that my children will be given curricular materials that testify to the existence of their race.
9. If I want to, I can be pretty sure of finding a publisher for this piece on white privilege.
10. I can be pretty sure of having my voice heard in a group in which I am the only member of my race.
11. I can be casual about whether or not to listen to another woman's voice in a group in which she is the only member of her race.

12. I can go into a music shop and count on finding the music of my race represented, into a supermarket and find the staple foods which fit with my cultural traditions, or into a hairdresser's shop and find someone who can cut my hair.

13. Whether I use checks, credit cards, or cash, I can count on my skin color not to work against the appearance of financial reliability.

14. I can arrange to protect my children most of the time from people who might not like them.

15. I do not have to educate my children to be aware of systemic racism for their own daily physical protection.

16. I can be pretty sure that my children's teachers and employers will tolerate them if they fit school and workplace norms; my chief worries about them do not concern others' attitudes toward their race.

17. I can talk with my mouth full and not have people put this down to my color.

18. I can swear, dress in second-hand clothes, or not answer letters without having people attribute these choices to the bad morals, poverty, or the illiteracy of my race.

19. I can speak in public to a powerful male group without putting my race on trial.

20. I can do well in a challenging situation without being called a credit to my race.

21. I am never asked to speak for all the people of my racial group.

22. I can remain oblivious of the language and customs of persons of color who constitute the world's majority without feeling in my culture any penalty for such oblivion.

23. I can criticize our government and talk about how much I fear its policies and behavior without being seen as a cultural outsider.

24. I can be pretty sure that if I ask to talk to "the person in charge," I will be facing a person of my race.

25. If a traffic cop pulls me over or if the IRS audits my tax return, I can be sure I haven't been singled out because of my race.

26. I can easily buy posters, post-cards, picture books, greeting cards, dolls, toys, and children's magazines featuring people of my race.

27. I can go home from most meetings of organizations I belong to feeling somewhat tied in, rather than isolated, out-of-place, outnumbered, unheard, held at a distance, or feared.

28. I can be pretty sure that an argument with a colleague of another race is more likely to jeopardize her chances for advancement than to jeopardize mine.

29. I can be pretty sure that if I argue for the promotion of a person of another race, or a program centering on race, this is not likely to cost me heavily within my present setting, even if my colleagues disagree with me.

30. If I declare there is a racial issue at hand, or there isn't a racial issue at hand, my race will lend me more credibility for either position than a person of color will have.

31. I can choose to ignore developments in minority writing and minority activist programs, or disparage them, or learn from them, but in any case, I can find ways to be more or less protected from negative consequences of any of these choices.

32. My culture gives me little fear about ignoring the perspectives and powers of peoples of other races.

33. I am not made acutely aware that my shape, bearing, or body odor will be taken as a reflection on my race.

34. I can worry about racism without being seen as self-interested or self-seeking.

35. I can take a job with an affirmative action employer without having my co-workers on the job suspect that I got it because of my race.

36. If my day, week, or year is going badly, I need not ask of each negative episode or situation whether it has racial overtones.

37. I can be pretty sure of finding people who would be willing to talk with me and advise me about my next steps, professionally.

38. I can think over many options, social, political, imaginative, or professional, without asking whether a person of my race would be accepted or allowed to do what I want to do.

39. I can be late to a meeting without having the lateness reflect on my race.

40. I can choose public accommodation without fearing that people of my race cannot get in or will be mistreated in the places I have chosen.

41. I can be sure that if I need legal or medical help, my race will not work against me.

42. I can arrange my activities so that I will never have to experience feelings of rejection owing to my race.

43. If I have low credibility as a leader, I can be sure that my race is not the problem.

44. I can easily find academic courses and institutions which give attention only to people of my race.

45. I can expect figurative language and imagery in all of the arts to testify to experiences of my race.

46. I can choose blemish cover or bandages in "flesh" color and have them more or less match my skin.

I repeatedly forgot each of the realizations on this list until I wrote it down. For me, white privilege has turned out to be an elusive and fugitive subject. The pressure to avoid it is great, for in facing it I must give up the myth of meritocracy. If these things are true, this is not such a free country; one's life is not what one makes it; many doors open for certain people through no virtues of their own. These perceptions mean also that my moral condition is not what I had been led to believe. The appearance of being a good citizen rather than a troublemaker comes in large part from having all sorts of doors open automatically because of my color.

A further paralysis of nerve comes from literary silence protecting privilege. My clearest memories of finding such analysis are in Lillian Smith's unparalleled *Killers of the Dream* and Margaret Andersen's review of Karen and Mamie Fields' *Lemon Swamp*. Smith, for example, wrote about walking toward black children on the street and knowing they would step into the gutter; Andersen contrasted the pleasure which she, as a white child, took on summer driving trips to the south with Karen Fields' memories of driving in a closed car stocked with all necessities lest, in stopping, her black family should suffer "insult, or worse." Adrienne Rich also recognizes and writes about daily experiences of privilege, but in my observation, white women's writing in this area is far more often on systemic racism than on our daily lives as light-skinned women.[2]

In unpacking this invisible knapsack of white privilege, I have listed conditions of daily experience which I once took for granted as neutral, normal, and universally available to everybody, just as I once thought of a male-focused curriculum as the neutral or accurate account which can speak for all. Nor did I think of any of these perquisites as bad for the holder. I now think that we need a more finely differentiated taxonomy of privilege, for some of these varieties are only what one would want for everyone in a just society, and others give license to be ignorant, oblivious, arrogant and destructive. Before proposing some more finely tuned categorization, I will make some observations about the general effects of these conditions on my life and expectations.

In this potpourri of examples, some privileges make me feel at home in the world. Others allow me to escape penalties or dangers which others suffer. Through some, I escape fear, anxiety, or a sense of not being welcome or not being real. Some keep me from having to hide, to be in disguise, to feel sick or crazy, to negotiate each transaction from the position of being an outsider or, within my group, a person who is suspected of having too close links with a dominant culture. Most keep me from having to be angry.

I see a pattern running through the matrix of white privilege, a pattern of assumptions which were passed on to me as a white person. There was one main piece of cultural turf; it was my own turf, and I was among those who could control the turf. I could measure up to the cultural standards and take advantage of the many options I saw around me to make what the culture would call a success of my life. *My skin color was an asset for any move I was educated to want to make.* I could think of myself as "belonging" in major ways, and of making social systems work for me. I could freely disparage, fear, neglect, or be oblivious to anything outside of the dominant cultural forms. Being of the main culture, I could also criticize it fairly freely. My life was reflected back to me frequently enough so that I felt, with regard to my race, if not to my sex, like one of the real people.

Whether through the curriculum or in the newspaper, the television, the economic system, or the general look of people in the streets, we received daily signals and indications that my people counted, and that others *either didn't exist or must be trying, not very successfully, to be like people of my race.* We were given cultural permission not to hear voices of people of other races, or a tepid cultural tolerance for hearing or acting on such voices. I was also raised not to suffer seriously from anything which darker-skinned people might say about my group, "protected," though perhaps I should more accurately say *prohibited,* through the habits of my economic class and social group, from living in racially mixed groups or being reflective about interactions between people of differing races.

In proportion as my racial group was being made confident, comfortable, and oblivious, other groups were likely being made inconfident, uncomfortable, and alienated. Whiteness protected me from many kinds of hostility, distress, and violence, which I was being subtly trained to visit in turn upon people of color.

For this reason, the word "privilege" now seems to me misleading. Its connotations are too positive to fit the conditions and behaviors which "privilege systems" produce. We usually think of privilege as being a favored state, whether earned or conferred by birth or luck. School graduates are reminded that they are privileged and urged to use their (enviable) assets well. The word "privilege" carries the connotation of being something everyone must want. Yet some of the conditions I have described here work to systemically overempower certain groups. Such privilege simply *confers dominance,* gives permission to control, because of one's race or sex. The kind of privilege which gives license to some people to be, at best, thoughtless and, at worst, murderous should not continue to be referred to as a desirable attribute. Such "privilege" may be widely desired without being in any way beneficial to the whole society.

Moreover, though "privilege" may confer power, it does not confer moral strength. Those who do not depend on conferred dominance have traits and qualities which may never develop in those who do. Just as Women's Studies courses indicate that women survive their political circumstances to lead lives which hold the human race together, so "underprivileged" people of color who are the world's majority have survived their oppression and lived survivors' lives from which the white global minority can and must learn. In some groups, those dominated have actually become strong through *not* having all of these unearned advantages, and this gives them a great deal to teach the others. Members of so-called privileged groups can seem foolish, ridiculous, infantile or dangerous by contrast.

I want, then, to distinguish between earned strength and unearned power conferred systemically. Power from unearned privilege can look like strength when it is in fact permission to escape or to dominate. But not all of the privileges on my list are inevitably damaging. Some, like the expectation that neighbors will be decent to you, or that your race will not count against you in court, should be the norm in a just society and should be considered as the entitlement of everyone. Others, like the privilege not to listen to less powerful people, distort the humanity of the holders as well as the ignored groups. Still others, like finding one's staple foods everywhere, may be a function of being a member of a numerical majority in the population. Others have to do with not having to labor under pervasive negative stereotyping and mythology.

We might at least start by distinguishing between positive advantages which we can work to spread, to the point where they are not advantages at all but simply part of the normal civic and social fabric, and negative types of advantage which unless rejected will always reinforce our present hierarchies. For example, the positive "privilege" of belonging, the feeling that one belongs within the human circle, as Native Americans say, fosters development and should not be seen as privilege for a few. It is, let us say, an entitlement which none of us should have to earn; ideally it is an *unearned entitlement.* At present, since only a few have it, it is an *unearned advantage* for them. The negative "privilege" which gave me cultural permission not to take darker-skinned Others seriously can be seen as arbitrarily conferred dominance and should not be desirable for anyone. This paper results from a process of coming to see that some of the power which I originally saw as attendant on being a human being in the U.S. consisted in *unearned advantage* and *conferred dominance,* as well as other kinds of special circumstances not universally taken for granted.

In writing this paper I have also realized that white identity and status (as well as class identity and status) give me considerable power to choose whether to broach this subject and its trouble. I can pretty well decide whether to disappear and avoid and not listen and escape the dislike I may engender in other people through this essay, or interrupt, take over, dominate, preach, direct, criticize, or control to some extent what goes on in reaction to it. Being white, I am given considerable power to escape many kinds of danger or penalty as well as to choose which risks I want to take.

There is an analogy here, once again, with Women's Studies. Our male colleagues do not have a great deal to lose in supporting Women's Studies, but they do not have a great deal to lose if they oppose it either. They simply have the power to decide whether to commit themselves to more equitable distributions of power. They will probably feel few penalties whatever the choice they make; they do not seem, in any obvious short-term sense, the ones at risk, though they and we are all at risk because of the behaviors which have been rewarded in them.

Through Women's Studies work I have met very few men who are truly distressed about systemic, unearned male advantage and conferred dominance. And so one question for me and others like me is whether we will be like them, or whether we will get truly distressed, even outraged, about unearned race advantage and conferred dominance and if so, what we will do to lessen them. In any case, we need to do more work in identifying how they actually affect our daily lives. We need more down-to-earth writing by people about these taboo subjects. We need more understanding of the ways in which white "privilege" damages white people, for these are not the same ways in which it damages the victimized. Skewed white psyches are an inseparable part of the picture, though I do not want to confuse the kinds of damage done to the holders of special assets and to those who suffer the deficits. Many, perhaps most, of our white students in the U.S. think that racism doesn't affect them because they are not people of color; they do not see "whiteness" as a racial identity. Many men likewise do not see themselves as having gendered identities. Insisting on the universal *effects* of "privilege" systems, then, becomes one of our chief tasks, and being more explicit about the *particular* effects in particular contexts is another. Men need to join us in this work.

In addition, since race and sex are not the only advantaging systems at work, we need to similarly examine the daily experience of having age advantage, or ethnic advantage, or physical ability, or advantage related to nationality, religion, or sexual orientation. Professor Marnie Evans suggested to me that in many ways the list I made also applies directly to heterosexual privilege. This is a still more taboo subject than race privilege: the daily ways in which heterosexual privilege makes married persons comfortable or powerful, providing supports, assets, approvals, and rewards to those who live or expect to live in heterosexual pairs. Unpacking that content is still more difficult, owing to the deeper imbeddedness of heterosexual advantage and dominance, and stricter taboos surrounding these.

But to start such an analysis I would put this observation from my own experience: The fact that I live under the same roof with a man triggers all kinds of societal assumptions about my worth, politics, life, and values, and triggers a host of unearned advantages and powers. After recasting many elements from the original list I would add further observations like these:

1. My children do not have to answer questions about why I live with my partner (my husband).
2. I have no difficulty finding neighborhoods where people approve of our household.

3. My children are given texts and classes which implicitly support our kind of family unit and do not turn them against my choice of domestic partnership.
4. I can travel alone or with my husband without expecting embarrassment or hostility in those who deal with us.
5. Most people I meet will see my marital arrangements as an asset to my life or as a favorable comment on my likability, my competence, or my mental health.
6. I can talk about the social events of a weekend without fearing most listeners' reactions.
7. I will feel welcomed and "normal" in the usual walks of public life, institutional, and social.
8. In many contexts, I am seen as "all right" in daily work on women because I do not live chiefly with women.

Difficulties and dangers surrounding the task of finding parallels are many. Since racism, sexism, and heterosexism are not the same, the advantaging associated with them should not be seen as the same. In addition, it is hard to disentangle aspects of unearned advantage which rest more on social class, economic class, race, religion, sex and ethnic identity than on other factors. Still, all of the oppressions are interlocking, as the Combahee River Collective statement of 1977 continues to remind us eloquently.[3]

One factor seems clear about all of these interlocking oppressions. They take both active forms which we can see and embedded forms which as a member of the dominant group one is taught not to see. In my class and place, I did not see myself as racist because I was taught to recognize racism only in individual acts of meanness by members of my group, never in invisible systems conferring unsought racial dominance on my group from birth. Likewise, we are taught to think that sexism or heterosexism is carried on only through individual acts of discrimination, meanness, or cruelty toward women, gays, and lesbians, rather than in invisible systems conferring unsought dominance on certain groups. Disapproving of the systems won't be enough to change them. I was taught to think that racism could end if white individuals changed their attitudes; many men think sexism can be ended by individual changes in daily behavior toward women. But a man's sex provides advantage for him whether or not he approves of the way in which dominance has been conferred on his group. A "white" skin in the United States opens many doors for whites whether or not we approve of the way dominance has been conferred on us. Individual acts can palliate, but cannot end, these problems. To redesign social systems we need first to acknowledge their colossal unseen dimensions. The silences and denials surrounding privilege are the key political tool here. They keep the thinking about equality or equity incomplete, protecting unearned advantage and conferred dominance by making these taboo subjects. Most talk by whites about equal opportunity seems to me now to be about equal opportunity to try to get into a position of dominance while denying that *systems* of dominance exist.

It seems to me that obliviousness about white advantage, like obliviousness about male advantage, is kept strongly inculturated in the United States so as to maintain the myth of meritocracy, the myth that democratic choice is equally available to all. Keeping most people unaware that freedom of confident action is there for just a small number of people props up those in power and serves to keep power in the hands of the same groups that have most of it already. Though systemic change takes many decades, there are pressing questions for me and I imagine for some others like me if we raise our daily consciousness on the perquisites of being light-skinned. What will we do with such knowledge? As we know from watching men, it is an open question whether we will choose to use unearned advantage to weaken hidden systems of advantage, and whether we will use any of our arbitrarily awarded power to try to reconstruct power systems on a broader base.

Notes

1. This paper was funded by the Anna Wilder Phelps Fund through the generosity of Anna Emery Hanson. I have appreciated commentary on this paper from the Working Papers Committee of the Wellesley College Center for Research on Women, from members of the Dodge seminar, and from many individuals, including Margaret Andersen, Sorel Berman, Joanne Braxton, Johnella Butler, Sandra Dickerson, Marnie Evans, Beverly Guy-Sheftall, Sandra Harding, Eleanor Hinton Hoytt, Pauline Houston, Paul Lauter, Joyce Miller, Mary Norris, Gloria Oden, Beverly Smith, and John Walter.
2. This paper was presented at the Virginia Women's Studies Association conference in Richmond in April, 1986 and the American Educational Research Association conference in Boston in October, 1986 and discussed with two groups of participants in the Dodge Seminars for Secondary School Teachers in New York and Boston in the spring of 1987.
3. Margaret Andersen, "Race and the Social Science Curriculum: A Teaching and Learning Discussion." *Radical Teacher,* November, 1984, pp. 17–20. Lillian Smith, *Killers of the Dream,* New York, 1949.
4. "A Black Feminist Statement," The Combahee River Collective, pp. 13–22. In Hull, Scott, Smith, eds., *All the Women Are White, All the Blacks Are Men, But Some of Us Are Brave: Black Women's Studies.* The Feminist Press, 1982.

Sexual Harassment

SUSAN M. DODDS ⬥ LUCY FROST
ROBERT PARGETTER ⬥ ELIZABETH W. PRIOR

Mary has a problem. Her boss, Bill, gives her a bad time. He is constantly making sexual innuendoes and seems always to be blocking her way and brushing against her. He leers at her, and on occasions has made it explicitly clear that it would be in her own best interests to go to bed with him. She is the one woman in the office now singled out for this sort of treatment, although she hears that virtually all other attractive women who have in the past worked for Bill have had similar experiences. On no occasion has Mary encouraged Bill. His attentions have all been unwanted. She has found them threatening, unpleasant and objectionable. When on some occasions she has made these reactions too explicit, she has been subjected to unambiguously detrimental treatment. Bill has no genuinely personal feelings for Mary, is neither truly affectionate nor loving: his motivation is purely sexual.

Reprinted by permission from *Social Theory and Practice* 14, No. 2 (Summer 1988), © copyright 1988. All Rights Reserved.

Surely this is a paradigmatic case of sexual harassment. Bill discriminates against Mary, and it seems that he would also discriminate against any other attractive woman who worked for him. He misuses his power as an employer when he threatens Mary with sex she does not want. His actions are clearly against her interests. He victimizes her at present and will probably force her to leave the office, whatever the consequences to her future employment.

Not all cases of sexual harassment are so clear. Indeed, each salient characteristic of the paradigmatic case may be missing and yet sexual harassment may still occur. Even if all the features are missing, it could still be a case of sexual harassment.

We aim to explicate the notion of sexual harassment. We note that our aim is not to provide an analysis of the ordinary language concept of sexual harassment. Rather we aim to provide a theoretical rationale for a more behavioral stipulative definition of sexual harassment. For it is an account of this kind which proves to be clearly superior for policy purposes. It provides the basis for a clear, just and enforceable policy, suitable for the workplace and for society at large. Of course ordinary language intuitions provide important touchstones. What else could we use to broadly determine the relevant kind of behavior? But this does not mean that all ordinary language considerations are to be treated as sacrosanct. Sexual harassment is a concept with roots in ordinary language, but we seek to develop the concept as one suitable for more theoretical purposes, particularly those associated with the purposes of adequate policy development.

In brief we aim to provide an account which satisfies three desiderata. The account should:

a. show the connection between harassment in general and sexual harassment
b. distinguish between sexual harassment in general and legitimate sexual interaction
c. be useful for policy purposes.

1. Sexual Harassment and Sexual Discrimination

It seems plausible that minimally harassment involves discrimination, and more particularly, sexual harassment involves sexism. Sexual discrimination was clearly part of the harassment in the case of Mary and Bill.

The pull towards viewing sexual harassment as tied to sexual discrimination is strengthened by consideration of the status of most harassers and most harassees. In general, harassers are men in a position of power over female harassees. The roles of these men and women are reinforced by historical and cultural features of systematic sexual discrimination against women. Generally, men have control of greater wealth and power in our society, while women are economically dependent on men. Men are viewed as having the (positive) quality of aggression in sexual and social relations, while women are viewed as (appropriately) passive. These entrenched attitudes reflect an even deeper view of women as fundamentally unequal, that is in some sense, less fully persons than men. Sexual harassment, then, seems to be just one more ugly manifestation of the sexism and sexual inequality which is rampant in public life.

MacKinnon sees this connection as sufficient to justify treating cases of sexual harassment as cases of sexual discrimination.[1] Sexual discrimination, for MacKinnon, can be understood through two approaches. The first is the "difference approach," under which a "differentiation is based on sex when it can be shown that a person of the opposite sex in the same position is not treated the same." The other is the "inequality approach," which "requires no comparability of situation, only that a rule or practice disproportionately burden one sex because of sex."[2] Thus, even when no comparison can be made between the situation of male and female employees (for example, if the typing pool is composed entirely of women, then the treatment a woman in the pool receives cannot be compared with the treatment of a man in the same situation), if a rule or practice disproportionately burdens women, because they are women, that rule or practice is sexually discriminatory. For MacKinnon all cases of sexual harassment will be cases of sexual discrimination on one or other of these approaches.

Closer consideration reveals, however, that while discrimination may be present in cases of harassment, it need not be. More specifically, while sexual discrimination may be (and often is) present in cases of sexual harassment, it is not a necessary feature of sexual harassment.

The fact that in most cases women are (statistically, though not necessarily) the objects of sexual harassment, is an important feature of the issue of sexual harassment, and it means that in many cases where women are harassed, the harassment will involve sexual discrimination. However, sexual harassment need not entail sexual discrimination.

Consider the case of Mary A and Bill A, a case very similar to that of Mary and Bill. The only relevant difference is that Bill A is bisexual and is sexually attracted to virtually everyone regardless of sex, appearance, age or attitude. Perhaps all that matters is that he feels that he has power over them (which is the case no matter who occupies the position now occupied by Mary A). Mary A or anyone who filled her place would be subjected to sexual harassment.

The point of this variant case is that there appears to be no discrimination, even though there clearly is harassment. Even if it is argued that there is discrimination against the class of those over whom Bill A has power, we can still describe a case where no one is safe. Bill A could sexually harass anyone. This particular case clearly defeats both of MacKinnon's conceptual approaches to sexual discrimination; it is neither the case that Bill A treats a man in Mary A's position differently from the way in which he treats Mary A, nor is it the case that (in Bill A's office) the burden of Bill A's advances is placed disproportionately on one sex, because of that person's sex (for the purpose of sex, perhaps, but not on account of chromosomes).[3]

A different point, but one worth making here, is that there is a difference between sexual harassment and sexist harassment. A female academic whose male colleagues continually ridicule her ideas and opinions may be the object of sexist harassment, and this sexist harassment will necessarily involve sexual discrimination. But she is not, on this basis, the object of sexual harassment.

2. Negative Consequences and Interests

Perhaps sexual harassment always involves action by the harasser which is against the interests of the harassee, or has overall negative consequences for the harassee.

However consider Mary B who is sexually harassed by Bill B. Mary B gives in, but as luck would have it, things turn out extremely well; Mary B is promoted by Bill B to another department. The long term consequences are excellent, so clearly it has been in Mary B's best interests to be the object of Bill B's attentions. One could also imagine a case where Mary B rejects Bill B, with the (perhaps unintentional) affect that the overall consequences for Mary B are very good.

Crosthwaite and Swanton argue for a modification of this view. They urge that, in addition to being an action of a sexual nature, an act of sexual harassment is an action where there is no adequate consideration of the interests of the harassee. They in fact suggest that this is both a necessary and sufficient condition for sexual harassment.[4]

We think it is not sufficient. Consenting to sex with an AIDS carrier is not in an antibody-negative individual's best interests. If the carrier has not informed the other party, the antibody-positive individual has not given adequate consideration to those interests. But this case need not be one of sexual harassment.

Nor is this condition necessary for sexual harassment. Of course Bill B may believe that it is in Mary B's interests to come across. (A sexual harasser can be deceitful or just intensely egotistical.) Bill B may believe that it would conform with Mary B's conception of her interests. And, as we noted earlier, it may even be objectively in her own best interests. Yet still we think this would not prevent the action of Bill B against Mary B—which is in other ways similar to Bill's actions against Mary—being a case of sexual harassment.

In general, harassment need not be against the interests of the harassee. You can be harassed to stop smoking, and harassed to give up drugs. In these cases the consequences may well be good, and the interests of the harassee adequately considered and served, yet it is still harassment. This general feature seems equally applicable to sexual harassment.

3. Misuse of Power

Bill has power over Mary and it is the misuse of this power which plays an important role in making his treatment of Mary particularly immoral. For, on almost any normative theory, to misuse power is immoral. But is this misuse of power what makes this action one of sexual harassment?

If it is, then it must not be restricted to the formal power of the kind which Bill has over Mary—the power to dismiss her, demote her, withhold benefits from her, and so on. We also usually think of this sort of formal power in cases of police harassment. But consider the harassment of women at an abortion clinic by Right-To-Lifers. They cannot prevent the women having abortions and indeed lack any formal power over them. Nonetheless, they do possess important powers—to dissuade the faint-hearted (or even the over-sensitive), and to increase the unpleasantness of the experience of women attending the clinic.

Now consider the case of Mary C. Bill C and Mary C are co-workers in the office, and Bill C lacks formal power over Mary C. He sexually harasses her—with sexual innuendoes, touches, leers, jokes, suggestions, and unwanted invitations. To many women Bill C's actions would be unpleasant. But Mary C is a veteran—this has happened to her so many times before that she no longer responds. It is not that she desires or wants the treatment, but it no longer produces the unpleasant mental attitudes it used to produce—it just rolls off her. She gives the negative responses automatically, and goes on as though nothing had happened.

It would still seem to us that Mary C has been sexually harassed. But what power has Bill C misused against Mary C? He has not used even some informal power which has caused her some significantly unpleasant experience.

Crosthwaite and Swanton also argue against the necessary connection between misuse of power and sexual harassment. They note that one case where there is a lack of power and yet harassment takes place (like the Mary C and Bill C case), is the case where there is a use of pornographic pictures and sexist language by work colleagues. They also note that there are cases in which a sexually motivated misuse of power leads to events advantaging the women in the long run. Misuse of power cannot in itself therefore constitute sexual harassment.[5]

4. Attitudes, Intentions and Experiences

In our discussions so far, it seems that we have not taken into account, to any significant extent, how Mary and Bill feel about things. It may be argued that what defines or characterizes sexual harassment is the mental state of the harasser, or harassee, or both.

Bill wanted to have sex with Mary. He perceived her as a sex object. He failed to have regard for her as a person. He failed to have regard for how she might feel about things. And his actions gave him egotistical pleasure. These attitudes, intentions and experiences may help constitute Bill's action as a case of sexual harassment.

Mary also had very specific kinds of mental states. She found Bill's actions unpleasant, and unwanted. She wished Bill would not act in that way towards her, and she disliked him for it. She was angry that someone would treat her in that way, and she resented being forced to cope with the situation. So again we have attributed attitudes and mental experiences to Mary in describing this case as one of sexual harassment.

We do not want to have to label as sexual harassment all sexual actions or approaches between people in formally structured relationships. Cases of sexual harassment and non-harassing sexual interaction may appear very similar (at least over short time intervals). It seems that in the two kinds of cases only the mental features differ. That is, we refer to attitudes, intentions or experiences in explaining the difference between the two cases. But attention to this feature of sexual harassment is not enough in itself to identify sexual harassment.

We will now consider one of the more salient features of the mental attitudes of Bill and Mary, and show that sexual harassment is not dependent on these or similar features. Then we shall describe a case where the mental experiences are very different, but where sexual harassment does, in fact, still occur.

Consider the claim that Bill uses (or tries to use) Mary as a sex object. The notion of sex object is somewhat vague and ill-defined, but we accept that it is to view her as merely an entity for sexual activity or satisfaction, with no interests in her attributes as a person and without any intention of developing any personal relationship with her.

This will not do as a sufficient condition for sexual harassment. We normally do not think of a client sexually harassing a prostitute. And surely there can be a relationship between two people where each sees the other merely as a sex object without there being harassment. Nor is viewing her merely as a sex object a necessary condition.[6] For surely Bill could love Mary deeply, and yet by pursuing her against her wishes, still harass her.

Now consider the claim that what is essential is that Mary not want the attentions of Bill. This is not a sufficient condition—often the most acceptable of sexual approaches is not wanted. Also a woman may not want certain attentions, and even feel sexually harassed, in situations which we would not want to accept as ones of sexual harassment.

Imagine that Mary D is an abnormally sensitive person. She feels harassed when Bill D comments that the color she is wearing suits her very well, or even that it is a cold day. Bill D is not in the habit of making such comments, nor is he in the habit of harassing anyone. He is just making conversation and noting something (seemingly innocuous) that has caught his attention. Mary D feels harassed even though she is not being harassed.

Perhaps this condition is a necessary one. But this too seems implausible. Remember Mary C, the veteran. She is now so immune to Bill C that she has no reaction at all to his approaches. He does not cause unpleasantness for her; she does not care what he does. Yet nonetheless Bill C is harassing Mary C.

Mary E and Bill E interact in a way which shows that sexual harassment is not simply a matter of actual attitudes, intentions or experiences. Bill E is infatuated with Mary E and wants to have sex with her. In addition to this, he genuinely loves her and generally takes an interest in her as a person. But he is hopeless on technique. He simply copies the brash actions of those around him and emulates to perfection the actions of the sexual harasser. Most women who were the object of his infatuation (for instance, someone like our original Mary) would feel harassed and have all the usual emotions and opinions concerning the harasser. But Mary E is different. Outwardly, to all who observe the public interactions between them, she seems the typical harassee—doing her best to politely put off Bill E, seeming not to want his attentions, looking as though she is far from enjoying it. That is how Bill E sees it too, but he thinks that that is the way women are.

Inwardly Mary E's mental state is quite different. Mary E is indifferent about Bill E personally, and is a veteran like Mary C in that she is not distressed by his actions. But she decides to take advantage of the situation and make use of Bill E's attentions. By manipulating the harassing pressures and invitations, she believes she can obtain certain benefits that she wants and can gain certain advantages over others. The attention from Bill E is thus not unwanted, nor is the experience for her unpleasant. In this case neither the harasser nor the harassee have mental states in any way typical of harassers and harassees, yet it is a case of sexual harassment.

Such a case, as hypothetical and unlikely as it is, demonstrates that the actual mental states of the people involved cannot be what is definitive of sexual harassment. They are not even necessary for sexual harassment.

5. A Behavioral Account of Sexual Harassment

The case of Mary E and Bill E persuades us that we require a behavioral account of sexual harassment. For a harasser to sexually harass a harassee is for the harasser to behave in a certain way towards the harassee. The causes of that behavior are not important, and what that behavior in turn causes is not important. The behavior itself constitutes the harassment.

But how then are we to specify the behavior that is to count as sexual harassment? We shall borrow a technique from the functionalist theory of the mind.

Functionalists usually identify mental states in terms of the functional roles they play. However some functionalist theories allow a variation on this. If we talk instead of the kind of mental state which *typically* fills a functional role or the functional role *typically* associated with a mental state, we maintain the functionalist flavor, but allow unusual combinations of kinds of inner states and kinds of functional roles to be accommodated. We shall follow a similar technique when describing the kinds of behavior associated with sexual harassment.

Consider the behavior which is typically associated with a mental state representing an attitude which seeks sexual ends without any concern for the person from whom those ends are sought, and which typically produces an unwanted and unpleasant response in the person who is the object of the behavior. Such behavior we suggest is what constitutes sexual harassment. Instances of the behavior are instances of sexual harassment even if the mental states of the harasser or harassee (or both) are different from those typically associated with such behavior. The behavior constitutes a necessary and sufficient condition for sexual harassment.

According to this view, the earlier suggestion that attitudes, intentions and experience are essential to an adequate characterization of sexual harassment is correct. It is correct to the extent that we need to look at the mental states typical of the harasser, rather than those present in each actual harasser, and at those typical of the harassee, rather than those present in each actual harassee. The empirical claim is that connecting these typical mental states is a kind of behavior—behavior not incredibly different from instance to instance, but with a certain sameness to it. Thus it is a behavior of a definite characteristic *type*. This type of behavior is sexual harassment.

This proffered account may at first appear surprising. But let us look at some of its features to alleviate the surprise, and at the same time increase the plausibility of the account.

Most importantly, the account satisfies our three desiderata: to show the connection between harassment in general and sexual harassment, to distinguish between sexual harassment and legitimate sexual interaction, and to assist in guiding policy on sexual harassment.

The relationship between harassment and sexual harassment is to be accounted for in terms of a behavioral similarity. This at first may seem to be a sweeping suggestion, since *prima facie,* there need be no descriptive similarity between sexual harassment, harassment by police, harassment of homosexuals, harassment of Jews, and so on. But the behavioral elements on which each kind of harassment supervenes will have enough in common to explain our linking them all as harassment, while at the same time being sufficiently different to allow for their differentiation into various kinds of harassment. The most plausible similarity, as we shall argue later, will be in the presence of certain behavioral dispositions, though the bases for these dispositions may differ.

Our approach allows for an adequate distinction between sexual harassment and legitimate sexual approaches and interactions. The approach requires that this be a behavioral difference. There is something intrinsically different about the two kinds of activity. Given that the typical causal origin of each of the kinds of behavior is different and so too is the typical reaction it in turn produces, it is to be expected that there would be a difference in the behavior itself. It is important to note that the constitutive behavior will be within a particular context, in particular circumstances. (The importance of this is well illustrated in cases such as a student and her lecturer at a university.[7]) Further it will include both overt and covert behavior (subtle differences count). In many cases it will also be behavior over a time interval, not just behavior at a time.

From the policy guiding perspective the account is very attractive. It is far easier to stipulate a workable, practical, defensible, and legally viable policy on harassment if it is totally definable in behavioral terms. Definition in terms of mental experiences, intentions and attitudes spells nothing but trouble for a viable social policy on sexual harassment.

The analysis we have offered entails that if there were no such characteristic kind of behavior there would be no sexual harassment. This seems to be right. In this case no legislation to ground a social policy would be possible. We would instead condemn individual actions on other moral grounds—causing pain and distress, acting against someone's best interests, misusing power, and so on.

In addition to satisfying these three desiderata, our account has numerous other positive features. First, our account is culturally relative. It is highly likely that the kind of behavior constitutive of sexual harassment will vary from culture to culture, society to society. That is, it will be a culture-relative kind of behavior that determines sexual harassment. In any culture our reference to the typical mental states of the harasser and harassee will identify a kind of behavior that is constitutive of sexual harassment in that culture. This kind of behavior matches well with the empirical observations. There is so much variation in human behavior across cultures that behavior which may be sexual harassment in one need not be in another. The same is true of other kinds of human behavior. In the Middle East, belching indicates appreciation of a meal. In Western society, it is considered bad manners. The practice of haggling over the price of a purchase is acceptable (indeed expected) in some societies, and unacceptable in others. But in almost any culture, some kind of behavior may reasonably be judged to be sexual harassment.

Second, while we have cast our examples in terms of a male harasser and female harassee, there is nothing in the account which necessitates any gender restriction on sexual harassment. All that is required is that the behavior is sexual in nature and has other behavioral features which make it an instance of sexual harassment. The participants could be of either sex in either role, or of the same sex.

We acknowledge that we use the notion of an action being sexual in nature without attempting any explication of that notion. Such an explication is a separate task, but we believe that for our purposes there is no problem in taking it as primitive.

Third, the account allows for the possibility of sexual harassment without the presence of the mental states typical of the harasser or the harassee. There is an important connection between these typical mental states and sexual harassment, but it does not restrict instances of sexual harassment to instances where we have these typical mental states.

Further, as the account focuses on behavior, rather than mental states, it explains why we feel so skeptical about someone who behaves as Bill behaves, yet pleads innocence and claims he had no bad intentions. The intentions are not essential for the harassment, and such a person has an obligation to monitor the responses of the other person so that he has an accurate picture of what is going on. Moreover, he has an obligation to be aware of the character of his own behavior. He also has an obligation to give due consideration to the strength and the weight of the beliefs upon which he is operating before he makes a decision to act in a manner that may have unpleasant consequences for others. Strength of belief concerns the degree of confidence it is rational to have in the belief, given the evidence available. Weight of belief concerns the quality of the evidential basis of the belief, and the reasonableness of acting on the evidence available.[8] If a person is acting in a way which has a risk of bad consequences for others, that person has an obligation to be aware of the risks and to refrain from acting unless he has gained evidence of sufficient strength and weight to be confident that the bad consequences will not arise. In the case of someone who wishes to engage in legitimate sexual interaction and to avoid sexual harassment, he must display a disposition to be alive to the risks and to seek appropriate evidence from the other person's behavior, as to whether that person welcomes his attentions. He must also display a disposition to refrain from acting if such evidence is lacking.

In the case of Mary E and Bill E, Bill E relies on the harassing behavior of other men as a guide to his actions regarding Mary E. Mary E has displayed standard forms of avoidance behavior (although she has ulterior motives). Bill E does not pay sufficient heed to the strength and weight of the beliefs which guide his actions, and it is just fortunate that Mary E is not harmed by what he does. Given Bill E's total disregard of Mary E's interests and reactions, it seems that his behavior could have caused, just as easily, significant distress to any other Mary who might have filled that role. A policy intended to identify sexual harassment should not rely on such luck, although the actual mental states (where they are as atypical as Mary E's) may mitigate blameworthiness. Bill E's harassing behavior should be checked and evaluated, regardless of any of Mary's actual mental states.[9]

Consider an example taken from an actual case[10] which highlights this obligation. Suppose Tom is married to Jane. He invites Dick (an old friend who has never met Jane) home to have sex with Jane. He tells Dick that Jane will protest, but that this is just part of the game (a game she very much enjoys). Dick forces Jane, who all the time protests violently, to have sex with him. Jane later claims to have been raped. Dick has acted culpably because he has acted without giving due consideration to the weight of the belief which guided his action, that is, to how rational it was to act on the belief given such a minimal evidential base. The only evidence he had that Jane did consent was Tom's say-so, and the consequences of acting on the belief were very serious. All of Jane's actions indicated that she did not consent.

In the case of Bill E and Mary E, Bill has an obligation to consider the strength and weight of the beliefs which guide his action before he acts. He is not justified in claiming that he is innocent, when he has been provided with signals that indicate that Mary does not welcome his attentions.

We acknowledge that it will be difficult in many situations to obtain sufficient evidence that a proposed act will not be one of sexual harassment. This will be true especially in cases where the potential harassee may believe that any outward indication of her displeasure would have bad consequences for her. The awareness of this difficulty is probably what has led others to promote the policy of a total ban on sexual relationships at the office or work place. While we acknowledge the problem, we feel that such a policy is both unrealistic and overrestrictive.

Fourth, the account allows an interesting stance on the connection between sexual harassment and morality. For consequentialist theories of morality, it is possible (though unlikely) that an act of sexual harassment may be, objectively, morally right. This would be the case if the long term good consequences outweighed the bad effects (including those on the harassee at the time of the harassment). For other moral theories it is not clear that this is a possibility, except where there are sufficiently strong overriding considerations present, such as to make the sexual harassment morally permissible. From the agent's point of view, it would seem that the probable consequences of sexual harassment (given the typical attitude of the typical harasser and the typical effects on the typical harassee) will be bad. Hence it is very likely, on any moral theory, that the agent evaluation for a harasser will be negative. The possible exceptions are where the harasser's actual mental state is not typical of a harasser, or the harassee's is not typical of a harassee.

Further, on this account many of the salient features of the case of Mary and Bill—such as misuse of power, discrimination, unfair distribution of favors, and so on—are not essential features of sexual harassment. They are usually immoral in their own right, and their immorality is not explained by their being part of the harassment. But the behavior characteristic of sexual harassment will be constituted by features which we commonly find in particular instances of sexual harassment. For sexual harassment must supervene on the behavioral features which constitute its instances, but there is a range of such behavior, no one element of which need be present on any particular occasion. Similarly the morality of an instance of sexual harassment (at least for the consequentialist) will supervene on the morality of those same features of behavior.

6. Objections to the Behavioral Account

It may be objected that we have made no significant progress. We acknowledged at the beginning of the paper that many different kinds of behavior were instances of sexual harassment, even though there seemed to be no specific kind of behavior commonly present in all these instances.

Our reply is to concede the point that there is no first order property commonly possessed by all the behaviors. However, other important similarities do exist.

The property of being an instance of sexual harassment is a second order property of a particular complex piece of behavior. It is a property of the relevant specific behavioral features, and these features may be from a list of disjunctive alternatives (which may be altered as norms of behavior change). Also, the behavior of a typical harassee will possess the property of being an instance of avoidance behavior. Avoidance behavior is a disposition. Hence, even if two lots of behavior are descriptively similar they may differ in their dispositional properties. Finally the behavior of the typical harasser will possess the property of being sexually motivated, which again is dispositional in nature.

A second objection goes as follows: couldn't we have the very same piece of behavior and yet have no sexual harassment? To take the kind of example well tried as an objection to behaviorism, what would we say about the case of two actors, acting out a sexual harassment sequence?

There are a variety of replies we may make here. We could "bite the bullet" and admit the case to be one of sexual harassment. On the model proposed, we may do this while still maintaining that the behavior in this case is not morally wrong. Or, instead, we could insist that certain kinds of behavior only become harassment when they are carried on over a sufficiently lengthy time interval, the circumstances surrounding the behavior also being relevant. The case of the actors would not count as an instance of harassment because the behavior has not been recurrent over a sufficiently long period of time, especially as the behavior before and after the acting period are significantly different. Also the circumstances surrounding an acting exercise would be typically different from those of an instance of sexual harassment.

Still another response to the acting example is to argue that if the actual mental states of "harasser" and "harassee" are sufficiently different from those of the prototypical harasser and harassee, there can be no sexual harassment as there will be behavioral differences. This is not a logical necessity, but a physical one given the causal relations which hold between the mental states and the behavior. We should also keep in mind that many of the features of sexual harassment are dispositional. Thus, even if such features of sexual harassment are not manifested in particular circumstances, they would in other circumstances, and it is in these other circumstances that the observable behavior would be significantly different if it is the manifestation of harassment from that which would be associated with non-harassment.[11]

A third objection to our behavioral account focuses on our use of the mental state *typical* of harassers and harassees. We have noted that it is possible that some instances of harassment will involve a harasser or harassee with mental states significantly different from those of the typical harasser or harassee. So it is possible that the harassee is not even offended or made to feel uncomfortable, and it is possible that the harasser did not have intentions involving misuse of power against, and disregard for the interests of, the harassee. It is even possible that one or both of the harasser and harassee could know about the atypical mental states of the other. Why, at least in this last case, insist that the behavior is sufficient for sexual harassment?

From our concern to provide an account of sexual harassment adequate for policy purposes, we would be inclined to resist this kind of objection, given the clear advantage in policy matters of a behavioral account. But there is more to say in reply to this objection. Policy is directed at the action of agents, and in all cases except where at least one of the agents involved has justified beliefs about the atypical actual mental states of the agents involved, it is clearly appropriate to stipulate behavior associated with the states of mind typical of harassers and harassees as sexual harassment. For agents ought to be guided by what it is reasonable to predict, and rational prediction as to the mental states of those involved in some kind of behavior will be determined by the mental states typically associated with that behavior. So only in cases where we have reliable and justified knowledge of atypical mental states does the objection have any substance at all.

But even in these cases it seems the behavior should not be regarded as innocuous. Instances of behavior all form parts of behavioral patterns. People are disposed to behave similarly in similar circumstances. Hence we ought not to overlook instances of behavior which would typically be instances of sexual harassment. Agents ought not be involved in such patterns of behavior. It is for similar reasons that while we allow for cultural relativity in the behavior constitutive of sexual harassment, this relativity should not be taken to legitimate patterns of behavior which do constitute sexual harassment but which are taken as the standard mode of behavior by a culture.[12]

There are three final notes about our account of sexual harassment. Provided that the kind of behavior so specified is characteristically different from behavior having other typical causes and effects, the desired distinction between sexual harassment and other kinds of sexual activity is assured.

The required connection between sexual harassment and other forms of harassment seems assured by a kind of behavioral similarity. Other forms of harassment are not sexual and vary in many ways from the pattern of behavior characteristic of sexual harassment. But there will be corresponding accounts for each kind of harassment in terms of typical causes and typical effects. The connection between all the different kinds of harassment may well be revealed by looking at these typical causes and typical effects. But despite the noted differences, the contention is that there will be an empirically verifiable behavioral similarity, and this will justify the claim that they are all forms of harassment. It may be that the relevant features of the behavior characteristic of the various forms of harassment are dispositional.

We have made two claims about behavior constitutive of sexual harassment, and we should now see how they relate. The behavior is identified in terms of its typical causes and typical effects, that is, in terms of the typical mental states of harassers and harassees. But harassment is recognized by reference to features of the behavior itself, and any legislation to ground social policy will also refer to such features. The philosophical claim is that there will be a range of such behavior features some combination of which will be present in each case of sexual harassment. The empirical job is to tell us more about the nature of such behavior and help determine the practical social policy and legislation.[13]

Notes

1. Catherine MacKinnon, *Sexual Harassment of Working Women*, (London: Yale University Press, 1979), Ch. 6.
2. MacKinnon, p. 225.

3. Given that sexual harassment is possible between men, by a woman harassing a man, among co-workers, and so on, MacKinnon's view of sexual harassment as nothing but one form of sexual discrimination is even less persuasive. It is also interesting that the problems which MacKinnon recognizes in trying to characterize the "offence" of sexual harassment (p. 162 ff.), indicate a need for a behavioral analysis of sexual harassment, like the one we offer.

4. Jan Crosthwaite and Christine Swanton, "On the Nature of Sexual Harassment," *Women and Philosophy: Australasian Journal of Philosophy*, supplement to 64 (1986): 91–106; pp. 100–101.

5. Crosthwaite and Swanton, p. 99.

6. If it is, it needs to be connected to a general view that women are sex objects, for pornographic pin-ups and sexist jokes and language may harass a women without anyone viewing *that* woman as a sex object. (See Nathalie Hadjifotiou, *Women and Harassment at Work*, (London: Pluto Press, 1983), p. 14.) Note that we have urged that sexual harassment should be a special case of harassment. But what is the general form of the sex object account? It seems implausible that for each form of harassment there is something corresponding to the notion of sex object.

7. See, for example, Billie Wright Dzeich and Linda Weiner, *The Lecherous Professor: Sexual Harassment on Campus*, (Boston: Beacon Press, 1984).

8. For a discussion of this concept of weight see Barbara Davidson and Robert Pargetter, "Weight," *Philosophical Studies* 49 (1986): 219–30.

9. Some might say that this behavioristic account of sexual harassment is similar to having strict liability for murder, that is to say, that mental states do need to be taken into account when judging and penalizing someone's actions. What we are arguing for is a way of *identifying* sexual harassment, not how (or even if) it should be *penalized*. The appropriate response to a case of sexual harassment may very well take mental states into account, along with the harm caused, or likely to be caused, and so forth. One advantage of our account is that it demands that potential harassers become aware of their behavior and to be alert to the responses of those around them. The response of Bill E (that he thought women liked to be treated that way) ought not be considered adequate especially in public life where a person's livelihood could hang in the balance.

10. This example is based on the British case, D.P.P. v. Morgan (1975), 2 All E.R. 347 (House of Lords): Morgan (1975), 1 All E.R. 8 (Court of Appeal); see also Frank Jackson, "A Probabilistic Approach to Moral Responsibility," in Ruth Barcam Marcus, *et al.* (eds.), *Logic, Methodology and Philosophy of Science VII* (North Holland, 1986), pp. 351–66.

11. For a useful account of dispositional properties, their manifestations, and their categorical bases, see Elizabeth Prior, Robert Pargetter and Frank Jackson, "Three Theses about Dispositions," *American Philosophical Quarterly* 19 (1982): 251–58.

The case of pressing solicitation by a prostitute towards a reluctant john can be viewed in the same manner as that of the actors. It is quite likely that there would be sufficient difference in the mental states of the pressing prostitute and the typical harasser to yield behavioral differences (for instance the prostitute is more interested in making money than having sex, so her behavior will reflect this insofar as, say, she would not keep on pressing if the john proved to have no money). The pressing behavior of the prostitute may be seen as a nuisance by the reluctant john, but it is not sexual harassment.

12. What will be culturally relative are types of behavior incidental to their being viewed as constituting sexual harassment in a particular culture. Acceptable standards concerning modes of address, physical proximity, touching, and so forth will vary among cultures, so the behavior patterns which will constitute sexual harassment will also vary. Of course we must be careful not to confuse socially accepted behavior with behavior which is not sexually harassing, especially in cultures where men have much greater power to determine what is to count as socially acceptable behavior. However, so long as there are typical mental states of harassers and harassees, the behavior which constitutes sexual harassment will be identifiable in each culture.

13. We acknowledge useful comments from Robert Young and various readers for this journal.

PART FOUR

International Business

Introduction

Ethical Relativism

Ethical relativism is the position that there are deeply irresolvable value differences. This is because there are no ultimate, universal, or absolute ethical principles that apply to everyone and to every situation. As Norman Bowie notes in "Relativism, Cultural and Moral," the ethical relativist is someone who believes that what is really right or wrong is what the culture says is right or wrong. Since there are no universal standards, one cannot judge the moral principles of another culture nor adjudicate between two clashing principles.

Ethical relativism frequently uses evidence provided by a closely related point of view known as cultural relativism. *Cultural relativism* is a descriptive view that emphasizes how the ways in which people reason about morality vary in different cultures because of different customs, religions traditions, methods of education, or beliefs about the world. But it requires an additional step to argue from cultural relativism to a position of ethical relativism. After noting the fact of cultural relativism and moral diversity, ethical relativism holds that no ethical assertion or set of assertions has any greater claim to objectivity or universality than any other. From the obvious empirical differences between cultures, an ethical relativist may go further to argue that all values and thus all value judgments are relative to particular contexts. Therefore the truth of ethical statements such as "bribery is wrong" is determined solely by the beliefs of the culture espousing or denying those claims. The case study "What Price Safety?" brings up the question of how to enforce what seem to be basically universal morally minimum standards of worker safety in a culture where local customs and value differences appear to question that standard. If values are merely relative, there is no satisfactory cross-cultural resolution to this issue.

Questions of ethical relativism challenge managers on an almost daily basis. The end of the Cold War has seen a massive growth of international business. Almost every corporation of any size conducts business multinationally. As managers increasingly work in international settings they face a multitude of questions of value differences. The Italian Tax Mores case discussed in Part One illustrates the difficulties managers face in deciding between home and host country practices. The case also illustrates that what a country does, its *accepted* practices, may not be what it holds to be *acceptable* or valuable. Most Italians find lying, bribery, and extortion to be abhorrent; they disapprove of the practices despite the fact that they occur. So even a relativist must be careful to distinguish between locally accepted from locally acceptable behavior in adapting a host country practice.

The development of transnational corporations that function globally without a "home" country of origin further complicates the job of managers. If there is no "home country" whose values and mores serve as a basis for moral judgments, the difficulty of sorting out practices and values of any particular country and between countries in transnational exchanges becomes even more exacerbated.

The relativity of value judgments can be an issue within a culture, as well. One can argue that values are not merely relative to particular cultures but also relative to particular spheres of activity. For example, although tackling in football is part of that game, it is not an accepted practice in other social interactions. If business itself is a game, as Albert Carr argues in Part One, then that sphere of activity has certain conventions and values that might not be acceptable in other spheres. According to this line of reasoning, the values of the medical community might differ from, say, those of certain religious groups, or the values espoused by corporations might differ from, and even conflict with, ideals espoused by nonprofit organizations. One could extend this argument to each of us as individuals. My religious values, for example, might clash with my work ethic, or the standards of behavior I adhered to as a teenager might be different from those I hold today.

One of the ways to challenge relativism, then, is to show that if all moral judgments are relative, this leads ultimately to the dead end of subjectivism. If all values are subject to change and challenge, even my own, then there is no basis for moral judgments except what one feels in a particular instance, a feeling that has no objective basis. Another and more obvious way to challenge ethical relativism is to argue that there are some values that are universal, that is, that apply in every case without exception. But while philosophers such as Norman Bowie and Richard De George find relativism implausible, nonetheless they recognize the difficulty of isolating universal truths. What those universal truths or standards are has been subject to philosophical debate since the beginning of human thinking, because the fallibility of human nature and diversity of human cultures preclude a final determination of absolute moral standards.

However, the process of moral reasoning involves making judgments that set or appeal to standards that cross individual, institutional, and even cultural boundaries. When one asserts that slavery is wrong, one ordinarily means that it was always wrong, and will always be wrong, no matter the circumstances. We appeal to notions of autonomy, community, freedom, and human rights in making such judgments, even though we have no final absolute knowledge of their universal validity. What we are doing is offering these values as candidates for universal moral standards, ones that we continue to challenge and refine. The United Nations Declaration of Human Rights sets out a list of basic rights as standards, as candidates for universal truths to be tested and perhaps even restated as we appeal to this set in making cross-cultural moral judgments and trying to resolve value differences in universal settings.

The conduct of multinational corporations has been under severe scrutiny in recent years. As a result of incidents involving sensitive payments, in 1977 the U.S. Congress passed the Foreign Corrupt Practices Act (FCPA). The FCPA is an attempt to legislate standards of conduct for multinational corporations by making it a crime for U.S.–based multinationals to offer or to acquiesce to sensitive payments to officials of foreign governments. The Act implies that what U.S. citizens in this country think is morally right should apply to their dealings in other countries. This position would be criticized by ethical relativists, since according to them, value differences between cultures preclude the justification of exporting the laws or moral principles of one country to another. Interestingly, however, despite the criticism by relativists, there are now attempts by a group of countries partnering with some of the large multinationals to formulate international standards for the restriction of sensitive payments.

Business Values away from Home

Levi Strauss, the manufacturer of world-famous jeans and other clothing, was faced with a dilemma. Company policies prohibit Levi Strauss from doing business in countries where there are persistent violations of what the company declares to be basic human rights. Given strong evidence of rights violations in China, the company was faced with the question of whether to continue to trade with, and expand its business in China, a country whose large population will provide a huge new market for its products.

The Levi Strauss case also illustrates how background social and political institutions often confound cross-cultural ethical pronouncements. As Richard De George argues, these background conditions often provide practical difficulties in specifying particular ethical principles that apply universally. "Some actions," he writes, "are wrong no matter which system of background institutions are in place." Still, ethical issues in business are always embedded in a socioeconomic and political background that helps to form and constrain moral decision making. Present circumstances in countries such as Russia and China mean that some policies or actions will appropriately be judged unethical when viewed from the assumption that *socialist* or *communist* background conditions are operative. The same policies or actions might appropriately be viewed as ethically justifiable when viewed from the assumption that *free market* conditions are operative. China's one-child-per-family policy might be one such example. The case study "Just When Is a 'Tip' Only Another Means to Insure Promptness?" also illustrates such a difficulty.

In his article, "Values in Tension: Ethics away from Home," Thomas Donaldson considers the vexing problems that arise when moral and legal standards vary between countries, especially between a multinational corporation's home and host countries. How, he asks, should highly placed multinational managers, typically schooled in home-country moral traditions, reconcile conflicts between their values and the practices of the host country? If host-country standards appear lower than home-country ones, should the multinational manager always take the "high road" and implement home-country standards? Or, does the "high road" sometimes signal a failure to respect cultural diversity and national integrity? The answer may be fairly obvious in the instance of South Africa (where acquiescing to racism and discrimination would surely be immoral), but would the answer be so obvious in other instances involving differences in wage rates, pollution standards, or "sensitive payments?"

To deal with these complex issues, Donaldson appeals to what he calls an *ethical threshold,* or a set of core values that cross cultural and country boundaries and are shared by most religious traditions. Respect for human dignity whether in a community or as individuals, respect for basic rights, and good citizenship are three values that set basic guidelines for developing corporate guidelines for conduct in international settings as well as "at home." These core values are not maximal absolutes. Rather, they set the moral minimums for integrity and business practice. At the same time, Donaldson recognizes that there are cultural differences and conflicts of traditions that cannot be adjudicated. Thus there is a "moral free space" within countries that allows for differences of business practice without challenging core values. Are core values at stake in Levi Strauss's decision, or are there merely less critical cultural differences between China and the United States that allow a moral free space in which Levi Strauss may operate in China?

Ethical Relativism

—➤ *Case Study* ➤—

What Price Safety?

This case takes place in 1995 in *Nambu,* an Asian nation with a centuries-old philosophical and ethical tradition emphasizing duty and harmony in all human relationships. In 1969 Motorola formed a joint venture (JV) partnership with a Nambunese multinational company to produce microelectronic products at a new facility in the city of *Anzen,* Nambu. Motorola's ownership share was 60 percent; the local partner company's, 40 percent. Many of the Anzen facility's key managerial personnel were Motorolans, while the lower-level associates were Nambunese citizens and employees of the partner company.

From its very beginning, the Anzen facility developed a strong tradition of safety consciousness. Even the most casual visitor to the Anzen plant would notice numerous signs and displays, in both Nambunese and English, urging associates to "Think and Act Safely," "Wear Protective Eyeglasses," "Report Dangerous Situations," etc.

Motorola also had other operations in Nambu. In charge of Human Resources for all these operations, including the Anzen joint venture, was Canadian *Stan Stark,* 47. Stan was based at Motorola headquarters, 300 kilometers north of Anzen. Since first assuming his position five years ago, Stan had made safety one of his top priorities. He took pride in the fact that during this period he had further reduced the Anzen facility's already-low rate of accidents and lost workdays.

Sharing in his pride was a Motorolan of Dutch nationality, *Henk Van Dyke,* 38. Henk had been at Anzen for three years, assigned by Motorola to serve as the Human Resources manager for the entire JV facility. He enjoyed working in Nambu, but was somewhat handicapped because he did not speak Nambunese. Henk reported to Stan.

One of the operations at the Anzen facility was "Final Test Assembly," carried out by three eight-person teams on each daily shift. These team members were all Nambunese employees of the partner company.

The employee relations manager for the Anzen facility was *Willard Wa.* Willard, an employee of the partner company, was born 54 years ago in a small village in northern Nambu, and had been assigned to the JV partnership since its very first day of operation. Willard reported to Henk.

The manufacturing manager for the Final Test Assembly operation was a Nambunese Motorolan named *Victor Min,* 49, whom Motorola had assigned to the JV partnership for this purpose. To all who knew him, Victor

From R. S. Moorthy, Thomas Donaldson, William S. J. Ellos, Robert Solomon, Robert B. Textor, eds., *Uncompromising Integrity: Motorola's Global Challenge: 24 Global Case Studies with Commentaries.* Copyright © 1998 Motorola, Inc. Used with permission of Motorola University Press, USA.

personified a deep dedication to traditional Nambunese cultural values of duty and obedience.

One of the most respected of the Final Test Assembly teams was Team Three, nicknamed the "*Morning Glory*" team. Members of this team were intensely proud of their performance in both productivity and safety, which was among the best in the entire facility. Morning Glory team members viewed this performance as the result not only of exceptional skill, but equally important, of an unusual degree of harmony and cooperation within their team.

When Victor took over management of the Final Test Assembly operation in 1994, he made an effort to get acquainted with everyone under his supervision. He soon felt comfortable with all the Morning Glory team members except one, namely *Tommy Tang*, 31. Tommy had been hired by the partner company only two years earlier, after having spent several years as a mountaineering guide. Compared with most Nambunese, Tommy's values leaned a bit more toward freedom and a bit less toward duty. He hated to wear the protective eyeglasses that all Final Test Assembly associates were required to wear on duty. When his teammates would urge him to put on his safety glasses, he would give a variety of reasons why he couldn't.

On several occasions Victor spotted Tommy in the Final Test Assembly Area without his protective eyeglasses. Each time he would counsel Tommy on the need to wear them. The last time he shouted, "Tommy, this is the last time I will see you here without your safety glasses. From now on, you will either wear them or else!"

Then, four weeks later, a terrible event occurred. Victor entered the Final Test Assembly Area and noticed Tommy working closely with his Morning Glory teammates. All of them were wearing their protective eyeglasses except Tommy. Suddenly Victor lost control of his temper. He jumped at Tommy and slapped him several times on both sides of the head, screaming, "This will teach you!" Tommy doubled over in pain, holding his ears. Then, despite his pain, he apologized over and over to Victor for not having complied with safety regulations. After two or three minutes of apology, Tommy went to see the facility's nurse.

The other seven Morning Glory members stood in shocked silence. Nothing like this had ever happened before at Anzen. None of them reported the incident. Nonetheless, rumors about it, both accurate and otherwise, spread instantly throughout the entire facility.

That night Victor had trouble sleeping. The following morning he went directly to see Tommy in the Final Test Assembly Area. He noted that Tommy was wearing the required eyeglasses. In the presence of several Morning Glory team members, Victor apologized and presented Tommy with a red envelope inside of which he had placed a substantial amount of his own money. Tommy accepted the envelope and the apology. The two men then shook hands and parted amicably.

Then, a few days later came some shocking news from the facility's doctor: Tommy had suffered permanent partial loss of his hearing as a result of the slaps he received from Victor. As a matter of standard procedure, the doctor reported this finding to both Stan Stark and Henk Van Dyke.

Stan was stunned. He sat silently for a moment. Then he placed a conference call to Henk and Willard, and questioned them about the incident and the doctor's report. Then Stan decided: "Both of you know that no Motorolan is ever allowed to physically assault a fellow associate. Could each of you please investigate this incident, and give me your recommendations within 48 hours."

Willard proceeded immediately to conduct the most thorough investigation he could. The first thing he discovered was that neither Tommy nor any of his teammates wanted to discuss the matter at all. They all felt that their team's harmony would be best served by treating the entire matter as if it had never happened. After all, Victor had apologized; Tommy had accepted the apology; and Tommy was now complying with all safety regulations. So, the only really important thing was to get on with the team's heavy workload. But Willard persisted. Finally he got some solid facts:

- Several Morning Glory members stated categorically that Victor had never before struck a subordinate or threatened to.
- These team members believed that Victor's outburst of temper was unique, and they considered any repetition unlikely. "Victor has learned his lesson," said one, "and from now on he will handle his stress better. We will help him."
- Victor's personnel file revealed nothing to suggest he was prone to losing his temper or "acting out" violently.
- Tommy, despite his impaired hearing, could still function effectively with his Morning Glory teammates.

Two days later Willard phoned Stan with his recommendations. "Frankly," said Willard, "I think the solution is pretty simple. I recommend that the JV partnership cover all of Tommy's medical costs and then quietly, without any ceremony, make a reasonable indemnification payment to him with our apologies. Beyond that, I recommend that we do nothing—except, of course, to keep monitoring the situation carefully. In my opinion as a former manufacturing associate, this would be the best solution, because it is now clear to me that the Morning Glory team is functioning well, and continuing to accept Victor's leadership."

A few minutes later, Stan got a call from Henk. "Well," said Henk, "I recommend that we terminate Victor right away. Victor is a Motorolan, and knows very well that he is not supposed to strike an associate. That would be a violation of the basic dignity to which every Motorolan is entitled, and to which I believe all JV partnership employees are also entitled. We cannot allow a Motorolan to enforce regulations for our associates' safety by violating that safety! That just doesn't make any sense at all. And while we are at it, we should pay Tommy's medical bills and terminate him, too."

Next Stan walked down the hall to consult *Cuthbert Kim,* senior counsel in the Motorola Law Department for Nambu. Stan carefully explained the facts of the case and then asked, "Cuthbert, what's the procedure if I decide to terminate Victor and Tommy?"

"Well, I'm afraid there is no such procedure," replied Cuthbert. "While it is true that under Nambunese law striking a subordinate is grounds for termination, it is also true that once an apology has been offered and accepted, the law determines that life can and should go on again, and that termination is not legally justified. So, you can't terminate him. And you can't terminate Tommy, either. But of course you could separate them from the company, provided you could manage to negotiate buy-out agreements that they would accept."

Stan found this hard to believe, but when he checked with an external Nambunese consulting attorney, he received essentially the same answer.

The next day, Stan asked Cuthbert to do some research and find out how much it would cost to buy the two associates out. Soon Cuthbert came back with the answer: "Since Victor still has about 11 years before he is due to retire from Motorola, he could probably bargain hard. My estimate is that the JV partnership would probably have to pay him about five years' worth of salary plus benefits and fringes. For Tommy, it might be three years' worth, because he is a relatively new employee."

"That's a huge amount of money," gasped Stan. "On the other hand, the behavior that both Victor and Tommy have modeled is certainly not the kind of behavior I want at Anzen. I'll think about it and then let you know my decision."

Relativism, Cultural and Moral

NORMAN E. BOWIE

Cultural relativism is a descriptive claim that ethical practices differ among cultures; that, as a matter of fact, what is considered right in one culture may be considered wrong in another. Thus truth or falsity of cultural relativism can be determined by examining the world. The work of anthropologists and sociologists is most relevant in determining the truth or falsity of cultural relativism, and there is widespread consensus among social scientists that cultural relativism is true.

Moral relativism is the claim that what is really right or wrong is what the culture says is right or wrong. Moral relativists accept cultural relativism as true, but they claim much more. If a culture sincerely and reflectively adopts a basic moral principle, then it is morally obligatory for members of that culture to act in accordance with that principle.

The implication of moral relativism for conduct is that one ought to abide by the ethical norms of the culture where one is located. This position is captured by the popular phrase "When in Rome, do as the Romans do." Relativists in ethics would say "One ought to follow the moral norms of the culture." In terms of business practice, consider the question, "Is it morally right to pay a bribe to gain business?" The moral relativist would answer the question by consulting the moral norms of the country where one is doing business. If those norms permit bribery in that country, then the practice of bribery is not wrong in that country. However, if the moral norms of the country do not permit bribery, then offering a bribe to gain business in that country is morally wrong. The justification for that position is the moral relativist's contention that what is really right or wrong is determined by the culture.

Is cultural relativism true? Is moral relativism correct? As noted, many social scientists believe that cultural relativism is true as a matter of fact. But is it?

First, many philosophers claim that the "facts" aren't really what they seem. Early twentieth-century anthropologists cited the fact that in some cultures, after a certain age, parents are put to death. In most cultures such behavior would be murder. Does this difference in behavior prove that the two cultures disagree about fundamental matters of ethics? No, it does not. Suppose the other culture believes that people exist in the afterlife in the same condition that they leave their present life. It would be very cruel to have one's parents exist eternally in an unhealthy state. By killing them when they are relatively active and vigorous, you insure their happiness for all eternity. The *underlying* ethical principle of this culture is that children have duties to their parents, including the duty to be concerned with their parents' happiness as they approach old age. This ethical principle is identical with our own. What looked like a difference in ethics between our culture and another turned out, upon close examination, to be a difference based on what each culture takes to be the facts of the matter. This example does, of course, support the claim that as a matter of fact ethical principles vary according to culture. However, it does not support the stronger conclusion that *underlying* ethical principles vary according to culture.

Cultures differ in physical setting, in economic development, in the state of their science and technology, in their literacy rate, and in many other ways. Even if there were universal moral principles, they would have to be applied in these different cultural contexts. Given the different situations in which cultures exist, it would come as no surprise to find universal principles applied in different ways. Hence we expect to find surface differences in ethical behavior among cultures even though the cultures agree on fundamental universal moral principles. For example, one commonly held universal principle appeals to the public good; it says that social institutions and individual behavior should be ordered so that they lead to the greatest good for the greatest number. Many different forms of social organization and individual behavior are consistent with this principle. The point of these two arguments is to show that differences among cultures on ethical behavior may not reflect genuine disagreement about underlying principles of ethics. Thus it is not so obvious that any strong form of cultural relativism is true.

But are there universal principles that are accepted by all cultures? It seems so; there does seem to be a whole range of behavior, such as torture and murder of the innocent, that every culture agrees is wrong. A nation-state accused of torture does not respond by saying that a condemnation of torture is just a matter of cultural choice. The state's leaders do not respond by saying, "We think torture is right, but you do not." Rather, the standard response is to deny that any torture took place. If the evidence of torture is too strong, a finger will be pointed either at the victim or at the morally outraged country: "They do it too." In this case the guilt is spread to all. Even the Nazis denied that genocide took place. What is important is that *no* state replies that there is nothing wrong with genocide or torture.

In addition, there are attempts to codify some universal moral principles. The United Nations Universal Declaration of Human Rights has been endorsed by the member states of the U.N., and the vast majority of countries in the world are members of the U.N. Even in business, there is a growing effort to adopt universal principles of business practice. In a recent study of international codes of ethics, Professors Catherine Langlois and Bodo B. Schlegelmich found that although there certainly were differences among codes, there was a considerable area of agreement (Langlois and Schlegelmich, 1990). William Frederick has documented the details of six international compacts on matters of international business ethics. These include the aforementioned U.N. Universal Declaration of Human Rights, the European Convention on Human Rights, the Helsinki Final Act, the OECD Guidelines for Multinational Enterprises and Social Policy, and the United Nations Conduct on Transnational Corporations (in progress) (Frederick 1991). The Caux Roundtable, a group of corporate executives from the United States, Europe, and Japan, are seeking worldwide endorsement of a set of principles of business ethics. Thus there are a number of reasons to think that cultural relativism, at least with respect to basic moral principles, is not true, that is, that it does not accurately describe the state of moral agreement that exists. This is consistent with maintaining that cultural relativism is true in the weak form, that is, when applied only to surface ethical principles.

But what if differences in fundamental moral practices among cultures are discovered and seem unreconcilable? That would lead to a discussion about the adequacy of moral relativism. The fact that moral practices do vary widely among countries is cited as evidence for the correctness of moral relativism. The discoveries, early in the century, by anthropologists, sociologists, and psychologists documented the diversity of moral beliefs. Philosophers, by and large, welcomed corrections of moral imperialist thinking, but recognized that the moral relativist's appeal to the alleged truth of cultural relativism was not enough to establish moral relativism. The mere fact that a culture considers a practice moral does not mean that it is moral. Cultures have sincerely practiced slavery, discrimination, and the torture of animals. Yet each of these practices can be independently criticized on ethical grounds. Thinking something is morally permissible does not make it so.

Another common strategy for criticizing moral relativism is to show that the consequences of taking the perspective of moral relativism are inconsistent with our use of moral language. It is often contended by moral relativists that if two cultures disagree regarding universal moral principles, there is no way for that disagreement to be resolved. Since moral relativism is the view that what is right or wrong is determined by culture, there is not higher appeal beyond the fact that culture endorses the moral principle. But we certainly do not talk that way. When China and the United States argue about the moral rights of human beings, the disputants use language that seems to appeal to universal moral principles. Moreover, the atrocities of the Nazis and the slaughter in Rwanda have met with universal condemnation that seemed based on universal moral principles. So moral relativism is not consistent with our use of moral language.

Relativism is also inconsistent with how we use the term "moral reformer." Suppose, for instance, that a person from one culture moves to another and tries to persuade the other culture to change its view. Suppose someone moves from a culture where slavery is immoral to one where slavery is morally permitted. Normally, if a person were to try to convince the culture where slavery was permitted that slavery was morally wrong, we would call such a person a moral reformer. Moreover, a moral reformer would almost certainly appeal to universal moral principles to make her argument; she almost certainly would not appeal to a competing cultural standard. But if moral relativism were true, there would be no place for the concept of a moral reformer. Slavery is really right in those cultures that say it is right and really wrong in the cultures that say it is wrong. If the reformer fails to persuade a slaveholding country to change its mind, the reformer's antislavery position was never right. If the reformer is successful in persuading a country to change its mind, the reformer's antislavery views would be wrong—until the country did, in fact, change its view. Then the reformer's antislavery view would be right. But that is not how we talk about moral reform.

The moral relativist might argue that our language should be reformed. We should talk differently. At one time people used to talk and act as if the world were flat. Now they don't. The relativist could suggest that we can change our ethical language in the same way. But consider how radical the relativists' response is. Since most, if not all, cultures speak and act as if there were universal moral principles, the relativist can be right only if almost everyone else is wrong. How plausible is that?

Although these arguments are powerful ones, they do not deliver a knockout blow to moral relativism. If there are no universal moral principles, moral relativists could argue that moral relativism is the only theory available to help make sense of moral phenomena.

An appropriate response to this relativist argument is to present the case for a set of universal moral principles, principles that are correct for all cultures independent of what a culture thinks about them. This is what adherents of the various ethical traditions try to do. The reader will have to examine these various traditions and determine how persuasive he finds them. In addition, there are several final independent considerations against moral relativism that can be mentioned here.

First, what constitutes a culture? There is a tendency to equate cultures with national boundaries, but that is naive, especially today. With respect to moral issues, what do U.S. cultural norms say regarding right and wrong? That question may be impossible to answer, because in a highly pluralistic country like the United States, there are many cultures. Furthermore, even if one can identify a culture's moral norms, it will have dissidents who do not subscribe to those moral norms. How many dissidents can a culture put up with and still maintain that some basic moral principle is the cultural norm? Moral relativists have had little to say regarding criteria for constituting a culture or how to account for dissidents. Unless moral relativists offer answers to questions like these, their theory is in danger of becoming inapplicable to the real world.

Second, any form of moral relativism must admit that there are some universal moral principles. Suppose a culture does not accept moral relativism, that is, it denies that if an entire culture sincerely and reflectively adopts a basic moral principle, it is obligatory for members of that culture to act in accord with that principle. Fundamentalist Muslim countries would reject moral relativism because it would require them to accept as morally permissible blasphemy in those countries where blasphemy was permitted. If the moral relativist insists that the truth of every moral principle depends on the culture, then she must admit that the truth of moral relativism depends on the culture. Therefore the moral relativist must admit that at least the principle of moral relativism is not relative.

Third, it seems that there is a set of basic moral principles that every culture must adopt. You would not have a culture unless the members of the group adopted these moral principles. Consider an anthropologist who arrives on a populated island: How many tribes are on the island? To answer that question, the anthropologist tries to determine if some people on some parts of the island are permitted to kill, commit acts of violence against, or steal from persons on other parts of the island. If such behavior is not permitted, that counts as a reason for saying that there is only one tribe. The underlying assumption here is that there is a set of moral principles that must be followed if there is to be a culture at all. With respect to those moral principles, adhering to them determines whether there is a culture or not.

But what justifies these principles? A moral relativist would say that a culture justifies them. But you cannot have a culture unless the members of the culture follow the principles. Thus it is reasonable to think that justification lies elsewhere. Many believe that the purpose of morality is to help make social cooperation possible. Moral principles are universally necessary for that endeavor.

Bibliography

Benedict, R. (1934). *Patterns of Culture.* New York: Penguin Books.

Bowie, N. (1988). The moral obligations of multinational corporations. In S. Luper-Foy (ed.), *Problems of International Justice.* (pp. 97–113). Boulder, CO: Westview Press.

Frederick, W. C. "The moral authority of transnational corporate codes," *Journal of Business Ethics.* 10 #3 (1991).

Harman, G. (1975). Moral relativism defended. *The Philosophical Review.* 84. 3–22.

Hatch, E. (1983). *Culture and Morality.* New York: Columbia University Press.

Krausz, M., and Meiland, J. (1982). *Relativism: Cognitive and Moral.* Notre Dame, IN: University of Notre Dame Press.

Ladd, J. (1973). *Ethical Relativism.* Belmont, CA: Wadsworth.

Langlois, C., and Bodo B. Schlegelmich, "Do corporate codes of ethics reflect national character? Evidence from Europe and the United States," *Journal of International Studies.* 21 #9 (1990). pp. 519–39.

Mackie, J. (1977). *Ethics: Inventing Right and Wrong.* Harmondsworth: Penguin Books.

Rachels, J. (1993). *The Elements of Moral Philosophy,* second edition. New York: McGraw-Hill, Inc.

Sayre-McCord, G. (1991). Being a realist about relativism (in ethics). *Philosophical Studies. 61.* pp. 155–76.

Wong, D. (1984). *Moral Relativity.* Berkeley: University of California Press.

The United Nations Declaration of Human Rights

Now, Therefore, The General Assembly *proclaims*

This universal declaration of human rights as a common standard of achievement for all peoples and all nations, to the end that every individual and every organ of society, keeping this Declaration constantly in mind, shall strive by teaching and education to promote respect for these rights and freedoms and by progressive measures, national and international, to secure their universal and effective recognition and observance, both among the peoples of Member States themselves and among the peoples of territories under their jurisdiction.

Article 1

All human beings are born free and equal in dignity and rights. They are endowed with reason and conscience and should act towards one another in a spirit of brotherhood.

Article 2

Everyone is entitled to all the rights and freedoms set forth in this Declaration without distinction of any kind, such as race, colour, sex, language, religion, political or other opinion, national or social origin, property, birth or other status.

Furthermore, no distinction shall be made on the basis of the political jurisdictional or international status of the country or territory to which a person belongs, whether it be independent, trust, non-self-governing or under any other limitation of sovereignty.

Article 3

Everyone has the right to life, liberty and security of person.

Article 4

No one shall be held in slavery or servitude; slavery and the slave trade shall be prohibited in all their forms.

Article 5

No one shall be subjected to torture or to cruel, inhuman or degrading treatment or punishment.

Article 6

Everyone has the right to recognition everywhere as a person before the law.

Article 7

All are equal before the law and are entitled without any discrimination to equal protection of the law. All are entitled to equal protection against any discrimination in violation of this Declaration and against any incitement to such discrimination.

Article 8

Everyone has the right to an effective remedy by the competent national tribunals for acts violating the fundamental rights granted him by the constitution or by law.

Article 9

No one shall be subjected to arbitrary arrest, detention or exile.

Article 10

Everyone is entitled in full equality to a fair and public hearing by an independent and impartial tribunal, in the determination of his rights and obligations and of any criminal charge against him.

Article 11

1. Everyone charged with a penal offence has the right to be presumed innocent until proved guilty according to law in a public trial at which he has had all the guarantees necessary for his defense.
2. No one shall be held guilty of any penal offence on account of any act or omission which did not constitute a penal offence, under national or international law, at the time when it was committed. Nor shall a heavier penalty be imposed than the one that was applicable at the time the penal offence was committed.

Article 12

No one shall be subjected to arbitrary interference with his privacy, family, home or correspondence, nor to attacks upon his honour and reputation. Everyone has the right to the protection of the law against such interference or attacks.

Article 13

1. Everyone has the right to freedom of movement and residence within the borders of each state.
2. Everyone has the right to leave any country, including his own, and to return to his country.

Article 14

1. Everyone has the right to seek and to enjoy in other countries asylum from persecution.
2. This right may not be invoked in the case of prosecutions genuinely arising from non-political crimes or from acts contrary to the purposes and principles of the United Nations.

Article 15

1. Everyone has the right to a nationality.
2. No one shall be arbitrarily deprived of his nationality nor denied the right to change his nationality.

Article 16

1. Men and women of full age, without any limitation due to race, nationality or religion, have the right to marry and to found a family. They are entitled to equal rights as to marriage, during marriage and at its dissolution.

2. Marriage shall be entered into only with the free and full consent of the intending spouses.

3. The family is the natural and fundamental group unit of society and is entitled to protection by society and the State.

Article 17

1. Everyone has the right to own property alone as well as in association with others.

2. No one shall be arbitrarily deprived of his property.

Article 18

Everyone has the right to freedom of thought, conscience and religion; this right includes freedom to change his religion or belief, and freedom, either alone or in community with others and in public or private, to manifest his religion or belief in teaching, practice, worship and observance.

Article 19

Everyone has the right to freedom of opinion and expression; this right includes freedom to hold opinions without interference and to seek, receive and impart information and ideas through any media and regardless of frontiers.

Article 20

1. Everyone has the right to freedom of peaceful assembly and association.

2. No one may be compelled to belong to an association.

Article 21

1. Everyone has the right to take part in the government of his country, directly or through freely chosen representatives.

2. Everyone has the right of equal access to public service in his country.

3. The will of the people shall be the basis of the authority of government; this will shall be expressed in periodic and genuine elections which shall be by universal and equal suffrage and shall be held by secret vote or by equivalent free voting procedures.

Article 22

Everyone, as a member of society, has the right to social security and is entitled to realization, through national effort and international cooperation and in accordance with the organization and resources of each State, of the economic, social and cultural rights indispensable for his dignity and the free development of his personality.

Article 23

1. Everyone has the right to work, to free choice of employment, to just and favourable conditions of work and to protection against unemployment.

2. Everyone, without any discrimination, has the right to equal pay for equal work.

3. Everyone who works has the right to just and favourable remuneration ensuring for himself and his family an existence worthy of human dignity, and supplemented, if necessary, by other means of social protection.

4. Everyone has the right to form and to join trade unions for the protection of his interests.

Article 24

Everyone has the right to rest and leisure, including reasonable limitation of working hours and periodic holidays with pay.

Article 25

1. Everyone has the right to a standard of living adequate for the health and well-being of himself and of his family, including food, clothing, housing and medical care and necessary social services, and the right to security in the event of unemployment, sickness, disability, widowhood, old age or other lack of livelihood in circumstances beyond his control.
2. Motherhood and childhood are entitled to special care and assistance. All children, whether born in or out of wedlock, shall enjoy the same social protection.

Article 26

1. Everyone has the right to education. Education shall be free, at least in the elementary and fundamental stages. Elementary education shall be compulsory. Technical and professional education shall be made generally available and higher education shall be equally accessible to all on the basis of merit.
2. Education shall be directed to the full development of the human personality and to the strengthening of respect for human rights and fundamental freedoms. It shall promote understanding, tolerance and friendship among all nations, racial or religious groups, and shall further the activities of the United Nations for the maintenance of peace.
3. Parents have a prior right to choose the kind of education that shall be given to their children.

Article 27

1. Everyone has the right freely to participate in the cultural life of the community, to enjoy the arts and to share in scientific advancement and its benefits.
2. Everyone has the right to the protection of the moral and material interests resulting from any scientific, literary or artistic production of which he is the author.

Article 28

Everyone is entitled to a social and international order in which the rights and freedoms set forth in this Declaration can be fully realized.

Article 29

1. Everyone has duties to the community in which alone the free and full development of his personality is possible.
2. In the exercise of his rights and freedoms, everyone shall be subject only to such limitations as are determined by law solely for the purpose of securing due recognition and respect for the rights and freedoms of others and of meeting the just requirements of morality, public order and the general welfare in a democratic society.
3. These rights and freedoms may in no case be exercised contrary to the purposes and principles of the United Nations.

Article 30

Nothing in this Declaration may be interpreted as implying for any State, group or person any right to engage in any activity or to perform any act aimed at the destruction of any of the rights and freedoms set forth herein.

Business Values
away
from Home

← *Case Study* →

Just When Is a "Tip" ONLY
"To Insure Promptness"?

Legend has it that the British invented the word "tip" as an abbreviation for "to insure promptness." The key question of this case is: When is it simply that, and when is it something more than that—enough "more" so that it verges on violating the Motorola Key Belief in Uncompromising Integrity?

The setting is the city of *Palatinsk,* capital of *Slavinia,* one of the Slavic-speaking republics that became independent when the USSR broke up. Motorola has recently established an office in downtown Palatinsk, and is eager to get going. But the going is not easy. Motorola must face remnants of the partially defunct Soviet culture, in which bribery was expected and tolerated. As if this were not enough, the corporation must also face the current Slavinia situation, in which even those Slavinians who strongly hold to the value that bribery is wrong, often find that they must engage in it to some extent merely to feed themselves and their families in the disorganized, inflation-ridden, crime-plagued reality that is Slavinia today.

One of the new hires at Motorola/Palatinsk is *Natasha Sakharov,* age 24. Natasha speaks native Slavinian, excellent Russian and adequate English. She is proud of her qualifications as an industrial engineer, openly disdainful of the unproductive Soviet past, and eager to make her contribution, through Motorola, to a "new Slavinia" where people will be rewarded on the basis of merit—NOT connections. True, the Slavinian job market is such that she would have taken a job even with a company not perceived as outstandingly ethical—but in her three months on the job she has obviously "bought into" the Motorola Culture, and proudly refers to herself as a Motorolan.

Enter *Bernard Yeats,* a senior Motorola manager out of Phoenix. Bernard arrives in Palatinsk on a Wednesday intending to stay six days and then leave for Germany—but on Thursday he suddenly receives a fax directing him to be in St. Petersburg, Russia, on Saturday to trouble-shoot a crisis.

Problem: Bernard must somehow get a Russian visa in time to leave on Friday. Most foreigners in Slavinia must wait two weeks to secure a Russian visa, during which they are forced to spend endless hours in the Outer Waiting Room of the Russian Embassy, located in downtown Palatinsk—ironically in the building that was once the headquarters of the Soviet Secret Police.

In an effort to assist Bernard, Motorola's Palatinsk office manager immediately tries to contact *Josef Fixzitup*. Fixzitup is a native Slavinian who speaks adequate Russian and broken English. He is a high school graduate and was recently superannuated out of the Soviet Army after 26 years, with the rank of senior sergeant of quartermaster. His pension is tiny, so he has become an independent "administrative broker" who specializes in getting governmental clearances for foreign companies.

Alas, at this moment Fixzitup is off on an errand for another of his foreign clients, *Burger Heaven*. Palatinsk does not yet have a paging system, so no one can find out exactly when Josef will be back.

Desperate, Bernard turns to Natasha. The latter, though knowing nothing about visas, is eager to establish herself as a "can-do" Motorolan. So, she jumps into a taxi with Bernard and off they career for the Russian Embassy.

There, in the Outer Waiting Room, reality confronts them. Fifty-seven foreigners of all nationalities, ages, and appearances are patiently waiting their turn to be admitted to the Inner Waiting Room, where they will have a good chance of receiving a visa within several days. Twenty make it, and then the door closes. The others are told brusquely: "Come back tomorrow."

Next problem: How to get Yeats into the Inner Waiting Room, even though the door has been closed? The key player is obviously the Russian guard, one *Igor Kipoutskii*, who speaks native Russian, minimal Slavinian, and virtually no English. Like most Russian government personnel, Kipoutskii's salary has been reduced by inflation to a mere pittance, and he could not possibly feed his family in high-cost Palatinsk unless he had additional sources of income.

Natasha quells her nerves and approaches Kipoutskii. She explains in Russian how important Motorola is to both Slavinia and Russia, and how important Yeats is to Motorola. Then she hands Bernard's visa application to Kipoutskii, along with an envelope from which a U.S. ten-dollar bill is slightly yet visibly protruding. Kipoutskii shakes his head vigorously to indicate that he is not interested in the envelope, but he immediately places Yeats' application in a special wire basket, and bids Yeats enter the Inner Waiting Room. There, after answering a few routine questions and paying the official $40 visa fee—no more—the dumbfounded Bernard receives his visa, all within 15 minutes!

As Bernard and Natasha are about to leave the embassy, in rushes Fixzitup. Eagerly, he learns from Natasha that Kipoutskii refused the ten-dollar bill. "Please give it to me," he barks, and immediately takes it to Kipoutskii who, after a sidelong glance or two, readily pockets it.

That evening, Yeats is having a vodka tonic with a group of Motorolans who have worked in various parts of the world. "Hey," he asks, "did Natasha and I violate Uncompromising Integrity?" The consensual answer was no.

"Why?" "Because, Bernie" replies *Dieter Weltlich* of Motorola/Latinia, "all you were doing was asking for promptness—not for something that they wouldn't have done for you anyway, sooner or later. What you did was legal, according to the U.S. Foreign Corrupt Practices Act."

"Legal, of course," pressed Yeats, "but was it ethical? And, to hell with Fixzitup and Kipoutskii, what I want to know is: Did I corrupt Natasha in the process?"

"Maybe, a little," interjected the scholarly *Lim Key-Boon* of Motorola/Hong Kong, "but I think it was OK nonetheless, because Natasha seems like a real serious post-Communist 'New Slavinian,' and probably sees her behavior as merely coping with a temporary situational norm, without endorsing it as a cultural value. As soon as the situation improves, she will no doubt act with Uncompromising Integrity. And furthermore, by helping Motorola in this way she is helping establish the corporation as a permanent player in Slavinia, and this in turn will help produce a future Slavinian culture in which people are rewarded for their merits and not their connections."

"Besides," added the demure *Kazuko Takeuchi* of Motorola/Sendai, "if you will excuse me for saying so shouldn't we remember that 'Uncompromising Integrity' is not the only value on our TCS Card? Don't we also need to take seriously the Key Initiative of 'Total Cycle Time Reduction'?"

Uncompromising Integrity

To maintain the highest standards of honesty, integrity, and ethics in all aspects of our business—with customers, suppliers, employees, governments, and society at large—and to comply with the laws of each country and community in which we operate.

FOR WHICH WE STAND

Motorola's Definition of Standards

Highest standards of openness, honesty, impartiality, fairness, and respect for basic human dignity in all our relationships within and outside Motorola.

➤ *Case Study* ➤

Levi Strauss & Co.: Global Sourcing (A)

LYNN SHARP PAINE ➤ JANE PALLEY KATZ

Levi Strauss & Co. has a heritage of conducting business in a manner that reflects its values. As we expand our sourcing base to more diverse cultures and countries, we must take special care in selecting business partners and countries whose practices are not incompatible with our values. Otherwise, our sourcing decisions have the potential of undermining this heritage, damaging the image of our brands and threatening our commercial success.

—LEVI STRAUSS & CO.
BUSINESS PARTNER TERMS OF ENGAGEMENT
AND GUIDELINES FOR COUNTRY SELECTION

"If we really are an aspirational company, shouldn't we be in there trying to make a difference?" asked one member of the China Policy Group at Levi Strauss & Co. (LS&CO.), the world's largest brand-name apparel manufacturer. Another responded, "We've got to be careful. There are some things we just can't be associated with—and still maintain our reputation."

The China Policy Group (CPG) had been chartered in late 1992 by CEO Robert D. Haas and Vice President of Global Sourcing Peter A. Jacobi specifically to consider whether LS&CO. should continue sourcing and purchasing fabric in China and whether it should make direct investments in marketing and manufacturing ventures there. The CPG had been asked to use the "principled reasoning approach" to make a recommendation based on the company's ethical values and global sourcing guidelines. Announced in March 1992, these guidelines were part of a comprehensive set of sourcing standards widely acknowledged to be among the most far-reaching of any adopted by a U.S. company.[1] (See Exhibits 1 and 2.) The CPG would report its recommendation to the nine-member Executive Management Committee, LS&CO.'s most senior decision-making group, early in 1993.

The CPG's leaders—Pete Jacobi, Lindsay Webbe, president of the Asia Pacific Division; and Robert Dunn, vice president of Corporate Affairs—had carefully identified and recruited nine others to join the group. They sought individuals with relevant knowledge and a range of perspectives informed by differences in experience, functional area, race, and gender.[2] Elissa Sheridan, a specialist on loan from Corporate Affairs, prepared voluminous background reports to aid the discussion. Once formed, the CPG reviewed its membership, studied the background materials, and identified additional information needed for its work. The group also decided to try for a consensus recommendation while reserving to anyone who disagreed the right to submit a minority opinion.

COMPANY BACKGROUND

LS&CO. traced its roots to the 1850s, when a Bavarian-born immigrant, Levi Strauss, came to San Francisco from New York and joined his brother-in-law's dry goods business. The company achieved early success producing and selling sturdy canvas trousers, the first jeans, to the many miners who arrived during the gold rush. In 1873, Strauss adopted the idea, from a Nevada tailor, to rivet the pockets for added strength. The double-arcuate pattern sewn on the hip pockets, the oldest apparel trademark in the United States, was added the same year. By the last half of the twentieth century, "Levi's®" had become synonymous with "jeans," while the spread of American popular culture—movies, television, and music—made the company's clothes a symbol of American values, sought after across the globe. Explained the vice president for Corporate Marketing, Levi's® jeans epitomized "freedom, originality, youthfulness and the spirit of America" in markets worldwide.[3] They were even included in the permanent collection of the Smithsonian Institute, a museum of U.S. history and culture located in Washington, D.C.

For the first 100 years of its history, LS&CO. was a private company. Family members owned nearly all of its stock, with employees holding most of the remaining shares. In 1971, needing funds for expansion, the company went public, although the Haas family retained a significant amount of the stock, with some of its members opposing the move.[4]

During the early 1980s, in response to a decline in the U.S. jeans market and a larger decline globally, LS&CO. closed 58 plants and laid off more than a third of its work force. In 1984, Robert D. Haas, the great-great-grand-nephew of founder Levi Strauss, became president and chief executive officer, following in the footsteps of both his uncle, Peter Haas, and his father, Walter Haas, Jr., who had previously served as president and chairman of the board, respectively, and as board members in 1993. In 1985, under Robert Haas's leadership, certain descendants of Levi Strauss's family repurchased publicly held shares for $50 a share—a 42 percent premium over the market price—or a total cost of $1.6 billion, at that time the biggest leveraged buyout in history.[5] In 1993, 95 percent of the company's stock was held by descendants of Levi Strauss and by certain non-family members of management. The remainder was held by the company's employee investment plans.

As the apparel industry became more competitive, with faster style changes and fewer, though larger, retail customers, LS&CO. reconceived itself from a manufacturer to a marketer. The company reorganized at the end of 1988, reducing layers of management and consolidating personnel, finance, and operations to advance its strategy of providing better and faster service to retail customers. Robert Haas became chairman of the board in 1989.

The Business in 1993

In 1992, LS&CO. recorded net earnings of $360 million on revenues of $5.6 billion, marking the sixth consecutive year of increased sales and earnings. . . . The company marketed products with the Levi's® brand name in more than 60 countries, using a variety of arrangements, including wholly owned and operated businesses, joint ventures, licensees, and distributors. Production and distribution facilities were located in more than 20 countries. LS&CO. employed 25,000 people in the United States and 9,000 people overseas. About half of its hourly work force was represented by the Amalgamated Clothing and Textile Workers Union (ACTWU) and the International Ladies Garment Workers Union (ILGWU).[6]

One estimate put the value of LS&CO., if publicly traded, at $5.5 billion.[7] When asked about the possibility of going public again, Tom Tusher, president and chief operating officer, replied, "We have no reason to go public. Being private helps us focus on long-term strategies. We don't have to worry about quarter-to-quarter results all the time. And we can take more risks."[8]

LS&CO. officials attributed the company's success of the late 1980s and early 1990s, in part, "to sales of jeans and related products outside the United States, principally in Europe and the Asia-Pacific region."[9] International sales had become a significant element of the business, accounting, in 1992, for 37 percent of total revenues and 53 percent of pretax profits. (See Exhibit 3 for data on worldwide operations.) The company credited higher foreign profit margins to foreign consumers' willingness to pay for the perceived high quality of Levis® clothing.[10] Overseas, a pair of jeans sold for up to $60 to $100—more than twice the average price in the United States. In some areas, a legal "grey market" surfaced in which jeans were bought in bulk off the shelves of U.S. retail stores, shipped to foreign countries, and sold in unauthorized outlets at cut-rate prices. The company estimated that the grey market cost it millions of dollars in sales each year and damaged the image of its product. Noted a spokesperson for LS&CO., "Our jeans are a premium product—and this damages their reputation and consumer confidence."[11]

To protect its brand name, the company registered its trademark, Levis®, in more than 150 countries, calling it "the most recognized apparel brand and one of the most famous consumer brand names in the world."[12] One study valued the Levis® brand at $4.811 billion, the top apparel brand measured.[13] Levis® was the market leader in every country where the company sold jeans.

In general, LS&CO. manufactured goods in the countries or regions where they would be sold.[14] Throughout much of its history, almost all manufacturing occurred in its own facilities or through a small number of contractors in the United States. However, like most U.S. apparel manufacturers, LS&CO. had moved an increased portion of its production to contract manufacturers, many of them offshore, to cut costs. (See Exhibit 4 for a comparison of labor costs and hours in selected countries.) By 1993, contractor sourcing around the world accounted for about half the company's global production. Company officials estimated that 45 percent of the LS&CO. apparel sold in the United States was made overseas, with 40 percent coming from contractors in Asia, and 60 percent from Central America, South America, and Mexico. Efforts were under way to consolidate and secure relationships with long-term contractors worldwide.

The loss of domestic jobs in the apparel industry was an ongoing concern for both labor unions and the consuming and voting public. An official from the ILGWU estimated that, in 1992, the apparel industry employed

816,000 production workers, down from 1,079,000 in 1980 and substantially lower than the industry's largest work force of 1,257,400 in 1973. The unemployment rate in the industry hovered around 11%, about twice as high as for the nation as a whole.[15]

When in early 1990 LS&CO. closed a 1,115-employee plant in San Antonio, Texas, and moved production to contractors in Costa Rica, it gave 90 days' notice, continued employee medical insurance, contributed $100,000 to local agencies, and gave $340,000 to the city of San Antonio to fund additional services and retraining programs for laid-off workers.[16] Instead of praise for its handling of the situation, LS&CO. faced harsh public criticism, a class-action lawsuit, a boycott of its products, substantial bad publicity, and even a small demonstration in front of its San Francisco offices. Judy Belk, vice president of Community Affairs, remarked on the San Antonio experience, "We were honest about what we were doing—work was going to be taken offshore—and we exceeded all the legal requirements in terms of severance. But the employees who were impacted did not think we were ethical in our attempts to make them whole."

In 1993, achieving preeminent customer service was a top priority at LS&CO. Management knew that continuing success would require ongoing development of new products and improved processes for getting goods into retail outlets. Based on intensive research begun in 1991, the company was reengineering the entire customer service supply chain, from the generation of new product ideas to the moment of purchase.

Company Philosophy

LS&CO. was known for its longstanding commitment to employees and the communities where they lived and worked. The company's founder had served as a board member of the California School of the Deaf and established 28 scholarships at the University of California; after his death, the tradition of corporate citizenship continued. Following the great San Francisco earthquake and fire of 1906, LS&CO. continued to pay its employees, even though there was no work for some of them for six months. During the Great Depression, it kept its workers on the payroll to install hardwood floors. The company desegregated its plants in the southern United States "before law or practice compelled them to do so."[17] In the 1970s, it set up the Community Affairs Department, which staffed the Levi Strauss Foundation and granted millions of dollars in its focus areas of AIDS, economic development, and social justice to institutions and groups in the communities it served.[18]

As LS&CO. contracted out more of its manufacturing, it also expanded its community affairs activities, recognizing that the new production arrangements did not extinguish its social responsibilities. In 1993, for example, it donated $127,000 toward maternal and child health care in Bangladesh, a valuable source of contract labor. The company received praise from the Amalgamated Clothing and Textile Workers Union, which represented its workers: "In an industry noted for sweatshops and abuses of workers' rights, LS&CO. has earned a reputation as a good employer in the United States. Its labor relations are among 'the best in the country.' "[19]

Until the late 1980s, LS&CO. managers had viewed the company's community and employee responsibilities "as something separate from how we ran the business." Noted Robert Haas, "We always talked about the 'hard stuff' and the 'soft stuff.' The soft stuff was the company's commitment to our work force. And the hard stuff was what really mattered: getting the pants out the door."[20] That view changed as the business environment of the 1980s changed. Increasing competition, new technology, corporate restructurings, the globalization of enterprises, greater consumer choice, and a new generation entering the work force led Haas and other LS&CO. managers to conclude that the "hard stuff and the soft stuff [were] becoming increasingly intertwined."[21] Haas saw values as the link.[22] He explained:

> In a more volatile and dynamic business environment, the controls have to be conceptual. They can't be human anymore: Bob Haas telling people what to do. It's the *ideas* of a business that are controlling, not some manager with authority. Values provide a common language for aligning a company's leadership and its people.[23]

LS&CO.'s top managers were convinced that values-based companies that honored their social responsibilities would ultimately achieve greater competitive success. Believing that a company's reputation had become increasingly important to customers, investors, employees, regulators, and other stakeholders, management reasoned that there was "not generally a conflict in the long term [between] doing good versus doing well.[24] Noted Toni Wilson, manager of the company's ethics initiative, "LS&CO. invites the whole person to the job. . . . Doing the right thing may cost in the short run, but in the long run it brings intangible benefits: trust, creativity, innovation. You can't buy trust, you have to earn it."

In 1987, under Haas's leadership, LS&CO. adopted a Mission and Aspirations Statement to communicate "where we wanted to go . . . [and] how we wanted to behave."[25] (See Exhibit 5.) Senior management defined the company's mission as "responsible commercial success," which was operationalized as "consistently meeting or exceeding the legal, ethical, commercial, and other expectations that society has of business."[26] In 1991, LS&CO. introduced a values-driven, principled approach to ethics, replacing its code of ethics (described by one manager as "very proscriptive—rules and regulations in a big binder") with a more open-ended statement of core principles (Exhibit 6). The company also articulated its environmental philosophy and principles.

Though LS&CO.'s Executive Management Committee saw a strong link between good ethics and good business over the long run, they recognized that particular decisions could pose difficult dilemmas. Senior management made it clear that ethics was to be a ground rule, not just a factor in decision making, and that ethical values would take precedence over nonethical values. Moreover, conflicts between and among ethical principles were to be resolved through an ethical process. As the paradigm for all of its decision making, the company adopted the "principled reasoning approach" (PRA), a thorough and explicit procedure that involved six discrete steps: (1) defining the problem, (2) agreeing on the principles to be satisfied, (3) identifying both high-impact and high-influence stakeholders and assessing their claims, (4) brainstorming possible solutions, (5) testing the consequences of chosen solutions, and (6) developing an ethical process for implementing the solution.

LS&CO. managers agreed that this process could be extremely exacting and time consuming, and some favored a more streamlined approach, especially for routine and medium-impact decisions. Yet most were convinced that understanding and applying the PRA was worth the effort. Bob Dunn explained,

> If there is anyone with a moral claim on the outcome [of a decision], their views have to be clear and present. The principled reasoning approach insists that we identify the ethical issues, the people who are affected, the possible solutions, and the ways to minimize harm. At the beginning, people are frustrated with the process, but at the end they feel it serves us well. It prevents the pressure of the moment, of personal involvement from getting in the way. Over time, people do it more naturally.

To support the new thinking and increase the organization's ability to do the right thing, LS&CO. managers developed a three-part core curriculum with a week of leadership training, four days of diversity training, and three days of ethics training, which introduced participants to the PRA. Management modified the criteria for performance evaluations, which were linked to compensation, basing a significant portion of the evaluation on adherence to aspirations and the rest on meeting business goals.

GLOBAL SOURCING GUIDELINES

In September 1991, after several managers expressed misgivings about the business practices employed by some of LS&CO.'s overseas contractors, top management set up a 12-person Sourcing Guidelines Working Group (SGWG) to determine what standards the company should expect of its contractors worldwide. Dunn explained, "As we expanded our operations to more diverse cultures and countries, we felt that we needed to set standards to ensure that our products were being made in a manner consistent with our values, that would not be damaging to our brand image."[27] In looking at both internal and external stakeholders, this senior-level, cross-functional working group would consider the full range of sourcing issues that could affect the company's assets, people, or products. As Dunn noted, they would in many cases be developing a vocabulary for issues previously left to individual discretion.

LS&CO.'s actions coincided with a rising public focus on the issue of supplier standards.

> Scrutiny by labor unions, activists and socially conscious investors is forcing importers to monitor not just their foreign subsidiaries but their far-flung networks of independent suppliers—and their suppliers' suppliers as well. . . . Socially conscious investors and mainstream religious groups promote the positive message that companies should extend their own high standards to all their business partners. Environmentalists and other activists tend toward the more direct pressure that comes from naming names. Union officials are taking a more investigative approach to locate human rights and other violations, including schemes in which foreign manufacturers, especially in China, circumvent U.S. textile quotas by misidentifying the country in which their goods were made.[28]

Some U.S. companies benefiting from questionable labor practices abroad had been targeted on television shows, such as NBC's news magazine

Dateline. At the same time, marketers were beginning to pay more attention to consumers who based their purchasing decisions, at least in part, on ethical concerns. Termed "vigilante consumers" by one British consultant, such consumers were interested not only in the products or services they bought but also "in the behavior of the company behind the brand and the way the product or service is developed."[29] Dunn agreed that consumers were increasingly "sensitive to goods being made under conditions that are not consistent with U.S. values and fairness.[30]

The Saipan Incident

LS&CO.'s sourcing initiative proved timely. The SGWG approved a set of guidelines in December 1991. In February 1992, before the guidelines were ratified by management, the media turned a spotlight on a company supplier in Saipan, a U.S. territory in the western Pacific, accused of paying workers substandard wages and forcing them to work long hours in fenced and guarded factories. In a suit filed four months earlier in October 1991, the U.S. Department of Labor charged that five garment manufacturers owned and operated by the Tan family recruited workers from China— mostly non-English-speaking women in their late teens and early twenties— and then seized their passports and kept them in padlocked and guarded barracks and factories for the duration of their employment contract. The government's investigation, which had begun in 1990, found that Tan employees worked up to 11 hours a day, seven days a week, for as little as $1.65 an hour, well below Saipan's minimum wage of $2.15.[31] The companies were cited also for deducting between $270 and $365 a month from workers' pay for room and board, "management fees," and other expenses.[32]

Saipan manufacturers, such as the Tans, were allowed to ship their goods to the United States, labeled "Made in the U.S.A.," without quota limits or duty. They were exempt from the U.S. minimum wage, but were legally required to comply with all other U.S. labor laws. According to government estimates, the Tan operations manufactured garments worth $100 million to be sold by U.S. clothing companies in the United States under brand names such as Perry Ellis, Eddie Bauer, Chaps Sportswear, Christian Dior, and Van Heusen, as well as private labels.[33]

When queried by LS&CO. managers in San Francisco in late 1991, Tan officials denied the charges and downplayed their seriousness. The media stories prompted LS&CO. to take a closer look. Within 48 hours of the February broadcast, LS&CO. suspended new business with the Tans and sent a team to investigate. As a result of the investigation, LS&CO. canceled its contract with the Tan family, incurring several hundred thousand dollars in contract penalties. Although LS&CO. investigators found the media's allegations of "slave labor" to be unwarranted, the Tan's practices did not conform to the company's new guidelines.

Later in May 1992, as part of a consent decree with the Labor Department, the five Tan companies agreed to pay $9 million in back pay and damages to contract employees who had worked for them from 1988 to 1992. Under the decree, in which the companies neither admitted nor denied breaking the law, they agreed to be monitored for four years.[34] According to Dunn, LS&CO.'s soon-to-be-ratified sourcing guidelines were "the best insurance policy we could have" to deal with the situation. Noted another manager, "If anyone doubted the need for guidelines, this convinced them."

Guidelines Announced

In March 1992, LS&CO. publicly announced its new global sourcing guidelines, which established standards in the areas of worker health and safety, employment practices, ethics, the environment, and human rights. Recognizing that some matters were under the control of individual contractors, whereas others were not, the SGWG had developed the guidelines in two parts: the Business Partner Terms of Engagement (see Exhibit 1) and the Guidelines for Country Selection (see Exhibit 2).

LS&CO. officials expected the standards, which were intended to be visionary and strategic, as well as practical, to result in higher production costs in 1993, affecting both 1993 net income and gross profit.[35] Noted Dunn, "Sourcing decisions that emphasize cost to the exclusion of all other factors will not best serve our long-term business interest. . . . Sometimes it costs a little more in the short term, but it really is possible to have your cake and eat it too."[36]

LS&CO. began an intensive communications program to inform employees and contractors worldwide about the guidelines. According to Sabrina Johnson, a corporate communications manager, the company took care to explain the reasoning behind the guidelines and to convey its willingness to cooperate with contractors in meeting them. Merchandisers, who were responsible for negotiating with and selecting contractors, received special briefings. Senior management indicated the possibility of "margin relief" for merchandisers whose bonuses might suffer if sourcing cost increases were necessary to meet the guidelines.

Business Partner Terms of Engagement

To implement the Business Partner Terms of Engagement, management sent audit teams to inspect the facilities of all the company's contractors. Training for these teams became a top priority. Richard Woo, at the time Community Affairs manager for the Asia Pacific region, was involved in designing and delivering the first training program, which was held in Singapore for employees from 13 Asian nations. Recalling that some managers wondered whether LS&CO. was imposing Western values on the rest of the world, Woo noted the challenge of "calibrating what was happening on the factory floor with the written standards," especially in differing cultural contexts. After refinement, the training program and audit instruments were introduced around the world.

Inspection teams visited more than 700 facilities in 60 countries. LS&CO. managers focused initially on sewing and finishing contractors and planned later to look at suppliers of fabric, sundries (e.g., buttons, thread), and chemicals. The auditors found 70 percent of the contractors to be in compliance. Another 25 percent, found lacking, made significant improvements in bathrooms, emergency exits, ventilation, and wastewater treatment equipment as a result of LS&CO.'s review. About 5 percent were dropped because of poor personnel practices, child labor, health and safety conditions, and trademark or other violations.

The sourcing guidelines introduced new factors into the process for selecting contractors, who had previously been chosen on the basis of price, quality, and delivery time from the pool of firms with available quota.[37] With adoption of the guidelines, LS&CO. began to require that potential contractors satisfy the Business Partner Terms of Engagement and the company's environmental principles, in addition to meeting the traditional selection criteria. LS&CO. sought long-term relationships and offered contractors large-volume orders and technical advice. Many contractors liked to have LS&CO. as a customer and took pride in their ability to meet the company's demanding quality standards. Having LS&CO. on a contractor's "resume" could help attract new business. At the same time, contractors resisted becoming too dependent on LS&CO. and claimed they could not make as much money on LS&CO. contracts as on some others.

Recognizing that certain improvements, particularly environmental ones, could be costly, LS&CO. sometimes accepted higher prices or offered contractors generous timetables, loans, and volume guarantees. However, contractors slow to upgrade their practices were reminded that LS&CO. would have to discontinue the relationship if changes were not made by the agreed-on deadline. In some instances, LS&CO. took extra steps to help contractors meet the guidelines. In Bangladesh, for example, two contractors employing underage workers agreed to send them to school—with pay—after LS&CO. offered to cover the cost of their books, tuition, and uniforms. The contractors agreed to rehire the children wishing to return when they turned 14. In both instances, the children represented less than 2 percent of the contractor's 200-person workforce.

Though a few contractors balked at making improvements, most were quite receptive. According to Y.S. Chan, manager of the Hong Kong branch of LS&CO.'s Asian sourcing organization,

> Most contractors don't mind spending money to make the improvements we recommend, since we try to be fair and reasonable, and we make it clear that we would like to work together. . . . We don't force things. . . . There are different ways to establish mutual understanding.

One approach was to show contractors video clips from television documentaries exposing shoddy conditions. A manager involved in training LS&CO. inspection teams around the world found that "regardless of whether they agreed with the media coverage or not, they understood [the relationship between the guidelines and the brand]."

Iain Lyon, vice president of Offshore Sourcing and, later, a member of the CPG, recalled his apprehension at the guidelines initiative. "This was America interfering with another country's business," he remembered thinking. But Lyon, English by birth, changed his mind after seeing the specifics of the company's approach and "how quickly contractors see the point and want to do the right thing." He added, "It's hard for anyone to say it's wrong to open up the fire exits, stop polluting, or give children an education." A relative newcomer to the company, Lyon found LS&CO.'s approach refreshing. He noted, "The vast majority [of sourcing managers outside LS&CO.] don't give a damn . . . Taking maximum advantage of contractors seems okay because they are foreigners. Getting away from that has been a great relief to me. . . ."

THE CHINA SITUATION

When the China Policy Group began its work in late 1992, LS&CO.'s presence in China was small. Though the company had been sourcing in China since 1986, sales remained "minuscule" since Levis® clothing was not mass marketed there. In early 1991, LS&CO. managers had decided in the "11th hour" of negotiations to forgo a China joint venture to produce clothes for sale in local markets after discovering that the venture would be responsible for enforcing China's one-child-per-family policy. In many parts of China, the work group was still the central organizing fact of life—where citizens received medical care and women registered their chosen form of birth control. Employers could be required to fine or dock the pay of workers who had second children. Some worker groups, it was reported, used physical force to "encourage" abortions and sterilization, even though such tactics were unlawful. Although support for the government's birth control policy was widespread in China, many LS&CO. managers found it abhorrent to risk involvement in family planning at this level. Operational concerns added to the troublesome nature of the venture.

Senior management put the China issue on hold, waiting until the company fully implemented its new principled reasoning approach (PRA) and global sourcing strategy. At that point, wrote the president of LS&CO.'s Asia-Pacific division, the company would be better prepared "to address the human rights issues in a full, responsible, [and] effective way." Meanwhile, LS&CO. made no direct investment in China, although Asia managers continued to investigate and hoped to enter the market at sometime in the future. By 1993, some of LS&CO.'s low-priced jeans competitors were beginning to become popular in China.

As for sourcing in China, LS&CO. purchased, either directly or indirectly through contractors, a large quantity of sundries (buttons, thread, and labels) and about eight million yards of fabric in China, which was increasingly popular as a site for fabric mills relocating from other parts of Asia.[38] The company also sourced about five million items of clothing (called "units"), totalling about $50 million, from Chinese sewing and laundry contractors.[39] More than half the units sourced in China were finished in Hong Kong and shipped to the United States with a "Made in Hong Kong" label as part of Hong Kong's legal quota.[40]

Any change in LS&CO.'s China stance would be felt most directly by employees in the Hong Kong branch of the company's Asian sourcing organization. Responsible for all Hong Kong and China sourcing, the 120-person office arranged for a total of 20 million to 22 million units from about 20 contractors in 1992. The Hong Kong branch was confident there would be no problem finding satisfactory contractors if LS&CO. expanded its China presence. In fact, the company's Chinese contractors were doing well under the Business Partner Teams of Engagement—better even than contractors in some other parts of Asia with whom LS&CO. had very successful relationships.

However, withdrawing from China was another matter. Even though China represented only about 10 percent of LS&CO.'s total Asian contracting (and 2% of worldwide contracting), it would not be easy to find alternative contractors with available quota at reasonable prices. In most Asian countries, the largest part of the quota was held by a few large contractors, with the remainder spread among many small ones. Moving production would mean increasing the number of contractors, sacrificing scale economies, and increasing auditing costs. Also, shifting production to other locations would add to the cost and complexity of transportation. (Items sourced in China could be transported relatively easily to Hong Kong, the preferred port for shipping to the United States.) Employment opportunities in the Hong Kong office would very likely diminish. It was estimated that moving production to other parts of Asia over a three-year period would raise costs between 4 percent and 10 percent, depending on the country.

Business Conditions

In contrast to LS&CO., many companies were rushing to establish an early foothold in China. Economic liberalization of the Chinese economy and a shift toward free markets which had begun in the late 1970s ushered in a period of rapid growth, estimated at more than 10 percent a year.[41] With retail sales rising an average of 15 percent per year since 1979[42] and a potential market of more than one billion customers, a U.S. Treasury Department official predicted that "China will soon have the world's second-biggest economy."[43]

Procter & Gamble, Johnson & Johnson, and H.J. Heinz were among the firms adding production facilities in 1993. Coca-Cola Co. Chairman Roberto C. Goizueta announced a deal to add 10 bottling plants to increase the total to 22, noting that the Chinese market had "virtually limitless long-term potential."[44] Total U.S. investment was expected to increase to $5 billion in 1993, up from less than $0.5 billion in 1990; U.S. exports rose from $5 billion to $9 billion during the same period.[45] In 1992, U.S. imports from China totaled $26 billion, mostly consumer goods such as clothing, shoes, and toys.[46] One commentator noted,

> If you don't take the dive into China, you may be missing the biggest sales opportunity of your generation. It could take years for your investment to bear fruit, but right now—while the market's still immature—may well be the time to make the jump. China may pitch into convulsions tomorrow, but that will always be a risk. And remember, that's also what people were saying about Japan in the 1950s.[47]

The apparel and textile industry was particularly active in China. With shipments totaling $7.3 billion a year, China was the largest supplier of textiles and apparel to the United States, accounting for 20 percent to 25 percent of U.S. textile and apparel sales.[48] The removal of trade quotas for Chinese-made apparel (likely to occur if China were admitted to GATT), would most certainly boost China's share even more.

Challenges

Nevertheless, China still posed difficulties for business. Outmoded infrastructure and tariffs meant it was difficult and expensive to transport goods across its vast distances. Though large, the China market was hardly unified; tastes and buying power varied greatly by region, and distribution systems were chaotic or nonexistent. Furthermore, economic growth had been accompanied by inflation and sharp rises in stock prices and property values, adding to the cost of doing business and the expense of stationing American workers in major Chinese cities. Restrictions on imports and currency convertibility created other problems. And, the threat of political instability was always present.[49] China experts consulted by the CGPG advised that the death of Deng Xiao Ping, China's then 88-year-old leader, could be followed by a period of chaos, probably with increased repression, social unrest, and anti-foreign sentiment. A coup or another "Cultural Revolution" could not be ruled out.

The CPG learned that foreign companies operating in China were under increasing pressure to accept government-backed Communist party representation on their boards and faced intensified levels of government inspections and audits. Though government-supported party organizing in the workplace was common, union organizing was illegal. Since 1989, companies' authority to hire, fire, and compensate employees as they wished had become more limited. The wages payable by joint ventures were capped at 150 percent of the amount paid by state-owned enterprises. To secure greater control over the workplace, some companies had chosen to establish wholly owned enterprises rather than joint ventures. Companies taking the joint venture route favored partnerships with private companies, collectively owned companies, or local government entities rather than national or provincial government entities.

The Chinese legal system remained a concern. Business laws and their enforcement lagged behind economic development, and the country still ran on power politics and personal relationships. Corruption was a problem, and public officials sometimes accepted bribes.[50] Laws and rules were vague and arbitrarily enforced. In the apparel industry, manufacturers were allowed to use false country-of-origin labels to avoid U.S. quotas.[51] If caught by U.S. Customs, these mislabeled goods were deducted from China's quota, reducing the quota amount that remained and potentially jeopardizing U.S. companies' ability to take delivery on contracted items. The Chinese government lacked clear policies on foreign investment, though officials eagerly courted foreign capital and technology. Withdrawal from joint ventures posed particular problems for foreign firms because dissolution required the Chinese partner's consent. Unable to secure such consent, some Western companies had been forced to abandon the assets of their ventures.

Protection of intellectual property, nonexistent under communist ideology, was a particular worry for many American businesses. Copyright and patent protection had existed on paper since 1979, but, according to the U.S. Embassy, "procedures for enforcement were still unclear." Legislation implementing trademark laws was not passed until 1987. The U.S. government called China "the single largest pirator of U.S. copyrights" and estimated the cost to American companies at $400 million in 1991.[52] In 1992, U.S. customs made 104 seizures of counterfeit merchandise worth $4.56 million in China, second only to its seizures of $5.85 million in goods from South Korea.[53] In January 1992, under pressure from the U.S. government, China agreed to improve protection of intellectual property by extending patent protection on chemicals and pharmaceuticals to 20 years, joining international copyright conventions, and agreeing to protect all existing copyrights on computers, software, books, and recordings. However, later that year, some companies still complained about a lack of "follow up."[54] LS&CO.'s legal department could find no reports of successful actions for trademark infringement in China.

As of May 1992, customs seizures had netted nearly two million pairs of counterfeit "501" jeans produced in China with "Made in the U.S.A." labels. Most were destined for Europe. According to David Saenz, LS&CO.'s director of Corporate Security, few consumers could detect the jeans failure to meet Levi's® standards. He noted also that Chinese authorities had been cooperative in investigating reports of false labeling.[55] However, their effectiveness was limited by China's size and the fragmentation of political power. In 1993, the problem of counterfeit jeans from China persisted; it remained unclear how aggressive U.S. and Chinese officials would be in trying to shut down factories making such goods.[56]

Human Rights

The CPG learned that leading human rights organizations considered China's human rights record among the worst in the world. Using the 1948 Universal Declaration of Human Rights as a benchmark, organizations such as the United Nations, Human Rights Watch, and Amnesty International, found human rights violations in China to be severe and persistent.[57] [*Note:* The Universal Declaration of Human Rights, adopted by the United Nations General Assembly, December 10, 1948, appears on p. 385 of this book.] Freedom House, for example, included China among the countries where political rights and civil liberties were absent or virtually nonexistent in 1992.[58] Since the Tiananmen Square attack on pro-democracy students in June 1989, the Chinese Communist Party had reportedly continued its harsh practices with the backing of its military and other security forces. There had never been a comprehensive public accounting of those detained after the Tiananmen demonstrations.

According to the U.S. State Department, China's human rights practices fell "far short of internationally accepted norms."[59] However, the State Department did note some "modest progress" in resolving a few individual human rights cases and reported that "rigid ideological controls reimposed after June 1989 were beginning to ease."[60] Human rights groups reported problems in three areas: the legal process, expression and association, and prison labor.

Legal Process. Trials of dissidents, religious figures, and other political offenders often violated China's own legal principles, as well as international standards of due process and fair-trial procedures. Trials were conducted rapidly, often in secret by judges, police, and prosecution working together; defendants had limited access to legal counsel; and many were threatened with a harsher sentence if they did not "show the right attitude" and confess. The country's security apparatus was responsible for numerous instances of arbitrary arrest, detention without formal legal proceedings, maltreatment, and torture. Furthermore, there were no independent Chinese organizations that publicly monitored human rights conditions, and authorities made it clear that they would not allow the existence of such groups.

Expression and Association. Although guaranteed by the Chinese Constitution, freedom of expression and association were severely restricted. Some well-known dissidents were not permitted to travel abroad. The press and academic institutions were tightly controlled, and the authorities extensively monitored personal and family life. Freedom of religion, also constitutionally guaranteed, became increasingly difficult in the 1990s, with government crackdowns on Christian, Buddhist, and Muslim religious groups that refused to practice their faith through government-supervised bodies particularly in Tibet and Mongolia, where cultural and religious groups were intertwined with forces for independence. Though laws existed to protect minorities and women, discrimination based on sex, religion, and ethnicity continued in practice in the areas of housing, jobs, and education.

Prison Labor. Although China had mostly ended its traditional use of massive forced labor to build public facilities, there was still some reliance on "mobilized" workers for security forces and public works. Moreover, imprisonment usually involved forced labor in prison or in the *laogai*,[61] a network of government "reeducation" camps where political and other offenders were compelled to work for little or no pay in tiring and often dangerous conditions. It was difficult to estimate accurately the extent of forced-labor production. A news article reported that one such prison facility consisted of 850 textile looms capable of producing sweaters worth "hundreds of millions of dollars" annually, all for export.[62] Chinese authorities valued prison labor production at about $500 million in 1990, not including output from the *laogai*. In 1991, the U.S. State Department found "substantial evidence" that China was exporting products produced with forced labor.[63] Since imports of products made by convict labor were prohibited under the Hawley-Smoot Tariff Act of 1930, the U.S. government responded by barring specific Chinese products known to be produced with prison labor from entry into the country.

In August 1992, the U.S. State Department and China's Ministry of Foreign Affairs signed an agreement prohibiting forced-labor exports and permitting the United States to inspect certain facilities to ensure compliance with the agreement.[64] Nonetheless, press accounts indicated that neither the suppliers in question nor the Chinese authorities could always be relied on to monitor abuses. Peter Yeo, an aide to the U.S. House of Representatives Subcommittee on Trade and the Environment, cautioned, "Don't trust your suppliers to tell the truth."[65] Harry Wu, a research fellow at Stanford University's Hoover Institute, and a dissident who had spent 19 years in China's prisons, claimed that guarantees provided by government officials were worthless.[66] In 1993, the U.S. Customs Department reported that the Chinese government had denied members of the U.S. Embassy access to all or parts of five factories, in violation of the earlier agreement. Monitoring difficulties were compounded because forced-labor exports were "often falsely labeled, mixed with other products and sold through intermediaries," according to the Customs Department's memorandum.[67]

Chinese Government's Response. The Chinese government rejected reports made by the U.S. State Department, Amnesty International, and Asia Watch on its human rights violations.

> Despite the [Chinese] Government's adherence to the United Nations Charter, which mandates respect for and promotion of human rights, Chinese officials do not accept the principle that human rights are universal. They argue that each nation has its own concept of human rights, grounded in its political, economic, and social system and its historical, religious, and cultural background. Officials no longer dismiss all discussion of human rights as interference in the country's internal affairs, but remain reluctant to accept criticism of China's human rights situation by other nations or international organization.[68]

However, Chinese officials had begun to promote academic study and discussion of concepts of human rights. Chinese research institutes organized centers and symposia on the subject and sent a group to France, Sweden, and the United Kingdom to study human rights practices there.

Engage or Withdraw. Thus, China presented a thorny problem; many considered it "the proverbial test case."[69] It was a country both "marred by systematic violations of fundamental rights, and at the same time . . . in massive need of support in reaching its development and modernization goals."[70] Human rights activists were divided as to whether socially responsible corporations should "remain and act as a progressive force or divest and withdraw."[71] Those advocating divestment argued that "economic growth and trade will merely finance a corrupt Communist elite"[72] and that the Chinese government would use the presence of reputable companies "to boost its image and maintain its grip on power." They argued that development and growth in Southern China's special economic zones had not been accompanied by human rights advances. Advocates for a presence in China believed that foreign corporations that were "actively engaged" with the Chinese economy were "helping to create power structures outside the government and state industries."[73] They stressed the dangers of isolating China, arguing that constructive engagement could contribute to human rights improvements. In South China, they said, people had become free to start their own businesses, to change jobs at will, and to talk and travel. . . .

THE DECISION

CPG members had met five times for a total of 19 days between November 1992 and February 1993. They had heard directly from a wide range of internal and external stakeholders, along with outside sources knowledgeable about the China situation. They included a former prisoner in China, a former head of the U.S.-China Business Council, and several China experts, as well as representatives of human rights organizations, the U.S. government, Chinese prodemocracy groups, U.S. labor unions, and other companies doing business in China. With the information and insights gained from these sources, the CPG was reviewing the company's global sourcing guidelines and working through the steps of the principled reasoning approach (PRA). Soon the group would have to settle on its recommendation to LS&CO.'s Executive Management Committee.

EXHIBIT 1.   Levi Strauss & Co. Global Sourcing Guidelines, Business Partner Terms of Engagement

---

BUSINESS PARTNER TERMS OF ENGAGEMENT

Our concerns include the practices of individual business partners as well as the political and social issues in those countries where we might consider sourcing.

This defines Terms of Engagement which addresses issues that are substantially controllable by our individual business partners.

We have defined business partners as contractors and suppliers who provide labor and/or material (including fabric, sundries, chemicals and/or stones) utilized in the manufacture and finishing of our products.

1. **Environmental Requirements**

    We will only do business with partners who share our commitment to the environment. (Note: We intend this standard to be consistent with the approved language of Levi Strauss & Co.'s Environmental Action Group.)

2. **Ethical Standards**

    We will seek to identify and utilize business partners who aspire as individuals and in the conduct of their business to a set of ethical standards not incompatible with our own.

3. **Health & Safety**

    We will seek to identify and utilize business partners who provide workers with a safe and healthy work environment. Business partners who provide residential facilities for their workers must provide safe and healthy facilities.

4. **Legal Requirements**

    We expect our business partners to be law abiding as individuals and to comply with legal requirements relevant to the conduct of their business.

5. **Employment Standards**

    We will only do business with partners whose workers are in all cases present voluntarily, not put at risk of physical harm, fairly compensated, allowed the right of free association and not exploited in any way. In addition, the following specific guidelines will be followed.

    (Continued)

EXHIBIT 1. *(Continued)*

- **Wages and Benefits**

  We will only do business with partners who provide wages and benefits that comply with any applicable law or match the prevailing local manufacturing or finishing industry practices. We will also favor business partners who share our commitment to contribute to the betterment of community conditions.

- **Working Hours**

  While permitting flexibility in scheduling, we will identify prevailing local work hours and seek business partners who do not exceed them except for appropriately compensated overtime. While we favor partners who utilize less than sixty-hour work weeks, we will not use contractors who, on a regularly scheduled basis, require in excess of a sixty-hour week. Employees should be allowed one day off in seven days.

- **Child Labor**

  Use of child labor is not permissible. "Child" is defined as less than 14 years of age or younger than the compulsory age to be in school. We will not utilize partners who use child labor in any of their facilities. We support the development of legitimate workplace apprenticeship programs for the educational benefit of younger people.

- **Prison Labor/Forced Labor**

  We will not knowingly utilize prison or forced labor in contracting or subcontracting relationships in the manufacture of our products. We will not knowingly utilize or purchase materials from a business partner utilizing prison or forced labor.

- **Discrimination**

  While we recognize and respect cultural differences, we believe that workers should be employed on the basis of their ability to do the job, rather than on the basis of personal characteristics or beliefs. We will favor business partners who share this value.

- **Disciplinary Practices**

  We will not utilize business partners who use corporal punishment or other forms of mental or physical coercion.

Note

Source: Company document.

EXHIBIT 2. Levis Strauss & Co. Global Sourcing Guidelines, Guidelines for Country Selection

---

GUIDELINES FOR COUNTRY SELECTION

The following country selection criteria address issues which we believe are beyond the ability of individual business partners to control.

1. **Brand Image**

    We will not initiate or renew contractual relationships in countries where sourcing would have an adverse effect on our global brand image.

2. **Health & Safety**

    We will not initiate or renew contractual relationships in locations where there is evidence that Company employees or representatives would be exposed to unreasonable risk.

3. **Human Rights**

    We should not initiate or renew contractual relationships in countries where there are pervasive violations of basic human rights.

4. **Legal Requirements**

    We will not initiate or renew contractual relationships in countries where the legal environment creates unreasonable risk to our trademarks or to other important commercial interests or seriously impedes our ability to implement these guidelines.

5. **Political or Social Stability**

    We will not initiate or renew contractual relationships in countries where political or social turmoil unreasonably threatens our commercial interests.

Note

Source: Company document.

EXHIBIT 3. Levi Strauss Associates Inc., U.S. and Non–U.S. Operations, 1990–1992 ($000s)

The following table presents information concerning U.S. and non-U.S. operations (all in the apparel industry).

	1992	1991	1990
Net sales to unaffiliated customers:			
United States	$3,482,927	$2,997,144	$2,560,662
Europe	1,367,783	1,209,428	1,032,404
Other non–U.S.	719,580	696,310	654,084
	$5,570,290	$4,902,882	$4,247,150
Sales between operations:			
United States	$139,652	$111,742	$121,134
Europe	28	67	383
Other non–U.S.	34,467	9,842	7,238
	$174,147	$121,651	$128,755
Total sales:			
United States	$3,622,579	$3,108,886	$2,681,796
Europe	1,367,811	1,209,495	1,032,787
Other non–U.S.	754,047	706,152	661,322
Eliminations	(174,147)	(121,651)	(128,755)
	$5,570,290	$4,902,882	$4,247,150
Contribution to income before other charges:			
United States	$460,218	$390,468	$312,697
Europe	362,174	334,220	295,954
Other non–U.S.	151,644	137,359	136,468
	$974,036	$862,047	$745,119
Other charges:			
Corporate expenses, net	$128,648	$99,310	$108,495
Interest expense	53,303	71,384	82,956
Stock option charge	157,964	—	—
Income before taxes and extraordinary loss:	$634,121	$691,353	$553,668
Assets:			
United States	$1,480,527	$1,346,033	$1,251,537
Europe	491,491	400,197	376,780
Other non–U.S.	273,355	317,284	272,549
Corporate	635,328	569,870	488,991
	$2,880,701	$2,633,384	$2,389,857

Source: Levi Strauss Associates Inc., Form 10-K/A Amendment No. 1, July 30, 1993.

Gains or losses resulting from certain foreign-currency hedge transactions are included in other expense, net, and amounted to losses of $10.2 million, $19.7 million, and $18.3 million for 1992, 1991, and 1990, respectively.

EXHIBIT 4. Labor Costs and Operator Hours, Production Workers in the Textile and Apparel Industries—Selected Countries, 1993

Country	Hourly Labor Cost Textile (in US$)	Hourly Labor Cost Apparel (in US$)	Normal Equivalent Days Worked Textile (per operator per year)
North America			
United States	11.61	8.13	241
Canada	13.44	9.14	237
Mexico	2.93	1.08	286
European Community			
Denmark	21.32	17.29	226
France	16.49	14.84	233
East Germany[a]	14.17	11.90	231
West Germany[a]	20.50	17.22	232
Greece	7.13	5.85	231
Holland	20.82	15.41	207
Ireland	9.18	7.44	243
Portugal	3.70	3.03	246
United Kingdom	10.27	8.42	234
Other European Countries			
Austria	18.81	14.30	231
Czech Republic	1.43	1.29	223
Finland	11.86	9.25	236
Hungary	1.80	1.62	233
Slovakia	1.29	1.14	230
Switzerland	22.32	18.08	227
Near East			
Israel	7.20	5.54	244
Syria	1.12	0.84	275
Turkey	4.44	3.29	300
Africa			
Egypt	0.57	0.43	288
Mauritius	1.42	1.04	285
South Africa	1.64	1.12	302
Tanzania	0.22	0.18	239
Tunisia	2.97	1.54	232
Zambia	0.32	0.24	249
Zimbabwe	0.47	0.35	278
South America			
Argentina	2.47	1.85	268
Brazil	1.46	0.73	274
Peru	1.43	1.00	276
Uruguay	3.09	2.35	288
Venezuela	1.90	1.48	245
Asia and Pacific			
Australia	10.84	8.67	229
Bangladesh	0.23	0.16	250

(Continued)

EXHIBIT 4. *(Continued)*

Country	Hourly Labor Cost Textile (in US$)	Hourly Labor Cost Apparel (in US$)	Normal Equivalent Days Worked Textile (per operator per year)
Peoples Republic of China	0.36	0.25	306
Hong Kong	3.85	3.85	294
India	0.56	0.27	289
Indonesia	0.43	0.28	297
Japan	23.65	10.64	261
South Korea	3.66	2.71	312
Malaysia	1.18	0.77	261
Pakistan	0.44	0.27	310
Philippines	0.78	0.53	288
Singapore	3.56	3.06	284
Taiwan	5.76	4.61	291
Thailand	1.04	0.71	341
Vietnam	0.37	0.26	287

aDesignations "East" and "West" are used for economic purposes only.

Source: Compiled by casewriter based on data from Werner International Management Consultants, New York, New York.

EXHIBIT 5. Levi-Strauss & Co. Mission Statement and Aspiration Statement

MISSION STATEMENT

The mission of Levi Strauss & Co. is to sustain responsible commercial success as a global marketing company of branded casual apparel. We must balance goals of superior profitability and return on investment, leadership market positions, and superior products and service. We will conduct our business ethically and demonstrate leadership in satisfying our responsibilities to our communities and to society. Our work environment will be safe and productive and characterized by fair treatment, teamwork, open communication, personal accountability and opportunities for growth and development.

ASPIRATION STATEMENT

We all want a company that our people are proud of and committed to, where all employees have an opportunity to contribute, learn, grow, and advance based on merit, not politics or background. We want our people to feel respected, treated fairly, listened to, and involved. Above all, we want satisfaction from accomplishments and friendships, balanced personal and professional lives, and to have fun in our endeavors.

When we describe the kind of LS&CO., we want in the future, what we are talking about is building on the foundation we have inherited: affirming the best of our Company's traditions, closing gaps that may exist between principles and practices, and updating some of our values to reflect contemporary circumstances. What type of leadership is necessary to make our Aspirations a Reality?

New Behaviors

Leadership that exemplifies directness, openness to influence, commitment to the success of others, willingness to acknowledge our own contributions to problems, personal accountability, teamwork, and trust. Not only must we model these behaviors but we must coach others to adopt them.

Diversity

Leadership that values a diverse work force (age, sex, ethnic group, etc.) at all levels of the organization, diversity in experience, and diversity in perspectives. We have committed to taking full advantage of the rich backgrounds and abilities of all our people and to promote a greater diversity in positions of influence. Differing points of view will be sought; diversity will be valued and honesty rewarded, not suppressed.

Recognition

Leadership that provides greater recognition—both financial and psychic—for individuals and teams that contribute to our success. Recognition must be given to all who contribute; those who create and innovate and also those who continually support the day-to-day business requirements.

Ethical Management Practices

Leadership that epitomizes the stated standards of ethical behavior. We must provide clarity about our expectations and must enforce these standards through the corporation.

Communications

Leadership that is clear about company, unit, and individual goals and performance. People must know what is expected of them and receive timely, honest feedback on their performance and career aspirations.

Empowerment

Leadership that increases the authority and responsibility of those closest to our products and customers. By actively pushing responsibility, trust, and recognition into the organization, we can harness and release the capabilities of all our people.

Note

Source: Company document.

EXHIBIT 6. Levi Strauss & Co. Code of Ethics and Ethical Principles

---

CODE OF ETHICS

Levi Strauss & Co. has a long and distinguished history of ethical conduct and community involvement. Essentially, these are a reflection of the mutually-shared values of the founding families and of our employees.

Our ethical values are based on the following elements:

- A commitment to commercial success in terms broader than merely financial measures.
- A respect for our employees, suppliers, customers, consumers and stockholders.
- A commitment to conduct which is not only legal, but fair, and morally correct in a fundamental sense.
- Avoidance of not only real, but the appearance of conflict of interest.

From time to time the Company will publish specific guidelines, policies and procedures. However, the best test whether something is ethically correct is whether you would be prepared to present it to our senior management and board of directors as being consistent with our ethical traditions. If you have any uneasiness about an action you are about to take or which you see, you should discuss the action with your supervisor or management.

ETHICAL PRINCIPLES

Our ethical principles are the values that set the ground rules for all that we do as employees of Levi Strauss & Co. As we seek to achieve responsible commercial success, we will be challenged to balance these principles against each other, always mindful of our promise to shareholders that we will achieve responsible commercial success.

The ethical principles are:

Honesty: We will not say things that are false. We will never deliberately mislead. We will be as candid as possible, openly and freely sharing information, as appropriate to the relationship.

Promise-Keeping: We will go to great lengths to keep our commitments. We will not make promises that can't be kept and we will not make promises on behalf of the Company unless we have the authority to do so.

Fairness: We will create and follow a process and achieve outcomes that a reasonable person would call just, even-handed and nonarbitrary.

Respect for Others: We will be open and direct in our communication and receptive to influence. We will honor and value the abilities and contributions of others, embracing the responsibility and accountability for our actions in this regard.

Compassion: We will maintain an awareness of the needs of others and act to meet those needs whenever possible. We will also minimize harm whenever possible. We will act in ways that are consistent with our commitment to social responsibility.

Integrity: We will live up to LS&CO.'s ethical principles; even when confronted by personal, professional and social risks, as well as economic pressures.

Note

Source: Company document.

Notes

1. For example, see "A stitch in time," *The Economist,* June 6, 1992, p. 27 ff.
2. Members were drawn from Human Resources, Levi Strauss International, Legal, Global Sourcing, the Asian Pacific Division, and Corporate Affairs.
3. Michael Janofsky, "Whether It's Bluejeans or Mini-Motors or Power Plants. . . : Levis Strauss, American Symbol with A Cause," *The New York Times,* January 3, 1994, p. C4 ff.
4. "Levi Strauss & Co. and the AIDS Crisis," HBS case No. 391-189, p. 5.
5. "Levi Strauss & Co. and the AIDS Crisis," p. 5.
6. Frank Swoboda, "Levi Strauss to Drop Suppliers Violating Its Worker Rights Rules," *The Washington Post,* March 13, 1992, p. D1 ff.
7. Kenneth How, "The Finance Lowdown on 25 Big Private Firms," *The San Francisco Chronicle,* September 23, 1993, p. D2 ff.
8. Gavin Power, "Levi's Plan to Sew up Europe Growth Aided by Rise of 42% in Yearly Profits," *The San Francisco Chronicle,* February 20, 1992, p. B1 ff.
9. "Apparel Business Unwrinkled by Retailing Slump" *San Francisco Business Times,* May 22, 1992, p. 5 ff.
10. John Eckhouse, "Record Profit as Levi's Sales Top $5 Billion," *The San Francisco Chronicle,* March 2, 1993, p. D2.
11. Ros Davidson, "Levi Strauss Sees Red Over Jeans Grey market," *Reuters,* September 10, 1993. Levi also feared that U.S. retailers, in clearing their shelves to grey-market buyers, might be unable to offer the full selection to regular customers. As a result, it raised U.S. prices to "narrow the gap" and asked U.S. retailers to limit the number of jeans sold to each shopper.
12. Levi Strauss & Co., *Fact Sheet,* company document, May 1993.
13. The study also valued the Nike brand (sneakers) at $3.497 billion. See "Brands," *Financial World,* September 1, 1993, p. 41.
14. Levi Strauss & Co., *Fact Sheet.*
15. Dr. Herman Starobin, research director, International Ladies Garment Workers Union, AFL–CIO, statement before the U.S. House of Representatives Ways and Means Committee, September 15, 1993.
16. Robert Levering and Milton Moskowitz, *The 100 Best Companies to Work for in America* (New York: Doubleday, 1993), pp. 501–502.

17. "Levi Strauss & Co. and the AIDS Crisis," p. 7.
18. "Levi Strauss & Co. and the AIDs Crisis," p. 6.
19. Louise Kehoe, "Bold Fashion Statement," *Financial Times,* May 8, 1993, p. 9 ff.
20. Robert Howard, "Values Make the Company," *Harvard Business Review,* September–October 1990, p. 134.
21. Robert Howard, p. 134.
22. Robert Howard, p. 138.
23. Robert Howard, p. 134.
24. Levi Strauss & Co., "Going Global," company document, January 31, 1994, p. 11.
25. David Sheff, "Mr. Blue Jeans," *San Francisco Focus,* October 1993, p. 128.
26. The LS&CO. definition of "responsible commercial success" was adapted from the work of Professor Archie B. Carroll, a management professor specializing in corporate responsibility at the University of Georgia.
27. Louise Kehoe, p. 9 ff.
28. John McCormack and Marc Levinson, "The Supply Police," *Newsweek,* February 15, 1993, p. 48 ff.
29. Nicole Dickenson, "Consumers Get Ethical With Choices," *South China Morning Post,* May 29, 1993, supplement.
30. Brian Dumaine, p. 10 ff.
31. "A Stitch in Time," p. 27 ff.
32. "U.S. Alleges Illegal Treatment of Garment Workers in Saipan," *Reuters,* October 1, 1991.
33. Frank Swoboda, p. D1 ff.
34. "Five Saipan Garment Manufactures to Pay $9 Million to Settle FLSA Suit," *BNA International Business Daily,* May 26, 1992.
35. Levi Strauss Associates Inc., *Form 10-K/A Amendment No. 1,* July 30, 1993, p. 3.
36. "Apparel Makers Can Do Well By Doing the Right Thing," *Apparel Industry Magazine,* September 1993, pp. 108–110.
37. The United States limited apparel and textile imports through quotas permitted by the MultiFiber Arrangement (MFA) under the auspices of the General Agreement on Tariffs and Trade (GATT). The MFA allowed the United States to set quotas, either by imposing them unilaterally or, more commonly, by negotiating bilateral agreements with other nations. Most Asian countries, including China, had an agreement with the United States which established that country's quota by product type and fiber content—men's cotton pants, men's noncotton pants, and so on. These agreements had some flexibility: there were usually provisions for category shifting, for borrowing against next year's quota, and for increasing the quota each year. Each government had the right to administer and divide that country's quota among local contractors on whatever basis they desired. Most countries distributed quota based on past shipping record; those contractors who had shipped large quantities in the past were most likely to get assigned large quota again, so as to minimize the risk of not shipping all allowable quota. Under serious consideration in 1993 was a proposal to phase out all textile and apparel quotas for GATT signatories over a 10-year period.
38. Levi did not contract directly with fabric mills for fabric purchases. Instead, the mill generally contracted with the sewing firm, which in turn, contracted with Levi.
39. Jim Carlton, "Ties With China Will Be Curbed by Levi Strauss," *The Wall Street Journal,* May 4, 1993, p. A3 ff.
40. This system of "outward processing," which was entirely legal, permitted apparel companies to take advantage of Hong Kong's large quota, while substantially bypassing its expensive wage rates.
41. "Cracking the China Market," *The Wall Street Journal,* December 10, 1993, p. R1.
42. Sally D. Goll and Yukimo Ono, "Consuming Passions," *The Wall Street Journal,* December 10, 1993, p. R15.
43. Joyce Barnathan, Lynn Curry, Owen Ullmann, "Behind the Great Wall," *Business Week,* October 25, 1993, p. 43.

44. Pete Engardio, Lynn Curry, Joyce Barnathan, "China Fever Strikes Again," *Business Week,* March 29, 1993, p. 46 ff.

45. Joyce Barnathan, Lynn Curry, and Owen Ullman, p. 43.

46. Daniel Southerland, "China Purchases Nearly $1 Billion in U.S. Goods; Recent Buying Spree Turned a Bid to Preserve Trade Status," *The Washington Post,* April 13, 1993, p. A23 ff.

47. "Cracking the China Market," p. R1.

48. David Skidmore, "U.S. Penalizes China Over Illegal Trade," *The Boston Globe,* January 7, 1994, p. 59.

49. China Supplement, *The Wall Street Journal,* December 10, 1993, p. R1 ff.

50. China Supplement, p. R1 ff.

51. John Maggs, "Levi's Get the Blues After Explosion of Fakes Hits the Market," *Journal of Commerce,* December 29, 1991, p. B8 ff.

52. Stuart Auerbach, "China, U.S. Reach Trade Accord; Beijing Agrees to Curb Piracy of Products, Safeguarded Material," *The Washington Post,* January 17, 1992, p. A24 ff.

53. Louise Lucas, "U.S. Brings War Against Copiers from H.K.," *South China Morning Post,* January 6, 1993, p. 3 ff. Officials believed that merchandise seized at customs represented only a fraction of all counterfeit goods because only a small portion of all imports were examined. As in the instances of mislabeled goods, the amounts seized were deducted from China's quota.

54. Nancy Dunne, "Patent Pirates 'Still Dodging the Rules': U.S. Complaints Over Enforcement of Anti-Counterfeiting Measures," *Financial Times,* December 3, 1992, p. 6 ff.

55. John Maggs, p. B8 ff.

56. Jim Doyle, "U.S. Crackdown on Bogus Levi's; Smuggling Ring Accused of Plot to Import Jeans Made in China," *The San Francisco Chronicle,* November 13, 1993, p. A17 ff.

57. For 1992, China appeared on the "worst country" lists prepared by Freedom House, the World Human Rights Guide, and the United Nations Commission on Human Rights.

58. Other countries on the list were Afghanistan, Burma, Cuba, Equatorial Guinea, Haiti, Iraq, North Korea, Libya, Somalia, Sudan, Syria, and Vietnam.

59. For a catalog of human rights practices in China, see, for example, *Country Reports on Human Rights Practices for 1992,* pp. 540–554.

60. *Country Reports on Human Rights Practices for 1992,* p. 540.

61. The term *laogai,* pronounced lau-guy, means "reform through labor."

62. Joyce Barnathan, "It's Time to Put Screws to China's Gulag," *Business Week,* December 30, 1991/January 6, 1992, p. 52 ff.

63. Daniel Southerland, "China Said to Still Use Forced Labor," *The Washington Post,* May 19, 1993, p. F3 ff.

64. Daniel Southerland, "China Said to Still Use Forced Labor," p. F3 ff.

65. Mark Veverka, "China Syndrome: Firms Struggle on Rights Issue," *Crain's Chicago Business,* July 5, 1993, p. 3 ff.

66. Mark Veverka, p. 3 ff.

67. Daniel Southerland, "China Said to Still Use Forced Labor," p. F3 ff.

68. *Country Reports on Human Rights Practices for 1992,* p. 549.

69. Diane F. Orentlicher and Timothy A. Gelatt, "Public Law, Private Actors: The Impact of Human Rights on Business Investors in China," *Northwestern Journal of International Law and Business* (Fall 1993), p. 98.

70. Diane F. Orentlicher and Timothy A. Gelatt, p. 69.

71. Simon Billenness and Kate Simpson, "Thinking Globally: Study of International Corporate Responsibility," *Franklin's Insight: The Advisory Letter for Concerned Investors,* Franklin Research and Development Corporation, September 1992, p. 11.

72. Simon Billenness and Kate Simpson, p. 12.

73. Simon Billenness and Kate Simpson, p. 12.

International Business Ethics and Incipient Capitalism: A Double Standard?

RICHARD T. DE GEORGE

The term "international business ethics" is ambiguous, and this ambiguity leads to some confusion and to a number of disputes. It is ambiguous because its referent is not clear. It may refer to the ethical rules that govern all business everywhere in the world. But in that case it is arguably reducible to the general or basic ethical norms that govern human behavior, irrespective of society. For it is doubtful that there are special rules of business that are so general as to be applicable everywhere. International business ethics might refer to the ethical rules that ought to govern multinational corporations; or to the rules that apply to business as well as to nations in speaking of global problems, such as global warming and depletion of the ozone level; or to the different ethical norms applicable in different countries because of different social, economic, political, and historical conditions.

The term also leads to a number of debates, the chief of which is a debate about moral relativism. Moral relativism has a long tradition apart from international business ethics, and in the modern period stems from cultural relativism documented by anthropological studies. If mores and customs vary from society to society, what rules should one follow when one leaves one's own society and goes to another? Is one bound by the sexual moral rules of one's own monogamous society if one goes to another which allows polygamy or polyandry? If such relativism holds with respect to sex, does it also hold with respect to business?

In some ways the term "international business ethics"—like the term "business ethics"—is misleading, because both seem to refer to something that is modeled on general ethics. If general ethical theories of the standard kinds are correct, they are not dependent on particular circumstances, even though one must consider particular circumstances in applying them. But utilitarianism and Kantianism do not depend on particular circumstances for their defense.

Business ethics is an area of applied ethics. What distinguishes it from general ethics is its application to specific kinds of activity, namely business activity. As such it necessarily depends heavily for its content on the structures that define business and in which business operates. It gains its specificity by taking into account particular socio-economic circumstances; the political system and existing laws that are intertwined with these; the level of economic development and the standard of living of a country; the local traditions, beliefs, and expectations of the people in a given society; and a host of other similar considerations. These taken together form what can be called the background institutions or conditions within which business, and so business ethics, operate and make sense.

Thus business ethics in a socio-economic-political system such as that found in the United States is very different from what might be called

Presented to the Society for Business Ethics, May, 1994. © by Richard T. De George. Reprinted with the permission of the author.

business ethics in a socialist system, to the extent that business is allowed in the latter.

What is allowed by legitimate legal structures varies from country to country and makes the practice of business vary accordingly. In a society in which social benefits for workers are mandated by law, the question of what ethics requires from employers with respect to the treatment of workers may be very different from a society in which such benefits are not mandated. If government provides health, old-age pension and other benefits to all its citizens, then the obligations of business in these regards are very different from a society in which these are not provided. If a country has a long tradition of business providing lifetime employment, the obligations of business are again different from a society which has no such tradition.

Business ethics as a movement and as an area of study had its birth in the United States. The issues that rose to the fore were those about which Americans were concerned. Business ethics in the United States developed within specifically American background institutions. As it was exported or as other countries followed America's lead in this area, business ethics texts written for America were often used as texts in other countries. It was not long before both business and those teaching business ethics saw the lack of fit in many areas. Because background institutions vary, so the issues of business ethics and specific applications vary. In a country such as Japan in the 1970s, when trading in the stock market was done almost exclusively by insiders, each of whom belonged to a system of interlocking companies, insider trading was not unethical, even though insider trading in the United States was both unethical and illegal. The same practice—or at least practices that went by the same name—was morally justifiable in the one case but not in the other. In Japan there was no unfairness, no one had advantages other traders did not equally enjoy, and the practice did not harm any of the participants. In the United States, however, insider trading did give insiders unfair advantage and did harm those who traded without access in principle to appropriate information. By the 1990s the situation had changed on the Tokyo exchange. Trading was done not only by insiders but significantly by small Japanese investors and by foreign investors. Hence the practice of insider trading came to be seen as unfair to non-insiders and the practice was eventually made illegal. Insider trading is neither ethical nor unethical in itself; it takes on a moral character only when considered in a specific social context.

Because background institutions vary to such a great extent, it is difficult to speak of international business ethics as if it were all of a piece. It cannot simply be American business ethics or German or Japanese or any other kind of business ethics, extended to an international level. But in one sense it is that. An American multinational must respect the ethical norms and values of the home company wherever the company is located. It must, of course, take into account local laws, traditions, and so on. But it cannot hire child labor, even if that is the local custom; nor can it discriminate against women, or follow apartheid laws, or buy goods made by slave labor, or fail to provide safe working conditions. The list goes on.

What might give one pause is my presenting these requirements as mandatory only for American companies, as if they were not required for all companies. After all, all companies must respect the human rights of workers, honor contracts, and not harm people by dumping toxic waste. Yet these are demanded not by any special ethics of business but by general moral norms, which apply in business as well as in every other realm in life.

As a test case for the thesis I have proposed, consider the differences, if any, between business in the United States on the one hand and in Russia at the present time on the other. The United States is the business leader of the world. It has a highly developed system of laws that control many of the socially negative tendencies of unrestrained capitalism. It has an educated citizenry conscious of its rights. It has critical and choosy consumers, who usually have the choice of which products to buy and which manufacturers to do business with. It has strong environmental protection groups. It has a tradition of business being expected to contribute to the welfare of the local community in which it operates. In sum, it has a host of well-defined background institutions, within which one can intelligently speak about business ethics and analyze practices from hostile buyouts to drug testing of employees to liability for dangerous products.

The background institutions in the United States did not come into place all at once. They developed slowly over time, often in response to abuses. The robber barons at the turn of the century are not a proud part of the history of American business, nor are the racketeers of the 1920s, or the sellers of snake oil, or the carpetbaggers in the South after the Civil War. Free enterprise is not as free as some of its early proponents would have wished. Government regulations aim to protect the public interest, promote health and safety, and keep competition fair. All of this developed within a democratic society with a free press. The history of capitalism in other countries with other background institutions is very different. Capitalism has been linked with dictatorships, with corrupt governments, with criminal elements, and with a variety of different background conditions and institutions. It is not all of a piece, and business ethics does not serve the same function or come up with the same evaluations of similar-sounding practices, often because the differing circumstances and legal backgrounds make the practices different in reality, despite the fact that they go by the same name.

What Americans consider just with respect to property transactions assumes the institution of private property, protected by law, and ethically justified within the system of free enterprise. In the former Soviet Union, in which private property was condemned as unethical and unjustifiable, there was no private ownership of the means of production and there was a very different notion of what justice with respect to property meant. A host of transactions that were legitimate and ethical in the United States were either not possible or were unethical in the former Soviet Union.

Because it is in transition between the state socialism under which it functioned for seventy years and some sort of still-to-be-defined free-market system, Russia at the present time makes for an interesting case study of the thesis that business ethics must take into account the existing background institutions in the societies in which business activities take place. Under existing conditions in Russia, which ethical rules can appropriately be applied to business?

In many instances the answer it not clear. But that does not mean that it is unclear in all instances. And I believe that with sufficiently careful analysis we can arrive at least at some tentative conclusions.

Russian Background

Since it is essential to keep the background conditions in mind, let me briefly sketch some of them. Under Soviet socialism there was no private ownership of the means of production. All productive resources were state owned. No individual was allowed to be in business for himself or to hire others, since that would constitute exploitation. The state employed all workers, and all able-bodied citizens were required to work. The state provided subsidized housing, free education and health care, old-age pensions, and a variety of other social benefits. Often these were provided by the factories at which people worked.

Bureaucracy was the rule, and centralized control dominated industry. Inefficiency was widespread. Without a market to determine supply and demand, the prices of goods, resources, and labor were more or less arbitrary.

The government sought to undermine traditional bourgeois morality and to replace it with a collectivist and state-oriented socialist morality. It succeeded in undermining traditional morality but failed in replacing it with an effective social morality. As a result, many Russians adopted a dualistic approach to morals.[1] Family, friends, and those with whom one was closely associated—often fellow workers—were treated according to standard rules of decency, concern, and respect. The system and those who represented it were seen as "them"—nameless and faceless and deserving no moral respect. Rules, which were too rigid and numerous to follow, were ignored or circumvented whenever possible. Since all property belonged in theory to everyone, one took what one could when and where one could. Invoices meant little. They were simply internal accounting procedures. There was little work discipline, since everyone was guaranteed employment by law, and there was no incentive for innovation or hard work. Reports were often falsified at all levels so as to meet paper production norms. The people felt that the government was a master of fabricating, slanting, distorting and suppressing the truth, and they followed suit in dealing with the government. The people were taught (and many people accepted) the claim that private property was exploitative and unethical, that large discrepancies in wealth were anti-social and represented the fruits of unethical activity, and that capitalism, despite the wealth it produced, was built on ethically unjustifiable principles.

It is from this background that Russia emerged in 1991. It moved from a communist type government to one that at least in theory was democratic. It moved from a socialist type economy to something else that at least in theory allowed free enterprise. It started privatizing its industry. But all its steps were tentative. Although background institutions must be developed in order to support the new way of life, these institutions have been slow in coming. Many of the large enterprises are still state owned, and of those that have been privatized, many still operate essentially the way they did before, including receiving subsidies from the government. The legal system is in disarray. A new constitution has only recently been adopted. But the legislature is divided and has not followed through with much of the legislation needed for a functioning market economy. The laws governing private enterprise are in a state of flux: they have been frequently rewritten during the past three years, and they are still not settled. Without laws, the judicial system cannot be expected to settle disputes. The enforcement apparatus of the government is also in disarray, and crime has burgeoned.

The Russians tend to distinguish business, which they consider is entrepreneurial activity on a relatively small level, from the running of factories and large enterprises. Laws have tended to favor large enterprises. Entrepreneurial activity, prohibited under socialism, has consisted of people opening small businesses, and to a large extent of importing and selling goods from abroad, acting as middlemen. Some have made quick fortunes. Those with money—and Russian TV now carries ads for Mercedes Benz and BMW, indicating there are quite a few such people—are looked at askance by the masses without much, who now live at a lower level than under socialism. The latter, given their own experience, feel that the nouveaux riches must be gangsters or members of the mafia, or exploiters, or former communist officials who were able to take advantage of their special position. The people were taught that capitalism is unethical, and those who take advantage of the market to amass wealth are unethical. Although the switch from socialism has made goods available in a quantity and of a quality not previously available, wages have not kept pace with costs, unemployment is rising, and the standard of living is falling.

Incipient Capitalism and Ethics

In such circumstances, what background institutions determine what is just, and how can one say what is fair or unfair, right or wrong, with respect to business? Failing to find any satisfactory answer, some claim that business ethics in this context is meaningless. Some characterize the situation as "wild" or primitive or incipient capitalism, reminiscent of conditions in the United States in the Wild West or under the robber barons. Many Russians, who were taught by their Marxist-Leninist teachers that capitalism is a rapacious system, think that the crime and corruption that has blossomed in Russia is a necessary price that goes together with the goods and higher standard of living that eventually capitalism will bring them. Is this so?

By way of response, I shall start with some broad generalizations. First, regardless of whether the characterization of wild or primitive or incipient capitalism is correct, the basic norms of morality apply to every society, whatever the background institutions. These norms are not dependent on particular background conditions. Murdering one's competitor, destroying the property of those who do not pay for protection, distributing poisoned food as pure—all such acts are unethical, no matter what the system. Hundreds of businessmen have been murdered by what has become known as the Russian mafia. This may resemble what took place as capitalism developed in 18th- and 19th-century Europe, but it is not a necessary stage on the way to a free-market economy today. Such behavior is clearly unethical. There are some acts that are wrong no matter what the background situation. Similarly, government officials who demand bribes to allow privileges that are legally restricted or who ignore violations of the law are unethical—no matter what the system. Such actions are generally and properly termed corrupt, no matter where practiced.

Second, although Russia will inevitably suffer the pangs of moving from a socialist economy to a free-market economy, it need not attempt to reinvent a market economy. Many rules necessary for its successful and efficient functioning have been developed elsewhere and need only be adopted. These include respect for private property and the honoring of contracts, among other norms. Without these, repeat business transactions will not take place or will be excessively costly. Efficient markets require rules, trust, enforcement mechanisms, and penalties for failure to perform.

Third, it is easier to control illegal and unethical behavior before it becomes a way of doing business, entrenched and powerful, than after it has become such. Hence there is no justification in terms of market development to allow unethical activity if it can be prevented.

Nonetheless, if we ask how Russia can move justly from a state-owned system to a privately owned system, the answer is anything but clear, and there may be no satisfactory answer. The reason is that what is just or fair depends in part on background institutions and assumptions, and these are systematically ambiguous in Russia with respect to privatization. Do the rules of socialism or of a free-market economy apply, for example, with respect to property rights? Under socialism, all property theoretically belonged to the people and was held and administered by the state. Property rights were not assigned to individuals. So if we ask who by right owns a particular factory or plant, the answer is not clear. Should the factory be turned over to the workers? But some factories were favored and are productive and worth a great deal, while others are for all intents and purposes worthless. Turning over a gold mine to the mine workers is different from turning over a university to its faculty. Should the rights to all state property be divided equally among all Russian citizens? An attempt to do just that consisted, in part, of giving each citizen vouchers worth 10,000 rubles ($40.00). But without a stock market to sell the vouchers and without information about how the system works, many quickly lost their share of Russian industry. Moreover neither approach brings in any new money, which is needed for many of the industries to function productively. To get new capital, some plants have been sold to non-Russian outside buyers. But such buyers are only interested in the more productive plants. No matter what method is chosen—and in Russia a variety of approaches to privatization have been used—each can be criticized as unjust to some group or portion of the population.[2]

Just as privatization cannot proceed justly because of different, changing and ambiguous background conditions, the difficulty spills over into other areas of economic life.

What then can we say about business ethics in Russia at the present time? As a start to answering this question I shall present and analyze four typical cases. I shall argue that these cases cannot be properly evaluated if we ignore the circumstances in which they are found, and that the evaluations that are justifiable may well be different from like-sounding cases in an American context. From the analyses I shall draw some tentative conclusions.

Four Cases

1. Consider the case of Ivan Ivanovich, a Russian manager of a large formerly state-owned factory. Although he has the new responsibility of running his factory in order to make a profit for the shareholders, he takes upon himself the obligation of paying the company's workers all the benefits the workers received under the communist system. The factory supplies them with housing, health care, and old-age pensions. In order to do this and still stay in business, Ivan ignores a number of laws that are not strictly enforced, and falsifies the factory's records so as not to incur any taxes. This is similar to what he did under the communist regime.[3] For the factory to be at all efficient, he should fire at least ten percent of his employees. But because they would have to join the growing army of the unemployed, he refuses to do so.

Ivan does not run the company for his own profit or that of the shareholders. He breaks a number of Russian laws, which are not enforced anyway, in order to provide the kinds of benefits that the workers of the factory have traditionally received under communism, and which the state has not taken over. He chooses to keep people employed rather than make the company efficient. Are his actions ethically justifiable? In this case, what Ivan does is unethical if he has an ethical obligation to obey the law and an ethical obligation to run the factory efficiently and profitably. But arguably the ethical obligation to obey the law holds only when the law is itself ethically justifiable and equitably enforced. Since both are open to question in the given circumstances in Russia—the first because of the ambiguity and contradictory nature of many of the laws and the second because of the lack of any effective enforcement—the ethical obligation to obey such laws is questionable at best. Nonetheless, Ivan opens himself up to possible legal prosecution. What of his obligation to increase shareholder wealth, which he is not doing by continuing worker benefits that are no longer legally mandated? From a long-range perspective, is he not also delaying the transition of the society to a true market economy? From an ethical point of view, whether the obligations to shareholders and to develop the new system take precedence over former obligations of the firm to its employees depends on how one interprets the background assumptions. And it is these that are mixed. I would argue (although restrictions of space and time prevent my doing so here) that his actions are ethically justifiable, given the circumstances.

2.   Since I have implied that it may not be unethical to ignore the law in Russia, let us turn to Alexander Alexandrovich, a Russian manager of a large aluminum manufacturing company, *A*, who together with other managers of the firm forms an independent company, *B*, which they privately own.[4] Company *A* is state-owned and subsidized. It sells its aluminum to company *B* at subsidized prices, the same as it does to other Russian companies. The managers of company *B*, as is the custom, pay an official for an export permit. They then export the aluminum they buy at subsidized prices and receive much higher world prices for their product. They siphon off most of their earnings to private Swiss bank accounts, returning to Russia only enough funds to cover their next purchase.

In forming Company *B*, Alexander and his colleagues did nothing illegal, and were fostering the advent of a free-market economy. *B* pays *A* the government subsidized prices, legally exports the aluminum, sells it at world prices, banks the profit abroad, and brings back sufficient capital to make the next purchase. No laws are broken. Firm *A* continues in business, the workers receive the same pay they did previously, and the managers, in good entrepreneurial fashion, take advantage of a situation to become millionaires. Did they do anything for which they can be ethically faulted? If legality equaled ethical permissibility, the answer would be no. Yet some questions arise.

The workers of the aluminum firm feel that some injustice is being done them. The managers have used their position and experience to create an independent company that reaps great rewards for the managers, while the workers are no better off than they were before. Is this unethical? The workers are no worse off than they were, and unlike many of their fellow Russians they still have their jobs and their wages. Of course they would be better off if the managers of the firm did not create the trading company and shared their profits with the workers. The question is whether the managers were ethically required to do this or ethically precluded from doing what they did. Do the rules and expectations of socialism operate here, in which case we have a violation of socialist solidarity; or do we adopt the rules of capitalism, which ignore such claims? If we adopt the rules of capitalism, do we have a conflict of interest—a concept unfamiliar to many Russians— and a failure of Alexander in his capacity as the manager of *A* to manage it for the best interests of that company rather than of *B*? Would the situation be different if company *A* had been privatized and was owned by the workers? In a mixed situation must one choose which set of background assumptions apply or may one choose among them, more accurately reflecting the actual situation? More importantly, it is not outside observers but the Russians who decide what should apply. And there seems to be little consensus on this issue in the present state of flux.

The managers paid the government bureaucrat who issued the export license. Is this a bribe or a facilitating payment? In either case, is it justifiable? The managers did not pay the official to do anything that the official was not supposed to do or to break any Russian law. If the official required a payment to issue the export permit, the question is whether officials who require such payment are more to blame than those who pay them. Many Russians feel that the bureaucracy and many of the rules bureaucrats enforce exist solely for the benefit of those who enforce them. In this situation exactly who is unethical is not always clear. The government's purpose in permitting exports is to bring back hard currency into Russia for the benefit of the country. But the government has not been able to control companies that trade abroad, or to enforce any type of accountability. Is Alexander ethically required to follow the intent of export controls or may he take advantage of loopholes in the law?

Finally Alexander takes advantage of the fact that Company *A* is subsidized in various ways by the government. This provides the owners of *B* with a product that costs them relatively little, which they sell at a handsome profit. Clearly the state does not subsidize the aluminum industry so that managers can become wealthy. Yet what the managers do is not illegal. Rather than invoke ethics, both the market and the government are responding to the situation. The Russian aluminum firms over the past three years exported in such quantity that they created a glut on the international market. The price of aluminum dropped sharply, as did the profits of the Russian exporters. The government in the meantime stopped subsidizing the cost of electricity, thus forcing the producing firm to bear its real costs and raise its selling price to *B*, as well as to all other firms.

One might argue that Alexander exploits the workers, the country, and the legal loopholes that exist so that he can reap enormous profits. I am inclined to argue this position against those who claim that Alexander and his fellow managers are just acting as entrepreneurs do and so are justified in their actions. But making out the case that their actions are unethical is difficult in the given circumstances. The reason is that it is unclear which sets of rules—socialist or capitalist—form the background against which to evaluate the entrepreneurial actions.

3. An entrepreneur, Aleksey Alekseyevich, joins a private electricians' cooperative. They wire houses and provide all the services generally provided by electricians. Since copper wire is in short supply and electrical fixtures go first to large state-owned factories, Aleksey can operate only by getting wire and fixtures where and how he can. Sometimes Aleksey buys them from suppliers—no questions asked. Sometimes he can, for a fee, get a shipment of supplies rerouted from its intended destination to the cooperative. He pays the local protection agency (part of the Russian mafia) a monthly fee to be allowed to continue operating.

This case is typical of a considerable number of small firms in Russia. The transition from state-owned factories and shops to privately owned ones has taken place without the distribution and allocation system being effectively replaced by the market.[5] Large state-owned and formerly state-owned industries still have priority claims on many resources. Although small enterprises are allowed and sometimes verbally encouraged, it is often extremely difficult for them to get the supplies they need to function. To some extent this is not new and is similar to conditions under communism.

When everything is said to belong to everyone, as was the case under socialism, there is often little concern for exactly who gets what. If a shipment goes to one firm rather than another, the second firm in a sense owns it as appropriately as the first, since it is common property. Such an attitude is found in the U.S. military in which inventoried items that are lost or misplaced or stolen are frequently made up by trading among property officers and clerks from different units. With this sort of background, what the entrepreneurs are doing, as well as what those who supply the goods may be doing, fits in with the way of doing business under the former system. The allocation system has not caught up with the free-market thrust of the economy. From the point of view of a market economy, the allocation system is distorted, given a move to a partially developed private-ownership system. Under these circumstances a small entrepreneur like Aleksey must either operate as the situation describes or not operate at all. Let us suppose that this is an accurate characterization of the situation. In such a case, may the entrepreneur get the material he needs as he can, and may he pay extortion in order to be allowed to operate?

We can make several distinctions. First, it is unethical for the suppliers of protection to charge extortion. Extortion is unethical, no matter what the system. But paying extortion is less bad than charging it; and it may be justifiable, at least temporarily, under certain circumstances. It is an evil because it tends to perpetuate extortion, and helps it to escalate, to the detriment of society. Yet paying extortion is the lesser of two evils for Aleksey, if the alternative is for him and all small entrepreneurs to be driven out of business and for there either to be no such services available or for only those who have no ethical compunctions to operate businesses.

Similarly, if the goods sold to the small business are stolen, we can fault those who steal. If they are diverted from their intended receiver but the producer is paid, then the harm done to the system might be grounds for ethical complaint, except that the system is chaotic, and determining which recipient produces more good or harm may be difficult to determine. Even if we ethically fault the supplier (as we should), the fault of the receiver is certainly less, and operating in the same fashion as under the communist system may be preferable once again to leaving all enterprise to the criminal element.

Both of these justifications are justifications only insofar as they are truly necessary and temporary, given the current state of affairs, and only insofar as they are the lesser of two evils.

4. A U.S. multinational, represented by John Jones, purchases a portion of a formerly state-owned enterprise that has been privatized. Its Russian co-owners tell the U.S. company that if they are to succeed, they should be ready to pay bribes to a variety of government officials.

This case demands a different analysis from the other three. Although the American multinational operates in the Russian system in which the laws are ambiguous and often unenforced, in which bribery is rampant and extortion the norm for small businesses, none of this justifies American companies acting as Russian firms might justifiably act. The reason is that American companies are in a very different situation from the Russian companies.

First of all, no American company is forced to operate in Russia. It always has the option of not operating there, and many American firms, given the ambiguity of the laws, the ambiguous status of property claims, the uncertainty of adjudication of disputes and the prevalence of corruption on both the governmental and the criminal levels, have decided not to venture into those circumstances. Those who do venture, do so knowing that they take enormous risks in the hope of gaining equivalent returns. But unlike their Russian counterparts they operate from a position of power. They have hard currency, which is in great demand. They can successfully refuse to pay bribes that are prohibited by the Foreign Corrupt Practices Act, and they can successfully refuse to pay extortion. If in some instances the costs of protecting their property and employees from violence is too great, they have the option of leaving. Hence they are not in a position of either being forced to engage in corrupt practices, thereby helping to sustain and promote them, or of not operating at all—even though they will not operate in Russia.

To the extent that they do operate in Russia, because of their powerful position, they have the obligation to help bring ethical practices into the marketplace and to help make the market fair. They are potentially in a position to exploit the people and the country with relative impunity. But not only is that not in the long-term interest of the company or of the development of a market economy in Russia, it is exploitation of a gross kind.

Does this mean that there are two sets of ethical rules, one for Russian companies and one for American (and other) multinational corporations? The answer is no, but this must be properly understood. It is no because the actual circumstances of the Russian and of American firms operating in Russia are different, despite the fact that both operate in the same place at the same time.

Does this imply that because of their different circumstances less is expected of Russian companies, or more is tolerated from an ethical point of view than of American companies? The answer is a qualified yes. There is no special set of lesser ethical rules that applies to conditions of incipient capitalism. But ethics never demands more than can reasonably be expected of people, in business just as in other areas of life. Moreover, business itself embodies and presupposes certain ethical norms without which it cannot and does not function. The limits of corruption that it can tolerate are not great. Nor are the limits of intentional misinformation, deceit, and exploitation. As these increase, business tends to retreat, being replaced by barter and more primitive forms of exchange. We are presently seeing this phenomenon in Russia and in some of the other former Soviet and communist states.

Corruption is not justifiable simply because it is rampant. But operating amidst corruption is not easy. The actual alternatives that are open to one are frequently decisive in determining whether certain practices—such as paying extortion—are justifiable. The conditions are different for local and foreign firms. American and other multinationals can serve a positive function by being the exemplars and bearers of ethical business practices, and this is as important and perhaps more important to the developing system than the goods or services such firms might provide.

Generalizations from These Cases

What conclusions can we draw from this discussion?

1.   Some actions are wrong no matter which system of background institutions are in place. Hence whether Russia's background institutions are socialist, free-market, mixed or chaotic, murder, extortion, violence and theft are unethical. The longer they are tolerated and become de facto part of the way of doing business, the more difficult it will be to achieve a reasonably efficient market.

2.   The U.S. business ethics literature and a U.S. perspective on particular business issues reflects American background conditions and cannot be superimposed on Russia. In the present circumstances in Russia some actions will appropriately be judged unethical when viewed from the assumption that socialist background conditions are operative, and will appropriately be viewed as ethically justifiable when viewed from the assumption that free-market conditions are operative. Since both are partially operative—or inoperative—it is not only practically difficult but in principle impossible to decide from some outside perspective the morality of some business practices.

3.   The discrepancies between aspects of the socialist system that are still in place—such as state subsidies—and the opportunities for profit by selling subsidized goods abroad under free-market rules is being exploited by some to their great advantage. Legislation and regulations that are rational, that are aimed at the common good, and that keep competition fair are essential. Russia can learn from the experience of developed countries what is required and need not learn only by trial and error.

4. The plight of the worker in Russia is worsening. Given the confusion about the role of the state in providing housing, health services, education, old-age benefits, and other social assistance, the obligations of industry and business to provide what was provided under the former socialist system are unclear. But business and industry cannot simply ignore the needs of their workers. How firms must treat employees, beyond respecting their basic human rights, is appropriately determined by considering the background conditions in which the firm operates. A pressing task is for Russia to determine and implement a clear policy. In the meantime Russian firms have some obligations to continue providing services that were formerly expected and considered entitlements.

5. American and other multinational corporations can serve an important function not only by economic joint ventures and economic activity, but also by adhering to the ethical standards that are expected at home and by helping guide the establishment of background institutions that are necessary for the long-run efficient and mutually beneficial development of business in Russia. Not only can they adhere to higher standards but they have the obligation to do so. This seemingly double set of ethical standards is justified by the fact that although operating in the same country, the circumstances of the foreign interest and of the local entrepreneur are different, and what is possible for each is different as well. Applying the principle of "ought implies can" yields different norms for foreign and for local businesses.[6]

Before closing, however, let me briefly extend the implications of my analysis to two other areas of international business ethics. I have discussed, first, business ethics within different countries (which one might call comparative international business ethics), and second, the possible difference between the obligations of multinationals and of indigenous businesses in a country like Russia. The third area is the area of mutual trade between or among countries.

If the thesis is correct that background institutions are necessary to the substantive norms of business ethics, then the background conditions of international trade and politics set the stage for international business and for international business ethics on this level. Here we frequently have negotiations not by multinationals but by the governments of countries. But in addition we have international codes, U.N. commissions, religious institutions, non-governmental organizations such as the Red Cross, and other similar groups and institutions that form part of the background. Expectations on the international level are also very different from on the national level. There is no effective redistribution mechanism among countries, no taxes for global redistribution, and so on. Issues of rich countries versus poor countries and of dependency versus independence form part of the background for trade negotiations, treaties, agreements, and the like for carrying on business. This area deserves more careful analysis and development for its ethical implications, problems, needs—especially the need for more effective background institutions—than it has received.

The fourth area is what I shall call the global area. There are some global issues—such as the depletion of the ozone level—that cannot be resolved and are not caused by individual companies or by companies from individual countries, but by countries and companies and people acting each in their own ways. With respect to the ozone level, to the extent that the problem is caused by chlorofluorocarbons, these are the results of modern chemistry, and are emitted by machines made by businesses—whether privately owned or government owned. No individual firm can solve the problem, nor can any individual country. The ethical responsibility falls collectively on all. Some contribute more to the problem than others. Some are able to do more to solve it than others. The background situation and conditions affect the obligations of different groups and different countries and different companies. The Rio Conference was a meeting of nations. Some American companies are ahead of the curve of the American government in their willingness to cut back on emissions; some poorer countries are unable to cut back as much as more affluent countries are. Are there two sets of norms here?

As in the case of Russia and incipient capitalism, it is possible to hold that some actions are simply wrong, no matter who does them; some actions are wrong, but may be tolerated in certain conditions as the lesser of two evils; and these same actions may be tolerated for some in certain conditions but not for others in other conditions. A greater burden falls on the industries in the developed countries than falls on the industries of developing countries both because the former are the greater cause of the degradation of the ozone level and because they have the financial and technological resources to do something to alleviate the problem. Similarly, affluent companies in developing countries have a greater responsibility to control their emissions than do struggling companies in such countries. The general rule to do no direct intentional harm plays out differently for different countries in different conditions. As we have seen, conditions may be different for two companies in the same country at the same time.

I started by noting the ambiguity of the term "international business ethics." It encompasses, I suggest, at least these four areas, although it is not exhausted by them. I also claimed at the start of this paper that even if general ethics had some claim to universality, business ethics, as an applied area, had much less, if any, such claim. As an applied area of ethics, it is always embedded in socio-economic-political conditions which form and engulf business. If this is correct, international business ethics is not more free from such constraints but equally tied to them, and is often more difficult because of the additional variables that one has to take into account.

Notes

1. See Richard T. De George, *Soviet Ethics and Morality*, Ann Arbor: Michigan University Press, 1969; Sheila M. Puffer, "Understanding the Bear: A Portrait of Russian Business Leaders," *The Academy of Management Executive*, Vol. 8, No. 1 (February 1994), pp. 41–54.
2. For a fuller discussion of privatization, see Richard T. De George, "International Business Ethics: Russia and Eastern Europe," *Social Responsibility: Business, Journalism, Law, Medicine*, Vol. XIX (1993), pp. 5–23.

3. Adi Ignatius, "Battling for Russia's Soul at the Factory," *The Wall Street Journal*, December 21, 1993, p. A6. In "Business Ethics of the Director of a Russian Industrial Enterprise," a paper presented at the 25th AAASS National Convention, Honolulu, November 12–22, 1993, Leonid Khotin describes such situations.

4. Ann Imse, "Russia's Wild Capitalists Take Aluminum for a Ride," *The New York Times*, February 13, 1994, p. F4.

5. See, among other sources, Alexander Filatov, "Unethical Business Behavior In Post-Communist Russia: Origins and Trends," *Business Ethics Quarterly*, Vol. 4, No. 1 (January 1994), pp. 11–15.

6. A somewhat similar analysis yields greater obligations to U.S. multinationals than to indigenous firms in less developed countries. See Richard T. De George, *Competing With Integrity in International Business*, New York: Oxford University Press, 1993.

Values in Tension: Ethics away from Home

Thomas Donaldson

When we leave home and cross our nation's boundaries, moral clarity often blurs. Without a backdrop of shared attitudes, and without familiar laws and judicial procedures that define standards of ethical conduct, certainty is elusive. Should a company invest in a foreign country where civil and political rights are violated? Should a company go along with a host country's discriminatory employment practices? If companies in developed countries shift facilities to developing nations that lack strict environmental and health regulations, or if those companies choose to fill management and other top-level positions in a host nation with people from the home country, whose standards should prevail?

Even the best-informed, best-intentioned executives must rethink their assumptions about business practice in foreign settings. What works in a company's home country can fail in a country with different standards of ethical conduct. Such difficulties are unavoidable for businesspeople who live and work abroad.

But how can managers resolve the problems? What are the principles that can help them work through the maze of cultural differences and establish codes of conduct for globally ethical business practice? How can companies answer the toughest question in global business ethics: What happens when a host country's ethical standards seem lower than the home country's?

Competing Answers

One answer is as old as philosophical discourse. According to cultural relativism, no culture's ethics are better than any other's; therefore there are no international rights and wrongs. If the people of Indonesia tolerate the bribery of their public officials, so what? Their attitude is no better or worse than that of people in Denmark or Singapore who refuse to offer or accept bribes. Likewise, if Belgians fail to find insider trading morally repugnant, who cares? Not enforcing insider-trading laws is no more or less ethical than enforcing such laws.

The cultural relativist's creed—When in Rome, do as the Romans do—is tempting, especially when failing to do as the locals do means forfeiting business opportunities. The inadequacy of cultural relativism, however, becomes apparent when the practices in question are more damaging than petty bribery or insider trading.

In the late 1980s, some European tanneries and pharmaceutical companies were looking for cheap waste-dumping sites. They approached virtually every country on Africa's west coast from Morocco to the Congo. Nigeria agreed to take highly toxic polychlorinated biphenyls. Unprotected local workers, wearing thongs and shorts, unloaded barrels of PCBs and placed them near a residential area. Neither the residents nor the workers knew that the barrels contained toxic waste.

We may denounce governments that permit such abuses, but many countries are unable to police transnational corporations adequately even if they want to. And in many countries, the combination of ineffective enforcement and inadequate regulations leads to behavior by unscrupulous companies that is clearly wrong. A few years ago, for example, a group of investors became interested in restoring the SS *United States,* once a luxurious ocean liner. Before the actual restoration could begin, the ship had to be stripped of its asbestos lining. A bid from a U.S. company, based on U.S. standards for asbestos removal, priced the job at more than $100 million. A company in the Ukranian city of Sevastopol offered to do the work for less than $2 million. In October 1993, the ship was towed to Sevastopol.

A cultural relativist would have no problem with that outcome, but I do. A country has the right to establish its own health and safety regulations, but in the case described above, the standards and the terms of the contract could not possibly have protected workers in Sevastopol from known health risks. Even if the contract met Ukranian standards, ethical businesspeople must object. Cultural relativism is morally blind. There are fundamental values that cross cultures, and companies must uphold them. . . .

At the other end of the spectrum from cultural relativism is ethical imperialism, which directs people to do everywhere exactly as they do at home. Again, an understandably appealing approach but one that is clearly inadequate. Consider the large U.S. computer-products company that in 1993 introduced a course on sexual harassment in its Saudi Arabian facility. Under the banner of global consistency, instructors used the same approach to train Saudi Arabian managers that they had used with U.S. managers: the participants were asked to discuss a case in which a manager makes sexually explicit remarks to a new female employee over drinks in a bar. The instructors failed to consider how the exercise would work in a culture with strict conventions governing relationships between men and women. As a result, the training sessions were ludicrous. They baffled and offended the Saudi participants, and the message to avoid coercion and sexual discrimination was lost.

The theory behind ethical imperialism is absolutism, which is based on three problematic principles. Absolutists believe that there is a single list of truths, that they can be expressed only with one set of concepts, and that they call for exactly the same behavior around the world.

The first claim clashes with many people's belief that different cultural traditions must be respected. In some cultures, loyalty to a community—family, organization, or society—is the foundation of all ethical behavior. The Japanese, for example, define business ethics in terms of loyalty to their companies, their business networks, and their nation. Americans place a higher value on liberty than on loyalty; the U.S. tradition of rights emphasizes equality, fairness, and individual freedom. It is hard to conclude that truth lies on one side or the other, but an absolutist would have us select just one.

The second problem with absolutism is the presumption that people must express moral truth using only one set of concepts. For instance, some absolutists insist that the language of basic rights provide the framework for any discussion of ethics. That means, though, that entire cultural traditions must be ignored. The notion of a right evolved with the rise of democracy in post-Renaissance Europe and the United States, but the term is not found in either Confucian or Buddhist traditions. We all learn ethics in the context of our particular cultures, and the power in the principles is deeply tied to the way in which they are expressed. Internationally accepted lists of moral principles, such as the United Nations' Universal Declaration of Human Rights, draw on many cultural and religious traditions. As philosopher Michael Walzer has noted, "There is no Esperanto of global ethics."

The third problem with absolutism is the belief in a global standard of ethical behavior. Context must shape ethical practice. Very low wages, for example, may be considered unethical in rich, advanced countries, but developing nations may be acting ethically if they encourage investment and improve living standards by accepting low wages. Likewise, when people are malnourished or starving, a government may be wise to use more fertilizer in order to improve crop yields, even though that means settling for relatively high levels of thermal water pollution.

When cultures have different standards of ethical behavior—and different ways of handling unethical behavior—a company that takes an absolutist approach may find itself making a disastrous mistake. When a manager at a large U.S. specialty-products company in China caught an employee stealing, she followed the company's practice and turned the employee over to the provincial authorities, who executed him. Managers cannot operate in another culture without being aware of that culture's attitudes toward ethics.

If companies can neither adopt a host country's ethics nor extend the home country's standards, what is the answer? Even the traditional litmus test—What would people think of your actions if they were written up on the front page of the newspaper?—is an unreliable guide, for there is no international consensus on standards of business conduct.

Balancing the Extremes: Three Guiding Principles

Companies must help managers distinguish between practices that are merely different and those that are wrong. For relativists, nothing is sacred and nothing is wrong. For absolutists, many things that are different are wrong. Neither extreme illuminates the real world of business decision making. The answer lies somewhere in between.

When it comes to shaping ethical behavior, companies must be guided by three principles.

- Respect for core human values, which determine the absolute moral threshold for all business activities.
- Respect for local traditions.
- The belief that context matters when deciding what is right and what is wrong.

Consider those principles in action. In Japan, people doing business together often exchange gifts—sometimes expensive ones—in keeping with long-standing Japanese tradition. When U.S. and European companies started doing a lot of business in Japan, many Western businesspeople thought that the practice of gift giving might be wrong rather than simply different. To them, accepting a gift felt like accepting a bribe. As Western companies have become more familiar with Japanese traditions, however, most have come to tolerate the practice and to set different limits on gift giving in Japan than they do elsewhere.

Respecting differences is a crucial ethical practice. Research shows that management ethics differ among cultures; respecting those differences means recognizing that some cultures have obvious weaknesses—as well as hidden strengths. Managers in Hong Kong, for example, have a higher tolerance for some forms of bribery than their Western counterparts, but they have a much lower tolerance for the failure to acknowledge a subordinate's work. In some parts of the Far East, stealing credit from a subordinate is nearly an unpardonable sin.

People often equate respect for local traditions with cultural relativism. That is incorrect. Some practices are clearly wrong. Union Carbide's tragic experience in Bhopal, India, provides one example. The company's executives seriously underestimated how much on-site management involvement was needed at the Bhopal plant to compensate for the country's poor infrastructure and regulatory capabilities. In the aftermath of the disastrous gas leak, the lesson is clear: companies using sophisticated technology in a developing country must evaluate that country's ability to oversee its safe use. Since the incident at Bhopal, Union Carbide has become a leader in advising companies on using hazardous technologies safely in developing countries.

Some activities are wrong no matter where they take place. But some practices that are unethical in one setting may be acceptable in another. For instance, the chemical EDB, a soil fungicide, is banned for use in the United States. In hot climates, however, it quickly becomes harmless through exposure to intense solar radiation and high soil temperatures. As long as the chemical is monitored, companies may be able to use EDB ethically in certain parts of the world.

Defining the Ethical Threshold: Core Values

Few ethical questions are easy for managers to answer. But there are some hard truths that must guide managers' actions, a set of what I call *core human values,* which define minimum ethical standards for all companies.[1] The right to good health and the right to economic advancement and an improved standard of living are two core human values. Another is what Westerners call the Golden Rule, which is recognizable in every major religious and ethical tradition around the world. In Book 15 of his *Analects,* for instance, Confucius counsels people to maintain reciprocity, or not to do to others what they do not want done to themselves.

Although no single list would satisfy every scholar, I believe it is possible to articulate three core values that incorporate the work of scores of theologians and philosophers around the world. To be broadly relevant, these values must include elements found in both Western and non-Western cultural and religious traditions. Consider the examples of values in Exhibit 1, "What Do These Values Have in Common?"

At first glance, the values expressed in the two lists seem quite different. Nonetheless, in the spirit of what philosopher John Rawls calls *overlapping consensus,* one can see that the seemingly divergent values converge at key points. Despite important differences between Western and non-Western cultural and religious traditions, both express shared attitudes about what it means to be human. First, individuals must not treat others simply as tools; in other words, they must recognize a person's value as a human being. Next, individuals and communities must treat people in ways that respect people's basic rights. Finally, members of a community must work together to support and improve the institutions on which the community depends. I call those three values *respect for human dignity, respect for basic rights,* and *good citizenship.*

Those values must be the starting point for all companies as they formulate and evaluate standards of ethical conduct at home and abroad. But they are only a starting point. Companies need much more specific guidelines, and the first step to developing those is to translate the core human values into core values for business. What does it mean, for example, for a company to respect human dignity? How can a company be a good citizen?

I believe that companies can respect human dignity by creating and sustaining a corporate culture in which employees, customers, and suppliers are treated not as means to an end but as people whose intrinsic value must be acknowledged, and by producing safe products and services in a safe workplace. Companies can respect basic rights by acting in ways that support and protect the individual rights of employees, customers, and surrounding communities, and by avoiding relationships that violate human beings' rights to health, education, safety, and an adequate standard of living. And companies can be good citizens by supporting essential social institutions, such as the economic system and the education system, and by working with host governments and other organizations to protect the environment.

The core values establish a moral compass for business practice. They can help companies identify practices that are acceptable and those that are intolerable—even if the practices are compatible with a host country's norms and laws. Dumping pollutants near people's homes and accepting inadequate standards for handling hazardous materials are two examples of actions that violate core values.

Similarly, if employing children prevents them from receiving a basic education, the practice is intolerable. Lying about product specifications in the act of selling may not affect human lives directly, but it too is intolerable because it violates the trust that is needed to sustain a corporate culture in which customers are respected.

Sometimes it is not a company's actions but those of a supplier or customer that pose problems. Take the case of the Tan family, a large supplier for Levi Strauss. The Tans were allegedly forcing 1,200 Chinese and Filipino women to work 74 hours per week in guarded compounds on the Mariana Islands. In 1992, after repeated warnings to the Tans, Levi Strauss broke off business relations with them.

Creating an Ethical Corporate Culture

The core values for business that I have enumerated can help companies begin to exercise ethical judgment and think about how to operate ethically in foreign cultures, but they are not specific enough to guide managers through actual ethical dilemmas. Levi Strauss relied on a written code of conduct when figuring out how to deal with the Tan family. The company's Global Sourcing and Operating Guidelines, formerly called the Business Partner Terms of Engagement, state that Levi Strauss will "seek to identify and utilize business partners who aspire as individuals and in the conduct of all their businesses to a set of ethical standards not incompatible with our own." Whenever intolerable business situations arise, managers should be guided by precise statements that spell out the behavior and operating practices that the company demands.

Ninety percent of all *Fortune* 500 companies have codes of conduct, and 70% have statements of vision and values. In Europe and the Far East, the percentages are lower but are increasing rapidly. Does that mean that most companies have what they need? Hardly. Even though most large U.S. companies have both statements of values and codes of conduct, many might be better off if they didn't. Too many companies don't do anything with the documents; they simply paste them on the wall to impress employees, customers, suppliers, and the public. As a result, the senior managers who drafted the statements lose credibility by proclaiming values and not living up to them. Companies such as Johnson & Johnson, Levi Strauss, Motorola, Texas Instruments, and Lockheed Martin, however, do a great deal to make the words meaningful. Johnson & Johnson, for example, has become well known for its Credo Challenge sessions, in which managers discuss ethics in the context of their current business problems and are invited to criticize the company's credo and make suggestions for changes. The participants' ideas are passed on to the company's senior managers. Lockheed Martin has created an innovative site on the World Wide Web and on its local network that gives employees, customers, and suppliers access to the company's ethical code and the chance to voice complaints.

Codes of conduct must provide clear direction about ethical behavior when the temptation to behave unethically is strongest. The pronouncement in a code of conduct that bribery is unacceptable is useless unless accompanied by guidelines for gift giving, payments to get goods through customs, and "requests" from intermediaries who are hired to ask for bribes.

Motorola's values are stated very simply as "How we will always act: [with] constant respect for people [and] uncompromising integrity." The company's code of conduct, however, is explicit about actual business practice.

With respect to bribery, for example, the code states that the "funds and assets of Motorola shall not be used, directly or indirectly, for illegal payments of any kind." It is unambiguous about what sort of payment is illegal: "the payment of a bribe to a public official or the kickback of funds to an employee of a customer. . . ." The code goes on to prescribe specific procedures for handling commissions to intermediaries, issuing sales invoices, and disclosing confidential information in a sales transaction—all situations in which employees might have an opportunity to accept or offer bribes.

Codes of conduct must be explicit to be useful, but they must also leave room for a manager to use his or her judgment in situations requiring cultural sensitivity. Host-country employees shouldn't be forced to adopt all home-country values and renounce their own. Again, Motorola's code is exemplary. First, it gives clear direction: "Employees of Motorola will respect the laws, customs, and traditions of each country in which they operate, but will, at the same time, engage in no course of conduct which, even if legal, customary, and accepted in any such country, could be deemed to be in violation of the accepted business ethics of Motorola or the laws of the United States relating to business ethics." After laying down such absolutes, Motorola's code then makes clear when individual judgment will be necessary. For example, employees may sometimes accept certain kinds of small gifts "in rare circumstances, where the refusal to accept a gift" would injure Motorola's "legitimate business interests." Under certain circumstances, such gifts "may be accepted so long as the gift inures to the benefit of Motorola" and not "to the benefit of the Motorola employee."

Striking the appropriate balance between providing clear direction and leaving room for individual judgment makes crafting corporate values statements and ethics codes one of the hardest tasks that executives confront. The words are only a start. A company's leaders need to refer often to their organization's credo and code and must themselves be credible, committed, and consistent. If senior managers act as though ethics don't matter, the rest of the company's employees won't think they do, either.

Conflicts of Development and Conflicts of Tradition

Managers living and working abroad who are not prepared to grapple with moral ambiguity and tension should pack their bags and come home. The view that all business practices can be categorized as either ethical or unethical is too simple. As Einstein is reported to have said, "Things should be as simple as possible—but no simpler." Many business practices that are considered unethical in one setting may be ethical in another. Such activities are neither black nor white but exist in what Thomas Dunfee and I have called *moral free space*. In this gray zone, there are no tight prescriptions for a company's behavior. Managers must chart their own courses—as long as they do not violate core human values.

Consider the following example. Some successful Indian companies offer employees the opportunity for one of their children to gain a job with the company once the child has completed a certain level in school. The companies honor this commitment even when other applicants are more qualified than an employee's child. The perk is extremely valuable in a country where jobs are hard to find, and it reflects the Indian culture's belief that the West has gone too far in allowing economic opportunities to break up families. Not surprisingly, the perk is among the most cherished by employees, but in most Western countries, it would be branded unacceptable nepotism. In the United States, for example, the ethical principle of equal opportunity holds that jobs should go to the applicants with the best qualifications. If a U.S. company made such promises to its employees, it would violate regulations established by the Equal Employment Opportunity Commission. Given this difference in ethical attitudes, how should U.S. managers react to Indian nepotism? Should they condemn the Indian companies, refusing to accept them as partners or supplies until they agree to clean up their act?

Despite the obvious tension between nepotism and principles of equal opportunity, I cannot condemn the practice for Indians. In a country, such as India, that emphasizes clan and family relationships and has catastrophic levels of unemployment, the practice must be viewed in moral free space. The decision to allow a special perk for employees and their children is not necessarily wrong—at least for members of that country.

How can managers discover the limits of moral free space? That is, how can they learn to distinguish a value in tension with their own from one that is intolerable? Helping managers develop good ethical judgment requires companies to be clear about their core values and codes of conduct. But even the most explicit set of guidelines cannot always provide answers. That is especially true in the thorniest ethical dilemmas, in which the host country's ethical standards not only are different but also seem lower than the home country's. Managers must recognize that when countries have different ethical standards, there are two types of conflict that commonly arise. Each type requires its own line of reasoning.

In the first type of conflict, which I call a *conflict of relative development,* ethical standards conflict because of the countries' different levels of economic development. As mentioned before, developing countries may accept wage rates that seem inhumane to more advanced countries in order to attract investment. As economic conditions in a developing country improve, the incidence of that sort of conflict usually decreases. The second type of conflict is a *conflict of cultural tradition.* For example, Saudi Arabia, unlike most other countries, does not allow women to serve as corporate managers. Instead, women may work in only a few professions, such as education and health care. The prohibition stems from strongly held religious and cultural beliefs; any increase in the country's level of economic development, which is already quite high, is not likely to change the rules.

To resolve a conflict of relative development, a manager must ask the following question: Would the practice be acceptable at home if my country were in a similar stage of economic development? Consider the difference between wage and safety standards in the United States and in Angola, where citizens accept lower standards on both counts. If a U.S. oil company is hiring Angolans to work on an offshore Angolan oil rig, can the company pay them lower wages than it pays U.S. workers in the Gulf of Mexico? Reasonable people have to answer yes if the alternative for Angola is the loss of both the foreign investment and the jobs.

Consider, too, differences in regulatory environments. In the 1980s, the government of India fought hard to be able to import Ciba-Geigy's Entero

Vioform, a drug known to be enormously effective in fighting dysentery but one that had been banned in the United States because some users experienced side effects. Although dysentery was not a big problem in the United States, in India, poor public sanitation was contributing to epidemic levels of the disease. Was it unethical to make the drug available in India after it had been banned in the United States? On the contrary, rational people should consider it unethical not to do so. Apply our test: Would the United States, at an earlier stage of development, have used this drug despite its side effects? The answer is clearly yes.

But there are many instances when the answer to similar questions is no. Sometimes a host country's standards are inadequate at any level of economic development. If a country's pollution standards are so low that working on an oil rig would considerably increase a person's risk of developing cancer, foreign oil companies must refuse to do business there. Likewise, if the dangerous side effects of a drug treatment outweigh its benefits, managers should not accept health standards that ignore the risks.

When relative economic conditions do not drive tensions, there is a more objective test for resolving ethical problems. Managers should deem a practice permissible only if they can answer no to both of the following questions: Is it possible to conduct business successfully in the host country without undertaking the practice? and Is the practice a violation of a core human value? Japanese gift giving is a perfect example of a conflict of cultural tradition. Most experienced businesspeople, Japanese and non-Japanese alike, would agree that doing business in Japan would be virtually impossible without adopting the practice. Does gift giving violate a core human value? I cannot identify one that it violates. As a result, gift giving may be permissible for foreign companies in Japan even if it conflicts with ethical attitudes at home. In fact, that conclusion is widely accepted, even by companies such as Texas Instruments and IBM, which are outspoken against bribery.

Does it follow that all nonmonetary gifts are acceptable or that bribes are generally acceptable in countries where they are common? Not at all. . . . What makes the routine practice of gift giving acceptable in Japan are the limits in its scope and intention. When gift giving moves outside those limits, it soon collides with core human values. For example, when Carl Kotchian, president of Lockheed in the 1970s, carried suitcases full of cash to Japanese politicians, he went beyond the norms established by Japanese tradition. That incident galvanized opinion in the United States Congress and helped lead to passage of the Foreign Corrupt Practices Act. Likewise, Roh Tae Woo went beyond the norms established by Korean cultural tradition when he accepted $635.4 million in bribes as president of the Republic of Korea between 1988 and 1993.

Guidelines for Ethical Leadership

Learning to spot intolerable practices and to exercise good judgment when ethical conflicts arise requires practice. Creating a company culture that rewards ethical behavior is essential. The following guidelines for developing a global ethical perspective among managers can help.

Treat corporate values and formal standards of conduct as absolutes. Whatever ethical standards a company chooses, it cannot waver on its principles either at home or abroad. Consider what has become part of company lore at Motorola. Around 1950, a senior executive was negotiating with officials of a South American government on a $10 million sale that would have increased the company's annual net profits by nearly 25%. As the negotiations neared completion, however, the executive walked away from the deal because the officials were asking for $1 million for "fees." CEO Robert Galvin not only supported the executive's decision but also made it clear that Motorola would neither accept the sale on any terms nor do business with those government officials again. Retold over the decades, this story demonstrating Galvin's resolve has helped cement a culture of ethics of thousands of employees at Motorola.

Design and implement conditions of engagement for suppliers and customers. Will your company do business with any customer or supplier? What if a customer or supplier uses child labor? What if it has strong links with organized crime? What if it pressures your company to break a host country's laws? Such issues are best not left for spur-of-the-moment decisions. Some companies have realized that. Sears, for instance, has developed a policy of not contracting production to companies that use prison labor or infringe on workers' rights to health and safety. And BankAmerica has specified as a condition for many of its loans to developing countries that environmental standards and human rights must be observed.

Allow foreign business units to help formulate ethical standards and interpret ethical issues. The French pharmaceutical company Rhône-Poulenc Rorer has allowed foreign subsidiaries to augment lists of corporate ethical principles with their own suggestions. Texas Instruments has paid special attention to issues of international business ethics by creating the Global Business Practices Council, which is made up of managers from countries in which the company operates. With the overarching intent to create a "global ethics strategy, locally deployed," the council's mandate is to provide ethics education and create local processes that will help managers in the company's foreign business units resolve ethical conflicts.

In host countries, support efforts to decrease institutional corruption. Individual managers will not be able to wipe out corruption in a host country, no matter how many bribes they turn down. When a host country's tax system, import and export procedures, and procurement practices favor unethical players, companies must take action.

Many companies have begun to participate in reforming host-country institutions. General Electric, for example, has taken a strong stand in India, using the media to make repeated condemnations of bribery in business and government. General Electric and others have found, however, that a single company usually cannot drive out entrenched corruption. Transparency International, an organization based in Germany, has been effective in helping coalitions of companies, government officials, and others work to reform bribery-ridden bureaucracies in Russia, Bangladesh, and elsewhere.

Exercise moral imagination. Using moral imagination means resolving tensions responsibly and creatively. Coca-Cola, for instance, has consistently turned down requests for bribes from Egyptian officials but has managed to gain political support and public trust by sponsoring a project to plant fruit trees. And take the example of Levi Strauss, which discovered in the early 1990s that two of its suppliers in Bangladesh were employing children under the age of 14—a practice that violated the company's principles but was tolerated in Bangladesh. Forcing the suppliers to fire the children would not have ensured that the children received an education, and it would have caused serious hardship for the families depending on the children's wages. In a creative arrangement, the suppliers agreed to pay the children's regular wages while they attended school and to offer each child a job at age 14. Levi Strauss, in turn, agreed to pay the children's tuition and provide books and uniforms. That arrangement allowed Levi Strauss to uphold its principles and provide long-term benefits to its host country.

Many people think of values as soft; to some they are usually unspoken. A South Seas island society uses the word *mokita,* which means, "the truth that everybody knows but nobody speaks." However difficult they are to articulate, values affect how we all behave. In a global business environment, values in tension are the rule rather than the exception. Without a company's commitment, statements of values and codes of ethics end up as empty platitudes that provide managers with no foundation for behaving ethically. Employees need and deserve more, and responsible members of the global business community can set examples for others to follow. The dark consequences of incidents such as Union Carbide's disaster in Bhopal remind us how high the stakes can be.

EXHIBIT 1.   What Do These Values Have in Common?

Non-Western	Western
Kyosei (Japanese):	Individual liberty
Living and working together for the common good.	
Dharma (Hindu):	Egalitarianism
The fulfillment of inherited duty.	
Santutthi (Buddhist):	Political participation
The importance of limited desires.	
Zakat (Muslim):	Human rights
The duty to give alms to the Muslim poor.	

Notes

1. In other writings, Thomas W. Dunfee and I have used the term *hypernorm* instead of *core human value.*
2. Thomas Donaldson and Thomas W. Dunfee, "Toward a Unified Conception of Business Ethics: Integrative Social Contracts Theory," *Academy of Management Review,* April 1994; and "Integrative Social Contracts Theory: A Communication Conception of Economic Ethics," *Economics and Philosophy,* spring 1995.

Contemporary Business Themes
Introduction

Previous parts in this book have treated broad concepts and broad categories of business ethics issues. Yet because each historical period is confronted by a swarm of unique challenges, those issues require attention. In Part Five we look closely at contemporary issues of marketing, strategy, and the environment.

Marketing

What are the ethics of selling? We are daily bombarded by brochures, TV commercials, direct-mail solicitations, and unsolicited phone calls. But what kind of selling behavior, if any, steps over the ethical line? And, consider *what* is being sold. Is it acceptable to sell products that are potentially harmful? Of course, automobiles are known to be some of the most harmful products, and yet we usually regard their utility as outweighing the disadvantages of their risk. But what happens when potential harm is not counterbalanced by substantial utility, or when the harm falls upon a particular, vulnerable group of people? Is it acceptable to claim that "Sugar Beanies" (the name of an imaginary breakfast cereal) is the "fun part of a nutritious breakfast?" To make this claim even when over half of the weight of the cereal is sugar, and when nutrition experts agree that too much sugar is harming today's children?

In her case study, "Joe Camel," Marianne Jennings explores a case study dealing with the sale of cigarettes to young people. Jennings describes the evolution of the cartoon character, Joe Camel, who proved during the 1980s to be a remarkably successful salesman for Camel cigarettes. The Joe Camel character, sporting sunglasses and a rebellious attitude, helped propel Camel cigarettes in a matter of years to a leading position in the youth market—a market, indeed, in which one of every three youth smokers came to smoke Camel cigarettes. Did the maker of Camel cigarettes, RJR Nabisco, violate tenets of business ethics? What obligations, if any, do cigarette manufacturers have regarding the style and material of their ads?

Roger Crisp, in his article "Persuasive Advertising, Autonomy, and the Creation Of Desire," argues that advertising can negatively affect people's freedom or autonomy. Crisp delves into the issues surrounding the question of whether advertising constitutes manipulation. Does advertising manipulate people? Or, rather, are people sufficiently sophisticated to elude advertising's powers? Crisp questions the claim that advertising does not affect one's autonomy. Persuasive advertising, in particular, he believes, creates desires, which in turn distract people from making clear choices. Advertising, he argues, can create images about lifestyles and values that at least peripherally affect one's self-image and choices.

In the ethics and advertising debate, subtleties abound. In the article "Ethical Myopia" by Alan Singer and others, the question of "framing" a message is addressed. Framing concerns not what an advertisement says directly, but what the "framing" or context is that surrounds the ad. Experiments have shown that people are often economically irrational in responding to choice situations when framed in selective ways. For example, when asked whether they would attend a theater performance, having arrived at the theater and lost an amount of money equal to the purchase price of the ticket, a high percentage of people say that they would, indeed, go ahead and attend the performance. But when asked whether they would go ahead and attend the theater performance, having lost the ticket itself (but in a situation where they could easily repurchase the ticket), many fewer people say that they would attend the performance. This and other experiments show that it is not just economic rationality, but psychological context, that often matters for customers.

This raises questions about how advertisers "frame" their message. A certain marketer may advertise a price in the newspaper, even as he fully intends to discount the price right away in order to "frame" the pricing attractively to the customer. The customer may not be directly misled, but she could be said to be *indirectly* misled insofar as she believes the price is below normal. Or, consider the practice of pricing with a "quantity surcharge" that relies upon the customer's expectation that if a pack is larger then the unit price is lower. Marketers have been known to exploit this presumption by selling *larger* packages while charging *more* per unit than in smaller packages.

Not only framing, but the nature of the audience for an advertisement can raise ethical issues. In his article "Marketing to Inner-City Blacks," George Brenkert examines the promotion of a new malt liquor, "PowerMaster," to inner-city blacks by Heileman Brewing Company. Here the issues are collective as well as individual in nature. For example, it is not the response of individual inner-city African-Americans that is at stake, but rather the health implications of alcohol use for the entire group.

Strategy

Increasingly ethical decisions intersect with strategic ones. The case study "Sears Auto Centers" describes Sears company's attempt to boost productivity through the use of structured incentive systems. Mechanics and other Sears employees were asked by Sears managers to meet specific targets or "quotas" for certain kinds of auto repairs. Critics believe that pushing employees to meet such quotas creates a conflict with certain ethical responsibilities. In the Sears case, many critics assert that Sears performed needless brake jobs and other auto repairs simply for the sake of meeting quotas.

Different elements of strategic thinking are covered in the readings. The well-known management consultant and writer, Peter Senge, discusses how today's challenges require leaders who place a special value on learning. Extending his recommendations even beyond individual learning, Senge argues for "organizational learning." And, in her article, "The Many Faces of the Corporate Code," Lisa Newton discusses the strengths and drawbacks of corporate codes of ethics.

Lynn Sharpe Paine's article "Managing for Organizational Integrity" suggests a comprehensive strategy for dealing with ethics in organizations. Paine contrasts an approach that relies exclusively on rules and hierarchy with one that reflects the deeper values of the organization. The values approach, she argues, is far more persuasive and successful. An overemphasis on compliance and policing ethics diminishes ethical motivation and frustrates cooperative ethical solutions.

The Environment

The final section in Part Five begins with one on the most explosive incidents in recent corporate history. The giant and well-respected European petrochemical company, Shell Oil, encountered in the mid-1990s a tragic situation in Nigeria. Local environmentalists who had complained about Shell's policies were tried, and finally hanged, by the Nigerian government. Some critics asserted that Shell could have done more to prevent the executions, and, in any event, needed to become more directly involved in the issues of the environment and human rights. Partly in response to the Nigerian episode, Shell announced later a series of changes in its famous "principles"—changes that dramatically reorder key values in the company. Shell became, for example, the first company to actively endorse the United Nations *Universal Declaration of Human Rights,* and it also explicitly included reference to human rights in its principles.

A heated controversy has occurred for the past three decades between those who see environmental issues as potentially catastrophic and demanding of radical changes in corporate and government policies, and those who believe that, however important, environmental issues have been exaggerated and are best addressed by market forces. Two essays in this section represent two starkly contrasting sides of this controversy. In his article "Scarcity or Abundance," Julian Simon critiques key assumptions of the environmental movement, arguing instead for a better economic understanding of the environmental phenomenon. There is more reason for optimism, he believes, than the environmental "doomsdayers" would have us believe. In sharp contrast, Ernest Partridge condemns the excessive optimism that he believes infects Simons's "cornucopianism." Simon, he argues, develops a worldview and proposes a policy that can only lead to ruin. Finally, moving away from the controversy and into the realm of practical action, Thomas Hellman, an environmental executive at Bristol-Myers Squibb Corp., proposes an alternative to "end of the pipe" controls. His company has undertaken "product life cycle" reviews that help it determine the best and most efficient ways to improve environmental standards. Hellman also explains how not only policies but culture needs attention in the corporation. For this reason Bristol-Myers Squibb has developed a special education program dealing with the environment.

Much of the analysis of environmental degradation and improvement is conducted in terms of its costs and benefits. Stephen Kelman questions the cost benefit analysis as a general rule for the evaluation of environmental concerns. He argues that there are nonmarket values that cannot be measured quantitatively, such as life, health, and liberty. Thus, in approaching environmental issues, we must clarify what we value in order to calculate the risks of pollution, the harm to future generations, and questions of sustainability.

Marketing

— *Case Study* —

Joe Camel: The Cartoon Character Who Sells Cigarettes

MARIANNE M. JENNINGS

Old Joe Camel, originally a member of a circus that passed through Winston-Salem, North Carolina, each year, was adopted by R. J. Reynolds (RJR) marketers in 1913 as the symbol for a brand being changed from "Red Kamel" to "Camel." In the late 1980s, RJR revived Old Joe with a new look in the form of a cartoon. He became the camel with a "Top Gun" flier jacket, sunglasses, a smirk, and a lot of appeal to young people.

In December 1991, the *Journal of the American Medical Association (JAMA)* published three surveys that found that the cartoon character Joe Camel reached children very effectively. Of children between the ages of three and six who were surveyed, 51.1 percent recognized Joe Camel as being associated with Camel cigarettes.[1] The six-year-olds were as familiar with Joe Camel as they were with the Mickey Mouse logo for the Disney Channel. The surveys also established that 97.7 percent of students between the ages of twelve and nineteen have seen Old Joe and 58 percent thought the ads he was used in were cool. Camel was identified by 33 percent of the students who smoke as their favorite brand.[2]

Before the survey results appeared in *JAMA*, the American Cancer Society, the American Heart Association, and the American Lung Association had petitioned the FTC to ban the ads as "one of the most egregious examples in recent history of tobacco advertising that targets children."[3]

In 1990, Camel shipments rose 11.3 percent. Joe Camel helped RJR take its Camel cigarettes from 2.7 percent to 3.1 percent of the market.[4]

Michael Pertschuk, former FTC head co-director of the Advocacy Institute, an antismoking group, said, "These are the first studies to give us hard evidence, proving what everybody already knows is true: These ads target kids. I think this will add impetus to the movement to further limit tobacco advertising."[5] Joe Tye, founder of Stop Teenage Addictions to Tobacco, stated, "There is a growing body of evidence that teen smoking is increasing. And it's 100 percent related to Camel."[6]

A researcher who worked on the December 1991 *JAMA* study, Dr. Joseph R. DiFranza, stated, "We're hoping this information leads to a complete ban of cigarette advertising."[7] Dr. John Richards summarized the study as follows, "The fact is that the ad is reaching kids, and it is changing their behavior."[8]

RJR spokesman David Fishel responded to the allegations with sales evidence: "We can track 98 percent of Camel sales; and they're not going to youngsters. It's simply not in our best interest for young people to smoke, because that opens the door for the government to interfere with our product."[9] At the time the survey results were published, RJR, along with other manufacturers and the Tobacco Institute, began a multimillion-dollar campaign with billboards and bumper stickers to discourage children from smoking but announced it had no intention of abandoning Joe Camel. The Tobacco Institute publishes a free popular pamphlet called "Tobacco: Helping Youth Say No."

Former U.S. Surgeon General Antonia Novello was very vocal in her desire to change alcohol and cigarette advertising. In March 1992, she called for the withdrawal of the Joe Camel ad campaign: "In years past, R. J. Reynolds would have us walk a mile for a Camel. Today it's time that we invite old Joe Camel himself to take a hike."[10] The AMA's executive vice president, Dr. James S. Todd, concurred:

> This is an industry that kills 400,000 per year, and they have got to pick up new customers. We believe the company is directing its ads to the children who are 3, 6 and 9 years old.[11]

Cigarette sales are, in fact, declining 3 percent per year in the United States.

The average Camel smoker is thirty-five years old, responded an RJR spokeswoman: "Just because children can identify our logo doesn't mean they will use our product."[12] Since the introduction of Joe Camel, however, Camel's share of the under-eighteen market has climbed to 33 percent from 5 percent. Among eighteen- to twenty-five-year-olds, Camel's market share has climbed to 7.9 percent from 4.4 percent.

The Centers for Disease Control reported in March 1992 that smokers between the ages of twelve and eighteen prefer Marlboro, Newport, or Camel cigarettes, the three bands with the most extensive advertising.[13]

Teenagers throughout the country are wearing Joe Camel T-shirts. Brown & Williamson, the producer of Kool cigarettes, began testing a cartoon character for its ads, a penguin wearing sunglasses and Day-Glo sneakers. Company spokesman Joseph Helewicz stated that the ads are geared to smokers between twenty-one and thirty-five years old. Helewicz added that cartoon advertisements for adults are not new and cited the Pillsbury Doughboy and the Pink Panther as effective advertising images.

In mid-1992, then-Surgeon General Novella, along with the American Medical Association, began a campaign called "Dump the Hump" to pressure the tobacco industry to stop ad campaigns that teach kids to smoke. In 1993, the FTC staff recommended a ban on the Joe Camel ads. In 1994, then-Surgeon General Joycelyn Elders blamed the tobacco industry's $4 billion in ads for increased smoking rates among teens. RJR's tobacco division chief, James W. Johnston, responded, "I'll be damned if I'll pull the ads." RJR has put together a team of lawyers and others it refers to as in-house censors to control Joe's influence. A campaign to have Joe wear a bandana was nixed, as was one for a punker Joe with pink hair.

Notes

1. Kathleen Deveny, "Joe Camel Ads Reach Children, Research Finds," *Wall Street Journal,* 11 December 1991, B1.
2. Walecia Konrad, "I'd Toddle a Mile for a Camel," *Business Week,* 23 December 1991, 34.
3. Deveny, B1.
4. Konrad, 34.
5. Deveny, B6.
6. Laura Bird, "Joe Smooth for President," *Adweek's Marketing Week,* 20 May 1991, 21.
7. Konrad, 34.
8. "Camels for Kids," *Time,* 23 December 1991, 52.
9. Ibid.
10. William Chesire, "Don't Shoot: It's Only Joe Camel," *Arizona Republic,* 15 March 1992, C1.
11. Ibid.
12. Konrad, 34.
13. "Selling Death," *Mesa Tribune,* 16 March 1992, A8.

Sources

Dagnoli, Judann. "RJR Aims New Ads at Young Smokers." *Advertising Age,* 11 July 1988, 2–3.

Lippert, Barbara. "Camel's Old Joe Poses the Question: What Is Sexy?" *Adweek's Marketing Week,* 3 October 1988, 55.

Persuasive Advertising, Autonomy, and the Creation of Desire

ROGER CRISP

In this paper, I shall argue that all forms of a certain common type of advertising are morally wrong, on the ground that they override the autonomy of consumers.

One effect of an advertisement might be the creation of a desire for the advertised product. How such desires are caused is highly relevant as to whether we would describe the case as one in which the autonomy of the subject has been overridden. If I read an advertisement for a sale of clothes, I may rush down to my local clothes store and purchase a jacket I like. Here, my desire for the jacket has arisen partly out of my reading the advertisement. Yet, in an ordinary sense, it is based on or answers to certain properties of the jacket—its colour, style, material. Although I could not explain to you why my tastes are as they are, we still describe such cases as examples of autonomous action, in that all the decisions are being made by me: What kind of jacket do I like? Can I afford one? And so on. In certain other cases, however, the causal history of a desire may be different. Desires can be

Kluwer Academic Publishers, *Journal of Business Ethics* 6 (1987) 413–418. © 1987 by D. Reidel Publishing Company. Reprinted with kind permission of Kluwer Academic Publishers.

caused, for instance, by subliminal suggestion. In New Jersey, a cinema flashed sub-threshold advertisements for ice cream onto the screen during movies, and reported a dramatic increase in sales during intermissions. In such cases, choice is being deliberately ruled out by the method of advertising in question. These customers for ice cream were acting "automatonously," rather than autonomously. They did not buy the ice cream because they happened to like it and decided they would buy some, but rather because they had been subjected to subliminal suggestion. Subliminal suggestion is the most extreme form of what I shall call, adhering to a popular dichotomy, persuasive, as opposed to informative, advertising, Other techniques include puffery, which involves the linking of the product, through suggestive language and images, with the unconscious desires of consumers for power, wealth, status, sex, and so on; and repetition, which is self-explanatory, the name of the product being "drummed into" the mind of the consumer.

The obvious objection to persuasive advertising is that it somehow violates the autonomy of consumers. I believe that this objection is correct, and that, if one adopts certain common-sensical standards for autonomy, non-persuasive forms of advertising are not open to such an objection. Very high standards for autonomy are set by Kant, who requires that an agent be entirely external to the causal nexus found in the ordinary empirical world, if his or her actions are to be autonomous. These standards are too high, in that it is doubtful whether they allow *any* autonomous action. Standards for autonomy more congenial to common sense will allow that my buying the jacket is autonomous, although continuing to deny that the people in New Jersey were acting autonomously. In the former case, we have what has come to be known in recent discussions of freedom of the will as *both* free will *and* free action. I both decide what to do, and am not obstructed in carrying through my decision into action. In the latter case, there is free action, but not free will. No one prevents the customers buying their ice cream, but they have not themselves made any genuine decision whether or not to do so. In a very real sense, decisions are made for consumers by persuasive advertisers, who occupy the motivational territory properly belonging to the agent. If what we mean by autonomy, in the ordinary sense, is to be present, the possibility of decision must exist alongside.

Arrington (1982) discusses, in a challenging paper, the techniques of persuasive advertising I have mentioned, and argues that such advertising does not override the autonomy of consumers. He examines four notions central to autonomous action, and claims that, on each count, persuasive advertising is exonerated on the charge we have made against it. I shall now follow in the footsteps of Arrington, but argue that he sets the standards for autonomy too low for them to be acceptable to common sense, and that the charge therefore still sticks.

(A) Autonomous Desire

Arrington argues that an autonomous desire is a first-order desire (a desire for some object, say, Pongo Peach cosmetics) accepted by the agent because it fulfils a second-order desire (a desire about a desire, say, a desire that my first-order desire for Pongo Peach be fulfilled), and that most of the first-order desires engendered in us by advertising are desires that we do accept. His example is an advertisement for Grecian Formula 16, which engenders in him a desire to be younger. He desires that both his desire to be younger and his desire for Grecian Formula 16 be fulfilled.

Unfortunately, this example is not obviously one of persuasive advertising. It may be the case that he just has this desire to look young again rather as I had certain sartorial tastes before I saw the ad about the clothes sale, and then decides to buy Grecian Formula 16 on the basis of these tastes. Imagine this form of advertisement: a person is depicted using Grecian Formula 16, and is then shown in a position of authority, surrounded by admiring members of the opposite sex. This would be a case of puffery. The advertisement implies that having hair coloured by the product will lead to positions of power, and to one's becoming more attractive to the opposite sex. It links, by suggestion, the product with my unconscious desires for power and sex. I may still claim that I am buying the product because I want to look young again. But the real reasons for my purchase are my unconscious desires for power and sex, and the link made between the product and the fulfilment of those desires by the advertisement. These reasons are not reasons I could avow to myself as good reasons for buying the product, and, again, the possibility of decision is absent.

Arrington's claim is that an autonomous desire is a first-order desire which we accept. Even if we allow that it is possible for the agent to consider whether to accept or to repudiate first-order desires induced by persuasive advertising, it seems that all first-order desires induced purely by persuasive advertising will be non-autonomous in Arrington's sense. Many of us have a strong second-order desire not to be manipulated by others without our knowledge, and for no good reason. Often, we are manipulated by others without our knowledge, but for a good reason, and one that we can accept. Take an accomplished actor: much of the skill of an actor is to be found in unconscious body-language. This manipulation we see as essential to our being entertained, and thus acquiesce in it. What is important about this case is that there seems to be no diminution of autonomy. We can still judge the quality of the acting, in that the manipulation is part of its quality. In other cases, however, manipulation ought not to be present, and these are cases where the ability to decide is importantly diminished by the manipulation. Decision is central to the theory of the market-process: I should be able to decide whether to buy product A or product B, by judging them on their merits. Any manipulation here I shall repudiate as being for no good reason. This is not to say, incidentally, that once the fact that my desires are being manipulated by others has been made transparent to me, my desire will lapse. The people in New Jersey would have been unlikely to cease their craving for ice cream, if we had told them that their desire had been subliminally induced. But they would no longer have voiced acceptance of this desire, and, one assumes, would have resented the manipulation of their desires by the management of the cinema.

It is no evidence for the claim that most of our desires are autonomous in this sense that we often return to purchase the same product over and over again. For this might well show that persuasive advertising has been supremely efficient in inducing non-autonomous desires in us, which we are unable even to attempt not to act on, being unaware of their origin. Nor is it an argument in Arrington's favour that certain members of our society will claim not to have the second-order desire we have postulated. For it may be that this is a desire which we can see is one that human beings *ought* to have, a desire which it would be in their interests to have, and the lack of which is itself evidence of profound manipulation.

(B) Rational Desire and Choice

One might argue that the desires induced by advertising are often irrational, in the sense that they are not present in an agent in full possession of the facts about the product. This argument fails, says Arrington, because if we require *all* the facts about a thing before we can desire that thing, then all our desires will be irrational; and if we require only the *relevant* information, then prior desires determine the relevance of information. Advertising may be said to enable us to fulfil these prior desires, through the transfer of information, and the supplying of means to ends is surely a paradigm example of rationality.

But, what about persuasive, as opposed to informative, advertising? Take puffery. Is it not true that a person may buy Pongo Peach cosmetics, hoping for an adventure in paradise, and that the product will not fulfil these hopes? Are they really in possession of even the relevant facts? Yes, says Arrington. We wish to purchase *subjective* effects, and these are genuine enough. When I use Pongo Peach, I will experience a genuine feeling of adventure.

Once again, however, our analysis can help us to see the strength of the objection. For a desire to be rational, in any plausible sense, that desire must at least not be induced by the interference of other persons with my system of tastes, against my will and without my knowledge. Can we imagine a person, asked for a reason justifying their purchase of Pongo Peach, replying: "I have an unconscious desire to experience adventure, and the product has been linked with this desire through advertising"? If a desire is to be rational, it is not necessary that all the facts about the object be known to the agent, but one of the facts about that desire must be that it has not been induced in the agent through techniques which the agent cannot accept. Thus, applying the schema of Arrington's earlier argument, such a desire will be repudiated by the agent as non-autonomous and irrational.

Arrington's claim concerning the subjective effects of the products we purchase fails to deflect the charge of overriding autonomy we have made against persuasive advertising. Of course, very often the subjective effects will be lacking. If I use Grecian Formula 16, I am unlikely to find myself being promoted at work, or surrounded by admiring members of the opposite sex. This is just straight deception. But even when the effects do manifest themselves, such advertisements have still overridden my autonomy. They have activated desires which lie beyond my awareness, and over behaviour flowing from which I therefore have no control. If these claims appear doubtful, consider whether this advertisement is likely to be successful: "Do you have a feeling of adventure? Then use this brand of cosmetics." Such an advertisement will fail, in that it appeals to a *conscious* desire, either which we do not have, or which we realise will not be fulfilled by purchasing a certain brand of cosmetics. If the advertisement were for a course in mountain-climbing, it might meet with more success. Our conscious self is not so easily duped by advertising, and this is why advertisers make such frequent use of the techniques of persuasive advertising.

(C) Free Choice

One might object to persuasive advertising that it creates desires so covert that an agent cannot resist them, and that acting on them is therefore neither free nor voluntary. Arrington claims that a person acts or chooses *freely* if they can adduce considerations which justify their act in their mind; and *voluntarily* if, had they been aware of a reason for acting otherwise, they could have done so. Only occasionally, he says, does advertising prevent us making free and voluntary choices.

Regarding free action, it is sufficient to note that, according to Arrington, if I were to be converted into a human robot, activated by an Evil Genius who has implanted electrodes in my brain, my actions would be free as long as I could cook up some justification for my behaviour. I want to dance this jig because I enjoy dancing. (Compare: I want to buy this ice cream because I like ice cream.) If my argument is right, we are placed in an analogous position by persuasive advertising. If we no longer mean by freedom of action the mere non-obstruction of behaviour, are we still ready to accept that we are engaged in free action? As for whether the actions of consumers subjected to persuasive advertising are voluntary in Arrington's sense, I am less optimistic than he is. It is likely, as we have suggested, that the purchasers of ice cream or Pongo Peach would have gone ahead with their purchase even if they had been made aware that their desires had been induced in them by persuasive advertising. But they would now claim that they themselves had not made the decision, that they were acting on a desire engendered in them which they did not accept, and that there was, therefore, a good reason for them not to make the purchase. The unconscious is not obedient to the commands of the conscious, although it may be forced to listen.

In fact, it is odd to suggest that persuasive advertising does give consumers a choice. A choice is usually taken to require the weighing-up of reasons. What persuasive advertising does is to remove the very conditions of choice.

(D) Control or Manipulation

Arrington offers the following criteria for control:

A person C controls the behaviour of another person P if
(1) C intends P to act in a certain way A
(2) C's intention is causally effective in bringing about A, and
(3) C intends to ensure that all of the necessary conditions of A are satisfied.

He argues that advertisements tend to induce a desire for X, given a more basic desire for Y. Given my desire for adventure, I desire Pongo Peach cosmetics. Thus, advertisers do not control consumers, since they do not intend to produce all of the necessary conditions for our purchases.

Arrington's analysis appears to lead to some highly counter-intuitive consequences. Consider, again, my position as human robot. Imagine that the Evil Genius relies on the fact that I have certain basic unconscious desires in order to effect his plan. Thus, when he wants me to dance a jig, it is necessary that I have a more basic desire, say, ironically, for power. What the electrodes do is to jumble up my practical reasoning processes, so that I believe that I am dancing the jig because I like dancing, while, in reality, the desire to dance stems from a link between the dance and the fulfilment of my desire for power, forged by the electrodes. Are we still happy to say that I am not controlled? And does not persuasive advertising bring about a similar jumbling-up of the practical reasoning processes of consumers? When I buy Pongo Peach, I may be unable to offer a reason for my purchase, or I may claim that I want to look good. In reality, I buy it owing to the link made by persuasive advertising between my unconscious desire for adventure and the cosmetic in question.

A more convincing account of behaviour control would be to claim that it occurs when a person causes another person to act for reasons which the other person could not accept as good or justifiable reasons for the action. This is how brain-washing is to be distinguished from liberal education, rather than on Arrington's ground that the brain-washer arranges all the necessary conditions for belief. The student can both accept that she has the beliefs she has because of her education and continue to hold those beliefs as true, whereas the victim of brain-washing could not accept the explanation of the origin of her beliefs, while continuing to hold those beliefs. It is worth recalling the two cases we mentioned at the beginning of this paper. I can accept my tastes in dress, and do not think that the fact that their origin is unknown to me detracts from my autonomy, when I choose to buy the jacket. The desire for ice cream, however, will be repudiated, in that it is the result of manipulation by others, without good reason.

———— • ————

It seems, then, that persuasive advertising does override the autonomy of consumers, and that, if the overriding of autonomy, other things being equal, is immoral, then persuasive advertising is immoral.

An argument has recently surfaced which suggests that, in fact, other things are not equal, and that persuasive advertising, although it overrides autonomy, is morally acceptable. This argument was first developed by Nelson (1978), and claims that persuasive advertising is a form of informative advertising, albeit an indirect form. The argument runs at two levels: first, the consumer can judge from the mere fact that a product is heavily advertised, regardless of the form or content of the advertisements, that that product is likely to be a market-winner. The reason for this is that it would not pay to advertise market-losers. Second, even if the consumer is taken in by the content of the advertisement, and buys the product for that reason, he is not being irrational. For he would have bought the product *anyway*, since the very fact that it is advertised means that it is a good product. As Nelson says:

> It does not pay consumers to make very thoughtful decisions about advertising. They can respond to advertising for the most ridiculous, explicit reasons and still do what they would have done if they had made the most careful judgements about their behaviour. "Irrationality" is rational if it is cost-free.

Our conclusions concerning the mode of operation of persuasive advertising, however, suggest that Nelson's argument cannot succeed. For the first level to work, it would have to be true that a purchaser of a product can evaluate that product on its own merits, and then decide whether to purchase it again. But, as we have seen, consumers induced to purchase products by persuasive advertising are not buying those products on the basis of a decision founded upon any merit the products happen to have. Thus, if the product turns out to be less good than less heavily advertised alternatives, they will not be disappointed, and will continue to purchase, if subjected to the heavy advertising which induced them to buy in the first place. For this reason, heavy persuasive advertising is not a sign of quality, and the fact that a product is advertised does not suggest that it is good. In fact, if the advertising has little or no informative content, it might suggest just the opposite. If the product has genuine merits, it should be possible to mention them. Persuasive advertising, as the executives on Madison Avenue know, can be used to sell anything, regardless of its nature or quality.

For the second level of Nelson's argument to succeed, and for it to be in the consumer's interest to react even unthinkingly to persuasive advertising, it must be true that the first level is valid. As the first level fails, there is not even a *prima facie* reason for the belief that it is in the interest of the consumer to be subjected to persuasive advertising. In fact, there are two weighty reasons for doubting this belief. The first has already been hinted at: products promoted through persuasive advertising may well not be being sold on their merits, and may, therefore, be bad products, or products that the consumer would not desire on being confronted with unembellished facts about the product. The second is that this form of "rational irrationality" is anything but cost-free. We consider it a great cost to lose our autonomy. If I were to demonstrate to you conclusively that if I were to take over your life, and make your decisions for you, you would have a life containing far more of whatever you think makes life worth living, apart from autonomy, than if you were to retain control, you would not surrender your autonomy to me even for these great gains in other values. As we mentioned above in our discussion of autonomous desire, we have a strong second-order desire not to act on first-order desires induced in us unawares by others, for no good reason, and now we can see that that desire applies even to cases in which we would *appear* to be better off in acting on such first-order desires.

Thus, we may conclude that Nelson's argument in favour of persuasive advertising is not convincing. I should note, perhaps, that my conclusion concerning persuasive advertising echoes that of Santilli (1983). My argument differs from his, however, in centering upon the notions of autonomy and causes of desires acceptable to the agent, rather than upon the distinction between needs and desires. Santilli claims that the arousal of a desire is not a rational process, unless it is preceded by a knowledge of actual needs. This, I believe, is too strong. I may well have no need of a new tennis-racket, but my desire for one, aroused by informative advertisements in the newspaper, seems rational enough. I would prefer to claim that a desire is autonomous and at least *prima facie* rational if it is not induced in the agent without his knowledge and for no good reason, and allows ordinary processes of decision-making to occur.

Finally, I should point out that, in arguing against all persuasive advertising, unlike Santilli, I am not to be interpreted as bestowing moral respectability upon all informative advertising. Advertisers of any variety ought to consider whether the ideological objections often made to their conduct have any weight. Are they, for instance, imposing a distorted system of values upon consumers, in which the goal of our lives is to consume, and in which success is measured by one's level of consumption? Or are they entrenching attitudes which prolong the position of certain groups subject to discrimination, such as women or homosexuals? Advertisers should also carefully consider whether their product will be of genuine value to any consumers, and, if so, attempt to restrict their campaigns to the groups in society which will benefit (see Durham, 1984). I would claim, for instance, that all advertising of tobacco-based products, even of the informative variety, is wrong, and that some advertisements for alcohol are wrong, in that they are directed at the wrong audience. Imagine, for instance, a liquor-store manager erecting an informative bill-board opposite an alcoholics' rehabilitation center. But these are secondary questions for prospective advertisers. The primary questions must be whether they are intending to employ the techniques of persuasive advertising, and, if so, how these techniques can be avoided.

References

Arrington, R.: 1982, "Advertising and Behaviour Control," *Journal of Business Ethics* I, 1.

Durham, T.: 1984, "Information, Persuasion, and Control in Moral Appraisal of Advertising Strategy," *Journal of Business Ethics* III, 3.

Nelson, P.: 1978, "Advertising and Ethics," in *Ethics, Free Enterprise, and Public Policy,* (eds.) R. De George and J. Pichler, New York: Oxford University Press.

Santilli, P.: 1983, "The Informative and Persuasive Functions of Advertising: A Moral Appraisal," *Journal of Business Ethics* II, I.

Seven Marketing Pitches

Consider the following seven marketing techniques:

1. An ad claiming that the Honda Accord has high satisfaction ratings among first-year owners.
2. A TV commercial in which James Garner exhibits the sporty, fun experience of driving the Mazda RX-7.
3. An ad for the Chevrolet Camaro presenting it as enhancing sex appeal by displaying the car among a group of attractive young men/women (your pick) in bathing suits.
4. An ad for Allstate life insurance that pictures two houses, one of which is fully involved in a fire, with a voice-over informing us that the real tragedy has just happened in the other house: The breadwinner died without sufficient life insurance to cover the mortgage.
5. An ad for a device which can summon medical assistance in an emergency; the ad shows an elderly woman falling down a flight of steps. Unfortunately, she is not wearing the device, and help arrives too late.
6. A Saturday morning TV ad for Smurf dolls; it is broadcast during a cartoon show starring the cute little creatures.
7. A subliminal message "Buy Coke" shown before intermission in a movie theater.

Which of these ads do you intuitively feel is a violation of the consumer's autonomy? If you feel as most people do, you will find the first ad unproblematic and the last ad to be a violation. If this is your response, you must identify the features of the subliminal technique that make it objectionable from the point of view of autonomy. You must also be consistent and willing to accept the consequences of your analysis. For instance, if the feature that makes the subliminal technique unacceptable is also present in the ad aimed at children, you must make the same judgment about both ads.

The most common explanation of the usual reaction to the seventh case relates the consumer's being unaware of the appeal. The subliminal technique is intended to manipulate consumers by making them less likely to resist the desire the ad may generate. (Note that this explanation makes the technique objectionable even if the consumer ultimately decides *not* to buy the product.)

Ethical Myopia: The Case of "Framing" by Framing

ALAN E. SINGER — STEVEN LYSONSKI
MING SINGER — DAVID HAYES

INTRODUCTION

Substantial recent research in management and marketing science has explored the practical implications of systematic patterns of bias and heuristic-use in human decision-making. Researchers have proposed several applications of the emergent cognitive models in administrative and marketing contexts. These applications have included:

- Using particular heuristics to influence subordinates' commitment to a proposal (Schwenk, 1986)
- Attempting to influence customers (i.e., consumers and corporate buyers) by appealing to framing-effects, reference-prices and other biases (Thaler, 1985; Puto, 1987; Urbany *et. al.,* 1988)
- Modelling aggregate-level equilibrium market processes (Russell and Thaler, 1985; Kahneman, *et. al.,* 1986)
- Explaining investors' preferences for cash dividends over capital gains, with implications for dividend policy (Sheffrin and Statman, 1984)
- Viewing negotiations as strategic interactions between faulty cognitive systems, with implications for bargaining tactics (Neale and Bazerman, 1985)
- Using framing effects to influence sequential investment decision-making processes (Whyte, 1986).

With only one exception, all of these applications of cognitive models have been proposed and investigated without any reference to the ethical issues involved, such as utilitarian justification, fairness, deception, or exploitation.

From *Journal of Business Ethics* 10:29–36, 1991. Copyright by Kluwer Academic Publishers. Reprinted with kind permission of Kluwer Academic Publishers.

The only recorded exception to this surprizing ethical myopia is Schwenk's (1986) observation that where senior management use techniques of persuasion based on subordinates' cognitive heuristic-use, like vivid but unrepresentative anecdotes, the practice possibly infringes the subordinates' rights.

Ethical myopia is particularly evident in some of the associated recent developments in marketing science. Recently, some sophisticated marketing techniques based on cognitive models have been described and implicitly advocated, without any reference to ethics, nor social responsibility. These new model-based techniques appeal to the imperfect but often systematic decision-making processes of individual buyers or consumers. In the underlying models, particularly Prospect Theory (Kahneman and Tversky, 1979) and Transaction Utility Theory (Thaler, 1985) the concepts of mental accounting, framing and transaction-utilities are employed. In the preliminary section of this paper, therefore, these concepts are described briefly with reference to examples of the associated marketing techniques. Some ethical issues surrounding proposed applications to marketing are then explored.

These ethical explorations are structured around three themes. First, the utilitarian justification for using the model-based techniques is considered. Given the original context in which the techniques were proposed, a plausible utilitarian justification could exist. However, in many other marketing contexts, where use of the same techniques could also increase the seller's profits, it is much more difficult to justify their use with reference to consequential costs and benefits. The second theme examined concerns the more general marketing practice of encouraging customers to hold false beliefs, or to make inappropriate inferences, when making purchasing decisions. Objections to that type of marketing practice then apply *a forteriori* to some of the proposed special applications of Prospect Theory (PT) and Transaction Utility Theory (TUT). Finally, there is a discussion of the claim that the new techniques and tactics are purely scientific and therefore value-free.

Mental Accounting, Framing and Utility

This section describes very briefly some of the new concepts employed in the marketing models.

Mental Accounting

The concept of a "mental account", as it is now used in consumer behavior theory, originated from Tversky and Kahneman's (1981) "Theatre Ticket" experiment. In that experiment, subjects were asked:

> Imagine that you have decided to see a play where admission is $10 per ticket. As you enter the theatre you discover that you have lost the $10 bill. Would you still pay $10 to see the play?

Responses obtained were "Yes", 88%; "No", 12%. Another group of subjects were then asked:

> Imagine that you have decided to see a play and paid the admission price of $10 per ticket. As you enter the theatre you discover that you have lost the ticket. The seat was not marked and the ticket cannot be recovered. Would you pay $10 for another ticket?

Responses obtained were "Yes", 46%; "No", 54%. Others have reported similar data in replications (e.g., Singer *et. al.,* 1986). The contrasting responses obtained to the two versions of the "Theatre Ticket" problem clearly demonstrate the effect of minor details or context on individual's preference and choice. The findings cannot be explained in terms of wealth-related outcomes alone, as in traditional economic models of rational individual choice. Instead, Tversky and Kahneman suggested that the differences could be explained in terms of mental or cognitive processes, specifically by assuming that "going to the theatre" is normally viewed as a transaction, in which the cost of the ticket is exchanged for the experience of seeing the play. Loss of the ticket would then mean debiting a "topical mental account" set up for the particular topic of play-going; whilst loss of the cash would not. According to this theory, the mental framing of the problem, or the structuring of these hypothetical mental accounts affects the purchasing decision.

In the light of these and similar concepts, like framing and transaction-utility, marketing scientists have been exploring ways of influencing the structure of customers' hypothetical mental accounts, for a given transaction, in order to influence behavior and increase the seller's profits (e.g., Puto, 1987; Urbany, 1988).

Framing

The particular concept of "Framing" also refers to the form of presentation of "risky" economic objects-of-choice, like gambles. In Kahneman and Tversky (1979), independent groups of subjects were offered the following two equivalent risky choices:

> 1. (Imagine that . . .) in addition to whatever you own you have been given $1000. You are now asked to choose between: "A 50–50 chance of $100 *or* $500 with certainty".

> 2. (Imagine that . . .) in addition to whatever you own, you have been given $2000. You are now asked to choose between: "A 50–50 chance of a loss of $1000 *or* A certain loss of $500."

For the first question, a clear majority chose the certain $500 alternative; but with the second question, a clear majority chose the risky gamble. This is a surprizing result because the objects-of-choice in the two versions are identical in terms of the wealth-related outcomes and the stated probabilities. This finding, often replicated, confirms that preferences are very much influenced by the presentation of a "deal" involving risk, rather than its objective economic substance. These findings, and many similar ones, are all accommodated and explained by the detailed decision models proposed in Prospect Theory and Transaction Utility Theory. These new models are variants of the subjective expected utility (SEU) model used to explain risky choice in economic theory, but they also include representations of cognitive processes, like the psychological editing of information.

Transaction Utility

The basic SEU model of consumer choice simply involves assigning quantitative utilities to the possible outcomes of decision, then taking expectations, or probability-weighted averages, of these utilities. According to this model, the alternative with the highest expected utility *should* be chosen. The basic model is viewed usually as a prescriptive model, yielding the rational choice alternative; but it may also be viewed as a descriptive model, capable of being falsified and modified through empirical testing. Subsequent modifications that improve the *predictive power* of the model then become useful as a base from which to develop practical marketing techniques.

Most variants and modifications of the basic SEU model are purely mathematical extensions, making no assumptions whatever about internal mental or cognitive processes (e.g., Schoemaker, 1982). However, Prospect Theory and Transaction Utility Theory are a radical departure from these black-box models and towards cognitive models involving hypothesized mental mechanisms. They may be said to "break the sacred boundary of the skin", in striving to accurately explain and predict consumer-choice. In the new models, cognitive or mental processes such as the *detection* and *editing* of information are represented. In addition, parameters of TUT include subjective mental constructs, such as a *perceived* reference-price, rather than *objective* prices (a distinction that has *ethical* implications to be explored later). Several specific empirical findings about behaviour may then be explained. For example, in addition to the robust results already described, the new models also accurately predict that:

- Most people, as consumers, would prefer "segregated gains" over combined gains of equivalent economic value. (e.g., Most people believe that a person would be "happier" to win $50 plus $25 in separate lotteries, rather than $75 in one; Thaler, 1985, p. 203).
- If a given dollar payment can be framed in the mind of a buyer (customer) as a reduction in a large gain (rather than an absolute loss) then the "displeasure" or loss-of-value associated with that payment will be small. This is deduced from the shape of the value function in the theories (Figure 1).

Marketing scientists have been quick to recognize the practical implications of such findings. Three examples are given here: First, the perceived value of a product could be increased by separately identifying the desirable features or attributes (reflecting the first finding above). Next, Thaler (1985,

FIGURE 1.   A hypothetical value function. *Source:* Kahneman and Tversky (1979)

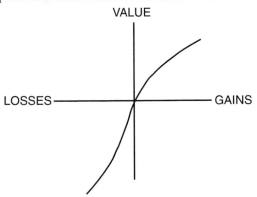

p. 209) has suggested that sellers might use "tie-ins" to increase their total sales, because the extra payment made for the minor item would be framed as only a small value-loss, because of the concave shape of the value function in the model. Finally, Puto (1987) has proposed that customers could be lured to a retail outlet through (sold-out or apparent) bargain offers so that a decision to buy nothing would be framed as a "loss" (a topical mental account with a debit balance) and them, according to the new theories, *risky* purchases would become more attractive to the customer.[1]

Market-clearing and Marketing Tactics

Although the new models were deduced from micro-level behavioral data, they have also subsequently been used to predict or explain some aggregate level market phenomena (e.g., Thaler, 1985; Russell and Thaler, 1985; Kahneman *et. al.*, 1986). The TUT model has enabled a specification of conditions under which consumer markets will fail to *clear* (i.e., where prices are such that supply and demand do not balance). Thaler (1985) explained the non-clearance of some markets, like the market for "superbowl" tickets in the U.S. (where demand is very high but official prices are only moderate) by pointing to the large negative transaction-utility associated with the very high price needed to clear the market. "Transaction utility" represents the idea that people often attach utility to a deal *per se*, that is independent of the economic value of the goods actually acquired. According to the theory, transaction utility is a function of the perceived reference price, which in turn depends on several factors, including the perceived fairness of a deal.

Therefore, according to TUT, marketing techniques aimed at manipulating the perceived reference price could facilitate the market-clearing process. That is, if the perceived reference price can somehow be raised, then people would be willing to pay the higher actual clearing price, without any loss of goodwill resulting from a "bad deal". Thaler (1985) offers the following examples of how, according to the theory, actual prices might be raised without reducing demand:

- raising the *perceived reference price* (for example, by discounting from an advertised retail price, a practice known as "double pricing", although there may be legal constraints),
- increasing the *perceived costs* incurred by the seller (as in the creation of an expensive image for the seller),
- obscuring the reference price (for example by changing the format of the product),
- using *minimum-purchases or tie-ins* (i.e. "integrate" the buyer's payments, to reduce the buyer's perceived value-loss from the total payment).

Thaler suggested that, for the purpose of applying the theory in this way, the metaphor of the consumer or buyer as a "pleasure-machine" is appropriate. Therefore the ethical case for or against the use of these and similar techniques rests partly on an acceptance of the pleasure-machine metaphor. The ethical issue surrounding the applications of these models are now explored, using three themes (i) utilitarian justification (ii) exploitation of cognitive habits, and (iii) scientific status.

(i) Utilitarian Justification

It seems reasonable to assume that facilitating the market clearing process by using these techniques would make a positive overall contribution to economic welfare. For example, balancing supply with demand through the price mechanism prevents the creation of "black markets", or other more arbitrary allocations of resources. So, there are at least some contexts where use of the model-based tactics might be ethically justified. However, these selling and marketing techniques can be applied also to a wide range of marketing situations, where the same justification is not available.

Thaler (1985) suggested the above tactics to facilitate market clearing. However, subsequent related research in consumer-behavior (e.g., Puto, 1987; Urbany *et al.,* 1988) has not been restricted to the originally discussed case of non-clearing markets. In fact, the same techniques for raising prices or profits might be employed by marketers in many different contexts. This includes cases where markets fail to clear because prices are already too *high* (so that raising reference prices further would artificially restrict the goods to an even wealthier minority) or in cases where the seller has effective market power over the supply of a good, including even basic goods like water, electricity, telecommunications, etc.

Marketers who are motivated purely to increase sales or profit in the short term have no pragmatic reason, relating to the nature of the market or the goods, to resist using these tactics for raising prices. From a marketer's perspective, these techniques can be used to increase profits for almost any given product or service. In the case of electricity, for example, the technique of shifting the reference price has been widely used in practice (by shortening the billing cycle). However, the utilitarian ethical argument is far less plausible in cases like electricity supply, than in cases like super-bowl tickets. For basic goods, it is the lack of *actual* (rather than perceived) ability of some consumer to *pay* for something they desperately need, that should be evaluated ethically (cf., Goldman, 1980). In essence, marketing tactics shaped around the new models may well induce a higher *perceived* reference price for, say, electricity, but this perception adds nothing to the less-wealthy customer's *real* ability to pay for the goods.

According to theories like TUT, the seller can increase the "value of buying a good" either by increasing the transaction-utility (by, for example, altering the reference price) or by increasing "acquisition utility", by re-framing the objects of choice. As ethical justification, it could be argued that reframing a "deal", or encouraging the setting up of a particular system of mental accounts, can actually make the customer feel better, or create happiness. This argument, however, is seriously flawed. First, the psychological phenomenon that "we value events under the descriptions we put on them" (cf., Schick 1987) does not automatically grant others a moral license to describe events for us, in clever pursuit of their own self-interest and at our possible economic cost! (This practice could even be described as "Framing by framing".) Second, precisely the same argument could license the use of *any* device, including outright lies, that deceptively increases perceived "value" for the buyer at the time of purchase.

A final obstacle to any attempted utilitarian ethical justification for these tactics, concerns the interpretations of "value" and "utility" in the new models.

The concept of "utility" in traditional SEU models arises from the need to satisfy particular abstract axioms, or postulates of "rationality" (such as transitivity of preferences). In contrast, the "Value-Function" of PT and the "Acquisition-Utility" of TUT, which operate after mental editing processes, can only be interpreted as measures of internal psychological states (i.e., using the pleasure-machine metaphor). Thus, when used in these new models, the meaning of "utility" has changed and now represents something like an internal-state parameter for the individual. This concept of utility in the "pleasure machine" metaphor contrasts markedly with the idea of measurable overall costs and benefit in ethical utilitarianism. Historically, ethical theory has considered these costs and benefits to be defined in terms of concepts like "happiness", "fulfillment", "human-potential" and even "friendship". Therefore all of these conceptions of utility in ethics are very remote from the new behavioral models and the data that has driven them.

(ii) Strategically Exploiting Cognitive Habits

A second basic theme in the ethical appraisal concerns the more general idea of exploiting another person's reasoning and cognitive habits. In order to structure the discussion of this theme, the buyer or consumer is considered here as a cognitive system having beliefs, goals and a capability of making inferences. Accordingly, attempts at influence or deception could be directed at (i) the buyer's beliefs and perceptions, or (ii) the buyer's use of general rules and cognitive heuristics. The relevant ethical issues and arguments then apply *a forteriori* to the use of the pleasure-machine metaphor in the marketplace, since the new marketing tactics are a special case of manipulating others' perceptions and cognitive mechanisms.

Buyer's Beliefs and Perceptions

First, a seller can focus on the buyer's beliefs. For example, a product might be falsely advertised or labelled (e.g., "waterproof" watches). Such false claims are obviously unethical and normally illegal. Gardner (1975) described them as "unconscionable lies". Yet ethically there may be little difference between deceiving someone with natural-language statements and deceiving them by creating an expensive "image" for a cheap product, in order to increase the perceived reference price, as suggested by the TUT model.

A related marketing tactic is where the seller conceals those facts about the product that could adversely affect the purchase decision. Such "nondisclosure" tactics often concern a product's operating characteristics (such as the high power-consumption of some cheap appliances). In making a purchase decision, the customer might completely overlook the non-disclosed product attribute; or alternatively might make inappropriate inferences about those characteristics, from the information that is readily available. There are many reported example of this form of deception:

- Claiming (truthfully) that a brand of washing powder "contains blue crystals", inviting the false inference that crystals improve cleaning power (Gardner, 1975).

- Pricing with a *quantity surcharge,* which exploits the (often appropriate) heuristic "If the pack is larger then price-per-unit is lower" (e.g., Nason and Della Bitta, 1983; Zotos, 1989).
- Marketing cheap brands of dishwashing liquids that are actually the most expensive in terms of price-per dish washed. "Some consumers confuse the mapping from price-per-bottle to price-per-dish-washed" (Russell and Thaler, 1985).
- Using nutritional labels on food products, to create a (false) impression that the product can provide protection against diseases such as cancer.

It is difficult to justify *these* particular non-disclosure tactics, ethically. They fail to meet conventional ethical criteria such as universalizability, fairness, etc. Moreover, even their legality has been debated in the U.S., with a view to making "affirmative disclosure" mandatory (cf., Buccholz, 1982). Yet these marketing tactics are also quite similar in spirit to those associated with the TUT model. Non-disclosure tactics, like some of the above tactics for raising prices, *all* involve "encouraging inappropriate inferences". For example, deliberately obscuring the reference price is basically similar in spirit to using a quantity surcharge. Thus the ethical objections apply with roughly similar force to both types of tactic.

Buyer's Cognitive Heuristics

There is a close parallel between deliberately encouraging a buyer or consumer to misuse common choice-heuristics and the new practice of targeting particular *cognitive* heuristics. Cognitive heuristics are hypothesized mental processes (procedures or mechanisms) that underlie quantitative judgments that in turn might affect buyer's preferences. Given the large and growing literature on behavioral decision theory and its applications, the absence of previous discussion of the ethical issues involved in exploiting cognitive heuristics seems particularly surprising.

The Availability Heuristic (Tversky and Kahneman, 1973) provides a clear illustration of these issues. This heuristic links the judged probability of an event to the ease of imagining that event. Marketers can exploit this cognitive heuristic to increase sales. For example, sales of earthquake insurance may be increased by furnishing vivid images of earthquakes. These messages, known as "fear-appeals", arouse anxiety; but they also act psychologically to make the event seem more likely than it actually is. The technique is not always completely unethical, since it could be used in the real interests of the customers and society, such as promoting the use of safety belts. However, there are several reasons why the *indiscriminate* and systematic targeting of such cognitive heuristics may be unethical.

First, Hamlin (1986) has noted that heuristic-use by the individual might be viewed as a "cognitive precommitment"; that is, the decision-maker has bound himself, like legendary Ulysses to his ship's mast, in order to save cognitive resources in the future. This means that targeting heuristic-use can be likened to "mugging" someone whose hands are tied, as compared with someone who is free to fight back. Second, cognitive errors do not arise from heuristic use *per se* but from a failure to realize that their use might be inappropriate in a particular context. Deliberate targeting of the misapplication of useful heuristics exploits that precise point of buyers' vulnerability, in a way that could be considered as predatory.

Finally, buyers who realize that their cognitive and choice heuristics are being systematically manipulated, might feel some resentment. They would be in a very similar position to informed victims of *subliminal* advertising (e.g., Crisp 1987) whose perceptual processes have been systematically targeted by marketers. Indeed, many of the ethical objections that have been voiced in connection with the commercial use of subliminal messages (manipulative, denial of autonomy, etc.) could also be directed to the targeting of cognitive heuristics. Although subliminal advertising is no longer practiced, it certainly provoked controversy and moral outrage when originally introduced on an experimental basis. It was widely condemned as being deceptive and unethical. It is also now illegal. Yet these ethical objections to targeting cognitive heuristics also apply to the targeting of the metaphorical "pleasure machine" with tactics like "obscuring the reference price". These marketing tactics deliberately target the buyers' frames (or percepts) and mental accounts (or heuristics).

(iii) Scientific Status as a Justification

The third and final overall theme in this ethical evaluation concerns the status of Prospect theory and Transaction utility theory within a scientific psychology of the individual. These modified SEU models seem to have all the appearance of normative or prescriptive decision models; but at some point in their development, prescription has given way to *prediction* as the "sole purpose" (Thaler, 1985). If the latter interpretation is accepted, it is then necessary to consider the overall social consequences of these behavioral predictions being made and used as a basis for marketing techniques.

First, in strategic contexts, such as interactions between buyers and sellers, the assumptions made by each party about the other's capabilities and preferences tend, over time, to exert a mutual influence on the actual behavior of both parties. If buyers are manipulated, they are more likely to respond with manipulative behavior of their own. Moreover, there seems to be a widespread tendency to underestimate the strength of such interactive effects in strategic contexts (e.g., Axelrod, 1984). Therefore, when marketing practitioners treat customers as though they were merely confused and predictable automata, by using tie-ins, obscuring the reference price, or by manipulating perceptions of the seller's cost, they could be actively contributing to degradation of the overall market environment.

Secondly, if marketers are going to view these models simply as a basis for purely scientific prediction, then "Science" itself will once more have become a mere tool or instrument for exerting control over others. There is a sense in which this attitude towards scientific developments could be compared to the application of nuclear physics to deliberately gain mastery or dominance over others. With the new marketing techniques, science is once again in some danger of being subverted, in the name of commercialism or profit, into a tool for exercising control. At the very least, therefore, it would be wrong to seek to justify the use of these techniques by claiming that they are "scientific and hence value-free".

Conclusions and Recommendations

In accordance with this ethical evaluation and appraisal of marketing techniques based on cognitive models, it is now recommended that:

- Legislators in consumer-protection should consider extending the concept of "deceptive practice" to include tactics shaped around cognitive models and heuristics, like (a) targeting the availability heuristic to promote overinsurance, (b) "obscuring the reference price" in markets where prices and profitability are already high, or (c) using unavailable loss-leaders to induce risky purchasing behavior in stores, etc.
- Teachers of marketing should emphasize the possible social consequences of indiscriminate application of the associated marketing techniques. They should not present the tactics as objectively scientific and value-free.
- Marketing experts could consider the possible benefits from consumer education programmes warning of these tactics [directly echoing Schwenk's (1986) suggestion that managers might defend themselves against manipulation].
- Researchers in consumer behavior could help to characterize those situations (if any) where the use of the above tactics *can* be broadly justified on social or economic grounds.

Finally, it is recommended that anyone who deliberately uses any device or technique that exploits the systematic but faulty cognitions of others, for their own advantage, should also consider the various distinctive ethical issues that have been outlined in this article.

Note

1. This argument invokes the PT value-function, noting the hypothesized risk-seeking tendency in the domain of *perceived* losses, indicated by the shape of the function (Figure 1). Similar arguments are found in Whyte, 1986.

References

Axelrod, R.: 1985, *The Evolution of Co-operation* (Basic Books, New York).

Buccholz, R. A.: 1982, *Business Environment and Public Policy* (Prentice Hall: Englewood Cliffs, N.J.).

Crisp, R.: 1987, 'Persuasive Advertising, Autonomy and the Creation of Desire', *Journal of Business Ethics* **6**, 413–18.

Gardner, D. M.: 1975, 'Deception in Advertising: A Conceptual Approach', *Journal of Marketing* **39**, 40–6.

Goldman, A. H.: 1980, 'Business Ethics: Profits, Utilities and Moral Rights', *Philosophy and Public Affairs*, 260–85.

Hamlin, A. P.: 1986, '*Ethics, Economics and the State*' (Wheatsheaf: Brighton).

Kahneman, D., Knetch, J., and Thaler, R.: 1986, 'Fairness as a Constraint on Profit-Seeking: Entitlements in the Market', *American Economic Review* **76**, 728–41.

Kahneman, D. and Tversky, A.: 1979, 'Prospect Theory: An Analysis of Decision under Risk', *Econometrica* **47** (2), 263–91.

Kahneman, D. and Tversky, A.: 1984, 'Choice, Values and Frames', *American Psychologist* **39**, 341–50.

Nason, R. W., and Della Bitta, A. J.: 1983, 'The Incidence and Consumer Perceptions of Quantity Surcharges', *Journal of Retailing* **59**(2), 40–54.

Neale, M. A. and Bazerman, M. H.: 1985, 'Perspectives for Understanding Negotiation', *Journal of Conflict Resolution* **29**(1), 33–55.

Puto, C. P.: 1987, 'The Framing of Buying Decisions', *Journal of Consumer Research* **14**, 301–15.

Russell, T. and Thaler R.: 1985, 'The Relevance of Quasi-Rationality in Competitive Markets', *American Economic Review* **75**(5), 1071–82.

Schick, F.: 1987, 'Rationality, a Third Dimension', *Economics and Philosophy* **3**, 49–66.

Schoemaker, P. J. H.: 1982, 'The Expected Utility Model: Its Variants, Purposes, Evidence and Limitations', *Journal of Economic Literature* **30** (June), 529–63.

Schwenk, C. R.: 1986, 'Information Cognitive Biases, and Commitment to a Course of Action', *Academy of Management Review* **11**, 298–310.

Sheffrin, H. M., and Statman, M.: 1984, 'Explaining Investor Preferences for Cash Dividends', *Journal of Financial Economics* **13**, 253–82.

Singer A. E., Singer, M. S. and Ritchie G.: 1986, 'The Role of Transactions in Mental Accounting', *Psychological Reports* **59**, 835–8.

Thaler R.: 1985, 'Mental Accounting and Consumer Choice', *Marketing Science* **4**, 199–214.

Tversky, A. and Kahneman D.: 1981, 'The Framing of Decisions and the Psychology of Choice', *Science* **211**, 453–58.

Tversky, A., and Kahneman D.: 1973, 'Availability: A Heuristic for Judging Frequency and Probability', *Cognitive Psychology* **5**(2), 207–32.

Urbany, J. E., Bearded, W. O. and Weilbaker, D. C.: 1988, 'The Effect of Plausible and Exaggerated Reference Prices on Consumer Perception and Price Search', *Journal of Consumer Research* **15** (June), 95–110.

Whyte, G.: 1986, 'Escalating Commitment to a Course of Action: A Reinterpretation', *Academy of Management Review* **11**(2), 311–21.

Zotos, Y.: 1989, 'The Incidence and Consumer Perceptions of Quantity Surcharge in Greece', Working Paper, University of Canterbury.

Marketing to Inner-City Blacks: PowerMaster and Moral Responsibility

GEORGE G. BRENKERT

I. INTRODUCTION

The nature and extent of marketers' moral obligations is a matter of considerable debate. This is particularly the case when those who are targeted by marketers live in disadvantaged circumstances and suffer various problems disproportionately with other members of the same society. An interesting opportunity to explore this difficult area of marketing ethics is presented by Heileman Brewing Company's failed effort to market Power-Master, a malt liquor, to inner-city blacks. The story of PowerMaster is relatively simple and short. Its ethical dimensions are much more complicated.

Excerpted from a paper to be published by *Business Ethics Quarterly*. Copyright © 1996 by George G. Brenkert. Reprinted by permission of the author.

In the following, I wish to consider the moral aspects of this case within the context of a market society such as the U.S. which permits the forms of advertising it presently does. To do so, I first briefly evaluate three kinds of objections made to the marketing of PowerMaster. I contend that none of these objections taken by itself clearly justifies the criticism leveled at Heileman. Heileman might reasonably claim that it was fulfilling its economic, social and moral responsibilities in the same manner as were other brewers and marketers. Accordingly, I argue that only if we look to the collective effects of all marketers of malt liquor to the inner-city can we identify morally defensible grounds for the complaints against marketing campaigns such as that of PowerMaster. The upshot of this argument is that marketers must recognize not only their individual moral responsibilities to those they target, but also a collective responsibility of all marketers for those market segments they jointly target. It is on this basis that Heileman's marketing of PowerMaster may be faulted. This result is noteworthy in that it introduces a new kind of moral consideration which has rarely been considered in discussions of corporate moral responsibilities.

II. HEILEMAN AND POWERMASTER

G. Heileman Brewing Co. is a Wisconsin brewer which produces a number of beers and malt liquors, including Colt Dry, Colt 45, and Mickey's. In the early 1990s, competition amongst such brewers was increasingly intense. In January 1991, Heileman was facing such economic difficulties that it filed for protection from creditors under Chapter 11 of the U.S. Bankruptcy Code (Horovitz, 1991b, D1). To improve its financial situation, Heileman sought to market, beginning in June 1991, a new malt liquor called "PowerMaster." At that time there was considerable growth in the "up-strength malt liquor category." In fact, "this higher-alcohol segment of the business [had] been growing at an explosive 25% to 30% a year" (Freedman, 1991a: B1). To attempt to capitalize on this market segment, Heileman produced PowerMaster, a malt liquor that contained 5.9% alcohol, 31% more alcohol than Heileman's top-selling Colt 45 (4.5% alcohol). Reportedly, when introduced only one other malt liquor (St. Ides) offered such a powerful malt as PowerMaster (Freedman, 1991a: B1).

Further, since malt liquor had become "the drink of choice among many in the inner city," Heileman focused a significant amount of its marketing efforts on inner-city blacks. Heileman's ad campaign played to this group with posters and billboards using black male models. Advertisements assured consumers that PowerMaster was "Bold Not Harsh." Hugh Nelson, Heileman's marketing director, was reported to have claimed that "the company's research . . . shows that consumers will opt for PowerMaster not on [the] basis of its alcohol content but because of its flavor. The higher alcohol content gives PowerMaster a 'bold not nasty' taste . . ." (Freedman, 1991a: B4).

In response, a wide variety of individuals and groups protested against Heileman's actions. Critics claimed that both advertisements and the name "PowerMaster" suggested the alcoholic strength of the drink and the "buzz" that those who consumed it could get. Surgeon General Antonia Novello criticized the PowerMaster marketing scheme as "insensitive" (Milloy, 1991: B3). Reports in *The Wall Street Journal* spoke of community activists and alcohol critics branding Heileman's marketing campaign as "socially irresponsible" (Freedman, 1991b: B1). "Twenty-one consumer and health groups, including the Center for Science in the Public Interest, also publicly called for Heileman to halt the marketing of PowerMaster and for BATF to limit the alcohol content of malt liquor" (Colford and Teinowitz, 1991: 29). A reporter for the *L.A. Times* wrote that "at issue is growing resentment by blacks and other minorities who feel that they are being unfairly targeted— if not exploited—by marketers of beer, liquor and tobacco products" (Horovitz, 1991: D6). Another reporter for the same paper claimed that "[a]nti-alcohol activists contend that alcoholic beverage manufacturers are taking advantage of minority groups and exacerbating inner-city problems by targeting them with high-powered blends" (Lacey, 1992: A32). And Reverend Calvin Butts of the Abyssinian Baptist Church in New York's Harlem said that "this [Heileman] is obviously a company that has no sense of moral or social responsibility" (Freedman, 1991a: B1).

Though the Bureau of Alcohol, Tobacco and Firearms (BATF) initially approved the use of "PowerMaster" as the name for the new malt liquor, in light of the above protests it "reacted by enforcing a beer law that prohibits labels 'considered to be statements of alcoholic content' " (Milloy, 1991: B3). It insisted that the word "Power" be removed from the "PowerMaster" name (Freedman, 1991b: B1). As a consequence of the actions of the BATF and the preceding complaints, Heileman decided not to market PowerMaster.

III. THE OBJECTIONS

The PowerMaster marketing campaign evoked three distinct kinds of moral objections:

First, because its advertisements drew upon images and themes related to power and boldness, they were criticized as promoting boldness, they were criticized as promoting satisfactions only artificially and distortedly associated with the real needs of those targeted. As such, the PowerMaster marketing campaign was charged with fostering a form of moral illusion.

Second, Heileman was said to lack concern for the harm likely to be caused by its product. Blacks suffer disproportionately from cirrhosis of the liver and other liver diseases brought on by alcohol. In addition, alcohol-related social problems such as violence and crime are also prominent in the inner-city. Accordingly, Heileman was attacked for its lack of moral sensitivity.

Third, Heileman was accused of taking unfair advantage of those in the inner-city whom they had targeted. Inner-city blacks were said to be especially vulnerable, due to their life circumstances, to advertisements and promotions formulated in terms of power, self-assertion and sexual success. Hence, to target them in the manner they did with a product such as PowerMaster was a form of exploitation. In short, questions of justice were raised.

It is important not only for corporations such as Heileman but also for others concerned with such marketing practices to determine whether these objections show that the PowerMaster marketing program was morally unjustified. The economic losses in failed marketing efforts such as PowerMaster are considerable. In addition, if the above objections are justified, the moral losses are also significant.

The first objection maintained that by emphasizing power Heileman was, in effect, offering a cruel substitute for a real lack in the lives of inner-city blacks. PowerMaster's slogan, "Bold not Harsh," was said to project an image of potency. "The brewers' shrewd marketing," one critic maintained, "has turned malt liquor into an element of machismo" (Lacey, 1992: A1). George Hacker, Director of the National Coalition to Prevent Impaired Driving, commented that "the real irony of marketing PowerMaster to inner-city blacks is that this population is among the most lacking in power in this society" (Freedman, 1991a, B1).

This kind of criticism has been made against many forms of advertising. The linking of one's product with power, fame, and success not to mention sex is nothing new in advertising. Most all those targeted by marketers lack (or at least want) those goods or values associated with the products being promoted. Further, other malt liquor marketing campaigns had referred to power. For example, another malt liquor, Olde English "800," claimed that "It's the Power." The Schlitz Red Bull was associated with the phrase "The Real Power" (Colford and Tenowitz, 1991: 1). Nevertheless, they were not singled out for attack or boycott as PowerMaster was.

Accordingly, however objectionable it may be for marketers to link a product with something which its potential customers (significantly) lack and which the product can only symbolically or indirectly satisfy, this feature of the PowerMaster marketing campaign does not uniquely explain or justify the complaints that were raised against the marketing of PowerMaster. In short, this objection appears far too general in scope of justify the particular attention given PowerMaster. Heileman could not have reasonably concluded, on its basis, that it was being particularly morally irresponsible. It was simply doing what others had done and for which they had not been boycotted or against which such an outcry had not been raised. It is difficult to see how Heileman could have concluded that it was preparing a marketing program that would generate the social and moral protest it did, simply from an examination of its own plan or the similar individual marketing programs of other brewers.

The second objection was that the marketers of PowerMaster showed an especial lack of sensitivity in that a malt liquor with the potency of PowerMaster would likely cause additional harm to inner-city blacks. According to various reports, "alcoholism and other alcohol-related diseases extract a disproportionate toll on blacks. A 1978 study by the National Institute on Alcohol Abuse and Alcoholism found that black men between the ages of 25 and 44 are 10 times more likely than the general population to have cirrhosis of the liver" (*N.Y. Times*, 1991). *Fortune* reported that "The Department of Health and Human Services last spring released figures showing a decline in life expectancy for blacks for the fourth straight year—down to 69.2 years, vs. 75.6 years for whites. Although much of the drop is attributable to homicide and AIDS, blacks also suffer higher instances of . . . alcohol-related illnesses than whites" (*Fortune*, 1991: 100). Further, due to the combined use of alcohol and cigarettes, blacks suffer cancer of the esophagus at a disproportional rate than the rest of the population. Similarly, assuming that black women would drink PowerMaster, it is relevant that the impact of alcohol use in the inner-city is also manifested in an increased infant mortality rate and by new born children with fetal alcohol syndrome (*The Workbook,* 1991: 18). Finally, a malt liquor with a high percentage of alcohol was expected to have additional harmful effects on the levels of social ills, such as violence, crime, and spousal abuse. As such, PowerMaster would be further destructive of the social fabric of the inner-city.

Under these circumstances, the second objection maintained, anyone who marketed a product which would further increase these harms was being morally obtuse to the problems inner-city blacks suffer. Accordingly, Heileman's PowerMaster marketing campaign was an instance of such moral insensitivity.

Nevertheless, this objection does not seem clearly applicable when pointed simply at PowerMaster. Surely inner-city blacks are adults and should be allowed, as such, to make their own choices, even if those choices harm themselves, so long as they are not deceived or coerced when making those choices and they do not harm others. Since neither deception nor coercion were involved in PowerMaster's marketing campaign, it is an unacceptable form of moral paternalism to deny them what they might otherwise wish to choose.

Further, those who raised the above complaints were not those who would have drunk PowerMaster, but leaders of various associations both within and outside the inner-city concerned with alcohol abuse and consumption. This was not a consumer-led protest. Reports of the outcry over PowerMaster contain no objections from those whom Heileman had targeted. No evidence was presented that these individuals would have found PowerMaster unsatisfactory. Argument is needed, for example, that these individuals had (or should have had) over-riding interests in healthy livers. Obviously there are many people (black as well as white) who claim that their interests are better fulfilled by drinking rather than abstinence.

Finally, argument is also needed to show that this increase in alcoholic content would have any significant effects on the targeted group. It might be that any noteworthy effects would be limited because the increased alcoholic content would prove undesirable to those targeted since they would become intoxicated too quickly. "Overly rapid intoxication undercuts sales volume and annoys consumers," *The Wall Street Journal* reported (Freedman, 1991a: B1). Supposedly this consequence led one malt brewer to lower the alcoholic content of its product (Freedman, 1991a: B1). Furthermore, malt liquor is hardly the strongest alcohol which blacks (or others) drink. Reportedly, "blacks buy more than half the cognac sold in the United States" (*The Workbook,* 1991: 18). Cheap forms of wine and hard liquor are readily available. Thus, it is far from obvious what significant effects PowerMaster alone would have in the inner-city.

One possible response to the preceding replies brings us to the third objection. This response is that, though inner-city blacks might not be deceived or coerced into drinking PowerMaster, they were particularly vulnerable to the marketing campaign which Heileman proposed. Because of this, Heileman's marketing campaign (wittingly or unwittingly) would take unfair advantage of inner-city blacks.

Little, if any attempt, has been made to defend or to explore this charge. I suggest that there are at least three ways in which inner-city blacks—or anyone else, for that matter—might be said to be specially vulnerable.

A person would be cognitively vulnerable if he or she lacked certain levels of ability to cognitively process information or to be aware that certain information was being withheld or manipulated in deceptive ways. Thus, if people were not able to process information about the effects of malt liquor on themselves or on their society in ways in which others could, they would be cognitively vulnerable.

A person would be motivationally vulnerable if he or she could not resist ordinary temptations and/or enticements due to his or her own individual characteristics. Thus, if people were unable, as normal individuals are, to resist various advertisements and marketing ploys, they would be motivationally vulnerable.

And people would be socially vulnerable when their social situation renders them significantly less able than others to resist various enticements. For example, due to the poverty within which they live, they might have developed various needs or attitudes which rendered them less able to resist various marketing programs.

Nevertheless, none of these forms of vulnerability was explored or defended as the basis of the unfair advantage which the PowerMaster marketers were said to seek. And indeed it is difficult to see what account could be given which would explain how the use of the name "PowerMaster," and billboards with a black model, a bottle of PowerMaster and the slogan "Bold Not Harsh" would be enough to subvert the decision making or motivational capacities of inner-city blacks. To the extent that they are adults and not under the care or protection of other individuals or agencies due to the state of their cognitive or motivational abilities, there is a prima facie case that they are not so vulnerable. Accordingly, the vulnerability objection raises the legitimate concern that some form of unjustified moral paternalism lurks behind it.

In short, if we consider simply the individual marketing program of PowerMaster, it is difficult to see that the three preceding objections justified the outcry against Heileman. Heileman was seeking to satisfy its customers. As noted above, none of the reported complaints came from them. Heileman was also seeking to enhance its own bottom line. But in doing so it was not engaged in fraud, deception or coercion. The marketing of PowerMaster was not like other morally objectionable individual marketing programs which have used factually deceptive advertisements (e.g., some past shaving commercials), taken advantage of the target group's special vulnerabilities (e.g., certain television advertisements to children who are cognitively vulnerable), or led to unusual harm for the group targeted (e.g., Nestlé's infant formula promotions to Third World Mothers). Black inner-city residents are not obviously cognitively vulnerable and are not, in the use of malt liquor, uniformly faced with a single significant problem such as Third World Mothers are (viz., the care of their infants). As such, it is mistaken to think that PowerMaster's marketing campaign was morally offensive or objectionable in ways in which other such campaigns have been. From this perspective, then, it appears that Heileman could be said to be fulfilling its individual corporate responsibilities.

IV. ASSOCIATED GROUPS AND COLLECTIVE RESPONSIBILITY

So long as we remain simply at the level of the individual marketing campaign of PowerMaster, it is doubtful that we can grasp the basis upon which the complaints against PowerMaster might be justified. To do so, we must look to the social level and the collection of marketing programs of which PowerMaster was simply one part. By pushing on the bounds within which other marketers had remained, PowerMaster was merely the spark which ignited a great deal of resentment which stemmed more generally from the group of malt liquor marketers coming into the inner-city from outside, aggressively marketing products which disproportionately harmed those in the inner-city (both those who consume the product and others), and creating marketing campaigns that took advantage of their vulnerabilities.

As such, this case might better be understood as one involving the collective responsibility of the group of marketers who target inner-city blacks rather than simply the individual responsibility of this or that marketer. By "collective responsibility" I refer to the responsibility which attaches to a group (or collective), rather than to the individual members of the group, even though it is only through the joint action (or inaction) of group members that a particular collective action or consequence results. The objections of the critics could then more plausibly be recast in the form that the *collection* of the marketer's campaigns was consuming or wasting public health or welfare understood in a twofold sense: first, as the lack of illness, violence, and crime, and, second, as the presence of a sense of individual self that is based on the genuine gratification of real needs. When the individual marketers of a group (e.g., of brewers) engage in their own individual marketing campaigns they may not necessarily cause significant harms—or if they do create harm, the customers may have willingly accepted certain levels of individual risk of harm. However, their efforts may collectively result in significant harms not consciously assumed by anyone.

Similarly, though the individual marketing efforts may not be significant enough to expose the vulnerabilities of individuals composing their market segment, their marketing efforts may collectively create a climate within which the vulnerabilities of those targeted may play a role in the collective effect of those marketing campaigns. Thus, it is not the presence of this or that billboard from PowerMaster which may be objectionable so much as the large total number of billboards in the inner-city which advertise alcohol and to which PowerMaster contributed. For example, it has been reported that "in Baltimore, 76 percent of the billboards located in low-income neighborhoods advertise alcohol and cigarettes; in middle and upper-income neighborhoods it is 20 percent" (*The Workbook*, 1991: 18). This "saturation advertising" may have an effect different from the effect of any single advertisement. Similarly, it is not PowerMaster's presence on the market as such, which raises moral questions. Rather, it is that alcohol marketers particularly target a group which not only buys ". . . more than half the cognac sold in the United States and . . . consume[s] more than one-third of all malt liquor . . ." (*The Workbook,* 1991: 18), but also disproportionately suffers health problems associated with alcohol. The connection between the amount of alcohol consumed and the alcohol related health problems is hardly coincidental. Further, if the level of alcohol consumption is significantly related to conditions of poverty and racism, and the consequent vulnerabilities people living in these conditions may suffer, then targeting such individuals may also be an instance of attempting to take unfair advantage of them.

Now to make this case, it must be allowed that individual persons are not the only ones capable of being responsible for the effects of their actions. A variety of arguments have been given, for example, that corporations can be morally responsible for their actions. These arguments need not be recited here since even if they were successful, as I think some of them are, the marketers who target inner-city blacks do not themselves constitute a corporation. Hence, a different kind of argument is needed.

Can there be subjects of responsibility other than individuals and corporations? Virginia Held has argued that under certain conditions random collections of individuals can be held morally responsible. She has argued that when it would be obvious to the reasonable person what a random collection of individuals ought to do and when the expected outcome of such an action is clearly favorable, then that random collection can be held morally responsible (Held, 1970: 476).

However, again the marketers of malt liquor to inner city blacks do not seem to fit this argument since they are not simply a random collection of individuals. According to Held, a random collection of individuals ". . . is a set of persons distinguishable by some characteristics from the set of all persons, but lacking a decision method for taking action that is distinguishable from such decisions methods, if there are any, as are possessed by all persons" (Held, 1970: 471). The examples she gives, "passengers on a train" and "pedestrians on a sidewalk," fit this definition but are also compatible with a stronger definition of a group of individuals than the one she offers. For example, her definition would include collections of individuals with no temporal, spatial or teleological connection. Clearly marketers of malt liquor to inner-city blacks constitute a group or collection of individuals in a stronger sense than Held's random collection of individuals.

Consequently, I shall speak of a group such as the marketers who target inner-city blacks as an associated group. Such groups are not corporations. Nor are they simply random collections of individuals (in Held's sense). They are groups in a weaker sense than corporations, but a stronger sense than a random collections of individuals. I shall argue that such groups may also be the subject of moral responsibility. This view is based upon the following characteristics of such groups.

First, an associated group is constituted by agents, whether they be corporate or personal, who share certain characteristics related to a common set of activities in which they engage. Thus, the marketers who target inner-city blacks share the characteristic that they (and no one else) target this particular market segment with malt-liquor. They engage in competition with each other to sell their malt-liquor according to the rules of the (relatively) free market. Though they themselves do not occupy some single spatial location, the focus of their activities, the ends they seek, and their temporal relatedness (i.e., marketing to the inner-city in the same time period) are clearly sufficient to constitute them as a group.

Second, though such associated groups do not have a formal decision-making structure which unites them, Stanley Bates has reminded us that "there are other group decision methods, [that] . . . are not formal . . ." (Btaes, 1971:345). For example, the brewers presently at issue might engage in various forms of implicit bargaining. These informal and implicit group decision methods may involve unstructured discussions of topics of mutual interest, individual group member monitoring of the expectations and intuitions of other group members, and recognition of mutual understandings that may serve to coordinate the expectations of group members (cf. Schelling, 1963). Further, brewers in the United States have created the Beer Institute, which is their Washington-based trade group, one of whose main purposes is to protect "the market environment allowing for brewers to sell beer profitably, free from what the group views as unfair burdens imposed by government bodies."[1] The Beer Institute provides its members with a forum within which they may meet annually, engage in workshops, discuss issues of mutual concern, agree on which issues will be lobbied before Congress on their behalf and may voluntarily adopt an advertising code to guide their activities. Such informal decision-making methods amongst these brewers and suppliers are means whereby group decisions can be made.

Third, members of associated groups can be said to have other morally relevant characteristics which foster a group "solidarity" and thereby also unify them as a group capable of moral responsibility (cf. Feinberg, 1974: 234). These characteristics take three different forms. a) Members of the group share a community of interests. For example, they all wish to sell their products to inner-city blacks. They all seek to operate with minimal restrictions from the government on their marketing activities within the inner-city. They all are attempting to develop popular malt liquors. They all strive to keep the costs of their operations as low as possible. b) Further, they are joined by bonds of sentiment linked with their valuing of independent action and successfully selling their products. Though they may try to out-compete each other, they may also respect their competitors when they perform well in the marketplace. c) Finally, they can be said to share a common lot in that actions by one brewer that bring public condemnation upon that brewer may also extend public attention and condemnation to the other brewers as well—as happened in the PowerMaster case. Similarly, regulations imposed on one typically also affect the others. Thus, heavy regulation tends to reduce all their profits, whereas light regulation tends to have the opposite effect.

The unity or solidarity constituted by the preceding characteristics among the various marketers would be openly manifested, for example, if the government were to try to deny them all access to the inner-city market segment. In such a circumstance, they would openly resist, take the government to court, and protest with united voice against the injustice done to them, both individually and as a group. In this sense, there is (at the least) a latent sense of solidarity among such marketers (cf. May, 1987: 37). When they act, then each acts in solidarity with the others and each does those things which accord with the kinds of actions fellow group members are inclined to take. All this may occur without the need for votes being taken or explicit directions given among the various brewers (cf. May, 1987:40).

Fourth, associated groups like inner-city marketers can investigate the harms or benefits that their products and marketing programs jointly do to those who are targeted. They can also study the overall effects of their own individual efforts. They could do so both as individual businesses and as a group. In the latter case, the Beer Institute might undertake such studies. Similarly, these marketers might jointly commission some other organization to study these effects. In short, they are capable both as individual businesses and as a group, of receiving notice as to the effects of their individual and collective actions. In short, communication amongst the group members is possible.

Finally, associated groups can modify their activities. They are not simply inevitably or necessarily trapped into acting certain ways. For example, the inner-city malt liquor marketers might voluntarily reduce the number of billboards they use within the inner-city. They might not advertise in certain settings or in certain forms of media. They might not use certain appeals, e.g., touting the high alcoholic content of their products. As such, they could take actions to prevent the harms or injustices of which they are accused. At present brewers subscribe to an advertising code of ethics which the Beer Institute makes available and has recently updated. The Beer Institute might even lobby the government on behalf of this group for certain limitations on marketing programs so as to eliminate moral objections raised against such marketing programs.

The preceding indicates that this group can act: it has set up the Beer Institute; it may react with unanimity against new regulations; it may defend the actions of its members; it may investigate the effects its group members have on those market segments which they have targeted. It does not act as a group in marketing particular malt liquors. The law prevents such collective actions. However, marketing malt liquor to particular groups is an action which this group may approve or disapprove. The group lobbies Congress on behalf of its members' interests. The group has organized itself such that through development and support of the Beer Institute its interests are protected. There is no reason, then, that such a group may not also be morally responsible for the overall consequences of its members' marketing.

Does the preceding argument suggest that the group of marketers would run afoul of concerns about restraint of trade? The above argument need not imply that inner-city marketers are always a group capable of moral action and responsibility—only that under certain circumstances it could be. Hence, the above argument does not suggest that this group constitutes anything like a cartel. In addition, the above argument does not suggest that marketers agree on pricing formulas, on reserving certain distributional areas for this or that marketer, or similar actions which would constitute classic forms of restraint of trade. Further, the preceding argument leaves open what mechanisms might be legally used whereby these moral responsibilities are discharged. It might be that individual marketers voluntarily agree to such actions as they presently do with their advertising code. On the other hand, they might collectively appeal to the government to approve certain general conditions such that the playing field within which they compete would be altered to alleviate moral objections to their marketing campaigns, but would remain relatively level in comparison with their situations prior to the imposition of such conditions.

If the preceding is correct, then given the assumption that basic items of public welfare (e.g., health, safety, decision-making abilities, etc.) ought not to be harmed, two important conclusions follow regarding the marketing of malt liquor to inner-city blacks.

First, malt liquor marketers have a collective responsibility to monitor the effects of their activities and to ensure that they jointly do not unnecessarily cause harm to those they target or trade on their vulnerabilities. Assuming that malt liquor does harm inner-city blacks and that the marketing programs through which malt liquor is sold to this market segment play some significant causal role in creating this harm, then they have an obligation to alter their marketing to inner-city blacks in such a way that the vulnerabilities of inner-city blacks are not exploited and that unnecessary harm does not come to them.

Second, where the collective consequences of individual marketing efforts create the harms claimed for alcohol among inner-city blacks, and marketers as a group do not discharge the preceding collective responsibility, then there is a need for some agency outside those individual marketers to oversee or regulate their actions. Obviously, one form this may take is that of an industry or professional oversight committee; another form might be that of government intervention.

V. IMPLICATIONS AND CONCLUSION

The implications of this social approach to the PowerMaster case are significant:

First, marketers cannot simply look at their own individual marketing campaigns to judge their moral level. Instead, they must also look at their campaign within the context of all the marketing campaigns which target the market segment at which they are aiming. This accords with Garrett Hardin's suggestion that "the morality of an act is a function of the state of the system at the time it is performed" (Hardin, 1968: 1245; emphasis omitted). It is possible that marketers could fulfill their individual responsibilities but not their collective responsibilities.

Second, when the products targeted at particular market segments cause consumers to suffer disproportionately in comparison with other comparable market segments, marketers must determine the role which their products and marketing programs play in this situation. If they play a contributory role, they should (both individually and as a group) consider measures to reduce the harm produced. One means of doing this is to voluntarily restrict or modify their appeals to that market segment. In the present case, industry organizations such as The Beer Institute might play a leading role in identifying problems and recommending countermeasures. Otherwise when harm occurs disproportionately to a market segment, or members of that segment are especially vulnerable, outside oversight and regulation may be appropriate.

Third, marketers have a joint or collective responsibility to the entire market segment they target, not simply for the effects of their own products and marketing campaigns, but more generally for the effects of the combined marketing which is being done to that segment. The protests against PowerMaster are best understood against the background of this collective responsibility.

Thus, when we think of responsibility in the market we must look beyond simply the responsibility of individual agents (be they personal or corporate). We must look to the responsibility of groups of persons as well as groups of corporations. Such responsibility is not personal or individual, but collective. Examination of the case of PowerMaster helps us to see this.

Accordingly, the preceding analysis helps to explain both why Power-Master was attacked as it was and also why it seemed simply to be doing what other marketers had previously done. Further, it helps us to understand the circumstances under which the above objections against marketing malt liquor to inner-city blacks might be justified. However, much more analysis of this form of collective harm and the vulnerability which is said to characterize inner-city blacks needs to be undertaken.

Finally, it should be emphasized that this paper advocates recognition of a new subject of moral responsibility in the market. Heretofore, moral responsibility has been attributed to individuals and corporations. Random collections of individuals have little applicability in business ethics. However the concept of associated groups and their collective responsibility has not been previously explored. It adds a new dimension to talk about responsibility within current discussions in business ethics.

Note

1. "The Beer Institute." *Encyclopedia of Associations,* Carolyn A. Fischer and Carol A. Schwartz (eds.), vol. 1 (New York: Gale Research Inc., 1995), p. 27.

Bibliography

Bates, Stanley (1971), "The Responsibility of 'Random Collections'," *Ethics,* 81, 343–349.

Benn, Stanley I. (1967), "Freedom and Persuasion," *The Australasian Journal of Philosophy,* 45, 259–275.

Brown, Jesse W. (1992), "Marketing Exploitation," *Business and Society Review,* Issue 83 (Fall), p. 17.

Colford, Steven W. and Teinowitz, Ira (1991), "Malt liquor 'power' failure," *Advertising Age,* July 1, pp. 1, 29.

Farhi, Paul (1991), "Surgeon General Hits New Malt Liquor's Name, Ads," *Washington Post,* June 26, pp. A1, A4.

Feinberg, Joel (1974), "Collective Responsibility," in *Doing & Deserving,* Princeton: Princeton University Press, pp. 222–251.

Fortune (1991), "Selling Sin to Blacks," October 21, p. 100.

Freedman, Alix (1991a), "Potent, New Heileman Malt Is Brewing Fierce Industry and Social Criticism," *Wall Street Journal,* June 17, pp. B1, B4.

_____ (1991b), "Heileman, Under Pressure, Scuttles PowerMaster Malt," *Wall Street Journal,* July 5, pp. B1, B3.

Hardin, Garrett (1968), "The Tragedy of the Commons," *Science,* 162, 1243–1248.

Held, Virginia (1970), "Can a Random Collection of Individuals Be Morally Responsible?," *The Journal of Philosophy,* 67, 471–481.

Horovitz, Bruce (1991), "Brewer Faces Boycott Over Marketing of Potent Malt Liquor," *L. A. Times,* June 25, pp. D1, D6.

Lacey, Marc (1992), "Marketing of Malt Liquor Fuels Debate," *L. A. Times,* December 15, pp. A32, A34.

May, Larry (1987), *The Morality of Groups.* Notre Dame: University of Notre Dame Press.

Milloy, Courland (1991), "Race, Beer Don't Mix, *The Washington Post,* July 9, p. B3.

New York Times, The (1991), "The Threat of PowerMaster," July 1, p. A12.

Schelling, Thomas (1963), *The Strategy of Conflict.* New York: Oxford University Press.

Teinowitz, Ira and Colford, Steven W. (1991), "Targeting Woes in PowerMaster Wake," *Advertising Age,* July 8, 1991, p. 35.

"The Beer Institute," *Encyclopedia of Associations* (1995), Carolyn A. Fischer and Carol A. Schwartz (eds.), vol. 1, New York: Gale Research Inc.

Workbook, The (1991), "Marketing Booze to Blacks," Spring, 16, 18–19.

Zimmerman, Michael J. (1985), "Sharing Responsibility," *American Philosophical Quarterly,* 22, 115–122.

Strategy

— *Case Study* —

Sears Auto Centers (A)

LYNN SHARP PAINE — MICHAEL A. SANTORO

On Friday, June 19, 1992, CEO Edward Brennan and other top executives of Sears, Roebuck & Co. were considering how to respond to allegations that the company's auto centers had been misleading consumers and charging them for unnecessary repairs for a period of more than three years.

A week earlier, on June 11, California's Department of Consumer Affairs had filed an administrative action to revoke the auto repair licenses of all 72 auto centers in California for violations of the state's Auto Repair Act. On the day of the announcement, the company's stock price fell 62.5¢ (Exhibit 1). Since that time, Sears had experienced a 15% drop in its auto center revenues nationwide and a 20% drop in California. Charges by New Jersey consumer affairs officials and Florida's attorney general had followed within a few days of the California action, though New York's Department of Motor Vehicles had gone on record as saying it did not believe there was a serious problem in that state.

COMPANY BACKGROUND

Chicago-based Sears, Roebuck & Co. traced its history to 1886 when Richard W. Sears, a Minnesota railway agent, founded a company to sell watches. In 1888, Sears published its first general catalog of mail-order consumer goods. The company offered low prices and money-back guarantees to the farmers who were its principal customers. Anticipating changes the automobile would bring to rural life, Sears opened its first retail store in 1924, serving farmers who could drive to town to buy merchandise. The next year, the company brought out a line of tires under the name Allstate. In 1931, the Allstate division expanded into auto insurance and, in 1957, into life insurance.

In 1981, Sears acquired the real estate broker and developer Coldwell Banker, and the stock brokerage firm of Dean Witter Reynolds. Under the Dean Witter umbrella, Sears launched the Discover credit card in 1985. In 1992, Sears was organized into four divisions: (1) the Merchandising group, which included the retail stores, appliance business, and auto centers; (2) Allstate; (3) Coldwell Banker; and (4) Dean Witter.

"Sears Auto Centers (A)" was prepared from public sources by Research Associate Michael A. Santoro under the supervision of Professor Lynn Sharp Paine. Copyright © 1993 by the President and Fellows of Harvard College. Harvard Business School Case 9-394-009 (Rev. May 31, 1996).

In 1992, the Merchandising group operated 868 department stores and 875 auto centers, nearly all of which were connected with a Sears department store. Through most of the twentieth century, by virtue of its penetration into the U. S. market, the Sears Merchandising group was the undisputed global leader in retailing. Its strategy was based upon selling high-quality Sears-label brands.

But in the 1980s, the Merchandising group's lead began to narrow. Attempting to reverse declining market share, Sears in 1988 restructured its retail division and acquired the 405-store Western Auto Supply Co. The company introduced an "everyday low pricing" policy and added non-Sears name brands in early 1989. Despite these measures, Sears suffered a 40% drop in earnings in 1990; earnings for the Merchandise group dropped 60%. The group slipped to the number three spot among retailers, after discounters Wal-Mart and Kmart.[1] (See Exhibit 2 for financials.) Edward Brennan, chairman of the company since 1985, instituted numerous cost-cutting measures, including a plan to eliminate 48,000 jobs by the close of 1992.

In the effort to spur performance, Sears introduced a productivity incentive for its auto mechanics in 1991. Of Sears's 13,500 mechanics, 9,000 had earned more than 17,000 certificates of Automotive Service Excellence, a nationally recognized standard for auto technicians. Many received training at one of Sears's four training centers. The new productivity incentive was comparable to a "piece rate" paid to a factory worker. Mechanics completing a job, such as installation of shock absorbers, within a specified period were paid a fixed dollar amount in addition to their base salary. A Sears mechanic described the change:

> On January 1, 1991 the mechanics, installers, and tire changers had their hourly wages cut to what Sears termed a fixed dollar amount, or FDA per hour which varied depending on the classification. At present, the mechanic's FDA amount is $3.25 which, based on current Sears minimum production quotas, is 17% of my earnings. What this means is that for every hour of work, as defined by Sears, that I complete, I receive $3.25 plus my hourly base pay. If I do two hours worth of work in one hour I receive an additional $3.25 therefore increasing my earnings. . . . Prior to this commission program when the mechanics were paid only an hourly wage, our production quotas were $35.00 per hour with the shop flat rate being $55.00 per hour. As of January 1, 1991 our quotas were changed to, and judged on, an FDA rate of $3.25 per hour. Since the FDA rate of $3.25 per hour is equal to one hour of shop flat rate work, the mechanic's quota was therefore increased $20.00 per hour.[2]

In the same year, Sears began the process of harmonizing the compensation of its California service advisors with that prevailing in the rest of the country. The company's 3,500 service advisors, who were responsible for processing repair orders, consulting with mechanics on a vehicle's condition, and advising customers on potential repairs and parts, were generally compensated by a base salary plus commission. Commissions had been introduced as part of the company's effort to improve sales in 1990.[3] Service advisors also had to meet certain product-specific sales quotas, such as a certain number of alignments per shift, and dollar volume quotas based on the value of goods and services sold per hour. Until 1991, California service advisors had been paid a straight salary.[4]

The Merchandising group continued to flounder in the early 1990s. Although its 1991 revenues of $31.4 billion were more than half of the company's $57.2 billion total, the Merchandising group contributed just $486 million ($393 million from credit operations) to Sears's $1.27 billion in profits. Sears auto centers serviced 20 million vehicles in 1991, employed some 34,000 people, and accounted for 9%, or $2.8 billion, of Sears's 1991 retail revenues. Automotive was the least profitable of Merchandising's three units, contributing some 5% of the division's profits.[5]

In February 1992, in the hopes of achieving efficiencies, Sears consolidated management responsibility for its Western Auto Supply subsidiary with its Sears auto centers. Western Auto's chairman and chief executive officer, John T. Lundegard, was put in charge of the newly consolidated nationwide automotive centers group. In addition to the 875 Sears automotive centers, the consolidated operations included 548 Western Auto Supply stores, of which 175 sold only tires. Lundegard reported to Forrest R. Hasselton, who had recently been promoted to president of Sears retail from vice president of Sears automotive.[6]

THE AUTO REPAIR INDUSTRY

Sears auto repair centers, the largest company-owned automotive service organization in the United States, focused on what were known as "undercar services"—mainly brake repair and replacing mufflers, shock absorbers, and struts. The undercar business absorbed about $26 billion of the $100 billion spent annually on auto parts and services by owners of the 187 million registered vehicles in the United States.[7] The auto repair industry consisted of four types of shops: dealerships, specialty shops, independents, and mass marketers like Sears.

Relative to services, such as engine tune-ups and transmission overhauls, that might take longer to perform—and that could be difficult to estimate—undercar services had volume profit potential because they could be performed reliably on a routine basis. Technicians, also known as mechanics, could deliver these services with little training and low levels of service equipment. Even so, some repair shop owners found it increasingly difficult to find good, trained technicians knowledgeable about increasingly complex auto systems.[8] A few mechanics were beginning to consider licensing schemes to raise competency levels and improve the industry's reputation.[9]

During the late 1980s and early 1990s, the auto repair industry was generally in a slump. During this period, competition in the undercar business intensified. Car dealerships were increasingly looking to the repair market for profits. Among dealers, profits from car repairs grew from 11% to 86% of total profits between 1983 and 1990. The brake repair market became especially competitive as the dealers and muffler specialists turned to brake repairs to cope with the lengthening useful life of tires and exhaust systems. During this time, the market for brake parts increased about 3% to 4% a year. Profit margins among those offering brake jobs were under increasing pressures.[10]

In 1991, the "magic number" for a brake job was $59.95 per axle. For that price, repair shops would change pads, inspect and fill the hydraulic system, resurface rotors or drums, and inspect calipers. Some in the industry questioned whether brake jobs could be conscientiously provided at this price. One car repair shop owner declared: "$59.95 is just a low-ball price. When the customer comes in, the shop tries to step him up to a higher-priced job. In fact, the job may wind up costing much more because the crew is told to find work: replace calipers, whether worn or not, sell a brake job for the second axle, and so on." Paul Corkins, vice president of marketing for Allied Signal Inc.'s Brake Division, commented: "A realistic price on a two-axle brake job is $175–$200. A price of $59.95 for a front-axle job is realistic if only the pads have to be replaced, and that's rare."[11]

Historically, a substantial percentage of brake jobs performed by Sears were the basic one-axle brake job. Commonly referred to as a "hang and turn" job, Sears's basic brake service included replacing pads, turning the rotors or drums, and repacking wheel bearings. Also, calipers and other brake parts were inspected at the time of service. Sears took special care in its advertising to put consumers on notice that brake jobs could sometimes be more complex and expensive than one might anticipate.[12] . . .

THE CALIFORNIA INVESTIGATION

The California Department of Consumer Affairs (DCA) action against the Sears auto centers resulted from a year-long investigation of the Sears shops by the DCA's Bureau of Automotive Repair (BAR). The investigation was part of a broader campaign against fraudulent repair shops, which, according to BAR, cost California motorists $2.2 billion each year. The BAR also pointed to a recent consumer survey: more than half of the respondents believed that repair shops were dishonest and did unnecessary repairs. Fraud-related complaints lodged with the BAR against the 40,000 registered repair dealers in California had increased 14% each year since 1985.[13] The BAR sought to target high-volume shops that had been the subject of complaints and to save California's 20 million motorists some $200 million a year in repair costs.

Citing a pattern of complaints against Sears, the BAR decided to investigate. According to a Sears official, however, the number of complaints against the company had increased only from 137 per year to 223 per year during the three-year period beginning in 1989, a small fraction of the 18,000 complaints received annually.[14]

Between December 1990 and December 1991, BAR conducted 38 undercover "runs" at Sears shops throughout California. According to the BAR, Sears employees recommended and performed unnecessary service or repairs in 34 of these runs. The overcharges averaged $223 and, in certain instances, amounted to as much as $550. According to the BAR, some cars left Sears in worse condition than when they had entered, and one left without any brakes[15] (Exhibit 3).

The BAR investigation focused on braking system repairs, a widely advertised service offered by the centers. Print ads offered a $48 (or, in some instances, $58) brake job (Exhibit 4). According to the BAR, when undercover operators brought vehicles requiring a simple brake job, they were often told that calipers, shock absorbers, coil springs, idler arms or master cylinders needed to be repaired or replaced, even though those parts were in good working order, usually with less than 20 miles of use. Jim Schoning, chief of the BAR, alleged that some Sears employees resorted to scare tactics to sell repairs. He commented that "one of our undercover operators was told that the front calipers on his car were so badly frozen that the car would fishtail if the brakes were applied quickly."[16]

To conduct the investigation, the BAR used vehicles needing minor brake repairs. Before taking a vehicle to Sears for repair, BAR employees disassembled the brakes and suspension and inspected, marked, and photographed the parts. A transport then moved the automobiles to a location near the shop, where they were dropped off to be driven by an undercover operator to the shop being investigated. Most shops displayed the Sears auto center slogan, "We Install Confidence." After arriving at Sears, the undercover investigator requested a brake inspection. In 34 of 38 instances, the investigator was told that additional, more expensive repairs were necessary. The undercover investigator authorized the repair and paid the amount due, after which the vehicle was transported back to a BAR facility for examination.[17]

The BAR investigation and results recalled a similar study done 50 years earlier by the *Reader's Digest*. In 1941, investigators for the *Digest* found that 75% of the garages asked to make repairs on cars with a defect created for the experiment misrepresented the defect and the work that was done. For a defect that should have cost 25¢ to repair, the average charge was $4, and some charged as much as $25.[18] Auto repair fraud had long been a main source of consumer complaints in many jurisdictions.[19]

In December 1991, before publicizing the results of its investigation, California Senior Assistant Attorney General Herschel T. Elkins wrote a letter that was hand-delivered to Sears CEO Brennan. Accompanying the letter were copies of the BAR investigation. Elkins informed Brennan that the investigation revealed "substantial problems" at Sears auto centers which "went deep" into the management structure.[20] The BAR and the attorney general's office discussed the results of the investigation with the Sears national service manager, national sales manager, senior counsel, and auto training manager.

Sears Challenges the Investigation[21]

Immediately after receiving the letter, Sears asked to meet with state officials in California and requested information about the investigation. The state provided two or three "examples" of runs conducted during its investigation. When the parties met later in December, the state was represented by the BAR, the Contra Costa district attorney, and the attorney general. The Contra Costa district attorney took the lead role at that time and throughout the negotiation period. At the meeting, Sears presented evidence that suggested there were significant problems with the way the BAR had prepared its vehicles for the runs and that these problems could have led mechanics to make good faith misdiagnoses. The Contra Costa district attorney and the attorney general's office suggested that the parties review their respective information. Sears asked for one month to conduct an internal investigation and report its findings. The request was granted.

Sears had several concerns about the BAR's investigatory methods. First, BAR took the position that no system or part should be repaired or replaced unless it had failed. Thus, it considered recommendations based on preventive maintenance inappropriate. Second, most of the vehicles the agency used were high-mileage, older models (1978–1986) with significant repair problems. BAR first repaired the vehicles by replacing failed parts with new parts, and then disguising the deed by "aging" the new parts so that they appeared to be original to the vehicle. Symptoms of the original repair problem(s) were, however, left on the vehicles. For example, BAR used a 1984 Chevrolet station wagon equipped with a trailer hitch on a number of runs. The vehicle exhibited symptoms of weak or inadequate rear springs, including: (a) undercarriage damage to the rear bumpers and exhaust system; and (b) clear evidence that the strike-out bumpers (rubber bumpers that protect the rear axle from damaging itself or the vehicle's frame when its springs are weak or inadequate) were hitting the vehicle's frame. Examples like these prompted Sears service advisors to recommend repairs based on the symptoms appearing on the vehicles.

Moreover, virtually all of BAR's runs involved brake jobs and raised the controversial question of whether brake calipers should be reconditioned at the time brake pads were replaced, especially if the pads showed highly significant wear, as did those in BAR-prepared vehicles. Some industry members, including Sears, thought that caliper reconditioning or replacement should be completed as a matter of course when brake pads were replaced in order to bring the entire system up to original standard. Others, including BAR, believed that only brake parts that had failed should be replaced.

BAR regulations recognized accepted trade standards as determinative of appropriate conduct under the law. Sears believed the caliper reconditioning issue should have been treated as a controversy over what constitutes "accepted trade standards," rather than as the basis for allegations of fraudulent overselling. During the negotiations, Sears took this position and suggested that BAR undertake an administrative rule-making to determine what should be classified as the accepted trade standard in this area. BAR had previously adopted rules dealing with ball joints in this manner.

A month after discussing its findings with Sears managers, BAR investigated 10 additional shops, where investigators found that Sears was no longer overselling springs, shocks, and front-end parts, but was continuing to oversell calipers[22] (Exhibit 4).

Negotiations

The parties spent several months meeting to see if a reasonable resolution to the controversy could be worked out. Again, the Contra Costa district attorney and the attorney general took the lead. Sears entrusted the handling of its negotiations to a San Francisco law firm known for its trial work.[23] After many meetings during several months of difficult negotiating, the parties agreed on a consent decree dealing with how business would be conducted. The decree was acceptable to all, including the Contra Costa district attorney, the California attorney general, BAR, and Sears. Negotiations then turned to reaching a financial settlement, but the parties could not reach agreement. BAR left the negotiating table just after a newspaper article entitled "Consumer Affairs Is Target of Budget Ax" appeared in the June 7 edition of the *Los Angeles Times*.[24]

Legal Actions

The administrative action filed by the DCA on June 11 sought to revoke the license of all 72 Sears auto centers in California for violating the state's Auto Repair Act. The complaint charged Sears with making fake or misleading statements, fraud, false advertising, failure to state clearly parts and labor charges on invoices, and willful departure from accepted trade standards (Exhibit 5).

The case was due to be heard by an administrative law judge in Sacramento. At the hearing, both sides could call witnesses and provide evidence. Although the judge had the power to recommend a permanent or temporary revocation of Sears's auto repair licenses or to dismiss the charges, the DCA had the authority to make the final decision. If the DCA ruled against Sears, the company could file an appeal with the California Superior Court.

Shortly after the filing of the revocation proceedings by the DCA, the California attorney general's office and the district attorney for the County of Contra Costa announced that they, too, were considering legal action. Unlike the DCA action, which could result only in a revocation of Sears' licenses, a civil lawsuit by the attorney general could lead to fines and other monetary damages against Sears.

Employee Perspectives

The BAR attributed the overselling at Sears auto repair centers to the employee compensation and monitoring systems. Current and former Sears employees told BAR investigators that they were instructed to sell a certain number of alignments, springs, and brake jobs during every eight-hour work shift. They were also pressured to sell a specified number of shock absorbers or struts per hour. At one store, employees were told to sell five front-end alignments, eight sets of springs, eight sets of shock absorbers, and two tires each day. These employees also told BAR that if they did not meet these goals, they often were cut back in their work hours or transferred to another Sears department.[25]

One mechanic, Jerry C. Waddy, who had worked in Sears's San Bruno, California, store, filed suit against Sears, claiming that he was fired for failing to meet his quota of 16 oil changes a day. Waddy, who sought $1 million from Sears in a wrongful discharge suit, claimed that his manager even advised him in the last week to cheat in order to save his job. Waddy reported that before being fired, "we talked about the pressure, pressure, pressure to get the dollars."[26] Another mechanic, who asked to remain anonymous, commented: "I'm torn between moral integrity, losing my job, and trying to figure out how to work all this out."[27] A service advisor at a Sears in Orange County said he had requested a transfer to another job because he "couldn't stomach the pressure to sell. It wasn't right. You sold things to people to meet your quota for that day, but you didn't feel right about doing it."[28]

Regulators' Perspectives

Some government investigators and law enforcement officials regarded Sears's compensation policy as a willful, systemic fraud upon consumers. "There was a deliberate decision by Sears management to set up a structure that made it totally inevitable that the consumer would be oversold," stated Roy Liebmen, a California deputy attorney general.[29] DCA director Jim Conran accused Sears of a "systematic effort to bilk and rip off consumers on auto repair sales and parts."[30] Compensation specialists noted that it was fairly common for automotive service employees to receive commissions, though it was less usual for service employees to have specific sales quotas. Nevertheless, similar quotas were reportedly used at Firestone, a Sears competitor.[31]

The auto centers were not the only Sears units to have experience with quotas. Although the Allstate insurance subsidiary had eliminated sales quotas several years earlier, one former employee who claimed he was fired for not meeting a $600 monthly quota for life insurance premiums, filed a complaint with Maryland regulators charging that his manager had pressured him to ignore underwriting guidelines to close a sale.[32]

State regulators were concerned also about the sale of maintenance agreements on expensive appliances. Such agreements generated up to 50% of a store's annual earnings and could cost more than 35% of an appliance's price. In March 1992, Sears changed its pay structure for its appliance salespeople, cutting base salaries and emphasizing commissions. One 30-year Sears salesman, who retired in Sacramento in 1992, reported that he had received a dozen letters in two years from his manager stating that he would be fired if he did not sell more maintenance agreements. The salesman declared, "An unhappy salesman who figures he's been shafted is going to shaft someone else." A saleswoman in Sears's Vernon Hills, Illinois, store commented that "the pressure is much greater today than it used to be."[33]

California's Department of Consumer Affairs

The Sears investigation helped to save the DCA from being closed because of the state's budget crisis. At a press conference that achieved wide coverage in June 1992, DCA Director Jim Conran announced the results of its 18-month undercover investigation. The announcement came just weeks after legislators had targeted the department for elimination as part of an effort to close an $11 billion shortfall in the state budget.[34]

The investigation was estimated to have cost between $300,000 and $500,000, including the purchase of 18 late-model cars used in the probe.[35] Shortly after the press conference, a *Los Angeles Times* editorial, citing the Sears investigation, noted that closing the department "would produce a direct savings of only about $2 million since most of the agency's budget comes from fees collected from the dozens of professions and trades it regulates. But the cost to Californians of this move—in dollars and consumer confidence—could be unacceptably high."[36]

Less than a week after the investigation was made public, the California legislators who sought to eliminate DCA announced that they had dropped their proposal.[37]

SEARS RESPONDS

In the first two days after the administrative action was filed, the responses of Sears management were varied. One unidentified spokesman denied the allegations and said that Sears would defend itself vigorously against them. He stated: "Our policy, in California and nationwide, has always been to put the safety of our customers first when recommending repairs to their vehicles." Another spokesman, Greg Rossiter, called the investigation "seriously flawed." He continued: "Our technicians are not paid at all in any way related to what is sold."[38]

Dirk Scheakkin, a San Francisco lawyer representing Sears, said: "I think it's disgraceful that [the state] is trying to portray this as a fraud. . . . There may have been some honest mistakes. But there was no fraud." The lawyer alleged that the BAR used older cars with signs of wear that tricked Sears's employees into thinking certain repairs were necessary. He denied that employees were driven to sell by quotas, conceding only that the company had established "modest" and "easy-to-attain" goals. He said that employees who were not meeting the goals were probably not providing enough "preventive maintenance" on the cars.[39]

Forrest R. "Woody" Hasselton, Sears's president of retail, commented that "for 105 years Sears has promised Americans "Satisfaction Guaranteed" when it comes to products and services. While we disagree with the allegations made about us in California, we will correct any mistakes that may have been made and will work in the coming months to resolve these issues. We immediately want to reassure our customers that this commitment to satisfaction continues unabated."[40]

DCA director Conran did not back down from his allegations in the face of Sears's denials: "They can say what they want. You can see the places where they screwed the public."[41]

On June 16, Sears published in major California newspapers an "open letter" from CEO Brennan. Brennan wrote: "With over two million automotive customers serviced last year in California alone, mistakes may have occurred. However, Sears wants you to know that we would never intentionally violate the trust consumers have shown in our company for 105 years." Brennan questioned the California investigation because it challenged the industry practice of replacing worn parts before they fail. He continued, "You rely on us to recommend preventive maintenance measures to help insure your safety, and to avoid more costly future repairs. This includes recommending replacement of worn parts, when appropriate, before they fail. This accepted industry practice is being challenged by the Bureau." Brennan also accused the Department of Consumer Affairs of trying to save itself from being eliminated by its high-profile attack upon Sears.[42]

The Probe Spreads to Other States

On June 15, the day before Brennan's open letter appeared in California newspapers, the New Jersey Division of Consumer Affairs charged Sears with systematically giving motorists inflated estimates for unnecessary repairs. The New Jersey investigation, which had been in progress for four months, covered Sears and non-Sears shops. Undercover investigators twice brought a late-model car with a disconnected alternator wire to 38 auto repair shops. Instead of simply reconnecting the wire, 23 shops at least once either incorrectly diagnosed the problem or recommended unnecessary repairs. Eleven shops did so both times. And all six Sears shops misdiagnosed the problem both times and gave some of the most expensive prescriptions, such as replacing the battery and the alternator at a cost of up to $406.[43]

A Sears spokesman said that the firm had requested further information about the allegations. He stated: "The charges made are of extreme concern to us. We are beginning an internal review as to what happened in each case and will work closely with New Jersey officials to resolve this situation as quickly as possible."[44]

A Sears official later elaborated on the New Jersey investigation. He explained that service advisors' preliminary assessment—alternator failure—resulted from the use of computerized machines for evaluating the vehicles' electrical systems. The computerized diagnostic systems, used by Sears as well as other large auto repair facilities, correctly reported that no electrical current was passing through the alternator. However, the machines could not detect the reason for the failure: the detachment by New Jersey officials of the incoming alternator lead, a wire located at the rear of the alternator and not readily visible. Because New Jersey officials refused to authorize work on vehicles brought in for repair, Sears mechanics had no opportunity to discover the detached leads and reconnect them. Citing General Motors, the Sears official noted that the likelihood of such a detachment was less than one-half of one percent. He also noted that, contrary to the state's allegations, Sears had in fact detected and reconnected the lead in one instance.[45]

On Thursday, June 18, two days after the New Jersey probe was announced, the Florida attorney general's office announced that it would be launching an investigation into Sears auto centers because of the large number of complaints. However, in New York, the Department of Motor Vehicles announced that it had found overcharging in only one of eight Sears shops investigated and that the department did not believe that there was a serious problem in New York.[46]

The Investigation and Publicity Continue

In the week following the filing of the administrative action, the California Consumer Affairs Department received more than 800 complaints about Sears auto centers.[47] Approximately two dozen Sears employees not involved in the original investigation came forward and provided statements to the department. Said one: "Employees at Sears auto centers deserve better treatment and the customers deserve better treatment than they've been getting." That same employee, a store manager, reported that the district manager ordered that customers be charged $5.99 for inspections of electrical systems during a battery installation, regardless of whether such an inspection was requested.[48] The California attorney general was reviewing the new charges coming forward and considering filing a separate civil lawsuit against Sears.

Publicity about the allegations spread throughout the nation. One analyst commented: "Sears is almost built on its guarantee of satisfaction.

Anything that undermines that trust is very serious."[49] David Letterman, the late-night television talk show host, turned Sears's problem into a national television joke with a list of "Top 10 repair jobs recommended by the Sears Automotive Department." Number 10 was "grease the ashtrays;" Number 1, "add a redwood deck."[50]

THE DECISION

As Brennan met with other Sears executives on June 19, he considered what the company's next step should be.

Notes

1. Stanley Ziemba, "Sears Slips to No. 3 in the Retail Kingdom," *Chicago Tribune*, February 21, 1991, Business Section, p. 1.
2. Letter from Chuck Fabbri, a Sears auto mechanic, Hearing Before the Subcommittee on Consumer [sic] of the Senate Committee on Commerce, Science, and Transportation, 102d Congress, 2d Sess., July 21, 1992 (S. Hrg. 102-972), p. 83. (Hereafter, "Hearing.")
3. Gregory A. Patterson, "Sears's Brennan Accepts Blame for Auto Flap," *The Wall Street Journal*, June 23, 1992, p. B1.
4. Richard J. Barnett, senior regulatory counsel, Sears, attachment to letter to case author, June 9, 1993.
5. Richard Ringer, "A President for Sears Automotive," *The New York Times*, April 13, 1993, p. D5.
6. "Sears Restructures Its Automotive Subsidiary," *Discount Store News*, February 17, 1992, Vol. 31, No. 4, p. 4.
7. Adam Bryan, "All About Dealer Repairs," *The New York Times*, January 26, 1992, Section 3, p. 10.
8. Edward L. Kaufman, "Competition Hotter Among Service Retailers for Undercar Business," *Automotive Marketing*, June 1991, vol. 20, No. 6, p. 15.
9. John R. White, "A Proposal to License Mechanics," *The Boston Globe*, November 30, 1991, p. 53.
10. Id.
11. Id.
12. Material in this paragraph was provided by Richard J. Barnett, senior regulatory counsel, Sears, attachment to letter to case author, June 9, 1993.
13. Department of Consumer Affairs/Bureau of Automotive Repair, Consumer Protection Initiative Fact Sheet, 1992.
14. Richard J. Barnett, senior regulatory counsel, Sears, attachment to letter to case author, June 9, 1993.
15. State of California, Department of Consumer Affairs, News Release, June 11, 1992.
16. Id.
17. Id.
18. Roger W. Rüs and John Patric, *The Repairman Will Get You If You Don't Look Out*, 1942.
19. Hearing.
20. Telephone interview with California Senior Assistant Attorney General Herschel T. Elkins, January 12, 1993.
21. Material in this section provided by Richard J. Barnett, senior regulatory counsel, Sears, attachment to letter to case author, June 9, 1993.
22. Patterson, "Sears Gets Harsh Lesson. . . . "
23. Gregory A. Patterson, "Sears Gets a Harsh Lesson from States in Handling of Auto-Repair Inquiries," *The Wall Street Journal*, October 2, 1992, p. B4A.

24. Unless otherwise indicated, material in this paragraph is from Richard J. Barnett, senior regulatory counsel, Sears, attachment to letter to case author, June 9, 1993.
25. State of California, Department of Consumer Affairs, News Release, June 11, 1992.
26. Julia Flynn, Christina Del Valle, and Russell Mitchell, "Did Sears Take Other Customers for a Ride?" *Business Week*, August 3, 1992, p. 25.
27. T. Christian Miller, "Sears Admits 'Mistakes' at Auto Service Centers," *The San Francisco Chronicle*, June 23, 1992, p. A1.
28. Denise Gellene, "New State Probe of Sears Could Lead to Suit," *Los Angeles Times*, June 12, 1992, Part D, p. 1.
29. *Business Week*, op. cit., August 3, 1992.
30. Michael Miller, "California Seeks to Shut Down Sears Auto Shops," Reuters, Los Angeles, June 11, 1992.
31. Letter from Mark Lewis, Hearing, pp. 86-87.
32. *Business Week*, op. cit., August 3, 1992.
33. Id.
34. Denise Gellene, "State Spares Consumer Department," *The Los Angeles Times*, June 17, 1992, Part D, p. 1.
35. Denise Gellene, "State to Seek to Lift Auto Repair License of Sears," *The Los Angeles Times*, June 11, 1992, Part A, p. 1.
36. Editorial, "A Case of Consumer Confidence; Sears Investigation, While Unresolved, Proves the Value of a State Agency," *The Los Angeles Times*, June 13, 1992, Part B, p. 7.
37. Denise Gellene, "State Spares Consumer Department," *The Los Angeles Times*, op. cit., June 17, 1992, Part D, p. 1.
38. T. Christian Miller, "Nine Bay Area Sears' Included in Overcharging Probe," *The San Francisco Chronicle*, June 12, 1992, p. **A23**.
39. Denise Gellene, "New State Probe of Sears Could Lead to Suit," *The Los Angeles Times*, June 12, 1992, Part D, p. 1.
40. "State Attorney General Probing Sears Auto Centers," UPI, Los Angeles, June 12, 1992.
41. Id.
42. "Sears Hits Back at California Probe," UPI, Los Angeles, June 16, 1992.
43. "Sears Charges More for Auto Work, New Jersey Consumer Watchdog Says," UPI, Newark, New Jersey, June 16, 1992.
44. Thomas Witom, "Sears Promises Quick Action on Auto Repair Flap," Reuters, Chicago, June 16, 1992.
45. Richard J. Barnett, senior regulatory counsel, Sears, attachment to letter to case author, June 9, 1993.
46. Denise Gellene and George White, "Florida Probes Sears' Car Repair Centers," *The Los Angeles Times*, June 19, 1992, Part D, p. 2
47. Id.
48. Id.
49. Denise Gellene, "New State Probe of Sears Could Lead to Suit," *The Los Angeles Times*, June 12, 1992, Part D, P. 1.
50. *Newsday*, June 28, 1992, op. cit.

EXHIBIT 1. Daily Closing Stock Price, Sears, Roebuck & Co. Common Stock, June 1–19, 1992 (344,924,000 shares outstanding)

June	1	43-2/8
	2	42-6/8
	3	42-4/8
	4	42-4/8
	5	42-4/8
June	8	42-1/8
	9	41-6/8
	10	42
	11	41-3/8
	12	40-4/8
June	15	40-7/8
	16	40-3/8
	17	38-4/8
	18	38-6/8
	19	38-1/8

Source: Standard & Poor's *Daily Stock Price Record: New York Stock Exchange*, April, May, June 1992, p. 434.

EXHIBIT 2. Financial Highlights (millions, except per common share data)

	1991	1990	1989	1988	1987
Sears, Roebuck and Co.					
Revenues	$57,242	$55,972	$53,794	$50,251	$45,904
Net income	1,279	902	1,509	1,454	1,633
Common share dividends	608	686	702	758	756
Per common share:					
Net income	3.71	2.63	4.30	3.84	4.30
Dividends	2.00	2.00	2.00	2.00	2.00
Investments	46,567	38,675	33,705	29,136	25,210
Total assets	106,435	96,253	86,972	77,952	75,014
Shareholder's equity	14,188	12,824	13,622	14,055	13,541
The Merchandising Group					
Revenues (millions)					
Total Merchandising group	31,433	31,986	31,599	30,256	28,085
Merchandising (excluding credit and international)	24,757	25,093	25,002	24,252	22,894
Net Income					
Total Merchandising group	486	257	647	524	787
Merchandising (excluding credit and international)	90	37	292	240	503

Source: Sears, Roebuck and Co., 1991 Annual Report.

EXHIBIT 3. Sears, Roebuck Case Summary—Initial Investigation and Random Runs

Location	Date of Run(s)	Estimated Oversell	Items Oversold
Los Angeles Metropolitan Area			
Brea (100 Brea Mall)	7-10-91	$350	front brake overhaul including calipers, struts and shocks
Canoga Park (6433 Falbrook Ave.)	6-12-91	130	front brake pads, turned rotors, rebuilt calipers
Covina (1414 N. Azusa Ave.)	3-30-91	136	adjust rear brakes, calipers
	4-07-91	307	front brakes, idler arms
	8-08-91	305	front brakes, rotors, calipers, shocks, idler arm
Hemet (25201 San Jacinto St.)	8-28-91	126	calipers
L.A. (2711 E. Olympic Blvd.)	7-11-91	170	rear springs, alignment, front calipers
Northridge (100 Northridge Fashion Ctr.)	7-10-91	480	coil springs, shocks, new calipers
City of Industry (100 Puente Hills Mall)	6-13-91	290	front/rear coil springs, repaired calipers
San Bernardino (100 Inland Center)	4-09-91	180	coil springs, calipers
	7-18-91	535	coil springs, calipers, four shocks
Santa Monica (302 Colorado Ave.)	8-29-91	230	caliper repairs, one rotor, four shocks
Fresno			
Fresno (3636 N. Blackstone Ave.)	7-08-91	328	head lamps charged for/not installed, front brakes, idler arms, new tires
Chico			
Chico (1982 East 20th St.)	10-30-91	275	calipers, master cylinder, front brake service
Redding			
Redding (1403 Hilltop Dr.)	7-25-91	229	replaced calipers, master cylinder, alignment
Visalia			
Visalia (3501 S. Mooney Blvd.)	8-08-91	106	calipers
San Francisco Bay Area			
Antioch (2600 County E. Mall)	3-13-91	158	oversold front pads, turned rotors
	4-04-91	126	idler arm
	6-19-91	275	shocks, struts
Concord (1001 Willow Pass Rd.)	1-31-91	100	front-wheel bearings, front calipers
	2-06-91	585	front brake pads, front and rear springs, control arm bushings
	2-13-91	185	master cylinder, charged for cylinder kits not installed

Fairfield (1549 Gateway Dr.)	7-31-91	$74	calipers
Hayward (660 W. Weston Ave.)	4-23-91	110	calipers
	6-13-91	306	front brakes, coil springs, radiator hoses, adjust steering box, tires, calipers
Mountain View (455 San Antonio Rd.)	4-23-91	265	calipers, rear springs
San Jose (2180 Tully Rd.)	8-22-91	430	calipers, shocks, coil springs
San Rafael (9000 Northgate)	6-13-91	340	calipers, wheel cylinders, rotors, wheel bearings
Santa Rosa (100 Santa Rosa Mall)	6-17-91	314	2 idler arms, 4 shocks
Monterey County Area			
Salinas (1100 Northridge Mall)	8-07-91	115	repaired left caliper, charged for right caliper and did not do, front seals, front brake pads
Sacramento			
Arden (1601 Arden Way)	4-23-91	376	calipers, rear drums, linings
Citrus Heights (5900 Sunrise Mall)	12-04-90	138	master cylinder, rear wheel cylinder
	12-19-90	85	rear brake repair
	2-02-91	187	calipers, spark plugs, bleeding of rear brakes

Source: California Department of Consumer Affairs, Bureau of Automotive Repair.

Summary of Investigations and Total Amounts Oversold

	Date(s) of Investigation	Total Oversold
Bay Area	March 1991–August 1991	$3,268
Chico	October 1991	275
Fresno	July 1991	328
Los Angeles	July 1991–August 1991	3,229
Redding	July 1991	229
Sacramento	December 1990–January 1992	786
Visalia	August 1992	106
Total amount oversold to BAR statewide:		$8,221

Source: California Department of Consumer Affairs, Bureau of Automotive Repair.

EXHIBIT 4. Sears, Roebuck Case Summary—Follow-up Runs

Location	Date of Run(s)	Estimated Oversell	Items Oversold
Costa Mesa (3333 Bristol St.)	1-18-92	$150	calipers replaced, rear brake service unnecessary
El Cajon (575 Fletcher Pkwy., #1)	2-05-92	129	calipers replaced
Glendale (236 N. Central Ave.)	1-17-92	130	calipers replaced, rear brake adjustment not needed
Hayward (660 W. Winston Ave.)	1-30-92	0	no unnecessary repairs
Oakland (2633 Telegraph Ave.)	2-03/92	22	lube charged for not provided, front rotors turned out of specification
Palmdale (1345 W. Ave.)	2-05/92	160	calipers, rear brake clean/ adjust, rear brake bleed charged/not done
Sacramento (1601 Arden Way)	1-02-92	50	caliper seals and dustboots replace unnecessarily
Salinas (110 Northridge Mall)	2-06-92	135	calipers replaced
San Luis Obispo (273 Madonna Rd.)	2-04-92	170	four shock absorbers, caliper seals and dustboots replaced unnecessarily
Visalia (3501 S. Mooney Blvd.)	1-21-92	0	no repairs performed

Source: California Department of Consumer Affairs, Bureau of Automotive Repair.

EXHIBIT 5. Sears, Roebuck Case—Business and Professions Codes Relating to Accusations

Business and Professions Codes		Related Accusation Examples
9884.7(1)(a)	False or misleading statements	Took vehicle with worn tires. No cord showing.
		Requested alignment advertised for $24.99 and a lube and oil change. Given estimate for $70. Told operator tires worn down to cords, required replacement. False statement—tires not worn to cord, in fact had usable tread left. (Citrus Heights)
		Operator asked for brake inspection. Respondent was advised that brakes were not releasing, which would cause the vehicle to fishtail. Advised the operator the vehicle needed front and rear brakes, that the rear drums were damaged and need replacement. Invoiced new calipers when in fact they were remanufactured. (Arden)
		Went to purchase four new tires. Told that she needed shocks and struts. Both were "blown out and leaking." Estimate $419.95. Second dealer said no sign of leakage, returned and discussed with manager who, with mechanic, reinspected and said nothing wrong. (Stockton)
		Vehicle taken to shop with worn pads. Advised vehicle needed front brakes, front struts, and rear shocks. Only brake pads needed repair. (Antioch)
		Recommended front brakes, right idler arms, and front and rear shocks. (Santa Rosa)
		In addition to front brakes, coil springs, and alignment, operator was told two new tires were needed because "they pull to the right or left." (Mountain View)
		New springs because riding low and shocks because these parts are rusty. (San Bernardino)
		Needed alignment "the front end that controls steering keeps pulling to the right." "The rear of the car is low and prevents alignment being properly set." Springs $79.99 a pair and $30 for labor. (Los Angeles)
		Needed shocks because they were old, cracked, leaking and the rubber was falling out. Had to turn rotors by California law. (Northridge)
9884.7(1)(d)	Fraud	Charged $34.95 for time saver oil change agreement without her knowledge or consent. Charged $54.99 for Road Handler. (Citrus Heights)
		Sold alignment, new cargo springs, and complete front brake job at a cost of $333, when all parts except brake pads were in good condition and vehicle did not need alignment. (Los Angeles)

EXHIBIT 5. *(Continued)*

Business and Professions Codes		Related Accusation Examples
9884.7(1)(d)	Fraud *(continued)*	Sold repair and replacement of front brakes, calipers, rotors turned, shock absorbers and idle arm, and an alignment, when all but worn brake pads were in good condition and did not require repair, adjustment or replacement. (Covina)
		Sold replacement idler arms and an alignment, when all parts except for brake pads and rotors were in good condition. Charged $22.50 to unnecessarily "clean and adjust rear brakes" without her consent. Charged $60 for a front brake kit, including brake caliper hardware—the only hardware installed were two mounting springs. (Covina)
9884.8	Failure to clearly state parts and labor on invoice	Incidence widespread.
9884.10	Failure to return parts	Failed to return old parts as requested. When asked, mechanic said they could not find them and asked what he could do to make it right. (Santa Rosa)

California Code of Regulations		Related Accusation Examples
3372.1	False advertising	Advertised that a customer could "save 10%-15%" on the purchase of tires. Advised operator that the Road Handler Response tires she requested were on sale for $54.99 each, but the tire was not in stock and that respondent would provide an upgrade for the same price, but charged $67.99 for each upgraded tire. (Citrus Heights).

Source: California Department of Consumer Affairs, Bureau of Automotive Repair.

The Leader's New Work:
Building Learning Organizations

Peter M. Senge

Human beings are designed for learning. No one has to teach an infant to walk, or talk, or master the spatial relationships needed to stack eight building blocks that don't topple. Children come fully equipped with an insatiable drive to explore and experiment. Unfortunately, the primary institutions of our society are oriented predominantly toward controlling rather than learning, rewarding individuals for performing for others rather than for cultivating their natural curiosity and impulse to learn. The young child entering school discovers quickly that the name of the game is getting the right answer and avoiding mistakes—a mandate no less compelling to the aspiring manager.

"Our prevailing system of management has destroyed our people," writes W. Edwards Deming, leader in the quality movement.[1] "People are born with intrinsic motivation, self-esteem, dignity, curiosity to learn, joy in learning. The forces of destruction begin with toddlers—a prize for the best Halloween costume, grades in school, gold stars, and on up through the university. On the job, people, teams, divisions are ranked—reward for the one at the top, punishment at the bottom. MBO, quotas, incentive pay, business plans, put together separately, division by division, cause further loss, unknown and unknowable."

Ironically, by focusing on performing for someone else's approval, corporations create the very conditions that predestine them to mediocre performance. Over the long run, superior performance depends on superior learning. A Shell study showed that, according to former planning director Arie de Geus, "a full one-third of the Fortune '500' industrials listed in 1970 had vanished by 1983."[2] Today, the average lifetime of the largest industrial enterprises is probably less than *half* the average lifetime of a person in an industrial society. On the other hand, de Geus and his colleagues at Shell also found a small number of companies that survived for seventy-five years or longer. Interestingly, the key to their survival was the ability to run "experiments in the margin," to continually explore new business and organizational opportunities that create potential new sources of growth.

If anything, the need for understanding how organizations learn and accelerating that learning is greater today than ever before. The old days when a Henry Ford, Alfred Sloan, or Tom Watson *learned for the organization* are gone. In an increasingly dynamic, interdependent, and unpredictable world, it is simply no longer possible for anyone to "figure it all out at the top." The old model, "the top thinks and the local acts," must now give way to integrating thinking and acting at all levels. While the challenge is great, so is the potential payoff. "The person who figures out how to harness the collective genius of the people in his or her organization," according to former Citibank CEO Walter Wriston, "is going to blow the competition away."

Reprinted by permission of the author, Peter M. Senge, Director of The Center for Organizational Learning at the MIT Sloan School of Management. "The Leader's New Work: Building Learning Organizations" by Peter M. Senge, *Sloan Management Review* 32 (Fall 1990) 7–23. Copyright © 1990 by Sloan Management Review Association. All rights reserved.

Adaptive Learning and Generative Learning

The prevailing view of learning organizations emphasizes increased adaptability. Given the accelerating pace of change, or so the standard view goes, "the most successful corporation of the 1990s," according to *Fortune* magazine, "will be something called a learning organization, a consummately adaptive enterprise."[3] As the Shell study shows, examples of traditional authoritarian bureaucracies that responded too slowly to survive in changing business environments are legion.

But increasing adaptiveness is only the first stage in moving toward learning organizations. The impulse to learn in children goes deeper than desires to respond and adapt more effectively to environmental change. The impulse to learn, at its heart, is an impulse to be generative, to expand our capability. This is why leading corporations are focusing on *generative* learning, which is about creating, as well as *adaptive* learning, which is about coping.[4]

The total quality movement in Japan illustrates the evolution from adaptive to generative learning. With its emphasis on continuous experimentation and feedback, the total quality movement has been the first wave in building learning organizations. But Japanese firms' view of serving the customer has evolved. In the early years of total quality, the focus was on "fitness to standard," making a product reliably so that it would do what its designers intended it to do and what the firm told its customers it would do. Then came a focus on "fitness to need," understanding better what the customer wanted and then providing products that reliably met those needs. Today, leading edge firms seek to understand and meet the "latent need" of the customer—what customers might truly value but have never experienced or would never think to ask for. As one Detroit executive commented recently, "You could never produce the Mazda Miata solely from market research. It required a leap of imagination to see what the customer *might* want."[5]

Generative learning, unlike adaptive learning, requires new ways of looking at the world, whether in understanding customers or in understanding how to better manage a business. For years, U. S. manufacturers sought competitive advantage in aggressive controls on inventories, incentives against overproduction, and rigid adherence to production forecasts. Despite these incentives, their performance was eventually eclipsed by Japanese firms who saw the challenges of manufacturing differently. They realized that eliminating delays in the production process was the key to reducing instability and improving cost, productivity, and service. They worked to build networks of relationships with trusted suppliers and to redesign physical production processes so as to reduce delays in materials procurement, production set up, and in-process inventory—a much higher-leverage approach to improving both cost and customer loyalty.

As Boston Consulting Group's George Stalk has observed, the Japanese saw the significance of delays because they saw the process of order entry, production scheduling, materials procurement, production, and distribution *as an integrated system.* "What distorts the system so badly is time," observed Stalk—the multiple delays between events and responses. "These distortions reverberate throughout the system, producing disruptions, waste, and inefficiency."[6] Generative learning requires seeing the systems that control events.

When we fail to grasp the systemic source of problems, we are left to "push on" symptoms rather than eliminate underlying causes. The best we can ever do is adaptive learning.

The Leader's New Work

"I talk with people all over the country about learning organizations, and the response is always very positive," says William O'Brien, CEO of the Hanover Insurance companies. "If this type of organization is so widely preferred, why don't people create such organizations? I think the answer is leadership. People have no real comprehension of the type of commitment it requires to build such an organization."[7]

Our traditional view of leaders—as special people who set the direction, make the key decisions, and energize the troops—is deeply rooted in an individualistic and nonsystemic worldview. Especially in the West, leaders are *heroes*—great men (and occasionally women) who rise to the fore in times of crisis. So long as such myths prevail, they reinforce a focus on short-term events and charismatic heroes rather than on systemic forces and collective learning.

Leadership in learning organizations centers on subtler and ultimately more important work. In a learning organization, leaders' roles differ dramatically from that of the charismatic decision maker. Leaders are designers, teachers, and stewards. These roles require new skills: the ability to build shared vision, to bring to the surface and challenge prevailing mental models, and to foster more systemic patterns of thinking. In short, leaders in learning organizations are responsible for *building organizations* where people are continually expanding their capabilities to shape their future—that is, leaders are responsible for learning.

CREATIVE TENSION: THE INTEGRATING PRINCIPLE

Leadership in a learning organization starts with the principle of creative tension.[8] Creative tension comes from seeing clearly where we want to be, our "vision," and telling the truth about where we are, our "current reality." The gap between the two generates a natural tension (see Figure 1).

Creative tension can be resolved in two basic ways: by raising current reality toward the vision, or by lowering the vision toward current reality. Individuals, groups, and organizations who learn how to work with creative tension learn how to use the energy it generates to move reality more reliably toward their visions.

The principle of creative tension has long been recognized by leaders. Martin Luther King, Jr., once said, "Just as Socrates felt that it was necessary to create a tension in the mind, so that individuals could rise from the bondage of myths and half truths . . . so must we . . . create the kind of tension in society that will help men rise from the dark depths of prejudice and racism."[9]

Without vision there is no creative tension. Creative tension cannot be generated from current reality alone. All the analysis in the world will never

FIGURE 1. The Principle of Creative Tension

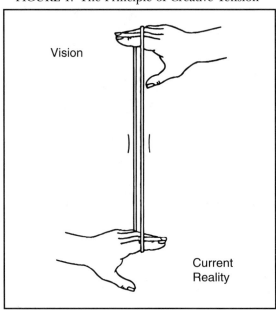

generate a vision. Many who are otherwise qualified to lead fail to do so because they try to substitute analysis for vision. They believe that, if only people understood current reality, they would surely feel the motivation to change. They are then disappointed to discover that people "resist" the personal and organizational changes that must be made to alter reality. What they never grasp is that the natural energy for changing reality comes from holding a picture of what might be that is more important to people than what is.

But creative tension cannot be generated from vision alone; it demands an accurate picture of current reality as well. Just as King had a dream, so too did he continually strive to "dramatize the shameful conditions" of racism and prejudice so that they could no longer be ignored. Vision without an understanding of current reality will more likely foster cynicism than creativity. The principle of creative tension teaches that *an accurate picture of current reality is just as important as a compelling picture of a desired future.*

Leading through creative tension is different than solving problems. In problem solving, the energy for change comes from attempting to get away from an aspect of current reality that is undesirable. With creative tension, the energy for change comes from the vision, from what we want to create, juxtaposed with current reality. While the distinction may seem small, the consequences are not. Many people and organizations find themselves motivated to change only when their problems are bad enough to cause them to change. This works for a while, but the change process runs out of steam as soon as the problems driving the change become less pressing. With problem solving, the motivation for change is extrinsic. With creative tension, the motivation is intrinsic. This distinction mirrors the distinction between adaptive and generative learning.

NEW ROLES

The traditional authoritarian image of the leader as "the boss calling the shots" has been recognized as oversimplified and inadequate for some time. According to Edgar Schein, "Leadership is intertwined with culture formation." Building an organization's culture and shaping its evolution is the "unique and essential function" of leadership.[10] In a learning organization, the critical roles of leadership—designer, teacher, and steward—have antecedents in the ways leaders have contributed to building organizations in the past. But each role takes on new meaning in the learning organization and, as will be seen in the following sections, demands new skills and tools.

Leader as Designer

Imagine that your organization is an ocean liner and that you are "the leader." What is your role?

I have asked this question of groups of managers many times. The most common answer, not surprisingly, is "the captain." Others say, "The navigator, setting the direction." Still others say, "The helmsman, actually controlling the direction," or, "The engineer down there stoking the fire, providing energy," or, "The social director, making sure everybody's enrolled, involved, and communicating." While these are legitimate leadership roles, there is another which, in many ways, eclipses them all in importance. Yet rarely does anyone mention it.

The neglected leadership role is the *designer* of the ship. No one has a more sweeping influence than the designer. What good does it do for the captain to say, "Turn starboard 30 degrees," when the designer has built a rudder that will only turn to port, or which takes six hours to turn to starboard? It's fruitless to be the leader in an organization that is poorly designed.

The functions of design, or what some have called "social architecture," are rarely visible; they take place behind the scenes. The consequences that appear today are the result of work done long in the past, and work today will show its benefits far in the future. Those who aspire to lead out of a desire to control, or gain fame, or simply to be at the center of the action, will find little to attract them to the quiet design work of leadership.

But what, specifically, is involved in organizational design? "Organization design is widely misconstrued as moving around boxes and lines," says Hanover's O'Brien. "The first task of organization design concerns designing the governing ideas of purpose, vision, and core values by which people will live." Few acts of leadership have a more enduring impact on an organization than building a foundation of purpose and core values.

In 1982, Johnson & Johnson found itself facing a corporate nightmare when bottles of its best-selling Tylenol were tampered with, resulting in several deaths. The corporation's immediate response was to pull all Tylenol off the shelves of retail outlets. Thirty-one million capsules were destroyed, even though they were tested and found safe. Although the immediate cost was significant, no other action was possible given the firm's credo. Authored almost forty years earlier by president Robert Wood Johnson, Johnson & Johnson's credo states that permanent success is possible only when modern industry realizes that:

- service to its customers comes first;
- service to its employees and management comes second;
- service to the community comes third; and
- service to its stockholders, last.

Such statements might seem like motherhood and apple pie to those who have not seen the way a clear sense of purpose and values can affect key business decisions. Johnson & Johnson's crisis management in this case was based on that credo. It was simple, it was right, and it worked.

If governing ideas constitute the first design task of leadership, the second design task involves the policies, strategies, and structures that translate guiding ideas into business decisions. Leadership theorist Philip Selznick calls policy and structure the "institutional embodiment of purpose."[11] "Policy making (the rules that guide decisions) ought to be separated from decision making," says Jay Forrester.[12] "Otherwise, short-term pressures will usurp time from policy creation."

Traditionally, writers like Selznick and Forrester have tended to see policy making and implementation as the work of a small number of senior managers. But that view is changing. Both the dynamic business environment and the mandate of the learning organization to engage people at all levels now make it clear that this second design task is more subtle. Henry Mintzberg has argued that strategy is less a rational plan arrived at in the abstract and implemented throughout the organization than an "emergent phenomenon." Successful organizations "craft strategy" according to Mintzberg, as they continually learn about shifting business conditions and balance what is desired and what is possible.[13] The key is not getting the right strategy but fostering strategic thinking. "The choice of individual action is only part of . . . the policymaker's need," according to Mason and Mitroff.[14] "More important is the need to achieve insight into the nature of the complexity and to formulate concepts and world views for coping with it."

Behind appropriate policies, strategies, and structures are effective learning processes; their creation is the third key design responsibility in learning organizations. This does not absolve senior managers of their strategic responsibilities. Actually, it deepens and extends those responsibilities. Now, they are not only responsible for ensuring that an organization have well-developed strategies and policies, but also for ensuring that processes exist whereby these are continually improved.

In the early 1970s, Shell was the weakest of the big seven oil companies. Today, Shell and Exxon are arguably the strongest, both in size and financial health. Shell's ascendance began with frustration. Around 1971 members of Shell's "Group Planning" in London began to foresee dramatic change and unpredictability in world oil markets. However, it proved impossible to persuade managers that the stable world of steady growth in oil demand and supply they had known for twenty years was about to change. Despite brilliant analysis and artful presentation, Shell's planners realized, in the words of Pierre Wack, that they "had failed to change behavior in much of the Shell organization."[15] Progress would probably have ended there, had the frustration not given way to a radically new view of corporate planning.

As they pondered this failure, the planners' view of their basic task shifted: "We no longer saw our task as producing a documented view of the future business environment five or ten years ahead. Our real target was the microcosm (the 'mental model') of our decision makers." Only when the planners reconceptualized their basic task as fostering learning rather than devising plans did their insights begin to have an impact. The initial tool used was "scenario analysis," through which planners encouraged operating managers to think through how they would manage in the future under different possible scenarios. It mattered not that the managers believed the planners' scenarios absolutely, only that they became engaged in ferreting out the implications. In this way, Shell's planners conditioned managers to be mentally prepared for a shift from low prices to high prices and from stability to instability. The results were significant. When OPEC became a reality, Shell quickly responded by increasing local operating company control (to enhance maneuverability in the new political environment), building buffer stocks, and accelerating development of non-OPEC sources—actions that its competitors took much more slowly or not at all.

Somewhat inadvertently, Shell planners had discovered the leverage of designing institutional learning processes, whereby, in the words of former planning director de Geus, "Management teams change their shared mental models of their company, their markets, and their competitors."[16] Since then, "planning as learning" has become a byword at Shell, and Group Planning has continually sought out new learning tools that can be integrated into the planning process. Some of these are described below.

Leader as Teacher

"The first responsibility of a leader," writes retired Herman Miller CEO Max de Pree, "is to define reality."[17] Much of the leverage leaders can actually exert lies in helping people achieve more accurate, more insightful, and more *empowering* views of reality.

Leader as teacher does *not* mean leader as authoritarian expert whose job it is to teach people the "correct" view of reality. Rather, it is about helping everyone in the organization, oneself included, to gain more insightful views of current reality. This is in line with a popular emerging view of leaders as coaches, guides, or facilitators.[18] In learning organizations, this teaching role is developed further by virtue of explicit attention to people's mental models and by the influence of the systems perspective.

The role of leader as teacher starts with bringing to the surface people's mental models of important issues. No one carries an organization, a market, or a state of technology in his or her head. What we carry in our heads are assumptions. These mental pictures of how the world works have a significant influence on how we perceive problems and opportunities, identify courses of action, and make choices.

One reason that mental models are so deeply entrenched is that they are largely tacit. Ian Mitroff, in his study of General Motors, argues that an assumption that prevailed for years was that, in the United States, "Cars are status symbols. Styling is therefore more important than quality."[19] The Detroit automakers didn't say, "We have a *mental model* that all people care about is styling." Few actual managers would even say publicly that all people care about is styling. So long as the view remained unexpressed, there was little possibility of challenging its validity or forming more accurate assumptions.

But working with mental models goes beyond revealing hidden assumptions. "Reality," as perceived by most people in most organizations, means pressures that must be borne, crises that must be reacted to, and limitations that must be accepted. Leaders as teachers help people *restructure their views of reality* to see beyond the superficial conditions and events into the underlying causes of problems—and therefore to see new possibilities for shaping the future.

Specifically, leaders can influence people to view reality at three distinct levels: events, patterns of behavior, and systemic structure.

Systemic Structure
(Generative)

↓

Patterns of Behavior
(Responsive)

↓

Events
(Reactive)

The key question becomes *where do leaders predominantly focus their own and their organization's attention?*

Contemporary society focuses predominantly on events. The media reinforces this perspective, with almost exclusive attention to short-term, dramatic events. This focus leads naturally to explaining what happens in terms of those events: "The Dow Jones average went up sixteen points because high fourth-quarter profits were announced yesterday."

Pattern-of-behavior explanations are rarer, in contemporary culture, than event explanations, but they do occur. "Trend analysis" is an example of seeing patterns of behavior. A good editorial that interprets a set of current events in the context of long-term historical changes is another example. Systemic, structural explanations go even further by addressing the question, "What causes the patterns of behavior?"

In some sense, all three levels of explanation are equally true. But their usefulness is quite different. Event explanations—who did what to whom—doom their holders to a reactive stance toward change. Pattern-of-behavior explanations focus on identifying long-term trends and assessing their implications. They at least suggest how, over time, we can respond to shifting conditions. Structural explanations are the most powerful. Only they address the underlying causes of behavior at a level such that patterns of behavior can be changed.

By and large, leaders of our current institutions focus their attention on events and patterns of behavior, and, under their influence, their organizations do likewise. That is why contemporary organizations are predominantly reactive, or at best responsive—rarely generative. On the other hand, leaders in learning organizations pay attention to all three levels, but focus especially on systemic structure; largely by example, they teach people throughout the organization to do likewise.

Leader as Steward

This is the subtlest role of leadership. Unlike the roles of designer and teacher, it is almost solely a matter of attitude. It is an attitude critical to learning organizations.

While stewardship has long been recognized as an aspect of leadership, its source is still not widely understood. I believe Robert Greenleaf came closest to explaining real stewardship, in his seminal book *Servant Leadership*.[20] There, Greenleaf argues that "The servant leader *is* servant first. . . . It begins with the natural feeling that one wants to serve, to serve *first*. This conscious choice brings one to aspire to lead. That person is sharply different from one who is leader first, perhaps because of the need to assuage an unusual power drive or to acquire material possessions."

Leaders' sense of stewardship operates on two levels: stewardship for the people they lead and stewardship for the larger purpose or mission that underlies the enterprise. The first type arises from a keen appreciation of the impact one's leadership can have on others. People can suffer economically, emotionally, and spiritually under inept leadership. If anything, people in a learning organization are more vulnerable because of their commitment and sense of shared ownership. Appreciating this naturally instills a sense of responsibility in leaders. The second type of stewardship arises from a leader's sense of personal purpose and commitment to the organization's larger mission. People's natural impulse to learn is unleashed when they are engaged in an endeavor they consider worthy of their fullest commitment. Or, as Lawrence Miller puts it, "Achieving return on equity does not, as a goal, mobilize the most noble forces of our soul."[21]

Leaders engaged in building learning organizations naturally feel part of a larger purpose that goes beyond their organization. They are part of changing the way businesses operate, not from a vague philanthropic urge, but from a conviction that their efforts will produce more productive organizations, capable of achieving higher levels of organizational success and personal satisfaction than more traditional organizations. Their sense of stewardship was succinctly captured by George Bernard Shaw when he said,

> This is the true joy in life, the being used for a purpose you consider a mighty one, the being a force of nature rather than a feverish, selfish clod of ailments and grievances complaining that the world will not devote itself to making you happy.

NEW SKILLS

New leadership roles require new leadership skills. These skills can only be developed, in my judgment, through a lifelong commitment. It is not enough for one or two individuals to develop these skills. They must be distributed widely throughout the organization. This is one reason that understanding the *disciplines* of a learning organization is so important. These disciplines embody the principles and practices that can widely foster leadership development.

Three critical areas of skills (disciplines) are building shared vision, surfacing and challenging mental models, and engaging in systems thinking.[22]

Building Shared Vision

How do individual visions come together to create shared visions? A useful metaphor is the hologram, the three-dimensional image created by interacting light sources.

If you cut a photograph in half, each half shows only part of the whole image. But if you divide a hologram, each part, no matter how small, shows the whole image intact. Likewise, when a group of people come to share a vision for an organization, each person sees an individual picture of the organization at its best. Each shares responsibility for the whole, not just for one piece. But the component pieces of the hologram are not identical. Each represents the whole image from a different point of view. It's something like poking holes in a window shade; each hole offers a unique angle for viewing the whole image. So, too, is each individual's vision unique.

When you add up the pieces of a hologram, something interesting happens. The image becomes more intense, more lifelike. When more people come to share a vision, the vision becomes more real in the sense of a mental reality that people can truly imagine achieving. They now have partners, co-creators; the vision no longer rests on their shoulders alone. Early on, when they are nurturing an individual vision, people may say it is "my vision." But, as the shared vision develops, it becomes both "my vision" and "our vision."

The skills involved in building shared vision include the following:

Encouraging Personal Vision.   Shared visions emerge from personal visions. It is not that people only care about their own self-interest—in fact, people's values usually include dimensions that concern family, organization, community, and even the world. Rather, it is that people's capacity for caring is *personal.*

Communicating and Asking for Support.   Leaders must be willing to continually share their own vision, rather than being the official representative of the corporate vision. They also must be prepared to ask, "Is this vision worthy of your commitment?" This can be difficult for a person used to setting goals and presuming compliance.

Visioning as an Ongoing Process.   Building shared vision is a never-ending process. At any one point there will be a particular image of the future that is predominant, but that image will evolve. Today, too many managers want to dispense with the "vision business" by going off and writing the Official Vision Statement. Such statements almost always lack the vitality, freshness, and excitement of a genuine vision that comes from people asking, "What do we reply want to achieve?"

Blending Extrinsic and Intrinsic Visions.   Many energizing visions are extrinsic—that is, they focus on achieving something relative to an outsider, such as a competitor. But a goal that is limited to defeating an opponent can, once the vision is achieved, easily become a defensive posture. In contrast, intrinsic goals like creating a new type of product, taking an established product to a new level, or setting a new standard for customer satisfaction can call forth a new level of creativity and innovation. Intrinsic and extrinsic visions need to coexist; a vision solely predicated on defeating an adversary will eventually weaken an organization.

Distinguishing Positive from Negative Visions. Many organizations only truly pull together when their survival is threatened. Similarly, most social movements aim at eliminating what people don't want: for example, anti-drugs, anti-smoking, or anti-nuclear arms movements. Negative visions carry a subtle message of powerlessness: people will only pull together when there is sufficient threat. Negative visions also tend to be short term. Two fundamental sources of energy can motivate organizations: fear and aspiration. Fear, the energy source behind negative visions, can produce extraordinary changes in short periods, but aspiration endures as a continuing source of learning and growth.

Surfacing and Testing Mental Models

Many of the best ideas in organizations never get put into practice. One reason is that new insights and initiatives often conflict with established mental models. The leadership task of challenging assumptions without invoking defensiveness requires reflection and inquiry skills possessed by few leaders in traditional controlling organizations.[23]

Seeing Leaps of Abstraction. Our minds literally move at lightning speed. Ironically, this often slows our learning, because we leap to generalizations so quickly that we never think to test them. We then confuse our generalizations with the observable data upon which they are based, treating the generalizations *as if they were data.* The frustrated sales rep reports to the home office that "customers don't really care about quality, price is what matters," when what actually happened was that three consecutive large customers refused to place an order unless a larger discount was offered. The sales rep treats her generalization, "customers care only about price," as if it were absolute fact rather than an assumption (very likely an assumption reflecting her own views of customers and the market). This thwarts future learning because she starts to focus on how to offer attractive discounts rather than probing behind the customers' statements. For example, the customers may have been so disgruntled with the firm's delivery or customer service that they are unwilling to purchase again without larger discounts.

Balancing Inquiry and Advocacy. Most managers are skilled at articulating their views and presenting them persuasively. While important, advocacy skills can become counterproductive as managers rise in responsibility and confront increasingly complex issues that require collaborative learning among different, equally knowledgeable people. Leaders in learning organizations need to have both inquiry *and* advocacy skills.[24]

Specifically, when advocating a view, they need to be able to:

- explain the reasoning and data that led to their view;
- encourage others to test their view (e. g., Do you see gaps in my reasoning? Do you disagree with the data upon which my view is based?); and
- encourage others to provide different views (e. g., Do you have either different data, different conclusions, or both?).

When inquiring into another's views, they need to:

- actively seek to understand the other's view, rather than simply restating their own view and how it differs from the other's view; and
- make their attributions about the other and the other's view explicit (e. g., Based on your statement that . . .; I am assuming that you believe . . .; Am I representing your views fairly?).

If they reach an impasse (others no longer appear open to inquiry), they need to:

- ask what data or logic might unfreeze the impasse, or if an experiment (or some other inquiry) might be designed to provide new information.

Distinguishing Espoused Theory from Theory in Use. We all like to think that we hold certain views, but often our actions reveal deeper views. For example, I may proclaim that people are trustworthy, but never lend friends money and jealously guard my possessions. Obviously, my deeper mental model (my theory in use), differs from my espoused theory. Recognizing gaps between espoused views and theories in use (which often requires the help of others) can be pivotal to deeper learning.

Recognizing and Defusing Defensive Routines. As one CEO in our research program puts it, "Nobody ever talks about an issue at the 8:00 business meeting exactly the same way they talk about it at home that evening or over drinks at the end of the day." The reason is what Chris Argyris calls "defensive routines," entrenched habits used to protect ourselves from the embarrassment and threat that come with exposing our thinking. For most of us, such defenses began to build early in life in response to pressures to have the right answers in school or at home. Organizations add new levels of performance anxiety and thereby amplify and exacerbate this defensiveness. Ironically, this makes it even more difficult to expose hidden mental models, and thereby lessens learning.

The first challenge is to recognize defensive routines, then to inquire into their operation. Those who are best at revealing and defusing defensive routines operate with a high degree of self-disclosure regarding their own defensiveness (e. g., I notice that I am feeling uneasy about how this conversation is going. Perhaps I don't understand it or it is threatening to me in ways I don't yet see. Can you help me see this better?)

Systems Thinking

We all know that leaders should help people see the big picture. But the actual skills whereby leaders are supposed to achieve this are not well understood. In my experience, successful leaders often are "systems thinkers" to a considerable extent. They focus less on day-to-day events and more on underlying trends and forces of change. But they do this almost completely intuitively. The consequence is that they are often unable to explain their intuitions to others and feel frustrated that others cannot see the world the way they do.

One of the most significant developments in management science today is the gradual coalescence of managerial systems thinking as a field of study and practice. This field suggests some key skills for future leaders:

Seeing Interrelationships, Not Things, and Processes, Not Snapshots. Most of us have been conditioned throughout our lives to focus on things and to see the world in static images. This leads us to linear explanations of systemic phenomenon. For instance, in an arms race each party is convinced that the other is *the cause* of problems. They react to each new move as an isolated event, not as part of a process. So long as they fail to see the interrelationships of these actions, they are trapped.

Moving beyond Blame. We tend to blame each other or outside circumstances for our problems. But it is poorly designed systems, not incompetent or unmotivated individuals, that cause most organizational problems. Systems thinking shows us that there is no outside—that you and the cause of your problems are part of a single system.

Distinguishing Detail Complexity from Dynamic Complexity. Some types of complexity are more important strategically than others. Detail complexity arises when there are many variables. Dynamic complexity arises when cause and effect are distant in time and space, and when the consequences over time of interventions are subtle and not obvious to many participants in the system. The leverage in most management situations lies in understanding dynamic complexity, not detail complexity.

Focusing on Areas of High Leverage. Some have called systems thinking the "new dismal science" because it teaches that most obvious solutions don't work—at best, they improve matters in the short run, only to make things worse in the long run. But there is another side to the story. Systems thinking also shows that small, well-focused actions can produce significant, enduring improvements, if they are in the right place. Systems thinkers refer to this idea as the principle of "leverage." Tackling a difficult problem is often a matter of seeing where the high leverage lies, where a change—with a minimum of effort—would lead to lasting, significant improvement.

Avoiding Symptomatic Solutions. The pressures to intervene in management systems that are going awry can be overwhelming. Unfortunately, given the linear thinking that predominates in most organizations, interventions usually focus on symptomatic fixes, not underlying causes. This results in only temporary relief, and it tends to create still more pressures later on for further, low-leverage intervention. If leaders acquiesce to these pressures, they can be sucked into an endless spiral of increasing intervention. Sometimes the most difficult leadership acts are to refrain from intervening through popular quick fixes and to keep the pressure on everyone to identify more enduring solutions.

While leaders who can articulate systemic explanations are rare, those who *can* will leave their stamp on an organization. One person who had this gift was Bill Gore, the founder and long-time CEO of W. L. Gore and Associates (makers of GoreTex and other synthetic fiber products). Bill Gore was adept at telling stories that showed how the organization's core values of freedom and individual responsibility required particular operating policies. He was proud of his egalitarian organization, in which there were (and still are) no "employees," only "associates," all of whom own shares in the company and participate in its management. At one talk, he explained the company's policy of controlled growth: "Our limitation is not financial resources. Our limitation is the rate at which we can bring in new associates. Our experience has been that if we try to bring in more than a 25 percent per year increase, we begin to bog down. Twenty-five percent per year growth is a real limitation; you can do much better than that with an authoritarian organization." As Gore tells the story, one of the associates, Esther Baum, went home after this talk and reported the limitation to her husband. As it happened, he was an astronomer and mathematician at Lowell Observatory. He said, "That's a very interesting figure." He took out a pencil and paper and calculated and said, "Do you realize that in only fifty-seven and a half years, everyone in the world will be working for Gore?"

Through this story, Gore explains the systemic rationale behind a key policy, limited growth rate—a policy that undoubtedly caused a lot of stress in the organization. He suggests that, at larger rates of growth, the adverse effects of attempting to integrate too many new people too rapidly would begin to dominate. (This is the "limits to growth" systems archetype explained below.) The story also reaffirms the organization's commitment to creating a unique environment for its associates and illustrates the types of sacrifices that the firm is prepared to make in order to remain true to its vision. The last part of the story shows that, despite the self-imposed limit, the company is still very much a growth company.

The consequences of leaders who lack systems thinking skills can be devastating. Many charismatic leaders manage almost exclusively at the level of events. They deal in visions and in crises, and little in between. Under their leadership, an organization hurtles from crisis to crisis. Eventually, the worldview of people in the organization becomes dominated by events and reactiveness. Many, especially those who are deeply commited, become burned out. Eventually, cynicism comes to pervade the organization. People have no control over their time, let alone their destiny.

Similar problems arise with the "visionary strategist," the leader with vision who sees both patterns of change and events. This leader is better prepared to manage change. He or she can explain strategies in terms of emerging trends, and thereby foster a climate that is less reactive. But such leaders still impart a responsive orientation rather than a generative one.

Many talented leaders have rich, highly systemic intuitions but cannot explain those intuitions to others. Ironically, they often end up being authoritarian leaders, even if they don't want to, because only they see the decisions that need to be made. They are unable to conceptualize their strategic insights so that these can become public knowledge, open to challenge and further improvement.

NEW TOOLS

Developing the skills described above requires new tools—tools that will enhance leaders' conceptual abilities and foster communication and collaborative inquiry. What follows is a sampling of tools starting to find use in learning organizations.

Systems Archetypes

One of the insights of the budding, managerial systems-thinking field is that certain types of systemic structures recur again and again. Countless systems grow for a period, then encounter problems and cease to grow (or even collapse) well before they have reached intrinsic limits to growth. Many other systems get locked in runaway vicious spirals where every actor has to run faster and faster to stay in the same place. Still others lure individual actors into doing what seems right locally, yet which eventually causes suffering for all.[25]

Some of the system archetypes that have the broadest relevance include:

Balancing Process with Delay. In this archetype, decision makers fail to appreciate the time delays involved as they move toward a goal. As a result, they overshoot the goal and may even produce recurring cycles. Classic example: Real estate developers who keep starting new projects until the market has gone soft, by which time an eventual glut is guaranteed by the properties still under construction.

Limits to Growth. A reinforcing cycle of growth grinds to a halt, and may even reverse itself, as limits are approached. The limits can be resource constraints, or external or internal responses to growth. Classic examples: Product life cycles that peak prematurely due to poor quality or service, the growth and decline of communication in a management team, and the spread of a new movement.

Shifting the Burden. A short-term "solution" is used to correct a problem, with seemingly happy immediate results. As this correction is used more and more, fundamental long-term corrective measures are used less. Over time, the mechanisms of the fundamental solution may atrophy or become disabled, leading to even greater reliance on the symptomatic solution. Classic example: Using corporate human resource staff to solve local personnel problems, thereby keeping managers from developing their own interpersonal skills.

Eroding Goals. When all else fails, lower your standards. This is like "shifting the burden," except that the short-term solution involves letting a fundamental goal, such as quality standards or employee morale standards, atrophy. Classic example: A company that responds to delivery problems by continually upping its quoted delivery times.

Escalation. Two people or two organizations, who each see their welfare as depending on a relative advantage over the other, continually react to the other's advances. Whenever one side gets ahead, the other is threatened, leading it to act more aggressively to reestablish its advantage, which threatens the first, and so on. Classic examples: Arms race, gang warfare, price wars.

Tragedy of the Commons.[26] Individuals keep intensifying their use of a commonly available but limited resource until all individuals start to experience severely diminishing returns. Classic examples: Sheepherders who keep increasing their flocks until they overgraze the common pasture; divisions in a firm that share a common salesforce and compete for the use of sales reps by upping their sales targets, until the salesforce burns out from overextension.

Growth and Underinvestment. Rapid growth approaches a limit that could be eliminated or pushed into the future, but only by aggressive investment in physical and human capacity. Eroding goals or standards cause investment that is too weak, or too slow, and customers get increasingly unhappy, slowing demand growth and thereby making the needed investment (apparently) unnecessary or impossible. Classic example: Countless once-successful growth firms that allowed product or service quality to erode, and were unable to generate enough revenues to invest in remedies.

The Archetype template is a specific tool that is helping managers identify archetypes operating in their own strategic areas (see Figure 2).[27] The template shows the basic structural form of the archetype but lets managers fill in the variables of their own situation. For example, the shifting the burden template involves two balancing processes ("B") that compete for control of a problem symptom. The upper, symptomatic solution provides a short-term fix that will make the problem symptom go away for a while. The lower, fundamental solution provides a more enduring solution. The side effect feedback ("R") around the outside of the diagram identifies unintended exacerbating effects of the symptomatic solution, which, over time, make it more and more difficult to invoke the fundamental solution.

FIGURE 2. "Shifting the Burden." Archetype Template

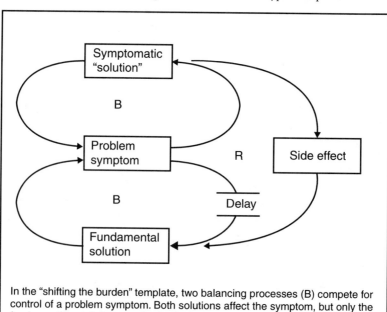

In the "shifting the burden" template, two balancing processes (B) compete for control of a problem symptom. Both solutions affect the symptom, but only the fundamental solution treats the cause. The symptomatic "solution" creates the additional side effect (R) of deferring the fundamental solution, making it harder and harder to achieve.

Several years ago, a team of managers from a leading consumer goods producer used the shifting the burden archetype in a revealing way. The problem they focused on was financial stress, which could be dealt with in two different ways: by running marketing promotions (the symptomatic solution) or by product innovation (the fundamental solution). Marketing promotions were fast. The company was expert in their design and implementation. The results were highly predictable. Product innovation was slow and much less predictable, and the company had a history over the past ten years of product-innovation mismanagement. Yet only through innovation could they retain a leadership position in their industry, which had slid over the past ten to twenty years. What the managers saw clearly was that the more skillful they became at promotions, the more they shifted the burden away from product innovation. But what really struck home was when one member identified the unintended side effect: the last three CEOs had all come from advertising function, which had become the politically dominant function in the corporation, thereby institutionalizing the symptomatic solution. Unless the political values shifted back toward product and process innovation, the managers realized, the firm's decline would accelerate— which is just the shift that has happened over the past several years.

Charting Strategic Dilemmas

Management teams typically come unglued when confronted with core dilemmas. A classic example was the way U. S. manufacturers faced the low cost–high quality choice. For years, most assumed that it was necessary to choose between the two. Not surprisingly, given the short-term pressures perceived by most managements, the prevailing choice was low cost. Firms that chose high quality usually perceived themselves as aiming exclusively for a high quality, high price market niche. The consequences of this perceived either-or choice have been disastrous, even fatal, as U. S. manufacturers have encountered increasing international competition from firms that have chosen to consistently improve quality *and* cost.

In a recent book, Charles Hampden-Turner presented a variety of tools for helping management teams confront strategic dilemmas creatively.[28] He summarizes the process in seven steps:

Eliciting the Dilemmas. Identifying the opposed values that form the "horns" of the dilemma, for example, cost as opposed to quality, or local initiative as opposed to central coordination and control. Hampden-Turner suggests that humor can be a distinct asset in this process since "the admission that dilemmas even exist tends to be difficult for some companies."

Mapping. Locating the opposing values as two axes and helping managers identify where they see themselves, or their organization, along the axes.

Processing. Getting rid of nouns to describe the axes of the dilemma. Present participles formed by adding "ing" convert rigid nouns into processes that imply movement. For example, central control versus local control becomes "strengthening national office" and "growing local initiatives." This loosens the bond of implied opposition between the two values. For example, it becomes possible to think of "strengthening national services from which local branches can benefit."

Framing/Contextualizing. Further softening the adversarial structure among different values by letting "each side in turn be the frame or context for the other." This shifting of the "figure-ground" relationship undermines any implicit attempts to hold one value as intrinsically superior to the other, and thereby to become mentally closed to creative strategies for continuous improvement of both.

Sequencing. Breaking the hold of static thinking. Very often, values like low cost and high quality appear to be in opposition because we think in terms of a point in time, not in terms of an ongoing process. For example, a strategy of investing in new process technology and developing a new production-floor culture of worker responsibility may take time and money in the near term, yet reap significant long-term financial rewards.

Waving/Cycling. Sometimes the strategic path toward improving both values involves cycles where both values will get "worse" for a time. Yet, at a deeper level, learning is occurring that will cause the next cycle to be at a higher plateau for both values.

Synergizing. Achieving synergy where significant improvement is occurring along all axes of all relevant dilemmas. (This is the ultimate goal, of course.) Synergy, as Hampden-Turner points out, is a uniquely systemic notion, coming from the Greek *syn-ergo* or "work together."

"The Left-Hand Column": Surfacing Mental Models

The idea that mental models can dominate business decisions and that these models are often tacit and even contradictory to what people espouse can be very threatening to managers who pride themselves on rationality and judicious decision making. It is important to have tools to help managers discover for themselves how their mental models operate to undermine their own intentions.

One tool that has worked consistently to help managers see their own mental models in action is the "left-hand column" exercise developed by Chris Argyris and his colleagues. This tool is especially helpful in showing how we leap from data to generalization without testing the validity of our generalizations.

When working with managers, I start this exercise by selecting a specific situation in which I am interacting with other people in a way that is not working, that is not producing the learning that is needed. I write out a sample of the exchange, with the script on the right-hand side of the page. On the left-hand side, I write what I am thinking but not saying at each stage in the exchange (see sidebar).

The left-hand column exercise not only brings hidden assumptions to the surface, it shows how they influence behavior. In the example, I make two key assumptions about Bill: he lacks confidence and he lacks initiative. Neither may be literally true, but both are evident in my internal dialogue, and both influence the way I handle the situation. Believing that he lacks confidence, I skirt the fact that I've heard the presentation was a bomb. I'm afraid that if I say it directly, he will lose what little confidence he has, or he will see me as unsupportive. So I bring up the subject of the presentation

---

The Left Hand Column: An Exercise

Imagine my exchange with a colleague, Bill, after he made a big presentation to our boss on a project we are doing together. I had to miss the presentation, but I've heard that it was poorly received.

Me: How did the presentation go?

Bill: Well, I don't know. It's really too early to say. Besides we're breaking new ground here.

Me: Well, what do you think we should do? I believe that the issues you were raising are important.

Bill: I'm not so sure. Let's just wait and see what happens.

Me: You may be right, but I think we may need to do more than just wait.

Now, here is what the exchange looks like with my "left-hand column":

What I'm Thinking	What Is Said
Everyone says the presentation was a bomb.	**Me**: How did the presentation goes?
Does he really not know how bad it was? Or is he not willing to face up to it?	**Bill**: Well, I don't know. It's to early to say. Besides, we're breaking new ground here.
	Me: Well, what do you think we should do? I believe that the issues you were raising are important.
He really is afraid to see the truth. If he only had more confidence, he could probably learn from a situation like this.	**Bill**: I'm not so sure. Let's just wait and see what happens.
I can't believe he doesn't realize how disastrous that presentation was to our moving ahead.	**Me**: You may be right, but I think we may need to do more than just wait.
I've got to find some way to light a fire under the guy.	

---

obliquely. When I ask Bill what we should do next, he gives no specific course of action. Believing he lacks initiative, I take this as evidence of his laziness; he is content to do nothing when action is definitely required. I conclude that I will have to manufacture some form of pressure to motivate him, or else I will simply have to take matters into my own hands.

The exercise reveals the elaborate webs of assumptions we weave, within which we become our own victims. Rather than dealing directly with my assumptions about Bill and the situation, we talk around the subject. The reasons for my avoidance are self-evident: I assume that if I raised my doubts, I would provoke a defensive reaction that would only make matters worse. But the price of avoiding the issue is high. Instead of determining how to move forward to resolve our problems, we end our exchange with no clear course of action. My assumptions about Bill's limitations have been reinforced. I resort to a manipulative strategy to move things forward.

The exercise not only reveals the need for skills in surfacing assumptions, but that we are the ones most in need of help. There is no one right way to handle difficult situations like my exchange with Bill, but any productive strategy revolves around a high level of self-disclosure and willingness to have my views challenged. I need to recognize my own leaps of abstraction regarding Bill, share the events and reasoning that are leading to my concern over the project, and be open to Bill's views on both. The skills to carry on such conversations without invoking defensiveness take time to develop. But if both parties in a learning impasse start by doing their own left-hand column exercise and sharing them with each other, it is remarkable how quickly everyone recognizes their contribution to the impasse and progress starts to be made.

Learning Laboratories: Practice Fields for Management Teams

One of the most promising new tools is the learning laboratory or "microworld": constructed microcosms of real-life settings in which management teams can learn how to learn together.

The rationale behind learning laboratories can best be explained by analogy. Although most management teams have great difficulty learning (enhancing their collective intelligence and capacity to create), in other domains team learning is the norm rather than the exception—team sports and the performing arts, for example. Great basketball teams do not start off great. They learn. But the process by which these teams learn is, by and large, absent from modern organizations. The process is a continual movement between practice and performance.

The vision guiding current research in management learning laboratories is to design and construct effective practice fields for management teams. Much remains to be done, but the broad outlines are emerging.

First, since team learning in organizations is an individual-to-individual and individual-to-system phenomenon, learning laboratories must combine meaningful business issues with meaningful interpersonal dynamics. Either alone is incomplete.

Second, the factors that thwart learning about complex business issues must be eliminated in the learning lab. Chief among these is the inability to experience the long-term, systemic consequences of key strategic decisions. We all learn best from experience, but we are unable to experience the consequences of many important organizational decisions. Learning laboratories remove this constraint through system dynamics simulation games that compress time and space.

Third, new learning skills must be developed. One constraint on learning is the inability of managers to reflect insightfully on their assumptions, and to inquire effectively into each other's assumptions. Both skills can be enhanced in a learning laboratory, where people can practice surfacing assumptions in a low-risk setting. A note of caution: It is far easier to design an entertaining learning laboratory than it is to have an impact on real management practices and firm traditions outside the learning lab. Research on management simulations has shown that they often have greater enter-tainment value than educational value. One of the reasons appears to be that many simulations do not offer deep insights into systemic structures causing business problems. Another reason is that they do not foster new learning skills. Also, there is no connection between experiments in the learning lab and real life experiments. These are significant problems that research on learning laboratory design is now addressing.

Developing Leaders and Learning Organizations

In a recently published retrospective on organization development in the 1980s, Marshall Sashkin and N. Warner Burke observe the return of an emphasis on developing leaders who can develop organizations.[29] They also note Schein's critique that most top executives are not qualified for the task of developing culture.[30] Learning organizations represent a potentially sig-nificant evolution of organizational culture. So it should come as no surprise that such organizations will remain a distant vision until the leadership ca-pabilities they demand are developed. "The 1990s may be the period," sug-gest Sashkin and Burke, "during which organization development and (a new sort of) management development are reconnected."

I believe that this new sort of management development will focus on the roles, skills, and tools for leadership in learning organizations. Un-doubtedly, the ideas offered above are only a rough approximation of this new territory. The sooner we begin seriously exploring the territory, the sooner the initial map can be improved—and the sooner we will realize an age-old vision of leadership:

> The wicked leader is he who the people despise.
> The good leader is he who the people revere.
> The great leader is he who the people say, "We did it ourselves."
>
> —LAO TSU

Notes

1. P. Senge, *The Fifth Discipline: The Art and Practice of the Learning Organization* (New York: Doubleday/Currency, 1990).
2. A. P. de Geus, "Planning as Learning," *Harvard Business Review*, March–April 1988, pp. 70–74.
3. B. Domain, *Fortune*, 3 July 1989, pp. 48–62.
4. The distinction between adaptive and generative learning has its roots in the distinction between what Argyris and Schon have called their "single-loop" learning, in which indi-viduals or groups adjust their behavior relative to fixed goals, norms, and assumptions, and "double-loop" learning, in which goals, norms, and assumptions, as well as behavior, are open to change (e. g., see C. Argyris and D. Schon, *Organizational Learning: A Theory-in-Action Perspective* (Reading, Massachusetts: Addison-Wesley, 1978)).
5. All unattributed quotes are from personal communications with the author.
6. G. Stalk, Jr., "Time: The Next Source of Competitive Advantage," *Harvard Business Review*, July–August 1988, pp. 41–51.
7. Senge (1990).
8. The principle of creative tension comes from Robert Fritz' work on creativity. See R. Fritz, *The Path of Least Resistance* (New York: Ballantine, 1989) and *Creating* (New York: Ballan-tine, 1990).

9. M. L. King, Jr., "Letter from Birmingham Jail," *American Visions*, January–February 1986, pp. 52–59.

10. E. Schein, *Organizational Culture and Leadership* (San Francisco: Jossey-Bass, 1985). Similar views have been expressed by many leadership theorists. For example, see: P. Selznick, *Leadership in Administration* (New York: Harper & Row, 1957); W. Bennis and B. Nanus, *Leaders* (New York: Harper & Row, 1985); and N. M. Tichy and M. A. Devanna, *The Transformational Leader* (New York: John Wiley & Sons, 1986).

11. Selznick (1957).

12. J. W. Forrester, "A New Corporate Design," *Sloan Management Review* (formerly *Industrial Management Review*), Fall 1965, pp. 5–17.

13. See, for example, H. Mintzberg, "Crafting Strategy," *Harvard Business Review*, July–August 1987, pp. 66–75.

14. R. Mason and I. Mitroff, *Challenging Strategic Planning Assumptions* (New York: John Wiley & Sons, 1981), p. 16.

15. P. Wack, "Scenarios: Uncharted Waters Ahead," *Harvard Business Review*, September–October 1985, pp. 73–89.

16. de Geus (1988).

17. M. de Pree, *Leadership Is an Art* (New York: Doubleday, 1989) p. 9.

18. For example, see T. Peters and N. Austin, *A Passion for Excellence* (New York: Random House, 1985) and J. M. Kouzes and B. Z. Posner, *The Leadership Challenge* (San Francisco: Jossey-Bass, 1987).

19. I. Mitroff, *Break-Away Thinking* (New York: John Wiley & Sons, 1988), pp. 66–67.

20. R. K. Greenleaf, *Servant Leadership: A Journey into the Nature of Legitimate Power and Greatness* (New York: Paulist Press, 1977).

21. L. Miller, *American Spirit: Visions of a New Corporate Culture* (New York: William Morrow, 1984), p. 15.

22. These points are condensed from the practices of the five disciplines examined in Senge (1990).

23. The ideas below are based to a considerable extent on the work of Chris Argyris, Donald Schon, and their Action Science colleagues: C. Argyris and D. Schon, *Organizational Learning: A Theory-in-Action Perspective* (Reading, Massachusetts: Addison-Wesley, 1978); C. Argyris, R. Putnam, and D. Smith, *Action Science* (San Francisco: Jossey-Bass, 1985); C. Argyris, *Strategy, Change and Defensive Routines* (Boston: Pitman, 1985); and C. Argyris, *Overcoming Organizational Defenses* (Englewood Cliffs, New Jersey: Prentice Hall, 1990).

24. I am indebted to Diana Smith for the summary points below.

25. The system archetypes are one of several systems diagraming and communication tools. See D. H. Kim, "Toward Learning Organizations: Integrating Total Quality Control and Systems Thinking" (Cambridge, Massachusetts: MIT Sloan School of Management, Working Paper No. 3037-89-BPS, June 1989).

26. This archetype is closely associated with the work of ecologist Garrett Hardin, who coined its label: G. Hardin, "The Tragedy of the Commons," *Science*, 13 December 1968.

27. These templates were originally developed by Jennifer Kemeny, Charles Kiefer, and Michael Goodman of Innovation Associates, Inc., Framingham, Massachusetts.

28. C. Hampden-Turner, *Charting the Corporate Mind* (New York: The Free Press, 1990).

29. M. Sashkin and W. W. Burke, "Organization Development in the 1980s" and "An End-of-the-Eighties Retrospective," in *Advances in Organization Development*, ed. F. Masarik (Norwood, New Jersey: Ablex, 1990).

30. E. Schein (1985).

The Many Faces of the Corporate Code

LISA H. NEWTON

INTRODUCTION

We seem to be in another of our code-writing phases. Interest in the development of corporate codes of ethics—by which term we encompass corporate Aspirations, Beliefs, Creeds, Guidelines and so on through the alphabet—has continued to rise since the 1970's, in tandem with the interest in the teaching and taking of ethics, in colleges and workplaces alike. In what follows, I take on some of the dominant themes in the codes of ethics literature, in an attempt to give a partial overview of the state of the art in the formulation of the corporate code.

The attempt turns out to be a study in multiple function. The much-recommended "corporate code of ethics" serves a diversity of functions, and must avoid a similar diversity of pitfalls. Some of these we will survey; to anticipate the end, we will discover that for maximum effectiveness and ethical validity, each code ought to meet three specifications:

1. In its *development and promulgation,* the code must enjoy the maximum participation of the officers and employees of the corporation (the principle of *participation*);
2. In its *content,* the code must be coherent with general ethical principles and the dictates of conscience (the principle of *validity*);
3. In its *implementation,* the code must be, and must be seen to be, coherent with the lived commitments of the company's officers (the principle of *authenticity*).

Clear and Present Need

Businesses ought to have codes of ethics, if for no other reason than to allay real doubts that businessmen are capable of morality at all. Leonard Brooks has recently taken note of the ". . . crisis of confidence about corporate activity. Many corporate representations or claims have low credibility, including those made regarding financial dealings and disclosure, environmental protection, health and safety disclosures related to both employees and customers, and questionable payments." That is quite a list of things to be distrusted about. If we were looking for a blanket indictment of business, that one ought to cover the ballpark.[1] Or as Michael Hoffman and Jennifer Moore put it somewhat more concisely, it is the opinion of many of our wiser heads that ". . . business faces a true crisis of legitimacy."[2]

We cannot, *pace* Milton Friedman, leave the governance of the corporation to the forces of the market. While the market may bring about economic efficiency, Gerald Cavanagh points out, it cannot guarantee that corporate performance will be ethically and socially sensitive. Here the responsibility lies with the Board of Directors and top management, and it is

"The Many Faces of the Corporate Code" by Lisa H. Newton. From *Institutionalizing Corporate Ethics Programs,* proceedings of the conference "Corporate Visions and Values," Fairfield University, November 1991, sponsored by the Connecticut Humanities Council and Wright Investors' Service of Bridgeport, CT. Reprinted by permission of the author.

"essential that board and management step up to the task," ascertain the ethical climate already prevailing and guide policy and decision in ethical directions. He adds as a final qualification that "while codes, structures and monitoring can encourage ethical decisions, it is even more important to have ethical people in the firm who want to make ethical judgments, know how to, and are not afraid to do so."[3] This is surely true: there is no structure or device in the universe, let alone within the capability of the American business community, that will keep people moral if they are determined to be immortal. But most people, at least most businesspeople, it seems are really neither one nor the other; they are prepared to be either, depending on the prevailing culture, and that is where the code can help.

There is nothing new in the aspiration to ethical codes. As early as 1961, Fr. Raymond Baumhart's survey of 2000 business managers showed two-thirds of them interested in developing codes of ethics, which they thought would improve the ethical level of business practice.[4] By the seventies, public attention reinforced that view. George Benson traces the current effort on codes to the revelations on foreign and domestic bribery in government investigations 1973–1976, lending to the Foreign Corrupt Practices Act of 1977.[5] In the mid-seventies, W. Michael Blumenthal, then CEO of Bendix, went so far as to propose that the business executives of America organize a professional association to develop a comprehensive code of ethics for business with a review panel to enforce it. The idea died at the time, but might be worth following up at some point.[6] To this day, the most highly placed businessmen support the development of codes of ethics. In a survey conducted by Touche Ross in October, 1987, 1,082 respondents concluded that the most effective way to encourage ethical business behavior was the adoption of a code of ethics—outscoring the adoption of further legislation by 19%.[7] Nor is this support surprising. Ethics pays, not just in public relations but in company work. As the Business Roundtable, an association of Chief Executive Officers of major U.S. companies, concluded in 1988,

> "It may come as a surprise to some that . . . corporate ethics programs are not mounted primarily to improve the reputation of business. Instead, many executives believe that a culture in which ethical concern permeates the whole organization is necessary to the self-interest of the company. . . . In the view of the top executives represented in this study, there is no conflict between ethical practices and acceptable profits. Indeed, the first is a necessary precondition for the second."[8]

To be sure, we can, at least in theory, behave like saints without a code to describe how we are behaving. But a written document reinforces an intention to be ethical—as a reminder, as a guide, and as a focus for the solidarity of the corporate officers in their attempts to run the company along the lines it lays down. And beyond this, there is the first concern mentioned: that the public is, probably justifiably, concerned over the proclivities of the business community and interested in seeing tangible proof of its intention to behave.

So a public commitment to ethics serves at least two functions: it addresses the concerns of the public and it reinforces (and clarifies) a bottom-line-justified interest in ethical behavior on the part of the officers. A third reason to take ethics seriously, address the subject explicitly, and articulate provisions to enforce it, is simple realism. As Freeman and Gilbert point out, as long as organizations are composed of human beings, no organizational task can proceed, nor can any cogent corporate strategy be formulated, without recognizing that these human beings have values. Their "First Axiom of Corporate Strategy"—"Corporate strategy must reflect an understanding of the values of organizational members and stakeholders"—is derived directly from the discovery that the human players in the corporate enterprise very often act in accordance with personal and cultural ethical imperatives. The corporation relegates itself to irrelevance if it fails to recognize this fact. Their second Axiom—"Corporate strategy must reflect an understanding of the ethical nature of strategic choice"—acknowledges the interaction between corporate direction and private value. It is essential that the choices made by management in strategic planning meet the ethical standards implicit in the stakeholders' values.[9] The authors note the current fashion for describing strategy formulation as if persons did not exist, and point out at some length the errors of such attempts.[10]

Why Codes Fail

We sometimes take note of "widespread skepticism" as to the effectiveness of codes and the motivation behind their development. That skepticism bears some examination. Oddly, the doubts do not seem to have their roots in the business community, whose opinions are captured above. It seems to originate in the academic community of the business schools, possibly due to misunderstandings on the nature of valid corporate codes. Larue Tone Hosmer states well the prevailing error:

> "Ethical codes are statements of the norms and beliefs of an organization. These norms and beliefs are generally proposed, discussed, and defined by the senior executives in the firm and then published and distributed to all of the members. Norms, of course, are standards of behavior; they are the ways the senior people in the organization want the others to act when confronted with a given situation."[11]

Again,

> "The beliefs in an ethical code are standards of thought; they are the ways that the senior people in the organization want others to think."[12]

With that understanding, no wonder that he must immediately insist that "[t]his is not censorship"! Although that insistence is hardly reinforced with his following, "the intent is to encourage ways of thinking and patterns of attitudes that will lead towards the wanted behavior."

And with both of those understandings in place, again it is not surprising that his evaluation of codes is negative: "Do ethical codes work? Are they helpful in conveying to all employees the moral standards selected by the board of directors and president? Not really."[13] The problem with the code he describes is not only that it is not effective—taking no essential account of the nature of the business, let alone the pre-existing commitments of the people to whom it is supposed to apply (how could it be?)—but that it is not ethical. The basis for its norms is, it appears, completely subjective, founded on the whim of whomever happens to be in the executive offices the day that it occurs to a CEO to write a code of ethics; its application is coercive, being conceived by a more powerful group to apply to a less powerful group (but not to themselves); and there is no built-in check to see that it will actually help the company and its employees achieve the ends of the business. In short, it fails by any standards of reasonableness, and why on earth any firm would be interested in such a code is puzzling beyond the norm for such writings. (As Richard De George points out, we are occasionally willing to allow short lists of rules to be simply imposed on us, as long as the author is reliably known to be God. Senior officers, even CEOs, are not God.)[14]

While we have Hosmer's example before us, we may take the opportunity to extract some more general ethical principles from the critique. The code he describes was brought into existence by a few people in a few remote offices, enlisting the energies of none of the lower-ranking employees of the company. For this reason it fails on any measure of democracy, that understanding of governance that holds participation in policy formulation to be a part of justice; and it fails on any estimate of likely relevance to the situation of those excluded employees. The temptations that beset the stockman and secretary are best known to them, and it is inherently unwise to draw up rules without drawing on their experience. To avoid both sets of failures, it is essential to include as many employees as possible in the development process. This imperative we may call the *principle of participation.*

Second, the content of the code is completely unspecified save by reference to its authors—its provisions are those that strike the CEO and his golfing buddies as good, at the time they write it. Given their understandings of justice (see above and below), we are not inspired to confidence in their intuitions, but that is quite beside the point. Subjective presentations of this type can never qualify as imperatives with the authority of ethics. The provisions of a code must be reasoned, logically consistent, defended by reasoned argument, and coherent with the usual understandings of ethics: they must demonstrate respect for the individual, a commitment to justice, and sensitivity to the rights and interests of all parties affected by corporate action. We may call this requirement the *principle of validity.*

Third, it is assumed that the code is written by the senior officers, but that they themselves are not bound by it, and are therefore by implication perfectly free to ignore it or defy it if that is what they want to do. No liberty could be more destructive. People will do not as they are told, but as it is modeled to them; the company's values are trumpeted in the acts of the highest ranking employees, and need appear nowhere else. Again there is a violation of justice, in the development of a set of rules from which a privileged few shall be exempt, and again there is gross inattention to effectiveness. Whatever we may not know about codes, we know for sure that the real culture of a corporation will be embodied in the behavior of the senior officers, especially the CEO, and that it is imperative to secure the allegiance and the compliance of those persons for a code to be taken seriously; we may call this imperative the *principle of authenticity.* Hosmer's understanding of a corporate code violates all three principles, and condemns itself to ineffectiveness through its violations.

In the limiting case, then, a purported "code" can be no more than some authority's attempt to impose whimsical rules, which are bound to fail. A second type of code that is doomed to failure is the oracular code, confined to bare rules or ideals, no matter how derived or promulgated, with no commentary or explanation grounding the rule in experience.

> "The difficulty with many codes is not that they prescribe what is immoral, but that they fail to be truly effective in helping members of the profession or company to act morally. To be moral means not only doing what someone says is right, but also knowing *why* what one does is right, and assuming moral responsibility for the action. How were the provisions of the code arrived at? On what moral bases do the injunctions stand?"[15]

The standard instruction at the end of such codes, to discuss any dilemmas with the legal office, won't do it; they don't know morality. Implicit in this objection is a strong suggestion that the code must serve an educational function. This is correct; we will come back to this point.

A third and common way for codes to fail is through failure of the highest executives to take the provisions seriously, not only as they apply to themselves (the principle of authenticity, above), but as they apply to the company's management policies (especially "management by objectives") and other standard procedures. If the CEO honestly believes in the provisions, and takes the lead in modeling and enforcing them, if top management follows suit, and if the company's reward and punishment structure reinforces those provisions consistently, the code may well achieve its purpose even if it fails as a model of logical coherence. If they do not do so, there is very little chance that anyone else will either, especially when no one is watching. "Management needs to understand the real dynamics of its own organization. For example, how do people get ahead in the company? What conduct is actually rewarded, what values are really being instilled in employees?"[16] And the modeling and enforcement must be spread throughout the company. As Andy Sigler, CEO of Champion International and initiator of one of the best corporate codes in existence, put it, "Making speeches and sending letters just doesn't do it. You need a culture and peer pressure that spells out what is acceptable and isn't and why. It involves training, education, and follow-up."[17] For example, the institutionalization of any code must include protection from retaliation by supervisors against whistleblowers.[18] Kenneth Arrow would go further, arguing that any effective code must not only be fused into the corporate culture," but "accepted by the significant operating institutions and transmitted from one generation of executives to the next through standard operating procedures [and] though education in business schools."[19]

How Codes Succeed

The first condition for success is a commitment to the promotion of ethical behavior in a company—not to better public relations, nor to more certain deterrence of Federal inspectors, nor to the terror of an occasional bad apple, but to make the whole company a better and finer employer, producer, resident and citizen. For starters, the business community must take a leaf from the book of the professions, who have seen themselves as moral communities from the outset.[20] Like the professions, the corporation must take its status as a moral agent seriously. (There is almost a note of surprise in Leonard Brooks' observation that nowadays, there is a public expectation that if managers are caught *in flagrante delicto*, as they sometimes are, they will be punished. "This is a significant change because it is signalling that our society no longer regards the interests of the corporation or its shareholders to be paramount in importance. Neither corporate executives nor professionals can operate with impunity any longer, because society now expects them to be accountable.")[21] It certainly does.

From that basic commitment should follow a commitment to a process aimed at gathering that ethos from, and infusing it throughout, the entire company. Our first and third specifications, the principle of participation and the principle of authenticity, are two phases of that process commitment. The whole company (starting from the top) must commit itself to the development of the corporate code; the whole company (including the most junior members) must contribute to the process of deliberation; and the whole company (again, especially the top) must be, and feel, bound to obey and to exemplify it.

The imperative of validity is no more than a remote test of the coherence of the content. In accordance with the examples set by the professions, it is not essential for a code to be a model of academic ethics. The requirement that the code be in conformity with theory does not mean that the code must explicitly signal the kind of reasoning that validates it. Earlier in this enterprise academicians were perhaps too insistent, and code-crafters too self-conscious, on this point; earlier discussions of the issue of corporate and professional codes were known to break down on the issue of "consequentialist vs. deontological moral reasoning." Both are necessarily included in the development of a corporate ethic. As Robin and Reidenbach point out, maintaining a certain kind of "ethical profile" (e.g. strong customer orientation for a sales-driven industry) is absolutely essential for the bottom line—there is no more utilitarian requirement. Yet the "core values" extracted from that profile (e.g. "Treat customers with respect and honesty, . . . the way you would want your family treated") can be derived from any system of primary duties, and are deontological in form and function. Any good formulation of a company's creed should be subject to verification by both kinds of moral reasoning.[22]

As Robin and Reidenbach emphasize, the code must be drawn to reflect the aims of the particular set of business practices with which the company is concerned. The ruling ideal of the code might equally be integrity of the practitioners, the excellence of craftsmanship, or the dedication to serve the client/customer, depending on the type of business it is. One of the first principles of "excellence" in the running of any company—the imperative to "stick to the knitting"—entails that a code for one industry, or one kind of company, need not apply with equal force to any others.

Along that line, be it noted that there are many reasons why a code cannot be all things to all people. Critics with certain key areas of interest, for instance, will often discover limits in codes that might not occur to the rest of us. Pat Werhane, for instance, complains that codes "usually tell the employee what he or she is not permitted to do, but they seldom spell out worker rights."[23] She goes on to argue that they tend to turn employees into legalists, obedient to the letter of the regulation but ignorant of its moral spirit.

The solution to both problems may lie in the shift of focus from dead rule to living dialogue. I am inclined to argue that the real value of the code does not lie in the finished product, rules with explanations that all must obey, but in the process by which it came to be. The first call for participation is an invitation to the employee to look into his conscience, discover his own moral commitments, and attempt to prioritize and formulate them. This may be the first time he has ever been asked to take on that job, and the educational value is enormous. The second phase of the participatory process includes the discovery of community consensus, a dialogue in which the employee must test his perceptions against those of others, re-examine and perhaps replace those that do not meet the test, and discover the defenses of those that do. However the code emerges, we will have much more articulate employees at the end of the process than we had at the beginning. And in this articulation is implicit genuine self-awareness: the employee now has his moral beliefs where he can see and get at them, and can be educated to apply them in new and creative ways should the situation around him change.

And it will change. Change was always a fact in the American business community, and very rapid, almost chaotic, change an occasional reality. Now, as Tom Peters points out, partly at his instigation, it has become a conscious policy. The continuation of that dialogue is needed especially as firms radically reorganize themselves, destroying the traditional departmental divisions and job descriptions. In the absence of traditional guides, all members of the corporation will need new and extraordinary norms to govern practice, and there is no substitute for a dialogical process in place as the change happens.[24]

Notes

1. Leonard J. Brooks, "Corporate Codes of Ethics," *Journal of Business Ethics* 8(1989):117–129. p. 119.
2. W. Michael Hoffman and Jennifer Mills Moore, *Business Ethics*, Second Edition. New York: McGraw-Hill, 1990. page 2.
3. Gerald F. Cavanagh, *American Business Values*, second edition. Englewood Cliffs, New Jersey: Prentice Hall, 1984. p. 159.
4. Raymond C. Baumhart. S. J., "How Ethical Are Businessmen?" *Harvard Business Review* 39(July–August 1961):166–71.
5. George C. S. Benson, "Codes of Ethics," *Journal of Business Ethics* 8(1989):305–319.p.306.
6. W. Michael Blumenthal, "New Business Watchdog Needed" *The New York Times*, May 25, 1975, Fl; and "R for Reducing the Occasion of Corporate Sin," *Advanced Management Journal* 42 (Winter 1977):4–13.
7. Touche Ross, *Ethics in American Business: An opinion survey of key business leaders on ethical standards and behavior*. New York: Touche Ross. 1988. page 14. The sample included only chief executive officers of companies with $500 million or more in annual sales, deans of business schools and members of Congress.
8. *Corporate Ethics: A Prime Business Asset* New York: The Business Roundtable, 1988. page 9.
9. R. Edward Freeman and Daniel R. Gilbert, Jr. *Corporate Strategy and the Search for Ethics*. Englewood Cliffs, New Jersey: Prentice Hall, 1988. pp. 6–7.
10. *Loc. cit.* See also p. 138, and p. 197, n. 3.
11. Larue Tone Hosmer, *The Ethics of Management*, Homewood, Illinois: Irwin, 1987, p. 153.
12. *Ibid.* p. 154.
13. *Loc. cit.* p. 154.

14. Richard T. De George, *Business Ethics* Third Edition. New York, Macmillan, 1990. p. 390.
15. De George, *op. cit* p. 391.
16. William H. Shaw, *Business Ethics*, Belmont, California: Wadsworth Publishing Company, 1991. p. 175.
17. Andrew Sigler, CEO of Champion International, cited in "Businesses are Signing Up for Ethics 101," *Business Week*, February 15, 1988. p. 56.
18. Leonard J. Brooks, "Corporate Codes of Ethics," *Journal of Business Ethics* 8(1989):117–129. p. 124.
19. Kenneth J. Arrow, "Social Responsibility and Economic Efficiency," *Public Policy* 21 (Summer 1973):42.
20. Mark S. Frankel, "Professional Codes: Why, How, and with What Impact?" *Journal of Business Ethics* 8(1989):109–115. p. 110.
21. Brooks, *op. cit.* p. 119.
22. Donald P. Robin and R. Eric Reidenbach, *Business Ethics: Where Profits Meet Value Systems.* Englewood Cliffs, New Jersey: Prentice Hall, 1989. p. 94–95.
23. Patricia H. Werhane, *Persons, Rights and Corporations*, Englewood Cliffs, New Jersey: Prentice Hall, Inc. 1985. p. 159.
24. See Tom Peters, "Get Innovative or Get Dead (part one)," *California Management Review* 33(Fall 1990):9–26.

Managing for Organizational Integrity

LYNN SHARP PAINE

Many managers think of ethics as a question of personal scruples, a confidential matter between individuals and their consciences. These executives are quick to describe any wrongdoing as an isolated incident, the work of a rogue employee. The thought that the company could bear any responsibility for an individual's misdeeds never enters their minds. Ethics, after all, has nothing to do with management.

In fact, ethics has *everything* to do with management. Rarely do the character flaws of a lone actor fully explain corporate misconduct. More typically, unethical business practice involves the tacit, if not explicit, cooperation of others and reflects the values, attitudes, beliefs, language, and behavioral patterns that define an organization's operating culture. Ethics, then, is as much an organizational as a personal issue. Managers who fail to provide proper leadership and to institute systems that facilitate ethical conduct share responsibility with those who conceive, execute, and knowingly benefit from corporate misdeeds.

Managers must acknowledge their role in shaping organizational ethics and seize this opportunity to create a climate that can strengthen the relationships and reputations on which their companies' success depends. Executives who ignore ethics run the risk of personal and corporate liability in today's increasingly tough legal environment. In addition, they deprive their organizations of the benefits available under new federal guidelines for sentencing organizations convicted of wrongdoing. These sentencing guidelines recognize for the first time the organizational and managerial roots of unlawful conduct and base fines partly on the extent to which companies have taken steps to prevent that misconduct.

Prompted by the prospect of leniency, many companies are rushing to implement compliance-based ethics programs. Designed by corporate counsel, the goal of these programs is to prevent, detect, and punish legal violations. But organizational ethics means more than avoiding illegal practice; and providing employees with a rule book will do little to address the problems underlying unlawful conduct. To foster a climate that encourages exemplary behavior, corporations need a comprehensive approach that goes beyond the often punitive legal compliance stance.

An integrity-based approach to ethics management combines a concern for the law with an emphasis on managerial responsibility for ethical behavior. Though integrity strategies may vary in design and scope, all strive to define companies' guiding values, aspirations, and patterns of thought and conduct. When integrated into the day-to-day operations of an organization, such strategies can help prevent damaging ethical lapses while tapping into powerful human impulses for moral thought and action. Then an ethical framework becomes no longer a burdensome constraint within which companies must operate, but the governing ethos of an organization.

How Organizations Shape Individuals' Behavior

The once familiar picture of ethics as individualistic, unchanging, and impervious to organizational influences has not stood up to scrutiny in recent years. Sears Auto Centers' and Beech-Nut Nutrition Corporation's experiences illustrate the role organizations play in shaping individuals' behavior—and how even sound moral fiber can fray when stretched too thin.

In 1992, Sears, Roebuck & Company was inundated with complaints about its automotive service business. Consumers and attorneys general in more than 40 states had accused the company of misleading customers and selling them unnecessary parts and services, from brake jobs to front-end alignments. It would be a mistake, however, to see this situation exclusively in terms of any one individual's moral failings. Nor did management set out to defraud Sears customers. Instead, a number of organizational factors contributed to the problematic sales practices.

In the face of declining revenues, shrinking market share, and an increasingly competitive market for undercar services, Sears management attempted to spur the performance of its auto centers by introducing new goals and incentives for employees. The company increased minimum work quotas and introduced productivity incentives for mechanics. The automotive service advisers were given product-specific sales quotas—sell so many springs, shock absorbers, alignments, or brake jobs per shift—and paid a commission based on sales. According to advisers, failure to meet quotas could lead to a transfer or a reduction in work hours. Some employees spoke of the "pressure, pressure, pressure" to bring in sales.

Under this new set of organizational pressures and incentives, with few options for meeting their sales goals legitimately, some employees' judgment understandably suffered. Management's failure to clarify the line between unnecessary service and legitimate preventive maintenance, coupled with consumer ignorance, left employees to chart their own courses through a vast gray area, subject to a wide range of interpretations. Without active management support for ethical practice and mechanisms to detect and check questionable sales methods and poor work, it is not surprising that some employees may have reacted to contextual forces by resorting to exaggeration, carelessness, or even misrepresentation.

Shortly after the allegations against Sears became public, CEO Edward Brennan acknowledged management's responsibility for putting in place compensation and goal-setting systems that "created an environment in which mistakes did occur." Although the company denied any intent to deceive consumers, senior executives eliminated commissions for service advisers and discontinued sales quotas for specific parts. They also instituted a system of unannounced shopping audits and made plans to expand the internal monitoring of service. In settling the pending lawsuits, Sears offered coupons to customers who had bought certain auto services between 1990 and 1992. The total cost of the settlement, including potential customer refunds, was an estimated $60 million.

Contextual forces can also influence the behavior of top management, as a former CEO of Beech-Nut Nutrition Corporation discovered. In the early 1980s, only two years after joining the company, the CEO found evidence suggesting that the apple juice concentrate, supplied by the company's vendors for use in Beech-Nut's "100% pure" apple juice, contained nothing more than sugar water and chemicals. The CEO could have destroyed the bogus inventory and withdrawn the juice from grocers' shelves, but he was under extraordinary pressure to turn the ailing company around. Eliminating the inventory would have killed any hope of turning even the meager $700,000 profit promised to Beech-Nut's then parent, Nestlé.

A number of people in the corporation, it turned out, had doubted the purity of the juice for several years before the CEO arrived. But the 25% price advantage offered by the supplier of the bogus concentrate allowed the operations head to meet cost-control goals. Furthermore, the company lacked an effective quality control system, and a conclusive lab test for juice purity did not yet exist. When a member of the research department voiced concerns about the juice to operating management, he was accused of not being a team player and of acting like "Chicken Little." His judgment, his supervisor wrote in an annual performance review, was "colored by naïveté and impractical ideals." No one else seemed to have considered the company's obligations to its customers or to have thought about the potential harm of disclosure. No one considered the fact that the sale of adulterated or misbranded juice is a legal offense, putting the company and its top management at risk of criminal liability.

An FDA investigation taught Beech-Nut the hard way. In 1987, the company pleaded guilty to selling adulterated and misbranded juice. Two years and two criminal trials later, the CEO pleaded guilty to ten counts of mislabeling. The total cost to the company—including fines, legal expenses, and lost sales—was an estimated $25 million.

Such errors of judgment rarely reflect an organizational culture and management philosophy that sets out to harm or deceive. More often, they reveal a culture that is insensitive or indifferent to ethical considerations or one that lacks effective organizational systems. By the same token, exemplary conduct usually reflects an organizational culture and philosophy that is infused with a sense of responsibility.

For example, Johnson & Johnson's handling of the Tylenol crisis is sometimes attributed to the singular personality of then-CEO James Burke. However, the decision to do a nationwide recall of Tylenol capsules in order to avoid further loss of life from product tampering was in reality not one decision but thousands of decisions made by individuals at all levels of the organization. The "Tylenol decision," then, is best understood not as an isolated incident, the achievement of a lone individual, but as the reflection of an organization's culture. Without a shared set of values and guiding principles deeply ingrained throughout the organization, it is doubtful that Johnson & Johnson's response would have been as rapid, cohesive, and ethically sound.

Many people resist acknowledging the influence of organizational factors on individual behavior—especially on misconduct—for fear of diluting people's sense of personal moral responsibility. But this fear is based on a false dichotomy between holding individual transgressors accountable and holding "the system" accountable. Acknowledging the importance of organizational context need not imply exculpating individual wrongdoers. To understand all is not to forgive all.

The Limits of a Legal Compliance Program

The consequences of an ethical lapse can be serious and far-reaching. Organizations can quickly become entangled in an all-consuming web of legal proceedings. The risk of litigation and liability has increased in the past decade as lawmakers have legislated new civil and criminal offenses, stepped up penalties, and improved support for law enforcement. Equally— if not more—important is the damage an ethical lapse can do to an organization's reputation and relationships. Both Sears and Beech-Nut, for instance, struggled to regain consumer trust and market share long after legal proceedings had ended.

As more managers have become alerted to the importance of organizational ethics, many have asked their lawyers to develop corporate ethics programs to detect and prevent violations of the law. The 1991 Federal Sentencing Guidelines offer a compelling rationale. Sanctions such as fines and probation for organizations convicted of wrongdoing can vary dramatically depending both on the degree of management cooperation in reporting and investigating corporate misdeeds and on whether or not the company has implemented a legal compliance program.

Such programs tend to emphasize the prevention of unlawful conduct, primarily by increasing surveillance and control and by imposing penalties for wrongdoers. While plans vary, the basic framework is outlined in the sentencing guidelines. Managers must establish compliance standards and procedures; designate high-level personnel to oversee compliance; avoid delegating discretionary authority to those likely to act unlawfully; effectively communicate the company's standards and procedures through training or publications; take reasonable steps to achieve compliance through audits,

monitoring processes, and a system for employees to report criminal misconduct without fear of retribution; consistently enforce standards through
appropriate disciplinary measures; respond appropriately when offenses are
detected; and, finally, take reasonable steps to prevent the occurrence of
similar offenses in the future.

There is no question of the necessity of a sound, well-articulated strategy for legal compliance in an organization. After all, employees can be frustrated and frightened by the complexity of today's legal environment. And
even managers who claim to use the law as a guide to ethical behavior often
lack more than a rudimentary understanding of complex legal issues.

Managers would be mistaken, however, to regard legal compliance as an
adequate means for addressing the full range of ethical issues that arise
every day. "If it's legal, it's ethical," is a frequently heard slogan. But conduct
that is lawful may be highly problematic from an ethical point of view. Consider the sale in some countries of hazardous products without appropriate
warnings or the purchase of goods from suppliers who operate inhumane
sweatshops in developing countries. Companies engaged in international
business often discover that conduct that infringes on recognized standards
of human rights and decency is legally permissible in some jurisdictions.

Legal clearance does not certify the absence of ethical problems in the
United States either, as a 1991 case at Salomon Brothers illustrates. Four top-
level executives failed to take appropriate action when learning of unlawful
activities on the government trading desk. Company lawyers found no law
obligating the executives to disclose the improprieties. Nevertheless, the executives' delay in disclosing and failure to reveal their prior knowledge
prompted a serious crisis of confidence among employees, creditors, shareholders, and customers. The executives were forced to resign, having lost
the moral authority to lead. Their ethical lapse compounded the trading
desk's legal offenses, and the company ended up suffering losses—including
legal costs, increased funding costs, and lost business—estimated at nearly
$1 billion.

A compliance approach to ethics also overemphasizes the threat of detection and punishment in order to channel behavior in lawful directions.
The underlying model for this approach is deterrence theory, which envi-
sions people as rational maximizers of self-interest, responsive to the personal costs and benefits of their choices, yet indifferent to the moral
legitimacy of those choices. But a recent study reported in *Why People Obey
the Law* by Tom R. Tyler shows that obedience to the law is strongly influenced by a belief in its legitimacy and its moral correctness. People generally feel that they have a strong obligation to obey the law. Education about
the legal standards and a supportive environment may be all that's required
to insure compliance.

Discipline is, of course, a necessary part of any ethical system. Justified
penalties for the infringement of legitimate norms are fair and appropriate.
Some people do need the threat of sanctions. However, an overemphasis on
potential sanctions can be superfluous and even counterproductive. Employees may rebel against programs that stress penalties, particularly if they
are designed and imposed without employee involvement or if the standards
are vague or unrealistic. Management may talk of mutual trust when un-
veiling a compliance plan, but employees often receive the message as a

warning from on high. Indeed, the most skeptical among them may view compliance programs as nothing more than liability insurance for senior management. This is not an unreasonable conclusion, considering that compliance programs rarely address the root causes of misconduct.

Even in the best cases, legal compliance is unlikely to unleash much moral imagination or commitment. The law does not generally seek to inspire human excellence or distinction. It is no guide for exemplary behavior—or even good practice. Those managers who define ethics as legal compliance are implicitly endorsing a code of moral mediocrity for their organizations. As Richard Breeden, former chairman of the Securities and Exchange Commission, noted, "It is not an adequate ethical standard to aspire to get through the day without being indicted."

Integrity as a Governing Ethic

A strategy based on integrity holds organizations to a more robust standard. While compliance is rooted in avoiding legal sanctions, organizational integrity is based on the concept of self-governance in accordance with a set of guiding principles. From the perspective of integrity, the task of ethics management is to define and give life to an organization's guiding values, to create an environment that supports ethically sound behavior, and to instill a sense of shared accountability among employees. The need to obey the law is viewed as a positive aspect of organizational life, rather than an unwelcome constraint imposed by external authorities.

An integrity strategy is characterized by a conception of ethics as a driving force of an enterprise. Ethical values shape the search for opportunities, the design of organizational systems, and the decision-making process used by individuals and groups. They provide a common frame of reference and serve as a unifying force across different functions, lines of business, and employee groups. Organizational ethics helps define what a company is and what it stands for.

Many integrity initiatives have structural features common to compliance-based initiatives: a code of conduct, training in relevant areas of law, mechanisms for reporting and investigating potential misconduct, and audits and controls to insure that laws and company standards are being met. In addition, if suitably designed, an integrity-based initiative can establish a foundation for seeking the legal benefits that are available under the sentencing guidelines should criminal wrongdoing occur. (See the insert "The Hallmarks of an Effective Integrity Strategy.")

But an integrity strategy is broader, deeper, and more demanding than a legal compliance initiative. Broader in that it seeks to enable responsible conduct. Deeper in that it cuts to the ethos and operating systems of the organization and its members, their guiding values and patterns of thought and action. And more demanding in that it requires an active effort to define the responsibilities and aspirations that constitute an organization's ethical compass. Above all, organizational ethics is seen as the work of management. Corporate counsel may play a role in the design and implementation of integrity strategies, but managers at all levels and across all functions are involved in the process. (See the chart, "Strategies for Ethics Management.")

During the past decade, a number of companies have undertaken integrity initiatives. They vary according to the ethical values focused on and the implementation approaches used. Some companies focus on the core values of integrity that reflect basic social obligations, such as respect for the rights of others, honesty, fair dealing, and obedience to the law. Other companies emphasize aspirations—values that are ethically desirable but not necessarily morally obligatory—such as good service to customers, a commitment to diversity, and involvement in the community.

When it comes to implementation, some companies begin with behavior. Following Aristotle's view that one becomes courageous by acting as a courageous person, such companies develop codes of conduct specifying appropriate behavior, along with a system of incentives, audits, and controls. Other companies focus less on specific actions and more on developing attitudes, decision-making processes, and ways of thinking that reflect their values. The assumption is that personal commitment and appropriate decision processes will lead to right action.

Martin Marietta, NovaCare, and Wetherill Associates have implemented and lived with quite different integrity strategies. In each case, management has found that the initiative has made important and often unexpected contributions to competitiveness, work environment, and key relationships on which the company depends.

Martin Marietta: Emphasizing Core Values

Martin Marietta Corporation, the U.S. aerospace and defense contractor, opted for an integrity-based ethics program in 1985. At the time, the defense industry was under attack for fraud and mismanagement, and Martin Marietta was under investigation for improper travel billings. Managers knew they needed a better form of self-governance but were skeptical that an ethics program could influence behavior. "Back then people asked, 'Do you really need an ethics program to be ethical?'" recalls current President Thomas Young. "Ethics was something personal. Either you had it, or you didn't."

The corporate general counsel played a pivotal role in promoting the program, and legal compliance was a critical objective. But it was conceived of and implemented from the start as a companywide management initiative aimed at creating and maintaining a "do-it-right" climate. In its original conception, the program emphasized core values, such as honesty and fair play. Over time, it expanded to encompass quality and environmental responsibility as well.

Today the initiative consists of a code of conduct, an ethics training program, and procedures for reporting and investigating ethical concerns within the company. It also includes a system for disclosing violations of federal procurement law to the government. A corporate ethics office manages the program, and ethics representatives are stationed at major facilities. An ethics steering committee, made up of Martin Marietta's president, senior executives, and two rotating members selected from field operations, oversees the ethics office. The audit and ethics committee of the board of directors oversees the steering committee.

The ethics office is responsible for responding to questions and concerns from the company's employees. Its network of representatives serves as a sounding board, a source of guidance, and a channel for raising a range of issues, from allegations of wrongdoing to complaints about poor management, unfair supervision, and company policies and practices. Martin Marietta's ethics network, which accepts anonymous complaints, logged over 9,000 calls in 1991, when the company had about 60,000 employees. In 1992, it investigated 684 cases. The ethics office also works closely with the human resources, legal, audit, communications, and security functions to respond to employee concerns.

Shortly after establishing the program, the company began its first round of ethics training for the entire workforce, starting with the CEO and senior executives. Now in its third round, training for senior executives focuses on decision making, the challenges of balancing multiple responsibilities, and compliance with laws and regulations critical to the company. The incentive compensation plan for executives makes responsibility for promoting ethical conduct an explicit requirement for reward eligibility and requires that business and personal goals be achieved in accordance with the company's policy on ethics. Ethical conduct and support for the ethics program are also criteria in regular performance reviews.

Today top-level managers say the ethics program has helped the company avoid serious problems and become more responsive to its more than 90,000 employees. The ethics network, which tracks the number and types of cases and complaints, has served as an early warning system for poor management, quality and safety defects, racial and gender discrimination, environmental concerns, inaccurate and false records, and personnel grievances regarding salaries, promotions, and layoffs. By providing an alternative channel for raising such concerns, Martin Marietta is able to take corrective action more quickly and with a lot less pain. In many cases, potentially embarrassing problems have been identified and dealt with before becoming a management crisis, a lawsuit, or a criminal investigation. Among employees who brought complaints in 1993, 75% were satisifed with the results.

Company executives are also convinced that the program has helped reduce the incidence of misconduct. When allegations of misconduct do surface, the company says it deals with them more openly. On several occasions, for instance, Martin Marietta has voluntarily disclosed and made restitution to the government for misconduct involving potential violations of federal procurement laws. In addition, when an employee alleged that the company had retaliated against him for voicing safety concerns about his plant on CBS news, top management commissioned an investigation by an outside law firm. Although failing to support the allegations, the investigation found that employees at the plant feared retaliation when raising health, safety, or environmental complaints. The company redoubled its efforts to identify and discipline those employees taking retaliatory action and stressed the desirability of an open work environment in its ethics training and company communications.

Although the ethics program helps Martin Marietta avoid certain types of litigation, it has occasionally led to other kinds of legal action. In a few cases, employees dismissed for violating the code of ethics sued Martin Marietta, arguing that the company had violated its own code by imposing unfair and excessive discipline.

Still, the company believes that its attention to ethics has been worth it. The ethics program has led to better relationships with the government, as well as to new business opportunities. Along with prices and technology, Martin Marietta's record of integrity, quality, and reliability of estimates plays a role in the awarding of defense contracts, which account for some 75% of the company's revenues. Executives believe that the reputation they've earned through their ethics program has helped them build trust with government auditors, as well. By opening up communications, the company has reduced the time spent on redundant audits.

The program has also helped change employees' perceptions and priorities. Some managers compare their new ways of thinking about ethics to the way they understand quality. They consider more carefully how situations will be perceived by others, the possible long-term consequences of short-term thinking, and the need for continuous improvement. CEO Norman Augustine notes, "Ten years ago, people would have said that there were no ethical issues in business. Today employees think their number-one objective is to be thought of as decent people doing quality work."

NovaCare: Building Shared Aspirations

NovaCare Inc., one of the largest providers of rehabilitation services to nursing homes and hospitals in the United States, has oriented its ethics effort toward building a common core of shared aspirations. But in 1988, when the company was called InSpeech, the only sentiment shared was mutual mistrust.

Senior executives built the company from a series of aggressive acquisitions over a brief period of time to take advantage of the expanding market for therapeutic services. However, in 1988, the viability of the company was in question. Turnover among its frontline employees—the clinicians and therapists who care for patients in nursing homes and hospitals—escalated to 57% per year. The company's inability to retain therapists caused customers to defect and the stock price to languish in an extended slump.

After months of soul-searching, InSpeech executives realized that the turnover rate was a symptom of a more basic problem: the lack of a common set of values and aspirations. There was, as one executive put it, a "huge disconnect" between the values of the therapists and clinicians and those of the managers who ran the company. The therapists and clinicians evaluated the company's success in terms of its delivery and high-quality health care. InSpeech management, led by executives with financial services and venture capital backgrounds, measured the company's worth exclusively in terms of financial success. Management's single-minded emphasis on increasing hours of reimbursable care turned clinicians off. They took management's performance orientation for indifference to patient care and left the company in droves.

CEO John Foster recognized the need for a common frame of reference and a common language to unify the diverse groups. So he brought in consultants to conduct interviews and focus groups with the company's health care professionals, managers, and customers. Based on the results, an employee task force drafted a proposed vision statement for the company, and another 250 employees suggested revisions. Then Foster and several senior managers developed a succinct statement of the company's guiding purpose and fundamental beliefs that could be used as a framework for making decisions and setting goals, policies, and practices.

Unlike a code of conduct, which articulates specific behavioral standards, the statement of vision, purposes, and beliefs lays out in very simple terms the company's central purpose and core values. The purpose—meeting the rehabilitation needs of patients through clinical leadership—its supported by four key beliefs: respect for the individual, service to the customer, pursuit of excellence, and commitment to personal integrity. Each value is discussed with examples of how it is manifested in the day-to-day activities and policies of the company, such as how to measure the quality of care.

To support the newly defined values, the company changed its name to NovaCare and introduced a number of structural and operational changes. Field managers and clinicians were given greater decision-making authority; clinicians were provided with additional resources to assist in the delivery of effective therapy; and a new management structure integrated the various therapies offered by the company. The hiring of new corporate personnel with health care backgrounds reinforced the company's new clinical focus.

The introduction of the vision, purpose, and beliefs met with varied reactions from employees, ranging from cool skepticism to open enthusiasm. One employee remembered thinking the talk about values "much ado about nothing." Another recalled, "It was really wonderful. It gave us a goal that everyone aspired to, no matter what their place in the company." At first, some were baffled about how the vision, purpose, and beliefs were to be used. But, over time, managers became more adept at explaining and using them as a guide. When a customer tried to hire away a valued employee, for example, managers considered raiding the customer's company for employees. After reviewing the beliefs, the managers abandoned the idea.

NovaCare managers acknowledge and company surveys indicate that there is plenty of room for improvement. While the values are used as a firm reference point for decision making and evaluation in some areas of the company, they are still viewed with reservation in others. Some managers do not "walk the talk," employees complain. And recently acquired companies have yet to be fully integrated into the program. Nevertheless, many NovaCare employees say the values initiative played a critical role in the company's 1990 turnaround.

The values reorientation also helped the company deal with its most serious problem: turnover among health care providers. In 1990, the turnover rate stood at 32%, still above target but a significant improvement over the 1988 rate of 57%. By 1993, turnover had dropped to 27%. Moreover, recruiting new clinicians became easier. Barely able to hire 25 new clinicians each month in 1988, the company added 776 in 1990 and 2,546 in 1993. Indeed, one employee who left during the 1988 turmoil said that her decision to return in 1990 hinged on the company's adoption of the vision, purpose, and beliefs.

Wetherill Associates: Defining Right Action

Wetherill Associates, Inc.—a small, privately held supplier of electrical parts to the automotive market—has neither a conventional code of conduct nor a statement of values. Instead, WAI has *Quality Assurance Manual*—a combination of philosophy text, conduct guide, technical manual, and company profile—that describes the company's commitment to honesty and its guiding principle of right action.

WAI doesn't have a corporate ethics officer who reports to top management, because at WAI, the company's corporate ethics officer *is* top management. Marie Bothe, WAI's chief executive officer, sees her main function as keeping the 350-employee company on the path of right action and looking for opportunities to help the community. She delegates the "technical" aspects of the business—marketing, finance, personnel, operations—to other members of the organization.

Right action, the basis for all of WAI's decisions, is a well-developed approach that challenges most conventional management thinking. The company explicitly rejects the usual conceptual boundaries that separate morality and self-interest. Instead, they define right behavior as logically, expediently, and morally right. Managers teach employees to look at the needs of the customers, suppliers, and the community—in addition to those of the company and its employees—when making decisions.

WAI also has a unique approach to competition. One employee explains, "We are not 'in competition' with anybody. We just do what we have to do to serve the customer." Indeed, when occasionally unable to fill orders, WAI salespeople refer customers to competitors. Artificial incentives, such as sales contests, are never used to spur individual performance. Nor are sales results used in determining compensation. Instead, the focus is on teamwork and customer service. Managers tell all new recruits that absolute honesty, mutual courtesy, and respect are standard operating procedure.

Newcomers generally react positively to company philosophy, but not all are prepared for such a radical departure from the practices they have known elsewhere. Recalling her initial interview, one recruit described her response to being told that lying was not allowed, "What do you mean? No lying? I'm a buyer. I lie for a living!" Today she is persuaded that the policy makes sound business sense. WAI is known for informing suppliers of overshipments as well as undershipments and for scrupulous honesty in the sale of parts, even when deception cannot be readily detected.

Since its entry into the distribution business 13 years ago, WAI has seen its revenues climb steadily from just under $1 million to nearly $98 million in 1993, and this in an industry with little growth. Once seen as an upstart beset by naysayers and industry skeptics, WAI is now credited with entering and professionalizing an industry in which kickbacks, bribes, and "gratuities" were commonplace. Employees—equal numbers of men and women ranging in age from 17 to 92—praise the work environment as both productive and supportive.

WAI's approach could be difficult to introduce in a larger, more traditional organization. WAI is a small company founded by 34 people who shared a belief in right action; its ethical values were naturally built into the organization from the start. Those values are so deeply ingrained in the company's culture and operating systems that they have been largely self-sustaining. Still, the company has developed its own training program and takes special care to hire people willing to support right action. Ethics and job skills are considered equally important in determining an individual's competence and suitability for employment. For WAI, the challenge will be to sustain its vision as the company grows and taps into markets overseas.

At WAI, as at Martin Marietta and NovaCare, a management-led commitment to ethical values has contributed to competitiveness, positive workforce morale, as well as solid sustainable relationships with the company's key constituencies. In the end, creating a climate that encourages exemplary conduct may be the best way to discourage damaging misconduct. Only in such an environment do rogues really act alone.

The Hallmarks of an Effective Integrity Strategy

There is no one right integrity strategy. Factors such as management personality, company history, culture, lines of business, and industry regulations must be taken into account when shaping an appropriate set of values and designing an implementation program. Still, several features are common to efforts that have achieved some success:

- *The guiding values and commitments make sense and are clearly communicated.* They reflect important organizational obligations and widely shared aspirations that appeal to the organization's members. Employees at all levels take them seriously, feel comfortable discussing them, and have a concrete understanding of their practical importance. This does not signal the absence of ambiguity and conflict but a willingness to seek solutions compatible with the framework of values.

- *Company leaders are personally committed, credible, and willing to take action on the values they espouse.* They are not mere mouthpieces. They are willing to scrutinize their own decisions. Consistency on the part of leadership is key. Waffling on values will lead to employee cynicism and a rejection of the program. At the same time, managers must assume responsibility for making tough calls when ethical obligations conflict.

- *The espoused values are integrated into the normal channels of management decision making and are reflected in the organization's critical activities:* the development of plans, the setting of goals, the search for opportunities, the allocation of resources, the gathering and communication of information, the measurement of performance, and the promotion and advancement of personnel.

- *The company's systems and structures support and reinforce its values.* Information systems, for example, are designed to provide timely and accurate information. Reporting relationships are structured to build in checks and balances to promote objective judgment. Performance appraisal is sensitive to means as well as ends.

- *Managers throughout the company have the decision-making skills, knowledge, and competencies needed to make ethically sound decisions on a day-to-day basis.* Ethical thinking and awareness must be part of every managers' mental equipment. Ethics education is usually part of the process.

Success in creating a climate for responsible and ethically sound behavior requires continuing effort and a considerable investment of time and resources. A glossy code of conduct, a high-ranking ethics officer, a training program, an annual ethics audit—these trappings of an ethics program do not necessarily add up to a responsible, law-abiding organization whose espoused values match its actions. A formal ethics program can serve as a catalyst and a support system, but organizational integrity depends on the integration of the company's values into its driving systems.

Strategies for Ethics Management

Characteristics of Compliance Strategy

Ethos	conformity with externally imposed standards
Objective	prevent criminal misconduct
Leadership	lawyer driven
Methods	education, reduced discretion, auditing and controls, penalties
Behavioral Assumptions	autonomous beings guided by material self-interest

Characteristics of Integrity Strategy

Ethos	self-governance according to chosen standards
Objective	enable responsible conduct
Leadership	management driven with aid of lawyers, HR, others
Methods	education, leadership, accountability, organizational systems and decision processes, auditing and controls, penalties
Behavioral Assumptions	social beings guided by material self-interest, values, ideals, peers

Implementation of Compliance Strategy

Standards	criminal and regulatory law
Staffing	lawyers
Activities	develop compliance standards
	train and communicate
	handle reports of misconduct
	conduct investigations
	oversee compliance audits
	enforce standards
Education	compliance standards and system

Implementation of Integrity Strategy

Standards	company values and aspirations, social obligations, including law
Staffing	executives and managers with lawyers, others
Activities	lead development of company values and standards
	train and communicate
	integrate into company systems
	provide guidance and consultation
	assess values performance
	identify and resolve problems
	oversee compliance activities
Education	decision making and values
	compliance standards and system

The Environment

— Case Study —

Shell and Nigerian Oil

William E. Newburry — Thomas N. Gladwin

> *The flames of Shell are flames of Hell,*
> *We bask below their light.*
> *Nought for us to serve the blight,*
> *Of cursed neglect and cursed Shell.*
>
> —Ogoni Song

Introduction

November 10, 1997, marked the second anniversary of the execution of Nigerian environmentalist Ken Saro-Wiwa and eight other Ogoni activists by the Nigerian government in Port Harcourt following a sentencing for allegedly inciting the murder of four Ogoni tribal leaders. Around the world, services of remembrance were held. However, in Ogoniland, Nigeria, it was doubtful that services would be possible. On the first anniversary of his death, no legal services were possible as gatherings of more than two people were banned in Ogoniland from October 1996 to January 1997 (Robinson, 1996). When services were held in violation of this ban, one person was killed and 46 were arrested.

The controversy over Ken Saro-Wiwa's death concerns not only the specific events of his arrest, trial and execution, but also several decades of incidents involving both the Nigerian government and Shell Oil Company. The trial, itself, was conducted by a Nigerian Civil Disturbances Special Tribunal (CDST), answerable only to Nigeria's military government. The executions, which were equated with "judicial murder" by numerous international observers, have led to massive international outcries against the military dictatorship of Nigeria. Additionally, international protests against Shell Oil Company have also been extensive, due to Shell's controversial oil operations in the Niger Delta of Nigeria and allegedly collusive ties with the Nigerian military government in suppressing Ogoni environmental and political autonomy movements. . . .

———•◆•———

A Brief History and Overview of Nigeria

The country of Nigeria represents the integration of an estimated 300+ ethnic groups under British colonial rule since its creation in 1914. Due to this vast number of groups under one government, with their own unique cultures and languages, the British had great difficulty maintaining control over Nigeria during its occupation. With 300 distinct ethnicities, there were countless disputes over (perceived or real) inequities.

Nigeria received independence from the United Kingdom on October 1, 1960. At this time, three states were established, each under the control of one of the country's three major ethnic groups: Hausa-Fulani, Igbo and Yoruba. It can be argued that this government arrangement served at a minimum to ignore the needs of the country's approximately 297 other ethnic groups, and at a maximum to exploit their resources in support of the needs of the three majority groups. This created an inherently unstable political situation, which resulted in a military coup d'etat on January 15, 1966 when the Federal Prime Minister and two other Regional Premiers (of the Yoruba and Hausa-Fulani regions) were killed and an Igbo Major General took control as ruler of Nigeria. At this point, the majority ethnic groups appeared to support the breaking up of the nation, but the minority groups "argued for the continued existence of the country and recommended the political re-structuring of the country through the creation of states" (Saro-Wiwa, 1992). When the minorities won, the result was an Igbo secession from Nigeria to form a new republic of Biafra in Eastern Nigeria (including the Ogoni territory). This in turn resulted in a three-year civil war where the resources of the minority ethnic groups (especially the oil of minorities such as the Ogoni) became the focus of some of the fiercest battles, resulting in many atrocities among these ethnic minorities.

Following the end of the Biafra Civil War, Nigeria remained under various forms of military rule for most of the 1970s and 1980s. Civilian government was scheduled to take over in 1993, following a general election, but the results were negated by General Babangida. A coup took place on 17 November 1993, when Sani Abacha announced himself as chief of state. The country's Senate and House of Representatives were suspended and General Abacha remained in power through the time of this case writing.

As reported by *The Economist* (11/18/95), "for all but nine of its 35 independent years, Nigeria has been ruled by soldiers. The current gang, under General Sani Abacha, are the worst: repressive, visionless and so corrupt that the parasite of corruption has almost eaten the host. These days the main activity of the state is embezzlement." Prior to Ken Saro-Wiwa's execution in 1995, the international monitoring organization, Freedom House (1995: 437) gave Nigeria its lowest possible political rights rating of 7, and downgraded the country's civil rights rating from 5 to 6 "because of the current government's declaration of commanding 'absolute power' and its disregard for basic human rights and civil liberties". In 1996, Freedom House downgraded Nigeria to its lowest possible human rights rating, deeming it a "most repressive state" similar to Iraq, North Korea, Sudan, Burma, Cuba, Libya, Syria, etc. . . . The U.S. State Department in March 1996 listed Nigeria as a major human rights abuser in its annual human rights report. Additionally, Transparency International, in its 1996 Internet Corruption Perception Index (ICPI), found that Nigeria is perceived to be the most corrupt country out of the 54 countries in their extensive survey (de Jonquieres, 1997). It can be argued that conditions in Nigeria violate nearly every provision of the Universal Declaration of Human Rights as adopted by the U. N. General Assembly in 1948 without a dissenting vote. In 1966, the United National General Assembly adopted the International Covenant on Civil and Political Rights, which transferred the original principals of the Universal Declaration of Human Rights into treaty provisions. By the beginning of 1991, this covenant had been ratified by 92 of the United Nations' 164 members.

Nigeria's land area is 910,770 sq. km., slightly more than twice the size of California. It is located in West Africa, bordering the Atlantic Ocean and lying between Benin and Cameroon. With an estimated population between 90 and 105 million, it is the most populous country in Africa. Moreover, the population of Nigeria has increased four-fold since 1958 and continues to rise rapidly. The general terrain consists of southern lowlands merging into central hills and plateaus. There are mountains in the southeast and plains in the north. The country's main natural resources are petroleum, tin, columbite, iron ore, coal, limestone, lead, zinc, and natural gas. While records are highly suspect, it is estimated that oil revenues account for between 43% and 90% of the country's GDP. Agriculture accounts for up to another 35%. 54% percent of the population is employed in agriculture. 31% of the land is arable. However, this percentage is threatened by soil degradation, rapid deforestation, desertification, and recent droughts in the north. Nigeria is also the passenger and cargo hub for drug trafficking in West Africa—of particular note are heroin from South East Asia and cocaine for South America. The main currency unit in Nigeria is the Naira. The exchange rate as of September 1996 was US\$1 = 85 Naira. 51% of the population age 15 and over can read and write. The average life expectancy is 55 years. . . .

The Ogoni

The Ogoni are a distinct ethnic group within Nigeria numbering approximately 500,000 and traditionally living in the Rivers state area, an area of approximately 600 miles near the Niger River delta (refer to Exhibit 1). The Niger River delta is home to approximately 6 million people. Historically, this area has been both fertile and highly populated. Due to its high fertility, this area has served as a major source of food for Nigeria. From early times, the Ogoni placed great value on the land where they lived (for both sustenance and spiritual reasons). They also placed a great value on nature and believed that "the soul of a man or woman has the power to leave its human form and enter into that of a beast, taking on the shape of an animal" (Saro-Wiwa, 1992: 12). Accordingly, they believed that causing harm to certain animals would also affect its human counterpart. Because of this, they were fierce defenders of their territory, which earned them the reputation of being cannibals. While located on the slave route of the Atlantic Slave Trade, there is no record of any Ogoni ever being taken into slavery. However, the slave trade did introduce firearms into the area and a series of wars in the late nineteenth century "virtually destroyed the fabric of the Ogoni society and the Ogoni were forced to survive in independent villages" (Saro-Wiwa, 1992: 14).

In 1901, the British claimed the Ogoni territory as a British protectorate. While the Ogoni resisted this intrusion for a number of years, they were eventually subjugated in 1914, the same year that Nigeria was created by Britain. For about 20 years, the Ogoni were ruled rather haphazardly, with a main emphasis on tax collection. In 1935, a road was completed from the Ogoni city of Kono to the town of Port Harcourt, opening up the Ogoni to contact with the outside world. In 1946, the Ogoni Division was established within the British administrative system of Nigeria, recognizing the Ogoni as a distinct ethnic group of considerable size. In 1950, the Ogoni State Representative Assembly was established, allowing the Ogoni a degree of self-determination and ethnic autonomy in government. These changes in government allowed the Ogoni to reestablish themselves as an ethnic civilization. At the same time, Ogoni leaders worked to pull the Ogoni into the 20th century by establishing schools (where Ogoni languages were taught), by translating the New Testament into an Ogoni language, and by building a general hospital with five local offices spread throughout the five Ogoni kingdoms (Saro-Wiwa, 1992).

Ken Saro-Wiwa estimated that the oil extracted from Ogoniland since 1958 is valued in excess of $30 billion. However, this figure more probably represents oil extracted from the Niger delta, which includes many different minority groups, including the Ogoni. An additional problem in determining the exact amount of oil in Ogoniland is that the area inhabited by the Ogonis has shrunk over time as this ethnic group has diminished in population, reportedly largely as the result of military actions. Saro-wiwa also stated that Ogoniland contains approximately 90% of Nigeria's oil resources. However, Shell officials reiterate that the oil extracted from Ogoniland is actually a relatively small portion of Shell's total operations in Nigeria. According to the World Council of Churches, Nigerian oil is located in the lands of several minority groups, including the Abriba, Andoni, Edo, Effik, Ibibio, Ijaw, Ika-Igbo, Ikwerre, Isekiri, Isoko, Kalabari, Ogoni and Urhobo (Robinson, 1996). The WCC adds that that these groups have small numbers, which gives them very little political power. Since all mineral rights in Nigeria are state-owned, the Ogoni people have reportedly received little compensation for the extraction of oil from their lands (see below). However, they have suffered the consequence of their land losing its fertility as a result of environmental damage, including oil spills and the release of toxic gases. Despite the oil revenues generated from the Ogoniland, most Ogoni currently lack running water, electricity, adequate schools or health care.

Since its inception, the Nigerian government has been continually unstable and prone to military governments as noted above. While initial protests against the Nigerian government by the Ogoni people occurred almost immediately after the government's inception, 12 elders of the Ogoni formed MOSOP, the Movement for Survival of Ogoni People, in 1990 to pressure the Nigerian government to accept responsibility for damage to the Ogoni homeland environment and to share Nigerian oil wealth with the Ogoni people. They soon after appointed Ken Saro-Wiwa, a successful author, playwright and businessman as their spokesperson.

Ken Saro-Wiwa and his MOSOP followers began to aggressively campaign for a greater share of oil revenues from the government, political self-determination and ownership of the oil beneath their land. In October of 1990, Saro-Wiwa (then as President of the Ogoni Central Union) authored and convinced the Chiefs and leaders of the Ogoni Kingdoms to endorse a

Bill of Rights (Saro-Wiwa, 1992) to submit to then Nigerian leader General Ibrahim Babangida and members of his Armed Forces Ruling Council. This Bill of Rights called for: (a) political control of Ogoni affairs by Ogoni people, (b) the right to control and use a fair proportion of Ogoni economic resources for Ogoni development (c), adequate and direct representation in all Nigerian national institutions, (d) the use and development of Ogoni languages in Ogoni territory and (e) the right to protect the Ogoni environment and ecology from further degradation. The Bill emphasized that the effort was not secessionist and that the proposed political autonomy would operate as part of The Federal Republic of Nigeria. With no response from the military government during the following year, an Addendum was added to the Bill of Rights in August of 1991 (also see Saro-Wiwa, 1992) and widely publicized to the United Nations Community.

In November of 1992, as the declared "Spokesperson for the Ogoni People," Saro-Wiwa introduced a motion at a meeting of the Ogoni Kingdoms that "called upon Shell, Chevron and the Nigerian National Petroleum Corporation (NNPC), the three oil companies operating in Ogoniland, to pay damages of U.S. four billion dollars for destroying the environment, six billion dollars in unpaid rents and royalties, and all within thirty days or it would be assumed that they had decided to quit the land. The resolution was unanimously carried in the six Kingdoms of Ogoni" (Saro-Wiwa, 1992, pp. 102–3). Saro-Wiwa went international with these demands in his 1992 book entitled "Genocide in Nigeria". By 1993, the movement had gained power to the point that a 300,000 person demonstration was held against Shell.

In a political speech in February of 1993, Saro-Wiwa claimed that:

> Today, the Ogoni people are involved in two grim wars. The first is the 35-year-old ecological war waged by the multinational oil companies, Shell and Chevron. In this most sophisticated and unconventional war, no bones are broken, no blood is spilled and no one is maimed. Yet, men, women and children die; flora and fauna perish, the air and water are poisoned, and finally, the land dies. The second war is a political war of tyranny, oppression and greed designed to dispossess the Ogoni people of their rights and their wealth and subject them to abject poverty, slavery, dehumanization and extinction. Taken together, both wars, waged against a defenseless and small people, amount to genocide and are a grave crime against humanity. Pitted against two deadly, greedy, insensitive and powerful enemies, the Ogoni people have refused to yield and are fighting doggedly and heroically for survival. And the war must be won, for the alternative to victory is extinction.

In February of 1993, Saro-Wiwa formed NYCOP, the youth wing of MOSOP. According to *The Economist* (11/30/95), "his youthful supporters soon deviated from the Ghandhian path, by displaying a taste for terror and extortion." Both the Nigerian government and Shell attributed many acts of sabotage against Shell operations in Ogoniland and other violent acts to NYCOP, in particular, and MOSOP, in general. While conclusive evidence is lacking, Ken Saro-Wiwa was deemed by Nigerian authorities to have taken part in these and other terrorist activities against Shell and the Nigerian government. According to Saro-Wiwa (1995), Shell, around this time, issued a "Briefing Note" accusing Saro-Wiwa of seeking "political self-determination" for the Ogoni people and using international criticism of Shell to reach this objective.

The *Wall Street Journal* (Brooks, 1994) characterized Ogoniland as "a ravaged environment," while The European Parliament later called the suffering of the Ogoni people "an environmental nightmare." A World Bank study report warned that "an urgent need exists to implement mechanisms to protect the life and health of the region's inhabitants and its ecological systems from further deterioration" (*The Guardian*, Nov. 17, 1995). Prior to such international attention, Ken Saro-Wiwa had described the environmental situation in 1992 as follows:

> Oil exploration has turned Ogoni into a waste land: lands, streams, and creeks are totally and continually polluted; the atmosphere has been poisoned, charged as it is with hydrocarbon vapors, methane, carbon monoxide, carbon dioxide and soot emitted by gas which has been flared twenty-four hours a day for thirty-three years in very close proximity to human habitation. Acid rain, oil spillages and oil blowouts have devastated Ogoni territory. High-pressure oil pipelines crisscross the surface of Ogoni farmlands and villages dangerously. The results of such unchecked environmental pollution and degradation include the complete destruction of the ecosystem. Mangrove forests have fallen to the toxicity of oil and are being replaced by noxious nypa palms; the rain forest has fallen to the ax of the multinational oil companies, all wildlife is dead, marine life is gone, the farmlands have been rendered infertile by acid rain and the once beautiful Ogoni countryside is no longer a source of fresh air and green vegetation. All one sees and feels around is death. Environmental degradation has been a lethal weapon in the war against the indigenous Ogoni people. (Saro-Wiwa, 1995, pp. 95–96)

'While it is not the place of a multinational company to interfere in the legal or political processes of any country, we will continue to promote humanitarian values and may on occasion feel it helpful to intercede, as in this case, either privately, or publicly'

MR. COR HERKSTRÖTER, CHAIRMAN OF THE ROYAL DUTCH/SHELL GROUP
AS QUOTED IN A JANUARY 30, 1996
SHELL INTERNATIONAL NEWS RELEASE (SHELL, 1996)

Shell Operations and Their Environmental Impact

Historical relationships between Shell and Nigeria date back to 1937, when Shell was granted its first exploration license, while Nigeria was still under British rule. Crude oil was first discovered in the mid-1950s, and in 1958, just prior to the establishment of Nigeria as an independent country, drilling operations began. The Shell Petroleum Development Company (SPDC) has by far the largest oil operations of any company operating in Nigeria (other companies include Chevron, Texaco and Mobil). The company is the result of a joint venture with equity currently divided amongst four joint venture partners, and recently reported as follows: the Nigerian National Petroleum Corporation (NNPC) (55% equity share), Shell (30% equity), Elf (10% equity) and Agip (5% equity) (Shell, 1995). Corzine and Goldman (1997) imply that NNPC's equity share is currently 49%. These equity positions have changed considerably over time, with NNPC maintaining a 35% equity share in 1973 and an 80% equity share throughout most of the 1980s. Gribben (1996) noted that Shell is currently trying to negotiate for a larger equity stake in the joint venture to allow more "financial headroom". Shell is already the dominant partner in terms of joint venture management. As noted by Shell (1997), "the margin of profit for the foreign partners in the Shell Petroleum Development Company (SPDC) operated joint venture is fixed over a wide range of oil prices, and amounts to US $1.00 a barrel shared between Shell, Elf and Agip."

Consistent with the underlying philosophies of joint ventures in other developing countries, the NNPC's major contribution to the joint venture was to allow Shell access to Nigeria's vast oil resources. SPDC was in charge of operating the joint venture. The joint venture is the largest Nigerian oil and gas exploration and production company with 94 producing oil fields and a 6,200-kilometer network of pipelines and flowlines spread over more than 31,000 square kilometers of the Niger Delta. SPDC's daily output from Nigeria in the early 1990s was approximately 910,000 barrels per day. This amounted to nearly half of Nigeria's OPEC crude oil quota. Of the other companies operating in Nigeria, "Chevron produces 380,000 barrels, compared with 310,000 by Mobil, 130,000 by Agip, 95,000 by Elf-Acquitaine and 60,000 by Texaco" (Billenness, Feb. 15, 1996). Nigeria represented approximately 14% of Shell's total worldwide oil production.

Between 1982 and 1992, an estimated 1.6 million gallons of oil were spilled from Shell's Nigerian fields in 27 incidents. 40% of all Shell oil spills worldwide were recorded to have been in Nigeria. According to Shell, "since 1989, SPDC has recorded an average of 221 spills per year in its operational area, involving a total of some 7,350 barrels of oil a year. Most of these spills involve volumes of less than eight barrels (one ton). In 1993 and 1994, 68 per cent of oil spills were smaller than eight barrels" (SPDC, May 1995: 3).

On January 25, 1995, Shell issued a detailed statement entitled "The Ogoni Issue," countering what the company deemed to be emotional and exaggerated accusations of environmental devastation made against its operations. Within this statement, Shell noted that "SPDC does not support violence and has frequently and publicly expressed its concern about the actions of both sides in the dispute. . . . There is no question of our staff carrying out their work under military protection. . . . we do believe that we need to protect ourselves against general crime, and that this protection should be enough to counter effectively the level of threat"(Shell, 1995). Regarding oil spills in Nigeria, Shell noted that "Some 75 percent of oil spills throughout our operations are from corrosion in older pipelines and other facilities, and from oil operations. Unfortunately, between 1989 and 1994 about 25 percent were the result of sabotage. In the Ogoni area, investigations show that 69 percent of all spills between 1985 and 1993 have been caused deliberately by the communities" (Shell, 1995).

> Compensation paid for spills and accidental damage between 1985–93 amounted to more than $575,000. The highly-publicized spill at Ebubu near Ogoni was a legacy of the civil war when a retreating army cut a main pipeline and set the crude oil on fire in the late 1960s. Nevertheless, SPDC has purchased the land at Ebubu and undertakes periodic clean-up as oil seeps to the surface. (Shell, January 25, 1995)

Shell admits having environmental problems, "but these do not add up to anything like devastation." A November 12, 1995 News Release from Shell explained part of its environmental problems as follows:

> In the Ogoni area—where Shell has not operated since 1993—the situation has been compounded by sabotage. Over 60% of the spills in the Ogoni area have been the direct result of sabotage, usually linked to claims for compensation. And when contractors have attempted to re-enter the area to deal with these problems, they have been forcibly denied access by activists. It is estimated that over U.S. $42 million of plant and equipment has been destroyed in Ogoni land since Shell withdrew in 1993.

Also relating to the cause of environmental damage in Ogoniland, Mortished (1996) presented another view of the Niger Delta environmental problem:

> The Niger Delta is suffering severe environmental damage, but the problem has more to do with people than oil rigs. The effect is most noticeable in Ogoni, the area abandoned by Shell in 1993 after attacks on staff, where the need for agricultural land by small farmers is causing deforestation. Population pressure has led to communities springing up around once remote oil installations—in the past farmers would sometimes use the heat from burning gas to dry cassava by laying the crop on the sand banks that surround the flare.

Shell announced that it was spending $100 million on environmental projects in Nigeria during 1995 and was also funding a $4.5 million environmental study of the Ogoni region in an effort to determine the extent to which the company was responsible for damage to the land. Senior Shell officials admitted off the record that it had been difficult to implement expensive environmental repair programs in Ogoniland because the Nigerian government (as its joint venture partner) was unwilling to match Shell's spending and would not countenance any reduction in its oil revenues (*The Guardian*, Nov. 16 & 18, 1995). Furthermore, as stated by Shell in its 1995 briefing on The Ogoni Issue (p. 7): "The need to safeguard the environment is universal, but the same action is not necessary or appropriate in every location. Ecological, technical, economic and other circumstances vary, so solutions may also vary." This adaptive view might be interpreted as being in contrast to the "Declaration of Principles on Human Rights and the Environment" issued by the Sierra Club Legal Defense Fund and other organizations (1994), which states in Part II, Paragraph 7, that "all persons have the right to the highest attainable standard of health free from environmental harm."

Corzine (1996a), reporting on a Shell visit to the Niger delta village of Omadina in the western delta "where nearly a quarter of Nigeria's total daily oil output of 2m barrels is produced," that while at first, "sullen youths in the village . . . listened in silence as a representative of Shell . . . outlined plans to build a new health clinic. . . . their anger soon broke through and they began barracking the Shell speaker. Such spending was too little too late, they shouted." However, elsewhere in the article, Corzine also added that "many locals admit privately that criticizing Shell is one of the few ways of gaining the attention of Nigeria's military rulers". Discussing the same visit to Omadina, Mortished (1996) added that "as the Shell delegation prepared to leave, a younger man shouted and pointed to the crumbling mud walls of the houses: 'Look at the buildings. This is a community that produces 20,000 barrels per day for Shell. What happened in Ogoni will happen here.' "

Following are excerpts from additional Shell statements regarding Shell's environmental responsibility, as documented in the company's corporate website (for additional Shell perspectives, see www.shellnigeria.com and www.shell.com):

> SPDC's policy is that all activities are planned and executed to minimize environmental impact. It strives for continuous environmental improvement and, like Shell companies world-wide, operates within the Royal Dutch Shell Group Statement of General Business Principles and the Policy Guidelines on Health, Safety and the Environment.

> The company recognizes the gap between its intentions and its current performance. It is working hard to renew aging facilities, reduce the number of oil spills in the course of operations, the amount of gas that is flared, and to reduce waste products. Improvements are being made in all these areas. There are unique challenges to operating 86 flowstations and some 6,200 km of pipelines and flowlines in 31,000 square kilometers of the Niger Delta in a variety of extreme habitats including humid swamp forest, mangrove swamp, seasonally-flooded forest and the sea.

> SPDC's current environmental performance should be seen in the context of Nigeria and its major social and economic problems and priorities. Though countries might all aim for the same environmental standards, at any one time they will be at different stages of development. Nigeria's environmental priorities are influenced by the social and economic circumstances which drive its development program. Companies operating in this setting are similarly affected. These realities are acknowledged in Principle 11 of the Rio Declaration from the Earth Summit of June 1992.

> Practices today are very different from those applied when most of SPDC's facilities and pipelines were constructed in the 1960s and 1970s. They were acceptable then, but they would not be built that way now.

According to *The Economist* (June 24, 1995), "Shell's return to shareholders over the past ten years out-performed both the stockmarket and most of its competitors, including giants such as BP, Exxon and Texaco. In a recent poll by Petroleum Economist, Shell was rated as the best-managed major oil company. . . . it is often held up as a model for managers of multinationals." According to *Time* (Hillebrand, 1996), "Royal Dutch/Shell Group, SPDC's parent, is the most profitable company on earth. Last year it earned $6.9 billion on revenues of $109.8 billion."

Military Operations in the Oil Drilling Area

Despite the largely nonviolent nature of the Ogoni struggle, Nigerian military and police intervention occurred on many occasions. In October of 1990, for example, the Etche people organized a peaceful demonstration at the village of Umuechem to protest Shell's pollution and lack of compensation for appropriated land. Allegedly, a Shell company manager, alarmed about the demonstration, sent an urgent message to the River State Police Commissioner requesting "security protection" to defend against an "impending attack" on company facilities. *The Ecologist* magazine (Nov. 1995) reported that Shell specifically requested the presence of the notorious Mobile

Police Force (MPF), known locally as the "kill and go bunch." The next day, the MPF carried out a "scorched earth" assault on Umuechem, brutally killing 80 people and destroying 495 homes according to Amnesty International. The MPF was again called upon to silence Shell's critics in 1992, when demonstrators against Shell's operations at the town of Donny were beaten and a few shot or killed. Shell defended its request for MPF operations claiming that "the request for police assistance was in strict accordance with legal requirements when an interruption to oil production may be caused" (*The Ecologist*, Nov. 1995).

According to the Sierra Club (December 17, 1996):

> Shell's payments to the military came in 1993, the year the Movement for the Survival of the Ogoni People (MOSOP), with Saro-Wiwa as its president, mobilized 300,000 people in a peaceful demonstration against the company. Since then, the military backlash against the Ogoni's has been devastating, with up to 1800 killed. Due to the ongoing unrest, Shell says it ceased operations in Ogoniland early in 1993.

> Despite its claims of withdrawal, Shell contracted the American firm Willbros to lay a pipeline through Ogoniland. In April 1993, Willbros started bulldozing farmland crops to make way for the pipeline, fomenting a protest of 10,000 peaceful demonstrators. The military opened fire on the rally, wounding at least 10 and leaving a mother of five in critical condition. The shootings prompted further demonstrations by the community, who, again, were shot at. One protester was killed and an additional 20 injured.

> Shell now admits that field allowances and transportation were provided for an army escort accompanying Willbros. However, Shell maintains that the Willbros army escort was not involved in any incident that caused injury to or the death of third parties.

The aforementioned incidents and subsequent ones were explained by the Nigerian government as communal clashes, i. e., "violence between the Ogoni and neighboring communities." Professor Claude Ake of the U.N. Commission on Development and Culture, after an investigation, however, found that "there was nothing in dispute in the sense of territory, fishing rights, access rights, discriminatory treatment, which are the normal causes of communal clashes." According to *The Earth Times* (11/30/95), "the sophistication of the weapons deployed against the Ogoni clearly indicate military involvement." As Human Rights organizations concluded, the attacks collectively killed 2,000 Ogoni, razed 27 villages and displaced 80,000 people who fled into the bush as refugees.

An intercepted memo signed by Major P. Okuntimo of the Rivers State Internal Security Task Force, dated May 11, 1994, stated "Shell operations still impossible unless ruthless military operations are undertaken to smooth economic activities to commence." The memo detailed that 400 soldiers should undertake "wasting operations" on Ogoni leaders who are "especially vocal individuals." It also advised putting "pressure on oil companies for prompt and regular inputs as discussed" (*The Ecologist*, Nov. 1995). Four Ogoni tribal leaders were killed nine days later and Ken Saro-Wiwa arrested the day after. Human Rights Watch documented hundreds of incidents of rape, torture and murder of Ogoni by marauding soldiers in the months which followed.

Once again, Shell denies involvement in the mobilization of violent repression in Ogoniland. Based on restricted military memos and verbal evidence from senior Nigerian military officers, however, *The Ecologist* (Nov. 1995) suggests that Shell may have funded some of the military operations against MOSOP. Allegations were offered that Shell representatives were meeting regularly with River State security officials, that Shell was paying for transportation salary bonuses of some troops, and that Shell was importing weapons into Nigeria for use by police forces protecting its installations. In February of 1996, Shell admitted that it had purchased weapons locally for use by the supernumerary police protecting its staff and facilities, but this had been initiated many years prior. Additional allegations regarding Shell's possible involvement in the military, legal, political, environmental and community affairs of Ogoniland have been made by the Body Shop, who have organized numerous campaigns against Shell and Nigeria in the past several years, including numerous editorials by Anita Roddick in newspapers around the world (e.g. Roddick, 1995a,b and c).

According to the U.S. State Department's latest "Country Reports on Human Rights Practices", issued on January 30, 1997, "the confrontation between the Government and the Ogoni remains violent." Robinson (1996) adds that between January and April 1996, over 1,000 Ogonis fled Nigeria to the neighboring Peoples Republic of Benin, with others traveling much farther. In Benin, most stay at the Come Refugee Camp, where they wait for a period generally over six months before a decision can be made whether to grant refugee status. Of the 200 cases for which evaluations have been completed, 20% have qualified for settlement in a third country and 60% have been granted refugee status and will remain under U.N. protection in Benin Republic.

> *"In Nigeria some $7 billion in oil money from Shell and other companies pours into the government treasury each year. Shell clears $220 million from the Delta."*
>
> *Time* (HILLEBRAND, 1996)

Who Has Benefited from Oil Exploitation to Nigeria

According to Shell estimates, oil revenues of about $10 billion per year were providing about 80% of Nigeria's Federal government's total revenue in the early 1990s. Oil revenues provided about 90% of Nigeria's foreign exchange. Statistics regarding the extent to which these benefits flowed down to particular ethnic groups within Nigeria, and particularly to groups disadvantaged by the oil operations, are less readily available.

The Economist (Nov. 18, 1995) claimed that the oil revenues provided to the Nigerian government were "systematically stolen and squandered" and the main activity of the state was "embezzlement." $12 billion of oil revenues were discovered to be missing from government accounts in 1994. According to The Body Shop, "profits from oil go almost exclusively to propping up the Nigerian military regime who use them to keep the population in a state of terror and oppression. Profits also go to foreign bank accounts controlled by Nigerian military leaders and their associates." This view was echoed by Tawo Akinola, head of The Campaign for Democracy in Nigeria who stated that "the oil money is not benefiting the people of Nigeria. It's used to finance tyranny." As a result, Nigeria's per capita income plunged from $1,000 a decade ago down to $280 as of 1995. The Nigerian state was supposed to direct 3% of its oil revenues back into the oil-producing communities. According to *The Earth Times* (Nov. 30, 1995), "in reality, little if any of that money has reached those in need."

Financial analysts variously estimate that Shell was earning Nigerian profits in the early 1990s of about $170 to $312 million a year, equal to nearly 10% of its total exploration and production profits. Shell claims that it cumulatively provided over $20 million of support for community projects in Ogoniland in the form of roads, health clinics, schools, water schemes, agricultural support projects (all detailed in Shell's January 1995 Ogoni briefing and updated in Shell's Internet Web Site discussion of the Ogoni situation. Ogoni activists dispute this amount and even Shell executives privately concede that many of the company's donations may have never reached their intended destination (Obe, 1995). As articulated in the Ogoni Bill of Rights (Saro-Wiwa, 1992), "in over 30 years of oil drilling, the Ogoni nationality have provided the Nigerian nation with a total revenue of 30 billion dollars . . . but in return for the above contribution, the Ogoni people have received NOTHING" . . . and our people wallow in "abject poverty and destitution." At best, according to Greenpeace, the Ogoni have received "just 0.000007 percent of the value of oil extracted" (*The Earth Times*, Nov. 30, 1995). The *Wall Street Journal* reported that just 88 of Shell's 5,000 Nigerian employees were Ogoni. Phil Watts (1997), group managing director for the Royal Dutch Shell Group recently stated that "Shell Nigeria runs one of the largest and most complex industrial operations in Africa—producing a million barrels of oil a day. It is an African company—97% of those who work in it are Nigerian." . . .

> "The future as dictated by Anita Roddick has seldom looked so unattractive. With her harsh call that 'political awareness and activism must be incorporated into business', she must raise shivers among lovers of democracy."
>
> D. VAN DEN BROEK, REGIONAL COORDINATOR,
> WESTERN HEMISPHERE AND AFRICA, SHELL CENTER, LONDON,
> AS QUOTED IN *The Independent*, DECEMBER 1, 1995

Ken Saro-Wiwa

Prior to becoming one of the key spokesman for the Ogoni movement in Nigeria, Ken Saro-Wiwa lived what would commonly be regarded as a fortunate life. He attended the University of Ibadan, in western Nigeria, in the mid-1960's. After graduating, he became a very successful writer, businessman, and political journalist who published novels, plays, poems and children's books. He was also writer and producer of Nigeria's most popular soap opera, *Basi & Co.* (Boyd, 1995). . . .

As time progressed, Ken Saro-Wiwa became increasingly concerned with the plight of his native Ogoni tribe. Eventually, he in effect gave up his business concerns so that he could concentrate on lobbying for the Ogoni cause. At this point in time, he was instrumental in establishing the group MOSOP (Movement for the Survival of the Ogoni People). In 1992, Ken was arrested and held for months without being charged by the Nigerian military, then under the command of General Ibrahim Babangida. This further promoted the situation in Ogoniland, leading to rallies, protests, and some acts of sabotage against Shell operations in Nigeria. Eventually, Ken Saro-Wiwa was released and Shell closed down its operations in Ogoniland in early 1993. As the result of a coup, General Babangida ceded control of Nigeria to General Abacha. Although a civilian election was held in 1993, elected President Chief Moshood Abiola was never allowed to take control of the country. Under General Abacha, military actions against the Ogoni intensified.

Although Mr. Saro-Wiwa has been widely portrayed as a gentle, pipe-smoking ecomartyr, he was a far more complex figure, an ambitious—Ogoni political rivals say ruthless—leader. His movement focused on ecological protection after calculating that this would have appeal in the West, but its main goals were to win the region autonomous power and a share of its oil revenues" (Lewis, 1996). North (1996) asked the question, "can you be sure of Ken Saro-Wiwa?" Within this article, he notes that Saro-Wiwa is "widely believed to have feathered his nest when managing the Niger delta oil port of Bonny during the (Biafran) civil war". The article questions Saro-Wiwa's motives for being involved with the Ogoni plight, stating that "Saro-Wiwa certainly believed that the campaign was a useful route to fame and wealth, and told friends that because it had an environmental dimension it pushed all the right buttons in the West.

In May 1994, Ken Saro-Wiwa was again arrested and publicly accused of incitement to murder (of the four tribal chieftains) by the Rivers State Military Administrator. Both the *New York Times* and *The Economist* reported these accusations to represent "trumped up charges." Ken was tried not by an ordinary court but by a Civil Disturbances Special Tribunal whose judge was the nominee of the Nigerian military government. The Tribunal refused to admit into evidence a videotape and transcript of a government news conference that contradicted important testimony against Saro-Wiwa and his co-defendants. It also rejected defense evidence in the form of sworn affidavits of the bribery of two key prosecution witnesses by the military (in the presence of Shell officials according to *The Ecologist*, Nov. 1995, something Shell denies) in order to have them testify against Saro-Wiwa. The legal team for Saro-Wiwa then resigned, convinced that the trial was pre-determined to find the defendant guilty.

The trial was widely condemned by international human rights organizations and independent legal experts as breaching both international law and Nigeria's own constitution. Amnesty International judged the trial to be "blatantly unfair" and declared Saro-Wiwa a prisoner of conscience. A senior British lawyer, Michael Birnbaum QC, who observed the trial, found the military Tribunal to be "neither independent nor impartial" and concluded that "the breaches of fundamental rights are so serious" that any trial before this Tribunal would be "fundamentally flawed and unfair."

The military-appointed Special Tribunal found Saro-Wiwa and eight other defendants guilty and sentenced them to death on October 31, 1995. In regard to Saro-Wiwa, the judge concluded that "although Mr. Saro-Wiwa was not directly involved in the killings, it was established beyond all doubt that he set up the machinery that consumed the four Ogoni leaders." The decision was vociferously and widely condemned around the world, including by the leaders of the British Commonwealth then assembled in New Zealand and by the U.S. White House, which urged the Nigerian government "not to carry out executions and to commute the death sentences."

Prior to the executions, Shell urged quiet diplomacy prior to the executions, rather than public condemnation and pressure, insisting that it would be "dangerous and wrong" for the company to intervene to have the judgments overturned, for "a commercial organization like Shell cannot and must never interfere with the legal processes of any sovereign state" (Shell, October 31, 1995). After massive international pressure, however, Mr. Herkströter, Chairman of the Committee of Managing Directors of the Royal Dutch/Shell group of companies did send a last-minute personal letter to the Head of State of Nigeria requesting clemency on humanitarian grounds for Ken Saro-Wiwa and his co-defendants. The nine defendants were executed by hanging a few days later on November 10, 1995. After the executions, the company stated "We believe our most useful role is helping Nigeria overcome its economic problems and creating wealth that will give the people of Nigeria a better living standard and open up for them more options for progress and development. We will continue to try to perform this role with efficiency and integrity without becoming involved in politics" (Shell, November 14, 1995). Additionally, Shell called for "clear thinking in troubled times" (Shell, November 19, 1995). . . .

Post-Execution World Reaction

Sanctions

Official international reactions to the executions were swift yet rather mild. The Commonwealth suspended Nigeria's membership for two years. European governments took some trivial measures against Nigeria such as banning sporting contracts, restricting visas for members of the regime, and expelling Nigerian military attaches and withdrawing their own. The U.S. and Britain halted military sales to Nigeria and withdrew their ambassadors. The World Bank retracted its support for a $100 million loan. Several Nobel Laureates circulated a "Call to World Conscience." The U. N. General Assembly, after five weeks, passed a resolution condemning Nigeria, but with no sanctions. Bills to impose sanctions against Nigeria, called the "Nigeria Democracy Act," were introduced in the U.S. House of Representatives and U.S. Senate in November 1995, but had gone nowhere as of March 1997.

Non-governmental reactions were more strident and radical. Many media editorials called for massive punishment of Nigeria and Shell (see, for example, Nixon, 1995; Porritt, 1995; Hoagland, 1995; Herbert, 1996). Fifty-four prominent African Americans urged President Clinton to impose an oil embargo and other punitive measures against the military dictatorship of Nigeria. Dr. Owens Wiwa (Ken's brother) urged the U.S. Congressional Human Rights Caucus and Congressional Black Caucus to take a range of extraordinarily tough actions. The Shell Boycott Campaign, described above, was revved up in Europe and the Sierra Club initiated a high profile Shell Boycott and Nigeria Embargo effort in the U.S.

In mid-March 1996, the Clinton Administration circulated a proposal for strong new economic sanctions intended to force the Nigerian military government to move toward democracy. These included banning all new foreign investment in Nigeria (which totaled $1.95 billion in 1994) and freezing the financial assets of Nigeria's leaders in western banks. The plan ruled out any embargo against Nigerian oil exports (44% of Nigerian exports go to the U.S. market). The proposal received a cool reception from Britain, France and the Netherlands and an even colder one from the Corporate Council on Africa, which represents 80 U.S. firms doing business there, which argued that "economic growth provides the best foundation for any successful transition to democratic government" and warned that "a collapsing Nigerian economy serves no one's interests, especially not the 100 million Nigerians" (*New York Times*, March 13, 1996). . . .

Nigeria

As for the Nigerian military government, General Sani Abacha remained indignant at the global outcry (see referenced press coverage in *The Economist*, the *New York Times International*, *The Guardian* and the *International Herald Tribune* for further details) and the Nigerian government went on a public relations offensive:

> "The Lagos government employed the services of nine U.S. public relations and lobbying firms spanning the American political spectrum. Among them were the law firm of Washington & Christian, run by liberal black Democrats, which reported receiving $600,000 from Nigeria for the first six months of the year, and Symms, Lehn & Associates, an Alexandria firm headed by former Idaho senator Steve Symms (R) and Alfred Lehn, former aide to Bob Dole, which reported receiving $300,000. Based on disclosure reports and other information, Nigeria's critics have estimated that the regime has spent more than $10 million in the United States on lobbying and public relations efforts since the hanging" (*Washington Post*, November 24, 1996).

On Monday, April 21, 1997, a special 16 page advertising supplement was included in the *Wall Street Journal*, as a further effort to educate the business community concerning the current conditions in Nigeria.

A video and book entitled "Not in Our Character" was also produced for external consumption in which General Abacha assured viewers that Nigeria's bad image was being projected by people who "have become instruments or tools of foreign propaganda, a foreign machine to undermine the survival, the stability and subvert the unity of the nation" (*The Economist*, December 9, 1995). Also, in November, "the Nigerian Government announced formation of a 170-member committee set up to raise the living standards of Nigeria's 100 million people" (*New York Times*, November 29, 1996). In October, 1996, General Abacha was awarded a gold medal by the World Intellectual Property Agency (a United Nations agency). This award has caused a "diplomatic row" at the U.N. (Williams, *New York Times*, November 1, 1996).

The Economist (April 6, 1996) noted that while Nigeria may have weakened already strained ties with many Western nations, the regime is cultivating new eastern friends. Trade with China and Hong Kong is increasing, and ties with North Korea getting closer, possibly through arms deals. Iran and Russia have sent high level delegations, Iran's specifically to look at the oil industry. .

Nor is the general isolated in Africa, despite criticisms from Nelson Mandela and others. Nigeria is still strong in the Organization of African Unity, and the biggest shareholder in the African Development Bank. Nearer home it has its client states—Liberia, the Gambia and Sierra Leone—and wields influence over . . . Niger, Chad and Guinea. . . . Relations with Togo and Ghana are good. Sudan sees Nigeria's problems with the West as an opportunity to secure more influence for its own brand of Islamic fundamentalism—a prospect that worries many Nigerians just as it does western governments.

Additionally, as of April 1997, another 19 Ogoni prisoners were being held on charges of murdering the same four Ogoni politicians in July 1994 as the Ogoni 9 were executed for. According to Nebehay (1997), two U. N. human rights investigators, who have been seeking access to Nigeria since November 1995, were recently invited by the Nigerian government to visit Nigeria. The investigators hoped to check out (among other things) the status of the 19 Ogoni. Nebehay quotes a U. N. source who told Reuters that "there is concern that the tribunal before which these people are appearing lack independence and impartiality. There are questions of access to legal counsel and other due process questions."

According to *The Guardian* (Black, 1997), Nigerian opposition groups are currently applying pressure to have Nigeria expelled from the Commonwealth at its upcoming November meeting in Britain.

Ambassador Carrington recently retired from his position as U.S. Ambassador to Nigeria. According to the *New York Times*, "throughout Carrington's tenure in Nigeria, senior officials of that country have interpreted the deep chill that permeates ties between Washington and the Nigerian capital, Abuja, as the reflection of Carrington's efforts to poison relations" (French, 1997). Just prior to Carrington's departure, "heavily-armed policemen burst into a well-attended reception in Carrington's honor in Lagos last week, threatened to shoot one speaker, and ordered the foreign guests, including the American ambassador, to leave at once" (French, 1997). On October 6, 1997, Representative Maxine Waters (1997) introduced a resolution to the 105th Congress "condemning the Nigerian dictatorship for its abuse of United States Ambassador Walter Carrington". Since returning to the United States, Carrington told a New York City Council that "he was 'convinced' that the Nigerian military dictatorship was responsible" for the murder of democracy leader Kudirat Abiola (wife of the 1993 elected president of Nigeria) in 1996 (Africa Fund, 1997).

Abacha "has promised to hold elections next year (1998) and hand power to a civilian government on October 1, 1998. . . . 'If he declares his intention to stand for the presidency, the Nigerian army will support him absolutely,'" according to a statement signed by an army spokesman (AP, 1997).

Shell

As for Shell, the company has refused to heed calls to pull out of Nigeria, although it has made some visible changes with respect to its operations within Nigeria. Just a few days after Saro-Wiwa and his colleagues were executed, Shell signed a contract (as a 25.6% shareholder and technical adviser) to build a $3.8 billion natural gas liquefaction plant at Donny, in eastern Nigeria, noting that "the project demonstrated the commitment of Shell and its partners to the long term future of Nigeria and its people" (Shell, Dec. 15, 1995). In 1999, the plant at Bonny will begin producing 7 billion cubic meters per year, about 8 percent of the output of the world's eight big producers (Adams, 1996). A British Labour MEP noted that Shell with this announcement had "shown a mind-boggling degree of insensitivity" (*The Sunday Times*, Nov. 19, 1995). In March of 1996, Shell announced a potentially significant discovery of oil in a deep-water area off the coast of Nigeria and a commitment to proceed with tests to see how large the discovery was and whether production was commercially feasible. As one news editor concluded, this announcement sent "a strong signal to human rights groups"—that Shell doesn't "care what you say" and is "going to carry on doing business" with the Nigerian military regime (Darnton, 1996). In addressing why Shell is "reluctant to walk away" from its substantial operations in Nigeria, Corzine (1996b) noted that "Shell's proven oil reserves in the delta will last for 100 years at current production rates, and the company is more than replacing its output with new reserves."

The New York-based Center for Constitutional Rights, has recently filed a lawsuit against Royal Dutch Petroleum Company and Shell Transport and Trading Company alleging that Shell was part of a conspiracy that led to the November 1995 hangings by the military government of Nigeria. The suit was filed on behalf of Ken Owens Wiwa, the son and brother of Ken Saro-Wiwa and Blessing Kpuinen, the widow of John Kpuinen, who was also executed with Mr. Saro-Wiwa. . . .

———————

As further evidence of the company's recent commitment to human rights and the environment, in March 1997, The Royal Dutch/Shell Group issued (1) the Royal Dutch/Shell Group Commitment to Health, Safety and the Environment and (2) the Royal Dutch/Shell Group Health, Safety and Environmental Policy. These are included in Exhibit 2, along with the company's newly revised Statement of General Business Principles. . . .

The August 4, 1997 issue of *Fortune* described Shell as a corporation that "looked at the future and didn't like the view. Now it is changing everything from the way its managers act to the way it does business" (Guyon, 1997: 121).

The September 24, 1997 issue of the *Financial Times* analyzed the most respected companies in Europe, noting in particular that "corporate reputation can be a matter of time-lags. The rise of BP versus Shell can be partly explained by a run of bad publicity on Shell's part, involving the Brent Spar environmental controversy, human rights in Niger and so forth." In this article, Shell was reported as the 11th most respected company by European senior managers, dropping from a position of third in 1994. In a related article (Jackson, 1997), Shell was listed as the third most respected company in the oil, gas and mining sector, behind British Petroleum (U.K.) and Total (France).

On October 16, 1997, Royal Dutch/Shell announced that they plan to invest $500 million over the next five years to establish a fifth of their business in renewable energy, under the auspices of a new business organization known as Shell International Resources (SIR). This organization will consolidate operations in solar, biomass and forestry. SIR hopes to capture 10% of world solar energy market, currently valued at $1 billion annually.

Goldman (1997a) noted that "ethnic groups are demanding bigger share of pie" with respect to Nigerian oil operations. The Shell-Nigeria-Action (1997) list recently reported that "The Western Division of Shell Pet. Dev. Co. has threatened to stop exploration and exploitation of oil in the Niger Delta if youths in its areas of operations continue to attack its facilities and personnel," allegedly according to an October 8, 1997 letter from Mr. A. D. Aramabi, Shell's Manager External Relations–West, to the Chairman of the Military Task Force on Warri Crisis.

Bibliography

Adams, P. 1996. Nigeria joins the club of LNG exporters. *Financial Times,* January 17.

Africa Fund. 1997. U.S. Ambassador 'convinced' Nigerian regime murdered opponent—New York City votes to honor slain democracy leader. October 27 press release.

Associated Press. 1997. Army vows to support Nigerian leader. September 26 dispatch.

Billenness, S. 1996. Nigeria's boiling oil: Oil companies resist an embargo. *Investing for a Better World,* February 15.

Black, I. 1997. Commonwealth urged to throw out Nigeria. *The Guardian,* October 18.

Boyd, W. 1995. Introduction to: Saro-Wiwa, K. 1995. *A Month and a Day: A Detention Diary.* New York: Penguin. (also published in the November 27, 1995 issue of *The New Yorker*)

Brooks, G. 1994. Slick alliance: Shell's Nigerian fields produce few benefits for regions villagers; Despite huge oil revenues, firm and government neglect the impoverished; How troops handle protests. *The Wall Street Journal,* May 6.

Business Ethics Magazine. 1994, September.

Corzine, R. 1996a. Shell faces up to distrust in troubled delta province. *Financial Times.* July 6.

Corzine, R. 1996b. Shell plays for high stakes in Nigeria. *Financial Times.* July 8.

Corzine, R. and A. Goldman. 1997. Backers seek talks over Nigeria energy sackings. *Financial Times.* June 6.

Darnton, J. 1996. Shell makes a big oil discovery off Nigeria. *New York Times.* March 12.

de Jonquieres, G. 1997. Nigeria seen as most corrupt nation. *Financial Times.* August 1: 4.

Daily Telegraph, The. 1995. Oil-rich Shell is morally bankrupt. *The Daily Telegraph,* Nov. 18: 4.

Donovan, P. 1996. Oil inflames delta of discontent. *The Guardian,* July 6.

Earth Times, The. 1995. *The Earth Times,* November 30.

Ecologist, The. *The Ecologist Magazine.* November 1995.

Economist, The. 1995. Shell on the rocks. *The Economist,* June 24.

Economist, The. 1995. Nigeria Foaming. *The Economist,* November 18.

Economist, The. 1995. Multinationals and their Morals. *The Economist,* November 18.

Economist, The. 1995. After the hangings. *The Economist,* November 18.

Economist, The. 1995. *The Economist,* November 30.

Economist, The. 1995. *The Economist,* December 9.

Economist, The. 1996. The general in his not-so-solitude. *The Economist,* April 6.

Economist, The. 1996. Abacha wins. *The Economist,* November 9.

Economist, The. 1997. Poetic injustice. *The Economist.* October 11: 107.

Financial Times. 1997. Europe's most respected companies: BP steals the limelight from Shell. *Financial Times.* September 24.

Freedom House. 1995. Freedom in the world 1994–1995: The annual survey of political rights and civil liberties, 1994–1995. New York: Freedom House.

French, H. W. 1995. Deadly logic in Nigeria. *New York Times.* November 12.

French, H. W. 1997. U.S. Envoy to Nigeria is given stormy farewell. *New York Times,* September 26.

Gladwin, T. N. and I. Walter. 1980. Multinationals and Human Rights. In: *Multinationals under fire: Lessons in the management of conflict.* New York: John Wiley (pp. 142–147).

Goldman, A. 1997a. Nigerian violence rattles oil giants: Ethnic groups are demanding bigger share of pie. *Financial Times,* May 1.

Goldman, A. 1997b. Nigerian military retires hurt: Botched intervention in Sierra Leone has left the army regime morally exposed. *Financial Times.*

Gribben, R. 1996. Shell fights to change oil deal with Nigeria. *The Daily Telegraph.* July 8.

Guardian, The. 1995. *The Guardian.* November 16 and 18.

Guyon, J. 1997. Why is the world's most profitable company turning itself inside out? *Fortune,* August 4: 120–125.

Herbert, B. 1996. Unholy alliance in Nigeria. *Liberal Opinion Week.* February 5.

Herkströter, C. 1997. Contributing to a sustainable future—The Royal Dutch/Shell Group in the global economy. Text of speech made at Erasmus University, Rotterdam, The Netherlands, March 17.

Hillenbrand, B. 1996. Seeing the light in Nigeria: No longer able to ignore criticism, Shell changes its tune in Nigeria. *Time,* November 25.

Hoagland, J. 1995. Big oil companies fuel rogue regimes. *Liberal Opinion Week.* December 11: 5.

Independent, The. 1995. December 1.

International Herald Tribune, The. 1996. Sanctions on Nigeria. *International Herald Tribune,* May. 7.

Jackson, T. 1997. European Business Challenges: East and west agree to differ. *Financial Times.* September 24.

Lewis, P. 1996. After Nigeria represses, Shell defends its record. *New York Times International,* Feb. 13.

Lewis, P. 1996. Nigerian group defends the execution of 9 Nigerian activists. *New York Times International,* December 7.

McGreal, C. 1995. Nigeria's hangman defends his country's honor. *The Guardian.* November 17: 1.

Mortished, C. 1996. No longer in glorious isolation. *The Times.* July 8.

Nebehay, S. 1997. Switzerland: UN rights envoys hope to see Nigeria's jailed Ogonis. Reuter's new release from Geneva, July 2.

New York Times. 1996. March 13.

New York Times. 1996. Nigeria's leader presses makeover of the economy and his image. *New York Times International.* November 29.

Nigeria. 1997. Nigeria. Advertising Supplement to the *Wall Street Journal.* April 21: D1–D16.

Nixon, R. 1995. The Oil Weapon. Nov. 17.

North, R. D. 1996. Can you be sure of Ken Saro-Wiwa. *The Independent,* November 8.

Obe, A. 1995. Sanction for Sanity. *The Guardian.* November 13.

Porritt, J. 1995. Oil-rich Shell is morally bankrupt. *The Daily Telegraph,* November 18: 4.

Reif, D. 1997. The threat of death: The ruin of Nigeria, the ruin of Africa. *The New Republic,* June 16.

Roddick, A. 1995a. Shell should speak out to help the Ogoni. *Financial Times,* November 1.

Roddick, A. 1995b. Shell not responsible in Nigeria? Get out of it! Open Editorial. November 21.

Roddick, A. 1995c. Shell must heed the danger. *The Independent,* November 28.

Robinson, D. 1996. *Ogoni: The struggle continues.* World Council of Churches: Geneva, Switzerland.

Royal Dutch/Shell Group of Companies. 1997. Statement of General Business Principals. March.

Saro-Wiwa, K. 1992. Genocide in Nigeria: The Ogoni tragedy (Chapter 7: The Autonomy Option, pp. 92–103). London: Saros International Publishers.

Saro-Wiwa, K. 1995. *A Month and a Day: A Detention Diary.* New York: Penguin.

Shell Petroleum Development Company. 1995. *Nigeria Brief: The Ogoni Issue.* The Shell Petroleum Development Company of Nigeria, Limited. January 25.

Shell Petroleum Development Company. 1995. *Nigeria Brief: The Environment.* The Shell Petroleum Development Company of Nigeria, Limited. May.

Shell. 1995. Construction contract signed for Nigeria LNG project. Shell Press release obtained at www.shellnigeria.com/news/prl19.html. December 15.

Shell. 1995. Clear thinking in troubled times. Shell Press release obtained at www.shellnigeria.com/news/prl12.html. November 19.

Shell. 1995. Execution of Ken Saro-Wiwa and his co-defendants. Shell Press release obtained at www.shellnigeria.com/news/prl15.html. November 14.

Shell. 1995. The environment and Ogoni land. Shell Press release obtained at www.shellnigeria.com/news/prl15.html. November 12.

Shell. 1995. Verdict on Mr. Ken Saro-Wiwa and Others. Shell Press release obtained at www.shellnigeria.com/news/prl18.html. October 31.

Shell. 1996. Shell reaffirms support for human rights and fair trial. Shell press release obtained at www.shellnigeria.com/news/prl10.html. January 30.

Shell. 1997. WCC Report "Ogoni - the struggle continues": Comments by Shell. Final draft for discussion with the World Council of Churches.

Shell Company Website: http://www.shellnigeria.com/

Shell-Nigeria-Action. 1997. Posting to the e-mail list shell-nigeria-action@essential.org on October 27.

Sierra Club Legal Defense Fund. The 1994 Draft Declaration of Principals on Human Rights and the Environment. The Sierra Club Legal Defense Fund and multiple other international organizations.

Sierra Club. December 17, 1996.

Sunday Times. 1995. November 19.

United Nations. 1948. Universal Declaration of Human Rights.

United Nations. 1966. International Covenant on Civil and Political Rights (ICCPR).

Wagstyl, S. and R. Corzine. 1997. Rights and wrongs. *Financial Times,* March 18.

Wall Street Journal, The. 1996. Shell earnings set a record. *Wall Street Journal,* May 10.

Washington Post, The. 1996. Nigeria mixes oil and money: A potent formula keeps U.S. sanctions at Bay. *Washington Post,* November 24.

Waters, Congresswoman M. 1997. Resolution condemning the Nigerian dictatorship for its abuse of United States Ambassador Carrington. Introduced to the U.S. House of Representatives on October 6.

Watts, P. 1997. A developing contribution - Shell companies in Africa. Speech made at 4th African–African American Summit, Harare, July 21–25.

Wheeler, D. 1995. Blood on British business hands.

Williams, 1996. *New York Times,* November 1.

EXHIBIT 1. Maps of Nigeria. *Source: The New York Times*

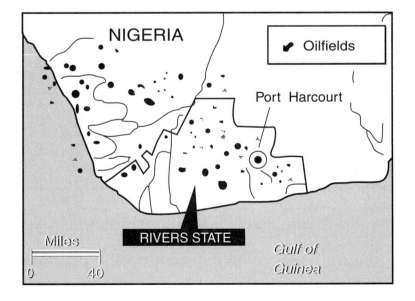

EXHIBIT 1. *(Continued)* Map of Shell Petroleum Development Company (SPDC) Nigerian Oilfields

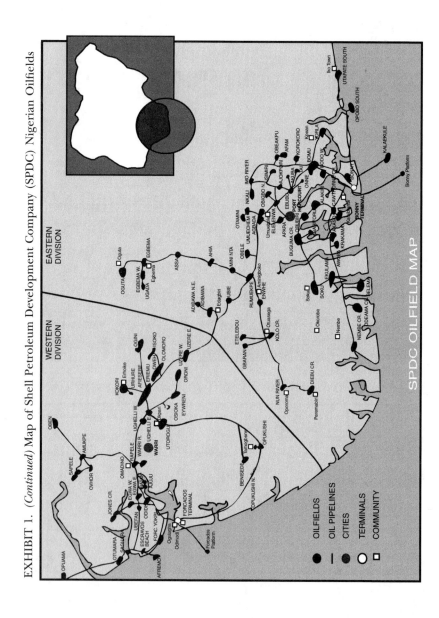

EXHIBIT 2. Royal Dutch/Shell Group Commitment
to Health, Safety and the Environment*

In the Group we are all committed to

- pursue the goal of no harm to people
- protect the environment
- use material and energy efficiently to provide our products and services
- develop energy resources, products and services consistent with these aims
- publicly report on our performance
- play a leading role in promoting best practice in our industries
- manage HSE matters as any other critical business activity
- promote a culture in which all Shell employees share this commitment.

In this way we aim to have an HSE performance we can be proud of, to earn the confidence of customers, shareholders and society at large, to be a good neighbour and to contribute to sustainable development.

ROYAL DUTCH/SHELL GROUP HEALTH, SAFETY AND ENVIRONMENTAL POLICY

Every Shell company

- has a systematic approach to HSE management designed to ensure compliance with the law and to achieve continuous performance improvement
- sets targets for improvement and measures, appraises and reports performance
- requires contractors to manage HSE in line with this policy
- requires joint ventures under its operational control to apply this policy and uses its influence to promote it in its other ventures
- includes HSE performance in the appraisal of all staff and rewards accordingly.

EXHIBIT 2. *(Continued)* Royal Dutch/Shell Group of Companies,
Statement of General Business Principles

INTRODUCTION

This document reaffirms the general business principles that govern how each of the Shell companies which make up the Royal Dutch/Shell Group of Companies conducts its affairs.

The Group is a decentralised, diversified group of companies with widespread activities, and each Shell company has wide freedom of action. However what we have in common is the Shell reputation. Upholding the Shell reputation is paramount. We are judged by how we act. Our reputation will be upheld if we act with honesty and integrity in all our dealings and we do what we think is right at all times within the legitimate role of business.

Shell companies have as their core values honesty, integrity and respect for people. Shell companies also firmly believe in the fundamental importance of the promotion of trust, openness, teamwork and professionalism, and in pride in what they do.

Our underlying corporate values determine our principles. These principles apply to all transactions, large or small, and describe the behaviour expected of every employee in every Shell company in the conduct of its business.

In turn, the application of these principles is underpinned by procedures within each Shell company which are designed to make sure that its employees understand the principles and that they act in accordance with them. We recognise that it is vital that our behaviour matches our intentions.

All the elements of this structure—values, principles and the accompanying procedures—are necessary.

Shell companies recognise that maintaining the trust and confidence of shareholders, employees, customers and other people with whom they do business, as well as the communities in which they work, is crucial to the Group's continued growth and success.

We intend to merit this trust by conducting ourselves according to the standards set out in our principles. These principles have served Shell companies well for many years. It is the responsibility of management to ensure that all employees are aware of these principles, and behave in accordance with the spirit as well as the letter of this statement.

1. Objectives

The objectives of Shell companies are to engage efficiently, responsibly and profitably in the oil, gas, chemicals and other selected businesses and to participate in the search for and development of other sources of energy. Shell companies seek a high standard of performance and aim to maintain a long-term position in their respective competitive environments.

2. Responsibilities

Shell companies recognise five areas of responsibility:

a. To shareholders
To protect shareholders' investment, and provide an acceptable return.

b. To customers
To win and maintain customers by developing and providing products and services which offer value in terms of price, quality, safety and environmental impact, which are supported by the requisite technological, environmental and commercial expertise.

c. To employees
To respect the human rights of their employees, to provide their employees with good and safe conditions of work, and good and competitive terms and conditions of service, to promote the development and best use of human talent and equal opportunity employment, and to encourage the involvement of employees in the planning and direction of their work, and in the application of these principles within their company. It is recognised that commercial success depends on the full commitment of all employees.

d. To those with whom they do business

To seek mutually beneficial relationships with contractors, suppliers and in joint ventures and to promote the application of these principles in so doing. The ability to promote these principles effectively will be an important factor in the decision to enter into or remain in such relationships.

e. To society

To conduct business as responsible corporate members of society, to observe the laws of the countries in which they operate, to express support for fundamental human rights in line with the legitimate role of business and to give proper regard to health, safety and the environment consistent with their commitment to contribute to sustainable development.

These five areas of responsibility are seen as inseparable. Therefore it is the duty of management continuously to assess the priorities and discharge its responsibilities as best it can on the basis of that assessment.

3. Economic Principles

Profitability is essential to discharging these responsibilities and staying in business. It is a measure both of efficiency and of the value that customers place on Shell products and services. It is essential to the allocation of the necessary corporate resources and to support the continuing investment required to develop and produce future energy supplies to meet consumer needs. Without profits and a strong financial foundation it would not be possible to fulfil the responsibilities outlined above.

Shell companies work in a wide variety of changing social, political and economic environments, but in general they believe that the interests of the community can be served most efficiently by a market economy.

Criteria for investment decisions are not exclusively economic in nature but also take into account social and environmental considerations and an appraisal of the security of the investment.

4. Business Integrity

Shell companies insist on honesty, integrity and fairness in all aspects of their business and expect the same in their relationships with all those with whom they do business. The direct or indirect offer, payment, soliciting and acceptance of bribes in any form are unacceptable practices. Employees must avoid conflicts of interest between their private financial activities and their part in the conduct of company business. All business transactions on behalf of a Shell company must be reflected accurately and fairly in the accounts of the company in accordance with established procedures and be subject to audit.

5. Political Activities

a. Of companies

Shell companies act in a socially responsible manner within the laws of the countries in which they operate in pursuit of their legitimate commercial objectives.

Shell companies do not make payments to political parties, organisations or their representatives or take any part in party politics. However, when dealing with governments, Shell companies have the right and the responsibility to make their position known on any matter which affects themselves, their employees, their customers, or their shareholders. They also have the right to make their position known on matters affecting the community, where they have a contribution to make.

b. Of employees

Where individuals wish to engage in activities in the community, including standing for election to public office, they will be given the opportunity to do so where this is appropriate in the light of local circumstances.

6. Health, Safety and the Environment

Consistent with their commitment to contribute to sustainable development, Shell companies have a systematic approach to health, safety and environmental management in order to achieve continuous performance improvement.

To this end Shell companies manage these matters as any other critical business activity, set targets for improvement, and measure, appraise and report performance.

7. The Community

The most important contribution that companies can make to the social and material progress of the countries in which they operate is in performing their basic activities as effectively as possible. In addition Shell companies take a constructive interest in societal matters which may not be directly related to the business. Opportunities for involvement—for example through community, educational or donations programmes—will vary depending upon the size of the company concerned, the nature of the local society, and the scope for useful private initiatives.

8. Competition

Shell companies support free enterprise. They seek to compete fairly and ethically and within the framework of applicable competition laws; they will not prevent others from competing freely with them.

9. Communication

Shell companies recognise that in view of the importance of the activities in which they are engaged and their impact on national economies and individuals, open communication is essential. To this end, Shell companies have comprehensive corporate information programmes and provide full relevant information about their activities to legitimately interested parties, subject to any overriding considerations of business confidentiality and cost.

---

*Endorsed by the Committee of Managing Directors. March 1997.

Scarcity or Abundance?

JULIAN L. SIMON

Is a big wheat harvest a good thing? Sometimes we read headlines such as "Good harvest, bad news"—the bad news being for wheat farmers, who face low prices. On balance a big harvest surely is better for society as a whole than a small harvest. Still, the headline is negative, as if a bad thing has happened.

Is the trend of black infant mortality rates discouraging? Take a look at Figure 1 and make your judgment, please. My own judgment is that the overall picture is good for blacks as well as for the community as a whole, because many fewer babies are dying nowadays than in earlier years and many fewer parents need to grieve. Unless you focus only on the *relative* positions of the two groups, there seems slim basis for judging the situation as bad, unless you enjoy being morally indignant.

This is the point of these examples: viewing the same facts, one person may be optimistic while the other is pessimistic. The contradiction often happens because persons judge from different points of view. Frequently the root of the difference is the length of the period you focus on—the short run or the long run. For many issues—and especially issues related to economic and population growth—the long-run effect is the opposite of the

FIGURE 1. Black and White Infant Mortality Rate (per 1,000 live births)

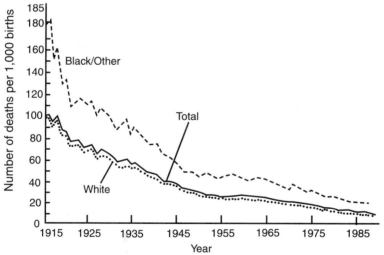

Source: U.S. Dept. of Commerce Bureau of the Census, *Historical Statistics of the United States: Colonial Times to 1970* (GPO, Washington, D.C., 1976); U.S. Dept. of Commerce Bureau of the Census, *Statistical Abstract of the United States* (GPO, Washington, D.C., various years).

short-run effect. More people are an economic benefit in the long run, though they are a burden in the short run.

My central proposition here is simply stated: Almost every trend that affects human welfare points in a positive direction, as long as we consider a reasonably long period of time and hence grasp the overall trend. . . .

I will first review some important absolute trends in human welfare. To repeat, my thesis is that just about every important measure of human welfare shows improvement over the decades and centuries.

Let's start with some trends and conclusions that have long represented the uncontroversial settled wisdom of the economists and other experts who work in these fields, except for the case of population growth. On that latter subject, what you read below was a minority viewpoint until sometime in the 1980s, at which point the mainstream scientific opinion shifted almost all the way to the position set forth here.

Length of Life

The most important and amazing demographic fact—the greatest human achievement in history—is the decrease in the world's death rate. We see that it took thousands of years for life expectancy at birth to increase from just over twenty years to the high 20s. Then, in just the past two centuries, the length of life you could expect for your newborn child in the advanced countries jumped from perhaps thirty years to about seventy-five years. It is this decrease in the death rate that is the cause of there being a larger world population nowadays than in former times. Is this not the greatest change that humankind has ever experienced?

Then, starting well after World War II, the length of life one could expect in the *poor* countries leaped upward by perhaps fifteen or even twenty years, caused by advances in agriculture, sanitation, and medicine. Are not these trends remarkably benign?

Agricultural Labor Force

The best simple measure of a country's standard of living is the proportion of the labor force that works in agriculture. If almost everyone works at farming, there can be little production of non-agricultural goods. We see the astonishing decline over the centuries in the proportion of the population working in agriculture in Great Britain to only about one person in fifty, and the same story describes the United States. This has enabled us to increase our consumption per person by a factor perhaps of 20 or 40 over the centuries.

Raw Materials

During all of human existence, people have worried about running out of natural resources—flint, game animals, what have you. Amazingly, all the evidence shows that exactly the opposite has been true. Raw materials—all of them—are becoming more available rather than more scarce.

Data clearly shows that natural resource scarcity—as measured by the economically meaningful indicator of cost or price for copper, which is representative of all raw materials—has been decreasing rather than increasing in the long run, with only temporary exceptions from time to time. In the case of copper, we have evidence that the trend of falling prices has been going on for a very long time. In the eighteenth century BCE in Babylonia under Hammurabi—almost 4,000 years ago—the price of copper was about 1,000 times its price in the United States now, relative to wages. And there is no reason why this downward trend might not continue forever.

The trend toward greater availability includes the most counterintuitive case of all—oil. The price rises in crude oil since the 1970s did not stem from increases in the cost of world supply, but rather cartel political action. The production cost in the Persian Gulf still is perhaps 25–75 cents per barrel (1993 dollars). Concerning energy in general, there is no reason to believe that the supply of energy is finite, or that the price of energy will not continue its long-run decrease forever. I realize that it seems strange that the supply of energy is not finite or limited, but if you want a full discussion of the subject, I hope that you will consult another of my books.[1]

Food

Food is an especially important resource. The evidence is particularly strong for food that we are on a benign trend despite rising population. The long-run price of wheat relative to wages, and even relative to consumer products, is down, due to increased productivity.

Famine deaths have decreased during the past century even in absolute terms, let alone relative to population, which pertains particularly to the poor countries. Food consumption per person is up over the last thirty years. Africa's food production per person is down, but by 1993 few people still believe that Africa's suffering has anything to do with a shortage of land or water or sun. Hunger in Africa clearly stems from civil wars and the collectivization of agriculture, which periodic droughts have made more murderous.

Human Life and Labor

There is only one important resource which has shown a trend of increasing scarcity rather than increasing abundance—human beings. Yes, there are more people on Earth now than ever before. But if we measure the scarcity of people the same way that we measure the scarcity of other economic goods—by how much we must pay to obtain their services—we see that wages and salaries have been going up all over the world, in poor as well as rich countries. The amount that you must pay to obtain the services of a manager or a cook has risen in India, just as the price of a cook or manager has risen in the United States over the decades. The increases in the prices of people's services are a clear indication that people are becoming more scarce economically even though there are more of us.

Cleanliness of the Environment

Ask an average roomful of people if our environment is becoming dirtier or cleaner, and most will say "dirtier." The irrefutable facts are that the air in the United States (and in other rich countries) is safer to breathe now than in decades past. The quantities of pollutants have been declining, especially particulates which are the main pollutant. The proportion of sites monitoring water of good drinkability in the United States has increased since the data began in 1961. Our environment is increasingly healthy, with every prospect that this trend will continue.

The Vanishing Farmland Crisis

The supposed problem of farmland being urbanized has now been entirely discredited, out-and-out disavowed by those who created the scare. This saga serves to illuminate many similar environmental issues.

The Greenhouse Effect, the Ozone Layer, and Acid Rain

What about the greenhouse effect? The ozone layer? Acid rain? I'm not a technical expert on the atmosphere. I can say with confidence, however, that on all of these issues there is major scientific controversy about what has happened until now, why it happened, and what might happen in the future. All of these scares are recent, and there has not yet been time for complete research to be done and for the intellectual dust to settle. There may be hard problems here, or there may not.

Even more important for people is that no threatening trend in *human welfare* has been connected to those phenomena. There has been no increase in skin cancers from ozone, no damage to agriculture from a greenhouse effect, and at most slight damage to lakes from acid rain. It may even be that a greenhouse effect would benefit us on balance by warming some areas we'd like warmer, and by increasing the carbon dioxide to agriculture.

Perhaps the most important aspect of the greenhouse—ozone-acid rain complex, and of their as-yet-unknown cousin scares which will surely be brought before the public in the future, is that we now have large and ever-increasing capabilities to reverse such trends if they are proven to be dangerous, and at costs that are manageable. Dealing with greenhouse–ozone–acid rain would not place an insuperable constraint upon growth, and would not constitute an ultimate limit upon the increase of productive output or of population. So we can look these issues squarely in the eye and move on.

ARE THESE PREDICTIONS SURE ENOUGH TO BET ON?

I am so sure of all these upbeat statements that I offer to bet on them, my winnings going to fund new research. Here is the offer: You pick (a) any measure of human welfare—such as life expectancy, infant mortality, the price of aluminum or gasoline, the amount of education per cohort of young people, the rate of ownership of television sets, you name it; (b) a country (or a region such as the developing countries, or the world as a whole); (c) any future year, and I'll bet a week's or a month's pay that that indicator shows improvement relative to the present while you bet that it shows deterioration.

1.   Here is the overarching theory that I offer you to explain why things happen exactly the opposite of the way Malthus and the contemporary Malthusians predict—and why I offer to bet that any measure of human welfare that you choose will show improvement rather than deterioration.

In 1951, Theodore Schultz published an article called "The Declining Economic Importance of Land." He showed that because of technological change, two related things were happening: Food production per person was going up, and the need for agricultural land was going down—even as population was growing very fast. In 1963, Harold Barnett and Chandler Morse showed that despite all the theory about limited quantities of raw materials, and reducing richness of the lodes that are mined, all the raw materials they studied had become less expensive and more available for the decades since the 1870s. A general process underlies these specific findings: Human beings create more than they use, on average. It had to be so, or we would be an extinct species. And this process is, as the physicists say, an invariancy. It applies to all metals, all fuels, all foods, and all other measures of human welfare, and it applies in all countries, and at all times. In other words, this is a theory of "everything economic," or really, a theory of economic history.

2.   Consider this example of the process by which people wind up with increasing availability rather than decreasing availability of resources. England was full of alarm in the 1600s at an impending shortage of energy due to the deforestation of the country for firewood. People feared a scarcity of fuel for both heating and the iron industry. This impending scarcity led to the development of coal.

Then in the mid-1800s, the English came to worry about an impending coal crisis. The great English economist W. S. Jevons calculated that a shortage of coal would bring England's industry to a standstill by 1900; he carefully assessed that oil could never make a decisive difference. Triggered by the impending scarcity of coal (and of whale oil, whose story comes next), ingenious profit-minded people developed oil into a more desirable fuel than coal ever was. And in 1993 we find England exporting both coal and oil.

Another element in the story: Because of increased demand due to population growth and increased income, the price of whale oil for lamps jumped in the 1840s, and the U. S. Civil War pushed it even higher, leading to a whale oil "crisis." This provided incentive for enterprising people to discover and produce substitutes. First came oil from rapeseed, olives, linseed, and camphene oil from pine trees. Then inventors learned how to get coal oil from coal. Other ingenious persons produced kerosene from the rock oil that seeped to the surface, a product so desirable that its price then rose from $0:75 a gallon to $2:00. This high price stimulated enterprisers to focus on the supply of oil, and finally Edwin L. Drake brought in his famous well in Titusville, Pennsylvania. Learning how to refine the oil took a while. But in a few years there were hundreds of small refiners in the United States, and soon the bottom fell out of the whale oil market, the price falling from $2:50 or more at its peak around 1866 to well below $1:00.

We should note that it was not the English or American governments that developed coal or oil, because governments are not effective developers of new technology. Rather, it was individual entrepreneurs who sensed the need, saw opportunity, used all kinds of available information and ideas, made lots of false starts which were very costly to many of those individuals but not to others, and eventually arrived at coal as a viable fuel—because there were enough independent individuals investigating the matter for at least some of them to arrive at sound ideas and methods. And this happened in the context of a competitive enterprise system that worked to produce what was needed by the public. And the entire process of impending shortage and new solution left us better off than if the shortage problem had never arisen.

Here we must address *another crucial element in the economics of resources and population*—the extent to which the *political-social-economic system provides personal freedom* from government coercion. Skilled persons require an appropriate social and economic framework that provides incentives for working hard and taking risks, enabling their talents to flower and come to fruition. The key elements of such a framework are economic liberty, respect for property, and fair and sensible rules of the market that are enforced equally for all.

3.   The world's problem is not too many people, but lack of political and economic freedom. Powerful evidence comes from pairs of countries that have the same culture and history, and had much the same standard of living when they split apart after World War II—East and West Germany, North and South Korea, Taiwan and China. In each case the centrally planned communist country began with less population "pressure," as measured by density per square kilometer, than did the market-directed economy. And the communist and non-communist countries also started with much the same birth rates. But the market-directed economies have performed much better economically than the centrally planned economies. This powerful explanation of economic development cuts the ground from under population growth as a likely explanation.

4.   In 1993 there is an important new element not present twenty years ago. The scientific community now agrees with almost all of what you have just heard. My comments today do not represent a single lone voice, but rather the scientific consensus.

The earlier remarks about agriculture and resources have always represented the consensus of economists in those fields. And now the consensus of population economists also is not far from what I have said to you.

In 1986, the National Research Council and the National Academy of Sciences published a book on population growth and economic development prepared by a prestigious scholarly group. This "official" report reversed almost completely the frightening conclusions of the previous 1971 NAS report. "Population growth at *most* a minor factor. . . . The scarcity of exhaustible resources is at most a minor constraint on economic growth," it now says. It found benefits of additional people as well as costs.

A host of review articles by distinguished economic demographers in the last three or four years have confirmed that this "revisionist" view is indeed consistent with the scientific evidence, though not all the writers would go as far as I do in pointing out the positive long-run effects of population growth. The consensus is more toward a "neutral" judgment. But this is a huge change from the earlier judgment that population growth is economically detrimental.

By 1993, anyone who asserts that population growth damages the economy must either be unaware of the recent economic literature on the subject, or turn a blind eye to the scientific evidence.

5.   There are many reasons why the public hears false bad news about population, resources, and the environment. Many of these matters are discussed in my earlier books. But lately I have come to emphasize the role of unsound logic and scientific understanding.

These are some of the elements of bad thinking that predispose people to doomsday thinking: (a) Lack of understanding of statistical variability, and of the consequent need for looking at a large and representative sample and not just a few casual observations. (b) Lack of historical perspective, and the need for looking at long time series and not just a few recent observations. (c) Lack of proportion in judgments. (d) Lack of understanding of the Hume-Hayek idea of spontaneously evolving cooperative social systems—Adam Smith's "invisible hand." (e) Seduction by exponential growth and the rest of Malthusian thinking. (f) Lack of understanding of Frédéric Bastiat's and Henry Hazlitt's one key lesson of policy economics—that we must consider not just the short-run effects of an action that we might take but also the effects well into the future, and not just the local effect but also the effect on faraway communities. That is, we must take into account not just the immediate and obvious impacts, but also the slow-responding adjustments which diffuse far from the point of initial contact and which often have the opposite result from the short-run localized effects.

6.   In response to questions about species extinction, the World Conservation Union (IUCN) commissioned a book edited by Whitmore and Sayer (1992) to inquire into the extent of extinctions that appeared after the first draft of this book. The results of that project must be considered amazing. All the authors are ecologists who express concern about the rate of extinction. Nevertheless, they all agree that the rate of *known* extinctions has been and continues to be very low. This is a sampling of quotations (with emphasis supplied), first on the subject of the estimated rates:

> . . . *60 birds and mammals are known to have become extinct between 1900 and 1950.* (Reid, 1992, p. 55)
>
> [F]orests of the eastern United States were reduced over two centuries to fragments totalling 1–2% of their original extent . . . during this destruction, only three forest birds went extinct—the Carolina parakeet (Conuropsis carolinensis), the ivory-billed woodpecker (Campephilus principalis principalis), and the passenger pigeon (Ectopistes migratorius). Although deforestation certainly contributed to the decline of all three species, it was probably not critical for the pigeon or the parakeet (Greenway, 1967). *Why, then, would one predict massive extinction from similar destruction of tropical forest?* (Simberloff, 1992, p. 85)
>
> IUCN, together with the World Conservation Monitoring Centre, has amassed large volumes of data from specialists around the world relating to

species decline, and it would seem sensible to compare these more empirical data with the global extinction estimates. In fact, these and other data indicate that *the number of recorded extinctions for both plants and animals is very small. . . .* (Heywood and Stuart, 1992, p. 93)

Known extinction rates are very low. Reasonably good data exist only for mammals and birds, and the current rate of extinction is about one species per year (Reid and Miller, 1989). If other taxa were to exhibit the same liability to extinction as mammals and birds (as some authors suggest, although others would dispute this), then, if the total number of species in the world is, say, 30 million, the annual rate of extinction would be some 2300 species per year. This is a very significant and disturbing number, but it is much less than most estimates given over the last decade. (Heywood and Stuart, 1992, p. 94)

. . . if we assume that today's tropical forests occupy only about 80% of the area they did in the 1830s, *it must be assumed that during this contraction, very large numbers of species have been lost in some areas. Yet surprisingly there is no clear-cut evidence for this. . . .* Despite extensive enquiries we have been unable to obtain conclusive evidence to support the suggestion that massive extinctions have taken place in recent times as Myers and others have suggested. On the contrary, work on projects such as Flora Meso-Americana has, at least in some cases, revealed an increase in abundance in many species (Blackmore, pers. comm. 1991). An exceptional and much quoted situation is described by Gentry (1986) who reports the quite dramatic level of evolution in situ in the Centinela ridge in the foothills of the Ecuadorian Andes where he found that at least 38 and probably as many as 90 species (10% of the total flora of the ridge) were endemic to the "unprepossessing ridge." However, the last patches of forest were cleared subsequent to his last visit and "its prospective 90 new species have already passed into botanical history," or so it was assumed. Subsequently, Dodson and Gentry (1991) modified this to say that an undetermined number of species at Centinela are apparently extinct, following brief visits to other areas such as Lita where *up to 11 of the species previously considered extinct were refound,* and at Poza Honda near La Mana where six were rediscovered. (Heywood and Stuart, 1992, p. 96)

. . . *actual extinctions remain low. . . . "Many endangered species appear to have either an almost miraculous capacity for survival,* or a guardian angel is watching over their destiny! This means that it is not too late to attempt to protect the Mediterranean flora as a whole, while still identifying appropriate priorities with regard to the goals and means of conservation." (Heywood and Stuart, 1992, p. 102)

. . . *the group of zoologists could not find a single known animal species which could be properly declared as extinct,* in spite of the massive reduction in area and fragmentation of their habitats in the past decades and centuries of intensive human activity. A second list of over 120 lesser-known animal species, some of which may later be included as threatened, show no species considered extinct; and the older Brazilian list of threatened plants, presently under revision, also indicated no species as extinct. . . . (Brown and Brown, 1992, p. 127)

Closer examination of the existing data on both well- and little-known groups, however, *supports the affirmation that little or no species extinction has yet occurred* (though some may be in very fragile persistence) in the Atlantic forests. Indeed, an appreciable number of species considered extinct 20 years ago, including several birds and six butterflies, have been rediscovered more recently. (Brown and Brown, 1992, p. 128)

And here are some comments from that volume on the lack of any solid basis for estimation:

... How large is the loss of species likely to be? *Although the loss of species may rank among the most significant environmental problems of our time, relatively few attempts have been made to rigorously assess its likely magnitude.* (Reid, 1992, p. 55)

It is impossible to estimate even approximately how many unrecorded species may have become extinct. (Heywood and Stuart, 1992, p. 95)

While better knowledge of extinction rates can clearly improve the design of public policies, it is equally apparent that *estimates of global extinction rates are fraught with imprecision. We do not yet know how many species exist, even to within an order of magnitude.* (Reid, 1992, p. 56)

... the literature addressing this phenomenon is relatively small.... Efforts to clarify the magnitude of the extinction crisis and the steps that can be taken to defuse the crisis could considerably expand the financial and political support for actions to confront what is indisputably the most serious issue that the field of ecology faces, and arguably the most serious issue faced by humankind today. (Reid, 1992, p. 57)

The best tool available to estimate species extinction rates is the use of species-area curves.... This approach has formed the basis for almost all current estimates of species extinction rates. (Reid, 1992, p. 57)

There are many reasons why recorded extinctions do not match the predictions and extrapolations that are frequently published.... (Heywood and Stuart, 1992, p. 93)

9.   The most important difference between my and ... the doomsters' approach to environmental issues is that I base my conclusions on the historical record of the past rather than Malthusian speculation that is inconsistent with the historical statistical record.

Note

1. See *The Ultimate Resource* (1981, or 2nd edition, forthcoming), chapters 1–3.

References

Brown, K. S., and G. G. Brown 1992. "Habitat Alteration and Species Loss in Brazilian Forests," in T. C. Whitmore, and J. A. Sayer, eds., *Tropical Forest and Species Extinction*, pp. 119–142.

Heywood, V. H., and S. N. Stuart 1992 "Species Extinctions in Tropical Forests," in T. C. Whitmore and J. A. Sayer, eds., *Tropical Deforestation and Species Extinction*, pp. 91–118.

National Academy of Sciences, *Rapid Population Growth: Consequences and Policy Implications*. Baltimore: Johns Hopkins University Press, 1971.

Reid, W. V., "How Many Species Will There Be?", in T. C. Whitmore and J. A. Sayer, eds., 1992. *Tropical Deforestation and Species Extinction*.

Simberloff, D., "Do Species-Area Curves Predict Extinction in Fragmented Forest?", in Whitmore and Sayer, eds., *Tropical Deforestation and Species Extinction*.

Simon, Julian L., *Economics of Population Growth*. Princeton: Princeton University Press, 1977; translated into Chinese, Beijing: Peking University Press, 1984.

———— , *The Ultimate Resource*. Princeton: Princeton University Press, 1981.

Whitmore, T. C., and J. A. Sayer, eds., *Tropical Deforestation and Species Extinction*. New York: Chapman and Hall, 1992.

Holes in the Cornucopia

ERNEST PARTRIDGE

INTRODUCTION

Why take Julian Simon seriously?

This economist has asked us to believe such things as the following:

- The supply of natural resources [is] really infinite![1]
- There is no reason to believe that at any given moment in the future the available quantity of any natural resource or service at present prices will be much smaller than it is now, or nonexistent.[2]
- "We now have in our hands—in our libraries, really—the technology to feed, clothe, and supply energy to an ever-growing population for the next 7 billion years . . . We [are] able to go on increasing forever."[3]
- "Even the total weight of the earth is not a theoretical limit to the amount of copper that might be available to earthlings in the future. Only the total weight of the universe . . .[4] [After all, alchemy is said to be] "preposterous because it is impractical now. But . . . so was electricity considered impractical a century ago."[5] "In the end, copper and oil come out of our minds. That's really where they are."[6]
- "Population density does not damage health or psychological and social well-being."[7]
- "There is no statistical evidence for rapid loss of species in next two decades."
- "The climate does not show signs of unusual and threatening changes."[8]

With such assertions flatly refuted by the preponderance of informed scientific evidence and opinion, why should we take Julian Simon seriously?

Because so many do. For instance, Simon's cornucopism is believed to deserve a hearing by such prestigious publications as *Science*, which published one of his papers, in 1980,[9] and also the *Bulletin of the Atomic Scientists* (1984),[10] and *New Scientist* (1986).[11] And his influential book, *The Ultimate Resource*, was considered significant enough to be published by Princeton University Press.

Moreover, among those who take Simon's views seriously are national and international leaders and legislators who are determining our environmental policy. In fact, "business as usual" in political economy treats cornucopism as an "as if" presupposition, that is, established private and political institutions in the world economy are acting "as if" they accepted cornucopism.

Few if any individuals who are well-informed about ecology, the atmospheric sciences, or thermodynamics can be much impressed by the cornucopian arguments. Nonetheless, it is very important that we understand these ideas and identify the presuppositions upon which they stand, and then set down a clearly articulated refutation thereof. For not only has Professor Simon received a respectful hearing among audiences of educated individuals who should know better, still worse, the general tenets of his view are, like it or not, the unarticulated assumptions behind the theory and practice of international commerce and politics.

Accordingly, we should take Julian Simon very seriously.

What is interesting about Simon's position is that the data that he cites are, in all probability, for the most part correct. The trouble is that these data are either irrelevant or partial, and as a result, do not sustain his cheerful worldview.[12] However, that worldview is supported by several presuppositions that are occasionally stated or hinted at but more often unacknowledged. And some of the more salient of these presuppositions can be inferred, not by the pattern of evidence that he cites, but by the patterns of significant information that he disregards.

The superficial plausibility of Simon's position is gained much more through his *exclusion* than through his citing of data. As we shall see, missing from Simon's cheerful prognoses is any acknowledgment or apparent comprehension of such fundamental ecological principles as nutrient cycling, feedback mechanisms, and limiting factors, or even that very foundation of physical science: *thermodynamics* and *entropy*. His perspective is confined to his own field of market economics. Herein is the trap that caught no less of a bioscientist than Paul Ehrlich, who, in 1980, carelessly consented to "wager" Simon that pending shortages in five designated metals would cause a rise in their prices during the next decade. Simon won that wager. Ehrlich's mistake was to consent to "play the game" according to the rules of Simon's discipline of economics. Recently, Ehrlich and his colleague, Stephen Schneider, challenged Simon to a new wager, this time utilizing indexes derived from atmospheric and soil science and also involving supplies of rice, wheat, and firewood, and additional factors such as AIDS mortality, ocean fisheries, male sperm counts, and species extinctions. Simon refused the offer, on the grounds that these indicators, based upon the biological and physical conditions, "have only indirect effects on people."[13]

I will not attempt in this essay to refute Simon's "cornucopism" point by point—a task that has been ably undertaken by individuals far more scientifically qualified than myself. Instead, this is an exercise in excavative analysis: that is, an attempt to search out the presuppositions of cornucopism—the axioms that must be assumed for Julian Simon's reassurances to stand up. If, as I hope to prove, at least a few of these presuppositions can be shown to be untenable, then so too are Professor Simon's reassurances.

If this analysis succeeds in overturning cornucopism, I cannot be entirely pleased with the accomplishment. I would like to believe that we can grow forever and that all environmental problems can be solved in short order by human ingenuity. It is a cheerful universe that Professor Simon describes for us. Unfortunately, as Richard Feynman used to remind his students, it is not the universe that we happen to live in, and for reasons that physicists like Feynman are especially well qualified to demonstrate.

Very well, then just what kind of universe *does* Simon describe?

The Essentials of Cornucopism

The fundamental tenets of Julian Simon's position appear to be the following:

- The supply of natural resources is infinite.
- Almost all trends in environmental quality are positive.

- History is a reliable guide to future possibilities.
- There is only one scarcity: Human brain power—"The Ultimate Resource."
- Accordingly, population growth rates are not a problem, except possibly in the sense of being too slow.

Let us spell out these claims in order.

The supply of natural resources is infinite.

Closer inspection shows that Simon means by this that "the supply of natural resources is not finite in any economic sense."[14] If shortages appear and prices begin to rise, "human ingenuity" gets to work and finds cheaper ways to extract or recycle the resource or else find alternative resources that provide the same "service"—for example, coal for whale oil, then petroleum for coal.[15] In the future, there is no practical limit to what human brain power will provide, not even, as we noted above, *alchemy*: the transmutation of elements.

Not content with this rather straightforward explanation of "non-finitude," Simon boldly ventures beyond the fringe. "Finitude," he reminds us, is a concept that "originates in mathematics." He then proceeds with an argument so strange that it must be quoted at some length, if we are to believe that he really means what he is saying:

> The length of a one-inch line is finite in the sense that it is bounded at both ends. But the line within the endpoints contains an infinite number of points; these points cannot be counted, because they have no defined size. Therefore, the number of points in a one-inch segment [of a line] is not finite. *Similarly*, the quantity of copper that will ever be available to us is not finite, because there is no method (even in principle) of making an appropriate count of it.[16] (my italics)

Note that word *similarly*. Clearly, Simon wishes to draw an inference from mathematics to the "real world." Unfortunately, such an inference is invalid, since:

> in the context of mathematics . . . all propositions are tautologous definitions. . . . But scientific subjects are empirical rather than definitional. . . . [Thus] mathematics is not a science in the ordinary sense because it does not deal with facts other than the stuff of mathematics itself, and hence such terms as "finite" do not have the same meaning elsewhere that they do in mathematics.[17]

This quotation is wholly consistent with the view of mathematics that is generally accepted by scientists, mathematicians, and philosophers today—as well as by Julian Simon, who is the author. In fact, of the two quotations just cited, the second appears just one page after the first. Remarkably, Simon seems quite unaware that he has thus totally demolished the conclusion that he painstakingly attempted to establish just three paragraphs previously.

But there is worse to come. In that same "points in a line" example, Simon equates (without supporting argument) the concepts of "indeterminate" and "not finite" (which he is willing to treat as "infinite"). Continuing: "The quantity of a natural resource that might be available to us . . . can never be known even in principle, just as the number of points in a one-inch line can never be counted even in principle. . . . Hence resources are not 'finite' in any meaningful sense."

I should find this very reassuring: for if the day of my death is indeterminate, then by Simon's reckoning I can assume that I am immortal. And since that drill hole on my property, left from a failed attempt at oil exploration, is of indeterminate depth, I can assume that it is infinitely deep. Absurd? Of course! But what else could he mean by his inference from "indeterminate" to "infinite"?

The remaining tenets of Simon's cornucopism can be stated briefly.

Almost all trends in environmental quality are positive.

This is the essential message of Simon's book, *The Ultimate Resource,* of his 1980 paper in *Science,* and indeed of most of his writings. In the anthology, *The Resourceful Earth,* coedited with Herman Kahn, he writes:

> If present trends continue, the world in 2000 will be *less* crowded (though more populated), *less* polluted, *more* stable ecologically, and *less* vulnerable to resource-supply disruption than the world we live in now. Stresses involving population, resources, and environment will be *less in the future than now.*[18]

History is a reliable guide to future possibilities.

To the objection that "history is not a good guide" to understanding the future, because "we are at a turning point in history," Simon replies:

> All throughout history people have felt that they are at a turning point, and it has not turned out to be so ... If we cannot base our judgments about the future largely on past experience, in conjunction with reasonable theoretical explanations of that experience, then all our experience and all our science are without value.[19]

As we shall see, it is just those "theoretical explanations of experience," provided by informed scientists, that are the undoing of Simon's optimism.

There is only one scarcity: Human brain power—"The Ultimate Resource."

Simon writes: "The main fuel to speed the world's progress is the stock of human knowledge. And the ultimate resource is skilled, spirited, hopeful people, exerting their wills and imaginations to provide for themselves and their families, thereby inevitably contributing to the benefit of everyone."[20] It then follows that,

Population growth rates are not a problem.

Except possibly in the sense of being too slow. The ultimate constraint upon our capacity to enjoy unlimited raw materials at acceptable prices is knowledge. And the source of knowledge is the human mind. Ultimately, then, the key constraint is human imagination and the exercise of educated skills. Hence an increase of human beings constitutes an addition to the crucial stock of resources, along with causing additional consumption of resources.[21]

Some Presuppositions of Cornucopism

This remarkable collection of assertions describes a worldview radically at odds with that of most biological and physical scientists. It is a view that, if true, would seem to rest upon a number of presuppositions equally at odds with "establishment science." In this section, I sketch what appear to me to be the presuppositions that are both most crucial to the cornucopian worldview and most vulnerable to scientific and conceptual criticism. The task of refuting these assumptions will occupy us throughout the remainder of this essay.

Many or most of these assumptions would be rejected by Simon and the cornucopians. But if I have done my work effectively, that rejection is so much the worse for cornucopism, since a rejection of these presuppositions entails a rejection of their worldview. So the challenge of this analysis is simply this: can the cornucopists carry forth their cheerful view of the world without the baggage of the seemingly absurd assumptions on which they rest? I submit that they cannot.

History assures us that human progress is perpetual. The essential parameters of historical development are invariable, and thus there are no essential discontinuities in history. Accordingly, since history discloses that human ingenuity has always eventually triumphed over environmental adversity in the past, there is no reason to doubt that it will do so in the future.

The question of what, if any, meaning and lessons might be drawn from history is one of the most profound and intractable issues in both philosophy and history. And that very fact undermines much of the cornucopian argument, which requires a naive and simplistic belief that history is a *reliable* predictor of the future.

The cornucopian argument rests, not only upon a false reading of history, but also on an over simplistic notion of induction: namely, that the long history of successful human "coping" with nature gives us inductive warrant to assume more of the same in the future.

By way of refutation, environmental alarmists like to tell the story of the optimist who falls off a high building and who reflects, two-thirds of the way down, "well, so far, so good!" I prefer another tale told by Bertrand Russell, which concerns a certain farmer and his turkey. From the point of view of the reflective turkey, the farmer will *always* greet him in the morning with a bucket of grain. Why? Because, by simple inductive reasoning, it follows that the more often this happens, the more secure he is in the belief that it will happen again—until, one morning, the farmer appears with an axe. Now from the farmer's better informed point of view, he knows that the more often the turkey gets the grain, the *less* likely it is that he will survive another day. Similarly, life underwriters adopt the farmer's point of view.

Eco-scientists, like the farmer, have the better informed point of view. They understand all too well that "business as usual," celebrated by the cornucopians, is undermining the physical-biotic structure that supports that "business," and that the more our industrial "business as usual" continues as it has, the less likely it is that we will be able to continue. We are, as eco-scientists like to put it, living off our biotic capital. All this is so, due to conditions in the real world well known to, and exhaustively studied by, these scientists—conditions systematically discounted and ignored by the cornucopians.

Nature is just inert "stuff," a warehouse of resources, on which we act and from which we take, but about which we need not give special notice. If nature causes us problems, we simply assemble our "best minds" and they will take care of it.

Prof. Simon's "nature" is a very strange place—almost a caricature of George Berkeley's subjective idealism; it exists only when we take note of it. "To be is to be a commodity." (More fairly: "to be of any concern to us, is to be a commodity.") Complete your transaction, turn your attention elsewhere, and nature will, for all practical purposes, just disappear until you next find need of it—infinitely and perpetually available. Moreover, nature is also an infinite "sink." When we throw something "away," it is really "away"—it never comes back. The chain of causation, which is very useful to us when we want resources from nature, somehow just stops when we cease taking note of it.

The Berkeleyan worldview goes even further: "to be is to be intended." It then follows that there are no "unintended consequences." In other words, after we enjoy the desired effect, there are no further causes. Pesticide residues "go away," never to appear again. The CO_2 produced by the burning of fossil fuels is of no further concern to us. Nor are the pesticides after they kill the pests and are thus miraculously rendered innocuous to songbirds.

Of course, the cornucopians will retort that this is an unfair caricature—and of course they are right. And yet, they act as if this were so. Cornucopians pay almost no attention to the complications and costs of unintended consequences, and they are quite unimpressed by the findings, even less the warnings, of scientists who study ongoing phenomena in uncommodified nature. And if they admit that causation continues unnoticed, they will then claim, "well never mind, we can fix all that—don't underestimate the power of human ingenuity, especially when motivated by the profit motive."

In short, cornucopians seem to be totally unconcerned by Commoner's law: *You can't do just one thing.* And they rarely bother to ask Hardin's query: *And then what?* All this is surpassingly strange since, despite their allegiance to free market theory, the cornucopians thus conveniently ignore that most fundamental of economic maxims: there is no such thing as a free lunch.

Nature (and, in particular the biosphere) is a mechanical order, not a systemic order.

This axiom of the cornucopian worldview is challenged by the late economist, Nicholas Georgescu-Roegen, who writes:

> . . . the founders of the neoclassical school set out to erect an economic science after the pattern of mechanics [and thus], analytic pieces that adorn the standard economic literature reduce the economic process to a self-sustained mechanical analogue. The patent fact that between the economic process and the material environment there exists a continuous mutual influence which is history making carries no weight with the standard economist.[22]

But while the "pattern of mechanics" is implicit in neoclassical economic theory, it is contrary to the principles of thermodynamics: "The opposition between the entropy law—with its unidirectional qualitative change—and mechanics—where everything can move either forward or backward while remaining self-identical—is accepted without reservation by every physicist and philosopher of science."[23] Georgescu-Roegen's enduring legacy is his demonstration that *entropy*, the cornerstone of physical science, challenges the very foundations of classical economic theory—even more, the reassurances of the cornucopians. We have much more to say about *entropy* shortly.

Simon's mechanistic view of physical reality is nowhere more evident than in his dismissal of concerns about global warming:

> ... no threatening trend in *human welfare* has been connected to [global warming]. ... It may even be that a greenhouse effect would benefit us on balance by warming some areas we'd like warmer, and by increasing the carbon dioxide to agriculture. ... [Moreover], we now have large and ever-increasing capabilities to reverse such trends if they are proven to be dangerous, and at costs that are manageable.[24] (Simon's italics)

Unfortunately, Simon offers not a word to identify these putative "means" to unscramble the atmospheric omelet.

Simon's view here of global atmospheric processes is astonishingly ill-informed. Brushing aside whole libraries of scientific data, he chooses to regard "global warming" as "global warming—*period.*" He acknowledges no changes in "warehouse Earth" except that everywhere things are a bit warmer. To Simon, "warming" the Earth is essentially no different than turning up the thermostat and warming up the house. He thus fails to recognize that the global climate is a *system.* Accordingly, global warming *in toto* would mean that some regions might in fact be cooler, some much hotter, some dryer, some wetter, some subject to more violent tropical storms, and so on, far beyond our reckoning. Ocean currents would likely change with dramatic consequences; for example, just a slight change of direction in the Gulf Stream could condemn Great Britain to a climate comparable to its latitudinal opposite, Labrador. (Of course, as we have seen, if scientists tell us that "we don't know the full effects" of something, Simon routinely interprets this to mean "there are no effects.") Also, Simon typically fails to comprehend the sensitivity of established ecosystems to such sudden climatic changes. For example, whole forest ecosystems, unable to migrate to more favorable climates, would collapse.

Because elementary matter cannot be destroyed, we'll never run out of resources. The dumps and sinks of today are the mines of tomorrow.

This seems to make superficial sense to the mechanist mind-set of reversible processes favored by the cornucopians. However, elemental resources that are scattered as garbage are often woefully beyond recovery. This is so due to some fundamental thermodynamic principles, to which we will return.

In particular, nature can be successfully managed. So-called biological services are fully replicable if not dispensable, once we put our engineering skills to the task.

Biological services, like so many basic concepts of the life and physical sciences, are totally ignored in Julian Simon's writings. Small wonder. To acknowledge these services is to admit that it just might be possible that the natural order that created and nurtured our species might be forever beyond our managerial capabilities. Yet such capabilities are implicit in Simon's cavalier assumption that any problems that might arise can be handled by human ingenuity.

Very well, cornucopians, manage *this*!

The biotic services that we can cite are endless: I will settle for two. First, the phytoplankton, whose production of atmospheric oxygen rivals that of the tropical rain forests. Next, consider permanent removal of CO_2 from the atmosphere by zooplankton, coral, and mollusks (which convert it into carbonates and eventually into limestone). And plankton, of course, is the base of the oceanic ecosystem and is thus utterly necessary if we are to be fed from the seas. And yet, the plankton are threatened by ultraviolet radiation from ozone depletion. Not to worry, Simon reassures us, since that increased UV radiation might improve our vitamin C intake, and the harmful effects might be overcome by wearing hats and sunglasses—and anyway, "if human interaction is causing the change, then human intervention can reverse it."[25]

Unfortunately, neither hats nor sunglasses are of much use to the plankton.

Then there are micro-invertebrates—what E. O. Wilson calls "the little things that run the world," including the mites, worms, and bacteria that transform "dirt" into *soil* and that transform the waste of completed life into nutrients for new life. Of these "little things," Wilson notes:

> . . . we need invertebrates but they don't need us. . . . If invertebrates were to disappear, I doubt that the human species could last more than a few months. . . . The earth would rot. As dead vegetation piled up and dried out, narrowing and closing the channels of the nutrient cycles, other complex forms of vegetation would die off, and with them the last remnants of the vertebrates. The remaining fungi, after enjoying a population explosion of stupendous proportions, would also perish. Within a few decades, the world would return to the state of a billion years ago, composed primarily of bacteria, algae, and a few other very simple multicellular plants.[26]

There is literally no end to an accounting of our debt to the other life forms that maintain the physical-chemical-biotic nexus that is the ecosphere—*Gaia*. But in Julian Simon's writings, there is scarcely a beginning of an acknowledgment of that debt.

In fact, we cannot manage the Earth, precisely because the planet is not an "inert warehouse"; rather, it is a lively place, more complex and wonderful (literally, full of wonders) than we can ever know or even imagine. It is all this, because it is, first and foremost, *systemic*, and thus it displays these features:

- *Energy* that *flows* and *nutrients* that *cycle* through the life forms of the trophic pyramids.
- Biotic and atmospheric action is *synergistic*, in ways that constantly surprise us and thus are out of our control. For example, photochemical smog, we have found, is more than just a soup of component air pollutants. It is a substance cooked into existence by those substances, through the catalytic action of sunlight.
- The biosphere displays numerous *feedback effects*: positive feedbacks that initiate runaway sequences, such as red tides or possibly, for that matter, the greenhouse effects; and negative feedbacks that are characteristic of stable ecosystems.

- We must also cope with *time-lag effects,* such as reforestation, or the so-called geological storage of toxic materials, or the slow spread of pollutants through aquifers.
- We are constantly surprised by *threshold effects* or "tipping effects," such as when a forest or a lake appears capable of absorbing pollutants without harm, until eventually a slight increase causes massive die-offs or eutrophication. (In popular parlance, this phenomenon is known as "the straw that breaks the back.")

Because of these mechanisms, and many more, the biosphere is, to paraphrase J. D. S. Haldane, not only more mysterious that we suppose, but more mysterious than we can suppose. Accordingly, the biosphere is *not* reliably "manageable."

Whatever problems may appear, human ingenuity will be equal to it. We've always solved our problems in the past, and we'll continue to do so long into the future.

Of course, most of this essay is an attempt to answer this cheerful reassurance, and our most systematic rejoinder will appear in the discussion of entropy, below. However, an epistemological note might be appropriate here, prefaced by a personal recollection.

Several years ago, I was engaged in a debate with a fundamentalist preacher. To his claims of the virtual existence of a heaven and hell, I protested that he was offering no evidence to support his claim. He replied, "just you wait—you are eventually going to encounter plenty of evidence, when you meet your Maker!"

His retort was not particularly useful at the time.

I submit that this oft reiterated claim, "human ingenuity will be equal to the task," is superempirical hand-waving of the same type. It is simply a secular eschatology—a kind of cargo cultism, which attempts to answer scientifically validated challenges with unverifiable promises.

In the meantime, human ingenuity *has* been at work—and in the very biotic, atmospheric, and other sciences that the cornucopians summarily dismiss. Their confidence in "gray matter" thus appears to be curiously selective. Never mind, they tell us, what ingenious humans in the sciences are telling us now, and kindly disregard the weight of evidence and the strength of inference amassed through this applied ingenuity. The cornucopians have faith that somehow, sometime, some other ingenious humans will eventually come along to prove that they are right. "Just you wait!" "*The facts speak for themselves.*"

To the anticipated criticism, "but what about the other side's data?" Simon boldly replies, "there are no other data." He continues. "I invite you to test for yourself this assertion that the conditions of humanity have gotten better." And he then refers the readers to the Census Bureau's *Statistical Abstract of the United States.* He concludes, "every single measure shows a trend of improvement rather than the deterioration that the doomsayers claim has occurred."[27]

No data? Perhaps he just has not bothered to look. Simon claims that "There is no documentation of further data produced by biologists since 1979 to demonstrate what Norman Myers was saying" about mass extinctions. Myers replies, "during those thirteen years, the number of papers published on the mass extinction crisis is over three hundred. . . . No documentation, no data, Professor Simon?"[28]

Simply put, Simon counts as data what he wants to use as data. The rest he simply disregards. As we stated at the outset, the problem with Simon's argument is not that the data he cites is not factual, but that it is partial or irrelevant. And it is that vast body of unacknowledged fact and theory that demolishes the cornucopian view.

"The facts speak for themselves" is the first refuge of the huckster posing as a scientist.[29] But as anyone even casually familiar with the philosophy of science knows full well, facts only speak to us *in context* of other facts, and guided by theory. This is what distinguishes sound scientific theory and ad hoc caricatures such as creation science and, I submit, cornucopism. In the case of science, theory arises out of observation of facts, effectively classified and organized. In caricatured science, the imposed theory selects facts and predetermines what is to count as a fact and as evidence. And finally, sound science is vulnerable to Karl Popper's "falsifiability principle;" that is, the principle that scientific theories must yield implications that can clearly and unequivocally be shown to be otherwise, if the world is *not* what the theory describes it to be. Political and religious apologists do not submit to such a test. Nor does Simon's worldview, for recall his stock-in-trade, unverifiable, superempirical plea: "human ingenuity will come up with an answer, sometime."

Facts do *not* speak for themselves. Give someone a carte blanche license both to pick any facts that he chooses and to disregard any others that he may find inconvenient, and he will be able to claim a demonstration of virtually anything under the sun. However, by violating the falsifiability rule, this self-concocted ability to prove anything whatever amounts to a capacity to prove nothing at all.

The preponderance of scientific opinion and theory, in the relevant disciplines of ecology, atmospherics, soils, demographics, and even physics, is simply wrong. Julian Simon and his friends know better. Furthermore, the well-known pessimism of environmental scientists is suspiciously motivated.

With this claim the cornucopians, quite frankly, display colossal *chutzpah.* For they contend, in effect, that the consensus opinion of entire fields of established sciences—ecology, atmospheric chemistry and climatology, demographics, agronomy, and so on—are fundamentally in error. All this scientific investigation and expertise is casually brushed aside in favor of historical analogies ("trends"), selected anecdotes, and abstract economic modeling. Still worse, at the close of his *Science* and *Bulletin of the Atomic Scientists* articles, and throughout the two books examined herein, Professor Simon practices unlicensed psychotherapy as he claims that the pessimism of "established science" is a conspiracy, motivated by careerism, competitive grantsmanship, a public fascination with bad news, and willingness to exaggerate in order to mobilize public activism.[30]

The Entropy Trap

The most fundamental error of the cornucopian worldview is that it takes no account of the laws of thermodynamics, and particularly of the condition known as *entropy*[31] And since these laws are at the foundation of modern physics and thus "no exception to [the thermodynamic laws] has ever been observed,"[32] it follows that the cornucopians must be dealing with a different physical universe than the one we happen to reside in.

While thermodynamics can be one of the most devilishly difficult branches of physics (and far beyond the comprehension of this writer), in its general, nonquantitative formulation, the second law is quite simple: "the free ["useful"] heat-energy of a closed system continuously and irrevocably degrades itself into bound ["useless"] energy. . . . Entropy (i. e., the amount of bound energy) of a closed system continuously increases or . . . the order of such a system steadily turns into disorder."[33]

Ehrlich, Ehrlich and Holdren express the second thermodynamic law as follows: "all physical processes, natural and technological, proceed in such a way that the availability of the energy involved decreases. . . . What is consumed when we use energy . . . is not energy itself but its availability for doing useful work." They then spell out five significant implications of the second law:

1. In any transformation of energy, some of the energy is degraded.
2. No process is possible whose sole result is the conversion of a given quantity of heat (thermal energy) into an equal amount of useful work.
3. No process is possible whose sole result is the flow of heat from a colder body to a hotter one.
4. The availability of a given quantity of energy can only be used once; that is, the property of convertibility into useful work cannot be "recycled."
5. In spontaneous processes, concentrations (of anything) tend to disperse, structure tends to disappear, order becomes disorder.[34]

This final formulation, linking *work and heat to structure, order, and probability*, is the most puzzling implication of the second law, and the implication that bears most heavily on the cornucopian worldview. An elaboration is in order.

The most memorable explanation, to my mind, comes from Isaac Asimov.[35] Consider a typical child's bedroom. When clean, it is orderly and improbable. Then entropy sets in, and it becomes disorderly and probable. Why probable? Because, for example, dirty socks belong in just one place— the laundry basket—but instead end up anywhere else, which is a more "probable" location than the basket. A made-up bed is just one improbable condition of numerous states of the bed; "unmade" is all the others.

Then Mother sees the entropic mess and says, "No dinner for you, young man, until you clean this up!" So what does it take to reverse entropy and achieve the improbably neat condition? Knowledge of where things belong (information) and *energy*.

Next, consider dispersion and probability. The tea in the tea bag disperses into the cup of hot water. Never does the tea in the cup return to the tea bag. Every pool game begins with a "break" of a racked triangle of fifteen balls. No game has ever succeeded in returning the scattered balls to a triangle. For that you need outside information and energy—a player racking them up. You will never shuffle a deck of cards into the order of suits. (Conceivably possible but virtually impossible.) "You can not unscramble an egg" (C. P. Snow). Once again, "all physical processes proceed in such a way that the entropy of the universe increases." "We can't win, we can't break even, and we can't get out of the game."[36]

In the realm of deliberate action, this means that *order, concentration, and useful energy is purchased at the expense of more disorder, dispersion, and lost potential.* You can't strike a match twice; water pressure having turned a turbine cannot turn it again, until solar energy has evaporated it, turned into rain again, and dropped it on the upstream watershed.

But if a local reversal of entropy ("negative entropy," or *negentropy*) must result in a net increase in systemic entropy, how then does life evolve toward greater complexity—from probable to improbable states? Simply because the entropy that drives the negentropy that is life and evolution comes to us from an external source: the sun. In short: the biosphere and human culture are entropy pumps powered by solar energy (in the case of human culture, solar energy stored in biomass and fossil fuels).

The implication for environmental policy and management is stark: *all our environmental "problems" are the result of prior "solutions"!* Think about it! The solution to premature death has resulted in the population explosion. The solution to mass transportation has led to air pollution. The solution of intensive agriculture has caused nitrate pollution of groundwater and the eutrophication of streams.

This undoing of our good intentions has received popular notice in Edward Tenner's new book, *Why Things Bite Back: Technology and the Revenge of Unintended Consequences.*[37] In his review of the book in *Science,* Langdon Winner cites some of these unintended consequences:

> Antibiotics marshaled against disease have spawned new varieties of highly virulent drug-resistant bacteria that pose new threats to human health. Methods for preventing forest fires have been so effective in preserving the dry underbrush that wildfires are now enormous conflagrations . . . Cleverly engineered structures that have altered the contours of rivers and beaches have unwittingly contributed to the lethal force of "natural disaster" that now vex civilization.[38]

Herein lies the fatal flaw in the cornucopians' attempt to extrapolate into the future, favorable trends (i. e., increased wealth and resources) from the past. While, in the past, we have exported our entropy cost to the environment as pollution, we have managed to get away with it. For, true to the traditional pioneer spirit, we have been able to use it up, then move on. But now, with the expanding population, there is no more "on" to move to, and still worse, the pollution sink that is the environment is nearing saturation, whereby the synergisms, feedbacks, and threshold effects begin to kick in. In fact, this has already happened in the Grand Banks fisheries and is likely happening in the atmosphere with ozone depletion and global warming. But don't expect the cornucopians to recognize any of this. *Entropy* and *thermodynamics* (along with *synergism, threshold,* and *feedback*) are missing from the indexes of the two Simon books on my desk, and I cannot recall encountering any of these concepts anywhere in Simon's writings.[39]

Finally, the principle that "order (negentropy) is purchased at the price of greater disorder (entropy)" may be the undoing of Simon's secular eschatology, that is, the faith that we'll think of something—don't underestimate the ingenuity of human beings. It is the irreparable hole in the cornucopia, since however we might manage to "fix" (reverse the entropy of) developing

environmental problems, these fixes are destined to create still more problems (entropy). (Remember: every environmental problem we now have is the
result of a prior solution.) Thus we are running a race with our shadow, with
the light source forever behind our backs. It won't do just to run faster. The
rules of that game forbid ultimate success: we can't win, we can't break even,
we can't leave the game. Perhaps the only acceptable option is cherish and
preserve the system that brought us here in the first place, namely, the ecosystem. If so, we might once again charge the entropy bill to the sun's account.

A Beautiful Theory and an Inscrutable World

An analysis of far-out examples is a useful and favorite trick of economists.
(Julian Simon)[40]

The Theory is Beautiful; It's Reality that Has Me Baffled. (Source unknown)

How can intelligent and well-educated individuals such as Julian Simon
arrive at such bizarre conclusions? John Ruggie, the moderator of Julian
Simon's debate with Norman Myers, offers an intriguing suggestion:

> The underlying ontology of [Myers's and Simon's] worlds . . . differs. Simon's
> world is made up of palpable and infinitely divisible units, existing within a field
> of discrete events. In contrast, Myers's world is made up of indivisible wholes,
> linked together by cycles and conjunctures that are subject to butterfly effects.
> If Simon's dominant metaphor is mechanical, Myers's is organic.[41]

As we have seen, the Simon worldview is an ontology in a Kantian sense:
it is a priori, and thus not the product of empirical investigation of the world,
but rather a theoretical construct that imposes his view upon the world, thus
dictating what will and will not count as evidence as to the nature of the
world. And since that worldview is presupposed, and refuting evidence is excluded a priori, this is an ontology that violates the most fundamental requirement of scientific inquiry, *falsifiability*; namely, the requirement that all
scientific hypotheses clearly indicate the type of evidence that would prove it
false. In simple terms, nothing will budge Simon's worldview, since he declares, at the outset, that nothing will be allowed to do so.

Clearly, Simon's ontology is derived from a dominant paradigm of his
discipline of economics: *the perfect market.* In theory, the perfect market has
these qualities:

An infinite (or very large) pool of potential buyers and sellers ("agents")

Radical autonomy: i. e., no collusion among the potential agents

All relevant information available to the agents

No transaction costs

No externalities, positive or negative, resulting from the transactions

Transactions, once completed, are final

All transactions are completely voluntary

"Pareto Optimality:" no transactions that leave a party worse off

All agents are solely motivated to maximize their personal utility, or "preference
satisfaction" (i. e., all parties are so-called "economic men"[42])

The perfect market thus aggregates autonomous agents, prepared to
exchange discrete items such as cash, goods, services, resources. It is this

theoretical construct that describes the mechanistic and atomistic world of Simon's ontology. It is also, let us note, a world wherein market incentives activate the human ingenuity that, Simon believes, can in principle overcome all obstacles—be they ecological or even thermodynamic.

As all economists (including Simon) would readily agree, the theoretical perfect market composed of economic agents is an ideal type, nowhere found in the real world. However, like ideal types in physics such as a frictionless machine, absolute zero, and perfect vacuum (also nowhere exemplified in nature), the perfect market and economic man are essential to the abstract quantified modeling that characterizes modern economic theory.[43]

This abstract worldview of autonomous, utility-maximizing rational agents is replicated in the political ideology of *libertarianism*, with its fundamental and inviolable rights to *life, liberty,* and *property,* and its concomitant denial of welfare rights and social duties. Accordingly, to the libertarian, the only legitimate functions of government are the protection of life, liberty, and property from external threats (the military), internal threat (the police), and civil disputes (the courts). To the libertarian, all else—education, welfare, promotion of the arts, protection of the environment, and so on—are solely the concern of private individuals, and no business of the government. Thus the libertarian repeats in his political theory, what the classical economist describes in his central paradigm: an aggregate of discrete, autonomous individuals, each owning items and parcels of property, totally encapsulated by title and well-defined boundary lines. To both, society is like a swap meet, composed of self-serving economic persons, all mutual strangers meeting on inert Newtonian space (which, *qua* inert, is totally unaffected by what transpires upon it).[44]

Classical, free-market economic theory, then, appears to be the foundation of Simon's atomistic worldview of autonomous individuals, inviolable property lines, and discrete events. From this idée fixe of the perfect market he moves outward to a theory of politics, libertarianism, and thence to a theory of physical reality—a view of a world of infinite resources, infinite possibilities, infinite growth, all this unhampered by such limitations and complications as feedbacks, synergisms, time lapses, and above all, *entropy*. In this Simonized world, nature is a passive theater whereupon we seek to maximize our individual utilities, all the while absorbing our assaults without consequences. By this account, in nature, just as in the market, when a transaction is agreed to and the exchange is made, then that's the end of it. All acts are disconnected. You *can* do just one thing! No need to ask Hardin's query: "and then what?" To Julian Simon, then, *economics* is the queen of sciences, according to which human endeavor and even physical reality is best interpreted. This point of view is not unique to Simon: for example, A. Myrick Freeman writes that "to the economist, the environment is a scarce resource which contributes to human welfare."[45] And William Baxter:

> All our environmental problems are, in essence, specific instances of a problem of great familiarity: how can we arrange our society so as to make the most effective use of our resources. . . . To assert that there is . . . an environmental problem is to assert, at least implicitly, that one or more resources is not being used so as to maximize human satisfactions. . . . Environmental problem are economic problems, and better insight can be gained by economic analysis.[46]

In short, in an audacious reversal of Copernicus, these economists are proposing to place humanity back at the center of the physical universe. In contradistinction, the economist Georgescu-Roegen insists that "the economic process is solidly anchored to a material base which is subject to definite constraints."[47] Gaylord Nelson puts the matter more bluntly: "the economy is a wholly owned subsidiary of the environment."[48]

Unfortunately, Julian Simon's ontology simply does not describe the world that we live in, since it is articulated with a fundamental disregard of basic ecological (which is to say natural) laws—not to mention the findings of behavioral science and the insights of moral philosophy (which we cannot elaborate in this space).[49] The surveyor can plot a property line within the inch, but that line has no meaning or significance to the conditions of nature that give that property its value—and that, for that matter, sustain our very lives. The atmosphere, the ocean, cycling nutrients, migrating birds, insects and spores, global pollution sinks and heat sinks—none of these are the least aware of property lines. None can be meaningfully contained within the confines, and thus within the concept, of "inviolable private property."

While Julian Simon's ontology selects, a priori, what is to count as data and evidence, it does not enjoy a priori immunity from the challenge of scientific facts. Nature, as discovered and articulated in the body of modern bioscience, talks back to Simon's ontology. Simon's reductive, atomistic worldview entails claims that are empirically falsifiable (thus scientifically meaningful), and furthermore, demonstrably false (thus scientifically refuted). Simply put, human ingenuity, exemplified by modern science, has persuasively demonstrated that in the real world, energy flows up trophic pyramids, nutrients recycle through and back into ecosystems, and entropy reigns supreme, and thus each solution generates new problems. Furthermore, science has taught us that the atmosphere, the oceans, and the soil, which support our lives, are in fact *systems* and not infinitely large and inert dumps. In short, life (including human life) and its supporting mechanisms are simply not what Julian Simon claimed them to be. Commoner's law—"you can't do just one thing"—is more than a slogan: it is a demonstrable fact.

CONCLUSIONS

Why, then, is Julian Simon taken seriously?

The dominant paradigm in the industrialized world requires constant growth. One might call this the shark economy since, like the shark, it has to move constantly in order to stay alive. Quiescence means death. The engine of the modern economy is return on investment, that is, growth. Steady-state and the end of growth (the sigmoid curve) are equally axiomatic in natural ecosystems. So the two economies, *natural* and *industrial*, are based upon logically contrary axioms.

Thus the economists' choice is simple and stark: either devise and defend a new economic theory that accommodates itself to the basic conditions of life as articulated by the life and physical sciences, or else simply elect to ignore these facts and deal instead with a fanciful world. Clearly, Simon chose the latter course and, in the face of both common sense and scientific evidence, posited, as he had to, a world of infinite resources that is supportive of perpetual growth.

I once heard Paul Ehrlich remark that if an engineer proposed a design for an aircraft with a constantly expanding crew, we would think him mad. And yet, when an economist defends a theory that posits a perpetually growing global economy, he is awarded a Nobel Prize. Notwithstanding that, perpetual growth is unknown in the natural world.

While I argue that there are severe limitations to the applicability of economic theory to the natural world, economic theory might nonetheless help to explain the successful promulgation of Professor Simon's ideas: There is a demand, lavishly rewarded, for an apologia for classical economic practice, for a justification of global industrial business as usual, and thus for a dismissal of the eco-scientists' warnings. Julian Simon met that demand with extraordinary wit and cleverness.

In short, if there had been no Julian Simon he would have to be invented.

But Simon posits a worldview and proposes a policy that can only lead to ruin. To paraphrase the wise and much-lamented physicist, Richard Feynman, "For a successful environmental policy, reality must take precedence over wishful thinking, for nature cannot be fooled."[50]

Notes

1. I take this to be a fair paraphrase, since it is taken from the title of Chapter 3 of Simon's book, *The Ultimate Resource*, "Can the Supply of Natural Resources Really Be Infinite? Yes!" (Princeton: Princeton University Press, 1981).
2. Ibid., 48.
3. Norman Myers and Julian Simon, *Scarcity or Abundance* (New York: Norton, 1994), 65.
4. Julian Simon, "Resources, Population, Environment: An Oversupply of False Bad News," *Science* 208 (June 1980): 1435–6.
5. Julian Simon, "Reply to Critics, Letters Section," *Science* 208, (December 19, 1980): 1306.
6. Myers and Simon, *Scarcity or Abundance*, 100. Norman Myers is here quoting Simon in *The Ultimate Resource*. Unfortunately, there is no page reference for Myers's citation.
7. Another chapter title (chapter 18) in Simon, *The Ultimate Resource*.
8. These last two from Julian Simon, "Bright Global Future," *Bulletin of the Atomic Scientists* (November 1984): 14.
9. "Resources, Population, Environment: An Oversupply of False Bad News," *Science* 208 (27 June 1980): 1431–37. This is not to say that this esteemed publication erred in choosing to publish Simon's paper. The paper is valuable for the significant policies that it supports and for its display of fallacies assembled in support of what, to many, are plausible conclusions. Equally valuable as the paper were the abundant criticisms that were to follow in the "Letters" section of *Science*.
10. "Bright Global Future," *Bulletin of the Atomic Scientists* (November 1984): 14–18. This article has its origin in a symposium at the 1984 annual meeting of the American Association for the Advancement of Science, "Knockdown-Dragout on the Global Future," which featured Prof. Simon.
11. "Disappearing Species, Deforestation and Data," *New Scientist* 110, (May 15, 1986): 60–63.
12. As an example of a non sequitur, consider Simon's dismissal of governmental concern about soil erosion, which he charges is a "fraud." On the contrary, he says (perhaps correctly) that soil loss has decreased by all of 6 percent (from 5.1 tons/acre to 4.8 tons/acre). But it does not follow from this that it is of no concern. Quite the contrary, he cites and does not contest Al Gore's observation that "eight acres of prime topsoil floats past Memphis every hour" and that half of the topsoil of Iowa has been lost to erosion. So the question he should ask, and doesn't is whether this allegedly "reduced" loss still

constitutes a problem. If so, then what is the "fraud?" (Myers and Simon, *Scarcity or Abundance*, 53). (Analogously, the FBI reports a 15 percent drop in murder rates last year. According to Prof. Simon's logic, it then follows that murder is no longer a problem in the United States.)

13. Charles Petit, "Two Stanford Scholars Take on Rosy Economist," *San Francisco Chronicle*, May 18, 1995, 15(A). The final quotation is from Petit, not Simon.

14. Simon, *The Ultimate Resource*, 42.

15. Simon, "Bright Global Future," 15.

16. Simon, "Bright Global Future," 47.

17. Simon, "Bright Global Future," 48.

18. Quoted by Simon in "Bright Global Future," 14.

19. Simon, "Bright Global Future," 16.

20. Myers and Simon, *Scarcity or Abundance*, 33. Philosopher Jan Narveson fully concurs: "Sustainability has become the buzz-word, the implication being that life as we currently know it and enjoy it is not sustainable. . . . Should we be impressed by that? . . . [T]he answer is no. Future generations will consist, after all, of rational animals, resourceful people like our ancestors and (I hope!) ourselves. They will be able to cope. The human species has made a decent or better than decent life for itself in an incredible variety of "ecologies." . . . It is astonishing how contemporary humans can overlook the resourcefulness of their fellows in all of this recent cant about ecology. . . . There is . . . no resource problem of consequence for the globe." (Jan Narveson, "Humanism for Humans," *Free Inquiry* (Spring 1993): 24.

21. Simon, "Resources, Population," 1435–36.

22. Nicolas Georgescu-Roegen, "The Entropy Law and the Economic Problem," in *Valuing the Earth: Economics, Ecology, Ethics*, ed. Herman E. Daly and Kenneth N. Townsend (Boston: MIT Press, 1993), 75.

23. Georgescu-Roegen, "Entropy, Economic Problem," 87–8.

24. Myers and Simon, *Scarcity or Abundance*, 18–19. Simon is referring here to acid rain and ozone depletion as well as the greenhouse effect. However, our focus of concern here is on global warming. About the ozone layer, Simon reports "there has been no increase in skin cancers from ozone." I doubt that he would be able to convince the Australians of this.

25. Myers and Simon, *Scarcity or Abundance*, 63.

26. Edward O. Wilson, "The Little Things That Run the World," *Conservation Biology* 1, no. 4 (December 1987): 344.

27. Myers and Simon, *Scarcity or Abundance*, 64.

28. Myers and Simon, *Scarcity or Abundance*, 129.

29. As an example, consider the recent NBC program on "The Mysterious Origins of Man," which has attracted the ire of *Science* magazine and the AAAS. In this strange compendium of kookery, we were told that dinosaurs and humans coexisted, that the sphinx was built 25,000 years ago, and that the site of Atlantis is now under a mile of Antarctic ice. At the close, the "host," Charlton Heston, urged us to "keep an open mind" and reminded us that "the facts speak for themselves."

30. Simon, "Resources, Population," 1436–37. See also, Simon, "Bright Global Future," 16. "The conspiracy of establishment science" is a recurrent theme among creationists, UFO-logists, and other pseudoscientific groups. The charge of "establishment conspiracy" was particularly prominent in the NBC-TV program, "The Mysterious Origins of Man," cited in the preceding note.

31. The title *The Entropy Trap* is "borrowed" from Kenneth Boulding. *The Meaning of the Twentieth Century* (New York: Harper Colophon, 1965), chap. 7. I can think of no better way to describe the significance of the concept of entropy to environmental policy.

32. Paul R. and Anne H. Ehrlich and John Holdren, "Availability, Entropy and the Laws of Thermodynamics," in Georgescu-Roegen, "Entropy, Economic Problem," 69.

33. The source of this formulation is Nicholas Georgescu-Roegen who, along with Herman Daly and Kenneth Boulding, is one of the few economists to take entropy seriously. Georgescu-Roegen, "Entropy, Economic Problem," 78.

34. Ehrlich, Ehrlich and Holdren, "Availability," 71.

35. I have long-since forgotten just where I read this. However, I am quite (though not totally) certain, that the source of this example is Isaac Asimov.

36. Ehrlich, Ehrlich, Holdren, *Availability*, 72.

37. New York: Knopf, 1966.

38. *Science* 224, (August 23, 1996): 1052.

39. The contrast between the economists' and the physicists' treatment of *heat* is instructive. In the taxonomy of classical economics, heat is a subset of *energy*, which in turn is a subset of the category of *economic resources*; that is, *heat* is just one of many economic *goods*. To the physicist studying the potentiality of all physical activity, heat is virtually everything. All work proceeds from heat differential (free energy), and the end product of all useful activity is useless or bound heat. In other words, according to the second law of thermodynamics, without heat differential, nothing happens.

40. Simon, *The Ultimate Resource*, 43.

41. John Ruggie, "Forward" to Myers and Simon, *Scarcity or Abundance*, xiv.

42. While I would prefer the politically correct *economic person*, the term *man* is used here to reflect an historically established gender preference: economic man (*homo economicus*).

43. If the physicist uses ideal types to advantage, then why not the economist? Because the difference between the disciplines is crucial: In physics, these ideal types are derived, one at a time, from carefully conducted experiments and measurements, and they are asymptomatic extrapolations from near perfect laboratory conditions end points of precisely measured empirical functions. And finally, in physics, unlike economics, these ideal types, when employed in the hypothetical-deductive methodology of physical science, yield falsifiable predictions and thence experimental verifications. None of this is true of the economists' ideal types. They are not extrapolated to zero, they are not the single controlled variables of experiments, but rather are bundled together in theoretical constructs. Furthermore, they posit, irrelevant to their theory, conditions which are in fact inalienable to human motives and economic activity: such things as transaction costs, externalities, collusion, restricted access, imperfect information, distributive injustice, self-transcending motivation, and communal loyalty.

44. For a more developed critique of libertarianism, see my "Environmental Justice and Shared Fate," *Human Ecology Review* 2, no. 2 (Winter/Spring 1996): 138–47.

45. "The Ethical Basis of the Economic View of the Environment," Center for the Study of Value and Social Policy, (Boulder: University of Colorado Press, 1983).

46. *People or Penguins: The Case for Optimal Pollution* (New York: Columbia University Press, 1974), 15–17.

47. Georgescu-Roegen, "Entropy, Economic Problem," 81.

48. "The Bankruptcy Files," *Wilderness* 58, (Summer 1994), 3.

49. But let this much suffice: First of all, human beings are in fact inalienably *social animals* and not the egoistic autonomous agents of the classical economic paradigm. Well-ordered societies can only exist and endure if the members thereof have concerns that transcend their personal "utility maximization." (I develop this notion at length in my essay, "Why Care About the Future?" in *Responsibilities to Future Generations*, ed. Ernest Partridge (Buffalo, NY: Prometheus Books, 1981). See also Mark Sagoff, *The Economy of the Earth* (Cambridge: Cambridge University Press, 1988), chaps. 2 and 3. Furthermore, perfect free market transactions, far from being exemplars of rational decision-making, often have little to do with rationality. We do not regard willingness to pay as relevant in the criminal or civil justice systems. Nor is this relevant in national defense or in education. Scientific and scholarly papers are not evaluated by pricing at the margin, nor are mathematical proofs or even economic theories. And moral issues are not properly settled by the free market, otherwise, we would still condone slavery. Clearly, the life of *homo economicus* is neither healthy, nor moral, nor even, in the final analysis, rational.

50. Originally, "for a successful technology, reality must take precedence over public relations, for nature cannot be fooled." This remark appeared at the close of Feynman's dissent from the report of the Challenger Committee.

Integrating the Environment Into Business Planning

THOMAS M. HELLMAN

Bristol-Myers Squibb is a large, diverse, decentralized company with a global focus. Total sales in 1992 exceeded $11 billion, with $2 billion in net earnings. Our products include pharmaceuticals, consumer and personal products, medical devices, and nutritionals. Approximately 43 percent of our sales come from outside the United States. We have about 50,000 employees worldwide and a commitment to include environmental concerns in our business plans.

An Alternative to "End-of-the-Pipe" Controls

Environmental management is changing in the 1990s. In the past, large corporations were primarily concerned with maintaining compliance with laws and regulations designed to control pollutants emitted into the air, discharged into water, and disposed of on land. Typically, these regulations focus on treating or controlling pollution after it has been created: that is, at the "end of the pipe." However, end-of-the-pipe controls, and the associated operational support, can be extremely expensive. Controlling pollution after it has been generated typically yields residuals that inevitably require disposal. The problem of environmental degradation is not solved, only transferred and delayed.

In the 1990s, an alternative to compliance-based end-of-the-pipe controls has emerged. Referred to as "prevention pollution," "waste minimization," "source reduction," or "continuous environmental improvement," its aim is to reduce or eliminate the generation of all forms of waste. When less waste is generated, the result should be reduced operational, transportation and handling costs; reduced risks to public health; reduced corporate liability; and reduced environmental degradation. For the first time, environmental management is being viewed not just as a necessary cost of doing business, but as a function of being an industry leader.

What has driven this change? First, our stakeholder expectations have changed. Today, our investors are keenly interested in how we manage our remedial liabilities, ensure ongoing compliance, prevent pollution and manage potential liabilities in a way that is consistent with sustainable competitiveness. Our employees care about the impact of our operations in terms of their own health and safety, as well as the effect on public health and environment. The communities in which we operate have become more educated about environmental issues. Our customers are demanding greater assurance that we are managing our environmental affairs in a responsible manner. And the consumer is placing greater importance on the environmental impacts of our products and packaging.

From *The Conference Board*, "Achieving Environmental Excellence", (February 1993) 15–17. Reprinted by permission.